JOB

THE NIV
APPLICATION
COMMENTARY

From biblical text . . . to contemporary life

THE NIV APPLICATION COMMENTARY

From biblical text . . . to contemporary life

JOHN H. WALTON
WITH KELLY LEMON VIZCAINO

ZONDERVAN.com/
AUTHORTRACKER
follow your favorite authors

ZONDERVAN

The NIV Application Commentary: Job
Copyright © 2012 by John H. Walton

This title is also available as a Zondervan ebook.
Visit www.zondervan.com/ebooks.

Requests for information should be addressed to:
Zondervan, *Grand Rapids, Michigan 49530*

Library of Congress Cataloging-in-Publication Data

Walton, John H.
    Job / John H. Walton with Kelly Lemon Vizcaino.
        p. cm. — (The NIV application commentary)
    Includes bibliographical references and indexes.
    ISBN: 978-0-310-21442-7 (hardcover)
    1. Bible. O.T. Job — Commentaries. I. Title.
    BS1415.53.W35 2012
    223'.1077 — dc23   2012001539

Printed in the United States of America

12 13 14 15 16 17 18 /DCI/ 24 23 22 21 20 19 18 17 16 15 14 13 12 11 10 9 8 7 6 5 4 3 2

To my son Jon,
who persuaded me to write this commentary,
then became thoroughly involved to improve it at every turn.
His contributions are immeasurable and my gratitude is unbounded.

The NIV Application Commentary Series

When complete, the NIV Application Commentary
will include the following volumes:

Old Testament Volumes

Genesis, John H. Walton

Exodus, Peter Enns

Leviticus/Numbers, Roy Gane

Deuteronomy, Daniel I. Block

Joshua, Robert L. Hubbard Jr.

Judges/Ruth, K. Lawson Younger Jr.

1-2 Samuel, Bill T. Arnold

1-2 Kings, August H. Konkel

1-2 Chronicles, Andrew E. Hill

Ezra/Nehemiah, Thomas and Donna Petter

Esther, Karen H. Jobes

Job, John H. Walton

Psalms Volume 1, Gerald H. Wilson

Psalms Volume 2, Jamie A. Grant

Proverbs, Paul Koptak

Ecclesiastes/Song of Songs, Iain Provan

Isaiah, John N. Oswalt

Jeremiah/Lamentations, J. Andrew Dearman

Ezekiel, Iain M. Duguid

Daniel, Tremper Longman III

Hosea/Amos/Micah, Gary V. Smith

Jonah/Nahum/Habakkuk/Zephaniah,
   James Bruckner

Joel/Obadiah/Malachi, David W. Baker

Haggai/Zechariah, Mark J. Boda

New Testament Volumes

Matthew, Michael J. Wilkins

Mark, David E. Garland

Luke, Darrell L. Bock

John, Gary M. Burge

Acts, Ajith Fernando

Romans, Douglas J. Moo

1 Corinthians, Craig Blomberg

2 Corinthians, Scott Hafemann

Galatians, Scot McKnight

Ephesians, Klyne Snodgrass

Philippians, Frank Thielman

Colossians/Philemon, David E. Garland

1-2 Thessalonians, Michael W. Holmes

1-2 Timothy/Titus, Walter L. Liefeld

Hebrews, George H. Guthrie

James, David P. Nystrom

1 Peter, Scot McKnight

2 Peter/Jude, Douglas J. Moo

Letters of John, Gary M. Burge

Revelation, Craig S. Keener

Contents

9
Series Introduction

13
General Editor's Preface

15
Author's Preface

16
Abbreviations

19
Introduction

49
Outline

50
Basic Bibliography on the Book of Job

55
Text and Commentary on Job

449
Technical Appendix

455
Scripture Index

464
Subject Index

NIV Application Commentary
Series Introduction

THE NIV APPLICATION COMMENTARY Series is unique. Most commentaries help us make the journey from our world back to the world of the Bible. They enable us to cross the barriers of time, culture, language, and geography that separate us from the biblical world. Yet they only offer a one-way ticket to the past and assume that we can somehow make the return journey on our own. Once they have explained the *original meaning* of a book or passage, these commentaries give us little or no help in exploring its *contemporary significance*. The information they offer is valuable, but the job is only half done.

Recently, a few commentaries have included some contemporary application as *one* of their goals. Yet that application is often sketchy or moralistic, and some volumes sound more like printed sermons than commentaries.

The primary goal of the NIV Application Commentary Series is to help you with the difficult but vital task of bringing an ancient message into a modern context. The series not only focuses on application as a finished product but also helps you think through the *process* of moving from the original meaning of a passage to its contemporary significance. These are commentaries, not popular expositions. They are works of reference, not devotional literature.

The format of the series is designed to achieve the goals of the series. Each passage is treated in three sections: *Original Meaning, Bridging Contexts*, and *Contemporary Significance.*

 THIS SECTION HELPS YOU understand the meaning of the biblical text in its original context. All of the elements of traditional exegesis—in concise form—are discussed here. These include the historical, literary, and cultural context of the passage. The authors discuss matters related to grammar and syntax and the meaning of biblical words.[1] They also seek to explore the main ideas of the passage and how the biblical author develops those ideas.

---

1. Please note that in general, when the authors discuss words in the original biblical languages, the series uses a general rather than a scholarly method of transliteration.

After reading this section, you will understand the problems, questions, and concerns of the *original audience* and how the biblical author addressed those issues. This understanding is foundational to any legitimate application of the text today.

 THIS SECTION BUILDS A bridge between the world of the Bible and the world of today, between the original context and the contemporary context, by focusing on both the timely and timeless aspects of the text.

God's Word is *timely*. The authors of Scripture spoke to specific situations, problems, and questions. The author of Joshua encouraged the faith of his original readers by narrating the destruction of Jericho, a seemingly impregnable city, at the hands of an angry warrior God (Josh. 6). Paul warned the Galatians about the consequences of circumcision and the dangers of trying to be justified by law (Gal. 5:2–5). The author of Hebrews tried to convince his readers that Christ is superior to Moses, the Aaronic priests, and the Old Testament sacrifices. John urged his readers to "test the spirits" of those who taught a form of incipient Gnosticism (1 John 4:1–6). In each of these cases, the timely nature of Scripture enables us to hear God's Word in situations that were *concrete* rather than abstract.

Yet the timely nature of Scripture also creates problems. Our situations, difficulties, and questions are not always directly related to those faced by the people in the Bible. Therefore, God's word to them does not always seem relevant to us. For example, when was the last time someone urged you to be circumcised, claiming that it was a necessary part of justification? How many people today care whether Christ is superior to the Aaronic priests? And how can a "test" designed to expose incipient Gnosticism be of any value in a modern culture?

Fortunately, Scripture is not only timely but *timeless*. Just as God spoke to the original audience, so he still speaks to us through the pages of Scripture. Because we share a common humanity with the people of the Bible, we discover a *universal dimension* in the problems they faced and the solutions God gave them. The timeless nature of Scripture enables it to speak with power in every time and in every culture.

Those who fail to recognize that Scripture is both timely and timeless run into a host of problems. For example, those who are intimidated by timely books such as Hebrews, Galatians, or Deuteronomy might avoid reading them because they seem meaningless today. At the other extreme, those who are convinced of the timeless nature of Scripture, but who fail to discern its timely element, may "wax eloquent" about the Melchizedekian priesthood to a sleeping congregation, or worse still, try to apply the holy wars of the Old Testament in a physical way to God's enemies today.

The purpose of this section, therefore, is to help you discern what is timeless in the timely pages of the Bible—and what is not. For example, how do the holy wars of the Old Testament relate to the spiritual warfare of the New? If Paul's primary concern is not circumcision (as he tells us in Gal. 5:6), what *is* he concerned about? If discussions about the Aaronic priesthood or Melchizedek seem irrelevant today, what is of abiding value in these passages? If people try to "test the spirits" today with a test designed for a specific first-century heresy, what other biblical test might be more appropriate?

Yet this section does not merely uncover that which is timeless in a passage but also helps you to see *how* it is uncovered. The authors of the commentaries seek to take what is implicit in the text and make it explicit, to take a process that normally is intuitive and explain it in a logical, orderly fashion. How do we know that circumcision is not Paul's primary concern? What clues in the text or its context help us realize that Paul's real concern is at a deeper level?

Of course, those passages in which the historical distance between us and the original readers is greatest require a longer treatment. Conversely, those passages in which the historical distance is smaller or seemingly nonexistent require less attention.

One final clarification. Because this section prepares the way for discussing the contemporary significance of the passage, there is not always a sharp distinction or a clear break between this section and the one that follows. Yet when both sections are read together, you should have a strong sense of moving from the world of the Bible to the world of today.

THIS SECTION ALLOWS THE biblical message to speak with as much power today as it did when it was first written. How can you apply what you learned about Jerusalem, Ephesus, or Corinth to our present-day needs in Chicago, Los Angeles, or London? How can you take a message originally spoken in Greek, Hebrew, and Aramaic and communicate it clearly in our own language? How can you take the eternal truths originally spoken in a different time and culture and apply them to the similar-yet-different needs of our culture?

In order to achieve these goals, this section gives you help in several key areas.

(1) It helps you identify contemporary situations, problems, or questions that are truly comparable to those faced by the original audience. Because contemporary situations are seldom identical to those faced by the original audience, you must seek situations that are analogous if your applications are to be relevant.

(2) This section explores a variety of contexts in which the passage might be applied today. You will look at personal applications, but you will also be encouraged to think beyond private concerns to the society and culture at large.

(3) This section will alert you to any problems or difficulties you might encounter in seeking to apply the passage. And if there are several legitimate ways to apply a passage (areas in which Christians disagree), the author will bring these to your attention and help you think through the issues involved.

In seeking to achieve these goals, the contributors to this series attempt to avoid two extremes. They avoid making such specific applications that the commentary might quickly become dated. They also avoid discussing the significance of the passage in such a general way that it fails to engage contemporary life and culture.

Above all, contributors to this series have made a diligent effort not to sound moralistic or preachy. The NIV Application Commentary Series does not seek to provide ready-made sermon materials but rather tools, ideas, and insights that will help you communicate God's Word with power. If we help you to achieve that goal, then we have fulfilled the purpose for this series.

The Editors

General Editor's Preface

THERE IS GOOD REASON why Christian theologians consider theodicy the unsolvable theological issue. The reason is this: It is unsolvable. Yet this does not stop generation after generation of theological scholars from trying to solve it. And the biblical text they most often reference in this Sysiphian task is the book of Job.

John Walton, author of this NIVAC commentary on Job, breaks the mold of these kinds of Job commentaries. To ask why God blesses, or doesn't bless, the righteous, or why God punishes, or doesn't punish, the wicked is to ask the wrong question when trying to understand this classic work. God's justice is ultimately unfathomable to us. God is just—we know that by faith—but we can't know *how* God is just. Thus, the book of Job does not answer that question, Walton avers; rather, it answers another question. Our task in reading Job is to read it as the answer to an unspoken question and then from the answer infer the correct question.

This approach seems to make superfluous a lot of folk theological wisdom we have learned about Job over the years. We learn a lot about Middle Eastern approaches to theodicy—all futile, of course. We have all gained some solace in knowing that undeserved suffering is not ours alone to bear—others experience it too. But the genius of Walton's exposition is that once we get the core question right, all of this other wisdom we have learned about Job remains just as meaningful to us, but with a slightly different twist and a more satisfying context—the context set by the right question.

I know. You probably want to know what the right question is. Patience. Have patience because in addition to Walton's groundbreaking insights regarding the right question, he tells us all we need to know about this somewhat enigmatic book. Unlike many books of the Bible, we don't know the author of Job or its date of composition. We do not really know whether it is based on historical events (and a historical person named Job) or whether it is a purely literary construction—a "thought experiment," as Walton labels it. We don't really know why the Hebrew language used in it is so complex. We recognize its genre as wisdom literature, but this is of little help because it is head and shoulders above other Near Eastern wisdom literature of this sort in terms of quality and sophistication. All of this Walton discusses expertly, and the reader comes away feeling informed.

Please notice that this is the only one of the forty volumes of the NIV Application Commentary published thus far that has a second author on the title page. Part of Professor Walton's convictions about this book is that even if it is a "thought experiment," it cannot be fully understood without relating it to real life—not just the legendary Job, but someone we know, here and now, in the twenty-first century. Enter Kelly Lemon Vizcaino. Kelly's relating of the lessons of Job to her own personal experiences of suffering appear throughout the book. "She has added an element of reality that is necessary for a work like this." Suffering is not, in the end, a philosophical, or even a theological problem, but a human problem. We all suffer, some more than others, but the quantity really doesn't matter. What matters is what suffering teaches us about God. But there I am getting dangerously close to telling you what the real question is, the one that Job answers.

So what's the right question that the book of Job answers? What is the right question we should be asking? Read the book—first the book of Job, and then this commentary.

Author's Preface

I HAVE HAD THE great privilege of having three marvelous teaching assistants while I was writing this commentary, all of whom were expert editors. I am grateful for their contribution in ensuring that I actually communicated the ideas that I wanted to get across. Ashley Edewaard and Kathryn Cobb both spent countless hours rewriting my sentences to make them effective and clear. Aubrey Buster did the same, but additionally read the manuscript numerous times providing critique of the ideas that I was trying to convey. Her input is reflected throughout the manuscript in more ways than I can recount. Many times, she was able to provide whole sentences that improved greatly on what I was trying to say. It was not uncommon that her wording corrected overstatements or logical non sequiturs. I am grateful and indebted to each for their conscientious work that served me well and will therefore serve the reader.

I would also like to thank Matthew Patton for preparing the indices.

Finally, I am very grateful that Kelly Lemon Vizcaino was willing to share her story, her life, and her struggles. As difficult as it was for her, she has added an element of reality that is necessary for a work such as this. Her courage is an inspiration to me, and I hope also to each reader.

Abbreviations

AB	Anchor Bible
ABY	Anchor Bible: Yale University Press
AfO	*Archiv für Orientforschung*
ANET	*Ancient Near Eastern Texts Relating to the Old Testament*. Ed. J. B. Pritchard
AOAT	Alter Orient und Altes Testament
As. Mos.	*Assumption of Moses*
BBR	*Bulletin of Biblical Research*
BETS	*Bulletin of the Evangelical Theological Society*
Bib	*Biblica*
BibInt	*Biblical Interpretation*
BJS	Brown Judaic Studies
BM	*Before the Muses*, 3rd ed. Ed Benjamin Foster
BSac	*Bibliotheca sacra*
BZAW	Beihefte zur Zeitschrift für die alttestamentliche Wissenschaft
CAD	*The Assyrian Dictionary of the Oriental Institute of the University of Chicago*
CANE	*Civilizations of the Ancient Near East*. Ed. J. Sasson
CAT	Commentaire de l'Ancien Testament
CBQMS	Catholic Biblical Quarterly Monograph Series
ConBOT	Coniectanea biblica: Old Testament Series
CTA	*Corpus des tablettes en cunéiformes alphabétiques découvertes à Ras Shamra-Ugarit de 1929 à 1939*. Ed. A. Herdner.
COS	*Context of Scripture*. Ed. W. W. Hallo
DCH	*Dictionary of Classical Hebrew*. Ed. D. J. A. Clines
DDD²	*Dictionary of Deities and Demons in the Bible*. Ed. K. van der Toorn et al. 2nd ed.
EBC	*Expositors Bible Commentary*
GKC	*Gesenius' Hebrew Grammar*. Ed. E. Kautzsch. Trans. A. E. Cowley.
HALOT	Koehler, L., W. Baumgartner, and J. J. Stamm, *The Hebrew and Aramaic Lexicon of the Old Testament*. Trans. and ed. M. E. J. Richardson
HMS	Harvard Semitic Monographs

HUCA	*Hebrew Union College Annual*
IBHS	*Introduction to Biblical Hebrew Syntax.* Ed. Bruce K. Waltke and M. O'Connor
JBL	*Journal of Biblical Literature*
JNES	*Journal of Near Eastern Studies*
JPS	Jewish Publication Society
JSOT	*Journal for the Study of the Old Testament*
JSOTSup	Journal for the Study of the Old Testament Supplement series
Jub.	*Jubilees*
KJV	King James Version
KTU	*Die keilalphabetischen Texte aus Ugarit.* 2nd ed. Ed. M. Dietrich, O. Loretz, and J. Sanmartín.
LXX	Septuagint
NASB	New American Standard Bible
NIBC	New International Biblical Commentary
NICOT	New International Commentary on the Old Testament
NIDOTTE	*New International Dictionary of Old Testament Theology and Exegesis.* Ed. W. VanGemeren
NIV	New International Version
NJPS	*Tanakh: The Holy Scriptures: The New JPS Translation according to the Traditional Hebrew Text*
NRSV	New Revised Standard Version
NSBT	Studies in Biblical Theology
OBO	Orbis biblicus et orientalis
OTL	Old Testament Library
PT	Pyramid Texts
PSCF	*Perspectives on Science and Christian Faith*
RIMA	The Royal Inscriptions of Mesopotamia, Assyrian Periods
RP	Retribution Principle
RSV	Revised Standard Version
SAA	State Archives of Assyria
SBLMS	Society of Biblical Literature Monograph Series
SBLWAW	Society of Biblical Literature Writings from the Ancient World
TDOT	*Theological Dictionary of the Old Testament.* Ed. G. Johannes Botterweck, Helmer Ringgren, and Heiz-Josef Fabry
TJ	*Trinity Journal*
TOTC	Tyndale Old Testament Commentaries

Abbreviations

TynBul	*Tyndale Bulletin*
WBC	Word Biblical Commentary
WTJ	*Westminster Theological Journal*
ZIBBCOT	*Zondervan Illustrated Bible Background Commentary: Old Testament.* Ed. J. H. Walton

Introduction[1]

Purpose of the Book

"IT WAS A DARK and stormy night. . . ." So begins the novel perpetually being attempted by Snoopy in the Peanuts comic strip. The humor is in the cliché. The cliché has its roots, I imagine, in the fact that novels want to draw the reader in by posing an intriguing scenario filled with danger and mystery. But when our lives are reading like that novel, the idle curiosity of a casual reader is replaced with the sorrow or abject fear of a person in crisis. No one is immune to "dark and stormy nights," and reading about Job's is designed to help us know how to think about our own.

The title character of the book of Job is caught in the ultimate "dark and stormy night" of a life gone tragically wrong. We should not mistakenly think that this book is just about Job, however; it is about all of us. Though the book does engage in extremes, it is not trying to minimize anyone else's suffering in comparison, for suffering cannot be measured objectively. Regardless of where anyone's experiences fit on the spectrum of pain and suffering, we are all prone to ask the same questions. These questions direct us to the central subject of the book, God himself, for he is the one to whom we direct our confused questions and perplexed musings. Archibald MacLeish, in his Pulitzer Prize winning play *J.B.*, frames it this way:

> Millions and millions of mankind
> Burned, crushed, broken, mutilated,
> Slaughtered, and for what? For thinking!
> For walking round the world in the wrong
> Skin, the wrong-shaped noses, eyelids:
> Sleeping the wrong night wrong city—
> London, Dresden, Hiroshima.
> There never could have been so many
> Suffered more for less. But where do
> I come in?[2]

---

1. For more detailed discussion about many of the issues addressed in this introduction, see J. Walton, "Job 1: Book of," in *Dictionary of the Old Testament: Wisdom, Prophets and Writings* (ed. T. Longman III and P. Enns; Downers Grove, Ill.: InterVarsity Press, 2008), 333–46.
2. A. MacLeish, *J.B.* (Boston: Houghton Mifflin, 1958), 13.

MacLeish had the same questions that we all direct heavenward, but as an existentialist, he had no answers. Like Job and like MacLeish, we are long on questions but short on answers. Does the book of Job offer any satisfaction? Many have thought not—that like MacLeish, the book simply restates the perennial and ubiquitous questions that plague humankind in a world full of pain and suffering.

I disagree. Perhaps we have not recognized the answers the book offers because we have asked the wrong questions—or, more accurately, the less important questions. When in Acts 3 the crippled beggar asks for money, Peter instead gives him healing. The beggar had not thought to ask for that. Sometimes what we ask for is too limited to do us any real good. We must learn to ask better questions so that we might find the more significant answers. To this end, the book of Job repeatedly shows us that what we thought were the most poignant questions are not significant enough, and it dismisses them. At long last it leads us to the most momentous questions by introducing a whole series of answers, answers that at first seem oblique. In fact, many have been willing to dismiss the answers as a mere smokescreen and turn away from the book disillusioned and disappointed. But if we allow the answers to prompt us to the right questions, we will discover the wealth that the book has to offer.

The book is not about Job, his friends, or the Challenger.[3] I have suggested it is about all of us, and ultimately about God.[4] Our questions about suffering inevitably lead to God, for when we go through difficult times in life, there is no one else to question—he is the one whose ways we seek to understand. When we ask "Why me?" we are in effect asking "How does God work?" We may start out asking why we deserved this, but ultimately the question we arrived at is, "What kind of God are you?" In all our difficult experiences, eventually we arrive at the place where it is no longer us, but God who is on trial.

As we examine the book in detail, it becomes clear that Job is not on trial. In fact, he is declared innocent from beginning to end by all parties. When the Challenger suggests that Job's motives may be self-interested, he has no evidence, only suspicions—possible explanations for Job's pris-

---

3. I am going to refer to Satan throughout as the "Challenger." For my reasoning and further information see discussion on 64–67.

4. Many have different opinions about this. Note W. Brown's confident assertion: "Job is *primarily* about Job and not someone else, even God, or something else, including theodicy. Job does not attempt to provide a solution to the universal problem of suffering" ("The Deformation of Character: Job 1–31," in *Character in Crisis* [Grand Rapids: Eerdmans, 1996], 51). I disagree with his view that the book intends to present Job as a role model, but I agree that it is not to give an answer to suffering or to provide a theodicy.

tine conduct. Job is thereby tacitly exonerated because there is no concrete evidence against him. When Job's friends go hunting for offenses, they likewise have no hard evidence to offer and can only suggest possible misdemeanors. Though Job and his friends may believe he is on trial, the prologue shows that this is a misunderstanding. Rather, it is God's policies that have been called into question, and he therefore takes the role of defendant.[5] Job becomes deeply enmeshed in this trial and is central to it, but he is not on trial.

This concept will be explored in greater depth in the commentary, but a summary here is apropos. The Challenger's question, "Does Job fear God for nothing?" (1:9) centers on Job's motivation for serving God and suggests that God's treatment of the righteous is the incentive for righteous conduct. The policy under scrutiny is known today as the Retribution Principle (RP): the righteous prosper and the wicked suffer. If this is a truism, then the motives of righteous-acting people may be corrupted by the lure of prosperity, because if such material gain is the inevitable result of righteousness, true righteousness becomes illusionary and elusive. The Challenger's claim is therefore that God's policy of rewarding the righteous actually undermines, if not subverts, the very righteousness that he seeks to foster.[6] In warfare, there is no true faithfulness in mercenaries. The RP has the potential of turning would-be righteous people into "benefit mercenaries" as it trains them to ask, "What's in it for me?" We might see the issue more clearly if we compare the criticism that some politicians have of entitlement programs: They claim that welfare, food stamps, and the like are bad policy because they make people lazy and dependent.

My son is an artist, and I noticed when he was grade school, still drawing dogs or dinosaurs, he used to either draw them upside down or draw the feet before he drew the rest of the figure. When I asked why, he replied that everything could be put in better proportion if he approached the drawing in this way. We find this same principle at work as we reflect on the literary artistry of the book of Job. The Challenger puts God's policies to the

---

5. Stated forthrightly, but undeveloped in P. L. Day, *An Adversary in Heaven* (Atlanta: Scholars, 1988), 80–1; N. Habel gets close to this, "It is God's integrity as the designer of the cosmos which is at stake" (*The Book of Job* [OTL; Philadelphia: Westminster, 1985], 65). But here it is still God's integrity rather than the legitimacy of his policies. Note also: "If we read Job 1–2 with the idea that the Satan has charged God with serious misconduct, then God is also subject to investigation" (F. R. Magdalene, *On the Scales of Righteousness: Neo-Babylonian Trial Law and the Book of Job* [BJS 348; Providence, R.I.: Brown Univ. Press, 2007], 117–18).

6. This focus emerges in 1:10 as the Challenger's language addresses what God has done ("Have you not put a hedge around him," etc.).

test by suggesting that it is counterproductive for God to bless righteous people, for it makes them less righteous (in motive, if not in action). Such an accusation gives the book an interesting twist, for while we might be inclined (along with Job and his friends) to spend time thinking about why righteous people suffer, the Challenger turns the question upside down and asks why they should prosper. It is drawing the picture upside down to put everything in better perspective. In this way the book gives us the answers we need rather than the answers we thought we wanted.

After God accepts the proposal of the Challenger, Job's suffering begins, which provides the other side of the dilemma. Even as the Challenger suggests it is bad policy for righteousness to result in prosperity (ethically counterproductive), Job presses his point that it is bad policy for God's most faithful people to suffer (theologically counterintuitive).[7] Caught on the horns of this dilemma, what is a God to do? This is what the book is going to sort out. Because the book is about God, the teaching that it offers is valuable to all of us. It does not tell us why Job or any of us suffer, but it does tell us a bit about how we should think about God when we are suffering. This is what we really needed to know anyway.

In summary, then, the purpose of this book is to explore God's policies with regard to suffering in the world, especially by the righteous or the innocent. In the process it seeks to revolutionize our thinking about God and the way that he runs the world. Most importantly, the book shifts our attention from the idea that God's *justice* (represented in the RP) is foundational to the operation of the world to the alternative that God's *wisdom* is the more appropriate foundation.[8] It does not offer a reason for suffering and does not try to defend God's justice. It does not answer the "why" question that we are so prone to ask when things go wrong. Instead, we are to trust God's wisdom and, in the process, to conclude by faith that he is also just.

In truth, we will never be in a position to evaluate God's justice. In order to appraise the justice of a decision, we must have all the facts, for justice can be derailed if we do not have all the information. Because we never have all the information about our lives, we cannot judge God when he brings experiences to us or make claims and demands. We cannot reach an

---

7. For the labels of "ethically counterproductive" and "theologically counterintuitive," see K. Ngwa, "Did Job Suffer for Nothing? The Ethics of Piety, Presumption and Reception of Disaster in the Prologue of Job," *JSOT* 33 (2009): 359–80, see 378.

8. A few commentators go in a similar direction but without going quite to this conclusion: "The design of God frees Job from a mechanical, blind submission to a moral law of retributive justice" (Habel, *Job*, 69; see also M. Weiss, *The Story of Job's Beginning* [Jerusalem: Magnes, 1983], 43).

affirmation about God's justice through our own limited insight or experiences. We affirm his justice by faith directed toward his wisdom. As we will see, God's speech at the end does not offer a defense of his *justice*, but of his *wisdom* and *power*.

The book, therefore, wants to transform how we think about God's work in the world and about our responses in times of suffering. Most people look at the book, thinking that it deals with the question of why righteous people suffer. Instead, the book sets out the question as, "Is there such a thing as disinterested righteousness?"[9] In this sense the book is about the nature of *righteousness*, not the nature of *suffering*. As the book unfolds, we are going to discover that Job's motives are indeed pure (he values righteousness over benefits), but his concept of God and his understanding of God's policies are going to need modification.

Author and Date

THE SHORT ANSWER IS that while we do not know the author or the date, this lack of information does not affect our interpretation of the book. Literary works in the ancient world were largely anonymous, and it was not unusual for them to go through development as they were transmitted from generation to generation. Scholars have traditionally placed the events of this book in the patriarchal period, citing the absence of any reference to covenant or law. Two facts join to support the conclusion that the book is set before the time of Moses: Job's service as the family priest and the lack of reference to a sanctuary. Against such an inference, we need only note that Job is not an Israelite (he is from the land of Uz, 1:1). We would therefore not expect any reference to covenant or law, priest, or temple.

We could explore some of the potential historical references in the book, such as to the Sabeans (1:15) and Chaldeans (1:17), but such studies do not yield consistent results. Many have also focused on the specialized language of the book, such as the arcane term *qesitah* (42:11), a unit of money found elsewhere only in early literature (Gen. 33:19; Josh. 24:32). But these give little to go on. Scholars do not contest that the

---

9. I am going to use this concept throughout the commentary so a brief qualification is necessary. I do not use it to refer to the total absence of self-interest—that is impossible. The "interests" that I refer to are those benefits or threats that consciously motivate us to certain behaviors. It concerns ulterior motives, not subconscious ones. It does not include existential benefits (such as an existentially satisfying epistemology that makes us content to have faith in a God). "Disinterested" should therefore be understood in relationship to the Retribution Principle: prosperity, wealth, health, respect, and status on the one hand; suffering, misfortune, illness, and death on the other.

---

book contains arcane features, but there is not sufficient information to date either the setting of the story or the composition of the book with any confidence. Even if we could provide such dates, it would make no difference in the book's interpretation.

We should also note that the language of the book has been the subject of much discussion. The book is uncontested for the complexity of its Hebrew. Scholars have attempted to identify it as a dialect or even as a translation, but no such suggestions have been substantiated or widely accepted.[10] All of this is to say that until we have more to go on, we cannot use the language of the book to determine its date.

Literature and History: The Genre of the Book of Job

WE MIGHT NEXT REASONABLY ask about the nature of the events. In the end this is a genre question. Is the author presenting the events of the book as actual occurrences? Was there such a man as Job? Did he suffer in these ways? Were there friends who came and discussed his plight with him? Is the book suggesting that there was such a scenario in heaven? Was there a divine appearance from the whirlwind?

All of these questions get at the same issue: How much of the book is literary artifice and how much is a journalistic reporting of real events?[11] Either option could be legitimate genres for canonical texts and could provide the authority for sacred writ. How important is this question and how should it be approached? Often we are guided by the claims we presume that the book makes for itself. We also are inclined to check any of these supposed claims by other authoritative, canonical sources. Along with all of this evidence, we are often also driven by our own presuppositions and traditions.

We might deduce from the fact that the book gives the names of Job's daughters at the end of the book (42:14) that the reader is expected to link them to known history, but any such connections are lost to us. Little else in the book suggests that the author is urging us toward a historical reading of the book. References to Job in the Old Testament (Ezek. 14:14, 20) and in the New Testament (James 5:11) have been used to argue that Job is an historical figure, but such reference could just as easily be made to a literary

---

10. For lengthy discussion, see M. Cheney, *Dust, Wind and Agony: Character, Speech and Genre in Job* (ConBOT 36; Lund: Almqvist & Wiksell, 1994).

11. I do not mean to set up a false dichotomy by suggesting that these are the only two possibilities—there may be numerous alternatives in between.

figure. Job's perseverance and righteousness could be drawn on effectively in either case, so these references prove nothing.

Before we move on too hastily, however, we might also inquire whether there *are* literary figures in the ancient world. We know that there are legendary figures, but there is no reason to believe that the legends are not built around historical persons (e.g., Gilgamesh, Adapa, Etana, Kirtu). How then would we establish that a character was simply a literary figure rather than an historical person? Perhaps the better question is whether this distinction really matters, for the argument of the book does not depend on the historicity of the main characters. This is different from the story of, say, Abraham. There the integrity of the text depends on whether there actually was a man named Abraham to whom God made certain promises. If there were no such man, there was no covenant. The situation in Job, however, is not the same.

Though there may be purely literary characters in the literature of the ancient world, ancient authors were more likely to construct their literature around epic figures of the distant past than to fabricate "fiction" as we understand it today.[12] This practice is illustrated in the Mesopotamian wisdom work known as *Ludlul bel nemeqi*, a first-person narration of someone who suffered greatly and did not know why. His name can be deduced from the work, and analysts do not hesitate to consider him a real person.[13] Weiss builds the case that the introduction of Job's name indicates syntactically that Job's character and reputation are familiar to all.[14] For these reasons, we may rightly assume that Job was a historical figure—a man who was righteous and suffered greatly.[15] We lose nothing by accepting Job's story as historical, and we gain nothing by concluding that he is a fabricated, fictional character.

Yet questions concerning the nature and genre of the book are far more complex than simply determining whether Job really existed and underwent such suffering. For example, even the most conservative and traditional of recent interpreters grant that the speeches of Job and his friends are literary artifice rather than journalistic transcripts. No stenographer would have

---

12. Fictional characters such as Jason Bourne, James Bond, or Indiana Jones have no precedent in ancient literature.

13. See the treatment by W. G. Lambert, *Babylonian Wisdom Literature* (Oxford; Clarendon, 1960), 21.

14. He shows that when the name comes first ("X is his name") rather than following ("His name was called X"), it is clear that everyone will recognize the name, rather than that a character is being introduced for the first time (Weiss, *Job's Beginning*, 19–21).

15. Note Weiss's indication of the consensus: "Scholars agree that the narrator did not invent Job" (ibid., 16).

been present; furthermore, people do not talk extemporaneously in such elevated prose. If we agree that the speeches are literary artifice, we must then ask which other parts of the book are in the same category; in fact, is every part of the book in the same category? If the speeches are literary constructions, are the friends themselves literary constructions? That is, are they designed to represent certain approaches to the question of suffering?

These questions are the same as those that surround other philosophical literature from the world of antiquity. For example, Socrates is a character in Plato's dialogues, in whose mouth Plato places his philosophy. The historical Socrates (and it is debated whether there was such a person) may not have said the things Plato has him say (the same goes for his [historical] interlocutors), may not have gone to trial in the same way, and may not have died the same way that Plato depicts. Ultimately, this makes no difference to Plato's philosophy; a discovery that there was no historical Socrates would not cast doubt on Platonism.

In approaching this question, we must keep foremost in our mind that this book is manifestly and unarguably in the genre category of wisdom literature, not historical literature.[16] As wisdom literature it makes no claims about the nature of the events. In that sense the discussion about whether the events are real events is misplaced. A second understanding that is important is that as wisdom literature, this book would fit easily into the classification "thought experiment."[17] In such a case the author is using the various parts of the book to pose a philosophical scenario that will be used to address the wisdom themes as we have articulated them above.[18] If the book of Job is a thought experiment, the reader is supposed to draw conclusions about God from the final point, not from every detail along the way. Consequently, for example, the opening scene in heaven is not intended to be used as a source of information about God's activities and nature. We

---

16. T. Longman notes that Maimonides is an example of rabbinic interpreters who considered the book of Job to be a parable (*Job* [Grand Rapids: Baker, 2012]).

17. I am grateful to my son, Jonathan Walton, for the earlier example of Socrates and for bringing this terminology and idea to my attention. Thought experiments can be used in many of the sciences. In both philosophy and science, hypothetical situations are explored for their philosophical value. The point is not to claim that the events in the thought experiment did happen, but they draw their philosophical strength from the realistic nature of the imaginative device. For explanation and example, see J. R. Brown, "Thought Experiments," *The Stanford Encyclopedia of Philosophy* (ed. Edward N. Zalta; Summer 2009), http://plato.stanford.edu/entries/thought-experiment. For discussion of science thought experiments and also the belief that Job may be one, see W. Brown, *The Seven Pillars of Creation* (Oxford: Oxford Univ. Press, 2010), 115.

18. Cf. J. Greenfield, "Reflections on Job's Theology," in *Studies in the Bible and Jewish Thought* (Philadelphia: JPS, 1995), 327–33, esp. 328.

would not rule out the possibility that such a scenario could happen, but we would be mistaken to think that author seeks to unfold a series of historical events. It is wisdom literature.[19]

The scene in heaven is not trying to explain why Job or any of us suffer. Job is never told about that scene, nor would he have derived any comfort from it. As I have taught Job to students over the years, the question frequently arises, "What sort of God is this who uses his faithful ones as pawns in bets with the devil?" I would suggest that we need not concern ourselves with this question. The scene in heaven, like the speeches of Job's friends, is part of the literary design of a thought experiment to generate discussion about how God runs the cosmos; it is not about trying to explain how Job got into such a difficult situation. The message of the book is offered at the end, in the speeches of God, not in the opening scenario, which only sets up the thought experiment.

As wisdom literature the book of Job seeks to give us appropriate foundations for understanding how the world works and how God works in the world. The book reveals how things work in the world, not how things work in heaven. If we are seeking to satisfy our curiosity about whether the Challenger has such access to heaven or whether there are such conversations concerning particular individuals, we cannot rule it out, but we should not think that the answers are provided here.

Shape and Structure

WE MIGHT THINK ABOUT the composition of the book of Job by using an analogy to some issues in the natural sciences. "Intelligent Design" has introduced the concept of "irreducible complexity" as one way to criticize Neo-Darwinism's adequacy as an explanation of origins. Irreducible complexity describes an organism in which all of the parts are essential to its operation such that the parts could not have developed independently or sequentially, for the organism could not survive if it were lacking any of them in their fully developed form.

A similar claim of irreducible complexity could be made for the book of Job. The book includes dialogues, discourses, narratives, hymns, and laments (to name a few of the major sections), and each one has a significant role to play. If any of them were absent, the book would not accomplish its purpose.

---

19. Compare the allegory of the cave in Plato's *Republic* (Book VII, 514a–520a). Plato/Socrates is making a point about knowledge, not relating a narrative about some people who were in a cave. Likewise, Job is making a point about God's policies, not about some characters who had a conversation in heaven.

Many recent commentators have proposed a history of composition of the book; some suggest, for example, that the Elihu speeches are later additions, or the speeches of Yahweh don't fit very well.[20] Some opine that an original narrative (the frame) was later embellished by the poetic speeches, while others propose that the speeches came first and the narrative frame was added later. Such discussions may have academic value, but in the end they can only result in speculation that has little impact on our reading of the book. Elihu's speeches cannot be discarded as redundant—they make a significant contribution as they take the argument into new territory. God's speeches are not superfluous, obtuse, or irrelevant. None of the pieces can be discarded from this carefully and artfully constructed book. The following table offers the structure of the book that I find most persuasive.

Narrative Frame: 1–3		
	Prologue: Heaven and Earth	1–2
	Job's Opening Lament	3
	Cycle One: 4–14	
	Eliphaz	4–5
	Job	6–7
	Bildad	8
	Job	9–10
	Zophar	11
	Job	12–14
Dialogue	Cycle Two: 15–21	
	Eliphaz	15
	Job	16–17
	Bildad	18
	Job	19
	Zophar	20
	Job	21
	Cycle Three: 22–27	
	Eliphaz	22
	Job	23–24
	Bildad	25
	Job	26–27

20. For a thorough analysis of the scholarly proposals and reasons for various parts of the book being included or excluded, see P. P. Zerafa, *The Wisdom of God in the Book of Job* (Rome: Herder, 1978), 12–54.

Interlude: Wisdom Hymn: 28		
Discourses	Series One: 29–31	
	Job: Reminiscences	29
	Job: Affliction	30
	Job: Oath of Innocence	31
	Series Two: 32–37	
	Elihu: Introduction and Theory	32–33
	Elihu: Verdict on Job	34
	Elihu: Offense of Job	35
	Elihu: Summary	36–37
	Series Three: 38–41	
	Yahweh: Maintaining roles and functions in cosmic order	38–39
	Yahweh: Harnessing threats to cosmic order	40:1–2; 40:6—41:34
Narrative Frame: 42		
	Job's Closing Statements	(40:3–5) 42:1–6
	Epilogue: Heaven and Earth	42:7–17

Note that there are three sets of speeches in the dialogue section (chs. 4–27), balanced by three sets of speeches in the discourse section (chs. 29–41). Leading into the dialogue section is Job's lament (ch. 3), which is balanced by Job's responses to God (esp. 42:1–6) coming out of the discourse section. Narrative frames the entire work. At the center of all this and most controversial is Job 28, which I have set off as the narrator's interjection that serves as a pivot for the book and a transition from the dialogues to the discourses.[21] Many commentators believe that chapter 28 is a speech of Job bridging from his last speech in the dialogue to his first speech in the discourses.[22] It is easy to understand how one would draw that conclusion, but a variety of reasons compel us to discard this option. N. Habel identifies the problem succinctly:

> For Job to return (in 28:28) to the traditional "fear of the Lord" would therefore mean returning to a posture of pious unquestioning submission which the friends had advocated all along and which he had repudiated time and again.[23]

21. Widely accepted and nicely presented by F. I. Andersen, *Job* (Downers Grove, Ill.: InterVarsity Press, 1976), 222–24. Cf. J. F. A. Sawyer, "The Authorship and Structure of the Book of Job," in *Studia Biblica 1978* (ed. E. A. Livingstone; Sheffield: JSOT, 1979), 253–57. For technical presentation, see Cheney, *Dust, Wind and Agony*, 42–45.

22. Cf. G. Wilson, *Job* (NIBC; Peabody, Mass.: Hendrickson, 2007), 7.

23. Habel, *Job*, 392–93.

Job's final speech in Job 27:7–23 shows a pessimistic, fatalistic despair that would be ill-matched to and arguably irreconcilable with chapter 28. Likewise, the speeches in 29–31 show no hint of the convictions expressed in chapter 28.[24] In his study of the forms and structure of Job, C. Westermann has concluded that the Wisdom hymn does not conform to any of the speeches by Job or his friends and therefore cannot derive from any one of them.[25] Habel summarizes the field as he observes that

> Job 28 is a brilliant but embarrassing poem for many commentators. It has been viewed as an erratic intrusion, an inspired intermezzo, a superfluous prelude, and an orthodox afterthought.[26]

In light of all of this, we may make the most sense of the text by viewing Job 28 as an interlude by the narrator.[27]

As a final observation, this bracketing out of Job 28 may also find some support in the speech formulas used in the book. Most of the speeches throughout all sections of the book are introduced by *wayya'an* ("he replied"). The only exceptions are Job 27:1; 29:1; and 36:1, where the text has *wayyosep* ("he continued"). The latter verb usually indicates continuing, repeating, or supplementing something that was done/said before. The placement and nature of these three speeches suggests that they should be taken as concluding summary remarks. Job 27 is Job's final statement regarding his friends' urgings and accusations. Job 29–31 is a summary of Job's position in the whole affair in relationship to his claim against God. Job 36–37 is Elihu's concluding summary statement. Unfortunately, the idea that a speech introduced by *wayyosep* can serve as a summary conclusion to a series of speeches introduced by *wayya'an* cannot be demonstrated by pointing to other contexts outside of Job. Extended dialogues are not common in the biblical text.[28] The structural points I would make are as follows:

---

24. Note the comments in that regard by E. Smick, "Job," *EBC* (ed. Frank E. Gaebelein; Grand Rapids: Zondervan, 1988), 4:974.

25. C. Westermann, *The Structure of the Book of Job* (Philadelphia: Fortress, 1981), 135–36.

26. Habel, *Job*, 391; for discussion, see H. H. Rowley, *The Book of Job* (Grand Rapids: Eerdmans, 1976), 179.

27. See the cogent defense by Cheney, *Dust, Wind and Agony*, 42–45. Many have decided that they cannot leave the text as is; cf. D. J. A. Clines, who proposes that ch. 28 is misplaced and is actually the conclusion of Elihu's speeches and serves as a transition to the speeches of Yahweh, see Clines, *Job 21–37* (WBC 18A; Nashville: Nelson, 2006), 907.

28. The only other comparable construction is found in Genesis 18 as Abraham speaks to the Lord about the destruction of Sodom. There *wayya'an* introduces Abraham's second remark as would be expected (Gen. 18:27) and *wayyosep* introduces his third remark (Gen. 18:29). Here this is not a summary conclusion, for negotiations continue through the end of the chapter.

1. We would not expect two *wayyosep* speeches back-to-back, making it unlikely that chapters 27–28 are one speech and chapters 29–31 are another.
2. Chapter 28 is so radically distinct from the end of chapter 27 that it would call for some introductory speech formula if it came from the mouth of Job.

If chapter 28 is put in the mouth of the narrator, it indicates that we have yet to hear true wisdom, even though we have now listened to extensive speeches from those characterized as the wisest in the ancient world. The accusation of the Challenger has been refuted even as the promptings and arguments of the friends have been rejected. Wisdom has yet to be heard, and Job's own claims have yet to be answered.

Job in the Ancient Near East

SEVERAL PIECES OF LITERATURE from the ancient Near East deal with the topic of individuals suffering for no apparent reason.[29] From a literary perspective none of these approach the topic with the subtlety and complexity of the book of Job. Though there is certainly no literary dependence in either direction, these pieces of literature are important because they show that this was a common philosophical discussion. They are also significant because they show the differences between the Israelite approach to the issue and that found in the surrounding cultures. Perhaps most importantly, by understanding what the typical ancient Near Eastern solutions were, we can see how the book of Job interacts with them and shows their inadequacy.

Primary Texts

DIFFERENT STUDIES INCLUDE A variety of different pieces, but here we will mention only the most similar literature containing discussion surrounding a pious but suffering individual. While dates are not always easy to determine,

---

29. Dozens of articles could be cited, but the most informative are: R. G. Albertson, "Job and Ancient Near Eastern Wisdom Literature," in *Scripture in Context II* (ed. W. W. Hallo, J. C. Moyer, and L. G. Perdue; Winona Lake, Ind.: Eisenbrauns, 1983), 213–30; D. P. Bricker, "Innocent Suffering in Mesopotamia," *TynBul* (2001): 121–42; J. E. Hartley, "Job 2: Ancient Near Eastern Background," in *Dictionary of the Old Testament: Wisdom, Poetry and Writings* (ed. T. Longman III and P. Enns; Downers Grove, Ill.: InterVarsity Press, 2008), 346–61; G. L. Mattingly, "The Pious Sufferer: Mesopotamia's Traditional Theodicy and Job's Counselors," in *The Bible in the Light of Cuneiform Literature: Scripture in Context III* (eds. W. W. Hallo, B. W. Jones, and G. L. Mattingly; Lewiston, N.Y.: Mellen, 1990), 305–48; and M. Weinfeld, "Job and Its Mesopotamian Parallels—A Typological Analysis," in *Text and Context: Old Testament and Semitic Studies for F. C. Fensham* (ed. W. Claassen; JSOTSup 48; Sheffield: JSOT, 1988), 217–26.

Mesopotamian Literature Compared with Job[30]

Literature	Status	Condition	Resolution	Outcome	Philosophy	Theology
A Man and His God[31] (Sumerian)	Ignorant of offense	Illness; social outcast	Sins confessed	Restored to health	No sinless child born	Results in hymn of praise
Dialogue between a Man and His God[32] (Akkadian)	Ignorant of offense	Illness	Text broken	Restored to health	None offered	Divine favor assured
Sufferer's Salvation[33] (Akkadian, from Ugarit)	No comment	Illness; death imminent; omens obscure	No indication	Restored to health	God brought his suffering then brought his healing	Results in hymn of praise to Marduk
Ludlul bel nemeqi[34] (Akkadian)	Conscientious piety; ignorant of offense	Social outcast; omens obscure; illness; protective spirits chased away; demon oppression	Dream appearance	Purification bringing appeasement; offenses borne away; demons expelled; restored to health	Gods are inscrutable	Results in hymn of praise to Marduk
Babylonian Theodicy[35] (Akkadian)	Claims piety	Family gone; poverty	none	none	Purposes of gods remote; RP unreliable	Gods make people with evil inclinations and prone to suffering
Job (Hebrew)	Claims righteousness and conscientious piety	Family taken; social outcast; illness; wealth taken	Yahweh offers new perspective based on wisdom	Restoration at all levels	RP unreliable; divine wisdom is foundation	God's justice is granted given his wisdom

generally speaking they range throughout the second millennium BC. The table on page 32 presents some analysis and comparison of these pieces.

Similarities

AS WE COMPARE THE principal pieces of Mesopotamian literature to Job, we find a number of superficial similarities. All feature an individual who is suffering, is baffled as to why he is suffering, and, in all but one case, is restored in the end. The sufferer in each case ponders his situation by laying his concerns before God or friends as he tries to understand the role of the gods in his plight. In that sense the scenarios are similar. As is often the case, however, when comparing the Bible to ancient Near Eastern exemplars, probing beneath the surface reveals many significant differences.

Differences

WHEN WE BEGIN TO penetrate beyond the superficial level of the general scenario, we find that Job differs on some important details as well as in its general philosophy and theology.

1. The nature of the suffering is different. In the ancient Near Eastern exemplars the major difficulty is health-related. Because of RP thinking, sudden serious illness was generally assumed to result from the gods' disfavor. Such illness inevitably led to social rejection, for if a god were angry with the sick individual, one would not want to be associated with that person. If a demon were causing the problem, it would likewise be best to keep one's distance. As the literature indicates, then, serious illness made one a social outcast. In contrast, Job loses his wealth and his family before he loses his health. The Mesopotamian pieces touch on poverty and lost family, but these are not presented as major issues.

---

30. I have used only Mesopotamian literature because, in my opinion, the Egyptian literature is not of a similar sort. The Dialogue Between a Man and his Ba is more reminiscent of Ecclesiastes, while the Admonitions pieces are about chaos at the society level more than about a single pious person's experiences with suffering. All of these pieces would have individual points of comparison, but overall are not the same sort of scenario faced by Job and the Mesopotamian sufferers.
31. *COS*, 1.179: 573–75.
32. *COS*, 1.151: 485
33. *COS*, 1.152: 486
34. *COS*, 1.153: 486–92.
35. *COS*, 1.154: 492–95.

2. The nature of the offenses considered in Job are never ceremonial. In the ancient Near East ritual offense was the most common sort of misdeed that a person could commit; though there were ritual expectations for the people, these were devised by society, not revealed by deity. Deity valued order in society, but moral responsibility was not understood as part of the people's responsibility toward the gods. Instead, humans were to care for the gods (through ritual), and they would incur the anger of the gods by failing to provide for them. One cannot, then, easily speak of "righteousness" in the ancient world, only of "piety" (by which I refer to conscientiousness in ritual activity). There was no orthodoxy (right belief), only orthopraxy (proper performance).

In the Mesopotamian pieces deity is eventually appeased, whether by prayers, laments, or rituals. This appeasement of the deity is necessary in these scenarios because the deity is presumed to be angry or inexplicably moody. In Job there is no appeasement of Yahweh, for Yahweh is not angry; furthermore, Job specifically rejects the path of appeasement urged by his friends (27:2–6). This refusal is important to the book of Job, for Job's pursuit of appeasement would demonstrate that the Challenger was right. Appeasement focuses on regaining benefits and tacitly denies the place of righteousness. The Challenger had made that precise claim—that supposedly righteous people weren't really righteous, but only behaved righteously to gain benefits.

The Mesopotamians pursued appeasement because they considered themselves to be in a symbiotic relationship with the gods. The gods had created people to serve their needs; in response to such service, the gods protected the faithful people and provided for them (e.g., fertile fields). This was the Great Symbiosis of religious thinking in the ancient world. It was benefit-based: the gods reaped benefits from the labor of humans, and the humans reaped benefits from the favor of the gods. This expectation was not based on the belief that the god was just, only that he or she was sensible. The gods needed what humans provided, and they in return were capable in most circumstances of providing protection. The system did not work this way because the gods were just, but because they were needy. The gods in the ancient world did not care about defending their character; they were concerned to preserve their prerogatives and their executive perquisites. When a god did not receive the cultic rites to which he was entitled, his status was threatened and his wrath and/or abandonment was predictable. Appeasement was a vital part of this system, and if Job had pursued appeasement, he would have showed himself a part of this system.

3. In the ancient Near Eastern exemplars, the sufferers stood ready to acknowledge offense if they could only be shown what it was. They claimed ignorance while Job claims innocence. This stance would be difficult to maintain in the ancient Near East, for the gods were the ones who decided where sacred spaces were and what rituals needed to be performed. People who lived in Mesopotamia never believed that their information on these issues was comprehensive. Job, in contrast, is confident in his innocence. He clearly uses different standards by which he makes his claims. Job never acknowledges any offense (unlike his Mesopotamian counterparts), and God does not offer forgiveness in the process of restoration.

4. We can identify a number of Mesopotamian pieces that belong to the declarative praise genre, a genre that likewise appears frequently in the biblical Psalms. This genre is characterized by a lament, a petition, a favorable response by God, and an ending of praise. This is far different from the book of Job, which includes no concluding praise of Yahweh. The Mesopotamian pieces seem designed to feature praise, while Job omits it entirely.

5. While the themes of justice (God's) and righteousness (Job's) are central to the book of Job, neither is present in the ancient Near Eastern exemplars. In the ancient world the gods were interested in justice being maintained in the human realm. Shamash, for example, was the god of justice, and kings were accountable to him to maintain justice in society. The gods desired an equitable society because a stable and prosperous community most effectively provided for their needs. It is more difficult to establish that the gods themselves were just or unjust. The gods did what they wished. They were not consistent or predictable. They were neither moral nor immoral.

Notice that the Mesopotamian pieces do not try to defend the justice of God (in the end, neither does the book of Job), nor do they question whether deity is just. The primary concern is the preservation of the parameters and rules of the

Great Symbiosis, not of justice. These pieces are all about the
relationship between piety and prosperity. The contrasts in
Job show it to be a work thoroughly immersed in the Israelite
theological system (see below).

6. Just as the gods were not necessarily just in the ancient world,
   neither were they necessarily responsible for evil or suffering.
   These elements were built into the fabric of the cosmos, but
   not by the gods or any other beings. Furthermore, demons
   or humans could be responsible for suffering or evil without
   necessarily involving the gods. In Israelite thinking God could
   not so easily be removed from the equation, though certainly
   humans could do evil.

7. The piety/prosperity matrix of the Great Symbiosis serves
   as the foundation of the Challenger's accusation against Job.
   If Job's response indicates that he is bound to this matrix,
   the Challenger has won his case. In other words, if Job is no
   different from all of the sufferers in the Mesopotamian literature,
   the Challenger has made his point. In this sense, while all of the
   Mesopotamian pieces end by affirming the traditional dogmas,
   in Job those very same traditional dogmas are voiced by the
   friends and persistently rejected by Job.

8. Job focuses on his own righteousness, not on the piety/
   prosperity matrix. While his Mesopotamian counterparts are not
   declared innocent at any point throughout the literature, Job is
   declared so from beginning to end. Unlike his Mesopotamian
   counterparts, Job never considers the option that he deserves
   what he is experiencing.

9. In the ancient Near East when one offended deity by some sort
   of ritual neglect or misstep, the deity might react by simply
   turning his back, leaving one vulnerable to demonic attack.
   In this way the deity was not the one actively bringing harm.
   These demons were not seen as doing the will of the deity;
   they were simply acting in character by attacking a vulnerable
   subject. The Challenger in Job, however, is not an independent
   agent opportunistically fulfilling its nature. Whatever he does,
   he does through the power of God; all the events of the book
   are understood as God's actions. Demons in their ancient
   Near Eastern role are absent from Old Testament theology,
   including Job.

10. Finally, it is evident that the philosophical and theological
    answers provided by the book of Job are far different from

those offered in the ancient Near Eastern exemplars. Job rejects the easy answers of Mesopotamia (divine inscrutability, inherent sinfulness of humanity, gods who make humanity crooked).[36]

For Job these premises are acceptable to a degree, but they are not the answers that the book offers. Mesopotamian literature concludes that pious people do sometimes suffer, but this suffering has nothing to do with divine injustice; it only means that one can never be fully comprehensive in one's ritual performance and therefore inadvertent offense is always possible. One can only increase one's piety and call out to the gods for mercy. Perhaps they will answer. Is there pious suffering? Yes. But it is no one's fault; it is just a possibility inherent in the very nature of the gods and the humans who blindly attempt to serve them in the Great Symbiosis. The texts from Mesopotamia consistently fail to affirm or defend the justice of deity. Instead they affirm pervasive and often ignorant offense by humans and the general inscrutability, or more likely, capriciousness of the gods.

> I wish I knew that these things were pleasing to one's god!
> What is proper to oneself is an offence to one's god;
> What in one's own heart seems despicable is proper to one's god.
> Who knows the will of the gods in heaven?
> Who understands the plans of the underworld gods?
> Where have mortals learnt the way of a god?[37]

The answer offered by the book of Job is different. Here the answer is that yes, sometimes righteous people suffer, but this fact should not be the basis for deducing that God is

---

36. Interestingly enough, a number of these views (or at least slight variations of them) have had currency in Christian theology as well. As early as Augustine one can find their expression in Christian forms; e.g., see his "Divine Providence and the Problem of Evil" (*De ordine*). Augustine would maintain that human suffering is not evil; rather, we just lack the proper perspective to understand it. Other views Augustine refutes. Inherent sinfulness is more common in discussions of atonement than as a reason for suffering, and inscrutability is more common in mysticism where it is not used for theodicy. The idea that God made humanity sinful is only in Christian contexts influenced heavily by Gnosticism. I am grateful to Jonathan Walton for this analysis.

37. *Ludlul bel nemeqi*, in *Babylonian Wisdom Literature* (ed. W. G. Lambert; Oxford: Oxford Univ. Press, 1960), 41.33–38.

unjust. Rather, it is a flawed philosophy to conclude that one's suffering or prosperity is directly related to one's behavior. The Great Symbiosis is not at the heart of human experience, but neither is the Retribution Principle. Instead, God's wisdom is at the heart of how the world operates and of what the resulting human experience is. In one sense this does suggest that God is inscrutable, but it is not capriciousness. Yahweh's inscrutability is a result of his infinite wisdom in contrast to our human limitations.

Ancient Near East as Foil

WITH SO MANY IMPORTANT differences, it is remarkable that some still speak of the book of Job as borrowing from the ancient Near Eastern exemplars. A more defensible model sees the ancient Near Eastern literature and mentality as a foil for the book of Job. Job's friends are the representatives of the ancient Near Eastern perspectives, and their views are soundly rejected. Nevertheless, we would have a poorer understanding of the book of Job if we did not look at it against its ancient Near Eastern backdrop. The world of the ancient Near East helps us to understand the way the book is framed and the issues it is dealing with. As we have become familiar with the literature of the ancient Near East, we have discovered the book of Job's conversation partners. Our understanding of Job is necessarily stilted if we have no awareness of the dialogue to which it contributes.

Distinctly Israelite Features in Job

IN CONCLUSION WE CAN summarize the distinctly Israelite features in Job:

- no symbiosis (God does not have needs, Job 22:3)
- interest in justice of God
- interest in righteousness as an abstract concept
- Job seems to have a sense of personal righteousness that goes beyond what the ancient world would have provided
- no ritual offenses considered or ritual remedies suggested or pursued
- no appeasement pursued
- worship of celestial deities considered an offense (Job 31:26–28), as it would not have been in the ancient Near East
- shape of RP different since God could not be absolved of role in bringing suffering

Theological Issues

Retribution Principle and Theodicy[38]

THE RETRIBUTION PRINCIPLE (RP) is the conviction that the righteous will prosper and the wicked will suffer, both in proportion to their respective righteousness and wickedness. In Israelite theology the principle was integral to the belief in God's justice. Since God is just, the Israelites believed it was incumbent on him to uphold the RP. Having a worldview in which God was absolutely just and compelled to maintain the RP, they developed the inevitable converse corollary, which affirmed that those who prospered must be righteous (i.e., favored by God) and those who suffered must be wicked (i.e., experiencing the judgment of God).

The RP was thus an attempt to understand, articulate, justify, and systematize the logic of God's interaction in the world. Because human experience often seemed to deny the tenets of the RP, the principle had to be qualified or nuanced in order to be employed realistically in the philosophical/theological discussion. How can God be just if he does not punish the wicked? In order to answer this question, the RP was frequently under discussion in Israelite theodicy (defense of God's justice in a world where suffering exists, which in modern terms extends into a philosophical discussion concerning the origin of evil), driven particularly by the context of ethical monotheism. The RP does not of necessity operate in the context of theodicy, but because of Israel's theological commitments this tendency is apparent in the Old Testament.

The literature of the ancient Near East continually demonstrates that people believed that the administration of justice in the human world was a concern and responsibility of the gods. The questions that swirl around the RP lose their philosophical urgency in the ancient world because injustice is often blamed on demons and humans rather than on the gods. In Mesopotamian thinking, evil was built into the fabric of the cosmos by means of the "cosmic laws,"[39] but even those were not established by the gods. Since evil existed outside of the jurisdiction of the gods, divine administration of justice did not necessarily eliminate suffering. Some misfortune came about simply because of how the world was.

In both Egyptian and Mesopotamian thinking, the gods were not considered responsible for evil in the world; therefore, the presence or

---

38. Much of this section is drawn from an article, "Retribution," that I did for the *Dictionary of the Old Testament: Wisdom, Prophets and Writings* (ed. T. Longman III and P. Enns; Downers Grove, Ill.: InterVarsity Press, 2008), 647–55.

39. For full discussion, see J. Walton, *Genesis 1 as Ancient Cosmology* (Winona Lake, Ind.: Eisenbrauns, 2011), 46–62.

experience of evil did not have to be resolved in reference to the justice of the gods (this in contrast to Israel, where nothing existed totally outside the jurisdiction of God's sovereignty; i.e., the rest of the gods were contingent, but he was not). In the Sumerian *Lament over the Destruction of Ur*, the city is destroyed not as an act of justice or injustice, but because it was time for kingship to be passed on. Likewise with regard to individuals, suffering can sometimes just be one's fate for the present. It is also clear that personal misfortune could result from offending the gods, even if that offense was committed innocently. In such cases, the gods were not unjust; they simply were not very forthcoming about communicating their expectations.

A sense and expectation of the RP at a basic level remains evident here, though the gods are relieved of responsibility because of the way their function in the cosmos is perceived. Even in the areas where the gods could be held responsible, they, like human judges, may be doing their best to administer justice, but do so imperfectly.

In this sense, though people of Mesopotamia might believe that the gods do indeed punish those who earn their wrath, this conviction cannot offer an explanation for all suffering. The notion that those who suffer must be wicked could not work because in the ancient Near Eastern worldview, much of the suffering that people experienced was not orchestrated by the gods. Suffering could be the result of the god's inattention, of simple circumstance, or of the nature of the world. Even if the gods abandoned a person because of some offense, they were not responsible for the ensuing evil; they simply did nothing to prevent it, having withdrawn their favor and protection.

Theodicy in its modern philosophical and existential guise concerns the origin and nature of suffering and evil. In theology proper (whether in mythology, in broad metaphysics, or in ethical monotheism), the philosophical question naturally focuses its attention on the divine role in suffering and the divine relationship to evil. The RP progresses from philosophy to pragmatism in trying to understand and formulate how deity acts in the world. To what extent can deity theoretically be considered responsible for the evil things that happen in this world? This question draws theodicy and the RP together in theological conundrum.

We have suggested above that the gods in the ancient Near East were somewhat relieved of responsibility because their role in the origin of evil was limited, and because they were often only indirectly considered the cause of suffering. This understanding of the role of deity, along with ambivalence regarding the god's inherent justice, nearly eliminates theodicy from the discussion. Though people continued to have deep concerns over a deity's actions in the world and therefore their interests in the

RP remained robust and vital, the RP could not be employed in theodicy. Given the above considerations, we would conclude that "theodicy" is a misnomer when applied to the ancient Near East. The origins of evil were impersonal and the gods were not just, nor did they take ethical responsibility for suffering.

In Israel the absence of any source of divine authority other than Yahweh limited the philosophical possibilities regarding the origin of evil and the source of suffering (1 Sam. 2:6; Isa. 45:7; Job 2:10; Eccl. 7:14). There existed no supernatural power alongside Yahweh or outside of Yahweh's sphere of power. At the same time Yahweh was considered powerful, good, and just. Thus one might say that the theodicy question bloomed in Israel, and in this hothouse of theological tension, the RP provided the traditional explanation, despite its obvious inconsistencies in accounting for human experience.

In considering the biblical position we need to recognize the tension between RP as *theodicy* and RP as *theology*. The affirmations of the RP in the text are intended to be *theological* in nature, and they serve well in that capacity. By this I mean they offer a picture of God's nature: He delights in bringing blessing to his faithful ones and takes seriously the need to punish the sinful. In contrast, the Israelites were inclined to try to wield that theology in service to *theodicy*, a role for which it was singularly unsuitable. That is, they wanted to apply it to their expectations and experiences in life, and in the process to understand God's justice and the reasons behind suffering. The role of the book of Job is to perform the radical surgery that separates theology from theodicy, contending that in the end Yahweh's justice must be accepted on faith rather than worked out philosophically. He does not need to be defended; he wants to be trusted. The entire constellation of God's attributes is at work in a complex coordinated manner. Justice is part of that constellation, but it does not trump all other attributes. Thus the RP cannot serve the purposes of theodicy.

In Israelite theology God is just and administers justice in the world. He employs the RP to disclose his character and to articulate the general parameters of his administration. This activity can be traced both on a *corporate* and *individual* level. Furthermore, the unique shape of the RP within Israelite thought is heavily influenced by two philosophical preconceptions: There is only one God, and there is no recognition of reward or punishment in the afterlife.

Corporate Level, Covenant Theme

ON A CORPORATE LEVEL this theology is expressed in the covenant blessings and curses. Consequently, it is also evident in the judgment oracles of the prophets, since they pronounce the doom that the Israelites have brought upon themselves by their covenant violations. The corporate aspects of the RP are worked out literarily by the Chronicler as he traces its effects through the history of the monarchy. On the corporate level, the RP provided for occasional tension (e.g., Psalm 44; Esther), but since it could be worked out over the long span of history, it carried less immediacy, urgency, or poignancy. Corporate RP in Israel is a covenant theme, and since covenant violation was rampant, the claim of innocence was difficult to maintain.

Individual Wisdom Theme

IN CONTRAST, THE RP on the individual level is a wisdom theme. This connection is laid out plainly in Psalm 1 and is confirmed repeatedly in the central role of the RP in wisdom literature. It is important to note, however, that the biblical text only offers affirmation of the main proposition ("the righteous prosper, the wicked suffer"), not of the deduced converse corollary ("the one who prospers is righteous; the one who suffers is wicked"). According to the principles of modern logic, the corollary could only be asserted if the main proposition is true universally and consistently. Nevertheless, the book of Job and the need for such a book imply that the Israelites did tend to extend their expectations to include the corollary. The tension of the book is created by the corollary as both Job and his friends conclude that his suffering can only be explained as punishment from God.

Connection to Monotheism and Afterlife

SINCE ISRAEL WAS TO believe in only one God who was responsible for every aspect of the cosmos, it was difficult to absolve him from responsibility for suffering. In order for him to be considered just, they believed that he must maintain the RP. If there were no opportunity for God to achieve final justice in the afterlife, then he was obliged to demonstrate his justice within the lifetime of the individual; note Psalm 27:13: "I am still confident of this: I will see the goodness of the LORD in the land of the living." These factors combined to pose the conundrum of the RP and human experience and led to RP's use for theodicy. It is in Israel, therefore, that we see the formulation of the inherent connection between the RP and theodicy, a formulation that becomes commonplace in the history of theological discourse.

Application to Job

THE BOOK OF JOB is all about God's policies and the role of the RP in those policies. Neither the RP nor Job is on trial, despite the fact that both he and his friends assume he is (though the book declares him righteous — from God's mouth — from the beginning). M. Tsevat has proposed that the tension in the book can be diagrammed by a triangle depicting the three elements to be defended by various proponents: God's justice, Job's righteousness, and the RP.[40] Given the situation that develops in the book, the proponents choose which element must be defended above all, and in the process must decide which of the three elements is expendable, for all three cannot be maintained simultaneously.

Job's three friends defend the RP and show themselves willing to deny Job's righteousness to support their defense. In the first round of speeches they focus on God's protection of the righteous (4:6–7; 5:18–27; 8:5–7). The destruction of the wicked is stated in brief principle (11:11) and alluded to as the problem of Job's sons (8:4). In the second round, the emphasis is entirely on the punishment that comes to the wicked (15:20–35; 18:5–21; 20:4–29), and this same theme is picked up from a different perspective in the third round (22:15–20). This is all defense of the RP, not defense of God or his justice, though Bildad gets the closest in his contention that God does not pervert justice (8:3). At occasional junctures other affirmations are made concerning God: He is more righteous than human beings (4:17), he exercises his power in the world to accomplish his will (5:8–16; confirmed by Job in 12:13–25), he effects the RP (8:20–22) as judge he sees and knows (22:12–14), and he establishes order in the cosmos (25:2).

As in the ancient Near Eastern literature, the friends fully believe in the RP but do not employ it for theodicy, though their view of God has more of an Israelite shape than an ancient Near Eastern one (specifically in that they do not treat God as having needs, nor do they see the solution in ritual terms). Nevertheless, they agree with the two basic tenets of ancient Near Eastern thinking regarding suffering: (1) they affirm human ignorance of what God demands and thus confirm innate human sinfulness (4:18–21; 22:5–9; 25:4–6); and (2) they likewise affirm the inscrutability of deity (11:7–9; 15:7–16).

Job chooses to defend his own righteousness, and since he sees no possibility of neutralizing the RP, he is left with suspicions about God. In Job's speeches we find an anti-theodicy (i.e., God is not just; e.g., 19:6; 24:12) as he refuses to defend God or make excuses for him. Indeed, this is what God reprimands Job for (40:8).

In contrast, Elihu distinguishes himself as the participant who actually offers a theodicy. His defense of God's justice falls under the category of "educative theodicy"—that is, suffering serves to bring potential problems to our attention so that they can be remedied. Elihu still believes in the RP and defends it, but it builds a case that suffering is not just God's response to past sin; it can also preempt future or potential sin. By choosing to defend

---

40. M. Tsevat, "The Meaning of the Book of Job," *HUCA* 37 (1966): 73–106.

God's corner of the triangle, he also calls Job's righteousness into question, but in a more nuanced way than the other friends. Elihu redefines the RP (preventive not remedial) and on the basis of that redefinition, he finds fault in Job's self-righteous response to suffering.

In God's speeches we find the true solution in a revised perspective on God's policies and practices, and in a revised vision of the RP. The triangle is too simplistic and reduces God's policies to a narrow system in which justice is the foundational attribute and the RP is law. God does not choose one of the three elements of the triangle to defend—rather, he discards the triangle model as artificial and inadequate.

The book thus offers a modified view of the RP that construes it in proverbial and theological terms. In other words, the RP is useful to describe what God is like and therefore serves as a basis for identifying general trends in human experience. However, the RP offers no guarantees. The book of Job in effect takes a contra-theodicy position (i.e., refuses to offer a theodicy) by defending God's wisdom rather than his justice. Though the book is not a theodicy, it is interested in the RP and its legitimacy. The RP is finally rejected as a foundation for divine activity in the human realm (i.e., as a theodicy), but it is reclaimed on the proverbial and anecdotal level as representing the character of deity (i.e., as a theology). God delights in bringing prosperity to the righteous, and he takes seriously the responsibility of punishing the wicked.

God's restoration of Job at the end of the book serves the important function of reemphasizing God's commitment to the RP properly understood as a theological principle. This principle cannot be employed to assess character—whether that of God (theodicy) or the individual. Thus the basic premise of the RP is retained (righteous prosper, wicked suffer), but since it does not represent a strict formula that always maintains, the corollary fails: One's wickedness cannot be inferred when one is suffering, nor can one's righteousness be inferred when one is prospering.

Israelite Theology versus Biblical Theology

DID THE ISRAELITES BELIEVE the RP and its converse? A sufficient number of texts imply that they knew it was not enforced moment by moment (e.g., Ps. 37:7, 25). That is, they realized that on certain occasions there might be a time lag before the books were balanced. With that caveat, they largely accepted the RP as true, and they were inclined to treat it as the main determining factor for God's activity. They also tended to accept the converse corollary as true and used it to shape their expectations and to formulate their theodicy.

In contrast to this Israelite theology, the biblical theology of the wisdom literature is more cautious and nuanced.[41] The text never affirms the converse corollary, so it cannot be framed as a biblical teaching. Furthermore, Proverbs couches the RP in proverbial language, Ecclesiastes casts suspicion on it, and the book of Job details its limitations. Thus wisdom literature rejects the RP as providing a theodicy, yet embraces it in its theology.

The contrast between the views of the character of Job and the teachings of Qoheleth in Ecclesiastes is instructive. We could imagine that Qoheleth would have much to say to Job had he joined the circle of Job's advisors. In fact, I often have had my students construct a conversation between Job and Qoheleth so as to draw out the issues. The following is one such dialogue.[42]

> Q: I see that in your despair you have buried yourself among the ashes. Trust me, Job, I will not ask you not to mourn in your tragedy, and neither will I claim that you are not righteous. But tell me, why do you heap sorrow on top of your sorrow?
>
> J: What do you mean? Can I give myself more sorrow than the hand of the Almighty has already poured on me?
>
> Q: Yes. For you grieve not only about your tragedy, but also because such tragedy has come to you. You wail not only because you have lost your sons, but because you have lost your dignity and status before men. Which do you consider more unfair?
>
> J: Both are unfair! I have lived a righteous life.
>
> Q: When has God promised to reward your righteousness? Or, more to the point: Is it the anticipation of reward that has given you meaning in life?
>
> J: I have no meaning in life because God has treated me as a wicked person. He has taken away everything in life that could have had meaning.
>
> Q: Ah ... so many are on a quest for meaning in life. I myself have pursued many different quests and found them all incapable of delivering self-fulfillment—meaningless vanity. Tell me, what is the nature of your quest? What held meaning in life before your tragedy? Was it your good wife?
>
> J: No.
>
> Q: Your camels and riches?

---

41. For understanding the distinction between Israelite theology (i.e., that which is evident in their practice as recorded in the Old Testament) and biblical theology (that which is taught as correct thinking in the Old Testament), note, for example, that Israelite theology was often syncretistic, while biblical theology seen in the prophets especially was monotheistic.

42. The framework and some of the wording was provided by Poul Guttesen, but I have added considerably to it to draw out more issues.

J: No

Q: Your children? Your health?

J: No, no, no—none of that!

Q: Then tell me, why do you grieve now? How can you say that your life has lost its meaning? What you have lost, though tragic, was not what you based your life on. What did you base your life on?

J: On God. But he has failed me.

Q: Certainly it is better for a man to base his life on God than on his hope for the benefits God can give. But in what way would you say that God has failed you?

J: Look at me—I've been made a fool! The God who promises to prosper the righteous and punish the wicked has raised his hand and lashed out at me. The God who I believed was just has failed me. That is why I am in despair.

Q: Do you think that God can be forced to act according to such expectations? Who has told you that God must punish all the wicked and withhold suffering from the righteous?

J: How can God be just if this is not so?

Q: I have never seen it like that. In my lifetime I have seen many righteous people oppressed under evil rulers.

J: Who is God then—a weakling who cannot oppose the wicked?

Q: No, he is the one who stands over all and in wisdom decrees how the world operates.

J: So, in this supposed wisdom, does your God not care about the righteous and wicked conduct of his creatures?

Q: On the contrary. It is in the character of God to prosper the righteous and punish the wicked. In the long run, I know that it will be well for those who fear God. But, Job, we are here on this earth, and we cannot see beyond the mountains that tower around us, nor do we know about tomorrow. There is a time for everything under the sun. So how can we know what is wisest? Since God is beyond all and sees all, might his wisdom sometimes look obscure to us?

J: How then shall we live?

Q: Take each day as it comes. When hardships come, endure them. When good things pass your way, seize them and enjoy them. And in all this continue to fear God and keep his commandments. You have looked for fulfillment in your own righteous standing before God, and now in your new quest you look for fulfillment in your vindication. Abandon the quest,

---

Job! There is nothing under the sun that brings the sense of self-fulfillment and meaning that you seem to think that you deserve. Forget thinking about what caused your tragedy—begin to think of what purpose it can serve. Your righteousness is your strength—live it out! Your desire for vindication and explanation is your weakness—leave it behind.

J: You are more tolerable to speak to than my other pitiful comforters, but your wisdom seems strange. How can God not work strictly according to the principle of retribution and still be counted just?

Q: We cannot have all the answers, Job; we don't even know all the questions. Though we may affirm that God is just, justice has not been built into the laws by which nature operates. We do not have enough information to critique God's justice. We must be content to accept his wisdom in our lives.

J: But I only wish I knew more of the wisdom of God, so I could affirm his justice!

Q: You have made much progress, Job. Until today you have been demanding your "rights"—that God appear and defend his justice; but "rights" too are vanity. Now you seek to learn more of his wisdom—a far more worthy goal, to which God is more likely to respond.

And in the distance they both could hear a rumble and see a disturbance on the horizon. They sat transfixed at the approach of the mighty whirlwind.

The RP continues to play a role in the theological discussion that persists into the New Testament. Jesus confronts it explicitly on two occasions. In John 9:1–3, the disciples pose the RP question when they ask why a man was born blind. Jesus' answer turns them away from the issue of theodicy (indicated by the question of cause) and toward an expanded theology: Suffering should not be evaluated in terms of its cause (actions in the past) but in terms of its purpose (God's ongoing plan). Thus his reply: "That the work of God might be displayed in his life." As in the book of Job, no explanation for suffering is forthcoming, possible, or necessary. More important is the need to trust God's wisdom and to seek out his purpose.

In Luke 13:1–5 the issue concerns whether those who had died in recent tragedies should be considered to have deserved their death. Again, Jesus turns the attention away from cause and even states that there is not a one-to-one correspondence between sin and punishment. As an alternative, Jesus tells his audience to view the incident as a warning. Consistent with John 9, he refuses to engage the question of cause and concentrates instead on purpose.

Paul weighs in on the RP question in Galatians 6:7: "A man reaps what he sows." Here he states the RP proverbially without neutralizing its theological impact. His statement can be interpreted this way based on the fact that his teaching regarding suffering in other passages does not embrace the converse corollary. In fact, the New Testament authors are more inclined to explain the suffering of the righteous as a participation in the sufferings of Christ and therefore a positive experience rather than a punishment of God.

Job and Open Theism

OPEN THEISM PROPOSES THAT the future is still unfolding and that God does not know what is going to happen since human choices have yet to unfold and have effect. Some outcomes remain undetermined (i.e., the future is open or unsettled in some details). God is still considered omniscient, but some things remain unknown because they have not yet happened. Scholars who argue for this theological perspective point to passages where God is "sorry" (Gen. 6:6–7), "changes his mind" (Jon. 3:10), or comes to "know something" (Gen. 22:12). Another example would include successful intercession by humans (e.g., Moses, Ex. 32).

Some assert that the scenario in Job supports open theism, in part to salvage God's reputation. It seems cruel for God to afflict Job if he already knew that Job would pass the test.[43] God's assent to the test proposed by the Challenger could only be justified if God did not know how it would turn out. This sort of thinking might have merit if it were true that God is testing Job's righteousness. As suggested above, however, I believe that God's policies are being tested rather than Job's righteousness, which is affirmed throughout. If it is correct that God's policies are being tested, then it does not matter whether God knows the outcome or not. The scenario must play out for God's policies to be vindicated.[44]

Another open theism question could be raised in connection with God's question to the Challenger concerning where he is coming from. As will be defended in the commentary in chapters 1 and 2, Yahweh's question simply opens the conversation by asking the Challenger, "What brings you here?" No occasion is therefore given in the book to suspect that the future remains open and unknown or that God's omniscience has such limitations.

---

43. Cf. comments to that regard in Magdalene, *On the Scales of Righteousness*, 118.

44. Furthermore, I am working under the premise that the book entails a thought experiment, in which case God's character cannot be deduced from his actions in this narrative context.

Outline of Job

I. Prologue (chs. 1–2)
II. Dialogues (chs. 3–27)
    A. Job's Opening Lament (ch. 3)
    B. Cycle 1: Consolation (chs. 4–14)
        1. Eliphaz (chs. 4–5)
        2. Job (chs. 6–7)
        3. Bildad (ch. 8)
        4. Job (chs. 9–10)
        5. Zophar (ch. 11)
        6. Job (chs. 12–14)
    C. Cycle 2: The Fate of the Wicked (chs. 15–21)
        1. Eliphaz (ch. 15)
        2. Job (chs. 16–17)
        3. Bildad (ch. 18)
        4. Job (ch. 19)
        5. Zophar (ch. 20)
        6. Job (ch. 21)
    D. Cycle 3: Specific Accusations (chs. 22–27)
        1. Eliphaz (ch. 22)
        2. Job (chs. 23–24)
        3. Bildad (ch. 25)
        4. Job (chs. 26–27)
III. Interlude: Wisdom Hymn (ch. 28)
IV. Discourses (29:1–42:6)
    A. Discourse 1: Job (chs. 29–31)
        1. Reminiscence (ch. 29)
        2. Affliction (ch. 30)
        3. Oath (ch. 31)
    B. Discourse 2: Elihu (chs. 32–37)
        1. Introduction and Theory (chs. 32–33)
        2. Verdict on Job (ch. 34)
        3. Offense of Job (ch. 35)
        4. Closing Statement of Summary (chs. 36–37)
    C. Discourse 3: God (chs. 38:1–40:2; 40:6–41:34)
        1. Speech 1 (chs. 38–39)
        2. Speech 2 (40:1–2; 40:6–41:34)
    D. Job's Closing Statements (40:3–5; 42:1–6)
V. Epilogue (42:7–17)

Basic Bibliography on the Book of Job

Commentaries

Alter, Robert. *The Wisdom Books*. New York: Norton, 2010.

Andersen, Francis I. *Job: An Introduction and Commentary*. Tyndale Old Testament Commentaries. Downers Grove, Ill.: InterVarsity Press, 1976.

Clines, David J. A. *Job 1–20*. Word Biblical Commentary. Vol. 17. Waco, Tex.: Word, 1989.

_____. *Job 21–37*. Word Biblical Commentary. Vol. 18A. Nashville: Nelson, 2006.

_____. *Job 38–42*. Word Biblical Commentary. Vol. 18B. Nashville: Nelson, 2011.

Dhorme, Édouard. *A Commentary on the Book of Job*. Translated by Harold Knight, with prefatory notes by H. H. Rowley and preface by Francis I. Anderson. Nashville: Nelson, 1984. Repr. London: T. Nelson, 1967. Translation of *Le livre de Job*. Paris: Victor Lecoffre, 1926.

Gordis, Robert. *The Book of Job: Commentary, New Translation and Special Studies*. Moreshet Series, Studies in Jewish History, Literature and Thought, vol. 2. New York: Jewish Theological Seminary of America, 1978.

Habel, Norman. *The Book of Job: A Commentary*. Old Testament Library. Philadelphia: Westminster, 1985.

Hartley, John E. *The Book of Job*. New International Commentary on the Old Testament. Grand Rapids: Eerdmans, 1988.

Janzen, J. Gerald. *Job*. Interpretation. Atlanta: John Knox, 1985.

Longman, Tremper, III. *Job*. Grand Rapids: Baker, 2012.

Pope, Marvin. *Job*. 3rd ed. Anchor Bible. New York: Doubleday, 1973.

Rowley, H. H. *Job*. New Century Bible. Greenwood, S.C.: Attic, 1976.

Smick, Elmer B., and Tremper Longman III (reviser). "Job." Pages 675–921 in *The Expositor's Bible Commentary*, rev. ed., vol. 4. Edited by Tremper Longman III. Grand Rapids: Zondervan, 2010.

Wilson, Gerald H. *Job*. New International Biblical Commentary: Old Testament Series 10. Peabody, Mass.: Hendrickson, 2007.

Other Books

Becton, Randy. *Does God Care When We Suffer and Will He Do Anything About It?* Grand Rapids: Baker, 1988.

Boyd, Gregory A. *Is God to Blame?* Downers Grove, Ill.: InterVarsity Press, 2003.

Brown, William P. "The Deformation of Character: Job 1–31"; "The Reformation of Character: Job 32–42." Pages 50–119 in *Character in Crisis: A Fresh Approach to the Wisdom Literature of the Old Testament*. Grand Rapids: Eerdmans, 1996.

Cheney, Michael. *Dust, Wind and Agony: Character, Speech and Genre in Job*. Coniectanea Biblica Old Testament Series 36. Lund: Almqvist & Wiksell, 1994.

Cornelius, Izak. "Job." Pages 246–315 in *The Zondervan Illustrated Bible Backgrounds Commentary: Old Testament*. Vol. 5. Edited by John H. Walton. Grand Rapids: Zondervan, 2009.

Fretheim, Terence E. *Creation Untamed*. Grand Rapids: Baker, 2010.

Fyall, Robert S. *Now My Eyes Have Seen You: Images of Creation and Evil in the Book of Job*. New Studies in Biblical Theology 12. Downers Grove, Ill.: InterVarsity Press, 2002.

Glatzer, Nahum N. *The Dimensions of Job: A Study and Selected Readings*. New York: Schocken, 1969.

Gordis, Robert. *The Book of God and Man: A Study of Job*. Chicago: University of Chicago Press, 1965; Phoenix ed. 1978.

Holbert, John C. *Preaching Job*. St. Louis: Chalice, 1999.

Janzen, J. Gerald. *At the Scent of Water: The Ground of Hope in the Book of Job*. Grand Rapids: Eerdmans, 2009.

Lo, Alison. *Job 28 as Rhetoric: An Analysis of Job 28 in the Context of Job 22–31*. Supplements to Vetus Testamentum 97. Leiden: Brill, 2003.

MacLeish, Archibald. *J.B.: A Play in Verse*. Boston: Houghton Mifflin, 1958.

Magdalene, F. Rachel. *On the Scales of Righteousness: Neo-Babylonian Trial Law and the Book of Job*. Brown Judaic Studies 348. Providence, R.I.: Brown Judaic Studies, 2007.

Newsom, Carol A. *The Book of Job: A Contest of Moral Imaginations*. New York: Oxford University Press, 2003.

Ticciati, Susannah. *Job and the Disruption of Identity*. London: T&T Clark/ Continuum, 2005.

Weiss, Meir. *The Story of Job's Beginning—Job 1–2: A Literary Analysis*. Jerusalem: Magnes, 1983.

Westermann, Claus. *The Structure of the Book of Job: A Form-Critical Analysis*. Translated by Charles A. Muenchow. Philadelphia: Fortress, 1981.

Whitney, K. William. *Two Strange Beasts: Leviathan and Behemoth in Second Temple and Early Rabbinic Judaism*. Harvard Semitic Monographs 63. Winona Lake, Ind.: Eisenbrauns, 2006.

Yancey, Philip. *Disappointment with God: Three Questions No One Asks Aloud*. Grand Rapids: Zondervan, 1988.

———. *Where Is God When It Hurts?* Grand Rapids: Zondervan, 1977.

Zerafa, Peter Paul. *The Wisdom of God in the Book of Job*. Studia Universitatis S. Thomae in Urbe 8. Rome: Herder, 1978.

Zuck, Roy B., ed. *Sitting with Job: Selected Studies on the Book of Job*. Grand Rapids: Baker, 1992.

Articles

Albertson, R. G. "Job and Ancient Near Eastern Wisdom Literature." Pages 213–30 in *Scripture in Context II*. Ed. W. W. Hallo, J. C. Moyer, and L. G. Perdue. Winona Lake, Ind.: Eisenbrauns, 1983,

Bricker, Daniel P. "Innocent Suffering in Mesopotamia." *Tyndale Bulletin* (2001): 121–42.

Dick, M. B. "The Neo-Assyrian Royal Lion Hunt and Yahweh's Answer to Job." *Journal of Biblical Literature* 125 (2006): 243–70.

Diewert, David A. "Job 7:12: *Yam, Tannin* and the Surveillance of Job." *Journal of Biblical Literature* 106 (1987): 203–15.

Gray, John. "The Book of Job in the Context of Near Eastern Literature." *Zeitschrift für die alttestamentliche Wissenschaft* 82 (1970): 251–69.

Handy, Lowell K. "The Authorization of Divine Power and the Guilt of God in the Book of Job: Useful Ugaritic Parallels." *Journal for the Study of the Old Testament* 60 (1993): 107–18.

Hoffman, Yair. "Ancient Near Eastern Literary Conventions and the Restoration of the Book of Job." *Zeitschrift für die alttestamentliche Wissenschaft* 103 (1991): 399–411.

Irvin, William A. "Job's Redeemer." *Journal of Biblical Literature* 81 (1962): 217–19.

Janzen, J. Gerald. "Another Look at God's Watch Over Job (7:12)." *Journal of Biblical Literature* 108 (1989): 109–16.

Mattingly, Gerald L. "The Pious Sufferer: Mesopotamia's Traditional Theodicy and Job's Counselors." Pages 305–48 in *The Bible in the Light of Cuneiform Literature: Scripture in Context III*. Eds. W. W. Hallo, B. W. Jones, and G. L. Mattingly (Lewiston, N.Y.: Mellen, 1990): 305–48.

Neville, Richard W. "A Reassessment of the Radical Nature of Job's Ethic in Job XXXI 13–15." *Vetus Testamentum* 50 (2003): 181–200.

Shields, Martin A. "Malevolent or Mysterious: God's Character in the Prologue of Job." *Tyndale Bulletin* 61 (2010): 255–70.

Tsevat, Matitiahu. "The Meaning of the Book of Job." Pages 1–37 in *The Meaning of the Book of Job and Other Biblical Studies*. New York: KTAV, 1980.

Von Rad, Gerhard. "Job xxxviii and Ancient Egyptian Wisdom." Pages 281–91 in *The Problem of the Hexateuch*. London: SCM, 1966.

Job 1

In the land of Uz there lived a man whose name was Job. This man was blameless and upright; he feared God and shunned evil. ²He had seven sons and three daughters, ³and he owned seven thousand sheep, three thousand camels, five hundred yoke of oxen and five hundred donkeys, and had a large number of servants. He was the greatest man among all the people of the East.

⁴His sons used to take turns holding feasts in their homes, and they would invite their three sisters to eat and drink with them. ⁵When a period of feasting had run its course, Job would send and have them purified. Early in the morning he would sacrifice a burnt offering for each of them, thinking, "Perhaps my children have sinned and cursed God in their hearts." This was Job's regular custom.

⁶One day the angels came to present themselves before the LORD, and Satan also came with them. ⁷The LORD said to Satan, "Where have you come from?"

Satan answered the LORD, "From roaming through the earth and going back and forth in it."

⁸Then the LORD said to Satan, "Have you considered my servant Job? There is no one on earth like him; he is blameless and upright, a man who fears God and shuns evil."

⁹"Does Job fear God for nothing?" Satan replied. ¹⁰"Have you not put a hedge around him and his household and everything he has? You have blessed the work of his hands, so that his flocks and herds are spread throughout the land. ¹¹But stretch out your hand and strike everything he has, and he will surely curse you to your face."

¹²The LORD said to Satan, "Very well, then, everything he has is in your hands, but on the man himself do not lay a finger."

Then Satan went out from the presence of the LORD.

¹³One day when Job's sons and daughters were feasting and drinking wine at the oldest brother's house, ¹⁴a messenger came to Job and said, "The oxen were plowing and the donkeys were grazing nearby, ¹⁵and the Sabeans attacked and carried them off. They put the servants to the sword, and I am the only one who has escaped to tell you!"

[16]While he was still speaking, another messenger came and said, "The fire of God fell from the sky and burned up the sheep and the servants, and I am the only one who has escaped to tell you!"

[17]While he was still speaking, another messenger came and said, "The Chaldeans formed three raiding parties and swept down on your camels and carried them off. They put the servants to the sword, and I am the only one who has escaped to tell you!"

[18]While he was still speaking, yet another messenger came and said, "Your sons and daughters were feasting and drinking wine at the oldest brother's house, [19]when suddenly a mighty wind swept in from the desert and struck the four corners of the house. It collapsed on them and they are dead, and I am the only one who has escaped to tell you!"

[20]At this, Job got up and tore his robe and shaved his head. Then he fell to the ground in worship [21]and said:

"Naked I came from my mother's womb,
     and naked I will depart.
The LORD gave and the LORD has taken away;
     may the name of the LORD be praised."

[22]In all this, Job did not sin by charging God with wrongdoing.

Job's Profile (1:1–5)

Uz. JOB'S HOMELAND HAS yet to be positively identified. Weiss points out that Uz is a region, not a city, and that "the East" is associated with the Syrian Desert stretching from Mesopotamia to Arabia.[1] In biblical genealogies, Uz is sometimes connected with Aram (Gen. 10:23; 22:21; 1 Chron. 1:17)[2] and at other times with Edom (Gen. 36:21, 28; 1 Chron. 1:42; Lam. 4:21; probably Jer. 25:20). Edom has been preferred over Aram,

---

1. Weiss, *Job's Beginning*, 23.
2. For the case for the area of Bashan and Hauran, see J. C. de Moor, "Ugarit and the Origin of Job," in *Ugarit and the Bible*, ed. G. J. Brooke, A. H. W. Curtis and J. F. Healey (Münster: Ugarit-Verlag, 1994), 242–45. He also offers his evidence for an association between Job and Ayyabu of Ashtartu known from the Amarna texts.

based on Edom's reputation for wisdom and Eliphaz the Temanite's origin from the area of Edom. In an appendix to the book of Job, the LXX locates Edom between Idumea and Arabia; thus, the earliest analysis situates it in the south.[3]

Regardless of its location, this detail is significant because it indicates that Job is not an Israelite. His non-Israelite status explains the absence of many key theological elements in the book, including law, covenant, temple, and references to Yahweh.[4] Intriguingly, however, the book frequently evidences an Israelite perspective,[5] which suggests that the story of the non-Israelite Job has actually been given its literary shape by an Israelite author for an Israelite audience. This secondary context gives the book a voice in the context of Israelite ideas about God and his expectations.[6]

Job's qualities. Weiss suggests that "blameless" (*tam*) refers to Job's character and "upright" (*yašar*) to his actions.[7] When we look at the use of the terminology elsewhere in the book of Job, we find that the opposites of *tam* are "proclaimed guilty" (ʿ*qš*, 9:20) and "wicked" (*rašaʿ*, 9:22). This verbal stem of ʿ*qš* occurs only four other times (Prov. 10:9; 28:18, both in contrast to *tam*; Isa. 59:8; Mic. 3:9, both in contrast to "justice," *mišpaṭ*) and specifically refers to something twisted or perverse. The noun *rašaʿ* is, in contrast, common (26x in Job), and refers generally to the wicked. The word *tam* denotes integrity and the resulting absence of blame or guilt. *Tam* is an appropriate description for people characterized by integrity when measured by general human standards. Note, for example, Abimelech, who asserts that he took Sarah in integrity of heart (NIV: "with a clear conscience" Gen. 20:5), and that God confirmed this assessment (20:6).

Second, Job is identified as "upright" (*yašar*), a term commonly used to describe people who behave according to God's expectations — specifically, kings faithful to Yahweh (e.g., Joash, 2 Chron. 24:2). An upright person gains God's favor (Deut. 6:18). God himself is upright (Deut. 32:4), and he made humankind upright (Eccl. 7:29), but people have gone in search of schemes. The Israelites each did what was (up)right in their own eyes (Judg. 17:6; 21:25) because they had no king and they were departing from faithfulness to God.

---

3. See É. Dhorme, *A Commentary on the Book of Job* (Nashville: Nelson, 1984), xxiii.

4. "Yahweh" is used consistently in the prologue (last occurrence in 2:7) and in the speeches of Yahweh at the end of the book (38:1; 40:1, 3, 6; 42:1, 7, 9–12). Other than these occurrences it is used only once (12:9), and on that verse some manuscripts have *ʾeloah* in its place. See there for further discussion.

5. See listing in the Introduction, 38.

6. See Introduction, 33–38.

7. Weiss, *Job's Beginning*, 25

Tam and *yašar* are desirable accolades, but they are achievable for humans who seek steadfastly to order their ways according to customary conceptions of godliness. But these terms do not describe people who live lives of sinless perfection; rather, they describe those who have found favor in the eyes of God and other humans (cf. Prov. 3:4).

Job is also described as one who "fears God" (*'elohim*). As we would expect in Job, the author does not identify him as one who "fears Yahweh" specifically. We can again turn to the description of the non-Israelite Abimelech and his people and the premature assessment made of them by Abraham (Gen 20:11).[8] In common Old Testament usage, to fear the Lord/God is to take God seriously. That can mean different things depending on what one knows of God. For the sailors in Jonah, fearing the Lord entailed a different response than the Israelites, who "feared the LORD" in response to the covenant. In a non-Israelite context, fearing God could refer to being ritually or ethically conscientious, and the context of Job requires nothing more than this definition. In sum, Job is a paragon of devotion and integrity.

Job's possessions and status. In verses 2 and 3 Job's prosperity is described in terms of his family and his possessions. The numbers all give indication of representing idealizations or stereotypes, but this is no evidence that they are contrived. Truth is stranger than fiction. Nevertheless, as suggested in the introduction, the book as wisdom literature would be expected to be the result of literary shaping. Everything about Job is ideal, which has the purpose of portraying him as the ultimate example of a person who is beyond reproach and who has achieved success by the highest standards.

Job's piety. A number of questions emerge from the short vignette in verses 4–6. One might first question why these feasts are the setting for the potential offense of cursing God. Note that these are not cultic feasts because the word used here usually denotes special celebratory occasions; other terminology designates a cultic feast. From a literary standpoint these feasts have significance because they provide the setting in which Job's sons and daughters eventually meet their demise (1:18–19).

This group setting might seem unnecessary at first glance since Job expresses his concern that they may have cursed God "in their hearts." Although this phrase often refers to the private thoughts of an individual, when a group of people are part of the scene, it can refer to corporate thinking shared confidentially (cf. Deut. 8:17; 18:21; Ps. 78:18). Tangentially, since just such a feast was taking place when Job's family was destroyed, one might ask whether their behavior at the feast may have

---

8. For another comparable use, see Gen. 42:18, where Joseph is pretending to be non-Israelite.

somehow brought this judgment on them (note that Bildad suggests exactly that in 8:4). In such a case, the death of his family could be interpreted by observers not as action against Job, but as action against his children. But the information here about Job's scrupulous purifying rituals argue against that suggestion.

Second, why does Job even imagine that his family might curse God in their private conversations at these feasts? Again, a first glance can be misleading. It would appear that this is an extreme offense that would be unlikely of this pious family, where we might expect an illustration that shows more subtlety. But that initial impression evaporates under scrutiny.

Strange as it may seem, the word translated "cursed" is the normal Hebrew word for "bless" (*barak*). The general consensus among interpreters is that the use of the opposite word is euphemistic so that the uncomfortable concept of cursing God is circumnavigated.[9] This unusual interplay between cursing and blessing becomes significant in the early sections of this book. In 1:11 (also 2:5) the Challenger suggests that Job will "bless" (= "curse") God to his face (in contrast to the fears Job had that his children might bless/curse God in their hearts). Instead, Job truly does "bless" God (1:21, same verb). Job's wife urges him to "bless" (= "curse") God blatantly and die (2:9). Job does not respond with blessing God after the second round, but neither does he curse God. Instead, he curses the day of his birth.[10]

Beyond this specific use of the terms in establishing a literary motif, we must also consider the underlying narrative framework. In the narrative God has blessed Job with children and possessions (1:10). But on the larger scale one could also say that God has orally blessed Job by praising him to the Challenger (sometimes blessing is accomplished by praise). As it turns out, the very nature of that oral blessing becomes a curse as it is made the basis for the challenge that leads to the loss of the material blessing. Eventually God restores and multiplies the material blessing (42:12). So the curse/bless antithesis stands as a significant motif in the book. Yet as important as this motif is, it fails to answer the question that we are pursuing.

The next level of investigation concerns what sort of statement would constitute "cursing God." In the Old Testament the matter of cursing (*qll*)

---

9. For euphemistic use outside of Job, see 1 Kings 21:10, 13; Ps. 10:3. The case against this euphemistic understanding is made by T. Linafelt, "The Undecidability of *barak* in the Prologue to Job and Beyond," *BibInt* 4 (1996): 154–72. See also Cheney, *Dust, Wind and Agony*, 58–77.

10. Here no euphemism need be used. A common verb for cursing, *qll*, is used. This verb usually has people as the grammatical subject and refers to the invocation of words of power against someone or something (cf. Ex. 22:28). When God is the object of the verb, it is often translated as "blaspheme" (cf. Lev. 24:11).

God is discussed explicitly in Leviticus 24:10–16 (see also the passing reference in Ex. 22:28 [27] and Isa. 8:21).[11] The offense is extreme (it carries the death penalty) and could be committed in a wide variety of ways. Cursing God could involve using God's name in a frivolous oath,[12] using God's name along with illicit words of power (e.g., hex),[13] using words of power against God, or speaking in a denigrating, contemptuous, or slanderous way about God—basically insulting God.[14] The last is the most likely in this context as most befitting the situation. We can identify some examples of this offense by moving beyond the actual occurrence of the term "curse" to exploring some of the offensive words people speak against God "in their hearts" in other passages:

- taking credit for what God has done (cf. Deut. 8:17)
- misjudging God's motives (Deut. 9:4)
- thinking that God will not act (Deut. 29:19 [18]; Isa. 47:8; Zeph. 1:12)
- expressing one's ambitions against God (Isa. 14:13)
- expressing one's arrogance (Isa. 47:10)
- stating that there is no God (Pss. 14:1; 53:1)

These examples all hold God in contempt by stating implicitly or explicitly that he is powerless to act, that God is corrupt in his actions or motives, that God has needs, or that God can be manipulated. These sorts of claims would constitute cursing God as they make God to be less than God. We thus discover that "cursing God" may not be as blatant and obvious an offense as first thought.

The way Job might curse God in response to his suffering would be to show contempt for God by suggesting that God is corrupt, irrational, or capricious. But it is unlikely that this is how his sons and daughters might curse God. They might be more inclined in their revelry to think that their

---

11. See lengthy discussion in J. Milgrom, *Leviticus 23–27* (AB; New York: Doubleday, 2001), 2107–9.

12. This is indirect since it involves cursing by God's name rather than directing a curse specifically at God. It would be included in ways that the Lord's name could be taken in vain. It can be included in the general practice of cursing God in that it fails to treat God with sufficient respect.

13. In the Old Testament enemies can be cursed in the name of Yahweh (see Josh. 6:26; 2 Kings 2:24).

14. "Curse" is therefore seen as failing to give honor (*kbd*), as when Shimei curses/insults David as he flees from Jerusalem (2 Sam. 16:5–13); see S. Tishchenko, "To Curse God? Some Remarks on Jacob Milgrom's Interpretation of Lev. 24:10–16, 23," in *Babel und Bibel* 3 (2006): 543–50, following suggestions put forth by H. C. Brichto, *The Problem of "Curse" in the Hebrew Bible* (SBLMS 16; Missoula, Mont.: Scholar's, 1963).

success has been achieved by their own hand and so fail to give God credit for the blessings they enjoy. Other possibilities exist, and we need not try to resolve this question, but it is important to realize the range of statements that could conceivably be considered "cursing God."

Nothing in the general wording here would indicate specifically either an Israelite or ancient Near Eastern way of thinking. Blasphemy is a recognized offense in either cultural setting. "Sins of the tongue" in Akkadian texts included making frivolous oaths and blasphemy (Akkad. *šillatu*).[15] The same verb could also be used of slander, insult, and insolence—in short, a wide variety of offensive speech.[16] It was considered a serious offense and sometimes identified as a possible cause of illness in medical diagnostic texts.[17]

With this information about the feast setting and the broad scope of what could entail "cursing God," we are finally in a position to ask and address the most important third question: Why does the author choose this sort of example to illustrate Job's piety? It is true that it offers a literary connection both to the death of his family (at such a feast) and to the option held out to Job to curse God. Perhaps that is sufficient reason, but it remains intriguing that the example of Job's blamelessness is not chosen from some of the areas that we might expect: e.g., how he used his wealth, how he protected the vulnerable classes, how he treated with respect those under his authority, or how he maintained ethical propriety. The text does not indicate that he loved God with all his heart, soul, mind, and strength. The example that the book gives is ritual in nature. Perhaps the intention is merely to indicate that among all of his other qualities, Job did not neglect ritual observance. But if that were the case, we would expect an illustration that focused on a minor point of ritual concerning a gray area of expectation. At first sight, "cursing God" seems the most blatant of acts, but as we have seen in the above study, a wide variety of statements could be so construed.

Could someone be accused of "cursing God" when they had no such intention at all? How sensitive will God be about categorizing what someone has said as "cursing God"? When we interact with someone whom we know to be sensitive, we will be careful about what we say. This is especially so if that person has some authority or power over us. We use the expression "walking on eggshells" to express how we seek to avoid offense with such people—perhaps a boss who is insecure. The

---

15. S. Paul, "Daniel 3:29—A Case of 'Neglected' Blasphemy," *JNES* 42 (1983): 291–94; reprinted in *Divrei Shalom* (Leiden: Brill, 2005), 133–38. See entry in *CAD* Š/2, 445–47.

16. K. van der Toorn, *Sin and Sanction in Israel and Mesopotamia* (Assen: Van Gorcum, 1985), 24–25.

17. Ibid.

question this example of Job's ritual fastidiousness raises is, "What does it say about Job's concept of God?" The example is not used to show what Job thought about his children; it is brought out to pose a question concerning what he thought about God. Job's repeated rituals do not suggest that he considered his children to be closet apostates hurling drunken insults heavenward. Instead, he considered that anytime such revelry occurred, the possibility existed that unguarded statements could be made that deity would take offense at despite the innocent intentions of the speaker.

In the ancient world outside of Israel the gods were considered to be unrealistic and almost childish in taking offense. For example, a Neo-Assyrian prayer expresses an individual's confusion over all that is going wrong in the author's life.[18] He begins listing all the unintentional ways that he might have offended some deity or other: Did he accidentally step on sacred space of some known or unknown god? Or did he perhaps eat some food forbidden by a known or unknown god? Is Job perhaps thinking of God in these terms?

In the ancient world, religious duty was more concerned with ritual than with ethics. In this view one could not really know what would please the gods, so people gave them gifts to keep them happy. This appeasement mentality carried with it the idea that deity was inclined toward irrational behavior. The gods had needs, and one tried to keep the gods content by meeting those needs (ritually).[19] Ethical behavior was not neglected, but it was not among the primary religious responsibilities. This question is important here because the chosen example clouds the issue of whether Job's behavior demonstrates an appeasement mentality toward an overly sensitive deity. In this way of thinking, God might suddenly get upset about someone committing some ritual offense in ignorance. The gods were often suspected of taking offense where none was intended. When Job begins to suffer, we see that he does consider that his troubles might be due to an overly attentive deity (7:17–21).

We can see, then, that the description of Job leaves no doubt that he is righteous. But the chosen example does not clarify his motives for being righteous and leaves unresolved what his picture of God is. Once we see the issue in this light, we can see how these two verses lead directly to the challenge posed by the Challenger, which was precisely on that point. If Job is engaged in the appeasement mentality of the Great Symbiosis, then it would be legitimate to question whether "Job serves God for nothing." If sacrilege can be inadvertent and if ritual is a shot in the dark in trying

---

18. Prayer to Every God, *ANET*, 391–92.
19. In the introduction we called this the "Great Symbiosis."

---

to appease any inadvertent word that deity may have taken offense at, deity has no integrity and the Great Symbiosis is the result. No motivation remains for righteousness except to reap benefits from a patronized god.

It is Job's fastidious ritual conduct that gives the opportunity for the question to be raised by the Challenger. We will find as we continue our analysis of this book that the Challenger's question has indeed identified a fundamental issue. It is not just *how* we act that is important; it is *why* we act that way. And our motives can only be sorted out in relationship to our concept of God and what we believe drives his policies on earth. The stage is set for the Challenger to raise the issue of Job's motives and through them to raise questions about God's policies.

First Conversation (1:6–12)

SONS OF GOD. THIS phrase (*bene 'elohim*) does not occur often in Scripture (Gen. 6:2, 4; Job 1:6; 2:1; 38:7),[20] but our understanding can be augmented by usage outside of the Old Testament (mostly the Ugaritic texts).[21] The designation relates to the idea of a divine council, where "the sons of God" are the functionaries who make up the council. This divine council meets to give reports and make decisions; it is where the business of heaven is done. In the ancient Near Eastern polytheistic cultures, this council was populated by the chief gods. Divine authority was distributed among these gods, and each had their area of jurisdiction.

In Old Testament monotheism this concept is revised but not eliminated. It is true that in biblical theology Yahweh needs no advice or consultants (Isa. 40:13–14), but it is his prerogative to discuss his plans with others as he wills and to delegate responsibility at his discretion. It is common today for the use of the divine plurals in Genesis 1:26; 3:22; and 11:7 to be explained as indicating involvement of the council.[22] Isaiah 6:8 also presents a view of the divine council in session. The most obvious passage portraying the divine council at work is 1 Kings 22. In these contexts, the council is not populated by other gods, but by the next lower tier of heavenly functionaries. We ought not call them "angels" because angels have a messenger function, not an administrative function. These administrative functionaries possess no independent divine authority, but they

---

20. These are the only occurrences of *bene 'elohim*. Comparable phrases include *bene 'elim* (Pss. 29:1; 89:7) and *bene 'elyon* (Ps. 89:7).

21. E. T. Mullen Jr., *The Divine Council in Canaanite and Early Hebrew Literature* (HMS 24; Missoula, Mont.: Scholars, 1980); L. Handy, *Among the Host of Heaven* (Winona Lake, Ind.: Eisenbrauns, 1994).

22. See discussion in J. Walton, *Genesis* (NIVAC; Grand Rapids: Zondervan, 2001), 128–30.

have delegated roles in the administration of Yahweh's authority.[23] In Psalm 82 the assembly is where God presides, and it is made up of *'elohim* (Ps. 82:1), but the psalmist makes clear that these *'elohim* are the "sons of the Most High" (*bene 'elyon*, 82:6). Other responsibilities of these sons of God apparently include representing the nations (Deut. 32:8).[24]

On the basis of this biblical and ancient Near Eastern background, we can conclude that Job 1 features a gathering of the divine council as the sons of God come together to give their reports and to do the work of heaven. Whether the conversation that follows with the Challenger takes place in session or not is of little concern, but the language suggests that he has come to give a report when Yahweh is holding open court. The thrust of the question is "What brings you here"? (2:2).[25]

The Challenger (*haśśaṭan*).[26] Because the Challenger comes among the sons of God, there has been some discussion as to whether he comes as a full-fledged member or as an interlocutor crashing the meeting.[27] The former would be supported by the casual way in which Yahweh engages him in conversation, asking from where he has come; God's question is an invitation to report, which suggests the Challenger has come to give just such a report. The verb that communicates the reason for his presence is also applied to the sons of God ("present themselves," Heb. *hityaṣṣeb*), which suggests that he is there in an official capacity, as courtier. We need

---

23. This can be derived from the first commandment, which indicates that there are no other gods in the presence of Yahweh. Divine authority is not distributed but delegated. See J. H. Walton, "Interpreting the Bible as an Ancient Near Eastern Document," in *Israel: Ancient Kingdom or Late Invention?* ed. D. I. Block (Nashville: Broadman & Holman, 2008), 298–327, specifically 305–8.

24. The Masoretic text indicates the division is according to the number of the "sons of Israel," but the more defensible variant says that it is according to the number of the "sons of God." See lengthy discussion in M. S. Heiser, "Deuteronomy 32:8 and the Sons of God," *BSac* 158 (2001): 52–74; M. S. Heiser, "Monotheism, Polytheism, Monolatry, or Henotheism? Toward an Assessment of Divine Plurality in the Hebrew Bible," *BBR* 18 (2008): 1–30.

25. *'e-mizzeh + bo'* inquires concerning motive or purpose. See Gen. 16:8; 2 Sam. 1:3; and discussion in Job 2 (p. 100).

26. Much information used in this section is abridged from J. Walton, "Satan," in *Dictionary of the Old Testament: Wisdom, Prophets and Writings* (ed. T. Longman III and P. Enns; Downers Grove, Ill.: InterVarsity Press, 2008), 714–17. Key sources for lengthy discussion include: Day, *Adversary*; N. Forsyth, *The Old Enemy* (Princeton, N.J.: Princeton Univ. Press, 1987); J. B. Russell, *The Devil* (Ithaca, N.Y.: Cornell Univ. Press, 1977); S. H. T. Page, *Powers of Evil* (Grand Rapids: Baker, 1995).

27. J. Hartley, *The Book of Job* (NICOT; Grand Rapids: Eerdmans, 1988), 72; D. J. A. Clines, *Job 1–20* (WBC 17; Dallas: Word, 1989), 18–19; Mullen, *Divine Council*, 190–244; Weiss, *Job's Beginning*, 31–33; Page, *Powers*, 25–26.

---

not infer from Yahweh's question that he is ignorant of what the Challenger's activities have been; it is simply a prompt to report.

So what can be said about this Challenger? The Hebrew word *satan* has traditionally been transliterated with capitalization as the proper name "Satan"; most translations follow tradition. This decision, in turn, leads casual readers to associate this Challenger with the devil, named as Satan in the New Testament. This conclusion is not necessarily valid and must be investigated closely.

The most important initial observation is that every time this word occurs in Job, it is preceded by the definite article (*hassatan*). This is strong evidence that *satan* is not a personal name, because Hebrew does not put a definite article in front of personal names. We might alternatively understand the word to indicate the office or function of the individual so designated. Therefore, we must conclude that the individual in Job 1–2 (and Zech. 3:1–2, where the article is also used) should be identified as "the Challenger" (description of function) rather than as "Satan" (proper name).[28] P. L. Day has demonstrated that the clear shift to using Satan as a proper name does not occur until the second century BC.[29]

Consequently, we must next consider what this designation conveys about the role of the Challenger. In the Old Testament, the word is used both as a verb and a noun. As a verb, it means generally "to oppose as an adversary" or "to accuse."[30] As a noun, it can be applied to a human being, thus designating him a challenger.[31] Finally, in the category of most interest to this study, the noun is applied to celestial beings.[32] This should lead us to revisit an assumption that is often carried blindly into the Old Testament, namely, that the technical term always applies to the same supernatural being, a single *satan*. Such an assumption is easily refuted by the fact that Numbers 22:22 and 32 refer to the angel of the Lord serving as a *satan*. So unless we posit that the Challenger in Job is the angel of the Lord, we must conclude that a variety of beings can serve this function. This means

---

28. The only case in the Old Testament where the word occurs without the definite article is 1 Chron. 21:1. For a discussion of whether there it should be read as a proper name or an indefinite Challenger, see S. Japhet, *1 & 2 Chronicles* (OTL; Louisville: Westminster John Knox, 1993), 374–75.

29. Day, *Adversary*, 128–29. She points to *Jub.* 23.29 and *As. Mos.* 10.1, both of which can be dated to the persecutions of Antiochus IV (ca. 168 BC). Tobit uses the name Asmodeus (Tob 3:8, 17) and in *1 Enoch* 6–11, the leader of the rebel angels is Shemihazah (later Asael).

30. Pss. 38:20; 71:13; 109:4, 20, 29; Zech. 3:1.

31. 1 Sam. 29:4; 2 Sam. 19:23; 1 Kings 5:4; 11:14, 23, 25; Ps 109:6.

32. Job 1–2 (14x); Zech. 3:1–2 (3x); also Num. 22:22, 32; 1 Chron. 21:1.

that the appearance of an individual with this function does not give us a specific identification of the individual.[33]

Job 1:6 would lead us to understand that a certain divine being whose precise identity is unimportant and who has the current and perhaps temporary status of Challenger is being introduced into the narrative. This interpretation is preferable because it is consistent with known Israelite (and Mesopotamian) legal practice, in that "Challenger" was a legal status that various people temporarily acquired in the appropriate circumstances, as opposed to a post or office.[34]

I conclude from the above description of this function that *śaṭan* refers to one who challenges. He might challenge someone by accusing them of a perceived wrongdoing. Alternatively, he might challenge as an adversary in court, in politics, or on the field of battle; he could challenge someone's status or someone's policies. Such a challenge could be made legitimately or presumptuously, with positive or negative intent, and it could be designed to preserve a system through accountability or to destabilize a kingdom.

Consequently, not only must we identify *śaṭan* here as a functional designation, we must now consider the possibility that, as a function, it is not intrinsically evil.[35] If we had no name for this individual (which, of course, we do not) and had to build his profile from the text of Job alone, what conclusions could we draw? It should be noted that the Challenger does not initiate the discussion about Job; he merely offers an alternative explanation of Job's righteous behavior. Though interpreters commonly portray the Challenger as one who seeks out human failings,[36] God's policies are the true focus of the challenge.[37] Job's character is only the test case. In this case, the Challenger serves as a "watchdog agency," meant to raise questions of accountability. The challenges issued are intended to promote the general good by putting potentially questionable policies and decisions under scrutiny.

The Challenger, therefore, does not necessarily imply some flaw in God or in Job. Some infer that the Challenger relishes the opportunity to strike

---

33. It is therefore possible that the individual designated as the Challenger in Job is not the same individual who plays that role in Zechariah or Chronicles. Though they may be the same individual, we cannot simply assume that they must be, or that the Israelites would have considered them to be the same individual. Pseudepigraphic literature refers to many *śaṭans* (e.g., the list of five *śaṭans* in *1 Enoch* 69.4–12 (1st cent. BC at the earliest); see D. S. Russell, *The Method and Message of Jewish Apocalyptic* [Philadelphia: Westminster, 1964], 254–55).

34. C. Breytenbach and P. L. Day, "Satan," *DDD²*, 728.

35. Weiss, *Job's Beginning*, 35–41.

36. Page, *Powers*, 26.

37. Day, *Adversary*, 80–81.

at Job. The text does not attribute to God or to the Challenger any personal emotional response to Job's tragedy; God carries more responsibility for striking Job than the Challenger (implied in 1:12 and 2:3),[38] and both lack any sympathetic response. It is arbitrary, therefore, to assume that the Challenger enjoys Job's suffering, while God sadly endures it. There is no expression of glee; there is no diabolical chuckle. Nothing personal, Job … there is a major philosophical issue on the line that supersedes individual circumstances.

Weiss concludes that nothing intrinsically evil emerges in the author's portrayal of the Challenger in Job. Certainly what he does has negative consequences for Job, a righteous man, but the text makes it clear that God is at least equally responsible for what happens to Job, thus freeing the actions from implicit evil.[39] There is no tempting, corrupting, depraving, or possessing.

The result of this profile is that we are not in a position to claim that the Challenger in Job should be identified with Satan as we know him in the New Testament. One cannot make the claim that they act the same way. In fact, there is little if any overlap between their two profiles. This does not prove that they are not the same individual; it merely reduces (if not eliminates) the basis for claiming that they must be equated. The profile of the Hebrew śaṭan in the book of Job does not answer to the same description as the Christian view of Satan in the New Testament. While the pictures are not contradictory, and they may even be complementary, we cannot consider them homogeneous.

Accolade. Yahweh praises Job (1:8), using the same language that the narrator has used in 1:1; everyone agrees that Job's conduct is impeccable. Furthermore, he prefaces his remarks with the assessment that Job stands as the most outstanding example of this righteous behavior among people on earth, a point we will explore further in Bridging Contexts. Most curious, however, is that Yahweh does not mention Job's ritual routines detailed in 1:5.

Challenge. We have suggested above that the challenge posed is not against Job per se, but against God's policies. In that vein, the existence of disinterested righteousness and the effect of a reward system on a person's motives are both legitimate issues. God does not scoff at the challenge or discount the legitimacy of the question. The Challenger is questioning God's blueprint for divine-human relations—the validity of a moral order in which the righteous unfailingly prosper, or what we have called the

---

38. Weiss, *Job's Beginning*, 37.
39. Ibid., 37; contra Page, *Powers*, 27–28.

Retribution Principle (RP). The test of true righteousness would be fear of God without the promise of reward or the threat of punishment.[40] The Challenger has no evidence for accusing Job of acting righteously only for reward. His point is that, given the system that Yahweh has set up, one cannot tell (notice all the second person subjects in 1:10, which show that God's policies are the target of accusations). Prospering the righteous, in the Challenger's view, is a questionable policy because it fosters corrupt motives. By pointing out all that Yahweh has done to bless and prosper Job, he raises the point that Job's motives are open to question: Is he truly righteous or just acting in ways that will gain him benefits?

As we have mentioned in the discussion of Job's fastidious ritual customs, not only is Job's motivation for righteous behavior subject to investigation, but his concept of God is open to question as well. The RP exposes God to criticism in that it could lead people to think that the world is founded on justice, that they can therefore expect predicted results to their behavior, and that when they experience anomalous or conflicting results, God's character may be misconstrued and his reputation compromised. It is difficult to fault the logic of this challenge. In fact, we find that Job does draw false conclusions about God's character and the nature of his operations of the world. God recognizes the legitimacy of the challenge and authorizes action against Job. It is important for God to clarify his character and the way he runs the world.

Curse/bless. In 1:11, as in 1:5, the word "bless" (*barak*) is again used euphemistically for "curse." In contrast to Job's sons and daughters, who might curse God privately, the Challenger expresses his pessimistic assessment that Job will curse God "to his face." The phrase used here typically refers to something that is done in the presence of another—not behind their back, covertly, privately or confidentially.[41] In contrast to the range of possibilities for Job's children (from subtle to blatant, inadvertent to rebellious contempt), this anticipated act of Job would be unambiguous and forthright.

It must be emphasized that the Challenger has no foreknowledge and can have no certainty. His claim stems not from some identified flaw in Job, but from his experience with human nature. He has no specific evidence that would impugn Job's character, though perhaps Job's ritual customs betray some crack in the façade. If he really had any evidence, the whole challenge would be invalid and fruitless. The Challenger's confidence is

---

40. Breytenback and Day, "Satan," 728.
41. Gen. 11:28; 23:3; 32:22; 50:1; Ex. 33:19; 34:6; Lev. 10:3; Num. 3:4; 1 Kings 9:7; 2 Kings 13:14; Job 4:15; 21:31; Ps. 9:20; Ezek. 32:10.

that God's policy is misguided and ill-advised, not wicked or corrupt. His confidence is that Job's motives are suspect and that Job's concept of God is vulnerable. There is no reason to believe that he takes delight in Job's ruin. If Job is as righteous as he appears, the Challenger is wrong, in which case the prosperity doesn't matter anyway. If righteousness is all that Job ultimately values, that cannot be taken away from him.

As a side note, we must remember that this is a thought experiment in a literary scenario. It is pointless to wring our hands over the sad fate of Job's innocent family, for the challenge does not focus on his family and their innocence, but on God's work in the world. The children simply represent the blessing of God, like Job's cattle. This is not to suggest they are no better than cattle; rather, it warns us that we are losing our way if we decide to advocate their cause and press a complaint against God on their behalf. Their fate is part of the challenge to God's policies, but not its focus.

Devastation of Job (1:13–22)

SABEANS AND CHALDEANS, FIRE of God and mighty wind. We can see that the Challenger uses all the resources at God's disposal — human foes, divine judgment from heaven, and "natural" disaster. These calamities occur in rapid succession, which thus dramatizes the literary scenario. The identification of the human foes is problematic. Verse 15 is usually translated as a reference to the Sabeans, though the lead consonant is *šin*, not *sin*; consequently, the raiders are from Sheba. In biblical and other literature from the ancient world, there was a Sheba in the south (same spelling; vicinity of modern Yemen, from where the Queen of Sheba traveled to learn of Solomon), but some have suggested a northern Sheba in the region of Edom. This suggestion is probable, given the towns listed in connection with Sheba and the improbability of raiders coming from a thousand miles away.[42]

The Chaldeans (Heb. *kaśdim*) represent a different problem. In Jeremiah and Ezekiel, they inhabit Babylonia and in fact are the ethnic group from which the Babylonian rulers, such as Nebuchadnezzar, are derived.

---

42. M. Pope, *Job* (AB; New York: Doubleday, 1973), 13. Note particularly the relationship between Sheba and Dedan in Gen. 25:3. The latter is located in the vicinity of Tema (descendant of Ishmael in Gen. 25:14). This same Sheba is mentioned in the inscriptions of Tiglath-pileser III (as Saba, each time with Tema), see H. Tadmor, *The Inscriptions of Tiglath-pileser III King of Assyria* (Jerusalem: Israel Academy of Sciences and Humanities, 1994), 143 (line 27'), 169 (line 3'), 201 (line 9'), 229 (§7). See I. Ephal, *The Ancient Arabs* (Jerusalem: Magnes, 1982), 88–89, 227–29. Most commentators still identify the Sabeans in Job as the southern Sabeans, cf. K. Kitchen, "Ancient Arabia and the Bible," *Archaeology in the Biblical World* 3 (1995): 26–34.

These Chaldeans first appear in ninth-century Assyrian inscriptions.[43] Some have offered a second millennium identification of *kasdim* in relationship to *kesed* in the area of Aram Naharaim among Abraham's relatives (Gen. 22:22),[44] but this seems too distant from Job's home territory.

As to the reference to divine judgment, the exact construction "fire of God" appears only in this passage. Other references to God sending fire from heaven make it clear that these are viewed as direct acts of judgment (Sodom, Gen. 19:24; Aaron's sons, Lev. 10:2; rebellious Israelites, Num. 11:1; 16:35; and king's messengers sent to take Elijah captive, 2 Kings 1:12).

Finally, a "mighty wind" destroys the house where Job's children had gathered and causes their death (1:19). Such destructive wind is elsewhere referred to in 1 Kings 19:11. Though nothing in the ancient world was perceived as "natural" (notice Hos. 13:15; Jon. 4:8), this mighty wind would be a meteorological phenomenon, which is not necessarily the case for the "fire of God." The point is that, even though all of these disasters come from the hand of God (notice Job 2:3), they fit into different categories — another way of showing the totality of the devastation.

One additional observation is that an Israelite audience would readily recognize all the disasters that overtake Job because they are among those delineated in the covenant curses for disobedience (Deut. 28:31–35).[45] This recognition would heighten the poignancy for the Israelite reader and would also evoke further connections with retribution theology — here on the corporate level.

Job's response. Job's initial response reflects the normal customs of mourning (tearing one's robe and shaving one's head, 1:20). Falling to the ground prostrate, however, is nowhere else included in mourning activities (for the closest, see 2 Sam. 1:2). Perhaps that is why the NIV has chosen to render the verb as "worship." When an act of worship is in view, however, the text generally specifies bowing down "before the LORD." The fact that Job does not address God in the succeeding lines argues against taking his prostration as an act of worship. Specifically, the verb refers to an act of prostration that may or may not be associated with worship; as often as not,

---

43. Ashurnasirpal II inscription from the Ninurta temple at Calah; see A. K. Grayson, *Assyrian Rulers of the Early First Millennium BC I (1114–859 BC)* (RIMA 2; Toronto: Univ. of Toronto Press, 1991), 214: iii.24.

44. J. A. Brinkman, *A Political History of Post-Kassite Babylonia 1158–722 B.C.* (Rome: Pontifical Biblical Institute, 1968), 260–67: "What slim evidence is presently available suggests a West Semitic relationship for the Chaldeans and possibly some kinship with the Arameans" (266).

45. S. Ticciati, *Job and the Disruption of Identity* (London: T&T Clark/Continuum, 2005), 61.

someone is prostrating oneself before someone of authority or higher rank.[46] Nevertheless, in any of these situations, the context typically specifies a person or group before whom one prostrates oneself. If this gesture does not signify mourning, deference, or worship, what are other alternatives?

We can gain some insight into Job's action from four other passages that use this verb (*ḥawah*) without designating an object. Genesis 47:31 and 1 Kings 1:47 are deathbed scenes (Jacob and David respectively), in which the subjects realize and acknowledge a significant act of God. Exodus 4:31 and 12:27 are scenes in which the Israelites have heard that God intends to deliver them from Egypt. None of these four contexts indicate that the subjects prostrate themselves before the Lord or engage in acts of worship. In each one, the prostration is a response to something remarkable that God has done and represents acknowledgment and acceptance.

In the same way, Job acknowledges by his prostration that God has performed a remarkable act, and Job accepts it as such; he abases himself in response to the great power that God has demonstrated. Presumably from his prostrate position, he utters his acceptance of God's actions. By ending his short speech with the invocation of blessing on the name of Yahweh, he has done exactly what the Challenger said he would and the exact opposite. The Challenger said he would "bless" (= euphemism for "curse") God to his face. Job does "bless" God to his face, but here, we must conclude, with no euphemistic connotation. Nevertheless, the multivalence and thus ambiguity of the term "bless" in these chapters keeps the reader alert to potential subtle nuances.[47]

The narrator concludes that Job does not attribute wrongdoing to God. The Hebrew word translated "wrongdoing" (*tiplah*) is used only two other times. In Job 24:12, we read that God had not held anyone accountable in that context of persecution. Jeremiah 23:13 uses it to refer to a travesty —prophets of Baal leading the Israelites astray. With so few uses of this word, certainty concerning its meaning is not possible, but the word appears in contexts where a person should be held accountable for wrongdoing. When this word is used of Job's response, it indicates that Job is not calling God to accountability; this accords with Job's words in verse 21: Whether God gives or takes away, he should be praised—God owes us nothing. This is not Job's final posture, but his reflection at this stage; we will later see that Job does call God to account. We will also see that all experiences cannot be accounted for as reflecting *God's* giving or taking away—that is too simplistic.

---

46. For more secular contexts, see Gen. 23:7; 33:3–7; 42:6, etc.
47. For in depth discussion, see Cheney, *Dust, Wind and Agony*, 58–77.

THE BRIDGING CONTEXTS SECTIONS of this commentary series have three specific functions. The first task is to discuss how the section under consideration fits into the argument of the book as a whole—that is, the rhetorical strategy. As the rhetorical strategy unfolds, it also leads to the message of the book—in this case, the answers that it offers regarding God's policies in this world and a proposed perspective on suffering. So, for example, below we will discuss the role of the prologue.

Second, in this section we can discuss the theological issues that arise in the book (whether or not the book intends to teach on that subject). So, for example, we will encounter material in Job that will lead us to examine theological concepts of creation or afterlife. We will try to address these issues throughout each unit.

Third, and most important, the Bridging Contexts section serves to identify the message that comprises the authoritative teaching of the text. Here, we would normally seek to identify the teaching of the book that applies to all audiences throughout time. This is problematic in Job because the book does not carry such a teaching in all its passages. Both Job and his friends are groping for answers and coming up short. In many of the sections of the book, there is no authoritative message, for eventually the book will reject the positions taken by the parties whose words have been offered. Consequently, we will often have to omit this discussion.

Rhetorical Strategy[48]

PURPOSE OF PROLOGUE. THE scene in heaven sets up a number of important issues in the book. First, it clearly indicates that Job is indeed innocent of wrongdoing.[49] This immediately eliminates the usual answers offered in the ancient Near East, in which there really is an offense of which the sufferer was unaware, or that God is simply capricious. This cleans the slate of tradition to make room for new explanations.

A second important point is that by acclaiming Job's righteousness from the beginning, the author makes clear, as we have noted, that Job is not on trial. This feature allows the book to focus on God's policy regarding the treatment of the righteous. Notice in the process that the book thus tackles the more difficult side of the retribution equation, for it is much easier to

---

48. Much information used in this section comes from Walton, "Job 1: Book of," 333–46.

49. M. Greenberg, "Reflections on Job's Theology," in *Studies in the Bible and Jewish Thought* (Philadelphia: JPS, 1995), 327–34, see 328.

discuss why the wicked prosper. By indicating that there is no one on earth like Job, the author also establishes the stark contrast between the height of his stature and the depth of his fall.

Third, the prologue reveals important information that is crucial to our understanding of the book. Because the conversation in heaven is never revealed to Job or his friends, they understandably misjudge precisely what is at stake. This hidden information is especially poignant because, as Job argues his case before God, he believes that he can "win" if he can force God into court to account for himself, to give an explanation for his actions. In reality, Job has nothing to win because he is not on trial. If, however, God were to give Job an explanation for his suffering—reasons why he acted the way that he did in the prologue—Job's challenge to God's policies (that it is bad policy for righteous people to suffer, see Introduction, p. 23) would be validated. In other words, if Job "wins" the case that he thinks he is in, God loses the case that the prologue sets up. If all suffering can be explained by the RP and the world operates on the foundation of God's justice, then it is bad policy or flawed execution when righteous people suffer.

Finally, the scene in heaven shows that, despite the role of the Challenger, God both initiated the discussion and approved the course of action.[50] This again avoids the easy solution that insulates God by inserting an independently wicked intermediary power. The book would be toothless without this introduction; it would be reduced to philosophical speculation, unable to rise above its contemporaries. In the same way, to view the prologue as suggesting that the book is the story of how a good man suffered because of a bet between God and Satan misses the point entirely.[51]

Theological Issues

THE GOD JOB FEARS.[52] The primary names used for God in the book of Job are *El*,[53] *Eloah*,[54] *Elohim*,[55] and *Shaddai*.[56] The characters in the book leave no room for the distribution of divine powers among a variety of entities, though the speakers refer to other known divine entities in a

---

50. Weiss, *Job's Beginning*, 37.

51. For discussion of some of the distorted views of God that have resulted from this misreading, see M. A. Shields, "Malevolent or Mysterious: God's Character in the Prologue of Job," *TynBul* 61 (2010): 255–70.

52. For lengthy analysis and discussion of the use of *'eloah* and *šaddai* in Job and the rest of the Old Testament, see Cheney, *Dust, Wind and Agony*, 233–42.

53. 57x, mostly in human speeches.

54. 41x, mostly in human speeches.

55. 11x in prologue, 5x in body, 1x in Yahweh speech (38:7, NIV: "angels").

56. 31x, all but one (40:2) in human speeches.

variety of places.[57] These indicate that Job inhabits the world of the ancient Near East, with all its mythologies, but he does not share the polytheistic worldview common to the region. Neither Job nor his friends specifically discuss Yahweh in their speeches to one another.[58] What is the significance of this? We have noted that Job is a paradox. The region of his home and the practices of his family clearly show his setting to be non-Israelite. This non-Israelite setting would find support in the use of divine names other than Yahweh. Yet, at the same time, Job is notably Israelite-like in his beliefs (see Introduction, p. 38). With the Prologue and Epilogue featuring Yahweh, an additional Israelite component is recognizable, but there is no attempt to insert Yahweh throughout the work.

Is Job being assessed in Israelite or non-Israelite terms? Again, there is a paradox that creates some tension in the book: a non-Israelite poly-theist could theoretically be described using the terms applied to Job by Yahweh ("blameless," "upright," "fearing God," "turning away from evil"), but it would be highly unusual for such a one to have risen above the Great Symbiosis (see explanation on p. 33–38), as must be the case if God's poli-cies are to be vindicated.

This paradox also extends to the way that the divine names are used in the book. Loyalty to Yahweh (as in the covenant) is not the issue under discussion; yet the divine epithets (as opposed to specific names of other gods) in the book allow no hint that Job worships another god. He uses all legitimate epithets for Israel's God. One of the issues particularly at stake in the book is whether Job's concept of God accords with the ancient Near Eastern models or with the ideal Israelite models. The ambiguity inherent in the use of divine names allows this tension to extend throughout the book.

The Challenger *(haśśaṭan)*. In the Original Meaning section, we adopted the following conclusions about the Challenger:

- He is one of the "sons of God" (a member of the divine council).
- He serves as a policy watchdog.
- He uses the ambiguity of Job's motives and concept of God to challenge God's policies.
- He does not act independently.
- He is not inherently evil.
- He cannot confidently be identified with Satan in the New Testament.

---

57. Besides the general category of the "sons of God," the list of possibilities includes Mot (Job 18:14), Shahar (3:9), Yam (3:8) and Shelah (33:18); see J. C. de Moor, "Ugarit and the Origin of Job," in *Ugarit and the Bible* (ed. G. J. Brooke, A. H. W. Curtis, and J. F. Healey; Münster: Ugarit-Verlag, 1994), 237.

58. Job does refer to Yahweh in 1:21. For the anomaly in 12:9, see discussion there.

In this section, then, we must discuss where this leaves us on two counts. (1) What is the theology surrounding the Challenger in the larger Old Testament context? (2) Does our doctrine of Satan need modification?

As indicated earlier, several Old Testament passages outside of Job use the noun *śatan* to refer to nonhuman beings, including Zechariah 3:1–2 and 1 Chronicles 21:1.[59] As in Job, Zechariah 3 also features the definite article; here the Challenger questions Joshua's right to play the role he has been given because he is covered with the stains of his and his people's guilt.[60] God responds by purifying him for the task. In Job, the policy of rewarding the righteous is questioned; in Zechariah, the policy of forgiveness and restoration is questioned.[61]

In 1 Chronicles 21 there is no definite article. This could mean that *śatan* is being used as a personal name, but it also could mean that it is simply indefinite (i.e., a *śatan*).[62] The role of the *śatan* here is somewhat different because the *śatan* is not challenging God's policies; rather, he is inciting David to take a census. In Job and Zechariah, the *śatan* acts in relation to God by challenging God's policies. In Chronicles (but also in Numbers) the *śatan* functions in relation to humans. As we consider 1 Chronicles 21, it is important to note that the parallel passage in 2 Samuel 24 gives no role to *śatan*; there the anger of God incites David to take a census.[63] This falls short of suggesting that God initiated the census; the passage makes no statement about agency.

In one possible scenario, God's anger against Israel would have been evidenced in some fashion (cf., e.g., 2 Sam. 21:1), and David may have been seeking to appease that anger by means of a census (which would eventuate in a head tax paid to the temple, "buying off" God, as it were). God takes offense at this pagan view of appeasement, and the subsequent plague is a further expression of his anger—both the original anger toward Israel and the unacceptable solution attempted by David.[64] The passage does not require that David's sin is the only object of punishment.

---

59. Num. 22:22, 32 use the term as an infinitive.

60. See this case made in Weiss, *Beginning of Job*, 36–37; C. and E. Meyers, *Zechariah 1–8* (AB; Garden City, N.Y.: Doubleday, 1987), 185–86. Note that one difference is that here the Challenger is rebuked.

61. Day, *Adversary*, 118–21.

62. See discussion in Japhet, *1 & 2 Chronicles*, 374–75.

63. Cf. the translation of the NASB. "Anger" is masculine, so this is grammatically acceptable.

64. In fact, the Chronicler adds yet another explanation of the punishment, suggesting that Joab was responsible because he failed to complete the numbering (1 Chron. 27:24, against NIV). If David had intended to "buy off" the Lord, it would make matters even worse if a lesser sum was involved.

In this interpretation of the Chronicles passage, then, the role attributed to *śaṭan* is not filled by God in the 2 Samuel 24 account. Rather, in Samuel the role is left unmentioned. Satan is now posited by the Chronicler as the intermediary responsible for David's decision to pursue the course of action he chose. The anger of the Lord created the circumstance; *śaṭan* is responsible for instigating the decision. In this way, his role is similar to that of the unnamed spirit in 1 Kings 22:19–23. It is interesting to note that in the Kings passage, though the course of action instigated by the spirit is punishable, the action is not urged to defy God; it is in fact approved by him.

How shall we view Chronicles' presentation of *śaṭan* as one who actively instigates the punishable behavior of human beings?[65] We should first notice that this is not the only passage where the anger of the Lord leads to the involvement of a *śaṭan*. First Kings 11:9–14 shows the Lord's raising up Hadad the Edomite as a human *śaṭan* against Solomon, when God becomes angry with him. Likewise, the angel of the Lord functions as *śaṭan* against Balaam, when the Lord becomes angry with him (Num 22:22). The pattern can now be seen as follows:

Passage	Agent of God's anger	Object of God's anger	Result of God's anger
1 Kings 11	Hadad the Edomite (a *śaṭan*)	Solomon	Rebellion
Num. 22	Angel of the Lord (a *śaṭan*)	Balaam	Near execution
1 Kings 22	Unnamed spirit working through false prophets	Ahab	Death in battle
2 Sam. 24/ 1 Chron. 21	a *śaṭan* working through David	Israel	Plague

The anger of the Lord is explicitly stated in each of these passages, with the exception of 1 Kings 22, though there the entire sequence of narratives has been emphasizing God's displeasure with Ahab. It is also noteworthy that, with the exception of 1 Kings 11, the immediate passage does not clarify what has caused God's anger.

The agents all function in the same way: They are instruments of God's punishment. In 1 Kings 11, the agent is human and described as a *śaṭan*; in Numbers 22 the agent is supernatural and likewise described as a *śaṭan*. The supernatural agent in the other two passages works indirectly by affecting a human agent who unwittingly initiates the punishment. We can observe here the parallel roles played by the unnamed spirit in 1 Kings 22

---

65. For further discussion of the relationship between the *śaṭan*'s function and the anger of Yahweh, see Day, *Adversary*, 33–34.

and the unnamed *śaṭan* in 1 Chronicles 21; in each case, the action instigated by the agent is something in itself displeasing to God (false prophecy
and the census).

Though the profiles in Job/Zechariah and Chronicles may differ from
one another, for our purposes it is important to note how different both
profiles are from that of the New Testament Satan. The New Testament
profile reflects the development of thought that took place throughout the
intertestamental period. J. B. Russell summarizes the development:

> Satan, Azazel, Belial, and Mastema were none of them in their
> origins a principle of evil, but in the apocalyptic literature they con-
> verge in that direction. What is important is the development of the
> concept of the principle of evil, with which the name of Satan was
> linked more closely than any other.[66]

Even though we do not view the literature of this period as inspired,
it evidences some of the progression in theological thinking that is later
affirmed by the New Testament. H. Ringgren summarizes those features
as follows:

> In the pseudepigraphic literature—and therefore primarily in the
> realm of apocalyptic—the development continues. As author and rep-
> resentative of evil we find here a prince of the evil spirits, who bears
> various names: Satan, Mastema (only in the *Book of Jubilees*), Belial
> or Beliar ("worthlessness"; primarily in the *Testaments of the Twelve
> Patriarchs* and the Qumran documents), and, in Greek, *diabolos* ("slan-
> derer"). He, together with his angels and powers, constitutes the realm
> of evil, and seeks to lead men to destruction and ruin. It was he who
> tempted the first human beings to sin; it was he who aided the Egyp-
> tians before and during the exodus of the Israelites; it is he who causes
> all evil and all sins. Through him death entered the world (Wisd. Sol.
> 2:24). He is the prince of lawlessness, the ruler of this world (*Mart. Isa.*
> 2.4); he stands in complete antithesis to God. At the end of the world,
> he will be conquered, bound, and destroyed by God.[67]

By the New Testament, much of this has been accumulated into the
profile of the being called Satan, the diabolical enemy leading the forces
of evil.

---

66. Russell, *Devil*, 189. For discussion of Asael and the Watchers in the Aramaic books of
Enoch, see Forsyth, *Old Enemy*, 160–81. For Mastema and the developments in the book
of *Jubilees*, see ibid., 182–91.

67. H. Ringgren, *Israelite Religion* (trans. D. E. Green; Philadelphia: Fortress, 1966),
313–14.

The New Testament Devil is a tempter, a liar, a murderer, the cause of death, sorcery, and idolatry; he hurts people physically, and he blocks and obstructs the teaching of the Kingdom of God wherever he can, assaulting us, possessing us spiritually, and tempting us to sin. In all this he is the enemy of the Kingdom of God.[68]

This sinister being has been viewed in many different ways throughout history. In some Jewish writings, he is the personification of the evil impulse in all of us. The more dualistic offshoots of Christianity (e.g., Manichaeism) understood him as the hypostasis of the dark side of God. Another variation, perhaps the most popular view in contemporary Christianity, posits him as the apotheosis of evil from within the world of demons.[69] This latter profile portrays Satan as a fallen angel. The Old Testament passages that mention śaṭan (discussed above) do not portray him as a fallen being (though neither do they explicitly deny his fallenness).

Two significant passages in the Old Testament that have been traditionally associated with the fall of Satan in Christian doctrine: Isaiah 14:12–15 and Ezekiel 28:12–19.[70] If Satan is truly a fallen being, this fact would significantly expand the possibilities for the interpretation of the Challenger in Job. Consequently, we must turn our attention to the tradition of the fall of Satan in these two passages.

Isaiah 14:12–15. From a contextual standpoint, this pericope concerns the king of Babylon and, accordingly, is placed among the oracles against the nations. It takes the form of a taunt (v. 5) anticipating the tyrant's imminent demise. His descent to the netherworld (vv. 9–11) is described with relish. Verses 12–15 refer to his downfall, despite his aspirations to divine grandeur.

Throughout most of church history, these verses have been applied to Satan. The earliest appearance of this association can be found in the writings of Origen.[71] Satan's fall had been discussed earlier by Tertullian and Justin Martyr, but with no obvious references to Isaiah 14. This is not surprising since Satan is mentioned nowhere in the passage. Jewish writings (cf. *2 En.* 29.4–5) had stories of the fall of Satan, but there is no evidence that Isaiah 14 was interpreted in relation to that fall.

The doctrine of Satan's fall and its association with Isaiah 14 passed into the mainstream of Christian theology through *Moralia* 34 by Pope

---

68. Russell, *Devil*, 240.

69. Ibid., 176–77.

70. A more detailed study could likewise consider the interpretations of Genesis 6 in *Enoch* and *Jubilees*, and of Genesis 3 in the *Apocalypse of Abraham*, but these have had less influence in Christian doctrine.

71. J. B. Russell, *Satan* (Ithaca, N.Y.: Cornell Univ. Press, 1981), 130. For a thorough discussion of the development of Origen's thought concerning Satan and his blending and use of the traditions available to him, see Forsyth, *Old Enemy*, 367–83.

Gregory the Great in the seventh century. Once part of popular belief, it easily passed into the great pieces of literature, such as Milton's *Paradise Lost*, which sustained its place in theology. The doctrine was also solidified by the way Isaiah 14 was handled in translation. Jerome, interpreting the difficult Hebrew term *helel* in v. 12 (NIV: "morning star") as a reference to Venus, used a Latin term for Venus, *luciferos*, to translate it. As the interpretation of the passage as a reference to Satan became popularized in the centuries following, Lucifer was adopted as a variant name for Satan — because that was what Satan was called in this passage!

> Tertullian and other fathers, Gregory the Great, and the scholastic commentators, regarding Luke x.18 as an explanation of this verse, apply it to the fall of Satan, from which has arisen the popular perversion of the beautiful name Lucifer to signify the Devil.[72]

By the sixteenth and seventeenth centuries, when the major English translations were being produced, the interpretation was so ingrained that "Lucifer" was retained, even in the KJV. This reinforced to the lay English reader that the passage explicitly concerned Satan.[73]

Despite the wide popular support for this interpretation, there was no lack of opposition. Neither Calvin nor Luther supports the idea that Isaiah 14 refers to the fall of Satan. Calvin is particularly undiplomatic as his heaps scorn on those who adopt such a noncontextual intrusion.

> The exposition of this passage, which some have given, as if it should refer to Satan, has arisen from ignorance; for the context plainly shows that these statements must be understood in reference to the king of the Babylonians. But when passages of Scripture are taken up at random, and no attention is paid to the context, we need not wonder that mistakes of this kind frequently arise. Yet it was an instance of very gross ignorance to imagine that Lucifer was the king of the devils, and that the prophet gave him this name. But as these inventions have no probability whatever, let us pass by them as useless fables.[74]

---

72. J. A. Alexander, *The Prophecies of Isaiah* (1846–47 in 2 vols.; repr., Grand Rapids: Zondervan, 1953), 295. Modern conservative commentaries also commonly reject any association between this passage and Satan. Cf. J. Oswalt, *The Book of Isaiah, Chapters 1–39* (Grand Rapids: Eerdmans, 1986), 320; E. J. Young, *The Book of Isaiah* (Grand Rapids: Eerdmans, 1972), 1:441; J. A. Motyer, *The Prophecy of Isaiah* (Downers Grove, Ill.: InterVarsity Press, 1993), 144. Motyer does not even mention the possibility of the passage referring to Satan.

73. For a summary of the use of the name Lucifer in medieval literature, see J. B. Russell, *Lucifer* (Ithaca, N.Y.: Cornell Univ. Press, 1984), 247.

74. John Calvin, *Commentary on Isaiah*, loc. cit.

From a hermeneutical standpoint one could hardly claim that Isaiah was intentionally addressing the issue of Satan's fall. Aside from not mentioning Satan, we have already seen how little the Israelite view of Satan would have accommodated such an understanding. Given our knowledge about what the Israelite audience knew (or did not know) about Satan, we would have no reason to assume that Isaiah would consider his audience automatically able to relate the information about the king of Babylon to Satan or his fall.

Lacking support in the author's intention, we would be equally hard pressed to sustain the suggestion that the passage refers to Satan, even though the author knew nothing of that association. Some have attempted this by invoking a *sensus plenior* related to a divine intention, much like the concept used to understand prophecy and fulfillment. However, we have no later revelation to support a connection between Isaiah 14 and the fall of Satan, so claiming "divine intention" is difficult. Those who seek to attach a *sensus plenior*, such as that invoked for other prophecy, face the difficulty that *sensus plenior* is only applied to future fulfillment and not to past events, such as the purported primeval fall of Satan. This is a different category altogether.

Those who continue to interpret Isaiah 14 as a reference to the fall of Satan base their beliefs on the statements made in vv. 13–14. They typically maintain that no human being could make such statements or seriously entertain such possibilities. Such assessments sadly underestimate the inclinations of rulers in the ancient world to make grandiose statements that would mock the label hyperbole as a vast understatement. One need not even read the inscriptional literature (though that would be instructive),[75] for ample evidence of royal hubris is even provided in biblical records such as Isaiah 47:8, where Babylon claims for itself, "I am, and there is none besides me!" (cf. Zeph. 2:15).

Moreover, we do not need to view Isaiah 14:13–14 as statements the king would actually make, for here the prophet is drawing a caricature, perhaps referencing well-known mythical material. This king, who takes his own mythology too seriously and even supposes himself capable of grandiose accomplishments like those sometimes enshrined in myth, will find himself instead in a similar situation to that portrayed in other mythology: the outcast, would-be usurper.

Ezekiel 28:12–19. In contrast to Isaiah 14, this passage has more obvious references to a primeval situation. Although it refers contextually to the king of Tyre, mention of the "garden of God" (v. 13) and the "cherub" (v. 14) have given interpreters sufficient basis to move beyond the stated context. Admittedly, it is within the function of metaphor to point to something

---

75. See, e.g., the royal inscriptions of Esarhaddon and Ashurbanipal, *ANET*, 289–301, and esp. the account of Nabonidus's rise to power, *ANET*, 308–11, and the Verse Account of Nabonidus, *ANET*, 312–15.

outside itself; yet the interpreter must still ask what the author intends the metaphor to relate to in this particular context.

Commentators have traditionally stated three reasons to support their claim that the king of Tyre should be understood as Satan: (1) the king is in the garden; (2) the king is identified as the cherub; and (3) the passage alludes to a fall from a blameless condition. As we examine each of these in light of Old Testament theology, however, the interpretation becomes increasingly difficult to maintain.

With regard to the first point, we must recognize that there is no indication in the Old Testament that the Israelites believed Satan was in the garden of Eden. No Old Testament passage either equates or relates the serpent and Satan, whether in Genesis or elsewhere (see below for further discussion). If Ezekiel 28 were phrased as instruction, suggesting that such an equation should be made, it would be another matter, but the Satan interpretation suggests that this passage refers to the fall of Satan metaphorically. For such a metaphor to work, it must make reference to well-known information. There is no evidence that Israel would have known that the serpent in Genesis 3 was a tool or representation of Satan. That being the case, they would not have placed Satan in the garden.

As to the second point, does any Scripture suggest that Satan was ever a cherub?[76] The cherubim are a specialized class of supernatural beings with specific functions. There is no basis for the speculation that Satan was once among their number, and certainly no reason to suggest that the Israelite audience would have recognized such a metaphorical allusion.

Finally, as suggested at the beginning of our discussion of Isaiah 14, the Old Testament nowhere portrays Satan as a fallen being.[77] Therefore, the fact that Ezekiel 28 refers to a fall would not suggest to the Israelite reader that the author was metaphorically invoking the fall of Satan for comparison to the fate of the king of Tyre.

Is there, then, any single datum in Ezekiel 28 that parallels information known about Satan in the Old Testament? I see none. If this is so, how can

---

76. Origen initiated the idea that Satan originally sang among the cherubs, but this only reflects his conclusion that Ezek. 28 was talking about Satan (*De Principiis* 1.5.4, 1.8.3; see Russell, *Satan*, 129). Subsequent to Dionysius's description of the celestial hierarchy (ca. AD 500), in which seraphs were considered the highest beings, Western writers generally assumed Satan had been a seraph prior to his fall; see Russell, *Lucifer*, 32. Gregory adopted the "cherub" view, ibid., 94. For the discussion among the scholastics, see ibid., 173 n. 36.

77. In Tertullian's context (and to a lesser extent, Origen's also), the existence of a "fallen being" is contrived as an anti-Gnostic cosmological argument. Not only are they reading a metaphorical passage literally, they are reading external assumptions into the account; the evil of Satan is Tertullian's premise, not his conclusion. I am grateful to Jonathan Walton for this observation.

we possibly understand Ezekiel as making use of the account of the fall of Satan as a metaphor to describe the impending fall of the king of Tyre?

But, the objection would arise, to whom else could the passage refer? What would we make of a story of a cherub in the garden who was created blameless but then rebelled? It must be some sort of metaphor, because no one suggests that Ezekiel thought the king of Tyre actually was a cherub in the garden.

One popular suggestion has been that verse 14 should be read as noting that this individual was with the cherub, but was not a cherub himself.[78] Such a reading opens up the possibility that the king of Tyre is being compared to primeval man, Adam.[79] This suggestion is problematic because, in the Genesis account, Adam is never with the cherub in the garden; the cherub is only stationed there after Adam and Eve were expelled. Those who maintain this identification are therefore obliged to posit a variant form of the Eden tradition in Ezekiel.

While the passage presents difficulties to all interpreters, scholars have made important progress on it in recent years. H. J. van Dijk and I. Goldberg have both noticed that verses 12b–15a feature very close parallelism:[80]

	vv. 12b–13	vv. 14–15a
Identification	You were the seal	You were ... a cherub
Description	of perfection full of wisdom perfect in beauty	anointed as a guardian ordained
Residence	You were in Eden, the garden of God	On the holy mount of God you walked
Position	every precious stone	among the fiery stones
Intrinsic quality	Your settings and mountings were made of gold; on the day you were created they were prepared	You were blameless in your ways from the day you were created

Given these parallels, two suggestions can be made. (1) There are two parallel metaphors in the passage rather than one single metaphor, as the other interpretations have assumed; (2) the metaphors do not extend to

---

78. This requires changing the pointing of the first word in v. 14 from *'at* (personal pronoun, "you") to *'et* (preposition, "with"); see NRSV.

79. See, e.g., W. Zimmerli, *Ezekiel* (Hermeneia; Philadelphia: Fortress, 1983), 2:90; and among conservative commentators, J. Taylor, *Ezekiel* (TOTC; Downers Grove, Ill.: InterVarsity Press, 1969), 196–97; and Douglas Stuart, *Ezekiel* (WBC; Dallas: Word, 1989), 273–74.

80. H. J. van Dijk, *Ezekiel's Prophecy on Tyre* (Rome: Pontifical Biblical Institute, 1968), 114; I. Goldberg, "The Artistic Structure of the Dirge over the King of Tyre" *Tarbis* 58 (1988–89): 277–81 (Hebrew).

the fall but only refer to the high station of the individual. The king of Tyre enjoyed a lofty status because of all that was entrusted to him; he was the guardian of extensive natural resources, just as the individuals in the two metaphors were.[81] Unfortunately, he was corrupted by them and was found to be treacherous and irresponsible. The metaphor ends where the parallelism ends, and from verses 15b–19 the king's conduct and punishment are addressed (though the end of v. 16 refers back to the metaphor). Thus, there is no reason to reach beyond the context and its metaphors for a sensible interpretation of the passage.

Conclusions regarding the fall of Satan. Some have contended that even though Satan is not mentioned in these passages, we know that they refer to Satan because they fit with everything else we are told about his fall. Without Isaiah 14 or Ezekiel 28, however, what do we know about his fall that would enable us to contend that it correlates with the information of these passages? Where do we receive inspired information about the cause of his fall or his status prior to the fall?

The New Testament information on the fall of Satan is extremely limited. In Luke 10:18, Christ remarks, "I saw Satan fall like lightning from heaven." It must be noted, however, that this is his response to the seventy-two's successful ministry, of which they observed, "Even the demons submit to us in your name" (10:17). It is therefore a possibility, if not a probability, that Christ is referring not to the primeval past, but to the recent triumphs of the seventy-two (cf. John 12:31), though he may be doing it through allusion to the distant past.

Revelation 12:9 is often invoked on the matter of Satan's fall, but here the reference is to the events of John's vision, which were still to take place in the future (whether our future or only his). Therefore, they offer no insight into occurrences of the past, such as a fall, though it is not improbable that parallels were seen to exist between a primeval fall (which would have been known through other contemporary literature, as noted above) and the future total defeat portrayed here.

In 2 Corinthians 11:14, Paul observes that Satan masquerades as an angel of light, but makes no suggestion that he once was an angel of light or, in fact, any other sort of angel. It is true that the New Testament authors show awareness of the existence of fallen angels (e.g., 2 Peter 2:4), but nowhere do they suggest that Satan was once among them, much less the leader of the rebellion.

---

81. This suits well with the understanding of the cherub as the guardian of the tree of life. The first metaphor concerns a "seal" if the text is taken as it stands, which may refer to a king as a "signet ring" (cf. Hag. 2:23). The metaphor is not drawn from myths, but from known literary motifs.

Finally, 1 Timothy 3:6 indicates that "the devil" has fallen under judgment because of his conceit. This is the most information that any passage offers, and we can see that it is scant. In addition to conceit, John 8:44 acknowledges Satan as the father of lies, but neither of these offenses is specifically identified as the sin that led to his fall.

In conclusion, the New Testament offers few details about the circumstances of Satan's fall or about his status prior to the fall.[82] Most of the details brought to bear on our theological discussion of the fall find their source in pseudepigraphic literature of the intertestamental period and the allegorical interpretation of the early church fathers, following the theories of Justin, Tertullian, Irenaeus, and Origen.[83]

Satan and the serpent. As mentioned in the discussion of Ezekiel 28, there is no hint in the Old Testament that the serpent of Genesis 2–3 was either identified as Satan or was thought to be inspired by Satan.[84] The earliest extant reference to any association is found in the Wisdom of Solomon 2:23–24 (1st cent. BC):

> For God created man for immortality,
> and made him the image of his own eternity,
> But through the devil's envy death came into the world,
> And those who belong to his party experience it.[85]

Even here, the devil is not given the name Satan and, in fact, was variously named in early literature.

This figure normally became Sammael in the Targum and in rabbinic tradition, but in a text known as the *Apocalypse of Abraham*, preserved only in Slavonic translation but datable to the same period that inspired the *Syriac Baruch* and the *Apocalypse of Ezra*, the seductive angel is called Azazel.[86]

---

82. It was Origen who was largely responsible for the concept that Satan fell as a result of pride prior to the creation of Adam and Eve; see Russell, *Satan*, 130. For a summary of the elaboration by Augustine, see ibid., 214; Forsyth, *Old Enemy*, 428–34.

83. For a summary of some of the early theories concerning the cause of Satan's fall, see Russell, *Devil*, 241–42. For an exhaustive summary of the thinking of the early church fathers, see his *Satan*.

84. Cf. G. J. Wenham: "Early Jewish and Christian commentators identified the snake with Satan or the devil, but since there is no other trace of a personal devil in early parts of the OT, modern writers doubt whether this is the view of our narrator" (*Genesis 1–15* [WBC1; Waco, Tex.: Word, 1987], 72).

85. Translation from J. E. Goodspeed.

86. Forsyth, *Old Enemy*, 224. Perhaps the earliest reference to Satan as the tempter (through the serpent) is in the *Apocalypse of Moses* 16–19 (properly titled *The Life of Adam and Eve*) contemporary to the New Testament. This text also links Isa. 14 to Satan's fall; see ibid., 232–38. In the writings of the church fathers, one of the earliest to associate the serpent with Satan was Justin, *First Apology* 28.1 (see ibid., 351).

Throughout the ancient world, the serpent was endowed with divine or semidivine qualities; it was venerated as an emblem of health, fertility, immortality, occult wisdom, and chaotic evil and was often worshiped. The serpent played a significant role in the mythology, the religious symbolism, and the cults of the ancient Near East.[87] In the context of Genesis, however, the serpent is merely one of the creatures God created. It is shrewd but not sinister. Unlike Christian theology, in Israel there was no inclination to embody all evil in a central figure or trace its cause to a single historical event.[88] Therefore, the Israelites were quite willing to recognize the serpent as representing an evil influence, without attempting to associate it with a being who was the ultimate source or cause of evil.

In fact, it would appear that the author of Genesis is intentionally underplaying the role or identification of the serpent; this would correlate with the other polemical elements of the early chapters of Genesis. It is important to remember that, in the ancient world, most cosmological models were built around a god taming or defeating the chaotic forces, often represented in the sea.[89] In Canaanite literature, this role of chaos was played by the serpentine Leviathan/Lotan. In contrast, the biblical narrative asserts that the great sea creature was simply another of the beasts God created (1:21). This demythologizing polemic may explain why the author avoids explaining the existence of evil with any conspiratorial uprisings theory.

We must therefore avoid importing into the Old Testament texts the idea that Satan was to be equated with the serpent. Likewise, we cannot rely on the narrative of Genesis 3 to enhance or inform our understanding of the Old Testament view of Satan. At the same time we can recognize that the New Testament eventually does offer some basis for connecting the serpent and Satan in Romans 16:20 and Revelation 12:9; 20:2.

In conclusion, the established occurrences of *śatan* in the Old Testament do not show the profile that we find developed in the intertestamental period and that reach full expression in the New Testament. None of these Old Testament passages attest to the fall of a being known as Satan; when we see a being who exercises the function of *śatan*, the text

---

87. Walton, *Genesis*, 203; N. Sarna, *Genesis* (Philadelphia: Jewish Publication Society, 1989), 24. For a brief summary of some of the supporting archaeological finds, see J. Scullion, *Genesis* (Collegeville, Minn.: Michael Glazier, 1992), 47; for more detail, see K. R. Joines, *Serpent Symbolism in the Old Testament* (Haddonfield, N.J.: Haddonfield, 1974), 19–29; J. Charlesworth, *The Good and Evil Serpent* (New Haven, Conn.: Yale Univ. Press, 2010).

88. Sarna, *Genesis*, 24.

89. Cf. J. Day, *God's Conflict with the Dragon and the Sea: Echoes of a Canaanite Myth in the Old Testament* (Cambridge: Cambridge Univ. Press, 1985).

---

gives no indication that the *saṭan* is intrinsically evil. The Old Testament theology surrounding the Challenger must be developed using only those passages in the Old Testament that make reference to this role. If we do this, we will find a far different profile than the one the New Testament or the church fathers would have brought. This new profile will then have significant impact on how we understand Job 1.

In terms of our doctrine of Satan, the study here is only the beginning of a much-needed investigation, including a renewed assessment of the ontology and nature of Satan. Is it possible that more of the Old Testament profile needs to be adopted as the backdrop for the New Testament profile? Is Satan less an immoral opponent of God and more an amoral agent, an instrument of God in a fallen world?[90] How much of Satan's portrayal in the ancient world accommodates Greco-Roman cultural views? How much were the church fathers influenced by intertestamental literature and the demonology of Hellenistic Judaism, imported from Assyria and Babylonian rather than from the Old Testament? These await careful study by those who maintain a strong doctrine of Scripture but are willing to reexamine traditions that may have insufficient scriptural basis.

IN THIS COMMENTARY SERIES, we have intentionally sought to draw out the contemporary significance of a passage from that which, in our best judgment, the author of the biblical text intends to teach. In other words, the method has been to move from the meaning of the text (determined by what the words mean and the sentences say = Original Meaning), to the universalized teaching of the text that comes with the authority of Scripture (= Bridging Contexts), to the identification of how we ought to believe and live in light of this teaching.

As I mentioned in the introduction to the Bridging Contexts section, this is problematic for the book of Job. Since not every pericope of the book has an authoritative teaching, not every pericope will have a contemporary significance that shows how that teaching ought to be lived out. The speeches of Job's friends, or even of Job himself, reflect flawed thinking and cannot be used as the foundation for scriptural teaching.

For this reason, I have decided to do Contemporary Significance in a different way. Many Christians experience significant suffering in their

---

90. Cf. the slaughtering angel in Ex. 12. Notice even in some of the most notorious passages, such as the temptation of Jesus in Matt. 4, it is the Spirit who leads Jesus into the wilderness to be tempted by the devil.

lives. In the end, the book of Job will help us sort out how we should think about suffering, but it will take a while for us to get there. In the meantime, before we begin to unfold some of the answers offered by the book, we can use the book of Job to consider our own experiences of suffering. The fact is, as we go through periods of suffering, we encounter many dead ends—well-meaning people whose counsel brings doubt and despair, our own struggles with doubt, and our questions about God. While many of us may be reluctant to think we have suffered as greatly as Job or to consider ourselves as righteous as Job, we can still see something of our own lives in Job's experiences.

Because I cannot claim to have suffered much in my life, it would be impossible for me to empathize with many readers whose life experiences have brought them pain. I have therefore recruited a friend for some help.

Kelly's Story

I FIRST ENCOUNTERED KELLY several years ago in my class on Old Testament Literature and Interpretation (a general education requirement for all students at Wheaton that introduces them to the Old Testament). I immediately saw that she had some disability related to her arm, but it took some time for me to hear her whole story—an inspiring one that helped bring the book of Job alive for me. In my course, I have the students choose a book of the Old Testament and write five short papers on that book, approaching it from different directions. Kelly chose the book of Job, and I have benefited from interacting with her over the book throughout the semester as she worked at applying the teaching of the book to her perspectives about her own situation.

Throughout the Contemporary Significance sections in this commentary, Kelly has agreed to share her story and her thoughts about suffering with the readers. Though she would strongly reject the idea that she was a modern-day Job (righteous in every way and wealth beyond imagining), through her eyes and experiences we will encounter the questions and doubts that Job encountered, along with all those since him who have suffered. This will help to draw us into the issues with which the book grapples.

In this chapter Kelly will begin by sharing her story: from the accident that disabled her arm to the medications, the surgeries, and the therapies that have characterized her life ever since, as doctors have sought to improve her quality of life.

JHW: Tell us what happened that day Kelly.

Kelly: July 29, 2000, has left a permanent mark—that day changed my life forever. I was an active twelve-year-old kid from Colorado, who loved theater and snowboarding and couldn't wait to start seventh grade. That summer I traveled with my family quite a bit, mostly to Sawyer, Michigan, to a small Christian community called Bethany Beach; I had spent time every summer of my life at this community. Our trip was coming to a close, and we needed to prepare for our long drive back home to Avon, Colorado. While we were packing up the car, we found out that the air conditioning was broken. This posed a significant problem for my mom, who was about to start a twenty-hour drive with three kids and trailer in the blasting heat and humidity of summer. We decided to sleep during the day and start our drive at night, when it was cooler. So we left at about 8:00 p.m. on July 28, 2000.

My sister, Jamie, my brother, J.D., and my mom, Heather, took shifts to split up the long drive. We had been driving through the whole night, and as the sun rose over the plains, we had driven midway through Nebraska. Jamie, 17, and I were sleeping in the back. I was lying down behind the passenger seat, with pillows, blankets, and a mini-TV to entertain us during the long drive. We had just stopped for gas and switched drivers, so my mom was in the passenger seat and J.D., 15, was driving. He had recently gotten his permit and needed more hours to get his license, so my mom told him that he could drive when we reached Nebraska, since we would be on Interstate 80 for hours and it was a straight shot home. J.D. and I were anxious to get back because we both had gotten good parts in the community theater musical *Guys and Dolls*, and rehearsal started at the beginning of August.

JHW: But then the unimaginable happened. What do you remember?

Kelly: Before getting back on the road I faintly remember J.D. asking, "Hey, do you guys want to stop for breakfast?" to which we mumbled, "Not yet, let's wait an hour or two." Jamie and I quickly drifted back to sleep. Suddenly I woke up to the most horrifying sound of my brother screaming and yelling profanities that I had never heard from his mouth. I sat up just in time to see the guardrail in front of me, and then everything went black. I woke up to the sound of sirens, with the world spinning around me, and seven paramedics hovering two feet above my face. When they noticed I had regained consciousness, they shouted, "She's awake!" "Can you feel your toes? Can you feel your fingers? How many fingers am I holding up?" In utter confusion, I screamed, "I don't care about my toes! What happened?! Who are you? Where is my family!?" One paramedic lowered his voice and said, "Kelly, everyone is alive. Everyone survived." "Survived! Survived what?!" I shouted using the only energy I had left. "Your family was in a serious car accident, but everyone is okay."

My mom is such a strong woman. As she came over to me, I could see her fighting back the tears and trying to keep her voice calm, "Kelly ... I am here. Can you feel your legs, honey?" I replied, "Yes, but mom, where is my arm? Where is it? I can't feel my arm! I can't move it! Is it attached?" Her voice began to crack as she looked at my arm, "Kelly, you just have a deep wound in your arm, and it probably hit a nerve, but don't worry — you'll be able to move it really soon." She did not know at the time that I would never again have a functioning right arm. I remember my mom's eyes watering as she said, "Kelly, you get to go on a helicopter ride! Isn't that cool?" As they hoisted me onto the gurney to be lifted into the Flight for Life helicopter, I fell back asleep.

JHW: So when you were finally able to reconstruct the event — what happened?

Kelly: We had been on the straight and monotonous Midwest roads for hours. Thirty minutes into J.D.'s driving shift, he began daydreaming about snowboarding, and two seconds later the Land Cruiser went off the road, down into the ditch. He turned the wheel with all his strength, but the weight of the trailer was too much. The car collided with the guardrail going 80 mph, hitting the passenger side door; the car flipped over the guardrail and rolled five times before it slid to a stop in the cornfield. At point of impact, my body shot out the side window, with my head breaking through the glass, and my body wrapped around the guardrail. As my head went through the window, the frame of the car smashed against my right shoulder on my way out, shattering the collarbone into dust and causing all five main nerves, also known as the brachial plexus (which controls that fourth of my body) to snap from the spinal cord. My right arm was torn at the armpit, causing significant blood loss. The paramedics, noticing the dangerously large amount of blood being lost for a young girl, called the Flight for Life helicopter. The accident broke my left collarbone (in addition to shattering the right), punctured my liver and spleen, broke all the bones in the left side of my face, and paralyzed one fourth of my body.

JHW: What about the rest of the family?

Kelly: That car accident on the morning of July 29, 2000, should have taken my life. It should have taken my sister's life. Jamie was ejected from the car after the third roll and thrown into the cornfield. She broke her neck in numerous places, but by God's grace, she recovered without any permanent damage outside of occasional neck pain. J.D. walked away with a cut on his shoulder. Miraculously, my mom saw the impact coming, brought her right leg to her chest, took the pillow from behind her head and put it in front of her — this act saved her right leg. She only sprained her ankle and broke three ribs. My family and I experienced a miracle that day; we learned how incredibly fragile is the gift of life.

JHW: But that was the beginning rather than the end. You now faced multiple surgeries. Can you tell us about them?

Kelly: I underwent my first surgery within hours of the accident. I had a deep wound on my arm because the glass went so deep; the bone and muscle were visible, so they grafted skin from my right hip to put over the hole so that it could heal. They were planning to operate on my punctured organs, but doctors were amazed to find that the organs were healing at an incredible pace, so that no surgery was needed—this was one of the blessings I received from the Lord. I was in the Intensive Care Unit in Nebraska for five days before they transferred me to Denver Children's Hospital, where I received numerous other surgeries. Since my right collarbone was shattered in the accident, the doctors wanted to operate immediately to try to rebuild my shoulder. They placed a metal plate over my collarbone and used screws to put the bone back together.

A couple of weeks after the surgery, we went to a neurologist to test the nerves in my right arm to see the damage that was done and what could be regained. As the doctor poked at different nerves and was moving certain muscles, he would ask, "Can you move this finger, Kelly? Really try hard." I tried with all my brainpower, but nothing moved. Not one muscle or nerve came out positive. "I am trying, but I can't! It won't move," I snapped. I stared down at my limp right arm and began to sob as I was hit with the gravity of my injury. The doctor shook his head and gave us the diagnosis. From my sternum to my shoulder all the way down to my pinky, my right side was completely paralyzed, which meant that all the nerves that control that fourth of the body were not just severed, but snapped from the brain stem. He explained that there was no way they could reattach the nerves because of the damage done to my spinal cord, and that only a serious nerve transplant could possibly restore any function or feeling.

My mom and I flew down to Texas, and on September 11, 2000, I underwent a thirteen-hour nerve transplant with the top brachial plexus specialist in the country. They took out two nerves in my legs that they told me were not completely necessary, then took out one nerve on the left side of my spinal cord and attached two nerves to that one socket. They threaded the nerves across my chest and into my armpit, where they attached them to other nerves in my right arm. When I woke up from surgery, I had never felt so much excruciating pain in my life; I remember sincerely and earnestly praying to God that he would take me home. Yet the Lord had a different plan in mind.

The doctor who grafted the two nerves said he hoped I would regain most of the feeling in the right arm and would be able to move my shoulder, biceps, triceps, wrist, and three fingers. Nerves regenerate a millimeter per month, so after the surgery, I would simply have to wait five years to see how my body would respond, hoping the muscles would work again before they completely atrophied. Since my muscles had no electrical stimulation from the brain, they would begin to atrophy and shrink, so we flew to Canada for my next surgery: to receive two electrical implants that would send stimulation to my biceps and triceps, in order to preserve the muscles until the nerve regenerated.

JHW: Beyond losing the use of your right arm, however, you had significant pain to deal with, as well as numerous surgeries intended to address those problems. How did that go?

Kelly: Adjusting to life without my right and dominant arm was not easy, but the chronic nerve pain that comes with paralysis is torturous. I began to realize that the nerve pain was seriously impacting all areas of my life. The pain can be so intense that my body will shut down, whether by collapsing to the ground in a classroom or going into convulsions. So my mom and I decided to go to a pain management clinic, where they suggested that I implant an electrical machine that would send signals throughout my right arm to override and weaken the pain. The first surgery was not too invasive, but it failed. The doctors scheduled another neck surgery, where they opened up my vertebrae to place the electrodes along the spinal cord, and then threaded wires down my back to attach to the battery they placed in my lower back. This surgery failed as well.

After I had undergone two failed surgeries and after months of wearing a neck brace, the doctors still insisted on a third surgery, where they would break apart my vertebrae and insert a small plate to hold the wires along my spinal cord. After spending thousands of dollars, wearing a neck brace for practically my whole sophomore year of high school, receiving scars all down my back, and suffering the pain from the surgeries, the device did nothing. The third surgery failed as well. The year that followed I went abroad to study in Ecuador and was happy to be away from the medical stress and numerous surgeries looming ahead. That same year I regained use of my back and chest, but it became clear that my arm was permanently paralyzed.

I took a couple years off from the operating room, hoping that time would bring some relief or even improvement; this reprieve lasted until November 2007, when I met with the brachial plexus specialist who had performed my nerve transplant seven years earlier. He was stopping in Chicago to speak with patients, and I jumped on the opportunity to meet with him, since he was incredibly difficult to contact. He only had time to meet with me for twelve minutes. My mind raced as I tried to think of all the questions I had—I didn't want to waste a minute. I told him I was considering amputation. He interrupted me and said:

"No, don't do that yet. Kelly, it is not your paralyzed arm that cripples you ... it's your nerve pain. You will have this pain for life. Normally the nerve pain fades within the first three to four years, but there are some patients for whom, because of the way the nerves were snapped from the brain stem, the pain becomes permanent. You have lived with the pain for seven years and it has not faded at all. I can see it in your eyes right now that you are trying to maintain your life in spite of the excruciating pain, and I'm telling you now that it will not go away. The surgeries you had never would have worked for your condition — those doctors should have known that. You need to have a spinal cord/brain stem surgery, take six months off from college, and then have numerous muscle transplants, moving muscles from your back and legs to your right arm. I'll call to schedule you for the spinal cord surgery in about three weeks, okay?"

I sat there in shock, trying to process all the information and began to cry. He sat there, surprised by my reaction and was confused as to why I was upset. He continued, "Kelly, I want you to sit here and picture a life without nerve pain. Nerve pain is one of the most painful things the human body can endure. Can you remember what it feels like to live without excruciating pain?" I shook my head. "Now the surgery has an 85 percent success rate for patients with your condition. Some wake up completely pain free and off their pain medication. Others wake up with significantly reduced pain, where the medication dose was cut in half. But there is a smaller percentage where it does not help with the pain, and it remains the same, but I think it is worth the shot."

After studying, analyzing, and praying for months, I decided to go ahead with the spinal cord surgery; I felt a life without pain was worth the risk. I just did not know how much I was risking. So on May 29, 2008, I reentered the operating room, more scared than I had ever been. The surgery entailed cutting five of my vertebrae in half and removing them, tearing the muscles around them in order to expose the spinal cord and brainstem. The surgeons drilled holes into the spinal cord and lasered the nerve endings and the right side of the spinal cord to create scar tissue, so that the pain signal from the brain would be blocked. After they finished the laser, they screwed my vertebrae back together and sealed up the eight-inch scar down my neck.

Six hours later I woke up and was in more pain than I had experienced in eight years since my nerve transplant. The nerve pain was horrifying; I curled into a ball on my hospital bed and sobbed; the pain was more intense than ever before. They told me that patients usually see results within the first two weeks. I went back for my checkup appointment only to find out that the doctor was not going to be there for the appointment or the appointment after that. I was so angry that the doctor could not take the time to spend a couple of minutes with me to explain what had happened to my body in the spinal cord surgery that he performed. So I met with his nurse and told her what I was experiencing and that my nerve pain was far worse than it was before the surgery. She tried to sound hopeful, but then explained softly, "You would have felt it by now if the operation was successful. I think you have memorized pain, which means that after your brain sends a pain signal for such a long time, the brain remembers it. No matter what operations you have to fix it, if your brain has memorized that signal and believes it is still there, there is nothing you can do." So the spinal cord surgery was a complete failure. It was not just that it did not help; rather, burning and lasering the nerve endings made my nerve pain worse permanently, so we had to double my medication dose to try to manage this new level of pain. Angry and confused, I tried to move on.

JHW: At this point you must have been feeling, like Job, that God had painted a target on your back. But it wasn't over yet, was it?

Kelly: Unfortunately, no. Three months later I left to study abroad in Spain for the fall semester of my junior year of college. Near the end of the semester I began to notice that my left hand was going numb for hours at a time. By the time I returned home to Colorado in December, my left hand was going numb for eight hours a day. I distinctly remember, as I was working as a snowboard instructor, that at the end of the day I was not able to check out my students because I could not pick up a pen; I stared at my limp left hand and the fingers would not respond. I assumed it had to be the cold temperatures, because I did not want to entertain the thought of what it might be. When I got home I jumped in the shower to warm up my body; as I raised my left arm to wash my hair, the arm lost all function — it flopped on my head and then fell to my side. I slid down the wall of the shower, sobbing. I had no idea what was causing this, but my left hand, the only hand I could use, was becoming paralyzed . . . or so it seemed.

When I came back to Wheaton College for my spring semester, I immediately sought out medical help from a chiropractor; he was eager and willing to assist me, and I consider him a gift from the Lord. We discovered that I had a spinal disc injury, in which the disc was sliding out of place and puncturing a nerve against the vertebrae. The injury was at my C6 and C7 vertebrae, meaning I was losing feeling in my whole hand and had already lost fine motor skills in my fingers as well as the strength in my forearm and triceps.

Over the course of my treatments (two to three visits every week for five months), we tried to address the problem with chiropractic, massage, and physical therapy. Throughout the semester there would be days I could not perform basic functions like typing, writing, buttoning my pants — which made my academic career at a rigorous college very difficult. Months later, by the Lord's grace, three out of five fingers began gaining strength and feeling, but my ring and pinky fingers were still not responding. The doctor realized that there was another injury that we had not detected before. During my final exam week I went to the hospital to get an MRI of my elbow. Sure enough, I had cubital tunnel, an injury where the ulnar nerve is entrapped by the surrounding tissues, cutting off connection to the brain. So my spinal disc injury caused my thumb, pointer finger, and middle finger to lose feeling and motor skills, while the cubital tunnel caused me to lose use of my ring and pinky finger.

When I went home for the summer, I saw an elbow specialist, who told me the injuries were completely unrelated, but their occurrence at the same time explained why I lost function in all five fingers. The specialist did not find a cause for the cubital tunnel and said, "Some people can get it randomly. You just really have bad luck." So on June 12, 2009, I was in the operating room once again, this time for my left arm. They decompressed the nerve by slicing the tissues surrounding the nerve, although they said that, because of the damage done to the nerve, it will take six months to two years to regain full motion and feeling in those fingers.

Over the next year I continued physical therapy trying to regain strength, but it is amazing how fast a muscle can atrophy when it loses connection to the brain for eight months. It was humbling, being an active girl from Colorado, to be lifting two-pound weights at the gym, especially since my left arm used to be so strong — the only arm that I used. I was grateful that for once, the medical situation was appropriately diagnosed and successfully treated.

After graduating from Wheaton College with my degrees in Spanish and Fine Art Photography, I moved back home to Colorado in May 2010. I had come to the conclusion that I would not try anything else medically because, as we had seen from my track record, it was doing more harm than good. About a year later, I began seeing a neurologist, and the topic of my nerve pain kept coming up. We tried new medications and varied the dosage, but I did not see any results. He finally said, "Kelly, I really want you to consider going to a nerve pain relief specialist in California. I really think he could do great things for you. He has the cutting-edge technology, and the sole purpose of his practice is to relieve chronic nerve pain." I was stubborn, but at every appointment he kept asking me, "What do you have to lose? He could be the one that finally makes a breakthrough and relieves you of this pain. No one should have to live with this pain the rest of their lives."

I finally decided that I would at least look into it, despite my weariness. I would wrestle back and forth between the thoughts, "I was told the same thing about the spinal cord surgery. I was told it would help my pain in amazing ways, but what did that do for me? It nearly paralyzed my left arm!" and "But what if this guy really is the best nerve pain relief specialist? That means he sees patients like me daily, right? What if he does have a treatment that works? Life without pain seems unimaginable."

After much prayer, I decided to call and see if they had an appointment available. I didn't want to drive out there alone, so I thought that I'd try to go the week of my husband Agustin's (fiancé at the time) spring break from grad school. They told me that this doctor is booked six months out and there is no way I can see him in a month. I put the decision on the back burner until I got a call saying they had a miraculous opening in the schedule, which happened to be the week of Agustin's spring break. Soon we were on the road to L.A. to see this nerve pain specialist.

After taking MRI images of my nerves and meeting with him, we talked about the damage done to the nerves and the possible solutions. He told me that my pain could either be coming from scar tissue build-up that was irritating the nerves under my collarbone or the pain source was in my brain, which means there was almost nothing we could do. He outlined a procedure that would give me the answer once and for all so I wouldn't have to keep trying treatments that were not addressing the actual problem. He said, "Why continue to have surgeries on the spinal cord if the pain source is the brain? That's a waste of time and money, and causes unnecessary pain." This test would detect the source of the pain by temporarily paralyzing my arm and all the nerves surrounding the initial spinal cord injury. Once medically anesthetized, if I did not have nerve pain, we would know the pain source was within the nerves that were paralyzed. But if I still had pain for that fifteen-hour trial period, we could conclude the pain source was in the brain.

The catch was that this test would cost $11,000. My jaw dropped when I heard the price. Since I had just graduated from a private Christian college and was planning my wedding, we would have to take a loan or set up a payment plan to even consider being able to pay that amount of money. Agustin and I discussed it. We decided that I had not taken a week off work and driven all the way to California to hear the suggestion and then turn it down. Plus, the amount of money that I have spent on surgeries that all failed surpasses that price. If we knew once and for all the source of the pain, we wouldn't have to consider treatment options that involved the spinal cord because we would know the source was in the brain — or vice versa. So we went ahead with the procedure.

Nothing happened. The medication given in the procedure to paralyze all the nerves failed. He said he gave me enough medication to paralyze a normal person's body almost entirely, and the medication had no effect. I still had the same feeling and motion. When I spoke with the doctor, they were still going to charge us the full $11,000. He also said that even though the test did not give us the result we were hoping for, we would go ahead and do the surgery. The nerves that were damaged in the car accident are encased in scar tissue. The surgery would remove scar tissue in hopes that the nerves would be able to breathe more and reduce nerve pain significantly. He strongly encouraged me to do the surgery, even though there was only a 50/50 chance that it would do anything for me at all.

I asked the doctor, "If the nerves are encased in scar tissue, is that possibly what holds them together? If we tear the scar tissue out, isn't there a risk it could tear the nerve too, causing me to lose the feeling and motion I gained?"

He recognized the risk but felt it was still worth it to move forward. The amount of pressure to move forward with the surgery, despite the lack of test results to detect the source of the pain, was unsettling. The surgery would cost us another $15,000. We decided not to do the surgery, and after a long stressful week of tests, a failed procedure, and countless hours of waiting to speak with the doctor, we decided to go home with a big stack of bills and no results. To say the trip was discouraging is a huge understatement. We found out weeks later that we were charged three times the amount that other doctors in that area charge for the same procedure. So we are currently trying to negotiate to lower the costs, for a procedure that did absolutely nothing, but we haven't had much success. In the end, we simply added one more procedure (that was guaranteed to work) which did nothing but add medical bills we will be paying for years.

JHW: That brings us up to the time of this writing, but let's backtrack a little. You were a Christian at the time of the accident; had yours been a faith embraced in early childhood?

Kelly: I would say it was. I grew up believing Christianity to be true, but I remember going to a worship concert in fifth grade and rededicating my life to Christ. I think that was when I really decided to make my faith my own, and I started to develop my own personal relationship with God.

JHW: Would you say that you had considered yourself a good person, an obedient girl (even if not in Joban proportions)?

Kelly: I would say I was a good kid, but maybe I should ask my mother. I had my bratty moments, but overall I think I considered myself a good person. I wanted to do the right thing, get good grades, and be nice. As I got older, around the age of ten, I started learning that good fruit only comes from my love for Christ; at that point I decided to intentionally pursue him.

JHW: How did your faith react in the aftermath of the accident? Were your responses anything like Job's (1:21; 2:10)?

Kelly: Immediately after the accident my response was not like Job's. I was not angry, but I wasn't praising the Lord for the event either. I was more confused than anything else. I knew the truth in the Scriptures that told me the Lord would bring good from the trials, but I just could not see it; nevertheless, I had to rest my faith on that truth. After about three years, my perspective began to change and I started to see the work that God was doing in me through the situation. I finally came to the point where I could praise him for his faithfulness in the events that took place.

We will follow Kelly's story from chapter to chapter and see more of her struggles trying to understand what God was doing in her life.

Before we conclude this contemporary significance section, however, we may also consider how the book of Job exposes unhelpful or untruthful thoughts concerning suffering. We expect to find some of these because the book functions, in part, to expose false thinking.

A reason for suffering? Many readers are disturbed by the discussion that occurs between Yahweh and the Challenger in the opening chapter. Does the text imply that such discussions occur frequently?[91] Might we find an explanation for our own suffering in such a scenario? I contend that we cannot. We must recall that the scene is not even given to Job as an explanation for his suffering. He never learns of it. If it does not serve as explanation for his suffering, we certainly should not entertain it as an explanation for our own.

One of the major points of this book is that we do not get any explanation for suffering; to expect such an explanation is folly. Explanations are not possible. How strange if we seized upon this scene to provide just that! Furthermore, the scene in heaven does not provide a reason for Job's suffering. There is no philosophical cause or reason for his suffering—just as there is none for ours. A scenario is not the same as a reason. This is not the same as inscrutability—a view that claims there *is* a reason, that it is just beyond our ability to understand.

A role model for response to suffering? A second thought might occur to the casual reader of Job 1: Should we understand Job 1:21–22 as an example of how to respond to suffering? Is Job supposed to be a role model for us? We might note two commendable aspects of Job's response. First, Job recognizes God's right either to give or to take; second, Job praises God instead of throwing accusations at him. Undeniably, these would be appropriate responses to catastrophes that might come upon us, but the

---

91. This premise is evident even in popular novels based on the book of Job, such as M. J. Ferrari, *The Book of Joby* (New York: Tor, 2007).

text cannot be upholding Job as a model response, because not all of his responses are commendable, and the text does not differentiate between what is acceptable and what is unacceptable. The text simply reports, as narratives often do.

Therefore, we should not conclude that the text is providing us with a biblically authorized response to suffering in the character of Job; we must maintain the distinction between description and prescription. Undoubtedly, God was pleased with Job's response (indicated by his repeated praise of Job in 2:3; see also Ezek. 14:14), but a variety of other responses may have been just as acceptable. This part of the book is not designed to detail "the" right response to suffering.

Questioning character. Finally, in the book of Job we find that suffering often results in someone questioning the character of someone else.[92] Job begins by offering sacrifices because he questions the character of his children; the Challenger questions the character of God and the motives of Job; Job's friends question his character; and Job questions the character of God. These questions reveal certain assumptions about character, and we will find the same is true in our consideration of suffering today. We might easily make unwarranted assumptions about the character of God, the character of those who suffer, or even about our own character when we suffer. Such doubts derive from our assumptions about the world and God's operation of the world, both often reflecting variations of the RP. As we proceed further into the book, we ought to suspend all such assumptions about character and open our minds that we might reconsider how much we truly know about God's administration of the world.

---

92. Ngwa, "Did Job Suffer for Nothing?" 359–80, see esp. 374–75.

Job 2

O n another day the angels came to present themselves before the LORD, and Satan also came with
them to present himself before him. ²And the LORD
said to Satan, "Where have you come from?"

Satan answered the LORD, "From roaming through the
earth and going back and forth in it."

³Then the LORD said to Satan, "Have you considered my
servant Job? There is no one on earth like him; he is blameless and upright, a man who fears God and shuns evil. And
he still maintains his integrity, though you incited me against
him to ruin him without any reason."

⁴"Skin for skin!" Satan replied. "A man will give all he has
for his own life. ⁵But stretch out your hand and strike his
flesh and bones, and he will surely curse you to your face."

⁶The LORD said to Satan, "Very well, then, he is in your
hands; but you must spare his life."

⁷So Satan went out from the presence of the LORD and
afflicted Job with painful sores from the soles of his feet to
the top of his head. ⁸Then Job took a piece of broken pottery
and scraped himself with it as he sat among the ashes.

⁹His wife said to him, "Are you still holding on to your
integrity? Curse God and die!"

¹⁰He replied, "You are talking like a foolish woman. Shall
we accept good from God, and not trouble?"

In all this, Job did not sin in what he said.

¹¹When Job's three friends, Eliphaz the Temanite, Bildad
the Shuhite and Zophar the Naamathite, heard about all the
troubles that had come upon him, they set out from their
homes and met together by agreement to go and sympathize
with him and comfort him. ¹²When they saw him from a distance, they could hardly recognize him; they began to weep
aloud, and they tore their robes and sprinkled dust on their
heads. ¹³Then they sat on the ground with him for seven
days and seven nights. No one said a word to him, because
they saw how great his suffering was.

Second Conversation (2:1–6)

THROUGH THE MIDDLE OF verse 3, this second conversation practically repeats Job 1:7–8; the only differences are the addition of three Hebrew words at the end of 2:1 (lit., "to present himself before Yahweh") and the word used for "from where" (*me'ayin* in 1:7; *'e mizzeh* in 2:2). In other occurrences, these two phrases used for "from where" function similarly.[1] The former (*me'ayin*) occurs in three different syntactical situations. When accompanied by a pronoun, it forms a question concerning a person's travels.[2] When accompanied by the verb "to come" (*bo'*), as here, it is used to inquire superficially about the location from where one has traveled, but is more interested in what brings the person there—that is, it is more a question concerning motives and purposes than travel itinerary.[3] When accompanied by a noun, it functions as an inquiry about the source from which something will be drawn.[4] The latter (*'e mizzeh*) evidences only two of these categories. It occurs with the verb *bo'* regarding motive or purpose,[5] and with a pronoun in contexts concerning place of origin.[6] We can therefore conclude that the two phrases are synonymous.

Job maintains his integrity. The text indicates that Job continues to cling to his integrity. The participle that I translate "cling to" is typically used to indicate grasping something firmly, sometimes even showing a response to grasp something more tightly when someone might be inclined to take that thing away—for instance, when a child tries to pull her hand away from her mother and the mother grips it more firmly (note Isa. 41:13). The word translated "integrity" is the same word that led off the sequence in the repeated accolade of Job ("blameless"). We can easily conclude that Job maintains not only his blamelessness but also his other commendable qualities. In short, Job's actions have revealed no flawed motive such as the Challenger earlier suggested.

Ruin without reason. We should analyze the language here to determine precisely who is responsible for Job's predicament: the Challenger or Yahweh. The close analysis provided in the appendix on the word trans-

---

1. *me'ayin* occurs 17x, *'e mizzeh* occurs 7x.

2. Gen. 29:4; Josh. 2:4; 2 Kings 5:25.

3. This is evident from the contexts of the questions and from the answers that are given: Gen. 42:7; Josh. 9:8; Judg. 17:9; 19:17; 2 Kings 20:14//Isa. 39:3; Jon. 1:8.

4. Num. 11:13; 2 Kings 6:27; Job 28:12, 20; Ps. 121:1; Nah. 3:7.

5. Gen. 16:8; 2 Sam. 1:3.

6. Judg. 13:6; 1 Sam. 25:11; 2 Sam. 1:13 (note different answer from where the other syntax was used in 1:3); 15:2.

lated "incited" (see p. 449–50) demonstrates that Yahweh is accountable and responsible despite the role that the Challenger plays.

Yahweh's statement that he has been incited to "ruin"[7] Job "without any reason" (Heb. *hinnam*) requires further clarification.[8] This same word (*hinnam*) was used in 1:9, when the Challenger raised the question about whether Job served God "for nothing [no reason]." While the term *hinnam* can refer to something done in vain (e.g., Ezek. 6:10), unnecessarily (e.g., 1 Sam. 25:31), or without compensation (e.g., Gen. 29:15; this is the meaning in Job 1:9), in most cases it refers to something done without cause — undeserved treatment (1 Sam. 19:5; 1 Kings 2:31). Job expresses this same assessment of what God has done in Job 10:7–8: "You know that I am not guilty ... will you now turn and destroy me?"

Such assertions confirm again that nothing that happens to Job can be construed as punishment for some offense; Job's righteousness continues to be confirmed from all sources. We should again emphasize that Job is not portrayed as totally sinless, but as one who does not deserve the tragedies that have befallen him. If the RP represents justice, it must be carried out in proportion: the punishment must suit the crime. In Job's case, no such proportionality can be sustained.

Affliction of Job and the Arrival of Counselors (2:7–13)

ADVANCED TRIAL. THE FIRST round of trials took away that which was positive in Job's life — that is, his prosperity; this second round adds the negative by causing physical suffering. The first round brought mental anguish associated with loss, while the second brings physical problems associated with pain.

Job first responded by acknowledging God's prerogative to take everything away (1:21), since all he had came from God in the first place. Thus, Job loses the "compensation" for his righteousness. The Challenger contends that Job will not be so sanguine if he believes that God is actually punishing him, despite his righteousness. The ancients did not think of good health as a benefit provided by deity, but they did think of sickness and disease as either punishments imposed by deity or, more likely, as the

---

7. The verb "ruin" (*bl'*) occurs 25x in the Piel and Pual stems. It conveys destructiveness, but in a variety of different ways. Destruction can come from being consumed (Ps. 21:9[10]); it can come from being devoured (i.e., taken in, Prov. 19:28; 21:20; Isa. 23:8); or it can come from being cut off from supply or resource (2 Sam. 7:16; Job 8:18). A number of passages are ambiguous (cf. Lam. 2:2, 5, 8, 16).

8. Note the telling combination of *bl'* and *hinnam* in Prov. 1:11–12, where an innocent is waylaid for no reason and, like Sheol, devoured indiscriminately.

result of God's abandoning the person to affliction from demons or ghosts.[9] Job allows no possibility that his affliction is caused by another party: the bad comes from God (2:10). In the first trial God took away the good (1:21); in the second, God brings the bad (2:10). Job accepts God's right to do both without cursing him.

Job's condition (*šeḥin*) does not yield confident diagnosis.[10] It is not the term that is sometimes translated as "leprosy"[11] and probably involves inflammation of the skin (if etymology leads the right direction). This skin disease would generally have resulted in his expulsion from the city. Though the reference to ashes recalls the common practice of mourners heaping dust and ashes on their heads, here Job has been relegated to sitting on the ash heap. The ash heap outside of town is like the city dump, which burned regularly.[12] The expansive translation of the LXX indicates that dung was one of the most common loads brought to the dump;[13] such a location confirms Job's outcast status.

Role of Job's wife. Several observations in verses 9–10 call for a fresh analysis of Job's wife. We need to sort out the possibilities, beginning at the level of text, because several possible interpretations of the wife's words have been suggested. Primarily we must decide between the traditional: "Are you still holding on to your integrity? Curse God and die!" and the variant: "Hold onto your integrity! Bless God and die" (i.e., continue blessing God and it will get you nothing but death). Our analysis will address four elements:

Discourse: the connection between the wife's and God's statements about Job
Syntax: the absence of the interrogative marker
Morphology: the forms of the verbs "bless" and "die"

---

9. The afflictions by ghosts, however, were not skin diseases, but headaches, eye and ear problems, and numerous other internal conditions. See J. Scurlock, *Magico-Medical Means of Treating Ghost-Induced Illnesses in Ancient Mesopotamia* (Leiden: Brill/Styx, 2006), 161–75.

10. For detailed textual and medical description of dozens of skin diseases known from Akkadian texts, see J. Scurlock and B. Andersen, *Diagnoses in Assyrian and Babylonian Medicine* (Urbana, Ill.: Univ. of Illinois Press, 2005), 208–41. Clines, *Job 1–20*, 48–49, has a fairly complete treatment of sources and suggestions, including the two uses of the cognate of this term in extrabiblical literature (Ugarit and the Qumran Prayer of Nabonidus), but none of these brings a resolution.

11. Note that even the word sometimes translated "leprosy" is probably not Hansen's disease.

12. See discussion in Clines, *Job 1–20*, 50.

13. LXX: *kopros*, though it is difficult to find evidence by which to affirm the interpretation of the LXX.

Lexical semantics: the meaning of the words *barek* (2:9) and
nebalah (2:10)

(1) In the discourse comparison, God's assessment of Job (2:3) is identical to the assessment of Job's wife (2:9), except for the insignificant and necessary change from third person to second person. The similarity could signal that we should read the two statements the same way, or the similarities could belie a contrast that the reader is supposed to pick up.[14]

(2) Regarding syntax, we must ask whether the first part of the wife's speech (2:9a) and the second part of Job's response (2:10b) are questions.[15] There are no interrogative markers, though, in Hebrew, an interrogative marker is not essential for a statement to be a question; sometimes only context will determine the reading. Nevertheless, the author has used the interrogative markers for questions of fact (1:8; 2:3) and for rhetorical questions (1:10) in this context. Furthermore, the speeches throughout Job are filled with rhetorical questions; yet there is not a single unarguable case where there is a question with no interrogative marker.[16]

(3) The morphological questions concern the verbal forms used by Job's wife. Both "bless" and "die" are imperatives, suggesting that they function as words of advice. If Job's wife intended to make general statements of principle, as some suggest, we would expect participles ("the one who blesses is the one who dies").

(4) The first semantic issue concerns whether the Hebrew word *barek* should be translated "curse" (i.e., understanding the verb euphemistically, as in ch. 1) or "bless" (as it stands). Here, context is our only guide, though the author might intend the verb to be ambiguous.

The second semantic issue concerns the characterization of the wife's words; Job labels them as words of "a foolish woman" (*nebalah*). The NIV note indicates that the term *"foolish* denotes moral deficiency," but others have suggested that the word is not limited to contexts of moral deficiency and can also refer to many forms of unconventional behaviors.[17] The word

---

14. In the near context we have seen that *hinnam* is used in two comparable speeches but with two different connotations. Elsewhere in Scripture this discourse art form can be observed in Isaac's blessing on Jacob masquerading as Esau and the almost identical words used for Esau's blessing later in the chapter (Gen. 27:28, 39 respectively).

15. Ngwa, "Did Job Suffer for Nothing?" 377.

16. A few of the major contested ones are Job 11:11; 32:16; and 37:24; but all of these have suitable explanations as statements rather than questions.

17. Ngwa, "Did Job Suffer for Nothing?" 378; J. Marböck, "נָבָל," *TDOT*, 9:167–71; his conclusion about the semantic location of the root is that it should be understood as "a breach or derangement of the bonds that unite human beings with each other or with God, whether expressed in status, attitude, word, or deed" (171).

nebalah, however, cannot be easily neutralized to simply refer to something unconventional. Elsewhere, it refers to a scandalous travesty, outrageous behavior—not simply unconventional, but violating all conventions of propriety (13x, almost half in the scandal passages of Gen. 34; Judg. 19–20; 2 Sam. 13). Yet even taking it as a scandalous suggestion leaves open the question about which part of what she says is scandalous. If the suggestion that blessing God will result in death rather than life (against the conventional wisdom), she is speaking what seems accurate given recent events, but what eventually is seen as a misrepresentation of the way God works. She claims that faithfulness leads to death—a world-upside-down scenario.[18] The friends are presumably also accused of speaking *nebalah* (42:8, though see comments there), which makes them liable to harsh treatment at God's hand, but their scandalous talk about God is expressed by an affirmation of the traditional philosophy.

The nature of Job's last statement in 2:10 drives the conclusions that I recommend. I cannot see any consistent way to render verse 9 as a statement rather than as a rhetorical question (despite the absence of the interrogative marker). If Job's last comment is a rhetorical question ("Should we not accept … trouble?"), then his wife's first statement could also be taken as a rhetorical question (as traditionally translated). The syntactical equivalence between verse 9 and God's statement in verse 3 is an example of contrast through similarity: Job's wife uses the same words but turns them to different purpose. If Job replies by saying that they ought to accept the bad from God, then she must have suggested that he do otherwise. Therefore, she could not have simply advised him to continue blessing God, even as it appears to be leading to death. She must have advised a contrary path of action (cursing God), an example of not accepting the bad. Job calls this advice foolishness because impious behavior is always outside the bounds of conventional propriety. In the end, then, linguistic analysis supports the traditional understanding as most likely. Job's wife has advised Job to capitulate to his tragic fate by cursing God and accepting the inevitable punishment of death.

The "trouble" ("bad"; Heb. *ra'*) that Job insists must be accepted is a term used repeatedly throughout the prologue.[19] It is what Job turns away from and now it is what he accepts from the hand of God. Moral evil is one possible denotation, but the term can be used for anything negative; here Job refers to all of the negative things that have come upon him. His

---

18. Notice that the *nabal* in Ps. 14:1 denies that there is a moral order maintained by God. Cf. Isa. 32:6–7, where the *nebalah* involves spreading evil about the Lord.
19. Job 1:1, 8; 2:7, 11.

words cannot be construed as labeling God as the source of moral evil, but the word leaves another ambiguity to be resolved as the book progresses. Contrary to "cursing God to his face," Job has not sinned with his lips. This still leaves unaddressed the question whether he has "cursed God in his heart," but nothing has indicated any wavering of his commitment.

The arrival of the friends. Eliphaz, Bildad, and Zophar now enter the picture. Eliphaz is from Teman, a well-known location in Edom, about half-way between the Dead Sea and the Gulf of Aqaba. Bildad is identified as a Shuhite, a designation that could either identify him as a descendant of Shuah, son of Abraham (Gen. 25:2), or a resident of the town of Suhu along the middle Euphrates. However, neither of these alternatives is conclusive—confidence is impossible at this stage. Zophar is a Naamathite; this location is even more uncertain. For modern readers, there is no information to be gleaned from the place names, though to the ancient reader they may have had significance.[20]

The friends come together by arrangement and with a specific purpose: to commiserate or sympathize and to offer condolences and assuage his grief. Clines may be right that the friends actually discard their good intentions once they encounter Job; he believes their mourning and seven days of silence indicate that they are treating Job as if he were already dead.[21] Thus it is left to Job to speak first.

TWO RHETORICAL ISSUES WILL be addressed in this section: (1) the contribution made by the second scene in heaven, and (2) the roles played by Job's wife and friends.

Second Scene in Heaven

THIS SECOND SCENE REAFFIRMS Job's righteousness and sets the stage for the second barrage of suffering. The conversation opens the same way as the first, and a similar exchange of information takes place. The second phase of suffering assures that Job has every opportunity to abandon God if his only motive for faithfulness has been to gain benefits. Tolerating pain is different from tolerating loss.

---

20. Clines locates the friends all in the vicinity of Edom (*Job 1–20*, 61), whereas Weiss suggests that they represent south, east, and north respectively (*Job's Beginning*, 75).

21. Clines, *Job 1–20*, 61.

Role of Job's Wife and Friends

JOB'S WIFE. THOUGH ONLY one verse is dedicated to the speech of Job's wife, she plays an important role. She makes no pretense of offering comfort or consolation; her comments offer instead a particular course of action. If Job listens to her advice, the Challenger wins the case. She believes that if Job has none of the benefits of his righteous living, his life has no value. If Job agrees, he would show that he has been living for the benefits—exactly what the Challenger suspected. This would demonstrate that God's policies corrupt the motives of righteous people.

The involvement of Job's wife accomplishes four purposes:

- It avoids the quick win for the Challenger. If Job is going to break, it will take more than this.
- It provides opportunity for Job to express his faithfulness yet again. Not only can God take away what he has given, but he can strike with pain and disease. Job remains steadfast.
- It serves as prelude and transition to the friends. The author will carry out the business of the book through the various solutions offered by humans trying to cope with crisis. Everyone has their perspectives and all will be considered.
- It proposes a solution opposite the direction the friends will go. They want to tell him how to live (with renewed benefits) while she tells him life is not worth living. Both assume that benefits are essential to the equation and therefore are pulling Job in the direction the Challenger has suggested he will go. They are unwitting agents for the Challenger.

Job's friends. A number of commentators have recognized that the friends function as representatives of the traditional views of the ancient Near East.[22] We can agree with that, but ask further whether they work together to offer a deeply nuanced picture or whether they each represent stereotypes of a particular view. Hartley has characterized each of the friends by the way that they argue their cases. He suggests that Eliphaz is a mystic who leans heavily on his experiences and observations (4:8, 12–16; 5:3); perhaps considering him a "spiritualist" would include his mysticism but also explain his consistent orientation to the spiritual realm. Bildad is a traditionalist (8:8) who relies on what he has been told. Zophar is a rationalist who depends on what his reason and logic tell

---

22. Mattingly, "Pious Sufferer," 332–33; Pope, *Job*, xxxvii; A. Cooper, "Reading and Misreading the Prologue to Job," *JSOT* 46 (1990): 67–79, see 71.

him.[23] In this way, the friends offer differing perspectives toward the problem of suffering. The following chart summarizes the viewpoints of the friends.

	Eliphaz	Bildad	Zophar
Philosophical solution	No mortal is righteous (4:17; 15:14).	We know nothing (8:9); no one can be righteous (25:4).	God is inscrutable (11:7–9).
Practical advice	Appeal to God (5:8) for restoration (5:17–19; 22:23) and remove wickedness (22:23) for renewed prosperity (22:21).	Plead your righteousness (8:5–6) to gain restoration (8:6–7).	Devote your heart and put away sin (11:13–14), and you will be restored (11:15–19).
Affirmation of RP	4:6–7; 15:20–35; 22:15–20	8:4–7; 18:5–21	11:11; 20:4–29

In their philosophical solutions, they reflect the common answers given in the ancient Near East.[24] It is therefore no surprise that they advise Job to deal with his offense, even though they cannot identify any particular sin he has committed. Eliphaz's catalog of Job's supposed transgressions in 22:5–9 is fishing—an attempt to offer suggestions. Even as they are fixated on uncovering Job's offense, their advice makes it clear that restoration of benefits is the goal. Eliphaz even goes so far as to claim that righteousness gives no pleasure to God (22:3). In this way, they are promoting the Challenger's case as they try to get Job to ignore the question of disinterested righteousness and instead pursue benefits. Though they do not propose ritual solutions, the core of their argument lies in the ancient Near Eastern appeasement mentality. They do not discuss at length how Job should appease God, but that end is their focus. They are more interested in outcome (benefits restored) than method. Even as the friends stand as representatives of the conventional thinking of the ancient Near East, more importantly, they are the Challenger's agents. If Job follows their advice,

---

23. Hartley, *Job*, 193. Though this can be helpful, we also must be cautious about using modernist categories. While differences between the friends would not be surprising, we also must recognize that there is considerable overlap among them.
24. See Introduction, 31–38.

the Challenger will win his case and God's policies will be shown to be flawed, as the Challenger has suggested.

In the Introduction we described briefly Tsevat's triangle of claims as a way of understanding the positions taken up in the book. The triangle illustrates the tension between three concepts that everyone believes should co-exist: the Retribution Principle, God's justice, and Job's righteousness. Given Job's calamities, one of the three has to be discarded. As we progress through the book, we will see that the various parties choose which corner is most important to them and which is no longer tenable. The friends act as a group in this; the most important corner for them is the RP, because that is the conventional thinking in the world of wisdom. It operates in a strict cause-and-effect manner with a benefits orientation. That means that as they set up their defense in that corner, they must question one of the other corners. Because they refuse to cast aspersions on the character of God,[25] Job is the weak link; his righteousness comes under automatic suspicion. As we proceed through the book, we will position others in relationship to this triangle.

The friends believe that Job is on trial — the defendant in a criminal case — and that he has been found guilty. But this is a backward trial. In their assessment, the judge has passed down the verdict, and now they, as the jury, need to try the case and find the evidence to uphold the verdict. To this end, Job is intensely cross-examined. In conclusion, then, the friends are the defenders of the RP, the agents of the Challenger, the representatives of the conventional thinking of the ancient Near East, and the jury trying the case in which, by virtue of his circumstances, Job is already presumed guilty.

Straddling the rhetorical issues and the theological issues is the contrast between the two uses of *ḥinnam* in Job 1–2, already discussed in Original Meaning. The two uses of *ḥinnam* interact to form a significant pair.[26] Job, as it turns out, was capable of fearing God *ḥinnam* ("without compensation") and God was incited to act against him *ḥinnam* ("without cause"). The two occurrences of *ḥinnam* bring into sharp relief the basic philosophical premises of the discussion, as well as the basic philosophical challenges directed toward God. The two philosophical premises are the Great Symbiosis[27] (if Job fears God *ḥinnam*, the Great Symbiosis does not affect Job's thinking — God owes him nothing) and the Retribution Principle[28] (if God brings evil on Job *ḥinnam*, the RP is not in effect in God's policies).

---

25. Cf. 4:17; 5:8–16; 8:3, 20–22; 22:12–14; 25:2.
26. Ngwa, "Did Job Suffer for Nothing?" 359–80.
27. People need gods to take care of them, and gods need people to take care of them.
28. The righteous prosper and the wicked suffer.

Job and the Challenger pose two opposite philosophical questions about God's policies. The Challenger questions whether Job would fear God if his service was *hinnam* ("without compensation"). Job questions whether it is good policy for God to ruin righteous people *hinnam* ("without cause"). By the end of the book, both the Great Symbiosis and the Retribution Principle are discarded as fundamental principles. This conclusion is already anticipated here as God affirms that he has ruined Job for no cause. As Clines observes, "the law of retribution has been broken!"[29] The word *hinnam* stands, therefore, at the heart of the book's focus on motive and cause. The characters concentrate on these, but the book will eventually contend that these are the wrong questions. But for now, they hold center stage and frame the coming discussions.

The main theological issue for us to address concerns the relative role of God and the Challenger in Job's suffering. Numerous verses clearly indicate that God is the cause of Job's suffering:

1:11; 2:5 — The Challenger says that God must stretch out his hand to strike Job.

2:3 — God indicates that he is the one who has brought Job's ruin without cause.

16:9 — God assails him.

19:21 — The hand of God has struck him.

42:11 — Job is consoled over all the trouble that Yahweh brought upon him.

No one in the book ever suggests any other agent as the cause of Job's suffering. When God places Job in the Challenger's hands (power, 1:12; 2:6), he is not absolving himself of responsibility but delegating authority to the Challenger. The Challenger's role is philosophical, not diabolical; he is a subordinate functionary, not an independent power for evil or the ruin of humanity. Anything approaching dualism would let God off the hook too easily; the book does not provide this option. It is trying to give a deeper understanding of God, not to somehow absolve him of responsibility.[30]

Is God cruel to accede to the challenge? The issue is presented poignantly by F. R. Magdalene, whose thoughts are worth quoting at length:

---

29. Clines, *Job 1–20*, 43.

30. This view is affirmed in L. K. Handy, "The Authorization of Divine Power and the Guilt of God in the Book of Job: Useful Ugaritic Parallels," *JSOT* 60 (1993): 107–18, where it is also demonstrated that this pattern is well-known in the ancient Near East, particularly Ugarit.

[God's] actions constitute a horrifically cruel deed if all that is at stake is a test of Job's faith. Surely God has other, less invasive and traumatic ways to gather such data. The theological view arising from a focus on the sovereignty and omnipotence of God that God must be in league with the Satan is deeply disturbing. If God is capable of destroying ten children and stripping Job of any human dignity on a bet—on a dare—then he is, to my mind, a very immature, highly insecure, and deeply troubled god, certainly no better than our worst view of the Satan. There is a better solution to the theological conundrum presented by the events in the Divine Council. If we read Job 1–2 with the idea that the Satan has charged God with serious misconduct, then God is also subject to investigation and must allow such investigation to proceed against his will. The withdrawal of all Job's blessings and the imposition of suffering are much more than an investigation of Job's state of mind; they are, more important, an investigation of God.[31]

If Yahweh's policies are to be investigated legitimately, he cannot simply say, "You're wrong," and be done with it. He allows his policies to be placed under thorough scrutiny.

Finally, I would again emphasize my belief that even though built on a forensic model, this is wisdom literature and is devised as a thought experiment, not as something that Yahweh actually did. It is designed to raise issues and discuss philosophical options. If so, we should not misguidedly enter into a discussion of whether Yahweh's action was justifiable or cruel.

Contemporary Significance

WE MUST NEVER ALLOW ourselves to believe that God is cruel. Job's response is appropriate: "Should we accept the good from God, and not trouble?" This is true regardless of whether we can identify cause. God acted against Job without cause. Does God sometimes act against us without cause? Does this make him cruel? Is there a difference between his acting without cause and his acting without purpose? That is, should we sometimes seek understanding of God's actions, not in light of just cause, but in light of wise purpose?

When life takes a turn for the worst, it is easy to blame God and to question what he is doing. It is easy for us to believe that he is making a mess of things and that we could do a better job of it, if given the chance; we will

---

31. Magdalene, *Scales of Righteousness*, 118.

discuss this further when God confronts Job with this very idea in 40:7–14. Whenever we raise questions about God's justice, we tacitly suggest that if we were given the chance, we would be more just. When we question God's love, we imply that we could be more loving. His grace, his mercy, his patience—name whatever attribute you will: If we think we can do them better than God, we have a defective view of God (not to mention an unrealistic conceit and a superficial and simplistic knowledge of the problem). Talk to any adult on the street and you would likely hear him or her express doubts about how unfair it is of God to do this or that. In today's climate of tolerance, we commonly hear that only an ogre of a God would so limit the range of salvation that only those who happened to hear of Jesus will benefit.

We all know that revelation is not exhaustive and our theology does not provide ironclad answers for every question. Where our revelation is silent and the logic of our theology fails, however, we are not without recourse; this is where faith begins.[32] Will not the Judge of all the earth do right? Of course he will. We don't have to worry that God is less fair, less just, less merciful, less loving, or less gracious than we would be. The "If I were God" option will always fall far short of letting God be God. This is our faith. We never have all the information and we are never wise enough to infallibly apply the information we have to whatever issue is at hand.

Kelly's Story[33]

OUR TENDENCY TO QUESTION God and his nature, motivations, and competency is especially evident when we suffer. In pain, grief, or loss, our unanswered cries become bewildered questions, then glares of disapproval, and finally accusations and even rejection of God and faith. Those who have suffered consider the answers of the faithful and the philosophical to be clichés that offer no solace and no sense of reality—well-intentioned but sadly superficial.

In order to make sure that we avoid the easy answers, Kelly is going to share some of her thoughts and struggles about God as she lived with the pain from her accident and the unsuccessful surgeries that sometimes made things worse rather than better.

JHW: Job expresses the philosophy that if we are willing to take good from the hand of God, we should also be willing to accept the bad. But

---

32. This is not to deny that faith has already been expressed as we accept the concept of revelation and the shape of theology.

33. Kelly interacts with parts of her story in each Contemporary Significance section. For the introduction to the details of her story, see Contemporary Significance in the commentary on ch. 1, pp.. 87–97.

many cannot face suffering with such stoicism. Can you share some of your thoughts about God's hand in all of your suffering?

Kelly: It has been a process of growth. I am still learning and being stretched when it comes to this topic. The accident happened over a decade ago, so I have gone through different stages in regards to my view on suffering and God's involvement. I have experienced times of anger, periods of confusion, and times of sorrow, curiosity, and joy. I do trust that God has a plan, but there are times where I have been confused as to what I am supposed to learn from it. The car accident is something that God allowed and for which I can praise him because I can see the fruit that has come from it. It is hard to praise him for the pain I am experiencing, when I can't see his purpose in it. Yet we are not guaranteed explanations. Even though I know God's will is better than my own, there are still some things I wrestle with and ask God about.

A good example of that is the result of my spinal cord surgery in May 2008. I had severe nerve pain for eight years, and it was something my friends and family were aware of. Yet when the surgery failed and the nerve pain increased dramatically, I was the only one who would feel the difference. So I asked, "God, what was the point of that? How did that strengthen my testimony? I could have dealt with the surgery failing and no improvement, but why did you allow the surgery to intensify the pain to the degree that it did? I had nerve pain before and that impacted my testimony; now I still have the same story, except that I am living in more pain." On days when I feel discouraged, I ask, "Lord, isn't my testimony strong enough? Aren't there enough trials in different areas of my life to encourage people from many walks of life? Now, could you extend me a little grace?" When I vocalize that, I see the faulty way of thinking, but I can't deny the questions that run through my head.

I vividly remember my conversation with God when I began to lose function in my left arm. As I sat in the shower looking at my two limp arms, I cried out in frustration. "God, you have already taken one arm and countless muscles in my body, please ... please don't take my left arm! Don't ... don't take it. You say you only give us what we can handle, and I can't handle having no arms! You've finally reached the limit of what I can take. I want to do things for your kingdom; please let me keep one hand!"

If I am truly honest with myself and think about my raw thoughts with God, I have realized that I have come to expect the worse—especially medically. I do not see my medical situation improving, yet I expect it to get worse as the years go on, to the point where I am no longer surprised by failed surgeries, but expect them. When things are calm in my life, I begin to wonder, "Okay, it has been relatively calm for too long. When does the next trial come? What will it be?"

It is a learning process. I unfortunately have seen how my trials have tainted my views of certain attributes of God and how my response to the suffering is not always biblical or praiseworthy, but in the times when I doubt or I am angry … I still go to him. I cry to him in my anger, sadness, or grief. Yet I am humbled because even though there are days when I am angry, there is still so much good that the Lord has brought from it. It is when I am thinking clearly that I can sincerely praise him for the life I have lived and the trials Christ has carried me through.

JHW: Though the book does not offer Job as a role model, his strength has been an encouragement to many over the centuries, and people have also been encouraged by your strength. Tell us about some of the opportunities you had to share the struggles you have been having and how that has affected people.

Kelly: Since I have a physical disability, it is one that everyone is aware of whether I talk about it or not. I wear a brace on my paralyzed right arm to protect it, so it looks like I sprained my wrist. So I get asked, "Oh, what did you do to your arm? Did you break your arm?" numerous times a day, whether it be the cashier at the grocery store, a waiter in a restaurant, or meeting a new friend. I get asked by almost every person I come into contact with, regardless of whether they know my name. I have numerous opportunities a day to share about his miracle in keeping my family alive through the car accident and his faithfulness to carry us through. Having a visual reminder on my body of the car accident opens doors of opportunity to share compassion and remind people that there is a living God. Not to say I take every single opportunity, but it is encouraging to see how the story of his faithfulness can encourage people.

I distinctly remember going to a spa to use a gift card for a massage. Within minutes of my session, my massage therapist was asking tons of questions about my car accident and then proceeded to ask how I was dealing with it emotionally. Now, as my face was smashed in the cradle of the massage table, I tried to articulate how through Christ's strength, you can endure through trials and with the right perspective you can learn, grow, and mature from them. So he started opening up and telling me that his girlfriend was in a car accident and was really emotionally distraught, but she felt as if no one understood how she felt. So he asked if I would be willing to meet with her. In other words, I walked in to get a massage and walked out with his business card and his girlfriend's cell phone to set up a coffee date. As I sat down to meet with her, I thought to myself, "Wow, what an incredible opportunity it is to sit here, one I would never have had without my disability." I met with her and simply listened to her story and affirmed her in how she was processing a traumatic event. Then I shared with her my experience and what God has done in my life, and she was encouraged by talking with someone who shared her trial and was still moving forward and living her life.

The Lord has graciously expanded my mission field, sometimes to areas where I feel like I am not equipped; yet those are the times I am reminded it isn't my words or work, but what he is doing through me. I can relate to numerous types of people and try to encourage them—which would be an unlikely opportunity, were it not for my disability. Since I am a kids' snowboard instructor around the holiday season, kids arrive and learn their instructor is snowboarding with only the use of one arm. So I have had the chance to encourage kids not to let a trial stop them from pursuing their passions. I can work with disabled kids and show them how they can modify sports, so they can participate. I have also been able to encourage the junior high girls about beauty. Since I have struggled with insecurities about appearance, with my surgery scars, I can relate to them and build their confidence in who we are as women and in the bodies God gave us.

I have a physical reminder of a very difficult trial. Because of that people from so many walks of life feel I can relate with them in what it feels like to have your world turned upside down. I started to realize that everyone has disabling events in their lives; mine you can just see.

In high school, I began recognizing that in the midst of the adversity, I was so blessed because I learned so many things from the accident and the years following. At an early age, I learned about the fragility of life, how each day is a gift we take for granted, and I learned to appreciate my family. That shift in perspective in junior high dramatically changed how I live my life and shaped me into a different person. I have had opportunities to talk in front of large groups on topics such as car accident awareness, overcoming trials, talking to God amidst adversity, and perseverance—all topics I still struggle with daily. Yet when I learn about how my testimony has affected someone, I can look back at the trials and say, "Okay, it is worth it."

JHW: God was also able to use you for the kingdom in a number of ways. Tell us about the foundation you were able to establish.

Kelly: After studying abroad in Quito, Ecuador, for my junior year of high school, I was challenged in new ways. I wanted to get out of my comfort zone. I was stretched and humbled that year and had my eyes opened to such poverty and suffering that I could not even fathom. It puts things in perspective. While living in Ecuador, I encountered poverty, which became a part of my life as I volunteered with different service groups and missionaries throughout that year. I saw an increasing problem of kids with disabilities being abandoned because their parents couldn't afford the medical costs.

When I returned to the U.S. for my senior year of high school, I wrestled with reverse culture shock. It was a tough transition, and I initially judged so many people around me for not appreciating their wealth and what they had. I was frustrated as I began realizing how much I had changed and how I no longer fit in the place I called home. Yet the Lord quickly humbled me and reminded me that I am just as guilty of materialism, and that he did not send me to Ecuador to come back and judge, but sent me to come back and share.

So I began working on what is now called the Ecuador Challenge. My parents and I went through the application process my senior year, and just after I turned eighteen the government approved it as a nonprofit foundation, allowing it to be tax deductible. I knew I wanted to raise support for different causes and to be transparent within the foundation about what I was doing, where the money was going, and how it was used. So in the first project, we raised support for an existing orphanage just outside Quito that specialized in caring for kids with disabilities. I was so impressed by the compassion of the workers and how they served the kids in that community that I wanted to raise financial support to help cover the costs of medical bills and care for these kids.

I expected to launch a small project within my high school, to expose high school students to the reality of poverty and to how they themselves could have an impact. I shared with the students that I was a high schooler like them, yet had been blessed with an opportunity to be challenged and changed by my experience in Ecuador. When the project launched, it took off. The Lord blessed it, and it has spread from one school to the next, to churches, businesses, media, and families. My goal had been to raise $2,000 in my high school. Within three short weeks with the additional help of the community, we raised $15,000. It was all in God's hands! So the day after I graduated in May 2006, I flew down to Ecuador bringing a friend, Jeff Hall, and a cousin, Elita Intini, with me to personally deliver the donation, letters, pictures, and gifts for the orphans.

I want the foundation to support and raise awareness for existing projects that are sustainable in Ecuador, but need financial support to continue serving their communities. The experience has radically changed me and given me a passion for serving. At the moment, the foundation is on standstill as I gain job experience to prepare me for what God has in store, but I am excited and praying about what the Lord will do in the future.

Kelly has shared with me on a number of occasions that as glad as she is for her pain and suffering to be an inspiration to others, she wouldn't mind sometimes if God would use someone else as an inspiration. Like Kelly (and unlike Job), for many the story has no end in this life. It is one thing to have a noble response to suffering when it first happens; it is another thing entirely to sustain that noble response through years and years of unending struggles. Many days are not good days and our resistance wears down. Job's did as well, and in the next chapter we will explore those days.

Before we move on, however, I offer a word of caution about how we think about God's role in our suffering. This topic is going to be addressed throughout the commentary from many different perspectives, but we need to introduce some of them here. Job assumed that his suffering came from the hand of God. Kelly likewise used active verbs to describe God's role (whether in sending or allowing things to happen). In Job's case the book tells us that God did indeed play an active role, but we must remember that the book is not trying to give us a model for how God is regularly involved in what people suffer.

What vocabulary should we use to describe God's involvement? Choosing terms inevitably becomes an expression of theology. I would suggest that one of the major lessons of the book of Job is that no such language suffices. Whenever we choose a verb to communicate God's relationship to suffering, we are proposing what can only be a simplistic understanding of what God does. Simplistic generalizations lead to flawed theology because God's role is beyond our comprehension and beyond our powers of explanation. In the scenario laid out in Job, he happened to be right—his circumstances were from the hand of God. But it would be reductionistic and inaccurate for us to characterize all suffering as coming directly from the hand of God. These issues will be unpacked gradually as we work through the book.[34]

---

34. Solutions that I have to offer are presented in the Bridging Contexts sections of the commentary on Job 38–41 and on Job 42.

Job 3

fter this, Job opened his mouth and cursed the day of
his birth. ²He said:

³"May the day of my birth perish,
and the night it was said, 'A boy is born!'
⁴That day—may it turn to darkness;
may God above not care about it;
may no light shine upon it.
⁵May darkness and deep shadow claim it once more;
may a cloud settle over it;
may blackness overwhelm its light.
⁶That night—may thick darkness seize it;
may it not be included among the days of the year
nor be entered in any of the months.
⁷May that night be barren;
may no shout of joy be heard in it.
⁸May those who curse days curse that day,
those who are ready to rouse Leviathan.
⁹May its morning stars become dark;
may it wait for daylight in vain
and not see the first rays of dawn,
¹⁰for it did not shut the doors of the womb on me
to hide trouble from my eyes.

¹¹"Why did I not perish at birth,
and die as I came from the womb?
¹²Why were there knees to receive me
and breasts that I might be nursed?
¹³For now I would be lying down in peace;
I would be asleep and at rest
¹⁴with kings and counselors of the earth,
who built for themselves places now lying in ruins,
¹⁵with rulers who had gold,
who filled their houses with silver.
¹⁶Or why was I not hidden in the ground like a stillborn child,
like an infant who never saw the light of day?
¹⁷There the wicked cease from turmoil,
and there the weary are at rest.

¹⁸Captives also enjoy their ease;
   they no longer hear the slave driver's shout.
¹⁹The small and the great are there,
   and the slave is freed from his master.

²⁰"Why is light given to those in misery,
   and life to the bitter of soul,
²¹to those who long for death that does not come,
   who search for it more than for hidden treasure,
²²who are filled with gladness
   and rejoice when they reach the grave?
²³Why is life given to a man
   whose way is hidden,
   whom God has hedged in?
²⁴For sighing comes to me instead of food;
   my groans pour out like water.
²⁵What I feared has come upon me;
   what I dreaded has happened to me.
²⁶I have no peace, no quietness;
   I have no rest, but only turmoil."

AS WE BEGIN THE poetic section of the book, we need to realize that the poetry of the book Job is the most difficult in the Hebrew Bible. The text is full of words with uncertain meaning, and commentaries are likewise full of suggestions for emendations. In a commentary such as this, we will not be able to spend time considering all of these words and the scholarly suggestions. I will choose those discussions that have most relevance to the typical user of this commentary series with accompanying apologies that so much is left unattended. Fuller discussion may be found in the more exhaustive classic commentaries such as those by Clines, Hartley, or Habel.

Job's lament has three discrete sections. In the first, 3:3–10, Job curses the day of his birth. The second (3:11–19) expresses his wish that he had never been born, that he had proceeded immediately from womb to the netherworld. The third (3:20–26) turns to the misery of his present life.

Cursing the Day of Birth (3:1–10)

JOB'S CURSING OF THE day of his birth is introduced by the usual Hebrew verb for "curse" (*qll*). The euphemism used in the prologue (*brk*, "bless") is not required when God is not the object of the verb. While the Challenger claimed that Job would curse God to his face (2:5), in this chapter we find the only curse Job utters, a curse that focuses on the day of his birth rather than on God. Some have wondered whether this is a difference without a distinction; after all, if Job recognizes God as the one responsible for the birth of each individual, Job is, in effect, cursing something that God did. Even if this were so, however, that one step removed constitutes an important difference. Throughout the book, Job gets desperately close to cursing God; in this sense, Job's lament introduces what later speeches will continue.

Some have wondered whether we see here a different Job from the character portrayed by the confident speeches of the prologue,[1] but I am not persuaded. The statements in the prologue concern Job's posture toward *God's rights*: God gave, so he has the right to take away (1:21); God has the right to give both good and bad (2:10). In contrast, chapter 3 begins to express Job's posture toward his own *circumstances*. Distress over one's circumstances is normal; therefore, we can hardly blame Job for his response. Though God is sovereign and Job therefore must hold him responsible, this is not the same as questioning God's rights. More importantly, even if Job were to question God's actions, this would not indicate that he counted benefits more important than righteousness. Notice that he does *not* say that his righteousness was useless or that he wishes he had never bothered, nor does he demand his benefits to be returned.

Chaos incantation. In 3:3, Job wishes not only that he had never been born, but that he had never been conceived.[2] As he moves to a discussion of that day in 3:4, he first says (lit.), "Let there be darkness," using wording that is the exact antithesis of Genesis 1:3, when God summons light to the first day. Thus begins what many interpreters identify as the undoing of creation. M. Fishbane refers to Job 3:3–13 as a "counter-cosmic incantation" that reverses the creation sequence of Genesis 1 — an undoing of order in favor of chaos.[3] Given the label "curse," which among other things

---

1. Clines (*Job 1–20*, 83) seems to support this as he cites the original suggestion by R. D. Moore uncontested.

2. Contrary to the NIV, in the second line of the verse, night proclaims that a man (already anticipating a mature man) has been conceived (Pual or passive Qal participle).

3. M. Fishbane, "Jeremiah IV 23–26 and Job III 3–13: A Recovered Use of the Creation Pattern," *VT* 21 (1971): 151–67, see 153 for the designation. In general, I agree with the assessment that Job 3 could use incantation language and is counter-creation in some sense, but I am not persuaded that Job is undoing each of the seven days or that Job 3 should be measured against Genesis 1. Light and darkness are the main foci. For point by point refutation of Fishbane, see R. S. Watson, *Chaos Uncreated: A Reassessment of the Theme of "Chaos" in the Hebrew Bible* (BZAW 341; Berlin/New York: Walter de Gruyter, 2005), 319–22.

can refer to the use of words of power against someone or something, it is appropriate for us to understand this passage as an incantation. As such, it is part of the vocabulary of the world of magical words, though Job is using them only to express a wish, not as actual words of power. Specifically, what is it that Job would like undone? Clines rightly observes that each day is called forth by God:[4]

> Job 38:12: God makes the dawn know its place and commands the morning.
> Isaiah 40:26: God calls the names of the stars to bring them into the night sky.

In Egyptian literature, creation recurred every day. Day was not simply summoned by deity; day had to overcome the hostility of the chaos creature Apophis, who attempted to swallow the sun to prevent it from rising from the netherworld, through which it traversed during the night. Though the role of Apophis has no correlate in Israelite thinking, we should understand the blackness, the unrealized day, and the extended treatment of the netherworld in relation to this cognitive environment. Even the wish that the night be barren (3:7) would make some sense here in light of Egyptian thinking since Nut, the sky god, gives birth to the sun every morning as it emerges from the netherworld.

If God were not to call forth the light, the sun, or the day, the day would not exist. The sequence of images expresses a variety of ways that the day could be negated; this is the thrust of 3:4–10. Such suggestions are contrary to creation and order, but here Job is not actually invoking words of power; rather, he is taking up an incantation genre to express his wish about the long past day of his birth—an obvious and effective rhetorical device.

Rousing Leviathan. Since this whole section concerns the fate of a particular day, we should not be surprised to read the word "day" in 3:8, but the verse is full of intriguing difficulties. Many have accepted the variant alternative reading of verse 8 as a reference to "Yam" (Heb. *yam*, the Sea, or the personality behind the Sea in Ugaritic texts) rather than "day" (*yom*). In support of this reading, the word occurs in parallel to Leviathan, a pairing that is attested in Ugaritic.[5] J. Day, however, has offered a convincing rebuttal of such an emendation, based on the fact that "cursing Yam" would be the opposite of rousing Leviathan, not a synonymous parallel.[6] Fur-

---

4. Clines, *Job 1–20*, 84.
5. See Baal and Anat I AB vi, 35–52 and as late as Aramaic Incantation texts in the Sassanian period. See Fishbane, "Jeremiah IV," 160.
6. Day, *God's Conflict with the Dragon*, 46–47.

thermore, it is logical that one might curse the day by rousing Leviathan, an opponent of day.[7] "Day" is a sign of order, and Leviathan is counterorder.[8] Rather than a "chaos creature," it might be more appropriate then to describe Leviathan as an "anti-cosmos figure," though it is important to determine whether Leviathan has differing roles in the Bible and in the ancient Near East. Besides the five passages in the Old Testament (elsewhere, Job 41; Pss. 74:14; 104:26; Isa. 27:1), Leviathan is present in Ugaritic literature as Litan/Lotan.[9] I will reserve fuller discussion of Leviathan for Job 41.

Here our main concern is to understand the rousing of Leviathan. The verb used here sounds the same as the verb in the first part of the sentence (rousing = ʿorer; cursing = ʾorer; both participles, the former singular, the latter plural). If we are going to understand the rousing of Leviathan, we need first to consider "those who curse the day." The root used for the cursing here (ʾrr) is different from the one that was used in verse 1 (qll). We have already noted above that qll refers to using words of power against someone or something (cf. Ex. 22:28); in contrast, ʾrr expresses removing someone or something from the protection and favor of God.[10] God is almost always the grammatical subject of this latter verb, though here such a reading seems unlikely, based on the use of the plural. When God is not the subject, the verb usually refers to someone who mediates on God's behalf (e.g., Balaam, Num. 22:6, 12; 23:7).[11] Understood as removing the day from God's favor or protection, this line parallels Job 3:4, where God does not "care" for the day.

Who are "those who curse the day?" In the human realm, those who curse would most naturally be diviners who specialized in such incantations; these would presumably be the same ones who could ritually arouse

---

7. R. Watson (*Chaos Uncreated*, 326) supports (though still with reservation) retaining the translation "day," but with the understanding that an ancient reader would have picked up the latent wordplay between *yom* and *yam*.

8. It would be particularly intriguing should Leviathan be proven to be a sun-devourer like Apophis, but such evidence does not currently exist.

9. The only two certain occurrences are in the Baal and Mot myth; for text see *COS*, 1.86: 265 (= *CTA* V/*KTU* 1.5.i.1,27). Literature on Leviathan is extensive. Some of the most helpful or foundational treatments are the following: C. Uehlinger, "Leviathan," *DDD²*, 511–15; E. Lipinski, "לִוְיָתָן," *TDOT*, 7:504–9; M. K. Wakeman, *God's Battle with the Monster: A Study in Biblical Imagery* (Leiden: Brill, 1973), 62–68; C. Kloos, *Yhwh's Combat with the Sea* (Leiden: Brill, 1986); Day, *God's Conflict with the Dragon*; Watson, *Chaos Uncreated*, esp. 319–27; C. H. Gordon, "Leviathan: Symbol of Evil," in *Biblical Motifs* (ed. A. Altmann; Cambridge, Mass.: Harvard Univ. Press, 1966), 1–10.

10. J. Scharbert, "אָרַר," *TDOT*, 1:409.

11. For possible exceptions, see Gen. 9:25; 27:29; Ex. 22:28.

Leviathan. The noun *'atidim* (NIV: "those who are ready") would then refer to those skilled in such incantations, though the term is obscure.[12] In the ancient Near Eastern context, Akkadian literature speaks of a class of scholars known as the *ummani le'uti* ("able scholars") who manifest one or more of five scholarly disciplines (*tupšarru*, "astrologer/scribe"; *baru*, "haruspex/diviner"; *ašipu*, "exorcist/magician"; *asu*, "physician"; and *kalu*, "lamentation chanter").[13] These *ummani* find their roots in the mythical sages, the *apkalli*—scholars and sages who ensured the correct functioning of the divine order;[14] it is less clear that they had the skills to disrupt that same divine order.

It is more likely, then, that Job is referring to a group in the divine realm. Deities, especially Enki/Ea, the god of divination, or his son, Marduk, are capable of powerful incantations.[15] The gods, however, are typically the ones who maintain order rather than disrupting it, though exceptions exist in destructive gods such as Erra (Nergal) and Namtar—both of whom set demons to their tasks. This leaves the primary candidates as beings who were considered more hostile, such as the seven, the Sebetti, primarily known from the Erra Epic.[16] These gods of war and destruction are seen, in one incantation text, as complicit in causing an eclipse.[17] Such an action could be considered the equivalent of rousing Leviathan, if Leviathan in Job 3 is bringing an eclipse as his attack against the day. Demons known as the *utukke lemnuti* also were considered responsible for disruption of order, and the *galle rabuti*, the great demons, were seen as responsible for eclipses, among other things.[18]

The book of Job makes no explicit references to demons, and nowhere do Job's friends or Job himself blame demons for Job's situation. Thus, we need not understand this passing reference to those who could disrupt order by combating the day of Job's birth as a reference to demons. In

---

12. Clines, *Job 1–20*, 86–87.

13. S. Parpola, *Letters from Assyrian and Babylonian Scholars* (SAA X; Helsinki: Helsinki Univ. Press, 1993), xiii.

14. Ibid., xx.

15. Many rituals to drive out demons invoke the power of Ea or Marduk to work through the specialist performing the incantation. This is evident, for instance, in the sixteen tablet sequence of the *utukku lemnutu* incantations; see M. J. Geller, *Evil Demons: Canonical Utukku Lemnutu Incantations* (SAA V; Helsinki: Neo-Assyrian Text Corpus Project, 2007).

16. Known in the Bible, as evident from Ezek. 9; see D. Bodi, *The Book of Ezekiel and the Poem of Erra* (OBO 104; Freiburg/Göttingen: Universitätsverlag Freiburg Schweiz/Vandenhoeck & Ruprecht, 1991), 95–110.

17. Geller, *Evil Demons*, 16.38–41 (pp. 58–63).

18. In the ancient Near East, these demons were considered the offspring of the gods ("Fashioned in the Netherworld, but spawned in Heaven" (see Geller, *Evil Demons*, 5.143) and they disrupt order at every level—from personal health to cosmic catastrophe.

the end I would view Job's statement as having an intentionally indefinite referent (i.e., "whoever curses days and rouses Leviathan, may they do so").

The Netherworld (3:11–19)

IN THESE VERSES, WE find one of the fullest treatments of the netherworld in the Old Testament. The alternative to being born, once that had been allowed by "the day," was to be stillborn or to die shortly after birth. Job expresses his belief that the netherworld would be a better place to be than his life on earth; he depicts the netherworld as a place of comfort, rest, ease, and tranquility. We should note that it is therefore a place of neither punishment nor reward. The fairly positive picture painted here gains its attractiveness because of the contrast to Job's circumstances on earth; the depiction is entirely relative, for such a positive view of the netherworld is not common in biblical perspective. In modern-day terms, someone who was starving might look forward to prison, where they could get three meals a day. As in the last section, this passage gains rhetorical force by the shocking pictures used to convey the desperation of Job's situation.

The Misery of Life (3:20–26)

THIS THIRD SECTION FOLLOWS in the sequence of the negative "if only" expressions: If only the day of my birth had never existed (3:3–10); but since it did, if only I had died upon birth and gone straight to the peaceful netherworld (3:11–19); but since it didn't, if only life were not my continuing portion (3:12–20) when it is so filled with misery and turmoil. Two statements here bear further examination.

God has hedged in (3:23). Job's choice of verb here is full of irony. He considers himself to be "hedged in" (Hiph. of *skk*) by his ignorance and impotence. In 1:10 the Challenger objected that God had hedged (*śuk*) Job in on every side.[19] The question concerns whether the hedge is protective shelter or restrictive barrier. To some extent, the answer will be determined by the perspective of those inside or outside, though it is possible that in the circumstances of the book, one sort of hedge has been replaced with another.[20] In the end perhaps one sort of hedge or another is inevitable.[21]

What I feared has come upon me (3:25). The question here is whether Job is thinking about the past or the present. Has that which he dreaded

---

19. The root *skk* (with the sibilant *samek*, *HALOT*, 754) used in 3:23 is fairly common, whereas the root *śuk* (with sibilant *sin*, *HALOT*, 1312) is used only one other time (Hos. 2:8). Both have related noun forms.

20. I am grateful to Ashley Edewaard for this observation.

21. I am grateful to Jonathan Walton for this observation.

throughout life come upon him? Or is he reflecting on a day-by-day experience; that is, at every turn is what he dreads becoming reality? The former is more likely, since in 31:23, Job clarifies that he specifically dreaded (*pḥd*) destruction from God. Job 1:4–5 shows that Job was fearful of actions that would cause him or his loved ones to lose the favor of God. His fears have been realized though he can imagine no actions of his that could have been the cause of his circumstances.

Both of the words for fear in this verse are different from the word used to express Job's "fear of the LORD" in the prologue. The first verb, *pḥd* (= "dread, terror"), usually has as its object or implied object a person or persons.[22] The verb in the second clause, *ygr* (= "fearful worry"), occurs elsewhere only four more times[23] and takes circumstances as its object. I am inclined to translate in paraphrastic style, "The inexorable foe of whom I am terrified has advanced and swept over me; the circumstances that I have long worried about have come to pass, as I anticipated they eventually would." This translation makes clear that the verb *pḥd* focuses on the source of the terror, while *ygr* focuses on the result.

We might ask yet again: When Job feared losing God's favor, did he fear forfeiting the benefits connected to God's favor, or simply losing his right standing before God? Job's words do not betray the reasons for his foreboding apprehension, and so the book remains ambiguous concerning Job's motives (and now his fears).

Rhetorical Issues

PURPOSE OF LAMENT. JOB'S lament builds the transition between the prologue and the speeches through the shift in genre (from narrative to direct discourse) and in theological emphasis. In the latter we see development from a confident Job (chs. 1–2) to a distraught, questioning Job. We begin to see the depth of Job's psychological despair as his speeches become less composed and dignified, which realistically reflects the scope of his loss. The author has portrayed Job as extraordinary in his

---

22. The noun *pḥd* may be used in Job as a personified reference to a supernatural being. See esp. 4:14, where it is parallel to "spirit," and 15:21, where the plural parallels the marauder. See R. Fyall, *Now My Eyes Have Seen You* (NSBT 12; Downers Grove, Ill.: InterVarsity Press, 2002), 120; See Clines, *Job 1–20*, 357, who suggests they are personified spirits of vengeance.

23. Deut. 9:19; 28:60; Job 9:28; Ps. 119:39.

piety and righteousness, but it would not do to leave the audience think-ing of him as superhumanly untouched by grief. The audience is able to sympathize with Job because in his place we would do the same; now Job is one of us.

Job's hopes. The lament also shows us Job's frame of mind. We can see already that he has no hope that death will lead to an eternity where all can be rectified. Neither life nor death offers him any hope, though death is preferable to life. We can also see that he has begun asking the "why" questions (vv. 11, 12, 16, 20, 23). Even as he does so, Job betrays no hint that he believes he deserves what he has gotten[24] or that the RP has been at work. Though he has not begun to blame God, he alludes to God's oppres-sive behavior in 3:23. Nevertheless, he has not yet launched his legal case.

Theological Issues

VIEW OF THE AFTERLIFE. In Job's lament we find the first of many refer-ences to death, afterlife, and the netherworld. While Christians enjoy an assurance of heaven as a place of reward for those who have received God's salvation, we cannot assume that the Israelites shared that confidence. We must explore the Old Testament to discover its concept of the afterlife at this stage of revelation. Did the Israelites believe that reward and judg-ment would occur in the afterlife? In their understanding, what possibili-ties existed after death? Did they look forward to an eternity with God? Answers to these questions are critical for understanding Israelite theology in general and Job's beliefs in particular. The possibility or impossibility of vindication in the afterlife will make a big difference in Job's understanding of God's justice.

"Sheol" (*šeʾol*) is the Hebrew designation for the place of the dead. Job does not use the term in this lament, but it occurs eight times throughout the book.[25] *Šeʾol* has no known antecedent in other cultures or religions of the ancient world; furthermore, the etymology of the word is uncertain and therefore unable to contribute to the discussion.[26] The most exten-sive section of the Old Testament concerning Sheol is Isaiah 14:9–11, in which the spirits of the dead come together to meet the recently demised king of Babylon, and the spirits of other deceased kings commiserate with him about their loss of power. This is similar to the picture given in Job 3:14–15, where we see the palaces of the kings lying in ruin; in Isaiah, the

---

24. Clines, *Job 1–20*, 104.

25. Job 7:9; 11:8; 14:13; 17:13, 16; 21:13; 24:19; 26:6.

26. For the most complete discussion and critique of etymological suggestions, see T. Lewis, "Dead, Abode of the," *ABD*, 2:101–2.

kings observe that their former pomp procures no status in Sheol, where they have only a maggot mattress and worm blankets. The figurative nature of these passages makes it difficult for us to make any conclusive statements about the details of life in Sheol, but the author successfully conveys the idea that it is not particularly pleasant. In this sense, Sheol is similar to the picture of the netherworld in Mesopotamian literature, though there kings are believed to retain some of their earthly status.[27] Compare, for instance, the description of King Urnammu's death:

> Here we find first a description of the king lying on his bier in his palace, mourned by his family and people. Then the scene changes, and Urnammu is in the underworld, where he presents gifts to its "seven gods" and sacrifices animals to its important dead; the gods receive the gifts in their respective palaces. So Urnammu comes to the place allotted to him, acquires certain of the dead as servants, and Gilgamesh explains the rules of life in the underworld. The next section describes how "after seven days, yea ten days" Urnammu hears the weeping and lamentation of those left behind, and responds to this by himself uttering a bitter lament.[28]

The term Sheol is often used metaphorically to refer to death or the grave (e.g., Isa. 28:15), a factor that complicates our ability to develop an understanding of Sheol as the netherworld. Because of its metaphorical usage, many passages that refer to Sheol become ambiguous. Sheol is spoken of as a place of decay (Ps. 16:10) to which someone would dig down (Amos 9:2). When Jacob speaks of going to Sheol (Gen. 37:35; 42:38; 44:29, 31), is he speaking of the netherworld or the grave? Some have maintained that the term never refers to the netherworld but always to the grave.[29] Difficulties with this view include:

1. In Psalm 55:15, the psalmist prays, "Let death take my enemies by surprise; let them go down alive to [Sheol], for evil finds lodging among them." The contrast between "death" in the first

---

27. We will not have occasion in this chapter to discuss the beliefs of the various peoples of the ancient Near East. A couple of the best discussions of this material can be found in K. Spronk, *Beatific Afterlife in Ancient Israel* (AOAT 219; Kevelaer: Butzon & Bercker; Neukirchen-Vluyn: Neukirchener Verlag, 1986), 86–236; D. Katz, *The Image of the Netherworld in Sumerian Sources* (Bethesda, Md.: CDL, 2003); and P. S. Johnston, *Shades of Sheol* (Downers Grove, Ill: InterVarsity Press, 2002).

28. H. Ringgren, *Religions of the Ancient Near East* (Philadelphia: Westminster, 1973), 46–47.

29. R. L. Harris, "The Meaning of the Word Sheol as Shown by Parallels in Poetic Texts," *BETS* 4 (1961): 129–35.

line and "alive" in the second warns us that these two phrases are not synonymous. It would be difficult to imagine that the psalmist hopes for his enemy to be buried alive.

2. In Psalm 139:8, as the psalmist speaks of the impossibility of fleeing from God, he observes, "If I make my bed in [Sheol], you are there." One could hardly contend that God is in the grave, but his access to the netherworld is appropriate and significant (see also Prov. 15:11; Amos 9:2).

3. As I already mentioned, both Job and Isaiah refer to kings. This would hardly be descriptive of the grave but fully appropriate to the netherworld.

These passages suggest that the concept of Sheol as the netherworld must be central to our understanding of the Israelite concept of afterlife.

Several observations from the text contribute to our understanding of the theology related to Sheol:

1. Those in Sheol are considered separated from God (Pss. 6:6; 88:3, 10–12; Isa. 38:18), though, as previously mentioned, God has access to Sheol.

2. Sheol is never referred to as the abode of the wicked alone.

3. While Sheol is never identified as the place where all go (though Eccl. 6:6 says that all go to the same place), the burden of proof rests on those who suggest that there was an alternative.[30]

4. Sheol is referred to in human speech as well as in divine speech (Deut. 32:22).

5. Sheol is a place of negation: no possessions, memory, knowledge, or joy.[31]

6. It is not a place where judgment or punishment takes place, though it is considered an act of God's judgment to be sent there prematurely. Subsequently, it is inaccurate to translate Sheol as

---

30. R. Rosenberg contends that Sheol and the pit are places for the "wicked dead"— those who suffer untimely or unnatural death. She sees the alternative as being gathered to one's ancestors ("The Concept of Biblical Sheol within the Context of Ancient Near Eastern Beliefs" [Ph.D. diss., Harvard Divinity School, 1981], 174–93). Nonetheless, her evidence is not able to rule out the idea that the untimely/unnatural death itself is the punishment of God, or that going down to the pit simply refers to improper burial. Additionally, verses like 1 Kings 2:6 suggest that one could go down to Sheol "in peace." Her explanation of this passage (240–41) is unconvincing.

31. N. J. Tromp, *Primitive Conceptions of Death and the Nether World in the Old Testament* (Rome: Pontifical Biblical Institute, 1969), 187–90. Tromp has the most thorough treatment of Sheol and other netherworld concepts.

"hell" in the Christian sense, for the latter is by definition a place of punishment.[32]

7. No reference suggests varying compartments in Sheol. "Deepest" Sheol (e.g., Deut. 32:22) refers only to its location ("beneath") rather than a lower compartment.[33]

8. Logically, one would not expect a distinction between a place of reward and a place of punishment at this juncture, since the ultimate criteria for the distinction as we understand it, the work of Christ, was not yet available.

I would agree with the summary of R. Martin-Achard:

> Sheol is not in fact a place of punishment reserved for the impious, the abode of the perished is not identical with Gehenna; all the departed are in it, and if in their existence in that place there is nothing of comfort, the evil-doer does not suffer eternal punishment there. It will not be until the period when the last of the Old Testament documents are appearing that the Jews, or at least some of them, will modify their ideas about the Beyond: Sheol will sometimes become a temporary abode where the dead are waiting for resurrection and judgment; to ensure the separation of the good and the evil, it will even be divided into several sections, of which one will be a place of bliss for the righteous, and another a place of suffering for the sinful.[34]

In potential contrast to these conclusions, three phrases occur in the Old Testament texts that scholars interpret as indications that the Israelites believed they would be with God when they died.

1. The reassurance that they will "see his face" (e.g., Ps. 11:7).
2. Various ways of expressing that the righteous person will not be "abandoned to Sheol" or will be "redeemed from Sheol" (e.g., Ps. 16:9–11).

---

32. Ibid., 190–94. This notwithstanding Rosenberg's etymological analysis. She offers a sound defense of Sheol as derived from the root *š'l*, meaning "to conduct an investigation" (found with this meaning also in Ugaritic, Akkadian, and Aramaic) and thus conveying a forensic concept of "call to account (= punish)" ("The Concept of Biblical Sheol," 9–12). She does not succeed, however, in demonstrating that the etymology has carried over into the concepts attached to the meaning of the term in Israelite usage.

33. E. F. Sutcliffe, *The Old Testament and the Future Life* (London: Burns Oates and Washbourne, 1947), 57–59.

34. R. Martin-Achard, *From Death to Life* (Edinburgh: Oliver and Boyd, 1960), 39–40. Though Enoch and Elijah are exceptional cases, we should note that the text does not indicate where they went in either instance. In Elijah's case he goes up to heaven, but "heaven" is also the word for "sky" in Hebrew; it is clear from the response of the other prophets (2 Kings 2:16) that they understand the word in that way (cf. Ezek. 3:14; 8:3).

3. The confidence that God will "receive" the psalmist (e.g., Pss. 49:15; 73:24, both using the same verb as with Enoch in Gen. 5:24).

We will examine each of these in turn to determine what they tell us about Israelite beliefs.

Seeing God's face. Psalm 11:7 proclaims that "upright men will see his face," and in Psalm 17:15, the psalmist is encouraged by the knowledge that "I—in righteousness I will see your face; when I awake, I will be satisfied with seeing your likeness." The second parallel statement in 17:15 confirms that the psalmist expects some tangible presence of God where he will be satisfied with the "likeness" of God. We could easily interpret this as a hope of seeing God face to face after death, but we must be careful to try to understand what the psalmist was expressing in these words. In both of these contexts, the Hebrew combines *hzh* and *panim*, a combination that occurs nowhere else in the Old Testament. We can compare this passage with Exodus 24:11, where the elders on Sinai *hzh* ("see") God rather than the face of God, referring to a theophany.

Additionally, and perhaps more significantly, some of the psalms speak of this sort of experience in the sanctuary. Psalm 63:2 says, "I have seen [*hzh*] you in the sanctuary and beheld your power and your glory." Likewise, Psalm 27:4 expresses the psalmist's desire to dwell in the house of the Lord "all the days of my life, to gaze [*hzh*] upon the beauty of the LORD and to seek him in his temple." In all these contexts, the psalmist seeks protection from God and deliverance from his enemies or troubles.

We must resolve whether this vision of God is to take place after death in heaven, or in the form of a theophany or oracle of deliverance[35] in the temple that will end the psalmist's troubles (Ps. 17:15). The crucial verb is "to awake" (Hiph. *qys*). Among the Reformers, Luther interpreted the verb as a reference to awaking in heaven from the sleep of death, while Calvin read it as awaking from the darkness and fatigue of persecution.[36] The verb refers to awaking from death in at least two places (Isa. 26:19; Dan. 12:2); the psalmist firmly attests to the motif of going to sleep besieged by enemies and awaking with an expectation of God's deliverance (e.g., 3:3; 63:3; 139:18).

Throughout the book of Psalms, the psalmists consistently expect vindication (deliverance from their enemies); they believe that the enemy will be destroyed, while they themselves will enjoy a long and happy life. They give no indication that they look for deliverance or vindication by being transferred to the presence of God. Such an event would not constitute vindication

---

35. H. J. Kraus, *Psalms 1–59* (Minneapolis: Augsburg, 1988), 334.
36. See the appropriate quotations in ibid., 250.

in their minds. It would not make sense to take this verb metaphorically when the motifs and contexts in these psalms make perfect sense without the metaphorical understanding. We certainly cannot use these passages to prove that the psalmists believed they would go to heaven to be with God when they died. They might allow an interpretation that hints at an alternative to Sheol, but the ambiguous terminology warns us against using these passages as the foundation of such a doctrinal understanding. They can all be easily understood within the "Sheol only" view. Since the verb "to awake" does not necessarily indicate an after-death experience, we certainly cannot use the references to "seeing the face of God" within the psalms to prove that the psalmists believed they would go to heaven to be with God when they died.

Redeemed from Sheol. Psalm 16:9–11 reads this way:

> Therefore my heart is glad and my tongue rejoices;
>   my body also will rest secure,
> because you will not abandon me to the grave,
>   nor will you let your Holy One see decay.
> You have made known to me the path of life;
>   you will fill me with joy in your presence,
>   with eternal pleasures at your right hand.

The phrase "abandon me to the grave [Sheol]" uses the Hebrew verb '*zb* followed by the preposition *le-*. This does not refer to the individual being abandoned *in* Sheol, but to his not being consigned to Sheol.[37]

Though this could mean that the psalmist expects an eternal destiny other than Sheol, it also could mean that he is confident that the Lord will allow him to live. The ambiguity is continued in the statement "You have made known to me the path of life." Though this might refer to life rather than death, some interpreters have seen the last line in verse 11 as clinching the matter by specifying "eternal" pleasures.

The Old Testament does not speak of the right hand of God as a place in the presence of God in heaven. Rather, the right hand of God acts to deliver the righteous and to judge the enemy; this is the position that the oppressed psalmist wants to enjoy. In Psalm 118:15–18, therefore, the Lord's right hand brings deliverance, which enables the psalmist to live rather than die. In Psalm 80:17, the man at the Lord's right hand is made an instrument of God's punishment against the wicked; this is often seen as the role of the king (Ps. 110:1). Furthermore, the Hebrew word translated

---

37. The combination is used elsewhere in Lev. 19:10; Job 39:14; Ps. 49:14; and Mal. 4:1, and in each case means "consign to." Even in Job 39:14, the ostrich does not "abandon" her eggs in the earth, but consigns them to the earth, which helps to protect them.

"eternal" (*nṣḥ* in Ps. 16:11) is used as an adjective only four other times, always in a temporal context to describe a perpetual condition.[38]

Consequently, we see Psalm 16 as expressing the psalmist's confidence that, rather than rejecting the psalmist, consigning him to death and the netherworld, God will protect his life by bringing his presence into the psalmist's life and providing perpetual deliverance from his enemies by the power of his right hand.[39]

> Like sheep they are destined for the grave,
>   and death will feed on them.
> The upright will rule over them in the morning;
>   their forms will decay in the grave,
>   far from their princely mansions.
> But God will redeem my life from the grave;
>   he will surely take me to himself. (Ps 49:14–15)

The NIV has correctly rendered the Hebrew term *nepeš* as "life" rather than "soul"; in fact, there is no place in the Old Testament where *nepeš* demonstrably refers to the soul in the theological sense. Rather, the *nepeš* refers to one's self or one's being and thereby can also represent one's life.[40] Several different verbs of rescue and deliverance take *nepeš* as their object, but none of these refer to eternal salvation the way that the New Testament means it.[41] Psalm 30:2–3 clearly demonstrates that to have one's *nepeš* redeemed from Sheol means to be preserved from death: "O LORD my God, I called to you for help and you healed me. O LORD, you brought me up from the grave [Sheol], you spared me from going down into the pit."[42]

---

38. Most occurrences use the word as the nominalized object of prepositions. The four occurrences similar to Ps. 16 are in Jer. 15:18 (perpetual pain); Amos 1:11 (perpetual anger of Edom against Israel); Ps. 13:2 (the Lord's apparent perpetual neglect of the psalmist); and Ps. 74:3 (the perpetual state of ruin of Jerusalem).

39. The New Testament use of Psalm 16:10 in Acts 13:35 cites Jesus as fulfilling this passage by his resurrection and the preservation of his body. This fulfillment should not be confused with the message of the psalm in its original context. For further discussion of the important distinctions between message and fulfillment, see A. Hill and J. Walton, *Survey of the Old Testament* (3rd ed.; Grand Rapids: Zondervan, 2009), 508–15.

40. See the excellent summary article by B. Waltke in *Theological Wordbook of the Old Testament* (ed. R. L. Harris, G. Archer, and B. Waltke; Chicago: Moody Press, 1980), 2:587–91, including his assessment that "the substantive must not be taken in the metaphysical, theological sense in which we tend to use the term 'soul' today."

41. E.g., Josh. 2:13; 1 Sam. 19:11; Pss. 6:5; 72:13.

42. Sutcliffe, *Old Testament and the Future Life*, 50–52. The Akkadian phrase *muballit miti* ("the one who gives life to the dead") is commonly used as epithets of gods and do not concern resurrection or the afterlife (see H. Ringgren, *Israelite Religion* [Philadelphia: Fortress, 1966], 245).

God "receiving" an individual. In Psalm 49:15 (cited above) the psalmist expresses his confidence that God "will surely take me to himself" (NIV). The verb "take" (*lqh*) is used of Enoch (Gen. 5:24) and also occurs in Psalm 73:23–24:

> Yet I am always with you;
>> you hold me by my right hand.
> You guide me with your counsel,
>> and afterward you will *take* me into glory. (emphasis added)

A few initial comments on the translation of these verses are necessary. In Psalm 49:15, the phrase reads simply "you will take me." The "to himself" has been added by the NIV translators without warrant (though it certainly reflects their interpretation). The NIV's translation of Psalm 73:24, then, leads us to the conclusion that "glory" is a synonym for heaven, since glory carries that connotation in English. We should note, however, that Hebrew never uses the word "glory" (*kabod*) as a synonym for heaven (the place of God's dwelling). Furthermore, there is no preposition "into" in 73:24, which suggests that we should treat the word as an adverb rather than a noun. The resulting translation would be along the line of the NRSV, "And afterward, you will receive me with honor"—or, to avoid the need of a preposition altogether, "honorably."[43]

In other words, neither Psalm 49:15 nor 73:24 suggests that the individual is being taken *somewhere*. But what else can the verb *lqh* suggest? A simple check of the concordance reveals how the psalmist uses the phrase.

> He reached down from on high and *took hold of me*;
>> he drew me out of deep waters.
> He rescued me from my powerful enemy,
>> from my foes, who were too strong for me.
> They confronted me in the day of my disaster,
>> but the LORD was my support.
> He brought me out into a spacious place;
>> he rescued me because he delighted in me. (Ps. 18:16–19, emphasis added)

The first line contains the exact same verbal form as that found in Psalm 49:15, and 73:24 is the same except for the change from third person to second person. Yet in Psalm 18, the phrase clearly means to deliver someone from their trouble. While the usage of the verb "to take" (*lqh*) in the Enoch narrative requires some ambiguity, its usage in Psalms tips the scales toward a more temporal deliverance.

---

43. Martin-Achard, *From Death to Life*, 162.

Thus, all three of the phrases that support an Israelite alternative to Sheol are ambiguous; furthermore, the various psalms (where references to Sheol are primarily found) suggest that the only alternative to Sheol is continued life on this earth. To substantiate the belief in an alternative to Sheol, we would need a clear, unambiguous passage. None of these offers that.

In conclusion, Job shows no deviation from the Israelite theology of the Old Testament. The Israelites believed that all persons would continue to exist after death in a place they called Sheol. This was not a place of reward or punishment; it was not a pleasant place, but there was no torment. God had access to Sheol, but those in Sheol had no access to God. While the Israelites may have believed in alternatives to Sheol, they did not profess to know anything about those alternatives, so they could only hope to be spared from Sheol for as long as possible. Thus, they saw God's blessing and reward in a long life. Revivification was within the power of God, as was translation from life, but neither were common or expected to be the lot of more than a select few. Unknown were: (1) the concept of spending eternity in heaven or with God; (2) the bodily resurrection of all people to their eternal place; (3) judgment by God in the afterlife to reward faithfulness and punish wickedness; (4) punishment of the wicked in hell.[44]

D. S. Russell identifies three major theological shifts that occurred between the Old and New Testament periods, as documented by the intertestamental literature.[45]

1. The dead are described as "souls" or "spirits" and are portrayed much more clearly as individual, conscious beings.
2. Doctrine was enhanced to include multiple chambers in Sheol to accommodate differing treatment for the righteous and the wicked. This is attested as early as *1 and 2 Enoch* in the early second century.[46] The LXX distinguishes between Hades and Gehenna, which, in early church history, were identified respectively as places of purgation and torment.[47] Evidence for two compartments also occurs in the parable of Lazarus and the rich man (Luke 16).

---

44. In one of the latest books of the Old Testament (Dan. 12:1–3), a separation is indicated between "some [who rise] to everlasting life, others to shame and everlasting contempt." See discussion of this important passage in the comments in Bridging Contexts section of chs. 15–21 (p. pp. 227–29).

45. Russell, *Method and Message of Jewish Apocalyptic*, 357–66. For detailed treatment of various traditions concerning resurrection during the intertestamental period, see G. W. E. Nickelsburg, *Resurrection, Immortality and Eternal Life in Intertestamental Judaism* (Cambridge, Mass.: Harvard Univ. Press, 1972).

46. J. J. Collins, *Daniel* (Minneapolis: Fortress, 1993), 396.

47. Russell, *Satan*, 120.

3. Sheol comes to be regarded as an intermediate state where the dead await the final resurrection and judgment.

A proper understanding of the Israelite doctrine of afterlife provides us with many insights into the Old Testament.

1. The Israelites did not construct their relationship with God around a hope of heaven. People often convert to Christianity because of fear; with heaven to gain and hell to avoid, conversion is logical. Likewise, we sometimes neglect our Christian life of faith because we have the assurance of heaven. To put it bluntly, our Christianity can be all one way: *What's in it for me?* This is precisely what the Challenger had claimed about Job's perspective. The dynamics of the Israelite faith operated on a totally different level. With no eternal gain in sight, their faith was inclined to be much more focused on God and less on self; this element also made their faith more concerned with the present than the future. They saw faith as something that existed in life and that lived on through generations, not that gave them heaven eternally.

2. We can now understand the Israelites' struggles with God's justice and recognize the importance of the RP. While they had no hope of heaven in eternity, their faith offered possible gain in the form of prosperity and long life. Just as we must avoid focusing our relationship with God on the possibility of heavenly gain, they had to avoid focusing on earthly gain. When earthly gain was not forthcoming, they asked distressed and probing questions about the justice of God (imagine how you would feel if after you died, you found out heaven was all a misunderstanding). For the Israelites, then, God's justice was a day-to-day concern.

God as a hedge-builder. Two varying concepts of God as a hedge-builder have emerged in the opening chapters of Job. In the first, the Challenger claims that God has built a protective hedge around Job so that no harm can befall him (1:10). In Job's lament, he complains that God's hedge limits human knowledge so that one cannot comprehend God's ways (3:23). As with nearly all theological statements in the book of Job, these need to be investigated to see if they represent God truthfully.

Regarding the protective hedge, we find affirmations throughout Scripture that God protects the faithful. Even as we pray for such protection, confident that he is able to provide it, we also know that such protection is not absolute. We have no reason to doubt that God did indeed set up a hedge around Job, but no such hedge is guaranteed to Job or to anyone else. Furthermore, a hedge may prevent intrusion from some but allow admittance to others.

Turning to the restrictive hedge, we must acknowledge that God has indeed left us in ignorance concerning his ways in our lives (Isa. 55:8–9). Job implies that the hedge goes beyond ignorance to oppression—God is turning the screws, tightening the noose. What does this suggest about God? We may accurately affirm that God has oppressed Job; since Job is unaware of the scene in heaven, he does not know the details of his particular situation. His statement adds specificity to his previous assertion in 2:10. Job unreservedly attributes responsibility to God for his negative experiences; if we maintain the traditional theology of a sovereign God in a monistic (rather than dualistic) system, we should do the same. As we incorporate that concept into our theology, we must remember that God's behavior toward us is undergirded with wisdom, not some arbitrary, cruel, uncaring, temperamental, or distracted aspect of his character. Our theology must always give God the benefit of the doubt.

GOD'S HEDGING IN. HOW do we perceive God's hedges? Perhaps we can best understand God's hedges when we consider how we, as parents, hedge in our children. When we raise children, we constantly wonder how much we should shield them from the "real" world and when we should "let them go." Some parents are obviously overprotective (perhaps in everyone's eyes but their own), producing a phenomenon today known as "helicopter parents." In contrast, other parents seem reticent to provide any parameters for the choices and behavior of their children. Yet others insist on tight regulation of control by rules that stifle the development of any discernment. Some kids want their parents to run interference for them well into their adult years, while others begin chafing under parental controls from an early age (expressed in the T-shirt message: "Parents for sale—two for the price of one!").

Our discussion here must not be about parenting, as interesting as that might be. Instead, the parent/child relationship illustrates God's role in our lives. Do we think that God is too protective? A hovering, "helicopter" God with short apron strings? People usually think of God as too restrictive rather than too protective. I don't know of anyone who would claim that God protects them too much from real life; in fact, many might wish for more protection. We know that his protection is qualified; else we would

not have to pray, "Deliver us from evil." Perhaps we are better off not knowing the many things from which God protects us.

Alternatively, some might believe that God draws the circle of expectations too tightly, regulating our lives ever more closely with the threat that
stepping outside that circle will reap dire consequences. In such circumstances it would be easy to feel spiritual claustrophobia—virtually smoth-
ered by attention and regulation.

What makes us think of God this way? Generally one of two possibilities (or a combination of them):

- We think that God has too many rules and we would rather have
  more freedom to do what we want.
- We think that difficult circumstances are punishment for failure
  to match up to God's too-demanding standards.

(1) We can address these two issues respectively through investigation of holiness and grace. For those who think that God has too many
rules that prevent them from having a good time, he becomes a spoilsport
who ruins all their fun; this legalistic view of God makes them resentful
and recalcitrant. For their benefit, we ought to emphasize the difference
between legalism and holiness. With all the laws in the Old Testament and
admonitions and exhortations in the New, some might easily draw the inaccurate conclusion that the Christian faith is all about rules. Indeed, many
churches and families treat it as exactly that; yet both Testaments seek not
to bind us with rules but to free us from our sinful inclinations so we might
become holy.

The laws and admonitions in the Bible help us understand what God
is like and how we can be like him. Even were we to follow every rule, we
would fall short of what God wants from us, because that is the wrong tactic. Though obedience is important, it is simply a means to a greater end.
The point is not to be perfect in our obedience, but to be perfect in our
imitation of God. We are not seeking the approval of a demanding parent,
but a relationship with a holy God as we reflect his character in our lives.
Christianity is about relationship, not about rules. The freedom that we
think we seek is often just a reflection of our intrinsic desires to live out
our fallenness. "Fun" is a misnomer, and too often a term to cover our self-
indulgence as we revel in our own depravity.

(2) Those who think that their misfortune comes from an oversensitive
deity who makes offenses too easy and consequences too severe ought to
become reacquainted with the God of grace who knows the weaknesses of
our humanity. Actually, there are two misconceptions behind this way of
looking at God: first, the flawed inference that the misfortunes we experi-

ence are God's punishment; second, our propensity to think of God as a harsh taskmaster rather than a gracious sovereign. The second depends on the first, and the first is a reflection of RP thinking. Like Job, we are too quick to attribute misfortune to offense—precisely the formula against which the book argues. God is not that sort of hedge-builder. When we misunderstand the nature of our misfortunes, we end up misconstruing God. The solution is to readjust our understanding of misfortune (a process the book is going to lead us through) and to trust the grace of God.

One more comment is necessary as we conclude this discussion. God also can use hedges that we perceive as negative but which are ultimately for our good—that is, disciplinary hedges. In Hosea 2:6[8], God builds a hedge around Israel to prevent her from finding her way. The hedge is intended to drive her back to her Lord, to prevent her from wandering. It manifests itself not in misfortunes, but in lack of success in worldly endeavors. When we experience these, we should reconsider our motives and our goals to pursue greater dependence on God.

Worry (3:25). God does not want us to live in fear, but to trust him. In the Sermon on the Mount, Jesus addresses one aspect of this straightforwardly as he admonishes the disciples not to worry about the basic needs of life; Job, however, worries about what circumstances might come his way. It is easy to find ourselves in the same situation. As the stock market tumbles, we worry about the shattered economy and the hardship it might bring. We worry about our health, either because we have troublesome symptoms, because we have a looming check-up or procedure, because we have a genetic predisposition to a particular disorder, or just because there are so many lurking diseases (cancer, heart problems, Alzheimer's, etc.). The fragility of Social Security causes us worry about retirement and whether we will have enough to sustain our old age. We worry about possibly losing our jobs and wonder how we will survive. We worry about relationships that are not as healthy as we would like. We worry about children who exhibit troubling tendencies. Worries can crowd out hope and undermine our trust in God. When some of these worries become realities, we find Job's words echoing through our minds: "What I dreaded has happened to me" (3:25).

Few people think they worry too much; they see their worries as legitimate concerns. How do we differentiate between responsible concern and paralyzing anxiety? When do our fears become obsessive? We know that worries can distract us and skew our focus in life; yet, as popular wisdom tells us, it is no good worrying over what we cannot change. In the parable of the sower, Jesus mentions those hounded by worry: "The seed that fell among thorns stands for those who hear, but as they go on their way they are choked by life's worries, riches and pleasures, and they do not mature" (Luke 8:14).

Of course, Job's lament is not intended to warn us against worry, nor does it offer any critique of Job's worries. It does not intend to push us in the opposite direction of fatalism either, though sometimes we might think that, though life has been going well, it will inevitably go sour.

Sermons could be preached on any of these approaches toward life, but if we want to ponder the issues raised in the text, we have to consider Job's wish for death. When people are going through periods of suffering, loss, and pain, they often begin to desire death. For those who have never been in such dire circumstances (myself included), it is difficult to imagine reaching such extremes—but many have and many do. MacLeish captures this all-too-common plight in the words of his actors:

> I've seen him.
> Job is everywhere we go
> His children dead, his work for nothing,
> Counting his losses, scraping his boils.
> Discussing himself with his friends and physicians,
> Questioning everything—the times, the stars
> His own soul, God's providence.[48]

In a later scene, the suffering reaches its inevitable conclusion, just as it does for the biblical Job, with the wish for death:

> Every human creature born
> Is born into the bright delusion
> Beauty and loving-kindness care for him.
> Suffering teaches! Suffering's good for us!
> Imagine men and women dying
> Still believing that the cuddling arms
> Enclosed them! They would find the worms
> Peculiar nurses, wouldn't they? Wouldn't they?
> What once was cuddled must learn to kiss
> The cold worm's mouth. That's all the mystery.
> That's the whole muddle. Well, we learn it.
> God is merciful and we learn it ...
> We learn to wish we'd never lived.[49]

So I have asked Kelly to address what it is like when suffering drives one to think that death is the best of all alternatives, and how one works through such morbid thoughts.

---

48. MacLeish, *J.B.*, 13.
49. Ibid., 49.

Kelly's Story: Wish for Death[50]

JHW: DID YOU WISH for death, Kelly?

Kelly: As I look back years ago, it is sad to say there was a time in my life that I prayed out to the Lord to take my life. I remember it vividly because it was immediately after my thirteen-hour nerve transplant in September of 2000. I woke up in more excruciating pain than I had ever experienced at the young age of twelve. My legs were burning, since they removed the long nerve that runs underneath your knee to your ankle, in both legs. So each leg was bandaged up past my knees and would burn if I straightened my leg because that would strain the nerve they took out. Then my neck was in so much pain, since they took out nerve from the spinal cord, causing my left arm to go numb for four months, and the nerve graft was threaded through my chest and into my armpit.

At the time it was the most pain I had ever experienced, and on top of that I had horrible phantom pains due to the trauma and stress of the surgery. So when I came out of the surgery, I remember lying down in the hospital bed, crying in pain, and praying, "Lord, why did you save my life in the car accident so that you would allow me to suffer to such a great degree? Lord, please take me home to be with you. Please allow me to fall asleep and wake up in your presence." Over the course of those days in the hospital, there were days that I screamed out loud in pain, pleading that the Lord would make it stop and bring me home.

JHW: How did you resist those wishes and eventually conquer them?

Kelly: Over time some of the pain subsided. The Lord gave me peace in my heart and assurance that he had plans for me. I felt the Lord saying, "I didn't miraculously save you from that accident, only to take you home a couple of months later. I want to use this trial, and I want to use you ... but you need to trust me." So I began trying to think of life on a day-to-day basis, trying to seek him for the strength to endure.

JHW: Was there consolation in the belief in heaven—an eternity with God?

Kelly: Definitely. My belief in Christ, God, heaven, and spending eternity with him dramatically impacted the growing process after the accident. I did not just simply want to end my life; rather, at the time I wanted God to take me to heaven—sooner rather than later. The pain and suffering I was experiencing seemed like too much to bear, so I yearned to be in heaven, in eternity with him.

---

50. Kelly interacts with parts of her story in each Contemporary Significance section. For the introduction to the details of her story, see Contemporary Significance on ch. 1, pp. 86–97.

JHW: Did such a hope help you feel any better about life and God?

Kelly: My hope in spending eternity with God did help knowing that there will be a day when I will not live in extremely excruciating pain; yet at times I was impatient and wanted that time to come now. Over time that hope did affect my thought process and did help me change my perspective on life.

JHW: Do you have any perspective to offer people who are suffering and desire death? What would you say to them?

Kelly: If I were speaking to someone who was in the midst of suffering to the point they desire death, I would first and foremost listen. I would intentionally listen to hope that I understood what they were trying to communicate before offering my opinion. Then I would try to encourage them to shift their perspective on how they view their trial—that instead of focusing on the "why" questions, they should seek the question, "Lord, what are you doing here and what do you want me to learn?" The Lord has a plan for their lives and isn't done yet, and he wants to carry them through the suffering. I would gently encourage them in how the Lord can use trials, such as: trials cause us to draw near to him, they test our faith, they can be used to move us to the place the Lord wants us to be, they can slow us down to focus on him, and trials can be used to show God's power, which he allows us to experience. We should take it day by day, and when we are called to be in his presence, it will be the right time; but until then, we are to seek him and offer our sufferings and our desire for death to him. For when do the stars shine the brightest? When the sky is the darkest and there is no other light in sight. When we are in dark times and can't see the light at the end of the tunnel, those are the times we seek Christ and experience him in a real way. Heaven will come in its time, but for now we are to take it one day at a time.

With Kelly's experience as a backdrop, perhaps in conclusion we should consider how our own beliefs in afterlife affect our response to suffering. Unlike Job, we have a hope beyond the grave. This could have an impact on a couple of different aspects of suffering. If we are concerned about the justice of God, a belief in an afterlife where there is reward and punishment can be used to "get God off the hook" in our belief that justice will be done. Yet that idea also needs to be qualified, because our eternal destiny is a matter of grace, not justice. We might spend our whole lives waiting to see a certain enemy receive what is coming in eternal judgment, only to find that they repent in the final moments of life. Eternity will not satisfy our desire for justice of that sort.

If, instead of the philosophical concerns of theodicy, we are thinking about the experience of our suffering, we might find the prospect of eternity to be small comfort. It is true that suffering will end, but that hope does not relieve our pain.

The important point I am trying to make is that the fact that we have hope in eternity does not eliminate the need for a strategy for dealing with pain and suffering. If the suffering is our own, the hope of heaven does not make it any easier to cope day by day, and it doesn't provide satisfactory answers to the "why" questions. It doesn't even help us focus on God's purposes. We need God's strength to do that, not just a hope for the future.

If the suffering is someone else's, we should not think that the only advice we need to give is that heaven is coming someday. As Kelly indicated, it is important to live in the now, not in the future. Taking one day at a time means looking to God for strength to persevere. With heaven before us, death can seem the easy way out, but God does not offer the easy way. I am reminded of the common comment by my friend Paul Wright of Jerusalem University College as we take students around the land of Israel: "To the left is the shortcut; we're going right." There are things we need to see and experience that will enrich our day that we will miss if we take the shortcut.

In C. S. Lewis's book *A Grief Observed*, he tells of how he found that all of his sage insights into dealing with suffering became nothing but so much meaningless rhetoric when he was faced with his wife Joy's suffering. We can't really understand suffering until we are involved in it; but we can prepare for it. In fact, we *must* do so. It is too late to learn a piano concerto when you walk onto the stage to perform it. It is past time to get into shape when you line up at the starting line for the marathon. In the same way, we try to prepare ourselves for suffering before it comes upon us. How do we prepare for suffering? By engaging in mental/theological exercises. It is a sound view of God and the world that can sustain us when the trials come, though we will still need God to undergird our resolve to honor him through it all.[51]

---

51. For more on this, see the Contemporary Significance on Job 38–41.

Job 4–14

Eliphaz

¹Then Eliphaz the Temanite replied:

²"If someone ventures a word with you, will you be
impatient?
But who can keep from speaking?
³Think how you have instructed many,
how you have strengthened feeble hands.
⁴Your words have supported those who stumbled;
you have strengthened faltering knees.
⁵But now trouble comes to you, and you are discouraged;
it strikes you, and you are dismayed.
⁶Should not your piety be your confidence
and your blameless ways your hope?

⁷"Consider now: Who, being innocent, has ever perished?
Where were the upright ever destroyed?
⁸As I have observed, those who plow evil
and those who sow trouble reap it.
⁹At the breath of God they are destroyed;
at the blast of his anger they perish.
¹⁰The lions may roar and growl,
yet the teeth of the great lions are broken.
¹¹The lion perishes for lack of prey,
and the cubs of the lioness are scattered.

¹²"A word was secretly brought to me,
my ears caught a whisper of it.
¹³Amid disquieting dreams in the night,
when deep sleep falls on men,
¹⁴fear and trembling seized me
and made all my bones shake.
¹⁵A spirit glided past my face,
and the hair on my body stood on end.
¹⁶It stopped,
but I could not tell what it was.
A form stood before my eyes,
and I heard a hushed voice:

¹⁷'Can a mortal be more righteous than God?
  Can a man be more pure than his Maker?
¹⁸If God places no trust in his servants,
  if he charges his angels with error,
¹⁹how much more those who live in houses of clay,
  whose foundations are in the dust,
  who are crushed more readily than a moth!
²⁰Between dawn and dusk they are broken to pieces;
  unnoticed, they perish forever.
²¹Are not the cords of their tent pulled up,
  so that they die without wisdom?'

^{5:1}"Call if you will, but who will answer you?
  To which of the holy ones will you turn?
²Resentment kills a fool,
  and envy slays the simple.
³I myself have seen a fool taking root,
  but suddenly his house was cursed.
⁴His children are far from safety,
  crushed in court without a defender.
⁵The hungry consume his harvest,
  taking it even from among thorns,
  and the thirsty pant after his wealth.
⁶For hardship does not spring from the soil,
  nor does trouble sprout from the ground.
⁷Yet man is born to trouble
  as surely as sparks fly upward.

⁸"But if it were I, I would appeal to God;
  I would lay my cause before him.
⁹He performs wonders that cannot be fathomed,
  miracles that cannot be counted.
¹⁰He bestows rain on the earth;
  he sends water upon the countryside.
¹¹The lowly he sets on high,
  and those who mourn are lifted to safety.
¹²He thwarts the plans of the crafty,
  so that their hands achieve no success.
¹³He catches the wise in their craftiness,
  and the schemes of the wily are swept away.
¹⁴Darkness comes upon them in the daytime;
  at noon they grope as in the night.

¹⁵He saves the needy from the sword in their mouth;
　　he saves them from the clutches of the powerful.
¹⁶So the poor have hope,
　　and injustice shuts its mouth.

¹⁷"Blessed is the man whom God corrects;
　　so do not despise the discipline of the Almighty.
¹⁸For he wounds, but he also binds up;
　　he injures, but his hands also heal.
¹⁹From six calamities he will rescue you;
　　in seven no harm will befall you.
²⁰In famine he will ransom you from death,
　　and in battle from the stroke of the sword.
²¹You will be protected from the lash of the tongue,
　　and need not fear when destruction comes.
²²You will laugh at destruction and famine,
　　and need not fear the beasts of the earth.
²³For you will have a covenant with the stones of the field,
　　and the wild animals will be at peace with you.
²⁴You will know that your tent is secure;
　　you will take stock of your property and find nothing
　　　　missing.
²⁵You will know that your children will be many,
　　and your descendants like the grass of the earth.
²⁶You will come to the grave in full vigor,
　　like sheaves gathered in season.

²⁷"We have examined this, and it is true.
　　So hear it and apply it to yourself."

Job
⁶:¹Then Job replied:

²"If only my anguish could be weighed
　　and all my misery be placed on the scales!
³It would surely outweigh the sand of the seas—
　　no wonder my words have been impetuous.
⁴The arrows of the Almighty are in me,
　　my spirit drinks in their poison;
　　God's terrors are marshaled against me.
⁵Does a wild donkey bray when it has grass,
　　or an ox bellow when it has fodder?
⁶Is tasteless food eaten without salt,
　　or is there flavor in the white of an egg ?

⁷I refuse to touch it;
  such food makes me ill.

⁸"Oh, that I might have my request,
  that God would grant what I hope for,
⁹that God would be willing to crush me,
  to let loose his hand and cut me off!
¹⁰Then I would still have this consolation—
  my joy in unrelenting pain—
  that I had not denied the words of the Holy One.

¹¹"What strength do I have, that I should still hope?
  What prospects, that I should be patient?
¹²Do I have the strength of stone?
  Is my flesh bronze?
¹³Do I have any power to help myself,
  now that success has been driven from me?

¹⁴"A despairing man should have the devotion of his friends,
  even though he forsakes the fear of the Almighty.
¹⁵But my brothers are as undependable as intermittent
      streams,
  as the streams that overflow
¹⁶when darkened by thawing ice
  and swollen with melting snow,
¹⁷but that cease to flow in the dry season,
  and in the heat vanish from their channels.
¹⁸Caravans turn aside from their routes;
  they go up into the wasteland and perish.
¹⁹The caravans of Tema look for water,
  the traveling merchants of Sheba look in hope.
²⁰They are distressed, because they had been confident;
  they arrive there, only to be disappointed.
²¹Now you too have proved to be of no help;
  you see something dreadful and are afraid.
²²Have I ever said, 'Give something on my behalf,
  pay a ransom for me from your wealth,
²³deliver me from the hand of the enemy,
ransom me from the clutches of the ruthless'?

²⁴"Teach me, and I will be quiet;
  show me where I have been wrong.
²⁵How painful are honest words!
  But what do your arguments prove?

²⁶Do you mean to correct what I say,
    and treat the words of a despairing man as wind?
²⁷You would even cast lots for the fatherless
    and barter away your friend.

²⁸"But now be so kind as to look at me.
    Would I lie to your face?
²⁹Relent, do not be unjust;
    reconsider, for my integrity is at stake.
³⁰Is there any wickedness on my lips?
    Can my mouth not discern malice?

⁷:¹"Does not man have hard service on earth?
    Are not his days like those of a hired man?
²Like a slave longing for the evening shadows,
    or a hired man waiting eagerly for his wages,
³so I have been allotted months of futility,
    and nights of misery have been assigned to me.
⁴When I lie down I think, 'How long before I get up?'
    The night drags on, and I toss till dawn.
⁵My body is clothed with worms and scabs,
    my skin is broken and festering.

⁶"My days are swifter than a weaver's shuttle,
    and they come to an end without hope.
⁷Remember, O God, that my life is but a breath;
    my eyes will never see happiness again.
⁸The eye that now sees me will see me no longer;
    you will look for me, but I will be no more.
⁹As a cloud vanishes and is gone,
    so he who goes down to the grave does not return.
¹⁰He will never come to his house again;
    his place will know him no more.

¹¹"Therefore I will not keep silent;
    I will speak out in the anguish of my spirit,
    I will complain in the bitterness of my soul.
¹²Am I the sea, or the monster of the deep,
    that you put me under guard?
¹³When I think my bed will comfort me
    and my couch will ease my complaint,
¹⁴even then you frighten me with dreams
    and terrify me with visions,

¹⁵so that I prefer strangling and death,
rather than this body of mine.
¹⁶I despise my life; I would not live forever.
Let me alone; my days have no meaning.

¹⁷"What is man that you make so much of him,
that you give him so much attention,
¹⁸that you examine him every morning
and test him every moment?
¹⁹Will you never look away from me,
or let me alone even for an instant?
²⁰If I have sinned, what have I done to you,
O watcher of men?
Why have you made me your target?
Have I become a burden to you?
²¹Why do you not pardon my offenses
and forgive my sins?
For I will soon lie down in the dust;
you will search for me, but I will be no more."

Bildad
^{8:1}Then Bildad the Shuhite replied:

²"How long will you say such things?
Your words are a blustering wind.
³Does God pervert justice?
Does the Almighty pervert what is right?
⁴When your children sinned against him,
he gave them over to the penalty of their sin.
⁵But if you will look to God
and plead with the Almighty,
⁶if you are pure and upright,
even now he will rouse himself on your behalf
and restore you to your rightful place.
⁷Your beginnings will seem humble,
so prosperous will your future be.

⁸"Ask the former generations
and find out what their fathers learned,
⁹for we were born only yesterday and know nothing,
and our days on earth are but a shadow.
¹⁰Will they not instruct you and tell you?
Will they not bring forth words from their understanding?

¹¹Can papyrus grow tall where there is no marsh?
   Can reeds thrive without water?
¹²While still growing and uncut,
   they wither more quickly than grass.
¹³Such is the destiny of all who forget God;
   so perishes the hope of the godless.
¹⁴What he trusts in is fragile;
   what he relies on is a spider's web.
¹⁵He leans on his web, but it gives way;
   he clings to it, but it does not hold.
¹⁶He is like a well-watered plant in the sunshine,
   spreading its shoots over the garden;
¹⁷it entwines its roots around a pile of rocks
   and looks for a place among the stones.
¹⁸But when it is torn from its spot,
   that place disowns it and says, 'I never saw you.'
¹⁹Surely its life withers away,
   and from the soil other plants grow.

²⁰"Surely God does not reject a blameless man
   or strengthen the hands of evildoers.
²¹He will yet fill your mouth with laughter
   and your lips with shouts of joy.
²²Your enemies will be clothed in shame,
   and the tents of the wicked will be no more."

Job
^{9:1}Then Job replied:

²"Indeed, I know that this is true.
   But how can a mortal be righteous before God?
³Though one wished to dispute with him,
   he could not answer him one time out of a thousand.
⁴His wisdom is profound, his power is vast.
   Who has resisted him and come out unscathed?
⁵He moves mountains without their knowing it
   and overturns them in his anger.
⁶He shakes the earth from its place
   and makes its pillars tremble.
⁷He speaks to the sun and it does not shine;
   he seals off the light of the stars.
⁸He alone stretches out the heavens
   and treads on the waves of the sea.

⁹He is the Maker of the Bear and Orion,
  the Pleiades and the constellations of the south.
¹⁰He performs wonders that cannot be fathomed,
  miracles that cannot be counted.
¹¹When he passes me, I cannot see him;
  when he goes by, I cannot perceive him.
¹²If he snatches away, who can stop him?
  Who can say to him, 'What are you doing?'
¹³God does not restrain his anger;
even the cohorts of Rahab cowered at his feet.

¹⁴"How then can I dispute with him?
  How can I find words to argue with him?
¹⁵Though I were innocent, I could not answer him;
  I could only plead with my Judge for mercy.
¹⁶Even if I summoned him and he responded,
  I do not believe he would give me a hearing.
¹⁷He would crush me with a storm
  and multiply my wounds for no reason.
¹⁸He would not let me regain my breath
  but would overwhelm me with misery.
¹⁹If it is a matter of strength, he is mighty!
  And if it is a matter of justice, who will summon him?
²⁰Even if I were innocent, my mouth would condemn me;
  if I were blameless, it would pronounce me guilty.

²¹"Although I am blameless,
  I have no concern for myself;
  I despise my own life.
²²It is all the same; that is why I say,
  'He destroys both the blameless and the wicked.'
²³When a scourge brings sudden death,
  he mocks the despair of the innocent.
²⁴When a land falls into the hands of the wicked,
  he blindfolds its judges.
  If it is not he, then who is it?

²⁵"My days are swifter than a runner;
  they fly away without a glimpse of joy.
²⁶They skim past like boats of papyrus,
  like eagles swooping down on their prey.
²⁷If I say, 'I will forget my complaint,
  I will change my expression, and smile,'

---

²⁸I still dread all my sufferings,
    for I know you will not hold me innocent.
²⁹Since I am already found guilty,
    why should I struggle in vain?
³⁰Even if I washed myself with soap
    and my hands with washing soda,
³¹you would plunge me into a slime pit
    so that even my clothes would detest me.

³²"He is not a man like me that I might answer him,
    that we might confront each other in court.
³³If only there were someone to arbitrate between us,
    to lay his hand upon us both,
³⁴someone to remove God's rod from me,
    so that his terror would frighten me no more.
³⁵Then I would speak up without fear of him,
    but as it now stands with me, I cannot.

¹⁰:¹"I loathe my very life;
    therefore I will give free rein to my complaint
    and speak out in the bitterness of my soul.
²I will say to God: Do not condemn me,
    but tell me what charges you have against me.
³Does it please you to oppress me,
    to spurn the work of your hands,
    while you smile on the schemes of the wicked?
⁴Do you have eyes of flesh?
    Do you see as a mortal sees?
⁵Are your days like those of a mortal
    or your years like those of a man,
⁶that you must search out my faults
    and probe after my sin—
⁷though you know that I am not guilty
    and that no one can rescue me from your hand?

⁸"Your hands shaped me and made me.
    Will you now turn and destroy me?
⁹Remember that you molded me like clay.
    Will you now turn me to dust again?
¹⁰Did you not pour me out like milk
    and curdle me like cheese,
¹¹clothe me with skin and flesh
    and knit me together with bones and sinews?

¹²You gave me life and showed me kindness,
    and in your providence watched over my spirit.

¹³"But this is what you concealed in your heart,
    and I know that this was in your mind:
¹⁴If I sinned, you would be watching me
    and would not let my offense go unpunished.
¹⁵If I am guilty—woe to me!
    Even if I am innocent, I cannot lift my head,
for I am full of shame
    and drowned in my affliction.
¹⁶If I hold my head high, you stalk me like a lion
    and again display your awesome power against me.
¹⁷You bring new witnesses against me
    and increase your anger toward me;
    your forces come against me wave upon wave.

¹⁸"Why then did you bring me out of the womb?
    I wish I had died before any eye saw me.
¹⁹If only I had never come into being,
    or had been carried straight from the womb to the grave!
²⁰Are not my few days almost over?
    Turn away from me so I can have a moment's joy
²¹before I go to the place of no return,
    to the land of gloom and deep shadow,
²²to the land of deepest night,
    of deep shadow and disorder,
    where even the light is like darkness."

Zophar
^{11:1}Then Zophar the Naamathite replied:

²"Are all these words to go unanswered?
    Is this talker to be vindicated?
³Will your idle talk reduce men to silence?
    Will no one rebuke you when you mock?
⁴You say to God, 'My beliefs are flawless
    and I am pure in your sight.'
⁵Oh, how I wish that God would speak,
    that he would open his lips against you
⁶and disclose to you the secrets of wisdom,
    for true wisdom has two sides.
    Know this: God has even forgotten some of your sin.

7"Can you fathom the mysteries of God?
    Can you probe the limits of the Almighty?
8They are higher than the heavens — what can you do?
    They are deeper than the depths of the grave — what can
        you know?
9Their measure is longer than the earth
    and wider than the sea.

10"If he comes along and confines you in prison
    and convenes a court, who can oppose him?
11Surely he recognizes deceitful men;
    and when he sees evil, does he not take note?
12But a witless man can no more become wise
    than a wild donkey's colt can be born a man.

13"Yet if you devote your heart to him
    and stretch out your hands to him,
14if you put away the sin that is in your hand
    and allow no evil to dwell in your tent,
15then you will lift up your face without shame;
    you will stand firm and without fear.
16You will surely forget your trouble,
    recalling it only as waters gone by.
17Life will be brighter than noonday,
    and darkness will become like morning.
18You will be secure, because there is hope;
    you will look about you and take your rest in safety.
19You will lie down, with no one to make you afraid,
    and many will court your favor.
20But the eyes of the wicked will fail,
    and escape will elude them;
        their hope will become a dying gasp."

Job
12:1Then Job replied:

2"Doubtless you are the people,
    and wisdom will die with you!
3But I have a mind as well as you;
    I am not inferior to you.
    Who does not know all these things?

4"I have become a laughingstock to my friends,
    though I called upon God and he answered —

a mere laughingstock, though righteous and blameless!
⁵Men at ease have contempt for misfortune
    as the fate of those whose feet are slipping.
⁶The tents of marauders are undisturbed,
    and those who provoke God are secure—
    those who carry their god in their hands.

⁷"But ask the animals, and they will teach you,
    or the birds of the air, and they will tell you;
⁸or speak to the earth, and it will teach you,
    or let the fish of the sea inform you.
⁹Which of all these does not know
    that the hand of the LORD has done this?
¹⁰In his hand is the life of every creature
    and the breath of all mankind.
¹¹Does not the ear test words
    as the tongue tastes food?
¹²Is not wisdom found among the aged?
    Does not long life bring understanding?

¹³"To God belong wisdom and power;
    counsel and understanding are his.
¹⁴What he tears down cannot be rebuilt;
    the man he imprisons cannot be released.
¹⁵If he holds back the waters, there is drought;
    if he lets them loose, they devastate the land.
¹⁶To him belong strength and victory;
    both deceived and deceiver are his.
¹⁷He leads counselors away stripped
    and makes fools of judges.
¹⁸He takes off the shackles put on by kings
    and ties a loincloth around their waist.
¹⁹He leads priests away stripped
    and overthrows men long established.
²⁰He silences the lips of trusted advisers
    and takes away the discernment of elders.
²¹He pours contempt on nobles
    and disarms the mighty.
²²He reveals the deep things of darkness
    and brings deep shadows into the light.
²³He makes nations great, and destroys them;
    he enlarges nations, and disperses them.

²⁴He deprives the leaders of the earth of their reason;
    he sends them wandering through a trackless waste.
²⁵They grope in darkness with no light;
    he makes them stagger like drunkards.

^{13:1}"My eyes have seen all this,
    my ears have heard and understood it.
²What you know, I also know;
    I am not inferior to you.
³But I desire to speak to the Almighty
    and to argue my case with God.
⁴You, however, smear me with lies;
    you are worthless physicians, all of you!
⁵If only you would be altogether silent!
    For you, that would be wisdom.
⁶Hear now my argument;
    listen to the plea of my lips.
⁷Will you speak wickedly on God's behalf?
    Will you speak deceitfully for him?
⁸Will you show him partiality?
    Will you argue the case for God?
⁹Would it turn out well if he examined you?
    Could you deceive him as you might deceive men?
¹⁰He would surely rebuke you
    if you secretly showed partiality.
¹¹Would not his splendor terrify you?
    Would not the dread of him fall on you?
¹²Your maxims are proverbs of ashes;
    your defenses are defenses of clay.

¹³"Keep silent and let me speak;
    then let come to me what may.
¹⁴Why do I put myself in jeopardy
    and take my life in my hands?
¹⁵Though he slay me, yet will I hope in him;
    I will surely defend my ways to his face.
¹⁶Indeed, this will turn out for my deliverance,
    for no godless man would dare come before him!
¹⁷Listen carefully to my words;
    let your ears take in what I say.
¹⁸Now that I have prepared my case,
    I know I will be vindicated.

¹⁹Can anyone bring charges against me?
    If so, I will be silent and die.

²⁰"Only grant me these two things, O God,
    and then I will not hide from you:
²¹Withdraw your hand far from me,
    and stop frightening me with your terrors.
²²Then summon me and I will answer,
    or let me speak, and you reply.
²³How many wrongs and sins have I committed?
    Show me my offense and my sin.
²⁴Why do you hide your face
    and consider me your enemy?
²⁵Will you torment a windblown leaf?
    Will you chase after dry chaff?
²⁶For you write down bitter things against me
    and make me inherit the sins of my youth.
²⁷You fasten my feet in shackles;
    you keep close watch on all my paths
    by putting marks on the soles of my feet.

²⁸ "So man wastes away like something rotten,
    like a garment eaten by moths.

^{14:1}"Man born of woman
    is of few days and full of trouble.
²He springs up like a flower and withers away;
    like a fleeting shadow, he does not endure.
³Do you fix your eye on such a one?
    Will you bring him before you for judgment?
⁴Who can bring what is pure from the impure?
    No one!
⁵Man's days are determined;
    you have decreed the number of his months
    and have set limits he cannot exceed.
⁶So look away from him and let him alone,
    till he has put in his time like a hired man.

⁷"At least there is hope for a tree:
    If it is cut down, it will sprout again,
    and its new shoots will not fail.
⁸Its roots may grow old in the ground
    and its stump die in the soil,

⁹yet at the scent of water it will bud
  and put forth shoots like a plant.
¹⁰But man dies and is laid low;
  he breathes his last and is no more.
¹¹As water disappears from the sea
  or a riverbed becomes parched and dry,
¹²so man lies down and does not rise;
    till the heavens are no more, men will not awake
    or be roused from their sleep.

¹³"If only you would hide me in the grave
  and conceal me till your anger has passed!
If only you would set me a time
  and then remember me!
¹⁴If a man dies, will he live again?
  All the days of my hard service
  I will wait for my renewal to come.
¹⁵You will call and I will answer you;
  you will long for the creature your hands have made.
¹⁶Surely then you will count my steps
  but not keep track of my sin.
¹⁷ My offenses will be sealed up in a bag;
  you will cover over my sin.

¹⁸"But as a mountain erodes and crumbles
  and as a rock is moved from its place,
¹⁹as water wears away stones
  and torrents wash away the soil,
  so you destroy man's hope.
²⁰You overpower him once for all, and he is gone;
  you change his countenance and send him away.
²¹If his sons are honored, he does not know it;
  if they are brought low, he does not see it.
²²He feels but the pain of his own body
  and mourns only for himself."

Eliphaz (Job 4–5)

ELIPHAZ'S FIRST EXHORTATION FOR Job occurs in the problematic verse 4:6, which the NIV renders, "Should not your piety be your confidence and your blameless ways your hope?" The syntax is complex, as we commonly find in Job, but even the words themselves present some challenges. The word translated "confidence" (*kislah*) is often rendered "folly," both for this form (Ps. 85:8[9]) and in a variety of derivative forms. When the root is contextually associated with trust, it is usually a vain or foolish trust (Job 8:14; 31:24; Ps. 49:13[14]; Eccl. 7:25). The only occurrences that suggest a different connotation are Psalm 78:7 and Proverbs 3:26; because God is the object of trust, the speaker cannot be foolish or vain.

We might account for this range of meaning by understanding the word as a designation of irrational trust, either because the object is not worthy of the trust (e.g., oneself, one's riches) or because it is born of faith with little or no supporting logic. If this is so, Eliphaz identifies Job's fear of God as an irrational confidence, since all the evidence now indicates that he lacks the requisite fear of God. Given Eliphaz's observations in verses 7–11, he seems to be accusing Job of denial in verse 6. In this interpretation, the translation should not be "Should not …," but something more like, "Is not your [self-proclaimed] piety the basis for this irrational confidence? Is your only hope really in the [presumed] blamelessness of your ways?" In Eliphaz's view, the incontestable RP (4:7–11) gives the lie to Job's delusion of righteousness and exposes his hope as vain.

Eliphaz's mystical experience (4:12–21) occurs in a vision (NIV "dreams"). This word (*hizzayon*) identifies prophetic visions (e.g., 2 Sam. 7:17; Joel 2:28; Zech. 13:4) as well as terrifying nightmares (Job 7:14) and sometimes both (Isa. 22:1, 5). Dreams and visions in the ancient world were not simply psychological experiences; they originated in the divine realm. The literature from Mesopotamia describes what people believed about dreams and their interpretation.[1] Job 33:15 also refers to visions derived from deep sleep (see also Abram's vision from a deep sleep in Gen. 15:12–21). The texts associates Zaqiqu, the dream god (also Ziqiqu) with the merest breath of wind (cf. the use of *ruah*, spirit/wind, in 4:15).[2] In

---

1. S. A. L. Butler, *Mesopotamian Conceptions of Dreams and Dream Rituals* (AOAT 258; Münster: Ugarit-Verlag, 1998); J-M. Husser, *Dreams and Dream Narratives in the Biblical World* (Sheffield: JSOT, 1999); A. L. Oppenheim, *The Interpretation of Dreams in the Ancient Near East* (Transactions of the American Philosophical Society 46/3; Philadelphia: American Philosophical Society, 1956).

2. Butler, *Mesopotamian Conceptions of Dreams*, 78–83. She points out that the word can be used for "ghost" and can also refer to a class of demons (78).

Ludlul bel nemeqi (one of the pious suffering pieces), the sufferer indicates that he appealed to a *zaqiqu*, "but he did not enlighten me."[3] Just as Eliphaz identifies a "form" that stood before him (4:16), "a remarkable young man of outstanding physique" brings the sufferer in *Ludlul* a message of imminent recovery.[4] Eliphaz is claiming revelation; in effect he says, "God gave me a message for you, Job."

The NIV renders 4:17 in the traditional way: "Can a mortal be more righteous than God? Can a man be more pure than his Maker?" This is a grammatically defensible interpretation, since the Hebrew uses a finite stative verb with the comparative *min*. This construction usually prefers an adjective rather than a finite verb, but the latter is attested (1 Sam. 10:23; Nah. 3:8).[5] Nevertheless, we should reject this translation on both lexical and rhetorical grounds. Lexically, it is not possible to compare a human's purity to God's because this term (*ṭhr*) is never used to describe God. It refers to a clean condition achieved from an unclean state—but because God cannot be unclean, God also cannot be designated as clean.

Rhetorically, many commentators have noted that if we follow the traditional rendering of this verse, Eliphaz has overplayed his case.[6] Would anyone need to be told that no one is more righteous than God? Certainly Eliphaz would need no mystical revelation to make such a point. Has Job implied that he is superior to God in these ways? In fact, the two verbs used here[7] have not yet been applied to Job's behavior; Job has not claimed these attributes for himself, neither has anyone attributed them to Job. A number of commentators have recognized this problem and translated the *min* preformative as "before" rather than as the comparative "better than,"[8] but the supporting evidence is weak; the Hebrew idiom would normally use the preposition *lipnê* to achieve that result rather than *min* (see Ps. 143:2).

We find a solution in other comparable syntactical arrangements, most importantly Psalm 139:12: "Even the darkness is not dark to you."[9] This verse clearly does *not* say that the darkness is not darker than God; rather, the darkness is not dark *from God's perspective*. This is still a comparative

---

3. Ibid., 81. Butler seems to favor this as a human expert rather than a divine mediator.

4. Lambert, *Babylonian Wisdom Literature*, 3.9.

5. GKC, §133b.

6. R. Whitekettle, "When More Leads to Less: Overstatement, *Incrementum*, and the Question in Job 4:17a," *JBL* 129 (2010): 445–48, retains the traditional "more than" rendering and defends Eliphaz's statement as intentionally hyperbolic rhetoric. I think the solution lies elsewhere.

7. "Righteous" (*ṣdq*) and "pure" (*ṭhr*).

8. Supported by Clines, *Job 1–20*, 132; Habel, *Job*, 116.

9. Imperfect of stative verb combined with comparative *min* with God as object of the preposition.

use of *min*, but the comparison is to God's perspective rather than to God himself. On the strength of this example, we may now confidently propose the reading of Job 4:17 as: "Can a mortal be righteous in God's perspective? Can a man be clean in the perspective of his Maker?" The rhetorical thrust is not much different from those who have translated, "Can a mortal be righteous before God," but the nuance is subtly different: meeting God's minimal standards for ritual acceptability ("before" God) versus meeting God's maximum standards in the broader moral/ethical realm ("in God's perspective"). The latter relegates Job's confidence to vanity. This interpretation is also confirmed by the "how much more ..." argument in 4:18–19, that even the angels cannot meet his standards.

We may note here that the angels charged with error need not refer to some great cosmic event; God commonly holds his messengers accountable and corrects them. Psalm 82 refers to just such an occasion, but Job 4:18 warrants close attention because it likely conveys Eliphaz's perspective of Job's situation. The combination of this verb (Hiph. of *'mn*) with the preposition *b-* (which here introduces the direct object [cf. Num. 20:12; Jon. 3:5]) indicates that God does not believe what his servants say. This does not suggest that God never believes them, but that he does not do so routinely without scrutiny. The second line is more difficult since the word NIV renders "error" (*tahalah*) occurs only here in the Old Testament. The verb + preposition in the sentence means to bring a formal charge; thus, this obscure noun may designate the charge that God brings against a person when he does not accept their account. This would then constitute Eliphaz's subtle accusation of Job.

Many scholars believe that the noun *tahalah* derives from a root *hll*.[10] Ecclesiastes uses other derivative forms of this root several times as synonyms for folly.[11] Of particular importance is Ecclesiastes 7:25, where the noun parallels the by-forms of the root *ksl*, which was used in Job 4:6 to describe Job's misplaced confidence. On this admittedly fragile basis, I tentatively suggest the following logical connections:

- In 4:18a God does not trust his servants unconditionally or accept their perspectives at face value.
- Instead, in 4:18b God does not hesitate to evaluate their assessments and conclusions as misguided or even foolish.

---

10. See the discussion in Clines, *Job 1–20*, 112 n. 18.c., and Hartley, *Job*, 114 n. 23. Both also list some of the more commonly suggested emendations. The most sensible emendation would be to *hattalah* (switch in the order of the first two Hebrew letters), which means "deception"—an appropriate parallel to God's lack of confidence in the angels' reports.

11. Eccl. 2:2; 7:7, 25; 10:13.

- By these observations, Eliphaz tacitly accuses Job of assessing his own situation dishonestly (the thrust of 4:17)...
- Which parallels Eliphaz's incredulity concerning (in his mind) Job's irrational confidence in 4:6.

Eliphaz's main point in 4:12–21 reflects ancient Near Eastern beliefs— namely, that the gods have far more regulations than humans know or recognize; there are so many ways one might offend the gods in one's ritual performance, one can never claim not to deserve what deity has sent. Such confidence would truly be irrational.

In 5:1 Eliphaz speaks of "the holy ones," another way of referring to members of the divine council (i.e., the "sons of God"). This is highly ironic, since the prologue has informed us that a member of the divine council initiated Job's current situation. Consequently, Eliphaz is more correct than he knows, for no appeal to the divine council will resolve this before its time. This is also the first suggestion of Job initiating legal action: the verbs "call" (*qr'*) and "answer" (*'nh*) are legal terms used for an official court summons and the appearance before the judging body in response to such a summons.[12] Job will later take up this idea of legal action and begin to call for an advocate to take up his case. Eliphaz, however, implies that summoning one of the council would be fruitless; perhaps his conviction goes back to 4:18, with his less-than-positive portrayal of God's servants.

Instead, Eliphaz counsels Job to appeal directly to God (5:8). The verb used for this appeal (*drš*) is used elsewhere of seeking an oracle. Sufferers often consulted oracles in an attempt to identify their offense or to discover a pathway to appeasement. For example, in the Babylonian piece *Ludlul bel nemeqi*, after the onset of the pious man's suffering, he says:

My omens were confused, they were contradictory every day.
The prognostication of diviner and dream interpreter could not
    explain what I was undergoing.[13]

After some time has passed, his situation has not improved and he laments:

I called to my god, he did not show his face,
I prayed to my goddess, she did not raise her head.
The diviner with his inspection did not get to the bottom of it,
Nor did the dream interpreter with his incense clear up my case.

---

12. See Deut. 25:8; 1 Sam. 20:9–14; and numerous others. For discussion see Magdalene, *Scales of Righteousness*, 141–42.
13. *COS* 1.153, I:51–52.

I beseeched a dream spirit, but it did not enlighten me,
The exorcist with his ritual did not appease divine wrath.[14]

Job has an entirely different idea in mind when he appeals to God, for rather than seeking an oracle from God to identify his offense, a path to appeasement, and restoration, he plans to appeal to God for a court appearance and ultimately vindication. He is not going to throw himself on the mercy of the court; instead, he is going to demand a hearing.

Eliphaz also points out that Job should look on his situation as the disciplinary correction of God (5:17). The verb that NIV translates "corrects" (Hiph. *ykḥ*) can refer to general reproof, but it is also a legal term for accusation.[15] Even more specifically, it can refer to the outcome of an accusation, the adjudication of a lawsuit that finds the defendant guilty as charged.[16] Again, Eliphaz obviously considers Job guilty, though he claims no insight into the nature of his offense. He counts Job among the fortunate because, having received God's attention in a negative way, Job can now have some confidence that God will also respond to Job's repentance and bring restoration. The rest of Eliphaz's speech anticipates this restoration (5:18 – 27); the climactic conclusion shows that Eliphaz sees restoration as the end goal, whereas Job ultimately desires vindication. If Job listens to Eliphaz and friends and seeks only restoration at any cost, he will confirm the Challenger's suspicions — that only prosperity is important, not righteousness itself. If, by contrast, he continues to pursue vindication, he shows that his righteous reputation is foremost in his thoughts.

Job (Job 6 – 7)

AFTER JOB AGAIN CALLS for his own death (6:8 – 9), he evaluates his stance, in which he takes consolation (6:10). This verse is pivotal but also difficult to understand. The NIV follows the LXX (as do most translations and commentaries), rendering the last clause, "denied the words of the Holy One." Unfortunately, the verb used here never elsewhere means "deny," and the expression "words of the Holy One" is opaque. We will briefly consider each in turn, beginning with the latter.

The phrase the NIV renders "words of the Holy One" (*'imrê qadoš*) occurs nowhere else in the Old Testament. The singular form of the

---

14. Ibid., II.4 – 9.

15. Notice the use of the verb and the noun in legal contexts throughout Job, particularly 6:25; 9:33; 13:3, 6; 22:4; 23:4; 40:2); Magdalene, *Scales of Righteousness*, 140 – 41.

16. Ibid., 141. She refers the reader to the detailed demonstration in P. Bovati, *Re-Establishing Justice: Legal Terms, Concepts and Procedures in the Hebrew Bible* (JSOTSup 105; Sheffield: Sheffield Academic, 1994), 42 – 48.

substantive (adjective/noun) for "holy" appears only here in Job; the plural is used twice, both times to speak of entities (5:1; 15:15). For this reason, the translators of the NIV chose to suggest an entity in their translation. The LXX and several translations, however, preferred to treat the word as an adjective and render the phrase "holy words," which I believe is preferable here, since no holy one has spoken. The holy words would refer to the traditional teachings of the fathers, frequently referred to in this book by other descriptions (e.g., 8:8; 15:18).

The verb in the clause (Piel of *khd*) is likewise problematic. Everywhere else this verb means "to conceal,"[17] but most interpreters find that meaning ill-fitting to this context. A careful analysis of the synchronic[18] data, however, yields promising results. In the fifteen occurrences of the verb in the Piel, the contexts always concern communication of words or feelings; these are all negated contexts—that is, indicating that words should *not* be concealed. A large percentage either state or clearly imply the person from whom words should not be concealed. Certainly one way to conceal words is to remain silent and not communicate at all, but these contexts illustrate that the choice is not between communication and silence, but how straightforwardly or guardedly one communicates.

People can hide words behind vague communication. We speak of full disclosure, not mincing words, telling it like it is, not beating around the bush, giving uncensored comments, laying the facts on the table—all of these are part of not hiding words. Rechecking all the uses shows that this nuance of the word fits perfectly. For example, Eli tells Samuel not to mince words as he demands to hear God's message (1 Sam. 3:17–18). David asks the woman of Tekoa to level with him and speak plainly about who sent her (2 Sam. 14:18). In Job 27:11, Job contrasts his own forthright words with the meaningless speeches of his friends (27:12); he then articulates his case with painful honesty. All of the examples fit.

Consequently, I offer the following interpretation of 6:10: Job consoles himself that he has not softened the blow of holy words (= traditional teaching) as Eliphaz did when he suggested that "everything's going to be OK" (5:18–27). Job is at least prepared to "face the facts" and wishes for death (both in his lament in ch. 3 and in his request in 6:8–9). As he expresses the misery of his condition, Job finds consolation only in his refusal to accept a sugar-coated view of reality (6:10). He is free to express himself without reservation because he views his situation as hopeless (6:11–13).

---

17. 15 occurrences: Gen. 47:18; Josh. 7:19; 1 Sam. 3:17 (2x), 18; 2 Sam. 14:18; Job 6:10; 15:18; 27:11; Pss. 40:10[11]; 78:4; Isa. 3:9; Jer. 38:14, 25; 50:2.

18. Synchronic lexical analysis works on the premise that meaning is determined by usage; a word should therefore be studied in all of its contexts in order to assess its meaning.

From this point, Job launches into his first full-scale verbal assault on his friends (6:14–30). He challenges them to cease their platitudes and reveal his specific offense (6:24). The word for offense (*šgh*) refers to an inadvertent or unintentional straying from the path of correct behavior (ritually or ethically). Not content with deduction (that Job *must* be guilty), Job wants his friends to identify definitive misdemeanor; by using this Hebrew word, Job implies his confidence that any such offense is unknown to him.

Job considers this important because his integrity is at stake (6:29). Job's demand of his friends is a bit stronger than the "relent/reconsider" of the NIV; he wants them to "take back"[19] their malicious words[20] because his "integrity is at stake" (NIV). This is Job's first claim to be righteous (*ṣdq*), a claim that he maintains to the end of the dialogue (cf. 27:6). Job in effect accuses his friends of slander. His righteousness describes his impeccable reputation for conscientious behavior in all things, and their barrage fails to gainsay it.

After another lament concerning his condition, Job finally — and for the first time — turns his attention and remarks directly to God (7:7–21). His words in verses 7–10 remind us of Ecclesiastes as he addresses the transience of life. These observations give him the confidence to complain boldly and lay out his case before God in one of the most poignant speeches in the book.

Job primarily accuses God of being overattentive and unrealistic in his expectations. Some in the ancient world might have viewed God as a distant being, such that trouble came on a person because of divine neglect. In contrast, Job claims that God scrutinizes him too closely. High-level scrutiny would be understandable for "the sea, or the monster of the deep" (7:12). The Hebrew word for "sea" (*yam*) is also the name of the personified Sea (Yamm), a chaos creature in Ugaritic mythological texts. Since this word is paralleled by another chaos creature (*tannin*, see Gen. 1:21), we should view both of these as creatures[21] that God keeps under watch as he maintains the orderly system. Job claims that, unlike the chaos creatures, he is no threat to order and therefore doesn't warrant constant attention. This concept is consistent with Old Testament theology expressed in passages where evil has come to God's attention (e.g., Sodom and Gomorrah, Gen. 18:20–21; Nineveh, Jon. 1:2).

Job continues in this vein as he asks, "What is man that you make so much of him?" (7:17). The reader immediately recalls Psalm 8, "What is

---

19. Hebrew *šub* ("return, turn back").
20. Hebrew *'wlh* is used both in vv. 29 and 30.
21. Note Ps. 74:13–14, where the two are mentioned together along with Leviathan.

man that you are mindful of him?" The only difference is the verb: in Psalm 8 God is "taking note" (Qal of *zkr*) of frail humanity; in Job 7 God is "considering him to be significant" (Piel of *gdl*). The verb in Psalm 8 conveys the marvelous and positive concept of God's care for humanity; the verse in Job 7 conveys the terrifying and negative prospect of God's singling out humanity as a whole — or worse still, a single person.

Job labels God a "watcher of men" (7:20, *noṣer ha'adam*). A class of beings known as the Watchers gained prominence in intertestamental literature, particularly in the book of *Enoch*. These were often fallen angels, but the term is also used for the archangels.[22] The designation occurs only once in the Old Testament (Dan. 4:13). But all of this is unrelated. Job does not use the same terminology and he is referring to God, not some group of angels, fallen or otherwise. Job uses a term that often bears a positive connotation, indicating care and protection, but, as so often in this speech, he ironically turns this positive language upside down.

Before we move from Job's first speech, we must consider whether Job continues to consider himself innocent of wrongdoing. While 6:29 suggests that he does, two statements at the end of this speech then become problematic. In 7:20, when he says, "If I have sinned ...," we must note that there is no "if" in the Hebrew text — scholars generally contend that the "if" is implied. But in 7:21, what is Job then referring to when he asks why God does not pardon his offenses? Job's posture regarding his status hinges on these verses. Job uses the same terminology in 13:23 to demand that God show him his offenses; his statements here are probably of the same sort.

Commentators have understood "offense" (*pš'*) as "an act that breaks relationship with God";[23] it occurs as an object of the verb "pardon" (*nś'*) seven other times.[24] The noun in legal literature refers to an indictable act that results in a trial. The phrase "forgive my sins" (*ta'abir 'et-'awonî*) uses a verb + noun combination that occurs only two other times (2 Sam. 24:10; Zech. 3:4). The reference in Zechariah 3:4 is of particular interest because it speaks of an imputed offense for which one potentially stands subject to accusation.

We can therefore explain the language in both clauses of 7:21 under the circumstances that Job views himself already in a trial and already undergoing punishment. The verse is a request for God to cease and desist his actions, which have presumed a trial and a guilty verdict. Job does not own up to such offenses, but he wants God to give up the prosecution of this

---

22. J. J. Collins, "Watcher," *DDD²*, 893 – 95.

23. H. Seebass, "פֶּשַׁע," *TDOT*, 12:143.

24. Gen. 50:17; Ex. 23:21; 34:7; Num. 14:18; Josh. 24:19; 1 Sam. 25:28; Ps. 32:1.

court action. The thrust of 7:20 is then, "I have sinned (= have somehow fallen out of favor), whatever I might have done to you."[25] Then 7:21 follows up with, "Why won't you pardon whatever I have done that you have judged as indictable and forgive whatever sin you have imputed to me, for which you are punishing me?" Job uses somewhat patronizing language toward this overattentive God.

Bildad (Job 8)

BILDAD SEES CLEARLY THE implication of Job's words and therefore launches into a speech of his own, a speech filled with rhetorical questions designed to affirm that God upholds justice. In these statements he denies that God would "pervert" (Piel of '*wt*) justice (*mišpaṭ*) and righteousness (*ṣedeq*) (8:3). The verb used in this sentence occurs only rarely;[26] it involves bending, twisting, or distorting, so "perverting" is a good translation. Elihu later echoes Bildad's claim that God does not pervert justice (34:12). In the second round of speeches, Job places God as the subject of this verb, but rather than the object being "justice" or "righteousness," it is Job himself (19:6; NIV: "God has wronged me" paralleled in the next verse when Job cries "violence!").

Is Bildad justified in his tacit accusation of Job, or is he caricaturing Job through hyperbole? Job has not charged God with perverting justice (yet), but in Bildad's view of the world, that would be the only logical conclusion if Job can sustain his claim of innocence (recall the triangle from the Introduction, pp. 42–44). Bildad is therefore confronting Job with the ultimate destination of the dangerous path he has taken.

Bildad clearly doubts Job's claims of innocence, reflected here in his words, "If you are pure and upright...." We have already encountered the word for upright (*yašar*, 1:1), but this is the first occurrence of the word for "pure" (*zak*; it is not the same as the adjective in 4:17).[27] The adjective occurs eleven times and the related verb form (*zkh*) another eight.[28] The uses in the Pentateuch refer to unadulterated or highest quality products (e.g., oil). In Job it is used as an adjective to describe teaching (11:4), prayer (16:7), and Job (33:9, parallel to "without sin"). Again, each occurrence refers to untainted or flawless behavior. The verb occurs in Job where both

---

25. Notice the use of the perfect form of the verb for "I have sinned" and the imperfect modal sense for "Whatever I might have done."

26. Besides here, Piel: Job 19:6; 34:12; Pss. 119:78; 146:9; Eccl. 7:13; Lam. 3:36; Amos 8:5; Pual: Eccl. 1:15; Hithpael: Eccl. 12:3.

27. Ex. 27:20; 30:34; Lev. 24:2, 7; Job 11:4; 16:17; 33:9; Prov. 16:2; 20:11; 21:8.

28. Job 15:14; 25:4; Pss. 51:6; 73:13; 119:9; Prov. 20:9; Isa. 1:16; Mic. 6:11.

Eliphaz and Bildad question whether any human could be so characterized (15:14; 25:4). Consequently here we find Bildad holding forth the possibility that God will restore Job, should Job show himself to be untainted; a few speeches later, however, Bildad reveals that no one can claim to be untainted. This shows that Bildad is simply patronizing Job in 8:6.

Bildad also has his own implied accusations as he unwraps the implications of the RP: "Surely God does not reject a blameless man or strengthen the hands of evildoers" (8:20). These convictions lead him to characterize Job implicitly as "godless" (*hanep*) and one who forgets God (8:13) — two ways to describe those who have departed from God's ways to follow their own.

Job (Job 9 – 10)

JOB IMMEDIATELY LATCHES ON to the idea of entering into legal action with God. This context compels us to understand his opening question differently than the NIV has rendered it. Job would not ask whether a mortal could be righteous because he believes that he is (29:14); rather, he is using the verb in its alternate sense of being declared righteous in a court of law — that is, being vindicated (see 13:18 for same verb in a clear context). Given God's power, he is now understandably worried about facing God in a courtroom setting.

Job's hymn (9:5 – 13) is an aside to explain why Job trembles at the thought of opposing God in court. Notice how Job's statements would flow smoothly from 9:4 directly to 9:14, but the introduction of God's superiority to the wise and the mighty warrants elaboration in the hymn.[29] These fascinating verses give a good sense of how Job thinks about the world and God's role in it.

Cosmic geography (9:5 – 9). The cosmic geography of the ancient world is generally founded on observation and experience, making one wonder what the author has in mind as he describes moving or overturning mountains (9:5). Close analysis reveals that the translation should go a different direction. The verb that NIV translates "moves" (Hiph. of '*tq*) only occurs a few times; in Genesis it refers to the movement of the patriarchs from place to place (Gen. 12:8; 26:22). The Hiphil is often, though not always, a causative verbal form — but the use of this verb in the Hiphil in Genesis is not. Therefore, we would not translate Job 9:5 as "God causes

---

29. The use of "wise of heart" (lit.) in 9:4 suggests that this is referring to human beings rather than to God. That is, even those humans who are wise or mighty cannot resist God and come out unscathed. See the detailed discussion of the phrase "wise of heart" at 37:24, pp. 370, 373).

mountains to move" (implied in NIV translation), but "God traverses the mountains."[30] This would parallel his treading on the seas in verse 8.

The next problem is to identify the subject of the verb "to know" ("He traverses mountains and they do not know," pers. trans.). Mountains are not sentient; likely the subject is those who resisted him in the previous verse. These resisters do not emerge unscathed, for God traverses the difficult passes of the mountains without his enemies' knowledge and thus overthrows them (the resisters, not the mountains).

The first clause of verse 6 contains terminology commonly used for earthquakes, but the second clause is more obscure. It begins with a reference to "the pillars" of the earth (cf. also Ps. 75:3[4]). Ancient peoples believed that the earth was a flat disk upheld by pillars; such a cosmic geography is portrayed on a boundary stone from the late second millennium. It is more difficult to understand what the pillars are doing, since the verb used (Hithpael of *plṣ*) occurs only here,[31] but the context gives us some confidence based on the parallel between the two lines. The earthquake continues the theme of punishment against those who resist.

The punishment theme moves heavenward in verse 7. In the first line, the sun is not simply obscured by an eclipse—it does not rise (Heb. *zrḥ*). Here Job returns to the concept first discussed in 3:8: God orders the cosmos day-by-day, not once for all. God's command causes the sun to rise or not to rise. This view is to be differentiated from Egyptian mythology in which the sun and the sun god are indistinguishable. In that view deity does not call forth the sun; rather, he rises as the sun, and chaos causes the sun to darken. This distinction provides additional evidence that Job's own thinking is more Israelite than not.

Job recognizes God as the one who seals off the stars in the second phrase of verse 7. Verbs of shutting, when used with the preposition *be‘ad*, mean to lock something in. The seal would be affixed to a closed door to make sure that what is inside is not disturbed. The ancients believed that the stars were engraved on the underside of the solid, rotating firmament,[32] and they moved along paths (in Akkadian literature, the paths of Anu, Enlil, and Ea).[33] To seal the stars would not be to inscribe them but to establish

---

30. The Akkadian cognate is *etequ* and has the same meaning (occurring many more times). The Akkadian *š* stem (equivalent to the Hebrew Hiphil) of the verb means to pass through difficult territory (*CAD* E, 393).

31. A derivative form of the root occurs in Isa. 21:4, apparently meaning to shudder with horror.

32. W. Horowitz, *Mesopotamian Cosmic Geography* (Winona Lake, Ind.: Eisenbrauns, 1998), 14–15.

33. Ibid., 154.

their paths so that they could not change. Such would be an act of creation, bringing order to the cosmos. Alternatively, we might understand the phrase as parallel to the first part of the verse—hence order is disrupted. Sealing the stars would refer to shutting them out so they could not enter the paths to shine in the heavens. In Isaiah 40:26, God leads forth the stars (cf. 45:12, where he commands their appearance); he does not do so here, but he keeps them shut behind sealed doors. We can read verse 7 as a continuation of God's cosmic judgment against those who resist him (9:4).

As translated by the NIV, verse 8 appears to concern God's creation, but close attention to the words shows otherwise. The two actions in the verse are related to theophanies in which God judges his enemies or his sinful people. Consider:

- *Psalm 144:5–6:* "Part [*nṭh*] your heavens, O LORD, and come down [*yrd*]; touch the mountains, so that they smoke. Send forth lightning and scatter the enemies, shoot your arrows and rout them."
- *Psalm 18:9/2 Samuel 22:10:* "He parted [*nṭh*] the heavens and came down [*yrd*]; dark clouds were under his feet."
- *Micah 1:3:* "Look! The LORD is coming from his dwelling place; he comes down [*yrd*] and treads [*drk*] the high places [*bomotey*] of the earth."
- *Job 9:8:* "He alone stretches out [*nṭh*] the heavens and treads [*drk*] the waves [*bamotey*] of the sea."

When we weave these overlapping verses together, we get the following composite profile for a judgment theophany: God "raises up" (*nṭh*) (the corner of) the heavens, comes down (*yrd*), and treads (*drk*) the heights (*bomotey*) of some part of the cosmos (earth, sea, clouds). Neither earth nor clouds are chaos creatures, so we would conclude that "sea" is not intended in that way either.

The first act refers not so much to stretching out the heavens, but to lifting them up. Two of the most common direct objects of the verb (*nṭh*) are "tent" and "hand/arm." Psalm 104:2 and Isaiah 40:22 make the metaphor explicit: "He pitched the heavens like a tent." In both cases the action is "lifting up" (note NIV translation of "pitch" one's tent, Gen. 12:8; 26:25; 33:19; etc. and of "upraised" hand, Isa. 9:12[11], 17[16], 21[20]). When the object is "heavens," as in the passage quoted above, we can see the idea of "lifting up" as God raises up the corner to step in under it.

The second half of verse 8 has been the subject of much discussion. The verb is clear enough, but the object is obscure; NIV translates "he treads on the waves of the sea." The phrase translated "waves of the sea" is *bamotey yam.*[34] Clines takes the line as a reference to Semitic mythology, where the deity treads on the back of Yamm (the sea god).[35] He supports this interpretation with the reference to stepping on the back (*bamah*) of one's enemies as a symbol of conquest (Deut. 33:29). Amos 4:13 refers to treading on the high places (Heb. *bamot*) of the earth—not places for worship, but the hills and mountains (cf. Hab. 3:19). Andersen and Freedman identify the form as a reference to the "rumpled surface of the earth consisting of both hills and valleys."[36] This understanding makes it logical that when the sea is the object, it would refer to the waves.[37] The famous Baal stele from Ugarit displayed in the Louvre shows the storm god walking on the waves of the sea as he strides forth with his lightning bolts in hand.

To interpret verse 9 we need a better understanding of constellations in the ancient world. Celestial omens from the ancient world are well-known; several sets of tablets give detailed information about the stars and constellations. There are many constellations, but three of the most prominent (judging by their place in the lists and the omens connected to them) are Pleiades (Akkad. *zappu*; Heb. *kimah*), Orion (Akkad. *šitadallu*, Heb. *kesil*), and Taurus (Akkad. *alû*, Bull of Heaven). We can identify these, along with the many other constellations in Akkadian and Sumerian texts, because of the technical information they include about the times of their rising and setting and their positions in the sky at various times during the year.

In contrast, we have much less information to determine the names of the Hebrew constellations; the Old Testament refers to constellations in only three contexts (here; 38:31 – 32; Amos 5:8). Scholars offer guesses concerning the identity of these constellations from commentary to commentary, based on comparative Semitic etymology[38] or the renderings of the earliest translations (e.g., Greek).

Regardless of which constellations Job 9 refers to, the more important question is why the constellations are brought into the discussion. Amos

---

34. For explanation of the strange form, see F. I. Andersen and D. N. Freedman, *Micah* (AB; New York: Doubleday, 2000), 164.

35. Clines, *Job 1– 20*, 230 – 31.

36. Andersen and Freedman, *Micah*, 164.

37. Andersen and Freedman (ibid., 164) postulate an original mythological referent in the phrase.

38. Cf. the suggestion that *kimah* is derived from Akkad. *kimtu* = family made by Mowinckel, also supported by an Ethiopic term for Pleiades, *kima*. See S. Paul, *Amos* (Minneapolis: Fortress, 1991), 168 n. 88. This has been verified in an Eblaite bilingual text, see W. Horowitz, "Some Thoughts on Sumerian Star-names and Sumerian Astronomy," in *An Experienced Scribe Who Neglects Nothing* (ed. Y. Sefati et al.; Bethesda, Md.: CDL, 2005), 163 – 178, esp. 173. The best accessible discussion of the possibilities and the reasons for them can be found in Clines, *Job 1– 20*, 231.

5:8 mentions the making of the constellations in a context of cosmic judgment. Similarly, scholars consistently agree that Job 9:5 − 8 refers to cosmic acts of judgment against those who resist God. If verse 9 simply expresses wonder over God's creative power, it is entirely inconsistent with the context; therefore, we should consider possible alternatives. As it turns out, constellations often are the subject of omens (for good or ill) in Akkadian literature. For example: "If Leo is dark: lions and wolves will rage and cut off traffic with the Westland."[39] Since God is the one who makes the constellations, he is the one who uses them to portend ominous events that are understood as acts of judgment.

The last two words of verse 9 continue the conundrum. The NIV translates them "constellations of the south," but the first word of that pair (*ḥdr*) usually refers to a room or chamber.[40] In Job 37:9 and 38:22 it refers to the storehouses from which the storm, snow, and hail issue. These are also used for judgment. The second word, *teman*, is also used in Psalm 78:26 as a reference for the destructive south wind.

Based on all of the analysis above, I would offer the following expansive translation for Job 9:5 − 9 after Job has posed the rhetorical question in 9:4, "Who can resist him and survive?"

> [5]He [God] traverses the mountains, but his enemies do not detect
>   him;
>   then he comes upon them [his enemies] in his anger and
>   overthrows them.
> [6]He causes the earth to tremble in its place
>   and makes its pillars sway.
> [7]He speaks to the sun and it does not shine [for them],
>   and he seals off the stars [from giving them light].
> [8]He raises the corner of the heavens by himself
>   [and comes down on them in judgment], treading the waves of
>   the sea.
> [9]He is the one who makes the constellations [as ominous signs
>   against them];
>   he makes the [destructive] south wind come from its chambers.

The point of the section is that God uses all of the cosmos as a weapon against those who would oppose him. Job sums this up in 9:10, giving the

---

39. H. Hunger, *Astrological Reports to Assyrian Kings* (SAA 8; Helsinki: Helsinki Univ. Press, 1992), 248 (437.6). This book is full of such omens.

40. In Job 38:32 the word translated "constellations" is a different Hebrew word. The NIV translation is based on a repointing of the word supported by Origen's *Hexapla*, see Clines, *Job 1 − 20*, 232.

impression that those wonders that he has named are only the beginning of what God can do. Though Job anticipates facing God in court rather than in combat, Job is justified in feeling apprehensive. In Job's perception, God's ways are imperceptible (10:11); he is accountable to none (10:12). The latter is again ironic in that God is allowing the Challenger to hold his policies accountable.

Even Rahab's consorts cower beneath God in verse 13. Rahab is another of the enemies of order generally connected to the sea (see Job 26:12; Ps. 89:11[10]; Isa. 51:9) and is historicized as a metaphor for Egypt (Ps. 87:4; Isa. 30:7).[41] In the Babylonian Creation Epic, Tiamat, the chaos creature associated with the sea, rebels against the gods with the aid of her consorts; Yamm also has a cohort in Ugaritic literature. This section shows God handily defeating even the most fearsome chaos creatures; if that is so, what chance does a human have in confronting God at any level?

This mode of thinking continues Job's characteristically deficient view of God, evident almost since the beginning of the book. He has viewed God as petty and overattentive, and now as one who is likely to abuse his power. Notice in 9:16, he does not believe that God will give him a fair hearing (perhaps no hearing at all); he worries that God will crush him even more without cause (9:17).[42] Not only does he see God as aloof in his power and lack of accountability; he even believes that God will twist Job's own words against him (9:20).

Job's rhetoric escalates as he throws caution to the winds (9:21) and makes his baldest statement yet: "He destroys both the blameless and the wicked" (9:22). We find a similar statement in Akkadian literature of the Erra Epic, where a violent, uncontrollable god boasts: "Like one who plunders a country, I do not distinguish just from unjust, I fell (them both)."[43] This kind of statement leads to God's rebuke of Job at the book's end (40:8). In one sense, his assertion here follows the train of thought already expressed in 2:10: God is the source of both good and bad. As he observes in 9:24, who else could it be? We will explore the theological implications of this train of thought under Bridging Contexts.

---

41. K. Spronk, "Rahab," *DDD²*, 684–86.

42. *ḥinnam* again, see discussion p. 101. Note also that the verb translated "crush" (9:17) here is the same as in Gen. 3:15 (and used elsewhere only in Ps. 139:11, "hide"). The context here and in Ps. 139 suggests the translation "attack," which also fits well in Gen. 3:15 (including Paul's choice of Greek verbs in Rom. 16:20).

43. Erra Epic, V.10, *COS* 1.113: 415; cf. P. Dion, "Formulaic Language in the Book of Job: International Background and Ironical Distortions," *Studies in Religion/Sciences religieuses* 16 (1987): 187–93.

Though Job identifies God as the source of destruction for all, he still believes there is a justice system, even if it is broken. This is evident in his contrasting statements in 9:21 and 9:29. In 9:21 he states, "I am innocent" (*tam*); yet in 9:29 he says, "I am guilty" (*'erša'*). The latter, however, does not reflect his own conviction about himself but expresses the state in which he finds himself (cf. 10:7). The fact that he can consider himself to be tried and found guilty (9:29) and that a courtroom scenario is possible (9:32) shows that there is still a justice system; Job has not claimed there is no justice — only that God is the sole target of his complaint. Job makes no allowance for the work of demons or other gods or a free agent (Satan).

Job requests a courtroom scenario in which an arbitrator will serve on his behalf (9:33) though he is not hopeful for such an exigency. This is Job's first reference to such a role, but this position becomes important in the remaining chapters of the book. Job uses a legal term (*mokiah*) that refers to one who argues a case and negotiates on behalf of another.[44] We will discuss this more fully in 16:19 – 21 and consider what sort of individual Job has in mind.

Chapter 10 shows us that Job continues to think the world ought to operate according to the RP (cf. 10:3). God as judge does not need to gather information like a human judge. Job questions God's omniscience as part of his defense. The psalmist presents this same sort of argument in Psalm 139:1 – 6, but an omniscient God cannot be lacking in the information needed to judge a case rightly.

In 10:8 – 12 Job wonders why God bothered making him at all if he only intends to destroy him. He uses language typical of the ancient world to describe his making: molded like clay (10:9a, *homer*). Genesis 2:7 tells us that humankind was formed from dust (*'apar*) and will return to the same upon death (Gen. 3:19, the same word used in Job 10:9b). Ancient Near Eastern accounts of human creation refer to clay more commonly than to dust:[45]

- Sumerian: Song of the Hoe (made in brickmold); *Enki and Ninmah*
- Akkadian: *Atrahasis* (made of clay mixed with the flesh and blood of a slain deity)
- Egyptian: Coffin Texts (fashioned on the potter's wheel by Khnum)

---

44. Elsewhere in Job this term is used in 32:12 (for Job's friends trying to make a case against him) and in 40:2 (for Job trying to make a case against God). For detailed analysis of the word, see Ticciati, *Job and the Disruption of Identity*, 119 – 37.

45. See full discussion in J. Walton, *Genesis 1 as Ancient Cosmology*, 74 – 77; see also idem, *Ancient Near Eastern Thought and the Old Testament* (Grand Rapids: Baker, 2006), 205 – 7.

The biblical and ancient Near Eastern accounts demonstrate the view that it was not just the first human who was made of dust/clay; every human is so made. Every human is molded by deity and every human returns to dust. We find this archetypal view throughout the ancient world.

Just when it seemed that Job could not get any bolder, he stunningly claims to know the mind of God (10:13). This brash and arrogant declaration shows once again Job's deficient view of God. God's statement about Job in 42:7–8 has inclined us to exonerate Job totally and consider his view of God to be accurate and appropriate, but how can we reconcile this inclination with the near blasphemous accusations he hurls against God in this chapter?

God's assessment of Job in 42:7–8 concerns speaking what is right to/about/on behalf of God (*dibber* + *neconah*, Niph. fem. ptc. of *kwn*). Rather than sorting out this language at the end of the commentary, we need to address it here so that we can rightly understand Job's position as we proceed. How did the friends speak what was not "right" and how did Job's statements differ? The adjective *neconah* has a variety of connotations, including describing something that is "appropriate" (Ex. 8:26[22]), and even a roof being supported by pillars (Judg. 16:26, 29). When the verb concerns something that is expressed or discovered, it connotes that what is said is sensible, logical, or able to be confirmed or verified. The message of Pharaoh's dream was valid because it came in two forms (Gen. 41:32). An accusation is investigated and born out by the evidence (Deut. 13:14 [15]). Saul asked the Ziphites to verify the location of David's hiding places (1 Sam. 23:23), and David confirmed the evidence that Saul had arrived (26:4). In these examples something is considered definite insofar as it can be investigated and supported by evidence. In other cases, a thing is declared definite by the consistency of the observable evidence, such as the rising of the sun (Hos. 6:3). The negation expresses that nothing can be verified or proven (Ps. 5:9[10]), as with the speech of the psalmist's deceitful enemies.

Bringing this evidence to Job 42, we conclude that Job has spoken on behalf of God that which was verifiable by experience and borne out by evidence: Job was drawing logical conclusions based on what had happened to him. In contrast to his friends, who were spouting unsubstantiable accusations based on theory (that God was punishing Job for his sins), Job describes the situation faithfully. Job believes that God is afflicting him without cause (9:17), a belief that God affirms is true (2:3); in contrast, Job's friends claim that God is afflicting Job with cause and press Job to confess his supposed crimes. This does not mean that Job's concept of God is unobjectionable or that all that he says of God is correct, but it does mean that Job has drawn logical conclusions, even if they don't happen to be true ones in this case.

We can understand this issue by looking at 2 Samuel 16:5 – 14. As David flees Jerusalem, driven from his capital city by his son Absalom, he is confronted by Shimei, a descendant of Saul's. Shimei throw rocks at David and curses him because he believes that David is getting what he deserves: punishment from God because of bloodshed against Saul's household. David's entourage takes offense and Abishai offers to execute the obnoxious opportunist for his presumptuous accusations. David's response is most interesting:

> "If he is cursing because the LORD said to him, 'Curse David,' who can ask, 'Why do you do this?'"
>
> David then said to Abishai and all his officials, "My son, who is my own flesh, is trying to take my life. How much more then this Benjamite! Leave him alone; let him curse, for the LORD has told him to." (2 Sam. 16:10 – 11)

David legitimizes Shimei's cursing, for Shimei has arrived at the most logical conclusion; given the circumstances, anyone would agree. In the same way God legitimizes Job's words because Job has arrived at the most logical conclusion. In this way, his words are considered verifiable. The conclusions of Job's friends were not born out by the evidence. Job's conclusions differed because they were.

However, we must make another important point. David does not believe that Shimei's assessment (however logical it may seem) will win out once time has run its course. He agrees that Shimei's logic legitimizes his chosen course of action, but he disagrees with Shimei's assessment of his character. In the same way, given the circumstances that Job is living through, God considers Job's conclusions legitimate, while those of his friends are not. Yet God is not content with Job's assessment of his character. Job's conclusions are understandable, but not correct. Just as Shimei's view of David is deficient despite the logic of his conclusions, Job's view of God is deficient despite the logic of his assessment. In both cases, only time will bring out the truth. The truth dawns on Job after the speeches of God — he then admits that he spoke of things that he did not understand (42:3).

Job finishes his speech of despair (over getting a fair trial) by wishing again for death (10:18 – 22), a reprise of his lament in chapter 3. Again we see his view of the netherworld with some clarity:

> Before I go to a place of no return,
>> to the land of gloom and deep shadow,

> to the land of deepest night,
>> of deep shadow and disorder,
>> where even the light is like darkness. (10:21 – 22)

The most interesting word is the one translated by the NIV as "disorder" (negated *sedarim*), which occurs only here in the Old Testament but is common in later biblical Hebrew, including the Dead Sea Scrolls.[46] The ancients commonly characterized the created world as "ordered." I have demonstrated elsewhere that "bringing order" is the most basic of creative activities in ancient literature, including the Old Testament.[47] In the created (= ordered) cosmos, there remain patches of disorder or chaos that are sometimes considered "nonexistent."[48] If "disorder" is an appropriate translation of the negated word *sedarim* in 10:22, it would suggest that the Israelites considered the netherworld a place untouched by the creative activity that brought order to the world of the living. This also explains the absence of light in Sheol.

Zophar (Job 11)

ZOPHAR ACCUSES JOB OF "idle talk" (11:3, *baddim*). This Hebrew word appears five other times in the Old Testament, always in the plural;[49] here it corresponds to the word translated "mock" (*l'g*). Job has accused God of mocking the innocent (9:23); according to the psalmist, God also mocks those who conspire against him (Ps. 2:4, NIV "scoff"). The innocent mock the wicked when the latter are punished (Job 22:19), and victims are mocked by their persecutors (Ps. 22:7[8]). We might then conclude that Zophar is characterizing Job's stance about his innocence as a farcical travesty.

When a politician gets caught abusing his power, extorting money from those desiring to work for the government, giving favors to relatives,

---

46. Occurs most commonly in the DSS in the War Scroll (1QM) in reference to battle formations or battle array. See listing in *DCH*, 6:122. Similar semantic range for this root is also attested in Aramaic, Syriac, and Akkadian. In the latter, the verb *sadaru* also refers to lining up in battle formation as well as doing anything with regularity or consistency (*CAD* S:11 – 14).

47. See Walton, *Ancient Near Eastern Thought*, 179 – 99, esp. 187; J. Walton, *The Lost World of Genesis One* (Downers Grove, Ill.: InterVarsity Press, 2009), 35, 38 – 53.

48. This is part of the functional ontology of the ancient world in which existence is predicated on functioning in an ordered system. In Egypt, places such as the desert and the cosmic sea were labeled nonexistent.

49. Job 41:4 (textually questionable); Isa. 16:6 and Jer. 48:30 (associated with Moab's prideful, insolent boasts); Isa. 44:25 and Jer. 50:36 (associated with diviners' worthless talk). In Ugaritic it refers to chanting, sometimes mournful.

and engaging in endless other crimes; or when the district attorney finally delivers the indictment, supported by wiretaps, dozens of witnesses, taped conversations, and boxes of incriminating documents, we are amazed to hear the politician claim his total innocence—with a straight face, as if he believes it: "The truth will come out in the trial" (cf. the words that Zophar puts in Job's mouth in v. 4). We can only sadly shake our heads at how such arrogance and presumption make mockery of justice. That is how Zophar characterizes Job: "We all know you are guilty Job. It's obvious! Why keep the charade going?"

As he wishes for God to address this subject, Zophar observes that "true wisdom has two sides" (11:6, *kiplayim letušiyyah*). The word *tušiyyah* occurs in 5:12 as "success" and in 26:3 as "insight" (parallel to "advice"). M. Fox defines it as "an inner resource, not specifically intellectual or moral, that can help one deal with a crisis."[50] He translates it "competence" or "resourcefulness" in Proverbs 3:21, a sense that works well in all its contexts.[51] The other word in the phrase, *kiplayim* (from the root *kpl*), occurs five times as a verb and three as the derivative noun. The root concerns doubling something (e.g., Ex. 26:9), and here uses a dual form typically applied to things that occur intrinsically in pairs. The combination is obscure, but working with what we do know of the words and analyzing them in the context of Zophar's conclusion (Job 11:6c), I would suggest an interpretation something like: "Competent, responsible thinking has to consider the other side of the equation; think of how much worse it could be if God decided to punish *all* your sins."

Zophar argues for God's inscrutability in 11:7 – 12. He thinks that Job takes too much on himself in supposing that he can match God in court. In one sense this anticipates part of what God will say when he appears in chapter 38: Job does not comprehend the vastness of God's wisdom. This again illustrates that the words of the friends are not utter foolishness. Their arguments derive power from the accepted, sound thinking on which they are based. The problem is often not a theology that is entirely wrong, but in drawing wrongheaded conclusions in a flawed assemblage of ideas or the intermixture of presuppositions that are not essential.

Zophar lays out his recommended course of action in 11:13 – 20. His advice in 11:13 is difficult to argue against—all followers of God should do such things. His assumption in 11:14, however, begins to show the deviation, and verses 15 – 20 reveal Zophar's perception of the goal. He

---

50. M. Fox, *Proverbs 1 – 9* (AB; New York: Doubleday, 2000), 163.
51. Eleven occurrences: Job 5:12; 6:13; 11:6; 12:16; 26:3; 30:22; Prov. 2:7; 3:21; 8:14; 18:1; Isa. 28:29; Mic. 6:9.

assumes that Job has indeed sinned and so brought this punishment down on himself—a flawed conclusion. The goal he holds out for Job is restoration of prosperity.

Job (Job 12–14)

DESPITE ZOPHAR'S CLAIM THAT Job is getting off easy (11:6), Job is not willing to look at his case in isolation; God should be concerned about those who are wicked and hold them in contempt (12:5–6). This observation rests on the premise that justice should be proportional and relative. The last phrase of 12:6 is somewhat difficult: What does it mean to "carry their god in their hands"? The most important grammatical question in this clause is whether "god/God" is the object or subject of the verb. The NIV presents an alternate: "To whom God brings by his hand." This rendering is preferable because the men referred to in 12:5–6 are represented in plural forms, while the verb and pronoun in 12:6c are masculine singular. If God is not the subject, there is no masculine singular subject available in the context. Job is therefore observing that even though these people provoke God, they are secure and continue to receive prosperity from him.

We may note in passing that 12:9 makes the only reference to Yahweh outside of the narrative frame and the Yahweh speeches in 38–41. Some manuscripts have "God" (*'eloah*), apparently concluding that Yahweh was a later scribe's slip. Nevertheless, those who make text critical decisions often prefer the unlikely reading. Since no interpretive matter hinges on the wording, we can leave it for now as a simple curiosity.

The hymnic section (12:10–24) expresses God's authority to revoke the power of corrupt or repressive leaders.

In chapter 13, Job turns his attention back to his desired court case, beginning with a rebuke to the friends (including his classic reference to them as "worthless physicians," v. 4). The more stinging complaint against them, however, comes as he accuses them of "speaking wickedly on God's behalf" (13:7). This wording will eventually find a partial echo in God's indictment of the friends (42:7). The preposition used here (*l*-; in 42:7, *'el* is generally considered to be equivalent and interchangeable) requires clarification. Do the friends speak ill *about* God, *to* God, or *on behalf of* God? The key to the decision is in the object of the verb describing what they speak, here "wickedness" (*'awlah*). This abstract noun occurs nine times in Job and other derivative forms occur six more times. Of particular significance are those occurrences that refer to speech in a court setting (Job 6:30; 27:4; Isa. 59:3).

- Job 6:30—Job asks rhetorically whether there is *'awlah* on his tongue in the context of whether he is lying about his integrity.
- Job 27:4—Job indicates that he would be speaking *'awlah* if he were to admit that his friends were right about his sinfulness.
- Isaiah 59:3—Israel has sinned because their tongues have spoken *'awlah*; this use parallels perjury in those who lack integrity (Isa. 59:4).

All of these refer to the crime of misrepresenting a case in court: offering as true testimony what is false. In 13:7 the friends are not giving testimony *to* God because they are not on trial; they are not giving false testimony *about* God, because they are not giving bad theology; they *are*, however, giving false testimony *on behalf of* God when they presume to represent God's testimony about Job and his supposed sin. The second clause of 13:8 confirms this interpretation when the same preposition questions whether the friends have the right to argue a case "for" ("on behalf of") God. Our conclusion will carry over to 42:7, where God accuses the friends of not speaking that which was verifiable on his behalf. "Verifiable" (*nekonah*; NIV "right") is the opposite of the misrepresentation (*'awlah*) here.

The next textual puzzle to solve is in the famous statement of Job in 13:15, "Though he slay me, yet will I hope in him." Unfortunately the most familiar and popular sections in Job are often among the most difficult; this verse is no exception, as a survey of translations and commentaries shows:

- NIV, NASB, KJV, Dhorme, Andersen, Hebrew Qere:[52] "Though he slay me, I will hope in him."
- RSV, Hebrew Ketiv: "Behold, he will slay me, I have no hope."
- Hartley: "If he were to slay me, I would have no hope."
- Gordis, Habel, Smick: "Yes, though he slay me, I will not wait [in silence]."

Does the last word (*yhl*) describe "hoping" or "waiting"? The impetus for interpreting the verb as "waiting in silence" concerns Elihu (Job 32:11, 16), who waited while the others spoke; the usage of the verb throughout Job confirms such an interpretation. The meaning of hope only comes in secondarily as those who are suffering often wait with hope for God to bring relief. I would therefore translate, "Even though he may slay me,[53] I

---

52. The Qere (that which is read, the Masoretic vocalization) has *lô* (= "in him"); the Ketiv (that which is written, the consonantal text) has *lō'* (= "not").

53. The word that leads off the verse (*hen*) is often used in Job to introduce a hypothetical condition. When construed with the imperfect, it conveys a subjunctive mood (9:11–12; 12:14–15; 23:8–9; 40:23; see also Ex. 4:1).

will not wait [in silence]"—that is, Job is going to continue pressing for the court appearance. The next line follows that same train of thought. This reading makes more sense than the traditional interpretation, both in terms of lexical semantics and in terms of the rhetorical and theological sense of the passage. As we have seen a number of times already and will encounter again, Job has no hope in the afterlife. In contrast, as we see in 13:18 – 19, Job does expect to receive vindication before he dies, though we need not think that he harbors any hope for a fair trial.

After concluding his plea for a legitimate hearing, he shifts to a discussion of human mortality and frailty (13:28 – 14). In 14:7 – 14 we find the strongest statements in the book about Job's beliefs concerning the afterlife, beliefs that prove bleak. Like everyone in the ancient world, Job believes that life continues after death, but such a belief offers little hope if life in the netherworld is dreary drudgery. Trees can resprout (14:7 – 9), but humans have no such prospects (14:10, 12)—they are more like the riverbed that simply dries up (14:11). Job wishes it were otherwise, that he could take refuge in the grave and then be brought back to life (14:13), but he realizes that such an option does not exist.

We must examine 14:14 closely to see how it fits in this sequence of thought. The rhetorical question in the first line expects a negative answer (as he has already indicated in 14:10). During the Old Testament period, the Israelites had no theologically formulated hope of resurrection; yet the end of the verse indicates that Job is waiting (same verb as in 13:15) for something, expressed in the words "for my renewal [*halipati*] to come" (NIV). The word in question is a noun derived from a Hiphil verbal form of the root *hlp*.[54] The abstract noun (*halipah*) appears twelve times in the Old Testament, eight as a reference to changes of clothes. Of the four remaining occurrences, one speaks of sending a troop of soldiers to relieve those in service (1 Kings 5:15[28]); the other (Job 10:17) speaks of one company of witnesses who are always ready to relieve the former set. The noun thus refers to someone or something coming to replace or relieve another; this suggests that in 14:14, Job is hoping that his turn will come. Job is the one replacing another (who theoretically is having his case heard).[55] This leads seamlessly into 14:15, where God will summon Job and Job will have the chance he has been looking for to have his case heard. As Job dreams of this new day, we should observe that his objective is restored relationship (14:15 – 17),

---

54. The verbal form has just been used in 14:7 for the resprouting of the tree.
55. In Ps. 55:19 – 20, there is no such opportunity coming for those who have no fear of God.

not restored benefits. This continues to be the most important aspect of Job's posture.

We need to clarify what Job is saying in 14:16 – 17 about his sins and transgressions. Is he now admitting to some? Some observations to begin:

- God's counting of one's steps is usually a negative sign of overattention.
- Not keeping track of one's sin (*šmr* + *ḥaṭṭa'āt*) is an act of mercy (Job 10:14).
- Sealing sins in a bundle or bag[56] reserves them for future punishment (Deut. 32:34 – 35; Hos. 13:12) — again, an operation of grace.
- Covering (*ṭpl*) over refers to smearing something with plaster or whitewash to hide it; when applied to sin, this act puts the sin out of sight.

All of these are still part of Job's dream for renewed relationship. In this new imagined setting, the offenses are all hypothetical. By "relationship" I do not refer to the Christian idea of relationship with God through Christ; that was neither available to Job nor was it present in his conceptual framework. I also do not refer to the relationship that Israel had with God through the covenant. Despite the fact that the audience of this book *is* the covenant people, Israel, Job is a non-Israelite, so that would not be fitting to apply to him. Finally, relationship cannot be thought of in ancient Near Eastern terms where it is framed by the Great Symbiosis. If relationship only meant restored favor, it could be mistaken for a desire for privileged status that would inevitably result in benefits. We have seen that Job is not motivated by this.

When Job thinks of restored relationship with God, he envisions a coming day after his reconciliation with God when he will be given the benefit of the doubt and will receive mercy based on a track record of good behavior, even if God is dogging his steps. His symbiosis with God is not driven by ritual performance and divine need (as in the ancient Near East); it is not driven by covenant stipulations and the *torah* (as in Israel); and it is not based on grace received by faith (as in Christian theology). Job's symbiosis with God is based on the idea that he will conduct himself in righteousness and that in so doing, he will gain the approval of God. That relationship would be encapsulated in the opening accolades in Job 1 in which God praised Job to the Challenger.

---

56. See discussion in Clines, *Job 1 – 20*, 334.

Rhetorical Issues

IN EACH OF THE three cycles of dialogue, the friend's speeches are interspersed with Job's replies. For the first cycle, the layout is as follows:

Eliphaz: chs. 4–5	Job: chs. 6–7
Bildad: ch. 8	Job: chs. 9–10
Zophar: ch. 11	Job: chs. 12–14

The friends' comments in the first dialogue cycle are comprised mostly of advice to Job: generalized statements accompanied by exhortations. Below I have summarized each speech and then focus in on a couple of important issues.

Eliphaz: You have counseled many in similar circumstances and you should take your own advice: Trust in your piety — the Retribution Principle will hold; it is the wicked who perish. Yet from God's perspective no mortal is righteous; appeal to God and accept his discipline.

Job: The extent of my misery justifies my outcry. I wish that he would put me to death; then I would die with the consolation that at least I had assessed the situation realistically. I feel so helpless, I am not sure I can continue, and my friends are of no help. I would be delighted if God could show me what I have done wrong. My miserable days will soon come to an end, so I may as well speak my mind: Why, O God, have you targeted me for such attention — no one could bear such scrutiny. Can't you show some tolerance before it is too late?

Eliphaz's first speech is restrained. Its central element is the mystical revelation that he claims (4:12–21). Imbedded in the heart of that revelation is the core of his argument in 4:17 — the ancient Near Eastern view that no one can be righteous from God's perspective. Most of the platitudes that he offers are theologically defensible, but we must also notice his reasoning: "Should not your piety be your confidence and your blameless ways your hope?" (4:6). What is the "confidence" and "hope" to which Eliphaz refers? It appears from the comments that follow that he is saying: "If you really have done nothing wrong, you have nothing to worry about." The hope to which he refers must be an expectation for vindication (as a result of his appeal to God, 5:8). Circumstantial prosperity is the only measure they have for vindication. From Eliphaz's perspective, Job's absolution would evidence itself in Job's recovery from illness and a restoration of his goods (5:17–26).

Job, however, wants vindication in the form of God asserting that he has done nothing to deserve his circumstances. This is a key difference because it hinges on the claims made by the Challenger. To have one's prosperity restored represents a different value than to have one's righteousness acknowledged. Though the former could be considered tacit evidence of the latter, we can see that Job draws a line of distinction between them. He never asks for God to return his prosperity or heal his illness; he wants God to declare him innocent and righteous.

Eliphaz begins lawsuit language (5:8). There has been a lot of discussion about whether Job is positioned as a defendant or a plaintiff.[57] I would propose that Job and his friends think that Job is a defendant in a criminal trial. Job launches a countersuit in an attempt to take the role of plaintiff. None of the characters know that Job is actually the star witness for the defense in the trial of God's policies.

Eliphaz's main statement (4:17) is not based on something like a Christian concept of human fallenness and a sin nature; his assertion concerns God more than humankind. No one can be righteous from God's perspective, not because people are inherently sinful, but because deity is non-communicative about his expectations and his standards are too complex for anyone to meet. This proclaimed inscrutability is the same sentiment expressed by the sufferer in *Ludlul bel nemeqi* (see p. 25): "When have mortals ever learnt the ways of a god?"

Eliphaz: Appeal to God and admit your offense.

Job: Stop treating me as guilty. Rather than appeal to God with false humility and trumped-up offenses, I will confront him with demands for vindication.

Bildad: How dare you suggest that God perverts justice! Your children undoubtedly sinned. Face the facts and come clean — then all will go smoothly for you. Traditional wisdom gives you all the information you need: the Retribution Principle. The wicked perish, but God does not reject a righteous man.

Job: How could anyone ever establish his righteousness before God? You can't argue with him and expect to win. Challenging him would be disastrous; he is too strong to overpower

---

57. See full discussion in Magdalene, *Scales of Righteousness*, 127–76.

and he is beyond being called to account. I have nothing left to live for, so I may as well say it outright: He is not just — both the blameless and the wicked are destroyed. I wish I had an advocate to speak on my behalf. Nothing makes any sense; I can't win. I wish God would just let me die.

In 8:5 Bildad continues the negotiation language that Eliphaz introduced. If Job lays out his case before God and if he is pure and upright (8:6), his plea will result in restoration (8:6 – 7). As always, the friends see this as the ultimate objective. Job, in contrast, sees acquittal as the paramount goal. Like Eliphaz, Bildad does not directly accuse Job of wrongdoing, but the wisdom observations that dominate his speech reek of implication that is far from subtle. Job, nevertheless, refuses to take the bait. He returns almost immediately to the issue of his court case with God and its prospects for success. Those who resist God are doomed, and if his cleverness does not overwhelm, his power can crush.

Job's statements drift among several postures:

1. I demand a hearing.
2. Any court case is doomed from the start.
3. Whatever else, I know I am innocent.
4. God is unjust (9:22 – 24).
5. I need an arbitrator.
6. Death is inevitable and desirable.

    Bildad: Take the traditional Retribution Principle seriously and recognize the inevitable conclusion.

        Job: I know the traditions are true, but I am not ready to admit the conclusions are inevitable. Yet I am without recourse.

    Zophar: What arrogance! You think you are so pure! Well, you haven't even begun to get what you deserve. Your understanding is miniscule compared to God. Give it up and repent of your sin so that all may go well for you.

        Job: You, my friends, mock me; if you would only show your wisdom by being silent. You offer no comfort in counsel and speak presumptuously and ignorantly on God's behalf. I suffer while the wicked escape scot-free. God is the fount of all wisdom and power. If only I could bring my case before him — I think I would have an airtight defense. I would request, however, that he cease and desist with the torment and terrors until the matter is settled. Given such a moratorium, I could concentrate on my case. Show me the evidence of my wrongdoing. This life is all I have, so I want to get this settled before it is too late.

Zophar takes offense at Job's claims and indignantly unleashes invectives against him. He considers Job to be foolish for thinking that he can stand up, look God in the face, and confront him with the details of the case. He does not actually refer to Job's desire for a hearing; instead, he expresses his wish that God will simply decide the matter and show Job his folly. In this speech Zophar makes the most forthright claim yet concerning Job's offense: "Put away the sin that is in your hand" (11:14). As this series of speeches reaches its conclusion, the gloves are off and subtle innuendo gives way to stark accusation. The summary conclusion again emphasizes restoration (11:15–20), which the friends see as the ultimate objective and which the Challenger contended was Job's primary motivation for righteous behavior.

Job likewise becomes more caustic as he replies with indignant sarcasm and appears to engage in wisdom one-upmanship. Then he returns to the issue of the hearing and accuses Zophar of speaking falsely on God's behalf. Job claims that it is not he but Zophar who deserves God's rebuke (13:9–10). Just as Zophar forthrightly accused Job of wrongdoing, Job replies that if anyone can bring specific charges, he will be silent and die (13:19). As he turns his attention away from Zophar toward God, we can see him move to the next level of thinking. In chapters 9–10 he was still worrying about the prospect of facing God in court. In 13:18 he declares that his case is ready and its outcome is sure. Before, litigation was the obstacle; now time is the obstacle. In contrast to the conclusion of the friends' speeches, where Zophar paints a lovely picture of Job's benefits being restored, Job concludes his series with first a beautiful dream of troubles being past and relationship with God restored (14:13–17) with his integrity being recognized and substantiated, but then the despair of his situation (14:18–22).

Zophar: Devote your heart to God and put away sin.

Job: You are badly misrepresenting God and me. I hope I can get my hearing and restore my relationship with God before I die.

Having addressed the rhetorical role of each of the speeches, we can now turn our attention to the rhetorical role of the series as a whole. Since the first half of the book is arranged in three series of dialogues (chs. 4–14; 15–21; 22–27), it is logical to assume that each series accomplishes something.[58] This conclusion derives from the belief that the book is designed carefully and intentionally. Consequently, as we assess the rhetorical strategy of each series, we should attempt to understand what the philosophical point is for the series and what the resolution is that closes that series and leads to the next.

In this first series, each friend's speech ends with painting a rosy picture of the benefits of righteousness (Eliphaz, 5:17–27; Bildad, 8:20–22; Zophar, 11:13–19). The main focus of this series is that the friends appeal to Job to think about getting his benefits back and doing whatever is necessary to accomplish that. The series comes to a conclusion when Job makes it clear that he has no hope for restoration and is not motivated by the desire that his friends have placed as the highest value (14:18–22). Once Job has refuted this argument and resisted this advice, the series comes to an end and the book moves on to the next philosophical issue.

Now we can turn our attention to the posture that Job adopts in this set and what its significance is in the scenario that the book unfolds. In the Introduction we described briefly Tsevat's triangle of claims as a way of understanding the characters' positions (pp. 42–43). The triangle illustrates the tension between three concepts that everyone in the book has ample reason to affirm: The Retribution Principle, God's Justice, and Job's Righteousness. Given Job's calamities, however, one of the three concepts has to be discarded. We noted in the discussion of Job 2 that the friends defended the corner represented by the RP and questioned Job's righteousness (p. 108). Their speeches in this first cycle repeatedly demonstrate this position as each one eloquently expounds on the judgment that comes to the wicked and the prosperity that comes to the righteous.

Job's place on the triangle is easy to discern: He defends his own righteousness (e.g., 9:20)—a position that forces him to choose between the RP and the justice of God. One of them has to go. Though he does not elaborate much on the RP in this set of speeches, his demand for a hearing carries the assumption that righteousness and suffering do not belong together. He also grants the RP as an acceptable premise (9:1) and does not argue its merits with his friends. Unfortunately this means that for Job, God's justice occupies the weak corner of the triangle, as we see in 9:17–24, most noticeably in Job's blunt statement: "He destroys both the blameless and the wicked" (9:22; see also 7:20–21; 10:3, 7).

By positioning himself in this way, he articulates the second aspect of the challenge to God's policies, as addressed in the Introduction (pp. 21–22).

---

58. This necessity was driven home to me in lengthy discussions with Jonathan Walton. It would be a last resort to conclude that there was simply repetition for rhetorical effect.

The Challenger suggested that bringing prosperity to righteous people was bad policy because it would eventually corrupt their motives and cause them to do right only to gain reward. This policy undermines and subverts true righteousness. The advice of Job's friends unwittingly would, if followed, prove the Challenger's point: If Job acknowledges his (fictional) sins with the ultimate goal of restoration, he will prove the Challenger's point.

Job's challenge of God is that it is bad policy for him to bring suffering to righteous people because that would undermine God's justice (as it has in Job's thinking). When we recall that the book is ultimately about God and his policies, not about Job and his suffering, we can see that all the pieces are in place. As the Challenger and Job both call God to account (to establish respectively true righteousness and true justice), the friends misrepresent God in their assessment of the situation.

What would Job, the star witness for the defense, have to do for God to lose this challenge? God would lose the case pressed by the Challenger if Job followed the advice of his wife or his friends. If Job were to follow either, he would demonstrate that he was only interested in restoration of benefits and that even *his* motives were corrupt. God could also lose the case pressed by Job if he were to give Job reasons for his suffering and thereby accept the cause-effect matrix of the unqualified RP. If God agrees to a court case to defend himself (theodicy) and offers Job an explanation, he tacitly admits that the system operates by justice, at which point he would have to admit that Job had not received justice in accordance with the parameters of the RP.

We must then evaluate how Job is doing. Has he cursed God? For us to maintain the proposed premise of the book, we must conclude that Job has not cursed God and that he never does curse God. Job has his best chance to curse God to his face when God comes to him in Job 38.[59] By that point the characters have exhausted all debate, and it seems that nothing is going to change; however, Job does not utter any formal curse against God in conclusion — in fact, he retracts (42:6). In the treatment of Job 1, I concluded that cursing God would entail speaking in a denigrating, contemptuous, or slanderous way about God (pp. 58–61). We considered examples such as taking credit for what God has done or attributing to God wrong motives; in general, suggestions that God is corrupt or powerless, or that God has needs or can be manipulated, qualify. Job has not suggested any of these. The Great Symbiosis operates on the premise that God's favor can be bought: If we do good for him, he will do good for us. Job does not believe God is powerless (exactly the opposite; God is

---

59. Observation made by Jonathan Walton.

the one acting), and he does not believe that God is corrupt (i.e., that his favors can be bought).[60]

Job *has*, however, called God's justice into question. Why does calling God's justice into question not constitute cursing God? The answer is to be found, I suggest, by investigating how and why he is questioning God's justice. Job does not doubt God's justice because he has lost his benefits, but rather because his own righteousness has been mitigated. His speeches have demonstrated that he cares little for restoration but greatly about righteousness. Job's priorities argue against the Challenger, who claimed there was no such thing as one who was concerned with righteousness apart from its connection with benefits. In fact, Job cares so much about his innocence and so little about his benefits that he is willing to risk all that remains to him (even life itself, which the Challenger is prevented from taking) in his suit against God. F. R. Magdalene has built a good case that Job sues God for abuse of power.[61]

> Job remembers the loving response of Yahweh. He therefore believes that God should call to him with loving-kindness instead of summoning him before a court. God should let him answer out of devotion instead of demanding a legal answer. God should look the other way when he commits infractions instead of expecting scrupulous conduct because such infractions could only have been unwitting, minor, or done in the folly of youth (6:24b; 13:26; and 19:4). God should treat him as the creature of God that he is (10:8a, 9–12; 12:9–10; 30:19; and 31:15) instead of treating him like a legal adversary worthy of inspection and destruction (13:24; cf. 10:8b). As Job understands it, God owes him a duty of care because he is God's creature; God is breaching that duty.[62]

As far as Job's stance goes, in the end there is little theological distinction between "both good and bad come from God" (2:10), and "he destroys both the blameless and the wicked" (9:22). God *must* be the one who destroys both the blameless and the wicked, for, in Job's mind, no one else can be held accountable for such destruction. In Genesis 18:25 Abraham

---

60. In fact, the Challenger was worried that Job's behavior could have been part of his desire to buy God's favor.

61. Magdalene, *Scales of Righteousness*, 145–57. She accepts R. Westbrook's suggestion that abuse of power is the thrust of the Hebrew root ʿšq, which occurs in Job 10:3. It particularly refers to an abuse of power where the deprivation of economic benefit or legal right results, 149. See R. Westbrook, *Studies in Biblical and Cuneiform Law* (Paris: Gabalda, 1988), 35–38.

62. Magdalene, *Scales of Righteousness*, 162.

objects to the Lord: "Far be it from you to do such a thing—to kill the righteous [*ṣaddiq*] with the wicked [*rašaʿ*], treating the righteous and the wicked alike. Far be it from you! Will not the Judge [*šopeṭ*] of all the earth do right [*mišpaṭ*]?" If we juxtapose Job 9:22 and Genesis 18:25 and set up a syllogism, we would have to conclude that Job is at least insinuating that God does not do right (*mišpaṭ*). Indeed, God's rebuke of Job in Job 40:8 suggests that it is precisely God's *mišpaṭ* that Job has questioned (cf. Job's claim in 19:7 that there is no *mišpaṭ* and his assertion in 27:2 that God has withheld *mišpaṭ* from him, cf. 34:5).[63]

All of these observations bring an important point to our attention. We are used to reading the book of Job to find encouragement from Job's exemplary response to suffering. We consider his patience, longsuffering, faithfulness, righteousness, and integrity all to make him an admirable character.[64] In our desire to preserve this pristine role model, we are perhaps sometimes too eager to eliminate or neglect anything that might compromise his stellar performance. This approach reads against the grain of the book's rhetorical strategy. The book is not trying to prove that Job's response to his situation is irreproachable; he is not held up as a paragon of virtue showing us how we ought to respond in suffering (though some of his responses are certainly admirable). The book is teaching us about God and his policies, not offering Job as a biblical paradigm for how to approach suffering. We will uncover the authoritative teaching of Scripture by unfolding its rhetorical strategy, not by imitating its characters. To say this another way, we will learn more about surviving crises by understanding God than by imitating Job.

Therefore we ought to be more discerning and allow Job his weaknesses: a flawed theology and a deficient view of God.[65] Such allowance is essential because we often share these shortcomings. Only one thing is required of Job in order for the book to accomplish its purpose: he must value his righteousness above his benefits. The Challenger has questioned whether God's policies allow anyone to preserve their integrity; God's policies will be vindicated as long as Job maintains that one conviction. It is not even important whether or not Job actually *maintains* his righteousness throughout the trial period—only that he *values* his righteousness above his benefits. The book is not trying to save Job's reputation, and we ought

---

63. Elihu asks nearly the same question as Abraham in Job 34:12, 17.

64. This profile is gleaned, at least in part, from James 5:11, though it should be noted that there it only mentions that Job persevered.

65. We have yet to unravel fully God's statement in Job 42 that Job has spoken of him what is right (though see an initial treatment earlier in this chapter, pp. 173–74). At this point I will only say that Job 42:7 is not as broad a commendation as it might seem.

not to read the book as if Job is the subject rather than God. Bad theology and a deficient view of God are not the same as cursing God. Questioning God's justice is not related to valuing righteousness over reward.

Theological Issues

IN THE LAST SECTION we actually already transitioned from rhetorical to theological issues since they inevitably overlap. I have chosen to examine three theological issues that arise in this series of speeches: (1) viewing God as petty; (2) accusing God based on logical conclusions about the system; and (3) understanding God's role in the cosmos. Again, from a methodological standpoint I want to emphasize that the book is not trying to teach us about these issues. The authoritative teaching of the text derives from its overall message; these are simply topics that command our attention as the book unfolds.

Viewing God as petty (7:17 – 21; 14:3 – 6). Job cannot consider his plight apart from the RP; nevertheless, the magnitude of his suffering cannot be explained by any observable behavior. His understanding at this point does not allow for flaw or inadequacy in the RP; he also confidently repudiates his friends' suggestions that he is guilty of great sins. Job is left to conclude that the standards of God's justice are too exacting. God has apparently lost all sense of proportion and forgotten how frail is the humanity that he himself created (cf. 10:4 – 8). Like the policeman who gives a ticket to the driver going 56 mph in a 55 mph zone, God appears to have too much time on his hands — maybe he should consider a hobby?

This trap in which Job has fallen is common enough today: God demands too much! Job has neglected or at least underestimated grace. By this I am not suggesting that Job should have seen how God's grace was evident in his circumstances. Instead, I refer to the necessity of understanding that God's actions are always infused with grace. In Job's view, justice is a runaway train and grace was left stranded at the station. Such thinking seriously misrepresents God's character. Unfortunately, many people have concluded that this petty, judgmental God dominates the Old Testament and that the God of grace and love only appears in the New Testament, in the person of Christ. This is dangerous theology. God knows our weaknesses. The God of the Old Testament is the very God that became incarnate in Jesus and is the very God whom Christ called people to follow.

The Old Testament is full of God's grace. Grace preserved humanity after the fall; grace led God to forge a covenant with Abraham as a means of revealing his plan to reconcile with sinful humanity. Grace provided the revelation of God's holiness in the law and allowed Israel a glimpse of how they could be holy. Grace characterized God's interaction with

Israel through centuries of rebellion and apostasy. Grace sent the prophets with warning and instruction. Grace prompted God to reveal himself in the Scriptures so that we might know him. We can then agree with the hymn writer: "'Twas grace that taught my heart to fear, and grace my fears relieved."

We have a deficient view of God, as Job did, if we believe that his attributes are manifested disproportionately or inappropriately. Mercy does not trump justice. Holiness does not trump grace. We cannot claim that love is the first and foremost of God's attributes; rather, it is one alongside of the rest that manifests itself in its proper place. We make the same mistake Job did when we fail to examine other options and prematurely cast a judgmental eye toward God, which leads us into the next topic.

Accusing God based on logical conclusions about the system. Job articulates his worst suspicions about God in 10:3. Job has allowed his beliefs about the world's operations to undermine his beliefs about the nature of God. He understands the RP as the foundation for God's involvement in the world: All experience must be explained by its tenets. He believes that if that is not so, God cannot be just. At the same time he believes that if the RP does not hold up, God's justice is open to question. The series of propositions goes like this:

1. If God is just, the RP is true.
2. If the RP is true, it is the foundation of how the world works.
3. If the RP is the foundation, one's experiences will be consistent with the RP.
4. If experience is not consistent with the RP, the RP is not the foundation.
5. If the RP is not the foundation, the RP is not true.
6. If the RP is not true, God is not just.

Here one's presuppositions about the way the world does or should work hold priority over one's understanding of God. Philosophy is valued above theology; experience is valued above revelation. The alternative is for faith to be the foundation of reason.

This problem evidences itself today in many people's beliefs. We commonly hear someone say, "I can't accept a God who would allow so much suffering in the world" (whether the topic is cancer or AIDS; hunger or poverty; war or terrorism). The question is whether we are prepared to let revelation and theology change our philosophy and shape our understanding of experience. Are we willing to give God the benefit of the doubt and question our own presuppositions instead of his character? This poignant question flows through the book of Job—we will encounter it time and again.

God's role in the cosmos. The poetic description of the cosmos in Job 9:5–14 accords with Old World Science; we also see a theological under-standing of God's pervasive role in the universe. His wisdom and power govern the cosmos moment by moment. Everything that happens is the work of God.

Unfortunately, our worldview, with its emphasis on empirical science, predisposes us to such a high interest in the mechanics and the processes of the universe that we easily neglect the one responsible for it all. The result of this is a practical deism that sees God as only remotely involved in the physical world. We think that he has set up "natural laws" and then flipped the switch to let them run. This is not the view suggested by Job in 9:7. We might claim that we are not bound by Job's theology, but we will find the whole of Scripture repeatedly affirm that same theology of cosmic operations.

In the ancient (and biblical) worldview, there was no divide between natural and supernatural.[66] One could not speak of "natural laws"; what we identify as natural laws only take on their "lawlike" quality because God acts so consistently in the operations of the cosmos. He has made the cosmos intelligible and has given us minds that can penetrate some of its mysteries.

Psalm 139:13 shows us the distinction. The psalmist declares to God: "You knit me together in my mother's womb." This act of creation is not instantaneous; it involves a process. Yet it is the work of God. The process is well understood by science: In the process of fertilization, conception, implantation, fetal development, and birth, scientists find that which is explainable, predictable, and regular. The field of science called embryol-ogy offers a complex sequence of naturalistic cause and effect for the devel-opment of a child; yet this blossoming of a life, which the Bible affirms as the work of God, remains full of mystery.

The activities of deity pervaded the ancient world; nothing happened apart from deity (or other beings outside the human realm such as demons or ghosts). In the minds of the ancients, the gods did not "intervene" because such thinking would assume a realm of activity apart from them, which they could step into and out of. The Israelites, along with everyone else in the ancient world, believed instead that every event was the act of deity; every plant that grew, every baby born, every drop of rain, and every climatic disaster was an act of God. No "natural" laws governed the cosmos; deity ran the cosmos or was inherent in it. There were no "miracles" (in

---

66. Sections of this discussion are adapted from Walton, *The Lost World of Genesis One.*

the sense of events deviating from that which was "natural"), only signs of the deity's activity (sometimes favorable, sometimes not). There is nothing "natural" about the world. Our theology needs to adjust to this alternative way of thinking in order for us to recover an appreciation of an active God.

THE NIV'S TRANSLATION OF Job 4:17 accurately represents my interpretation of Eliphaz's viewpoint, as discussed in Original Meaning: "Can a mortal be righteous in God's perspective? Can a man be clean in the perspective of his Maker?" This is good New Testament theology (cf. Rom 3:23), but even so, we must realize that it does not provide the answer to the sufferer's conundrum. We need the work of Christ to cleanse us from sin because we all stand guilty before God. Eliphaz, however, is not dealing with our need for redemption; he is offering an explanation for suffering. This is a good example of sound theology improperly applied, resulting in false conclusions.

We suffer because we are a part of a fallen world that God, in his wisdom, has allowed to exist. The world is fallen because no one meets God's standard of righteousness;[67] suffering is an inherent consequence of the fall, not divine retribution for a list of tallied offenses.

This means suffering should not lead us to look back on our behavior in search of a cause; rarely is there any identifiable one-to-one correspondence. Occasionally there might be (someone embezzles funds and finds themselves caught and imprisoned; a man and a woman get entangled in an affair and ruin two families), but such cases are obvious and don't require any guesswork.

Those who speculatively link behavior to suffering often conclude that God is petty. Such thinking may constitute a motivation for legalism. While some adopt legalism in order to earn salvation or grace, others see it as a means of maintaining God's favor, believing that God requires minute observance of obscure demands. Ancient Near Eastern thought closely corresponds to this view, as people believed that God has many unknown, untold, unidentifiable requirements that he holds people responsible to observe.

I was a business-economics major in college; my introductory accounting courses were taught by an adjunct with his own accounting firm. He was a friendly and competent professor, but we students were all stunned

---

67. Or perhaps the converse, if Augustine is right.

when he drew test after test from the CPA qualifying examination. We were just beginning students! How could he hold us to such high criteria? It was no surprise that average scores were in the 20–30 percent range. The professor did not do this to be mean, vindictive, or unfair; he simply believed that even budding accountants needed to be responsible for this material. However, there was no way he could communicate the necessary knowledge to us students. Thus, we were left to struggle with material that was beyond our capacity to understand.

Nietzsche viewed God much as we students viewed our accounting professor; his criticisms have been accepted by many today, whether in their formal philosophical form or their more popular permutations. He discusses this view under the question of God's honesty.

> A god who is all-knowing and all-powerful and who does not even make sure that his creatures understand this intention—could that be a god of goodness? Who allows countless doubts and dubieties to persist, for thousands of years, as though the salvation of mankind were unaffected by them, and who on the other hand holds out the prospect of frightful consequences if any mistake is made as to the nature of the truth? Would he not be a cruel god if he possessed the truth and could behold mankind miserably tormenting itself over the truth?... Must he not then endure almost the torments of Hell to have to see his creatures suffer so ... for the sake of knowledge of him, and *not* be able to help and counsel them, except in the manner of a deaf-and-dumb man making all kinds of ambiguous signs when the most fearful danger is about to fall on his child or his dog?[68]

A similar view of God appears in classic literature as John Milton crafts the word of the serpent's temptation of Eve in *Paradise Lost*:

> Or will God incense his ire
> For such a petty Trespass, and not praise
> Rather your dauntless vertue, whom the pain
> Of Death denounc't, whatever thing Death be,
> Deterrd not from atchieving what might leade
> To happier life, knowledge of Good and Evil;
> Of good, how just? of evil, if what is evil
> Be real, why not known, since easier shunnd?
> God therefore cannot hurt ye, and be just;

---

68. F. Nietzsche, *Daybreak: Thought on the Prejudices of Morality* (ed. M. Clark and B. Leiter; Cambridge Texts in the History of Philosophy; Cambridge: Cambridge Univ. Press, 1997), 1.91. I am grateful to my colleague L. Miguelez for this reference.

Not just, not God; not feard then, nor obeyd:
Your feare it self of Death removes the feare.
Why then was this forbid? Why but to awe,
Why but to keep ye low and ignorant,
His worshippers.[69]

Nevertheless, this view is not limited to godless philosophers and literary constructs of Satan. People in our world and in our lives share this same opinion. We reveal it any time we respond to misfortune by seeking out some small, insignificant lapse to blame for our circumstance, as if God were keeping close account of our every activity, then assigning demerits for the minutest peccadillo. Yes, God knows the number of hairs on our head and our every thought, but, in his grace, he also recognizes our frailty.

People whose lives are full of tragedy and suffering often may find themselves accusing and finally rejecting God. Such a scenario provides the basis of the novel *Till We Have Faces*, in which C. S. Lewis tells the story of Orual, queen of Glome. The novel depends most prominently on the Greek myth of Psyche and Cupid, but certain aspects also depend on the story of Job, in that Lewis frames the book as a letter of complaint to the gods. Orual knows only the mysterious god Ungit, who lives in the dark and devours human blood. The queen complains of many things, but most especially the trauma of being born with disarmingly grotesque facial features, and the impact of a wise Greek slave who taught her to distrust the gods. Her life of loneliness and disappointment is relieved only by her beautiful and kind younger half sister, Psyche, who loves her. Orual complains most virulently when the gods take away her beloved Psyche.

As Orual bitterly recounts her experiences in the pages of her book to the gods, she yearns, as Job does, for the opportunity to look the gods in the face and throw her accusations at their feet, to receive an accounting of their actions. She feels justified in her anger and self-righteously vilifies the god's motives. At the end of the book she, like Job, finally finds herself in the presence of the deity with the opportunity to file her complaint. Her closing arguments summarize her grievance:

> You stole her [Psyche] to make her happy, did you? Why, every wheedling, smiling, cat-foot rogue who lures away another man's wife or slave or dog might say the same. Dog, now. That's very much to the purpose. I'll thank you to let me feed my own; it needed no tidbits from your table. Did you ever remember whose the girl was? She was mine. *Mine*. Do you not know what the word means?

---

69. John Milton, *Paradise Lost*, 9.692 – 705.

Mine! You're thieves, seducers. That's my wrong. I'll not complain (not now) that you're blood-drinkers and man-eaters. I'm past that.[70]

At this point Orual is interrupted and realizes that she has been repeating her complaint over and over. But she also realizes that the voice that read it was strange to her—it was her real voice. And in the silence of the court she found the answer.

> The complaint was the answer. To have heard myself making it was to be answered. Lightly men talk of saying what they mean. Often when he was teaching me to write in Greek the Fox [her tutor] would say, "Child, to say the very thing you really mean, the whole of it, nothing more or less or other than what you really mean; that's the whole art and joy of words." A glib saying. When the time comes to you at which you will be forced at last to utter the speech which has lain at the center of your soul for years, which you have, all that time, idiot-like, been saying over and over, you'll not talk about joy of words. I saw well why the gods do not speak to us openly, nor let us answer. Till that word can be dug out of us, why should they hear the babble that we think we mean?[71]

Orual's specific accusation against the motives of deity have little connection with Job, but her situation finds resolution in the same way that Job's eventually will. That resolution is found in her next sentence, the one that gives us the title of the book: "How can they meet us face to face till we have faces?"

Like Orual, we have our complaints that, though they reflect real suffering, fail to account adequately for the true nature of God. We are the ones who have misconstrued him, preferring to think of him as less than he is. We are the ones who have imagined him with human motives and appetites. We are the ones who have created the word "Mine" and then rage against him for stealing away that to which we thought we had a right or believed we owned. If God seems petty to us, it is because we have chosen to create a false picture of him in our minds rather than to adopt by faith the picture given in the Bible. Like Job and Orual, perhaps we have persuaded ourselves that only this picture of a flawed God makes sense, but such a persuasion only shows how little sense we are capable of making. Orual and Job both needed to find a face before they could meaningfully meet God face to face—and we are no different.

---

70. C. S. Lewis, *Till We Have Faces* (Grand Rapids: Eerdmans, 1956), 292.
71. Ibid., 294.

Kelly's Story[72]

JHW: I AM SURE that you have encountered many people who offered encouragement and advice — perhaps, like Job's friends, meaning well, but in the end detrimental. Can you tell us about some of those?

Kelly: I have an outward trial, a trial that I wear on my sleeve and that is exposed and vulnerable for everyone to see whether I want that or not. Some people simply offer their encouragement, support, or prayers, which I deeply appreciate. Yet I am actually surprised by how many encounters I have had in which people try to explain my "life of suffering," with good intentions, and all too quickly offer advice or the remedy to my ailment.

The first year after my accident I went to a prayer service, where people were discussing healings and God's will for the lives of Christians. After the short message, two women approached me and said, "We believe that you are supposed to be healed today ... there is a demon inside of you paralyzing your right arm and giving you this nerve pain!" They proceeded to pat my back forcefully, encouraging me to cough out this demon ... I began to sob. Nothing happened, and there was an awkward silence. They looked at me and said, "Kelly, you need to believe that God can heal you, and with Jesus' power remove this demon from your body." What a horrifying experience for a twelve-year-old girl who was already wrestling with confusion about God's involvement in the trials that were taking place.

Over the next few years, periodically someone would tell me that I needed to strengthen my faith, but I had never had so many encounters as in the spring semester of 2009, when I was in the midst of a very hard trial period when I was losing control of my left arm. I came back to Wheaton after being away for eight months for my semester abroad, and I returned to campus in a dire state. My nerve pain had radically increased, they were worried about the lack of calcium in my bones due to my recent diagnosis of Osteopenia, and out of the blue my left arm started paralyzing itself. People around me began to feel extremely uncomfortable, confused, and nervous as my situation got worse every day.

During that semester I had seven separate encounters with people who spoke with the right intentions, yet their words were hurtful and detrimental. A woman heard my story and told me that I had a demon of adversity that was attacking my life, because there was no other explanation of why everything in my life would go so wrong. She told me that God wants to bless the children that follow him, so I must be under the attack of a

---

72. Kelly interacts with parts of her story in each Contemporary Significance section. For the introduction to the details of her story, see Contemporary Significance in the commentary on ch. 1, pp. 87 – 97.

demon. I also encountered numerous situations where people would see my right arm in a brace and ask if they could pray with me. They would usually start by saying that they strongly believed that I was supposed to be fully healed in that moment. So they would pray over me, and nothing would happen and they would respond frustrated with me that I was keeping this miracle from happening that they so strongly felt was supposed to happen at that moment through their prayers. Throughout the semester I had numerous encounters like these, and the effects were frustrating, confusing, and hurtful rather than encouraging or challenging. They would cause me to question my faith, God's involvement, and myself.

JHW: Eliphaz claims in effect that God has given him a message for Job. People who are going through difficult circumstances will often find those ready to share their "message from God." Did you encounter some of that?

Kelly: Yes, a few of the people who have approached me have done so from that perspective. I have experienced people who come to me saying, "Kelly, I have been praying for you diligently, and I truly believe that God has told me to share with you that you are going to be healed today, so have faith and trust in his power that the message is true!" Others have communicated their thoughts in the forms of messages from God, such as the conversations when they gently tell me that it is my lack of faith that is holding me in this place and that God so eagerly wants me to be freed of these trials, but he is waiting for me to really trust him. It would sadden me when the people did not get the outcome they had wanted. I wanted to encourage them to pray and to be seeking God's voice, but first acknowledge that his power is only manifested in his divine will. So in that spring semester in particular, I began praying for wisdom and patience in how to respond in those situations, since I know that many times their intentions were pure.

JHW: Job's friends continually held out false hopes. How do you deal with false hopes?

Kelly: False hope is a difficult subject and is an area in which I still struggle. When people pray over me, telling me to believe that God will heal me, my emotions are so torn, because at times I allow my mind to think, "Maybe he does want to heal me. Maybe I do need to believe." Yet every time, nothing happens. It is really hard to enter the emotional rollercoaster. My thoughts become conflicted, and I start thinking that maybe they are right and I could be healed. False hopes then lead to entertaining the thought of how amazing it would be to live a day without pain, yet when nothing changes I am left feeling disappointed and dumb for allowing myself to think that maybe God's plan was different from what I had thought.

This struggle does not only apply to miraculous healings, but also ones in the advanced medical field. Understandably, people would encourage me that without a doubt God would allow a surgery to be successful in reducing my pain, and every surgery has failed, even if there was only a 2 percent chance of failure. So if I am honest, it has come to the point where I no longer listen to false hopes, because I do not want to risk the pain of being reminded of the outcome. I feel that God has given his answer in my pursuit to remove the excruciating nerve pain from my body; that answer is no. I do not even pray for my right arm anymore. At times I'll still pray concerning my nerve pain or my left hand, but I pray with caution. I don't doubt that God has the power to work; I just think he has already given his answer.

So those are my raw thoughts and feelings regarding false hopes, yet I see the flaws in this way of thinking. God has told us to pray the cries of our heart, but should we continue to pray even after God has so evidently given his answer? Perhaps that is a larger question for another time. I know I need to grow in this area, but I believe my heart has become guarded and has decided that if I have low expectations, there is less of a chance that I will get hurt or disappointed.

In conclusion, the book of Job forces us to consider what values motivate our faith. Kelly has struggled with those constant suggestions that healing is the reward of faith. She has struggled as well to sustain a strong faith even when healing was not forthcoming. Job's friends similarly placed the highest value on material reward, and the Challenger's contention was that this exigency was the inevitable result of God's policies of blessing righteous people. Job has succeeded thus far in maintaining righteousness as his highest value as he hopes for renewed relationship with God rather than a restoration of his possessions.

Can there be true righteousness without the promise of reward? Or, in Kelly's case, can there be true faith without the reward of healing? Are we able to look beyond a consideration of what is in it for me to an unqualified desire for righteous lives that will bring us into close relationship with God? How can we tell what our motivations are?

Plato considered this question of how true righteousness could be identified. In the *Republic* the question concerning what motivates justice is posed by Glaucon to Socrates considering what would characterize a man who was superlatively just:

> A simple and noble man, who, in the phrase of Aeschylus does not wish to seem but be good. Then we must deprive him of the seeming. For if he is going to be thought just he will have honours

and gifts because of that esteem. We cannot be sure in that case whether he is just for justice' sake or for the sake of the gifts and honours. So we must strip him bare of everything but justice.... Though doing no wrong, he must have the repute of the greatest possible injustice, so that he may be put to the test as regards justice through not softening because of ill repute and the consequences thereof. But let him hold on his course unchangeable even unto death, seeming all his life to be unjust though being just.... Such being his disposition, the just man will have to endure the lash, the rack, chains, the branding iron in his eyes, and finally, after every extremity of suffering, he will be crucified; and so will learn his lesson that not to be but to seem just is what we ought to desire.[73]

In this view, true justice (or we might say righteousness) can only be detected if there is no reward for it. When all is taken away and death is the final result, true righteousness will show its true colors.

In the same way we must ask whether our faith can be sustained when our desires are not granted, when healing does not come, when broken homes are not restored, when the goals we pursue remain beyond our reach.

As Christians we must first conclude that being motivated by righteousness and faith rather than by benefits should be our goal. For some they never get there. They only think of Christianity as a benefits system, and if there is nothing in it for them, they lose all motivation. Yet Christ has told us that the cost of discipleship is high. We lose our lives, not gain them. Once this course is set, we must determine that righteous behavior earns us nothing and that even if it gains us nothing, God is worthy of this life response. He is a righteous God and has created us with the capacity to imitate him. It is in the imitation of him that we find relationship with him—our highest joy. Our faith and its accompanying righteousness ought not to be self-serving. Righteousness should have its desired end in relationship with God, not in gaining reward from God. This is the teaching of the book of Job, and it is a lesson we still desperately need to learn.

---

73. Plato, *The Republic*, 2.361B–D; 361E–362A (trans. P. Shorey; Loeb Classical Library).

Job 15–21

*E**liphaz*
¹Then Eliphaz the Temanite replied:

²"Would a wise man answer with empty notions
  or fill his belly with the hot east wind?
³Would he argue with useless words,
  with speeches that have no value?
⁴But you even undermine piety
  and hinder devotion to God.
⁵Your sin prompts your mouth;
  you adopt the tongue of the crafty.
⁶Your own mouth condemns you, not mine;
  your own lips testify against you.

⁷"Are you the first man ever born?
  Were you brought forth before the hills?
⁸Do you listen in on God's council?
  Do you limit wisdom to yourself?
⁹What do you know that we do not know?
  What insights do you have that we do not have?
¹⁰The gray-haired and the aged are on our side,
  men even older than your father.
¹¹Are God's consolations not enough for you,
  words spoken gently to you?
¹²Why has your heart carried you away,
  and why do your eyes flash,
¹³so that you vent your rage against God
  and pour out such words from your mouth?

¹⁴"What is man, that he could be pure,
  or one born of woman, that he could be righteous?
¹⁵If God places no trust in his holy ones,
  if even the heavens are not pure in his eyes,
¹⁶how much less man, who is vile and corrupt,
  who drinks up evil like water!

¹⁷"Listen to me and I will explain to you;
  let me tell you what I have seen,
¹⁸what wise men have declared,
  hiding nothing received from their fathers

¹⁹(to whom alone the land was given
   when no alien passed among them):
²⁰All his days the wicked man suffers torment,
   the ruthless through all the years stored up for him.
²¹Terrifying sounds fill his ears;
   when all seems well, marauders attack him.
²²He despairs of escaping the darkness;
   he is marked for the sword.
²³He wanders about—food for vultures;
   he knows the day of darkness is at hand.
²⁴Distress and anguish fill him with terror;
   they overwhelm him, like a king poised to attack,
²⁵because he shakes his fist at God
   and vaunts himself against the Almighty,
²⁶defiantly charging against him
   with a thick, strong shield.

²⁷"Though his face is covered with fat
   and his waist bulges with flesh,
²⁸he will inhabit ruined towns
   and houses where no one lives,
   houses crumbling to rubble.
²⁹He will no longer be rich and his wealth will not endure,
   nor will his possessions spread over the land.
³⁰He will not escape the darkness;
   a flame will wither his shoots,
   and the breath of God's mouth will carry him away.
³¹Let him not deceive himself by trusting what is worthless,
   for he will get nothing in return.
³²Before his time he will be paid in full,
   and his branches will not flourish.
³³He will be like a vine stripped of its unripe grapes,
   like an olive tree shedding its blossoms.
³⁴For the company of the godless will be barren,
   and fire will consume the tents of those who love bribes.
³⁵They conceive trouble and give birth to evil;
   their womb fashions deceit."

Job
^{16:1}Then Job replied:

²"I have heard many things like these;
   miserable comforters are you all!

³Will your long-winded speeches never end?
    What ails you that you keep on arguing?
⁴I also could speak like you,
    if you were in my place;
I could make fine speeches against you
    and shake my head at you.
⁵But my mouth would encourage you;
    comfort from my lips would bring you relief.

⁶"Yet if I speak, my pain is not relieved;
    and if I refrain, it does not go away.
⁷Surely, O God, you have worn me out;
    you have devastated my entire household.
⁸You have bound me—and it has become a witness;
    my gauntness rises up and testifies against me.
⁹God assails me and tears me in his anger
    and gnashes his teeth at me;
    my opponent fastens on me his piercing eyes.
¹⁰Men open their mouths to jeer at me;
    they strike my cheek in scorn
    and unite together against me.
¹¹God has turned me over to evil men
    and thrown me into the clutches of the wicked.
¹²All was well with me, but he shattered me;
    he seized me by the neck and crushed me.
He has made me his target;
    ¹³his archers surround me.
Without pity, he pierces my kidneys
    and spills my gall on the ground.
¹⁴Again and again he bursts upon me;
    he rushes at me like a warrior.

¹⁵"I have sewed sackcloth over my skin
    and buried my brow in the dust.
¹⁶My face is red with weeping,
    deep shadows ring my eyes;
¹⁷yet my hands have been free of violence
    and my prayer is pure.

¹⁸"O earth, do not cover my blood;
    may my cry never be laid to rest!
¹⁹Even now my witness is in heaven;
    my advocate is on high.

²⁰My intercessor is my friend
    as my eyes pour out tears to God;
²¹on behalf of a man he pleads with God
    as a man pleads for his friend.

²² "Only a few years will pass
    before I go on the journey of no return.
¹⁷:¹My spirit is broken,
    my days are cut short,
    the grave awaits me.
²Surely mockers surround me;
    my eyes must dwell on their hostility.

³"Give me, O God, the pledge you demand.
    Who else will put up security for me?
⁴You have closed their minds to understanding;
    therefore you will not let them triumph.
⁵If a man denounces his friends for reward,
    the eyes of his children will fail.

⁶"God has made me a byword to everyone,
    a man in whose face people spit.
⁷My eyes have grown dim with grief;
    my whole frame is but a shadow.
⁸Upright men are appalled at this;
    the innocent are aroused against the ungodly.
⁹Nevertheless, the righteous will hold to their ways,
    and those with clean hands will grow stronger.

¹⁰"But come on, all of you, try again!
    I will not find a wise man among you.
¹¹My days have passed, my plans are shattered,
    and so are the desires of my heart.
¹²These men turn night into day;
    in the face of darkness they say, 'Light is near.'
¹³If the only home I hope for is the grave,
    if I spread out my bed in darkness,
¹⁴if I say to corruption, 'You are my father,'
    and to the worm, 'My mother' or 'My sister,'
¹⁵where then is my hope?
    Who can see any hope for me?
¹⁶Will it go down to the gates of death?
    Will we descend together into the dust?"

Bildad
^{18:1}Then Bildad the Shuhite replied:

²"When will you end these speeches?
  Be sensible, and then we can talk.
³Why are we regarded as cattle
  and considered stupid in your sight?
⁴You who tear yourself to pieces in your anger,
    is the earth to be abandoned for your sake?
    Or must the rocks be moved from their place?

⁵"The lamp of the wicked is snuffed out;
  the flame of his fire stops burning.
⁶The light in his tent becomes dark;
  the lamp beside him goes out.
⁷The vigor of his step is weakened;
  his own schemes throw him down.
⁸His feet thrust him into a net
  and he wanders into its mesh.
⁹A trap seizes him by the heel;
  a snare holds him fast.
¹⁰A noose is hidden for him on the ground;
  a trap lies in his path.
¹¹Terrors startle him on every side
  and dog his every step.
¹²Calamity is hungry for him;
  disaster is ready for him when he falls.
¹³It eats away parts of his skin;
  death's firstborn devours his limbs.
¹⁴He is torn from the security of his tent
  and marched off to the king of terrors.
¹⁵Fire resides in his tent;
  burning sulfur is scattered over his dwelling.
¹⁶His roots dry up below
  and his branches wither above.
¹⁷The memory of him perishes from the earth;
  he has no name in the land.
¹⁸He is driven from light into darkness
  and is banished from the world.
¹⁹He has no offspring or descendants among his people,
  no survivor where once he lived.
²⁰ Men of the west are appalled at his fate;
  men of the east are seized with horror.

²¹ Surely such is the dwelling of an evil man;
  such is the place of one who knows not God."

Job
¹⁹:¹Then Job replied:

²"How long will you torment me
  and crush me with words?
³Ten times now you have reproached me;
  shamelessly you attack me.
⁴If it is true that I have gone astray,
  my error remains my concern alone.
⁵If indeed you would exalt yourselves above me
  and use my humiliation against me,
⁶then know that God has wronged me
  and drawn his net around me.

⁷ "Though I cry, 'I've been wronged!' I get no response;
  though I call for help, there is no justice.
⁸He has blocked my way so I cannot pass;
  he has shrouded my paths in darkness.
⁹He has stripped me of my honor
  and removed the crown from my head.
¹⁰He tears me down on every side till I am gone;
  he uproots my hope like a tree.
¹¹His anger burns against me;
  he counts me among his enemies.
¹²His troops advance in force;
  they build a siege ramp against me
  and encamp around my tent.

¹³"He has alienated my brothers from me;
  my acquaintances are completely estranged from me.
¹⁴My kinsmen have gone away;
  my friends have forgotten me.
¹⁵My guests and my maidservants count me a stranger;
  they look upon me as an alien.
¹⁶I summon my servant, but he does not answer,
  though I beg him with my own mouth.
¹⁷My breath is offensive to my wife;
  I am loathsome to my own brothers.
¹⁸Even the little boys scorn me;
  when I appear, they ridicule me.

¹⁹All my intimate friends detest me;
   those I love have turned against me.
²⁰I am nothing but skin and bones;
   I have escaped with only the skin of my teeth.

²¹"Have pity on me, my friends, have pity,
   for the hand of God has struck me.
²²Why do you pursue me as God does?
   Will you never get enough of my flesh?

²³"Oh, that my words were recorded,
   that they were written on a scroll,
²⁴that they were inscribed with an iron tool on lead,
   or engraved in rock forever!
²⁵I know that my Redeemer lives,
   and that in the end he will stand upon the earth.
²⁶And after my skin has been destroyed,
   yet in my flesh I will see God;
²⁷I myself will see him
   with my own eyes—I, and not another.
   How my heart yearns within me!

²⁸"If you say, 'How we will hound him,
   since the root of the trouble lies in him,'
²⁹you should fear the sword yourselves;
   for wrath will bring punishment by the sword,
   and then you will know that there is judgment.'"

Zophar
²⁰:¹Then Zophar the Naamathite replied:

²"My troubled thoughts prompt me to answer
   because I am greatly disturbed.
³I hear a rebuke that dishonors me,
   and my understanding inspires me to reply.

⁴"Surely you know how it has been from of old,
   ever since man was placed on the earth,
⁵that the mirth of the wicked is brief,
   the joy of the godless lasts but a moment.
⁶Though his pride reaches to the heavens
   and his head touches the clouds,
⁷he will perish forever, like his own dung;
   those who have seen him will say, 'Where is he?'

⁸Like a dream he flies away, no more to be found,
    banished like a vision of the night.
⁹The eye that saw him will not see him again;
    his place will look on him no more.
¹⁰His children must make amends to the poor;
    his own hands must give back his wealth.
¹¹The youthful vigor that fills his bones
    will lie with him in the dust.

¹²"Though evil is sweet in his mouth
    and he hides it under his tongue,
¹³though he cannot bear to let it go
    and keeps it in his mouth,
¹⁴yet his food will turn sour in his stomach;
    it will become the venom of serpents within him.
¹⁵He will spit out the riches he swallowed;
    God will make his stomach vomit them up.
¹⁶He will suck the poison of serpents;
    the fangs of an adder will kill him.
¹⁷He will not enjoy the streams,
    the rivers flowing with honey and cream.
¹⁸What he toiled for he must give back uneaten;
    he will not enjoy the profit from his trading.
¹⁹For he has oppressed the poor and left them destitute;
    he has seized houses he did not build.

²⁰"Surely he will have no respite from his craving;
    he cannot save himself by his treasure.
²¹Nothing is left for him to devour;
    his prosperity will not endure.
²²In the midst of his plenty, distress will overtake him;
    the full force of misery will come upon him.
²³When he has filled his belly,
    God will vent his burning anger against him
    and rain down his blows upon him.
²⁴Though he flees from an iron weapon,
    a bronze-tipped arrow pierces him.
²⁵He pulls it out of his back,
    the gleaming point out of his liver.
Terrors will come over him;
    ²⁶total darkness lies in wait for his treasures.
A fire unfanned will consume him
    and devour what is left in his tent.

²⁷The heavens will expose his guilt;
    the earth will rise up against him.
²⁸A flood will carry off his house,
    rushing waters on the day of God's wrath.
²⁹Such is the fate God allots the wicked,
    the heritage appointed for them by God."

Job
²¹:¹Then Job replied:

² "Listen carefully to my words;
    let this be the consolation you give me.
³Bear with me while I speak,
    and after I have spoken, mock on.

⁴"Is my complaint directed to man?
    Why should I not be impatient?
⁵Look at me and be astonished;
    clap your hand over your mouth.
⁶When I think about this, I am terrified;
    trembling seizes my body.
⁷Why do the wicked live on,
    growing old and increasing in power?
⁸They see their children established around
            them,
    their offspring before their eyes.
⁹Their homes are safe and free from fear;
    the rod of God is not upon them.
¹⁰Their bulls never fail to breed;
    their cows calve and do not miscarry.
¹¹They send forth their children as a flock;
    their little ones dance about.
¹²They sing to the music of tambourine and harp;
    they make merry to the sound of the flute.
¹³They spend their years in prosperity
    and go down to the grave in peace.
¹⁴Yet they say to God, 'Leave us alone!
    We have no desire to know your ways.
¹⁵Who is the Almighty, that we should serve him?
    What would we gain by praying to him?'
¹⁶But their prosperity is not in their own hands,
    so I stand aloof from the counsel of the
            wicked.

¹⁷"Yet how often is the lamp of the wicked snuffed out?
How often does calamity come upon them,
the fate God allots in his anger?
¹⁸How often are they like straw before the wind,
like chaff swept away by a gale?
¹⁹It is said,₎ 'God stores up a man's punishment for his sons.'
Let him repay the man himself, so that he will know it!
²⁰Let his own eyes see his destruction;
let him drink of the wrath of the Almighty.
²¹For what does he care about the family he leaves behind
when his allotted months come to an end?

²²"Can anyone teach knowledge to God,
since he judges even the highest?
²³One man dies in full vigor,
completely secure and at ease,
²⁴his body well nourished,
his bones rich with marrow.
²⁵Another man dies in bitterness of soul,
never having enjoyed anything good.
²⁶Side by side they lie in the dust,
and worms cover them both.

²⁷"I know full well what you are thinking,
the schemes by which you would wrong me.
²⁸You say, 'Where now is the great man's house,
the tents where wicked men lived?'
²⁹Have you never questioned those who travel?
Have you paid no regard to their accounts—
³⁰that the evil man is spared from the day of calamity,
that he is delivered from the day of wrath?
³¹Who denounces his conduct to his face?
Who repays him for what he has done?
³²He is carried to the grave,
and watch is kept over his tomb.
³³The soil in the valley is sweet to him;
all men follow after him,
and a countless throng goes before him.

³⁴"So how can you console me with your nonsense?
Nothing is left of your answers but falsehood!"

THE SECOND SET OF speeches turn even greater attention to the fate of the wicked. Job is accused of responding arrogantly and failing to face the facts, but not of specific sins committed prior to his calamities. The speeches get shorter as the dialogue continues.

Eliphaz (Job 15)

JOB 15:1 – 16 contains Eliphaz's rebuke of Job and 15:17 – 35 offers his wisdom sayings about the fate of the wicked. Though Eliphaz evaluates Job's arguments as nonsense, he more importantly accuses Job of sinful words. He uses terminology that we have already encountered to confront what he considers effrontery to God. He makes six accusations in three parallel pairs (15:4 – 6).

Eliphaz first says that Job "undermines piety" (*prr* + *yir'ah*). As in 4:6, Eliphaz uses "piety" (= "fear"[1]) without an accompanying genitive (i.e., not "fear of God" or "fear of Shaddai"). I previously offered the translation, "Is not your [self-proclaimed] piety the basis for this irrational confidence? Is your only hope really in the [presumed] blamelessness of your ways?" The verb *prr* is also used in Eliphaz's first speech (5:12), where he says that God "thwarts" the plans of the crafty. The translation "undermine" is probably not strong enough — the sense of the word is more accurately conveyed by "nullify." This verb occurs only one other place in this book, when Yahweh accuses Job of "nullifying" his justice (40:8). In 15:4, then, Eliphaz does not accuse Job of nullifying piety itself, but of negating his own claims to piety by contradicting himself.

The second phrase indicates that Job has "hindered devotion to God" (*gr'* + *śiḥah*). The verb *gr'* generally concerns reduction and is used again in the second part of 15:8. The noun *śiḥah* is more obscure, occurring only here and twice in Psalms (Ps. 119:97, 99). Another noun form (*śiḥ*) from the same root occurs fourteen times and the verbal derivative (*śiḥ*) semantically associated with *śiḥah* occurs another twenty times; thus, the amount of synchronic data allows us to determine meaning. The root generally refers to deep thought and is sometimes related to anguish and complaint, but it is often more neutral or even positive as a reference to meditation. However, because Job has already used the related verb and noun forms referred to above several times to define his formal complaint against God (7:11, 13; 9:27; 10:1), it seems likely that Eliphaz is saying that Job's words have not only nullified his claims to piety, but they have effectively reduced the persuasiveness of the

---

1. "Piety" can be reflected merely in conscientious performance of ritual requirements, but can also include righteous behavior, depending on whose perception is involved.

claim[2] that he would make against deity. In this phrase, "undermine" works better than in the first phrase. Eliphaz claims that Job's response has weakened his case considerably and undermined the respect of his peers.

The second pair of accusations (15:5) concern Job's motives and methods. Eliphaz first claims that "your sin prompts your mouth" ('awon + 'lp, Piel). The noun 'awon can refer to either sin or guilt—in Job, usually the former. The verb 'lp occurs only four times, three in Job.[3] Though there are not enough occurrences to confidently determine subtle nuances, they can arguably be understood to refer to a process of learning that occurs through ongoing observation. If this is the meaning Eliphaz has in mind, he is suggesting that Job has rationalized his sins so much so that he is not aware of them. That is, the sinful deeds he has committed have taught his mouth how to rationalize so that the sins are not recognized for what they are.

The second line in 15:5 follows up on this course of thinking by suggesting that Job has adopted "crafty" ('arumim) language to accomplish his rationalization. Though Eliphaz has used the adjective before (5:12) in a negative sense, the term is often used positively in Proverbs. Perhaps 'arumim is most widely known for its description of the serpent in Genesis 3:1. It expresses an awareness of the subtleties and complexities in carefully crafted words. When we combine this understanding with the first line's probable allusion to rationalization, we can conclude that Eliphaz is accusing Job of what we today call "spin."

In the third parallel set (15:6) Eliphaz expresses his assessment of Job's current position—he stands condemned by his own words. Eliphaz uses legal language to identify Job's mouth as both the source of his verdict (not the indictment that started the trial, but the pronouncement that ends it) and the witness that has provided testimony to arrive at that verdict. This is close to what Job has said that God would do to him in court—to make his own mouth pronounce the verdict (9:20, using the same verb).

Eliphaz then attacks what he assesses as Job's arrogance. He clearly identifies "the first man ever born" as a person of great wisdom (15:7), but this identification does not come out of the biblical tradition (though eventually interpreters characterized Adam and Eve as very wise, and some found it as early as Ezek. 28:12).[4] Eliphaz's portrayal has more in common with the

---

2. Magdalene makes a persuasive case that the word carries legal force as a "petition" (*Scales of Righteousness*, 206).

3. Piel here and twice in Elihu's speeches, 33:33; 35:11. The Qal occurs only once, Prov. 22:25.

4. Note that in Gen. 2–3 they are lacking what the Tree of the Knowledge of Good and Evil (= wisdom) provide.

Mesopotamian tradition of Adapa, the first of the seven *apkallu* sent by the gods to teach humans the arts of civilization. These beings were considered sages of great wisdom, servants of the kings who ruled before the flood.[5]

As readers, we detect the irony of Eliphaz's rhetorical question concerning Job's involvement in God's heavenly council (15:8), since it was the meeting of the council that precipitated Job's situation. Had Job been privy to the discussions in the divine council, he would have understood his predicament more fully.

One wonders what Eliphaz has in mind when he speaks of God's "consolations" (*tanḥumot*) in 15:11. The noun occurs only one other time (21:2), but context indicates that it retains its close association to the root (*nḥm*).[6] What words of comfort or consolation has God offered Job? Since God has not spoken, commentators generally conclude that Eliphaz considers his own words to be the consolations of God, presumptuous as that may sound. More specifically Eliphaz may refer to the revelation that he divulged in 4:12–21. This speech would be considered a consoling word because it suggested that Job was not alone—all humanity shares his deficiency of righteousness (4:17).

Just before Eliphaz explicates the fate of the wicked, he returns to a theme addressed in previous speeches. His opening line in 15:14 alludes to Job's question in 7:17 ("What is man ...?"). These two Job passages share many similarities with Psalm 8:4[5]:

> Job 7:17—*mah-ʾenoš ki tegaddelennu*: "What is man that you elevate him?"
> Job 15:14—*mah-ʾenoš ki yizkeh*: "What is man that he could be unflawed?"
> Psalm 8:4[5]—*mah-ʾenoš ki tizkerennu*: "What is man that you take note of him?"

All of these point out, but refrain from evaluating, the distance between God and mortal humanity. This statement in 15:14 returns to the key point in Eliphaz's first speech (4:17). Here, as in 4:18, he follows his initial statement with an assertion concerning God's lack of trust in his holy ones (15:15). Eliphaz uses the same verb in both 15:15 and 4:18 to indicate that God routinely scrutinizes his heavenly servants. In this sense the verb may well follow the Akkadian cognate that refers to freedom from claim or obligation.[7] Even God's heavenly servants are accountable.

---

5. For more information, see J. C. Greenfield, "Apkallu," *DDD*[2], 72–74; F. A. M. Wiggermann, "Theologies, Priests, and Worship in Ancient Mesopotamia," *CANE*, 1865.

6. Job uses the same root when he refers to his friends as comforters (see 16:2).

7. *CAD* Z, 25–32, specifically in legal contexts, see 26–27.

His second line in 15:15, however, departs from the pattern of chapter 4 as he indicates that "even the heavens are not pure," using a similar verb (*zkk*) as in the first phrase of 15:14 (*zkh*). The verb in 15:15 typically refers to objects, whereas that of 15:14 refers to people. In Job 25:5 Bildad refers to the stars not being unobstructed (*zkk*), parallel to the moon not shining brightly. The Akkadian cognate verb (*zakû*) is also used to describe the heavens and the moon.[8] The point does not concern ritual purity, nor does it personify the heavens or the stars; rather, Eliphaz is suggesting that even those things that seem to be unblemished from our perspective are not so to God. This leads him to the "how much less" conclusion of 15:16, where he notes the intrinsic corruption of humanity.

We cannot pause to consider each detail of 15:17 – 35, but a few matters stand out. The speech primarily focuses on the destiny of the wicked man rather than on his acts (15:20). In 15:25, however, Eliphaz states specifically that his subject is the man who "shakes his fist at God and vaunts himself against the Almighty." This statement unequivocally places Job in the category of the wicked, but it does not require Eliphaz to prove specific acts of injustice or violence. Finally we also should note that Eliphaz sees prosperity and other benefits as the ultimate payoff and greatest potential loss. He still does not seem to comprehend that Job is not concerned with these things.

Job (Job 16 – 17)

FOLLOWING HIS USUAL TENDENCY, Job turns his attention increasingly toward/about God as the dialogue progresses. He continues to delineate new charges against God. Though he voices accusations in 16:11 – 14, his main charge is summarized in 16:9. Three verbs portray God as a savage, predatory beast: "assails" (*trp*, tearing up prey), "tears" (*śṭm*, acting hostile), and "gnashes his teeth" (*ḥrq*, expressing the aggression of enemies). Again Job accuses God of making him a target, but here he uses different terminology; in 7:20 Job used *mipgaʿ* while here in 16:12 he uses *maṭṭarah*. The former only occurs once, but judging from the etymology (an unreliable guide, but that's all we have in this case) it is more like a punching bag (or we might say, a tackling dummy) while the latter is a target for archers (cf. 1 Sam. 20:20; Lam. 3:12).

---

8. *CAD* Z, 23 – 24. The term *zakû* is used in eclipse omens to describe that part of the moon that is not eclipsed; see H. Hunger, *Astrological Reports to Assyrian Kings* (SAA 8; Helsinki: Helsinki Univ. Press, 1992), text 300, reverse line 6 and text 4 line 2. The term is used of the heavens when they are being described as made of jasper that is crystal clear, as opposed to jasper that is translucent (an overcast sky), see Horowitz, *Mesopotamian Cosmic Geography*, 14.

Having noted the pitiless attacks of God and his own mourning and innocence, Job turns again to his long-desired court case. As in 9:33 he anticipates some help in his litigation. There we noted that Job used a legal term (*mokiah*) in referring to one who argues a case or negotiates on another's behalf. In 16:18–21 we see a variety of terms:

- cry (*za'aqah*)[9]
- witness (*'ed*)
- advocate (*śahed*)
- intercessor (*meliṣ*)
- one who pleads (*yokah*, from the same root as *mokiah* used in 9:33)[10]

Clines appeals to the first term here in the list and uses it as the determinative factor in identification of the focus of Job's hope.[11] Since the "cry" is nonpersonal, he sees the other terms as personifications of Job's cry that hovers in the air, awaiting an answer. Other interpreters have commonly seen God himself as the mediator.[12] As Clines points out, however, it would be strange to posit God as the mediator between Job and himself. This would set up precisely the kind of kangaroo court that Job has feared.

The other alternative is that Job is expecting a third party to step up and represent him, testify on his behalf, and advocate for his innocence. Theoretically such a third party could be a human being or someone from the divine council. Ironically, Job's predicament actually began when God advocated for him before the divine council; in fact, one who could potentially call God to account (the Challenger) precipitated Job's calamities.[13] Though all of this is unknown to Job, it shows that the last thing Job really needs is someone else calling God to account.

Thus far we have been led to believe that Job has no relative at hand to serve as his advocate,[14] and that even if such a person were available, they could not hope for access to the heavenly court. This leaves us the option that Job desires an advocate from the divine council.[15] While interpreters have accurately pointed out that Eliphaz previously suggested that Job should not count on such an option (5:1), we need not take this too seriously.

---

9. Note how in Gen. 4:10 the blood of Abel cries out for vengeance and justice.

10. For full discussion of the options, see J. B. Curtis, "On Job's Witness in Heaven," *JBL* 102 (1983): 549–62; F. R. Magdalene, "Who Is Job's Redeemer? Job 19:25 in Light of Neo-Babylonian Law," *Zeitschrift für altorientalische und biblische Rechtsgeschichte* 10 (2004): 292–316.

11. Clines, *Job 1–20*, 389–90, 459; accepted tentatively by Wilson.

12. Hartley, Dhorme, Gordis, Rowley, Andersen, Driver.

13. Day, *Adversary*, 89–90.

14. Note Job 19:13–14.

15. An option supported by Pope, Smick and Habel; cf. Fyall, *Now My Eyes Have Seen You*, 40; Magdalene, *Scales of Righteousness*, 221–22, suggests that the specified role is "second accuser"—someone to stand alongside Job and second his accusation.

Job does not hesitate to dismiss other points made by Eliphaz; for example, Job still pursues the idea of a hearing, though Eliphaz told him before to drop the idea altogether. Furthermore, Elihu later identifies just such a role, using one of the terms that appears in 16:20 (*meliṣ*, 33:23 in reference to an angel).

We must examine the terms to arrive at the best explanation. The use of witness (*'ed*) and arbitrator (*yocah/mokiah*) have already positioned this individual in legal terms. "Advocate" (*śahed*) occurs only here in Hebrew, but several of the cognate Semitic languages (particularly Aramaic) attest to the meaning "witness."[16] The last term (*meliṣ*) occurs only four other times. The passages show different roles, but each refers to someone who speaks on behalf of another, a middleman or go-between ("interpreter," Gen. 42:23; "envoys," 2 Chron. 32:31; "spokesmen," most likely prophets and priests, Isa. 43:27). If we combine information from the context of Job, the Old Testament, and court documents from the ancient Near Eastern cultural background, we can infer that Job hopes for a member of the divine council to call God to account on his behalf.

In chapter 17 Job returns to the topic of death. Again it is clear that he sees no vindication after the grave; he cannot return from the grave (16:22) and death offers no relief (17:1, 13). In 17:15 — 16 he again makes it clear that he has no hope in the afterlife. As we discussed in detail earlier (p. 125 – 34), the Old Testament indicates that the Israelites as a whole (until Dan. 12) and Job in particular had no revelation of reward or judgment in the afterlife and viewed the netherworld as a place where all relationships (human and divine) were ruptured. The NIV interprets the Hebrew as a reference to the "gates of death" (= Sheol). Such an understanding is reminiscent of Mesopotamian literature, particularly the famous myth This Descent of Ishtar; this work recounts the journey of the goddess, who must pass seven gates before she can enter the netherworld. Nevertheless, the Hebrew word never means gates; rather, it refers to poles or shoots. The NIV has apparently chosen to interpret the poles of Sheol as "bars" and then associate those bars with gates that can be locked shut.[17]

---

16. It occurs in the Sefire Inscriptions, Ahiqar, and the DSS as well as in Laban's Aramaic name for the pile of stones that stood as witness between him and Jacob (Jegar Sahadutha, Gen. 31:47).

17. Though the bars of a gate are everywhere else expressed by the Hebrew word *beriah*, see Job 38:10. If the situation can only be resolved by speculation, one might wonder whether the Hebrew consonants *bdy(m)* in the text might be a transcription error for *bby(m)* since in the earliest Hebrew scripts *b* and *d* look quite similar. Then the noun *bab* could be read as the Akkadian word, *babu*, "gate" well-known as part of the name for Babylon (*bab-ili*, "gate of the gods"). It should be noted, however, that no remnant of the Akkadian word *babu* is evident in Hebrew lexicography. Combining a transcription error and an otherwise unknown borrowed term would be a radical solution, but in some ways no more radical than the alternatives proposed by others.

Chapter 17 also affirms Job's tenaciously held and accurate view of righteousness. In light of all of the abuse that he has suffered at the hands of friends and strangers, his declaration is 17:9 makes his position clear: "Nevertheless, the righteous will hold to their ways, and those with clean hands will grow stronger." Not one whisper comes from Job about the righteous getting all their prosperity back. Truly righteous people are concerned about their integrity, not the rewards they receive.

Bildad (Job 18)

WHEN BILDAD SPEAKS OF the earth's abandonment and the rocks' removal, he is speaking metaphorically to convey how radically Job is challenging traditional wisdom. Bildad, the traditionalist in the group, reasserts traditional wisdom concerning the plight of the wicked. In so doing he illustrates what the friends have done all along in their interpretation of the RP. It is one thing to say that the wicked will suffer, but it is quite another to conclude that anyone who is suffering must be wicked; this, however, is the inference drawn by the friends. For one to conclude that only the wicked suffer, it is necessary to believe that wickedness always results in suffering and that only wickedness can bring about suffering. Those are monumental assumptions not essentially part of the RP, yet they were regularly included as corollaries.

Bildad's litany concerning the doom of the wicked contains a particularly obscure statement: "Death's firstborn devours his limbs" (18:13b). The description speaks not of a slowly progressing disease, but of the total destruction of the body in the grave. The more intriguing question concerns the identity of the "firstborn of death." The Hebrew word *mawet* is personified and said to have a firstborn. Mot, the god of death, plays a prominent role in Ugaritic literature. Unfortunately, the extant literature ascribes no offspring to Mot. J. B. Burns considers the merits of identifying Resheph (the plague god in Ugaritic text) as Mot's firstborn, but he finally prefers a Mesopotamian connection. He summarizes this option as follows:

> Namtar is the god of plague and pestilence. He is described as *sukallu irṣiti*, the "vizier of the underworld." He is also the *ilitti* ᵈ*ereškigal*, the "offspring of Ereshkigal," who was the queen of the underworld. In Mesopotamian mythology the first-born, if male, was generally the vizier of his parent.... As Namtar was both the offspring of Ereshkigal and the vizier of the underworld, he was, most probably, her first-born. The First-born of Death is the god of plague and pestilence.[18]

---

18. J. B. Burns, "The Identity of Death's First-Born (Job XVIII 13)," *VT* 37 (1987): 362–64.

Clines considers all the evidence in detail and prefers to interpret Death's offspring as a vague reference to a demon rather than to any particular mythological tradition.[19] He considers the subject nouns in 18:12 (NIV: "calamity" and "disaster") also to be demons,[20] but we must tread carefully here since the Old Testament offers so little of belief in or reference to demons.[21] Abstractions can be personified literarily without being demonized.

Bildad ends on a stinging insinuation. He has described the plight of the wicked using a number of statements that coincide with Job's experiences, and in 18:21 he concludes that such things happen to those who do not know God. Has it come to this? Not only is Job considered guilty of wicked deeds, but now Bildad tacitly suggests that he has no knowledge of God. It matters little whether Bildad means that Job lacks a relationship with God or accurate information about God (or both) — this is a devastating judgment.

Job (Job 19)

IT IS NO SURPRISE that Job feels crushed by the words of Bildad. His sense of abandonment leads him to reiterate that his friends have deserted him and to claim blatantly that God has wronged him (*'iwwetani*, 19:6). The root *'wt* occurs eleven times in the Old Testament and has already been used incredulously by Bildad in Job 8:3.[22] There it was translated "pervert" since the nature of the verb concerns bending, twisting, or distorting. Here, however, rather than having an abstraction as the direct object of the verb (*mišpaṭ* and *ṣedeq* in 8:3), Job himself is the object (for other occurrences where people are the object of the verb see Ps. 119:78; Lam 3:36). The verb does not pertain to moral wrongdoing, but just making a mess of things. God has made Job's life wreckage (note 19:21: "The hand of God has struck me"). This begins a series of accusations specifying how God has brought disaster, which parallels Bildad's litany of the plight of the wicked. Job, however, still refuses to admit that this treatment might be God's response to his behavior.

---

19. Clines, *Job 1–10*, 418. See also the detailed discussion of T. Lewis, "First Born of Death," *DDD²*, 332–35.

20. Clines, *Job 1–10*, 418.

21. J. Walton, "Demons in Mesopotamia and Israel: Exploring the Category of Non-Divine but Supernatural Entities," in *The Biblical World and Its Impact: Essays on Precept and Praxis in Honor of Samuel Greengus* (ed. B. Arnold et al.; Winona Lake, Ind.: Eisenbrauns, forthcoming).

22. See p. 165.

This leads us into one of the most familiar yet controversial sections of the book. In 19:25 we find the much beloved declaration, "I know that my Redeemer lives" (NIV, "redeemer" = Heb. *go'el*), immortalized in Handel's *Messiah*. Even more than 13:15, this verse stands in many people's minds as representing the posture and hope of Job. A christological interpretation is clearly indicated by those translations that capitalize "Redeemer" despite the fact that the New Testament never integrates this verse into its own Christology or suggests this was a prophecy fulfilled in Christ.

Unfortunately, in the analysis that follows, we will see little that is certain in 19:23–27. As we sort through the problems in translation, we must also seriously consider how these verses fit with what Job and his friends are saying throughout the rest of the book. These verses ought not be interpreted as an inexplicable departure from the context.

The issues with the Hebrew text are myriad and complex; we will address the problems as they arise in the following close lexical, syntactical, and grammatical analysis.

Job 19:23–24. Because Job does not expect to be around much longer to present his case personally, he wishes for a permanent record of his sufferings and claims for posterity. The Behistun Inscription is one example of an engraving filled with lead, but lead tablets are also known.

Job 19:25. The word *go'el* fits into the same semantic category as the variety of words discussed in 16:19–20 (advocate, witness, etc.; see p. 214). A *go'el* is also one who enters a legal situation on behalf of another. Scenarios include gaining release from debt slavery (Lev. 25:25), avenging a murder (Num. 35:19; Deut. 19:6–12), marrying a brother's widow (Ruth), and purchasing land (Jer. 32:7–8). It is not unusual to see God identified as the *go'el* of his people (Pss. 19:14; 78:35; Isa. 44:6; 49:7, 26, etc.). The job of the *go'el* is to recover losses and to salvage the dignity of one who has suffered loss. It is not surprising, then, to hear Job speak of a *go'el* who might act on his behalf. We will return to the question of who might serve as this *go'el* after the other language issues are addressed.

Job is persuaded that his *go'el* is alive (i.e., help is on the way), and that this one will arise to take a stand. The verb *qwm* can be used in a legal sense of someone being called to testify (e.g., Job 16:8; Ps. 27:12; Zeph. 3:8) or to render judgment (Ps. 76:9[10]). The former is more likely here because that is what the *go'el* is supposed to do. The questions here are when and where. The timing is addressed in the word *'aharon* (NIV: "in the end").[23]

---

23. The word has been interpreted personally as an epithet for God (cf. Isa. 48:12), eschatologically (at the last day), temporally (afterwards or last in the dispute), or logically (at last).

Job is anticipating the end of his ordeal, and this word introduces what Job thinks will happen in the climactic final scenes. The place is stipulated as *'al-'apar* (NIV: "upon the earth").

The general interpretation offered by the NIV is not likely, given the specific word that was chosen (support could be given based on Job 41:33[25], but the syntactical context is quite different). The word *'apar* designates the substance from which humans were made and to which they will return (Gen. 3:19); in Job, it has aptly been used to reference the place of death (e.g., 7:21; 10:9; 16:15; 17:16; 20:11; 21:26; 34:15). In a synchronic study, we should first match all the essential elements as closely as possible. In this case we can look for all occurrences that feature the following similarities to Job 19:25: human subject + verb + preposition *'al* + *'apar* with no further construct element. Five of the six matching constructions occur in Job (Job 17:16; 20:11; 21:26; 34:15; 42:6; also Isa. 47:1), referring to the place where one dies or mourns. This evidence suggests that Job expects his *go'el* to arrive and testify at the place where he is mourning and where he has expected to lie down and turn to dust—his dung heap (2:8),[24] his expected grave.[25]

Job 19:26. Three major theories have been posited concerning Job's understanding of *when* the *go'el* will appear in relation to his death.[26]

- *Resurrection.* Job believes that God will raise him from the grave to witness his vindication. This view is supported strongly in church history (e.g., Clement, Origen, Jerome, Luther), but is problematic because it seems to contradict Job's earlier affirmations that the grave is permanent. Furthermore, resurrection is not a tenet of Job's belief before or after this chapter, nor is it part of Israelite doctrine throughout most of the Old Testament.
- *Posthumous vindication.* Job expects to witness his vindication as a bodiless spirit from the grave. This view finds support in Jewish interpreters as early as *Jubilees* 23:30–31. Unfortunately it also contradicts Job's earlier affirmations (e.g., 14:12) and proves to be a less-than-definitive vindication.
- *Last-minute reprieve.* Job expects God to intervene and vindicate him before he dies (e.g., Hartley, Habel). Clines favors a variation of this by differentiating Job's expectation (death) from his hope (reprieve). This reprieve solution finds a parallel in the last minute healing in the Babylonian *Ludlul bel nemeqi* (2.114–15). The

---

24. Job's dung heap is the word *'eper* (NIV, "ashes"), similar to the word for dust (*'apar*) and the two are used together in Job 42:6.

25. Day, *Adversary*, 99.

26. Developed in Hartley, *Job*, 295–96.

author reports that the grave was already opened and the funerary goods prepared—in other words, the formal mourning had already taken place, even though he had not yet died. It was at that point that the deity intervened and brought healing.

Verse 26 starts with a temporal adverb, "after," and sets the time of the action subsequent to Job's skin being "destroyed" (NIV; Piel of *nqp*). The verb occurs only in one other context (Isa. 10:34), where it refers to cutting down thickets. A derivative noun form occurs in Isaiah 17:6 and 24:13 to refer to olives harvested from an olive tree.[27] Major lexicons and commentaries can only speculate about the meaning,[28] but all approach the same conclusion. Does Job expect still to be alive at this point? I view this as intentional hyperbole that plays on the words with the next clause, expressed by this expanded paraphrase: "Even after I have to flay off all my skin this way (i.e., with his scraping potsherd), yet in my flesh I will see God." Skin may be all but gone, but he still retains his fleshly frame. This paraphrase takes the last controversial word in 19:26 (*mibbeśari*) as introduced with the usual meaning of the Hebrew preposition *min*, "from" (note same form and meaning in 19:22).

It is fitting to the context and to Job's other statements in the book that he expects to see vindication before he dies. So far in this interpretation, the *go'el* is currently alive (not one yet to come) and is expected to arrive at the climactic moment to the place of Job's mourning. Though he loses more skin by the hour, Job expects to live to see God. In this context, to "see God" would be to receive an audience with him, presumably to regain his favor and restore the relationship. This verb (*ḥzh*) usually takes a vision as the direct object, but in five other contexts it occurs with deity in this position (Ex. 24:11; Pss. 11:7; 17:15; 27:4; 63:2). In each of these latter instances, the verb refers to the favored status of one enjoying relationship with God. Job is not expecting this to happen in heaven—we have seen throughout the book that he has no hopes for the afterlife. If Job believed in resurrection, or even in judgment and reward in the afterlife, certainly one must wonder why those issues do not figure more prominently in his understanding of God's justice and practices. In fact, statements such as those found in 14:12 suggest that he had no such hope.[29]

---

27. In the Mishnah (*Giṭṭin* 5:8) the verb is understood to refer to knocking off olives (as opposed to picking them off).

28. E.g., *HALOT*, 722: "flay"; *DCH*, 753−54: "strip off".

29. For an excellent treatment of understanding Job 19 within the context of the entire argument of the book of Job, see Sutcliffe, *Old Testament and the Future Life*, 131−37; see also Martin-Achard, *From Death to Life*, 179.

Job 19:27. Job's statement in 19:27, "I myself will see him with my own eyes" (NIV), further substantiates the idea that Job will enjoy restored favor with God in his own flesh. The phrase in the middle of the verse (*lo'-zar*, NIV: "not another"), however, is problematic. The word *zar* usually refers to an outsider—someone foreign, unauthorized, a stranger. Does Job mean that he will see the God he has long been familiar with rather than the God of his recent experience, who seems to be a stranger? This understanding is unlikely, for God would not be appropriately classified as an outsider. Does Job mean that he himself will see God, rather than a stranger standing in for him? This is also improbable, because a person standing in for him would be authorized to do so. Does Job mean that he will not be a stranger to God or perhaps that God will no longer treat him as a stranger? I consider this last idea the most likely, as it parallels nicely the idea of being received back favorably into God's presence; no longer an outsider, Job is welcomed back into fellowship.

Finally, the last clause of this difficult sequence (NIV: "How my heart yearns within me!") refers to Job's deepest yearnings. The word that the NIV translates "heart" is actually "kidneys" (*kilyot*, for anatomical use, see Ex. 29:13), which he locates in his bosom (*heq*, NIV: "within me"). In the ancient world many of the internal organs were considered to be involved in cognitive intellectual and emotional processes. The ancients were unaware of the physiology and role of the brain. Translators, understanding the cognitive connotation of the word, often translate it "mind" (cf. NIV in Ps. 7:9; Jer. 11:20; 17:10; 20:12), and other times as "inmost being" (Ps. 139:13; Prov. 23:16). The verb (*klh*) in the Qal stem refers to something coming to an end, fading away, failing, or perishing. Job would not be talking about kidney failure here, but the failure of his mind and spirit. He is mentally exhausted, emotionally drained. Despite the strong convictions he expresses in the first part of the verse, Job knows that he cannot hang on much longer.

In summary of this technical analysis, I would offer the following expanded paraphrase:

> "I firmly believe that there is someone,[30] somewhere, who will come and testify on my behalf right here on my dung heap at the end of all this. Despite my peeling skin, I expect to have enough left to come before God in my own flesh. I will be restored to his favor and no longer be treated as a stranger. This is my deepest desire!" (prosperity has nothing to do with it).

---

30. Perhaps from the divine council, but unspecified.

Zophar (Job 20)

FINALLY THE THEOLOGIAN SPEAKS—but his words can only echo what the mystic and the traditionalist have already asserted: It is the wicked who suffer. Eliphaz made his case based on his observation and experience (15:17). Bildad, as the traditionalist, couched his observations in aphorisms; now Zophar grounds his argument in God's actions against the wicked: He takes away their riches (20:15), rains down blows on them (20:23), and carries away all that they have (20:28–29). The reader knows that even though Job has experienced these things, they do not result from the wrath of God, as Zophar suggests (20:28). Zophar indirectly accuses Job of pride (20:6) and of concealing evil (20:12). As always, the friends observe Job's circumstances but draw illegitimate conclusions about God's motives and Job's conduct.

Job (Job 21)

IN RESPONSE TO THESE three speeches about the plight and destiny of the wicked, Job offers his own observations about the wicked—diametrically opposed to the neat and tidy perspective of the friends. Job confronts them with evidence that contradicts the traditions they have been spouting: The wicked often prosper (21:7–33).[31] This is information that they all know but prefer to ignore. Job is preparing his case that the system is broken, for whether people have a secure and prosperous life or a miserable life of destitution, they all die (21:26). This sentiment picks up a theme well-known from Ecclesiastes. We will explore this in greater detail under Bridging Contexts.

Bridging Contexts

Rhetorical Issues

THE SECOND SET OF speeches is dominated by discussions of the fate of the wicked. The antagonism of Job's friends and his hostile responses escalate, and the idea of comfort (2:11) slips away. They have reached an impasse, but the dialogue continues, drawing out the inevitable conclusions to the reasoning that the speeches employ. Even as Job's antagonism toward his friends grows, so too does his antagonism toward God. He turns more and more of his attention toward God as he stridently demands his day in court.

---

31. For some detailed analysis of the Hebrew text of 21:22 see the Original Meaning section connected to Job 22, pp. 244–45.

The second cycle takes the following pattern:

Eliphaz: ch. 15	Job: chs. 16 – 17
Bildad: ch. 18	Job: ch. 19
Zophar: ch. 20	Job: ch. 21

Below I summarize each speech and then focus on a couple of important issues.

> *Eliphaz:* Your bluster is a disgrace; you are merely digging a deeper hole for yourself. What makes you think you are so much better than everyone else? Stop railing against your circumstances and accept that what has come upon you is the result of the corruption shared by all humanity. Since wicked people are ferreted out, you ought to consider how much you have in common with them.
>
> *Job:* Talk is easy, Eliphaz, but I would be more encouraging if I were you. Meanwhile, God, why are you attacking me? You have abandoned me to be tormented by enemies and then you pitilessly join in yourself. If you can't respond to my misery, I need someone to stand up for me. As for me, I am determined to stay the course of righteousness, though death is all I have to look forward to.

By elaborating on what God does to the wicked, Eliphaz insinuates that Job is to be counted in their number. This differs from his first speech, in which he counseled Job to have confidence in his piety (4:6). Now he accuses Job of undermining piety (15:4) and no longer allows that Job should continue his posture of righteousness. Furthermore, in the first set of speeches the friends counseled Job to appeal to God (Eliphaz, 5:8; Bildad, 8:5), but when Job does so (beginning in 9:14), Zophar responds with disdain, dismissing the claim's legitimacy (11:5). In the second set of speeches, Job becomes increasingly fixated on pressing the legal case, while the friends neither encourage nor discourage that course of action. As Job more persistently pursues a legal resolution, his accusations against God also become more strident.

> *Eliphaz:* Recognize your guilt by comparing how God treats the wicked to how he is treating you. You have nullified your own piety.
>
> *Job:* I need protection from God's attacks and call for an advocate to take up my case.

> *Bildad:* God's judgment of the wicked is severe, and those who are
> subject to it (including you, Job) can be classified as those
> who do not know God.
>
> *Job:* Despite your accusations, I have done nothing; yet God, in
> his inexplicable anger, has made a mess of my life. I am an
> outcast, despised by all. I am confident that someone will
> come to help and that just when all seems finally lost, I will
> be vindicated. You supposed friends are in more jeopardy
> than I am.

Bildad's speech is easier to relate to Job's response to him in the first cycle
(chs. 9 – 10) than to Job's reply to Eliphaz (chs. 16 – 17). Job had referred to
cosmic effects of judgment (9:5 – 9), and Bildad here speaks of shaking the
earth and moving rocks (18:4). Furthermore, his tacit classification of Job
as one who does not know God (18:21) would be a logical response to Job's
many statements about the nature of God in his reply to Bildad in chapters
9 – 10 (esp. 10:13; these elements are largely absent in 16 – 17).

Job's reply shows that his bereavement is fueled by more than the loss
of family, possessions, and health; he has lost his self-respect and standing
in society. This set of speeches furthers the argument of the book as Job
increases his rhetoric against God and continues to assert unflaggingly that
he will be vindicated.

> *Bildad:* Give up the pretense; the wicked are doomed. You are among
> those who do not know God.
>
> *Job:* It is God who has messed up my life, not me; a defender will
> arise and vindicate me from your insinuations.

> *Zophar:* You offend me. You know how the rules work. Your self-
> righteousness betrays you, for all know that such pride char-
> acterizes the wicked.
>
> *Job:* I realize that I am risking a lot by pressing legal action against
> God. Do you realize how many wicked people prosper
> despite their arrogance against God? He does nothing about
> it! In such a world it is a complex and terrifying thing to try to
> call God to account. If God does not consistently punish the
> wicked, couldn't we conclude that he does not consistently
> protect and prosper the righteous?

Zophar refers to a rebuke that dishonors him (20:3), which again takes
us back to Job's answer to Zophar in chapters 12 – 14 (note particularly

12:2 – 3). This speech, like the others in the second cycle, primarily elaborates on the fate of the wicked.

Zophar: Your sin is pride, and God has judged you as wicked.
Job: The system (= God's policies) is broken.

The second cycle as a whole has focused on the premise of the RP that God judges the wicked. The associated inferences insinuate that those who are apparently under judgment must indeed be wicked. Job's last speech gets as close as ever to rejecting the RP, though he does not find resolution of the triangle of tension in this direction. The friends have lost their confidence in Job, and Job's view of God continues to deteriorate though he unwaveringly insists on his own righteousness. He rejects the confession and appeasement resolution proposed by the friends as his desire for a legal resolution escalates. Job continues to insist on vindication rather than restoration, while his friends consider vindication an unrealistic and vain expectation. In their view, Job needs to identify with the wicked since his experiences indisputably place him into that category.

In cycle 2, the differences between Job and his friends become intractable. Job likewise moves further from God as the deity increasingly becomes the object of Job's suspicions; God's unresponsiveness to Job's pleas suggests his continued distance from Job.

As we track the philosophical focus and resolution of each series, we see that the reasoning of this second sequence centers on the RP. Each of the friends spends a major proportion of his speech affirming that the wicked demonstrably and inevitably suffer the judgment of God. The first series broached this topic, but turned it to a consideration of what Job could do to regain his benefits and favored status. In this second series it is the very validity of the RP that is under discussion. After Job's friends have each elaborated on it at length, Job denies that the suffering of the wicked is either demonstrable or inevitable. The friends have argued for the integrity of a system; Job, convinced of his own integrity, rejects the system as spurious. This stands as the philosophical resolution to the second series and leads into the third, where accusation will replace insinuation.

Theological Issues

CHRIST AS OUR MEDIATOR. The New Testament unequivocally affirms that Christ is our mediator (1 Tim. 2:5; Heb. 8:6; 9:15; 12:24), but we are not free to read even a true doctrine into any text we wish. We desire for our interpretation to reflect the authoritative teaching of the text, and the text cannot mean to us what it never meant to the author or audience.

Job was not looking for a priestly mediator to ritually resolve his sin. This is the role that Jesus fills: He offered his blood for our sin. Job was looking for a legal advocate to take up and argue his case before God. We have nothing to argue before God; we stand guilty and condemned to death. Job was not arguing his sinlessness, but the injustice of his treatment. We cannot argue that God is unjust because we now know all have sinned and death is the penalty of sin. Jesus is our Mediator because he has taken our sin upon himself. Job was not looking for someone to do that for him because he did not see sin as the problem. His redeemer was supposed to defend his legal rights; ours pays the debt that is due.

It would be a total contradiction to think that Job suddenly believed that he had a debt to pay and sins to be cared for. Jesus does not mediate for us by arguing for our innocence; he contends before the Father that we have been justified by his blood. Yes, Christ is our Mediator, but to impose that imagery on the thoughts or words of Job is to misrepresent the case Job is making as well as the doctrine of authority that we hold dear.

Resurrection.[32] Some interpreters of Job 19:25–26 believe that Job is expressing a confidence in resurrection.[33] We have already noted in the Original Meaning section that there is reason to doubt such an interpretation; it contradicts many other statements Job makes throughout the book. At this stage in the discussion, however, we should explore the extent of the Israelite belief in resurrection in case that may come into play in the development of the book.

To begin, we must phrase the question more carefully. Resurrection may be viewed in three different categories. (1) There is resurrection that represents an individual's return to physical life. Several Old Testament passages refer to such an occasional occurrence (1 Kings 17:22; 2 Kings 4:35; 13:21). (2) We could speak of a corporate resurrection: a people being brought back into existence from apparent extinction. This is represented in Ezekiel's vision of the valley of the dry bones, where Israel as a nation

---

32. For treatments of the concept of resurrection in the Old Testament, see L. J. Greenspoon, "The Origin of the Idea of Resurrection," in *Traditions in Transformation* (ed. B. Halpern and J. Levenson; Winona Lake, Ind.: Eisenbrauns, 1981), 247–321; Johnston, *Shades of Sheol*, 218–39; Spronk, *Beatific Afterlife in Ancient Israel*; Sutcliffe, *Old Testament and the Future Life*.

33. Evident as early as Jerome's expansive translation in the Vulgate ("On the last day I shall arise from the earth"). It should be noted that the church fathers were not unanimous in their support of this interpretation. In numerous works John Chrysostom denies that Job has knowledge of the resurrection (e.g., *Hom. In Matt.* 33.7, on Matt. 10:22).

is brought back to life (Ezek. 37). (3) There is the doctrine of individual resurrection of the body in the afterlife; we might call this "eschatological" resurrection. The first and second types of resurrection are demonstrably consistent with the beliefs of ancient Israel, but what about the third?

Passages such as Isaiah 26:19 and Daniel 12:1–2 are most easily connected to eschatological resurrection. Additionally, some claim that certain Hebrew terms carry a technical meaning compatible with the concept of resurrection.

> But your dead will live;
> > their bodies will rise.
> You who dwell in the dust,
> > wake up and shout for joy.
> Your dew is like the dew of the morning;
> > the earth will give birth to her dead. (Isa. 26:19)

Isaiah 26:19 is replete with textual difficulties. The second line of the text, contrary to the NIV reproduced above, reads, "my corpse will arise." Not only is the switch from "your" in line 1 to "my" a problem, but the confusion compounds with the singular noun, "corpse," and the plural verb "will arise." The antecedents to all the pronouns are questionable, and to crown the whole passage, the very end of the verse introduces the controversial *repa'im* ("the dead"; "shades"?).

Isaiah 26:19 must be understood in contrast to 26:14, a passage that uses much of the same terminology and expresses the idea that the lords who once exercised power over Israel will not rise; instead, they have been punished and brought to ruin. In other words, Isaiah 26:14 has a corporate sense that concerns restoration of a group to life in this world. In 26:15 the author begins to contrast the prosperity brought to the nation Israel. This would lead us to conclude that the passage is concerned with national resurrection (type 2 above), comparable to Ezekiel 37.[34] Though the grammar and text of 26:19 remain enigmatic, 26:14 provides an appropriate context for interpretation.

> At that time Michael, the great prince who protects your people, will arise. There will be a time of distress such as has not happened from the beginning of nations until then. But at that time your people — everyone whose name is found written in the book — will be delivered. Multitudes who sleep in the dust of the earth will awake: some to everlasting life, others to shame and everlasting contempt. Those who are wise will shine like the brightness of the heavens, and those who lead many to righteousness, like the stars for ever and ever. (Dan. 12:1–3)

---

34. J. J. Collins, *Daniel* (Hermeneia; Minneapolis: Fortress, 1993), 395.

Daniel 12:1–2 is the only passage to speak forthrightly about differing destinies for the righteous and the wicked. But we must not jump too quickly to the standard Christian doctrine of the resurrection. A few observations are in order. (1) The text says "many" (NIV: "multitudes") will awake, not "all"; so this is not a general resurrection.

(2) The text speaks of those who sleep in "the land of dust" ('*admat-ʿapar*; NIV: "dust of the earth"). This is the only occurrence of this phrase in the Old Testament, but since it refers specifically to a "land" and since Sheol is often connected with dust (e.g., Job 17:16), one could deduce that it is a reference to Sheol, the netherworld. If this is the case, both classes of individuals are to be found in Sheol.

(3) The phrase translated "everlasting life" (*hayye ʿolam*) occurs only here in the Old Testament, but similar phrases occur (in Greek) in pseudepigraphic literature such as *1 Enoch* and the *Sibylline Oracles*.[35] In these contexts it is equated to periods such as 500 years (*1 Enoch* 10:10).[36]

(4) Finally, we must observe that the text conveys nothing concerning the place of resurrection; that is, it does not speak of lasting life *in heaven* or of lasting contempt in any particular locale. In fact, it does not clarify whether the resurrection to which it refers is an afterlife condition or a restoration to life on earth. Additionally, notwithstanding the reference to the "wise" and "those who lead many to righteousness" in verse 3, it does not offer any qualifying criteria for resurrection that would coincide with Christian doctrine.

What then is this passage saying? What belief does it reflect? The author anticipates that numerous individuals will be brought back to life. He does not indicate whether they will be brought back to life in this or another world, though no Old Testament passage speaks clearly of a bodily existence in a world to come. In this resurrected life they will enjoy an extension to their life (as a reward for their faithfulness?) or will suffer ongoing humiliation (as punishment for their treachery?). G. Nickelsburg still sees this passage as most concerned about the reconstitution of the nation:

> For Daniel, judgment is the prelude to the reconstitution of the nation. Verse 1 mentions the register of the citizens of new Israel. The resurrected righteous of verse 2 are not isolated individuals; they

---

35. R. H. Charles, *Eschatology* (New York: Schocken, 1963), 212–13, n. 3.

36. The Hebrew term *ʿolam* ("everlasting") has been recognized as less abstract than the philosophical concept of eternity. Discussions include J. Barr, *Biblical Words for Time* (London: SCM, 1969), 73–74, 93, 123–24; D. Howard "The Case for Kingship in the Old Testament Narrative Books and the Psalms," *TJ* 9 (1988): 29 n. 38; A. MacRae, "ʿôlam," in *Theological Wordbook of the Old Testament* (eds. R. L. Harris, G. Archer, B. Waltke; Chicago: Moody Press, 1980), 2:672 (#1631).

are raised to participate in this new nation.... The dead apostates are raised so that their bodies can be exposed in the Valley of Hinnom.[37]

While this relatively late passage exceeds any other statements in the Old Testament, it remains basic and does not approach the fully developed doctrine of the New Testament. While interpreters struggle to define the precise shape of Israel's doctrine and often arrive at vastly different conclusions, most would agree that Israelite beliefs differed substantially from the doctrine eventually formulated in New Testament theology and church history. Consequently, this later theology should not be read into Job's statements.

What then should we think concerning the long traditions in the church's seeing Job 19:25–26 as messianic prophecies of Christ the Redeemer and as expressing hope in the resurrection? Do the existence and truth of these New Testament doctrines supersede the contextual analysis of Job's words? If any of the New Testament authors commented on Job's statements here and offered an interpretation of it, we would have a more difficult riddle to solve. But since that is not the case, we only argue against our own interpretive imagination, not against Scripture. If neither the Old nor the New Testament suggests that Job 19:25–26 ought to be interpreted as a reference to Christ or the resurrection, we have no authority for such a conclusion. Though we respect the opinion of the church fathers, they do not carry intrinsic authority; furthermore, they are of mixed opinions on this passage.

We can, of course, continue to enjoy Handel's *Messiah*, even though we might disagree with the interpretation of Job that led to it. *Our* Redeemer does live (though Job is not referring to him), and we will see him in resurrected bodies (though Job did not foresee such a possibility). When we preach or teach a certain passage, we ought to carefully avoid imposing our own agenda on that passage; rather, we should allow it to speak from its own context. Laxity on this matter only encourages the people we teach to employ the same methods, which can lead to naive or even dangerous flights of fancy. The danger is not in the doctrine but in the method, which, when applied without restraint, can result in tragic mishandling of the text.

Job's view of God. Do we see any movement or development in Job's view of God in his second set of speeches? In this analysis we move beyond statements of what God has done to Job's deductions and inferences about the nature of God. In Job 4–14 we saw that Job conceives of God as petty. Just as the friends' attacks on Job escalate in the second set, in the same way Job's statements against God grow stronger.

---

37. Nickelsburg, *Resurrection, Immortality and Eternal Life*, 23.

- God is angry (16:9; 19:11).
- God is pitiless (16:13).
- God attacks violently (16:14).
- God fails to judge the wicked (21:30–31).

Whereas the accusation of pettiness in previous speeches was based on Job's assessment of God's judging criteria, the accusations in this set are based on Job's assessment of how God acts on those criteria. Job has experienced what he can only conclude is God's anger. His previous assessment was that God's system of evaluation needed adjustment to take account of human frailty. Now he has concluded that the system is broken.

Job is wrong about God's anger—we know this from the prologue. His conclusion about the brokenness of the system shows a glimpse of insight, but he takes this in the wrong direction. Yes, the system as Job understands it is unsalvageable. But this problem with the system concerns only Job's perception, not the actual system that God has set up. Job and his friends have deduced a system based on the RP, and when it does not hold up under scrutiny, Job assumes that God is incompetent or unconscionable. God is neither; he is being held accountable to a system that he did not set up and that does not accurately represent him. It is no wonder that Job finds such a system inadequate; it has been devised by humans and is intrinsically flawed. Job's situation reminds us of what we often experience when our world falls apart: Our faulty and inadequate understanding of God suddenly comes to the forefront and is exposed, and this is what creates a spiritual crisis.

Job's focus is unchanged. He values his righteousness most of all. He still expresses no wish of regaining his benefits. Unfortunately, in his desire to vindicate his own righteousness, Job has let his theological guard down. We will have to reconcile this with Job 42:7–8, in which God asserts that Job has spoken that which was "right" about him.

Contemporary Significance

THE FORCE OF THE argument in this second series of dialogues concerns the suffering of the wicked. Job's friends insist that the wicked do suffer, and Job's concluding speech questions whether experience affirms such consistency. What should we think about this, and how does it factor into our own worldview?

Certainly both Old and New Testaments encourage us to think that God delights in good behavior and that he will judge the wicked. We reap what we sow (Gal. 6:7). Yet our own experiences and observations lead us to share in Job's skepticism. In the Introduction we treated the RP (p. 21 – 23) at length, and I will not repeat that here. I proposed that we should adopt a modified view of the RP, understood in proverbial and theological terms. In other words, the RP is useful to describe God's nature, and it therefore helps us to identify general trends in human experience, but it offers no guarantees and cannot be applied consistently or universally in this fallen world.

This interpretation suggests several important conclusions:

- We cannot draw conclusions about people's behavior from their circumstances.
- We should not expect wicked people to get their just punishment in this life.
- We should never rejoice in the misfortune of an enemy, though we may take consolation that justice is sometimes served in this world.

On the last point we would distinguish between judicial actions and personal circumstances. In the former case, justice is vindicated when a corrupt politician is caught, indicted, tried, and punished for his or her crimes. Without indulging vindictive feelings, we can rejoice that justice was served and that the system worked. However, we should not respond gleefully when someone we consider an enemy or a wicked person suffers personal tragedies (i.e., they lose a loved one or contract a serious disease). We should rather defer to Christ's teaching that we love even our enemies, and we cannot legitimately assess their circumstances as God's judgment of wickedness.

When we or our loved ones suffer, we also question the purpose and cause of the suffering. We like to believe that some sort of logic undergirds the events of our lives, a logic that we can somehow work out. I wanted Kelly to talk about how she has experienced and coped with this inclination.

Kelly's Story[38]

JHW: As MULTIPLE DIAGNOSES revealed increasingly gloomy prospects for recovery, did you try to work out why this was happening to you and what God was doing?

Kelly: To be honest, that is a hard question. I feel there have been different points in the past ten years where I would start overanalyzing the outcome of these failed surgeries and began drawing conclusions that it was

---

38. Kelly interacts with parts of her story in each Contemporary Significance section. For the introduction to the details of her story, see Contemporary Significance in the commentary on ch. 1, pp. 87 – 97.

not God's will that I might be healed and that I should stop trying. These types of thoughts caused a lot of confusion because I began wondering if I should proceed and try the next medical "miracle" if God did not want it to happen, because he would ensure it wouldn't. I told my mother that I didn't think it was wise for me to continue to fight against God's will, since obviously he wants me in this physical state; but that was a hard thing for a mother to accept as she watched her daughter in so much pain.

More recently I am in a place where I don't see each failed surgery as a sign from God that I am not supposed to be healed, but as I have mentioned, this process is not only about physical healing but emotional healing as well. My physical, emotional, and spiritual state has changed over time, and I have also matured a lot over the course of this process, and that has greatly impacted my perspective at different points in my life. My view on suffering and God's will for my life when I was twelve does differ from my view at age eighteen or in my early twenties. As I continue to grow in my maturity as a Christian and as a woman, my thoughts on these difficult topics continue to evolve, but that does not mean that I will not have days where I feel weak and fall back into drawing big conclusions that are connected to my experiences.

JHW: Did people prompt you to identify reasons for your suffering?

Kelly: At times, I think the answer would be yes. Sometimes I felt that God wanted to use my testimony in some amazing way to bring him glory, so that was why he would not allow any medical treatment to work. At times I felt encouraged by that and other times angry. In the beginning of 2009, when my left arm began to paralyze itself and no doctor could detect why, I began thinking that God was simply adding something extra to my testimony to make it more exciting, so that I would encourage others and through that give him the glory, but at my expense. I had an ongoing dialogue with God. "Now you are going to take away my other arm too? And with no medical explanation? Well, you say you only give us what we can handle, and I can't handle having no arms! You've finally reached the limit of what I can take."

Then after things continued to get worse, I'd find myself thinking, "God, isn't this enough? You have used my testimony; do you have to keep adding to it?" I think overall, even though this is inaccurate, your mind tells you how encouraging it is to know the reasons behind your suffering so that you don't feel as if you are just simply unlucky and got dealt a bad hand of cards. When you are in that time of suffering, no matter what the circumstance, you feel you need to believe there is a purpose and reason behind the pain you are going through.

JHW: How successful were you at contriving rationalizations?

Kelly: Very. But as I said, my thoughts and perspective came in seasons. Oftentimes when I was in the heat of the storm, I would find myself creating reasons and false rationalizations for why God was allowing these things to happen. I did not always like the reason I came up with, but I felt comforted that there was at least a reason behind it.

JHW: How did you get past the rationalization stage? What new ways of thinking about your own experiences helped you avoid that trap?

Kelly: Over the course of my life, I have had numerous trial periods, and the healing process varied for each one: in the way that I handled it and the length of time that I was in this stage of rationalizing my pain. Even though my age at the time of the trial and my maturity in my faith greatly impacted what the healing process looked like, I continued to learn that my pride and my lack of trust would cause me to not fully depend on God. I didn't expect him to be there. With a slightly bitter tone, I would puff up my chest and say, "Well then, I'll just make it on my own." But, of course, over time my own strength would grow weary and faint until I came to a completely broken state, where I couldn't walk alone any longer. I would cry out to God in despair, not fully trusting that he was listening: "Jesus, I need you! I can't do this alone. Carry me through." Christ would do just that.

I saw a change in my heart and mind. My circumstances didn't always change; in fact they usually never did, but Christ doesn't promise to remove the thorn, he promises to give us the strength to endure. I don't have the clear answer for how to avoid the painful stage of searching for some rhyme or reason for your suffering, but I learned a good place to start was in complete humility at Christ's throne. The sooner I humbled myself before him and the sooner I realized I am *not* strong enough to handle it, the sooner my perspective of my experience grew.

Besides seeking to establish fault (reasons), we also tend to seek help (remedies/solutions). Depending on the nature of the crisis, these could be medical, legal, political, or spiritual. In an effort to resolve the crisis, we look for experts who can help. As Kelly discovered, some potential resolutions made things worse, and others turned out to be ineffective. When faced with these obstructions, we sometimes don't know how to pray; other times we despair.

Job sought recourse in making a legal appeal to God and looked for a specialist to help—someone who could call God to account (16:19–21). Job didn't know that his crisis was instigated by the Challenger calling God to accountability. In this case, the solution he envisioned was not a solution at all. It is not unusual that we envision the wrong or inadequate solutions because we misunderstand the problem. When this is so, our prayers for these imagined solutions are misguided. We might pray to be physically cured when we actually need emotional or psychological healing. Sometimes our thinking might need to change more than our circumstances. In such a case we ought to ask God to change our thinking rather than our circumstances. Even if a crisis is never resolved, our attitude toward the crisis can improve, thus changing our perspective and ability to cope. At this point we must hear from Kelly again.

JHW: Have your prayers changed over the years? If so, how?

Kelly: My prayers have changed over the years along with my thoughts on my own experiences. Over time, I realized that I had stopped praying for my arm, my pain—healing of any sort. I found myself conflicted between accepting something that may be a reality for the rest of my life (like Paul, who did not have his thorn removed) and knowing that we are called to pray the cries of our hearts and believe in the power of prayer. So how do I pray for healing or for being released from the pain that I endure daily, when my experiences have shown that this will not change? Should I keep praying for the same thing, or has God given me the answer "no"?

Many times during a season of trial, I would pull back from God and not pray because I was hurt and felt that God had abandoned me, but during this last season of extreme trials my prayer life did change dramatically. I began meeting with professors, mentors, and pastors to confront God. I was angry and burned out. I thought I had already experienced the most painful period of my life and felt so much despair to be in a place so much worse. So, like I said, my tendency was to pull away—and initially I did; but then I felt the emptiness and could not carry on without his strength … I had met my limit. So I turned to God and said, "God, I am afraid to ask these questions about suffering in my life, because I am afraid of what the answer will be. I am afraid to pray, in fear that you won't answer or that the answer will always be 'no.' I am afraid to confront how my experiences have formed a distorted view of you."

After that I realized how my prayer life had been so radically impacted, and I sought out professors, like you, and mentors to speak into my life. Slowly my prayers began to shift from praying for healing for my body to healing in my heart, and instead of praying for the thorn to be removed, I started praying for the strength to endure and the wisdom to have the right perspective. He has responded to those prayers and answered "yes."

JHW: Could you share with us any "Aha!" moments you have experienced concerning the way you think about your circumstances?

Kelly: Well, I think when I started changing how I prayed, that slowly began to change how I thought about my circumstances. I realized that

I needed to confront the emotional pain behind this physical disability. I have been learning over the course of this past year how our emotions are connected to what we believe. For example, if we believe that a robber is in the house, that will instill fear; or if we believe the robber is gone, that instills peace. So I began thinking about my experiences and how I formed lies about myself and about God, which have allowed me to carry deep emotional pains. I realized that I believed the lie that God did not love me and that he would hurt me for the benefit of others. So every time I had something else go wrong with my health, I would hear that lie in my head . . . that God did not love me. When I brought that lie to light and was willing to hear what Christ had to say about that, emotional healing was taking place. So that was an "Aha!" moment for me since I realized how my experiences with my health had been influencing my beliefs about God. I'm still in a process of growing, pruning, and healing, but confronting how our trials change our view of God can be an incredible step to take in the process of healing.

In conclusion, from the analysis of 17:9 in Original Meaning I observed: "Truly righteous people are concerned about their integrity, not the rewards they receive." We have partly treated this in the Contemporary Significance section of the first series of speeches (p. 199). Here we will move to the next step in this line of argument: Aren't there always benefits? Even if the benefits are not material, we can think of emotional, psychological, and spiritual benefits. Being in relationship with God can be considered a benefit; joy in worship can be a benefit; fellowship with God's people can be a benefit; even a sense of contentment or confidence that we have done what is right and pleasing to God can be a benefit. How are we supposed to think about righteousness in relationship to these sorts of benefits?

The question cannot be whether or not there *are* benefits, but to what extent we are motivated by benefits (the Great Symbiosis—I will do for God and he will do for me). Put another way, might there come a point when we feel the benefits are just not worth it and we set our faith aside saying in effect, "This is not for me—count me out?" To what extent do we think about the cost/benefit ratio? Do we base our participation on foreseen benefits? These questions help us to think about the import of Job for our own lives. The book is not suggesting that there are not/should not be benefits to our faith, but it asks us to evaluate our priorities and motivations.

Christianity cannot just be a way of cashing in or making a profit. If our faith is only a means by which we gain heaven, avoid hell, win material prosperity, or avoid illness, we are in it for all the wrong reasons.

What does the alternative look like? The alternative is the "for better, for worse" commitment. Righteousness matters because God matters. God matters because he is worthy. What we get or don't get is beside the point. Our integrity is measured by our consistency in following these principles. There can be no "what's in it for me?" element. As the book of Ecclesiastes teaches, when life is going well and benefits abound, thank God for his good gifts (Eccl. 5:19). When frustration, pain, suffering, and disappointment fill day after day, recognize that such adversity also comes from the hand of God and can shape you like nothing else will (7:19). God offers no guarantees concerning our experiences.

This perspective is consistently supported by the New Testament. Jesus warns us to count the cost of discipleship; Hebrews instructs us to persevere through hardship; Peter and Paul teach us to endure hardship for the sake of Christ and to partake in his suffering. From each of these texts we learn that Christianity is the way of hardship (the narrow path), not of ease.[39] Our goal is stated in Philippians 3:8, "I consider everything a loss compared to the surpassing greatness of knowing Christ Jesus my Lord, for whose sake I have lost all things. I consider them rubbish, that I may gain Christ." There can be no doubt that "gaining Christ" should be considered a benefit, but it is a far different sort of benefit than that envisioned in the Retribution Principle.

---

39. Matt. 5:11–12; 19:21–30; Luke 6:35; 14:26; John 16:33; Acts 14:22; 2 Cor. 12:9–10; Phil. 1:29–30; 3:10; Heb. 10:32–34; 11:32–40; 12:7; James 1:2–4; 1 Peter 2:19–21; 3:14–17; 4:12–19.

Job 22–27

᭐

Eliphaz

E ¹Then Eliphaz the Temanite replied:

²"Can a man be of benefit to God?
   Can even a wise man benefit him?
³What pleasure would it give the Almighty if you were
      righteous?
   What would he gain if your ways were blameless?

⁴"Is it for your piety that he rebukes you
   and brings charges against you?
⁵Is not your wickedness great?
   Are not your sins endless?
⁶You demanded security from your brothers for no reason;
   you stripped men of their clothing, leaving them naked.
⁷You gave no water to the weary
   and you withheld food from the hungry,
⁸though you were a powerful man, owning land—
   an honored man, living on it.
⁹And you sent widows away empty-handed
   and broke the strength of the fatherless.
¹⁰That is why snares are all around you,
   why sudden peril terrifies you,
¹¹why it is so dark you cannot see,
   and why a flood of water covers you.

¹²"Is not God in the heights of heaven?
   And see how lofty are the highest stars!
¹³Yet you say, 'What does God know?
   Does he judge through such darkness?
¹⁴Thick clouds veil him, so he does not see us
   as he goes about in the vaulted heavens.'
¹⁵Will you keep to the old path
   that evil men have trod?
¹⁶They were carried off before their time,
   their foundations washed away by a flood.
¹⁷They said to God, 'Leave us alone!
   What can the Almighty do to us?'
¹⁸Yet it was he who filled their houses with good things,
   so I stand aloof from the counsel of the wicked.

¹⁹"The righteous see their ruin and rejoice;
   the innocent mock them, saying,
²⁰'Surely our foes are destroyed,
   and fire devours their wealth.'

²¹"Submit to God and be at peace with him;
   in this way prosperity will come to you.
²²Accept instruction from his mouth
   and lay up his words in your heart.
²³If you return to the Almighty, you will be restored:
   If you remove wickedness far from your tent
²⁴and assign your nuggets to the dust,
   your gold of Ophir to the rocks in the ravines,
²⁵then the Almighty will be your gold,
   the choicest silver for you.
²⁶Surely then you will find delight in the Almighty
   and will lift up your face to God.
²⁷You will pray to him, and he will hear you,
   and you will fulfill your vows.
²⁸What you decide on will be done,
   and light will shine on your ways.
²⁹When men are brought low and you say, 'Lift them up!'
   then he will save the downcast.
³⁰He will deliver even one who is not innocent,
   who will be delivered through the cleanness of your
       hands."

Job
^{23:1}Then Job replied:

²"Even today my complaint is bitter;
   his hand is heavy in spite of my groaning.
³If only I knew where to find him;
   if only I could go to his dwelling!
⁴I would state my case before him
   and fill my mouth with arguments.
⁵I would find out what he would answer me,
   and consider what he would say.
⁶Would he oppose me with great power?
   No, he would not press charges against me.
⁷There an upright man could present his case
       before him,
   and I would be delivered forever from my judge.

⁸"But if I go to the east, he is not there;
  if I go to the west, I do not find him.
⁹When he is at work in the north, I do not see him;
  when he turns to the south, I catch no glimpse
      of him.
¹⁰But he knows the way that I take;
  when he has tested me, I will come forth as gold.
¹¹My feet have closely followed his steps;
  I have kept to his way without turning aside.
¹²I have not departed from the commands of his lips;
  I have treasured the words of his mouth more than my
      daily bread.

¹³"But he stands alone, and who can oppose him?
  He does whatever he pleases.
¹⁴He carries out his decree against me,
  and many such plans he still has in store.
¹⁵That is why I am terrified before him;
  when I think of all this, I fear him.
¹⁶God has made my heart faint;
  the Almighty has terrified me.
¹⁷Yet I am not silenced by the darkness,
  by the thick darkness that covers my face.

^{24:1}"Why does the Almighty not set times for judgment?
  Why must those who know him look in vain for such
      days?
²Men move boundary stones;
  they pasture flocks they have stolen.
³They drive away the orphan's donkey
  and take the widow's ox in pledge.
⁴They thrust the needy from the path
  and force all the poor of the land into hiding.
⁵Like wild donkeys in the desert,
  the poor go about their labor of foraging food;
  the wasteland provides food for their children.
⁶They gather fodder in the fields
  and glean in the vineyards of the wicked.
⁷Lacking clothes, they spend the night naked;
  they have nothing to cover themselves in the cold.
⁸They are drenched by mountain rains
  and hug the rocks for lack of shelter.

⁹The fatherless child is snatched from the breast;
    the infant of the poor is seized for a debt.
¹⁰Lacking clothes, they go about naked;
    they carry the sheaves, but still go hungry.
¹¹They crush olives among the terraces;
    they tread the winepresses, yet suffer thirst.
¹²The groans of the dying rise from the city,
    and the souls of the wounded cry out for help.
    But God charges no one with wrongdoing.

¹³"There are those who rebel against the light,
    who do not know its ways
    or stay in its paths.
¹⁴When daylight is gone, the murderer rises up
    and kills the poor and needy;
    in the night he steals forth like a thief.
¹⁵The eye of the adulterer watches for dusk;
    he thinks, 'No eye will see me,'
    and he keeps his face concealed.
¹⁶In the dark, men break into houses,
    but by day they shut themselves in;
    they want nothing to do with the light.
¹⁷For all of them, deep darkness is their morning;
    they make friends with the terrors of darkness.

¹⁸"Yet they are foam on the surface of the water;
    their portion of the land is cursed,
    so that no one goes to the vineyards.
¹⁹As heat and drought snatch away the melted snow,
    so the grave snatches away those who have
        sinned.
²⁰The womb forgets them,
    the worm feasts on them;
evil men are no longer remembered
    but are broken like a tree.
²¹They prey on the barren and childless woman,
    and to the widow show no kindness.
²²But God drags away the mighty by his power;
    though they become established, they have no assurance
        of life.
²³He may let them rest in a feeling of security,
    but his eyes are on their ways.

²⁴For a little while they are exalted, and then they are gone;
 they are brought low and gathered up like all others;
 they are cut off like heads of grain.

²⁵"If this is not so, who can prove me false
 and reduce my words to nothing?"

Bildad
^{25:1}Then Bildad the Shuhite replied:

²"Dominion and awe belong to God;
 he establishes order in the heights of heaven.
³Can his forces be numbered?
 Upon whom does his light not rise?
⁴How then can a man be righteous before God?
 How can one born of woman be pure?
⁵If even the moon is not bright
 and the stars are not pure in his eyes,
⁶how much less man, who is but a maggot—
 a son of man, who is only a worm!"

Job
^{26:1}Then Job replied:

²"How you have helped the powerless!
 How you have saved the arm that is feeble!
³What advice you have offered to one without
 wisdom!
 And what great insight you have displayed!
⁴Who has helped you utter these words?
 And whose spirit spoke from your mouth?

⁵"The dead are in deep anguish,
 those beneath the waters and all that live in them.
⁶Death is naked before God;
 Destruction lies uncovered.
⁷He spreads out the northern ⌞skies⌟ over empty space;
 he suspends the earth over nothing.
⁸He wraps up the waters in his clouds,
 yet the clouds do not burst under their weight.
⁹He covers the face of the full moon,
 spreading his clouds over it.
¹⁰He marks out the horizon on the face of the waters
 for a boundary between light and darkness.

¹¹The pillars of the heavens quake,
    aghast at his rebuke.
¹²By his power he churned up the sea;
    by his wisdom he cut Rahab to pieces.
¹³By his breath the skies became fair;
    his hand pierced the gliding serpent.
¹⁴And these are but the outer fringe of his works;
    how faint the whisper we hear of him!
    Who then can understand the thunder of his
        power?"

²⁷:¹And Job continued his discourse:

²"As surely as God lives, who has denied me justice,
    the Almighty, who has made me taste bitterness of soul,
³as long as I have life within me,
    the breath of God in my nostrils,
⁴my lips will not speak wickedness,
    and my tongue will utter no deceit.
⁵I will never admit you are in the right;
    till I die, I will not deny my integrity.
⁶I will maintain my righteousness and never let go of it;
    my conscience will not reproach me as long as I live.

⁷"May my enemies be like the wicked,
    my adversaries like the unjust!
⁸For what hope has the godless when he is cut off,
    when God takes away his life?
⁹ Does God listen to his cry
    when distress comes upon him?
¹⁰Will he find delight in the Almighty?
    Will he call upon God at all times?

¹¹"I will teach you about the power of God;
    the ways of the Almighty I will not conceal.
¹²You have all seen this yourselves.
    Why then this meaningless talk?

¹³"Here is the fate God allots to the wicked,
    the heritage a ruthless man receives from the Almighty:
¹⁴However many his children, their fate is the sword;
    his offspring will never have enough to eat.
¹⁵The plague will bury those who survive him,
    and their widows will not weep for them.

¹⁶Though he heaps up silver like dust
    and clothes like piles of clay,
¹⁷what he lays up the righteous will wear,
    and the innocent will divide his silver.
¹⁸The house he builds is like a moth's cocoon,
    like a hut made by a watchman.
¹⁹He lies down wealthy, but will do so no more;
    when he opens his eyes, all is gone.
²⁰Terrors overtake him like a flood;
    a tempest snatches him away in the night.
²¹The east wind carries him off, and he is gone;
    it sweeps him out of his place.
²²It hurls itself against him without mercy
    as he flees headlong from its power.
²³It claps its hands in derision
    and hisses him out of his place.

THIS THIRD SERIES OF speeches concludes the dialogue section. As we will see, the friends have much less to say: Bildad has only six verses and Zophar is silent, leaving Eliphaz to carry the main thrust of the sequence.

Eliphaz (Job 22)

ELIPHAZ'S OPENING LINE SETS the tone for the remainder of his speech as he targets the issue that Job has been holding as his defense. Unfortunately, the Hebrew is extremely difficult. If we follow the NIV translation, Eliphaz is suggesting that it doesn't matter to God whether a person is righteous/blameless or not; God derives no benefit from moral behavior. This interpretation is out-of-character for Eliphaz and does not fit well with the rest of his speech. We are not surprised, then, at the numerous lexical, grammatical, and syntactical problems in verses 2 and 3.

A look at some of the major technical commentaries will confirm the uncertainties.

> NIV: "Can a man be of benefit to God? Can even a wise man benefit him? What pleasure would it give the Almighty if you were righteous? What would he gain if your ways were blameless?"

Habel: "Can a hero endanger El? or a sage endanger the Ancient
One? Is it a favor to Shaddai if you are righteous, or his gain if
you perfect your ways?"

Hartley: "Can a man benefit God, that a wise man should be in
harmony with him? What asset is it to Shaddai that you are
innocent, or gain that you claim that your ways are blameless?"

Clines: "Can a human be profitable to God? Can even a sage
benefit him? Is it an asset to the Almighty if you are righteous?
Does he gain if your conduct is blameless?"

I would propose the following translation:

"Can a wise mediator do any good for a human being [serving] on
behalf of God? Can such a mediator bring a human any benefit?
Will God respond favorably when you justify yourself? Will there
be a gain when you give full account of your ways?"[1]

In 22:2–3 Eliphaz is in effect saying, "A mediator will do you no good;
your proposed lawsuit would have no chance of success." In 22:4 this rhetoric is continued with: "Is it for your piety that he argues his case against
you?" Of course not! Circumstances have made it clear to Eliphaz that Job
has no piety, so he should not press this lawsuit idea or expect that it would
succeed if he did manage to get a hearing. Eliphaz concludes his point in
22:5 with the rhetorical question that offers the alternative: "[Instead] isn't
your wickedness great?" This then leads to the enumeration of Job's many
sins (all presumed, not observed).

In 22:6–9 we find the friends' only attempt to accuse Job of specific
sins. The list alleges injustice toward three vulnerable classes: the debtor
(22:6), the hungry/thirsty (22:7–8), and the widow/orphan (22:9). We
know that these are generic offenses (rather than demonstrably Israelite in
nature) from the standpoint of ancient Near Eastern legal texts that regularly address the obligations of society to care for these vulnerable people.

Knowing that the accusations of injustice are speculative and unfounded,
we must also question the validity of Eliphaz's claims concerning Job's
speech. In 22:13 he alleges that Job has said, "What does God know? Does
he judge through such darkness?" These do not match up with any words
that Job has actually spoken, so we must take them as Eliphaz's synthesis of
what Job has "in effect" said. Such an inference could be made from 21:22:
"Does he [the wicked man][2] teach knowledge on behalf of God, when he

---

1. For those who want to see the technical support, consult the appendix (pp. 450–53).

2. The subject of this sentence is represented only by the third person singular verbal
form. The NIV uses the universal "anyone" whereas I favor picking up the antecedent from
the previous discussion.

[God] is the one who judges even the highest?" This is one of the verses that I used as a comparison for 22:2, and on the basis of which I offered my alternate translation. The reference to judging (*špṭ*) the highest (*ramim*) in 21:22 and to the lofty (*rmm*) stars and God's judging (*špṭ*) in 22:12 – 13 support my comparison.

This suggests that there is a further connection between the wicked teaching knowledge in 21:22 and questioning what God knows in 22:13. In 21:13 – 16, the wicked enjoy the fruits of their wickedness, but in 21:22 Job claims that they cannot communicate information regarding divine judgment because God judges universally and impartially.[3] Job thus asserts that the defiant prosperity of the wicked should not be interpreted as a reflection of God's policies, which are too complex to be sorted out (21:23 – 26). Yet 21:31 – 33 suggest that (in Job's mind) God is shirking his duties. These statements would lead Eliphaz to assert that Job has accused God of overlooking the wicked. Such an affirmation does not indicate an underlying deism, because Job has already indicated in 7:17 – 21 that God was, at the same time, paying too much attention to him.

As Eliphaz continues his discourse, we see further connections to Job's last speech. In 22:15 he is urging Job not to think that he can follow the path of the wicked that Job has just described. His comments in 22:17 – 18 contain the same wording that Job attributes to the wicked in 21:14 – 16.[4]

In 22:21 Eliphaz begins his exhortation to Job and picks up the verb *skn* ("submit") that he used in 22:2, except now it is in the Hiphil stem.[5] Based on a cognate in the Akkadian letters from Amarna and the contexts of the three biblical passages where this form occurs, it is likely that the verb signifies showing awareness, taking an informed position, paying attention — engaging with someone.[6] If this is so, Eliphaz advises Job to pay attention to God — to reengage with him and stop arguing.[7] Eliphaz's understanding of reengaging with God is, however, far different from Job's understanding.

Concluding his final speech, Eliphaz turns from his exhortation to the anticipated results. Here he emphasizes restored favor with God

---

3. In 38:15 God breaks the upraised (*ramah*) arm of the wicked. The root can refer to both positive ("exalted") and negative ("haughty") behavior.

4. Clines (*Job 21 – 37*, 560) is certainly correct in his assessment that as a result of these parallels, Eliphaz's statement in 22:17b should be translated "What can the Almighty do *for* us?" instead of the NIV (emphasis added) "What can the Almighty do *to* us?"

5. The only other occurrences of the Hiphil are in Num. 22:30 and Ps. 139:3.

6. The donkey in Num. 22:30 had never before shown awareness or paid any attention to Balaam's intentions, and in Ps. 139:3, God does show awareness and pay attention to the psalmist's movements.

7. This understanding is based on the observation that the imperative verb (*šelam*) occurs in the Qal ("be at peace") rather than in the Hiphil ("make peace").

(22:25–27) but with the twist that renewed favor will put Job in a position to influence God. This is a more subtle temptation for Job to respond in anticipation of benefits, rather than retain righteousness for righteousness' sake (as Job has maintained all along). The lure of possessions has now been displaced by the lure for power: "Think of all the good you can do!" We see the ironic contrast between Eliphaz's prognosis here (Job's influence with God will enable him to help the downcast) and his previous accusation (that Job has abused this same class of people).

The last verse (22:30) is unfortunately problematic. The NIV follows the primary and traditional path, indicating that Job could even deliver the one who is "not innocent" (*'i-naqi*). Though *'i* is not used as a negative particle elsewhere in the Hebrew Bible, it is known from postbiblical Hebrew and other Semitic cognate languages (e.g., Phoenician and Ethiopic).[8] It is curious that the author uses this awkward construction rather than one of the many available words for "guilty." This oddity has caused many commentators to propose textual emendations, none of which are particularly persuasive.[9] If we retain the meaning of "where" (established in 1 Sam. 4:21), we might surmise that Eliphaz refers to a category of individuals who are caught in the legal system. Accused of guilt and unable to establish innocence (not unlike Job), this person's reputation and integrity have come under suspicion. Perhaps Eliphaz is suggesting, then, that when Job is restored, he could help people who are suffering the same thing he has endured. Presumably he could urge them to return to God, just as Eliphaz has urged him.

Job (Job 23–24)

IN JOB 23 JOB ponders his status before God. He is torn between optimistic confidence (23:6b–7, 10) and frustrated attempts at justification (23:8–9). He is filled with continuing plans for his legal defense (23:4–5) and affirmations of his righteousness (23:11–12). Both his suffering (23:1) and his terror of God (23:13–17) remain.

In chapter 24 Job turns his attention to the injustice in the world as he wonders why God does not respond. Many of Job's friends predicted the inevitable doom of the wicked. In Job 21 Job elaborated on the prosperity of the wicked—a situation that seemed to him unfair. His charge against God progresses from "unfair" to "unjust"[10] as he enumerates the many ways

---

8. *'i* is known only elsewhere in the Hebrew Bible in the personal name Ichabod (1 Sam. 4:21, *'i-kabod*, "where is the glory?"),

9. See listing in Clines, *Job 21–37*, 547, n. 30a.

10. Job also initially accused God of treating him unfairly (Job 7) and then accused God of dealing with him unjustly (Job 9).

in which the wicked oppress the vulnerable. In Job 1 the narrator noted that Job did not sin by charging God with wrongdoing (1:21); in contrast, Job here complains, "God charges no one with wrongdoing" (24:12).

Job 24:13–17 identifies the characteristics of those who love the dark ("rebel against the light"). Murderers, adulterers, and thieves comprise the three categories of offenders (reflecting commandments 6–8 in the Decalogue, though that is not Job's referent).

In light of 24:12c, Job's continuing speech in 24:18–25 seems problematic. Job has not yet elaborated the coming judgment of the wicked. For this reason, many commentators attribute this speech to one of the friends (especially Zophar, who has no last speech).[11] If the speech truly does belong in the mouth of Job, it would confirm that he still clings to the RP in theory, in spite of general observation and his own experiences, which do not bear it out. Job's claim of disinterested righteousness rests on his commitment to the RP, insofar as it is the RP that distinguishes between righteousness for its own sake and righteousness for reward. Without the RP there is no "interested righteousness," for no gain could be expected or anticipated.

We have mentioned already that the Hebrew of the book of Job is the most difficult in the Old Testament; worse still, this section of Job 24 is often considered the most obscure in this book. Before exploring specific lexical issues, we must address the sometimes confusing use of singulars and plurals in this section.

Singular/plural in 24:13–24. Readers comparing translations will notice some variability on the representation of singulars and plurals throughout this section. The difficulty of the section is partly responsible for this, but gender policies also come into play as translations seek to avoid gender-specific pronouns when gender is not the issue. To sort out the interpretation of the section, we need to sort out the use of singular and plural forms.

Job 24:13 uses the plural to introduce a group of criminals who operate at night. Singulars are used to discuss two criminal classes: the murderer (24:14) and the adulterer (24:15). A third class, those who break into houses, returns to the plural. All of these criminals are again grouped together using plural forms in 24:17–19, and at the end they are collectively referred to in the plural as sinners.

In 24:20 the text introduces a second category of unsavory character, using a singular abstract noun to represent a stereotype (*'awlah*).[12] This

---

11. See discussion in Clines, *Job 21–37*, 661–62, 667–69. While this kind of misplacement is not impossible, such an interpretation should be our last resort.

12. The transition is admittedly rough because the Hebrew text only introduces the subject, *'awlah*, in the last word of the verse.

word was discussed in the treatment of Job 13:7 (pp. 177–78), where I proposed that this noun essentially signifies misrepresentation. In that same vein, but in contrast to the outright criminals of 24:13–19, Job here describes those in positions of power who pretend to be ethical but who actually oppress and manipulate others. Just as 24:14 used singular forms to identify specific types from the larger class of criminals, so 24:21 uses singular forms to identify typical behaviors of these powerful tyrants.[13] These include the individual who preys on the vulnerable (24:21) as well as the individual who manipulates the aristocracy (24:22).

In conclusion, the text uses the plural forms of 24:24 to summarize the destiny that awaits these tyrants as a group, just as it used the plurals to summarize the previous group in 24:18–19.

Lexical issues. Job's characterization of the wicked in 24:13–20 shows that he is not at all tempted to imitate them, and he has repeatedly refused to identify himself as one of them. He neither admits to personal deficiencies nor abandons his commitment to righteousness. That path has no future. In 24:21 the wicked are the ones who do what Eliphaz had accused Job of doing (22:9)—victimizing the vulnerable. As we have seen in previous chapters, Job continues to characterize the ways of the wicked in deplorable terms.

Up to this point we have seen nothing that would be out of place in Job's mouth or in the flow of his argument. Job would not hesitate to suggest that the wicked die like everyone else. A problem would occur only if Job specifically refers to God's judgment of the wicked, because he has been denying this all along (24:12, "God charges no one with wrongdoing"). Job 24:22 (NIV: "God drags away the mighty") poses just such a potential contradiction. It is therefore important to note that the subject of 24:22 is not specified in the Hebrew text; "God" has been supplied by the translators. After a detailed analysis of verses 22–23 we must reconsider whether this is the best choice.

umašak 'abbirim bekoho yaqum welo'-ya'amin baḥayyin.
yitten-lo labeṭaḥ weyišša'en we'enehu 'al-darkehem.

> NIV: But God drags away the mighty by his power; though they become established, they have no assurance of life. He may let them rest in a feeling of security, but his eyes are on their ways.

---

13. The noun *'awlah* from v. 20 is not technically the subject of the verbs in vv. 21–22 because then they would take the feminine form like *tiššaber* in v. 20. This is because noun abstractions use the feminine ending. Thus, the singular subjects in vv. 21–22 refer to categories of people.

The addition of "God" as the subject in verse 22 is followed in most all translations and commentaries.[14] This single factor causes these statements to sound foreign to the mouth of Job. I propose it is unnecessary either to supply "God" as the subject or to significantly emend the text to arrive at a suitable translation. I suggest the following paraphrase for 24:22–23:

> He (a wicked person) uses his power to draw along the mighty;
> he rises (to positions of influence), but his life is in constant
> jeopardy. Though he has provided for his own security, he has to
> keep his eyes on them (the mighty) all the time.[15]

In this analysis, Job observes that wickedness offers no advantage, but he does not suggest that the wicked are called to account by God. They fall prey to their own schemes and to their own mortality. This sort of statement would not be out of place in the mouth of Job.

Bildad (Job 25)

BILDAD'S LAST SPEECH IS only six verses long. This brevity is defensible in light of his entrenched traditionalism, which, at this point in the dialogue, has reduced him to platitudinous reiteration of his major salient points: God is unimaginably great; humans are intrinsically flawed and, in the grand scheme of things, are of little consequence.[16] He believes in an ordered world, and as we have seen previously, that order is founded on the RP.

Job (Job 26–27)

AFTER INTRODUCTORY COMMENTS FILLED with biting sarcasm (26:1–4), Job launches into another of his hymnic orations of God's cosmic power (see 9:4–10) that extends through the remainder of the chapter and leads to the statement of his final position in ch. 27. God is never mentioned by name in the Hebrew text of this hymn (v. 6 has only a pronoun), though the chapter is full of activities that can only be attributed to God.[17]

---

14. Clines, *Job 21–37*, 657 n. 22b indicates that v. 22 takes "the wicked" as the subject. Gordis and Habel take "the mighty" as the subject, but they have the problem that the verbs are singular while "the mighty" is plural. A. De Wilde (*Das Buch Hiob*, 1981) and G. Bickell (late nineteenth century) take "the wicked" as the subject and "the mighty" as the object, but both emend the latter to a different word entirely (each with a different suggestion). The NJPS takes "wicked" as the subject and "mighty" as the object, but suggests a different root for the verb.

15. For those who want to see the technical support, consult the appendix (pp. 453–54).

16. For discussion of the "purity" of the stars, see treatment of 15:14–15, p. 213.

17. Clines accounts for this by interpreting 26:5–14 as belonging to Bildad's speech, in which the moon and stars are mentioned toward the end.

Job 26:5–6. These verses describe the dead and the netherworld. The subject of the first sentence is the group known as the *repa'im* (NIV: "dead"). This is the word used occasionally in the Hebrew Bible for the shades of the dead[18] and more specifically in Ugaritic for the shades of perhaps deified royal ancestors.[19] It is more difficult to understand what engages the Rephaim in their dwelling place beneath the sea. The translation "deep anguish" (NIV) is based on an identification of the verbal form (*yeholalu*) as a Polal of the root *ḥyl*; all the other uses of this form in biblical Hebrew describe the writhing of a woman in labor. The Akkadian myth The Descent of Ishtar to the Underworld recounts Ishtar's passage through the seven gates of the netherworld. As each gate opens for her, Ishtar is required to forfeit another piece of her garments of splendor and power until at last she is left naked. Even so, Ereshkigal, the queen of the netherworld, trembles (Akkad. *ra'ābu*)[20] at her presence.[21]

It is intriguing to see all of these elements (the opening of the netherworld, nakedness, and trembling) grouped together in both Job and the The Descent, but the contexts are very different. In *Enuma Elish* one of the fifty names of Marduk is *Nari-lugal-dimmer-ankia*, which designates him as the one who set up the dwelling places for the various levels of deity. It is said that at his name, "the gods shall tremble and quake in their dwellings."[22] From these examples we see that it is common to praise a deity as one at whose name or presence other beings of power tremble fearfully.

The phrase "beneath the waters" (*mittaḥat mayim*) uses the same terms as Genesis 1:7 (*hammayim 'ašer mittaḥat laraqia'*) to reference the cosmic waters. One can also enter the netherworld through these waters, not just through the grave (Job 38:16–17; Jon. 2:2[3]). The dead (both the Rephaim and the other inhabitants) live beneath the cosmic waters because Sheol is deeper than anything. Even as the most awesome tremble in God's presence, the most mysterious, Sheol and Abaddon (here used in synonymous parallelism), are subject to his scrutiny and control (see NIV text note). "Abaddon" is used only four other times in the Old Testament (Job 28:22; 31:12; Ps. 88:11[12]; Prov. 15:11), but that it refers to the place of the dead is clear enough from its contexts and its association with known cognate roots.

It is unclear how these verses connect to Job 26:7–13, in that the latter verses refer to creation events in primordial time—probably not the time

---

18. Ps. 88:10[11]; Prov. 2:18; 9:18; 21:16; Isa. 14:9; 26:14, 19.

19. For discussion, see H. Rouillard, "Rephaim," *DDD²*, 692–700, and W. Pitard, "The *Rpum* Texts," in *Handbook of Ugaritic Studies* (Leiden: Brill, 1999), 259–69.

20. *CAD* R, 2–3.

21. *COS*, 1.108, line 64.

22. *BM*, 475 (6.146).

---

frame for 26:5−6. The other alternative is that 26:5−6 continue the sarcasm of the previous verses. Job has referenced some anonymous source for Bildad's supposed words of wisdom. As mentioned above, the NIV, along with most others, has provided "God" as the subject of discussion in the first line of 26:6, but the Hebrew text has only a third masculine singular suffix on the preposition. Theoretically, then, the "him" could be this unnamed source. Even the mighty ones in the netherworld are simply quivering over the wisdom of this wellspring, and in fact, all the mysteries of death and the netherworld are like an open book to this dynamo. I suggest this only tentatively as an alternative consideration.[23] The switch to participial forms discussing primordial time in 26:7 would then indicate when God becomes the unspecified but self-evident subject.

Job 26:7. If we follow the traditional understanding of 26:5−6, the hymn moves from God's control of the realm of the dead and powerful spiritual or cosmic creatures to his control of the upper cosmos. The cosmic geography expressed in 26:7 has attracted considerable attention, since some have asserted that it reflects some modern, scientific models that conceive of the earth suspended in space.[24] Careful attention, however, shows this not to be the case. The key terms to explore are *tohu* (NIV: "empty space") and *belyi-mah* (NIV: "nothing").

Tohu is used twenty times—more than half in Isaiah (mostly Isa. 40−49,[25] with the other occurrences scattered between Job [3x][26] and Gen. 1:2; Deut. 32:10; 1 Sam. 12:21; Ps. 107:40; Jer. 4:23). Elsewhere I have argued that *tohu* refers to that which is nonfunctional.[27] Genesis 1:2 begins by describing everything as *tohu*, and as creation unfolds, God assigns function. Egyptian literature describes the nonfunctional as nonexistent; just as it categorizes the desert as nonexistent (nonfunctional), so too the Hebrew Bible characterizes the desert as *tohu* (Deut. 32:10; Job 6:18; 12:24; Ps. 107:40; Isa. 24:10; 45:19). Just as the Egyptian pharaoh discuss the doom of those they destroy in terms of nonexistence, Hebrew

---

23. We might even wonder whether the supernatural source of Bildad's might hints at a character from mythology who would be considered feeble in contrast to the power of the Creator God.

24. This view can be found in some of the older commentaries such as M. Buttenweiser, *The Book of Job* (New York: MacMillan, 1922), but is also asserted in those Bible and Science books that are inclined to a concordist interpretation of the Old Testament, e.g., W. Kaiser, "bālâ," *Theological Wordbook of the Old Testament* (ed. R. L. Harris, G. L. Archer, and B. K. Waltke; Chicago: Moody Press, 1980), 1:111. For full discussion, see R. J. Schneider, "Does the Bible Teach a Spherical Earth?" *PSCF* 53 (September 2001): 159−69.

25. Isa. 24:10; 29:21; 34:11; 40:17, 23; 41:29; 44:9; 45:18, 19; 49:4; 59:4.

26. Job 6:18; 12:24; 26:7.

27. Walton, *Lost World of Genesis One*, 47−53.

uses *tohu* to talk about the destruction of order and civilization (cf. Jer. 4:23). Job 26:7 is the best example of *tohu* as a reference to nonfunctional cosmic realms. None of the uses of *tohu* suggest anything about form or its absence. Whether speaking of geographical areas, nations, cities, people, or idols, *tohu* refers to that which is nonproductive, nonfunctional, of no purpose. These conclusions are fully supported by the contexts and by the words used in parallel.

The usage in Ugaritic[28] resembles the Hebrew passages that reference a trackless waste, but, significantly, in the Ugaritic passage *thw* is used parallel to *ym*, the sea. All of this suggests that neither "trackless" nor "waste" are the most germane operative concepts; the Egyptian concept of "nonexistence" more accurately conveys the sense.

This connection is particularly intriguing in Job 26:7: *noṭeh ṣapon 'al-tohu toleh 'ereṣ 'al- beliy-mah*. Hebrew uses the word *ṣapon* for "north"; however, the significance of the word lies not in its orientation with the points of the compass, but in its use as a reference to Zaphon, the sacred mountain known from Ugaritic literature.[29] In Canaanite mythology, this mountain is the location of Baal's palace and (in their cosmic geography) was probably the center of the world. Typically the ancients pictured the cosmic mountain, like the alternate image of the cosmic tree, with its foundations in the netherworld and its heights in the heavens. As such, it marks the meeting place of heaven and earth. The cosmic mountain also served as the convening place for the assembly of the gods and was thus their dwelling place (heaven).

The author's use of the verb "spreads out" (*noṭeh*) suggests that he is talking about "the heavens," since this verb usually takes "heaven" as its object in biblical cosmology contexts.[30] If that is the case, we can understand *tohu* as a reference to the "nonexistent" (= nonordered, nonfunctional) cosmic waters above, over which the heavens were stretched (cf. Ps. 104:2–3).[31]

In Job 26:7 *tohu* parallels the unique phrase *beliy-mah*.[32] Most commentators consider the latter a reference to the void—that is, the matterless

---

28. *KTU* 1.5; Baal and Mot i.15–16; see S. Parker, *Ugaritic Narrative Poetry* (SBLWAW; Atlanta: Scholars, 1997), 142.

29. H. Neihr, "Zaphon," *DDD²*, 927–29; R. Clifford, *The Cosmic Mountain in Canaan and the Old Testament* (Cambridge, Mass.: Harvard Univ. Press, 1972); J. J. M. Roberts, "ṢĀPÔN in Job 26, 7," *Bib* 56 (1975): 554–57.

30. Job 9:8; Ps. 104:2; Isa. 40:22; 42:5; 44:24; 45:12; 51:13; Jer. 10:12; 51:15; Zech. 12:1.

31. Hartley, *Job*, 365–66, also considers *tohu* to refer to the cosmic waters citing Gen. 1:2, but does not make the connection to the "nonexistent."

32. Even-Shoshan's concordance lists this as a single word without *maqqeph*. Also listed as a variant in *HALOT*. See Dhorme, *Job*, 371.

space in which earth is suspended. This interpretation largely derives from our modern material ontology, which is concerned with the material. The ancients, however, were more concerned with functions.[33] In the context of Job and the ancient Near East, the statement makes more sense when compared to the cosmology underlying the Egyptian sense of the nonexistent, referring to that which lacks function.[34]

The verb in the second clause, "suspends" (*tlh*), most often refers to a form of execution ("hanged," Gen. 40:19, 22; 41:13; Deut. 21:22–23; Josh. 8:29; 10:26; 2 Sam. 4:12; 18:10; often in Esther). In many of these references, *tlh* occurs in collocation with the preposition '*al* (as in Job 26), nearly always with the object '*eṣ* (tree, or, more likely, wooden pole/pike, since in ancient practice the corpse was impaled as a means of exposure and a denial of proper burial). These cases would be better translated "suspended on" (not "over"). Four other contexts use the combination *tlh* '*al* (2 Sam. 4:12, to hang next to; Song 4:4, to affix shields to a wall; Isa. 22:24, to bear the family honor; Ezek. 15:3, to hang on a peg).

With all the difficult words in this verse, one might think that at least the word "earth" ('*ereṣ*) is straightforward—but unfortunately this is not the case. Though the word means earth in hundreds of passages, in a few instances (both from the Hebrew Bible and from ancient Near Eastern cognate languages) it can also refer to the netherworld.[35] I favor the translation "netherworld" here instead of "earth," primarily because this poem does not begin discussing the earth until verse 10 (see discussion there). Furthermore, the netherworld would be more appropriate as the opposite extreme of Zaphon. Support for "earth," however, could be found in passages that speak of the earth as "founded on the waters" (cf. Ps. 24:1; 136:6).

From this profile we conclude that Job 26:7 indicates what the '*ereṣ* is suspended on. In the ancient functional ontology, people saw the earth/ netherworld as suspended on the functionless cosmic waters below,[36] parallel to the heaven stretched out over the upper cosmic waters. This understanding finds support in early versions (such as the Targum) when

---

33. See my demonstration of this in *Lost World of Genesis One*, 23–36; cf. Walton, *Ancient Near Eastern Thought*, 87–91, 179–99.

34. E. Hornung, *Conceptions of God in Ancient Egypt* (Ithaca, N.Y.: Cornell Univ. Press, 1982), 172–85; S. Morenz, *Egyptian Religion* (Ithaca, N.Y.: Cornell Univ. Press, 1973), 171–74. See my extensive treatment in *Genesis 1 as Ancient Cosmology*, 24–26.

35. Ex. 15:12; 1 Sam. 28:13; Job 10:21–22; Eccl. 3:21; Isa. 26:19; Jon. 2:6. Akkadian: *erṣetu*; Ugaritic: '*arṣ*; J. Sasson, *Jonah* (AB; New York: Doubleday, 1990), 188–89; N. Tromp finds many more examples, many of which are ambiguous at best (*Primitive Conceptions of Death*, 23–46).

36. Also supported by Hartley, *Job*, 366.

the material ontology was not quite so firmly established: "Over the *water* without anything supporting it."[37] This is not to say that *tohu* and *beliy-mah* are actually words for the waters above and waters below. Rather, they describe the nonexistent, and the cosmic waters fit into the category of the nonexistent.[38]

Job 26:8. The imagery of cloud-enveloped waters likewise fits the ideas current in the ancient world; note in *Enuma Elish* 5.49, "[Marduk] collected it and rolled it into clouds."[39] An Assyrian artifact in the British Museum provides our only graphic representation of this phenomenon. It depicts the winged deity with drawn bow in the skies, flanked by bags containing hail or rain.[40] The two words for "cloud" used in this verse (*'ab* and *'ann*) both occur commonly. The former occurs mostly in poetic texts to describe dense rain clouds (of the cumulus varieties) rather than the wispy cirrus type.[41] This term is used most often in theophanies, accompanied by imagery associated with the storm god, the divine warrior who rides on the clouds (e.g., Isa. 19:1).

The second noun, *'ann*, occurs more often in prose contexts. Many of its eighty-seven occurrences refer to the pillar of cloud in the wilderness and the cloud of Yahweh's presence in sacred space.[42] It is used in reference to meteorological phenomena only a few times.[43] This noun often describes clouds that obscure or shroud something in contrast to clouds that bring the blessing of rain or the threat of storm. Aside from Job 26, *'ab* and *'ann* occur together only two other times: Exodus 19:9 (odd combination of the two in construct relationship: *be'ab he'anan*, "in the storm cloud of the cloud cover") and Isaiah 44:22 (both metaphorical references to sins). The point of their inclusion in Job 26 is largely self-evident as it speaks of God's control: He does not allow the bags to burst under the weight of the water.

Job 26:9. This verse begins with a familiar verbal root *'ḥz*; however, this particular form (the Piel, D stem) occurs nowhere else in the Old Testament. The Akkadian cognate *aḫāzu* may offer helpful comparison; it shares a simi-

---

37. Cited in Dhorme, *Job*, 371.

38. An interesting parallel also occurs between the affirmation of God's work in Job 26:7 and the thirty-second name of Marduk in *Enuma Elish* 7.83: Agilimma: "Creator of the earth above the waters, establisher of the heights."

39. Here what is being collected is not just water, but the spittle of Tiamat.

40. For illustration, see I. Cornelius, "Job," *ZIBBCOT*, 5:294.

41. B. Holmberg, "עָב," *TDOT*, 10:372.

42. These are never expressed with *'ab*.

43. Gen. 9:13–16; Isa. 44:22; Jer. 4:13; Ezek. 32:7; Job 3:5; 7:9; 37:11, 15; 38:9. See discussion in H.-J. Fabry et al., "עָנָן," *TDOT*, 11:253–57.

lar semantic range with the Hebrew root '*ḥz*, and it does have attested uses of the D stem (*uḫḫuzu*), which may eventually assist us. The noun (*kisseh*) that serves as direct object of '*ḥz* is equally problematic. The NIV has followed a medieval tradition in reading this as a reference to the full moon (from noun *kese*'; see Ps. 81:3[4]; Prov. 7:20).[44] Other interpreters have chosen another emendation, *kisse*', a word commonly translated "throne."[45] At least one Akkadian text uses the verb *uḫḫuzu* to describe the adorning (edging) of a throne with special stone; based on this occurrence, I would be inclined to translate verse 9 as: "the one edging the surface of [his] throne by spreading his cloudbank over it."[46] The word translated "spread" is not a Hebrew verb (four radicals, *pršz*) but I believe this rendering is still the best guess.[47]

Job 26:10. God's power over the sea is a familiar theme in poetic literature, both in reference to creation and to the deliverance at the Red Sea. The following passages speak of the sea's cosmic boundaries:

> But at your rebuke the waters fled,
>> at the sound of your thunder they took to flight;
> they flowed over the mountains,
>> they went down into the valleys,
>> to the place you assigned for them.
> You set a boundary they cannot cross;
>> never again will they cover the earth. (Ps. 104:7–9)

> I was there when he set the heavens in place,
>> when he marked out the horizon on the face of the deep,
> when he established the clouds above
>> and fixed securely the fountains of the deep,
> when he gave the sea its boundary
>> so the waters would not overstep his command,
> and when he marked out the foundations of the earth.
>> (Prov. 8:27–29)

---

44. A meaning supported by the Akkadian cognate, *kussu*.

45. In 1 Kings 10:19 the Hebrew word for throne is spelled this way.

46. Unquestionably this rendering is still a bit awkward, in that covering with clouds hardly seems to be "edging," but it makes no less sense than covering the full moon, which would ill fit with all the other actions of creation.

47. In Hebrew, both *prš* and *prz* mean to spread out. Possibly a scribe included both in a transition. There are two other alternatives: We could take it as a four radical loanword (none comparable known) or assume that one of the letters was miscopied at some stage (but which one? Most likely the first letter should be a *b* instead of a *p*, and therefore be a preposition, though the remaining three letters do not form any known word either).

I made the sand a boundary for the sea,
an everlasting barrier it cannot cross.
The waves may roll, but they cannot prevail;
they may roar, but they cannot cross it. (Jer. 5:22)

Who shut up the sea behind doors
when it burst forth from the womb,
when I made the clouds its garment
and wrapped it in thick darkness,
when I fixed limits for it
and set its doors and bars in place,
when I said, "This far you may come and no farther;
here is where your proud waves halt"? (Job 38:8–11)

Vocabulary similarities between the passages include the following:

- inscribe/decree (*hoq*) a limit (Job 28:10; 38:10; Prov. 8:27, 29; Jer. 5:22)
- barriers (doors and bars,[48] Job 38:8, 10) that cannot be passed (Job 38:11; Prov. 8:29; Ps. 104:9; Jer. 5:22).
- set a boundary (*gebul*, Ps. 104:9; Jer. 5:22; *taklit*, Job 28:10)
- inscribe the circle (*hug*) of the earth (Job 26:10; Prov. 8:27; cf. also Isa. 40:22)

Though these verses indicate that God has established a boundary for the sea,[49] it is not certain that Job 26:10 alludes to that event. The inscribed circle here (also in Prov. 8:27) is likely not the horizon, but the entire land disk—the earth. Isaiah 40:22 uses this same terminology ("circle of the earth") to describe a disk rather than a sphere. Anyone who gets an unobstructed view of the horizon can easily see the circular shape of the earth, and this observation led the ancients to believe that heaven, earth, and netherworld were all disk-shaped.[50] For example, the speaker in the

---

48. See Akkadian *šigaru nahbalu tâmti*, "the bolt named 'Net of the Sea'" discussed in Horowitz, *Mesopotamian Cosmic Geography*, 326–27; W. G. Lambert and A. Millard, *Atra-hasis: The Babylonian Story of the Flood* (Oxford: Clarendon, 1969), 116–21, lines i.6, i.10, ii.4, ii.11, ii.18, ii.34; and *hargullu*, "Lock of the Sea," Horowitz, *Mesopotamian Cosmic Geography*, 327. For other examples of locks on the sea, see *CAD* T, 157 (*tâmtu*).

49. Though this concept is clear enough in the Old Testament, this element of cosmic ordering is not found in the ancient Near East. Mesopotamian literature speaks of limiting the seas to their place in *Atrahasis* and *Enuma Elish*, and neither have much connection to the biblical expressions mentioned above. The Sumerian piece Bird and Fish says vaguely that "Enki ... collected all the waters, established their dwelling places."

50. Akkadian uses the term *kippatu*, see *CAD* K, 399; see Horowitz, *Mesopotamian Cosmic Geography*, 334.

Babylonian Hymn to Shamash proclaims: "You suspend the circle of the lands[51] from the center of the sky." In Job 26 and Proverbs 8 the earth is inscribed as a boundary between heaven and the deep (or netherworld), not between the land and the sea.[52] This is precisely what is said in the second half of Job 26:10 — the land-disk forms the boundary between light and darkness; when the sun passed under the earth into the netherworld, there was darkness.

Job 26:11. This verse contains the only reference in the Old Testament to "the pillars of the heavens" (but see "pillars" of earth in Job 9:6). Just as the earth is supported by pillars, so too are the heavens — or, more specifically, the dome of heaven. The pillars may refer to mountains, since some mountains were believed to intersect the sky and perhaps hold it up. Ancient Near Eastern texts from Mesopotamia (e.g., *Enuma Elish*) make no mention of what holds up the sky. Egyptian iconography portrays the sky god Shu holding up the heavens from earth, while Pyramid Text 1040c says that the mountains hold up the sky.[53]

In the context of Job 26, why do these pillars "quake" (*rpp*)[54] and stand "aghast" (*tmh*)?[55] What is the "rebuke" (*g'rh*) all about? Judging from other Old Testament cosmological passages, the rebuke is most likely directed against the sea. The sense of the verbal root includes rebuke, reprimand, and threat. It is likely onomatopoetic (sounding like a snarl or growl).[56] The sea retreats at God's rebuke.[57] This action creates a natural transition into the next verses.

Job 26:12 – 13. Here Job continues his hymnic description of God's primordial ordering of the cosmos. The churning (*rg'*) of the sea has been generally considered an element of the typical mythical scene in which the restless cosmic ocean disturbs the creatures (monsters, beasts) that represent

---

51. Akkad. *kippat* KUR.KUR (= *matati*).

52. Fox, *Proverbs 1 – 9*, 284.

53. P. Seely, "The Geographical Meaning of 'Earth' and 'Seas' in Gen. 1:10," *WTJ* 59 (1997): 233; see also Pyramid Text 299a (see *The Pyramid Texts* [trans. S. A. B. Mercer: New York: Longmans, Green & Co., 1952]). If wordplays are to be taken seriously, the Egyptians may have believed that the heavens were made of meteoric iron, since pieces of it occasionally fell to earth. See L. Lesko, "Ancient Egyptian Cosmogonies and Cosmology," in *Religion in Ancient Egypt* (ed. B. Shafer; Ithaca, N.Y.: Cornell Univ. Press, 1991), 117.

54. Occurs only here in the Old Testament but is used in later Hebrew with this meaning.

55. Conveys a combination of stupification and astonishment.

56. Think here of Aslan's growling roar in the Chronicles of Narnia.

57. Can refer to the primordial retreat (cf. Ps. 104:7) when the land emerged from the water, to the retreat of the waters of the Red Sea for the Israelite crossing (Ps. 106:9), or to cosmic judgment (2 Sam. 22:16/Ps. 18:15; Isa. 50:2; Nah. 1:4).

chaos and disorder. For instance, in *Enuma Elish*, Anu creates the four winds that stir up Tiamat.[58] Bringing this understanding to Job, the cosmic creature Rahab (discussed in connection to Job 9:13, p. 171) is roused by the agitation of the sea. God's power enables him to stir up the sea, but it is his understanding (*tebunah*) that gives him victory. This same understanding enabled him to set the heavens in place (Prov. 3:19; Jer. 10:12). M. Fox describes the word as skill expressed specifically in a functional capacity.[59] The presence of this word might suggest that, regardless of our translation of the Hebrew verb *mhs*, we ought to understand God's action toward Rahab as a positive act of ordering rather than a negative act of destruction.[60]

In *Enuma Elish*, Marduk divides Tiamat's body and uses the two halves to form the waters above and the waters below. The NIV's translation of *mhs* as "cutting in pieces" is problematic because most other uses of this verb are not this specific.[61] Something more along the line of "smite" is more probable, given the other occurrences in the Old Testament and the usage in Ugaritic, as in the story of Baal and Mot, col 1, line 1: *ktmhs. ltn.btn.brh:* "As you smote Litan, the fleeing servant."[62] Contexts suggest someone dealing a deathblow. We might well wonder how such smiting could be an act of ordering. One could propose that God's understanding is involved because it takes specialized skill to dispatch a great cosmic creature like Rahab. This reading finds comparative support in the Akkadian stories *Enuma Elish* and The Tale of Anzu, wherein the victor god needs to possess special knowledge and weapons in order to defeat the chaos opponent.

To resolve the conundrum of this verse, I tentatively follow Clines in taking the verb *rg* not as "churn" but as the *rg*[2], "to still" (cf. Jer. 50:34).[63]

---

58. Dan. 7:2 (this Aramaic portion of Daniel uses the verb *gwh*; see Isa. 51:15 and the mention of Rahab being cut to pieces a few verses earlier in 51:9; *Enuma Elish* 1.105–110.

59. Fox, *Proverbs 1–9*, 159.

60. In Isa. 51:9 the form is the strikingly similar *mhsbt*, putatively a participle from the root *hsb*, though the Vulgate and 1QIsaᵃ read it as *mhst*, from the same root used in Job. The versions were probably attempting to harmonize with Job because nothing in the context explains the addition of the *b*. The verb in Job, *mhs*, usually means "crush" while the one in Isaiah, *hsb*, usually means "dig" or "hew." Consequently, neither is easily understood as "cut in pieces." The cognates of these two verbs are used in parallel in Ugaritic, in the Baal cycle concerning Anat's battle (*CTA* 3/*KTU* 1.3 II.5–6, 29–30), see Parker, *Ugaritic Narrative Poetry*, 107–8 or *COS*, 1.86, p. 250.

61. Num. 24:8, 17; Deut. 32:39; 33:11; Judg. 5:26; 2 Sam. 22:39; Job 5:18; Pss. 18:38; 68:21[22], 23[24]; 110:5, 6; Hab. 3:13.

62. *COS*, 1.86, p. 265.

63. Clines, *Job 21–37*, 623; though unquestionably the use of the same verb refers to churning up the waves in Isa. 51:15 and Jer. 31:35, mitigating any confidence we can have in this solution.

In this interpretation God stills the sea by his strength—and he does so by dealing a deathblow to Rahab (using his great skill). Thus, like all the other statements in the cosmological hymn, this is an act of bringing order, which particularly fits with the parallel defeat of "the gliding serpent" (*naḥaš bariaḥ*), another chaos creature mentioned in the next verse. Though we must observe the use of this word for serpent in Genesis 3, we should more importantly recognize the connection with Isaiah 27:1, where Leviathan is described as a *naḥaš bariaḥ* in a group of terms cataloguing chaos creatures. Note also the same phrasing in the Ugaritic text cited in the previous section. More difficult questions surround the first line of verse 13: "By his breath the skies became fair" (NIV). Most interpreters have understood that the line indicates God's overcoming another chaos creature connected with storm. Thus in verse 12 he stills the sea and in verse 13 he calms the storm; both acts of ordering are accomplished by overcoming chaos creatures.[64]

Job 27:1–6. These verses are extremely significant, for they contain Job's final response to the case of his friends, who have argued from the converse logic of the RP that if the wicked suffer, those who suffer must be wicked. By urging Job to confess blindly in order to regain prosperity, they have unwittingly become representatives of the Challenger.

The oath formula that begins Job's speech, "As surely as God lives," shows that Job is not simply making a serious statement but is delivering an ultimatum to his friends—further debate will be useless.

Job's next two statements concern what God has done to him: "denied me justice" (Hiph. *sur* + *mišpaṭ*) and "made me taste bitterness of soul" (Hiph. *mrr* + *nepeš*). Though at one level they can be affirmed, these two statements summarize Job's flawed view of God, which he has expressed before: God has not provided justice for Job (either in the initial strikes or in Job's requests for legal proceedings), and God has caused his suffering. The flaw is not in the blunt facts (Job's suffering at God's hand), but in what he implies about God's character as he reiterates those facts.

The first phrase uses the same root that described Job's devotion in the early chapters of the book: He "shunned evil" (1:1). Here, however, God has caused justice to turn aside. In particular, Job probably means that God has denied him the right to defend himself in court. The second phrase resembles Naomi's expression in Ruth 1:20, when she indicates that God has caused her calamities.

---

64. Unfortunately, the word that the NIV translates "became fair" (*šiprah*) is uncertain, but cannot be further clarified at this point.

Job expresses his lifelong commitment in six phrases, each of which is discussed below.

- "My lips will not speak wickedness [*'awlah*]." The term used here has occurred at several key points in the book (see 24:20 and esp. 13:7). Job previously insisted that there was no wickedness on his lips (6:30). We have found that the word concerns misrepresentation, best describing one who is two-faced or hypocritical.

- "My tongue will utter no deceit [*remiyyah*]." This statement parallels the previous line. The two nouns *'awlah* and *remiyyah* were also used in parallel in 13:7, but there they concerned the friends' depiction of God. Here Job uses them in reference to his own reputation. "Deceit" is a good translation. Job is insisting that his words align with his behavior.

- "I will never admit you are in the right [Hiph. *ṣdq*]." We have seen Job use this verb many times, referring to his righteousness or his desire to be vindicated, but this is the only time he uses the Hiphil form.[65] In the Hiphil stem, this verb indicates an action of declaring someone righteous or innocent, legally acquitting them of guilt or blame. Job is refusing to allow that his friends have accurately assessed his character.

- "I will not deny my integrity [*tmm*]." This statement uses the vocabulary that has characterized Job since the first chapter; he has been proclaimed blameless or innocent at every turn. The verb used here also occurs in 27:2 (Hiph. *sur*). Though God has denied his rights, Job will not deny his integrity. It is important to reiterate that "integrity" is not an all-inclusive category. Job has not committed any sins that would explain or deserve his treatment, but this does not mean that he is free of all sin or offense. It also does not mean that his concept of God is wholly accurate or that he is justified in all of the accusations that he has hurled at God. Job has made mistakes in assessing the situation, but he has never given up his belief in the intrinsic value of disinterested righteousness. Had Job demonstrated that he was not primarily interested in righteousness for its own sake, he would have forfeited his integrity. If he had been willing to blindly confess to unknown crimes to regain his

---

65. The Hiphil form of the verb occurs in a handful of other passages: Ex. 23:7; Deut. 25:1; 2 Sam. 15:4; 1 Kings 8:32; 2 Chron. 6:23; Ps. 82:3; Prov. 17:15; Isa. 5:23; 50:8; 53:11; Dan. 12:3.

prosperity (as his friends suggested), that integrity would have been forfeited.

- "I will maintain my righteousness [*ṣdq*]." This line confirms the manner in which he is maintaining his integrity. He is neither clinging to his rights nor to his losses. He is not demanding restoration of his prosperity.
- "My conscience [heart] will not reproach me [*ḥrp*]." This verb occurs only five times in the Qal stem and can refer to a variety of denigrating taunts.[66] Though none of the other occurrences feature the heart as the subject, this context makes Job's assertion clear enough: His outward denials of wrongdoing do not contradict his inmost knowledge. He harbors no secret sins.

At a basic level, our interpretative task would have been simpler if Job had stopped after verse 6. Job 27:7–23 now sounds anticlimactic, and it is easy to see why some ascribe these verses to one of the friends. But our procedure has been to grapple with the text as it stands, and we will treat this section in that same way.

Job begins (27:7–10) by cursing his enemies, defined in 27:7b as those who stand (Hith. of *qwm*)[67] against him. By this point in the book we might well imagine that Job counts his three "advisors" as enemies, in that they have opposed and condemned him. This understanding follows naturally from 27:1–6. Just as they have implicitly condemned him, he now does the same to them. Anyone who opposes him, a godly man, would naturally be considered godless (*ḥanep*)[68] — if the shoe fits. . . .

In 27:11–12 he again addresses the friends directly. Job initially asked for their instruction (6:24), which they offered in the form of teaching (8:10). Now Job again turns the tables, assessing their instruction as nothing but "meaningless talk." Here Job uses the term that forms the theme of Ecclesiastes (*hebel*). I interpret the word as referring to that which is incapable of bringing ultimate satisfaction or contentment.[69]

Job now returns to a discussion of God's interaction with the wicked (27:13–23). Unlike his previous treatment of this topic (24:18–24), Job here specifically mentions God's retributive action (though God is only

---

66. Besides here, 2 Sam. 23:9, taunting the enemy; Ps. 69:10, insulting God; Ps. 119:42, accusers taunting; Prov. 27:11, adversaries taunting.

67. Four other occurrences of *qwm* in the Hithpael: Job 20:27; Pss. 17:7; 59:[12]; 139:21.

68. Previous uses in Job 8:13; 13:16; 15:34; 17:8; 20:5.

69. Job has considered his own life to be *hebel* (7:16), his attempts to find justice as *hebel* (9:29), and the advice of his friends to be *hebel* (21:34). In a later chapter Elihu will label Job's talk as *hebel* (35:16).

named in v. 13). Still, in this context, Job only speaks of a general fate allotted by God, not a specific act of judgment; thus, he does not contradict his statement in 24:12.

Bridging Contexts

AS WE CONTINUE TO trace the rhetorical development through the series of speeches, the brevity of the third series shows that most of the arguments have been covered. The friends have tried seducing Job into appeasement by holding out the hope of restoration (cycle 1) and by humiliating Job with the insinuations inherent in the RP (cycle 2). All that is left is outright accusation. Because the Challenger's case depends on Job's admission of guilt (as proof that Job is only interested in benefits), the friends continue to abet the Challenger by urging Job to confess. The friends advocate this response because their entire worldview depends on the RP (remember, that is the corner of the triangle where they have staked their claim). If Job is suffering for something other than wrongdoing, there is no equity or stability in the world. For them, such a concession would necessitate nihilism.

Rhetorical Issues

IN THIS THIRD CYCLE of dialogues, the spiritualist, Eliphaz, is left to enumerate the offenses in the indictment (22:5–11). Bildad the traditionalist has nothing new to say, as his mere six verses attest. He is left blithering the unsatisfying conclusion, "OK, man is nothing more than a maggot." Zophar, the rationalist, has nothing at all to say in the third series. The absence of a speech by Zophar reveals that rationalism has been silenced, not that the text has been corrupted. The series concludes in chapter 27 as Job defiantly rejects all accusations; he will never budge from his integrity.

The third series is laid out as follows:

Eliphaz: ch. 22	Job: chs. 23–24
Bildad: ch. 25	Job: chs. 26–27
Zophar: no speech	

Eliphaz: All your talk of a mediator and a hearing is hollow — a smokescreen. God obviously knows your wicked deeds of injustice — you have gotten what you deserve, and I for one am glad of it. Your best course of action is to start listening and stop arguing; when you do, just imagine all the benefits and favor you will again enjoy.

Job: If only I could find God! I fantasize about what that would be like, but it is hopeless. I *am* innocent and *he* knows it. What a terrifying position to be in! Why doesn't God do something about this mess? Oppressive people do whatever they want without any accountability while poor people trying to scrape out a living suffer under their unchecked tyranny. Criminals go about their business unrestrained, but I am still convinced that there is no future for such people—their wickedness will catch up to them eventually.

The main rhetorical progress in this series is found in Eliphaz's direct accusation against Job. After dismissing Job's attempts at legal action as ridiculous, he accuses him of injustice. Why does Eliphaz select these particular charges? In the Original Meaning section we noted that these are generic offenses, evident throughout the ancient Near Eastern legal literature. The gods expected order within society, and the king (as appointee of the gods) was responsible for establishing such order. Furthermore, just behavior was also one of the most basic responsibilities of citizens of the ancient world, a universal expectation.[70] At the same time, though justice could be evident in one's public life, private life also held many opportunities to be just or unjust. Eliphaz's accusations address Job's private offenses in individual situations that would have had no witnesses but the voiceless victims.

Eliphaz's first speech advised Job to appeal to God (5:8), and Zophar's first speech urged Job to put away whatever sin he might have committed (11:13–14). But in both of these, the actual presence of sin was hypothetical. Against the NIV, 11:14 says, "If there is sin in your hand, renounce it."[71] Here Eliphaz uses similar vocabulary but revised syntax as he finally calls Job to repent. "Look at all you will get out of it and all the good you can do! You will be able to help people just like you (caught in an ambiguous situation and thus exposed to accusation)." This speech therefore suggests that Job, by virtue of repentance, could take his place among those who are able to advise by experience. His testimony of sin, judgment, repentance, and restoration could provide great encouragement to others.

---

70. For discussion, see Walton, *Ancient Near Eastern Thought*, 149–61, 283.

71. Cf. Clines, *Job 1–20*, 253 and note on 256. The "if" is with sin, not with the verb as the NIV has it. The verb is an imperative form, not a second masculine singular imperfect as apparently emended by the NIV.

Job, however, insists on his innocence (23:12) and envisions an entirely different scenario. In contrast to Eliphaz's confidence that everything will turn out fine in the end, Job envisions a world awaiting reconciliation to the ideal; he is powerless to set things right. Job is looking beyond his own circumstances to the disharmony that is evident throughout the world. Eliphaz wants Job to focus on himself; Job is more concerned about a world run amok. But even in the dissonance, Job finds a glimmer of hope: If the wicked can prosper for a time, isn't it possible that the righteous can suffer for a time? Temporary circumstances cannot evidence one's moral character. This constitutes a potential chink in the RP.

Eliphaz: Repent, be restored, and go on the lecture circuit.

Job: Look around you! Who can think about self when the world is so out of sync?

Bildad: God is unimaginably great; humans are intrinsically flawed and don't ultimately matter anyway.

Job: Your position is preposterous and totally unpersuasive. You have referred to God as establishing order, but you haven't begun to grasp the immensity of God's work. Yet for all of the order that he has established in the cosmos, he has brought nothing but disorder to my life. Nevertheless, I will *never* follow the advice that all of you have offered. My righteousness is all I have and I will cling to it until the end. You have become my enemies, and therefore God's enemies, so we all know what is in store for you.

Job's last speech expresses a combination of his awe of God (26:7−14), his resolve (27:1−6), and his despair (27:11−23). His hymn is one of the most extensive creation hymns in Scripture. It functions rhetorically to indicate our negligible knowledge of the order that God has established. I draw this conclusion from 26:14, where Job characterizes his reports as but a "faint whisper."[72] If little is known and if displays of God's power are difficult to understand, one should then expect that not everything will make sense. Interestingly, God later demonstrates this point to Job even more powerfully in his own speeches.

---

72. The translation of this word (*šemeṣ*) as "faint whisper," as we have found so often with terms used in the book of Job, is far from certain (appears only here and in 4:12), but most agree on this general direction, which also derives some support from cognates and later Hebrew.

Job's determination in 27:1–6 forms the climax of the dialogue section of the book. It proves that Job's righteousness *is* disinterested and that the Challenger's contention against God's policies will not stand scrutiny. Job makes no mention of getting his benefits back but shows every intention of clinging to his integrity. *His integrity is demonstrated in his resolve to live according to righteousness, whether it pays or not.* He believes that righteousness can be objectively defined, unlike the ancient Near Eastern view that righteousness is randomly determined by the gods. The people of the ancient world believed that they could know that they were doing right when they experienced the favor of the gods; alternately, they knew that they had committed some offense when the gods withdrew their favor and subjected them to oppression. Such a system cannot conceive of righteousness for righteousness' sake. Disinterested righteousness would be an oxymoron.

This mind-set is what we have been calling the Great Symbiosis: People meet the needs of the gods and the gods meet the needs of the people. Needs define the system. "Doing right" means meeting the needs of the gods, and you know you have done right when they meet your needs. Righteousness is tangential—secondary at best. Given this information, the book of Job would have made no sense to a Canaanite or Babylonian. Who could think of serving a god for nothing? Why would you? How could you know you were serving him? The book of Job is thus a stunning literary monument in the history of theological development.

If Job intends the last section (27:7–23) as a virtual curse on his friends, his imprecations suggest what fate they will/should suffer.[73] Rather than Job joining their circles as an adviser (implication of Eliphaz's speech in ch. 22), Job suggests that they will join his circle as victims—a message of despair for them, but also for him since he does not imagine a way out of his predicament. Job may well be teaching about the fate of the wicked from his own experience of being treated by God as if he were wicked. His statement in 27:11 could be paraphrased, "You think you can explain God's power? I have *experienced* the power of God and I will tell you all about it."

Bildad: Face the facts that tradition knows well.

Job: God's immense power has brought order to the cosmos but not to my life. I am God's victim and you will be too. Here I stand with only my righteousness to cling to.

---

73. Smick, "Job," 972.

The philosophical focus and resolution in this series of speeches hinges on whether or not Job will admit to sin. Eliphaz explicates his accusations, which Job resolutely denies. This series completes the friends' role. Job is not seduced by the prospect of renewed benefits (series 1, Job 4 – 14), he concludes that the system known as the RP is broken (series 2, Job 15 – 21), and he refuses to admit wrongdoing as the cause of his calamity (series 3, Job 22 – 27). He has proven that his righteousness is not founded on the expectation of reward. As star witness for the defense, he has demonstrated that there *is* such a thing as disinterested righteousness. Job thus disproves the Challenger's claim that God's policy of rewarding the righteous was counterproductive. The friends, who represented the Challenger's case, have been silenced. Case dismissed.

But what about Job's claim? God's policies have not only been questioned by the Challenger ("counterproductive for righteous people to be rewarded") but also by Job ("irrational for righteous people to suffer"). The remainder of the book will address this other side of the dilemma.

Theological Issues

AS IN THE PREVIOUS sections, we will explore some of the theological issues suggested by these speeches, though we fully realize that the book has not adopted these as its message. The friends and Job all have pieces of truth, but their views do not carry the authority of the text. However, we can explore their perspectives to see whether we share some of the same shortsightedness about God and the world.

Eliphaz's theological warnings. Eliphaz begins with the difficult statement concerning Job's inability to resolve his predicament, using the tactics he had adopted (22:2 – 3). The NIV's translation has Eliphaz questioning whether anything that humans could do would bring pleasure to or benefit God. Though I feel that such a translation cannot be sustained, it suggests an interesting discussion. Since I have gone a different direction with the translation, I will not elaborate my position further, except to say that, while we cannot benefit God (i.e., complete a deficiency or meet a need), he does take pleasure in our righteousness and faithfulness.

My preferred translation portrays Eliphaz asking Job whether God will respond favorably to Job's course of action. Job's procedure has involved (1) denying any wrongdoing (justifying himself), (2) requesting a mediator, and (3) demanding God to appear in court. Eliphaz's two questions are: (1) Will a mediator do any good? and (2) Will God be pleased that you justify yourself at his expense? These rhetorical questions suggest negative answers with which we could find reason to agree. We will look at each one individually.

Will a mediator do any good? In Job's case this is ironic; he wants someone to hold God accountable—precisely the role that the Challenger has played. Rather than resolving Job's predicament, the mediator instigated it. But this is not Eliphaz's point. He implies that even skillful negotiators could not represent God to our benefit. Eliphaz considers God too remote from even the angels for any being to intervene adequately.

Moving beyond the understanding of Eliphaz and Job, we must consider God's remoteness as a theological concept. People today commonly think of God as too remote to care, yet the revelation of both Old and New Testaments contradict this notion. The testimony of the incarnation in the New Testament is enough, but even the Old Testament makes the case clearly, as the following samples attest:

1. "What other nation is so great as to have their gods near them the way the LORD our God is near us whenever we pray to him?" (Deut. 4:7)
2. "The LORD is close to the brokenhearted and saves those who are crushed in spirit." (Ps. 34:18[19])
3. "The LORD is near to all who call on him, to all who call on him in truth." (Ps. 145:18)
4. "'Am I only a God nearby,' declares the LORD, 'and not a God far away?'" (Jer. 23:23)

Furthermore, one of the most important theological foundations of the Old Testament, the covenant, is based on the nearness of God.[74]

Beyond the issues of revelation and God's presence, the center of the New Testament speaks of God's provision of a mediator (1 Tim. 2:5). I hasten to add that this was not the kind of mediator that Job and Eliphaz were discussing. Job wanted a mediator to explain God's actions in relation to his personal circumstances and to represent his righteousness to God. Christ's mediation for us in the New Testament consists, not of representing our righteousness before God, but of offering a sacrifice for our sin and interceding for us. This development moves far beyond Job's imagination or interest.

Will God be pleased that you justify yourself at his expense? The short answer, of course, is "No," and God expresses his displeasure over Job's attempt to do so in 40:8. Theologically, only a flawed view of God would allow anyone to suggest that they are in the right, thereby necessitating that God is in the wrong. Yet it is natural for fallen humans to mistrust God and to doubt his attributes.

---

74. Cf. J. Walton, *Covenant: God's Purpose, God's Plan* (Grand Rapids: Zondervan, 1994).

Christians easily talk about the authority of the Bible, but they often neglect to think through the implications of this concept. I think that most Christians see the authority of the text in terms of its content/nature (truth) and their response (obedience). Both of these concepts proceed from authority: truth, because the speaker's words reflect his character; obedience, because God has the right to tell us what to do. This concept of truth often becomes part of the argument for the historical accuracy of the Bible: What it says happened, happened; people who it says lived, lived.

Without desiring to take anything away from those two important perspectives, I suggest there is a third aspect that is actually more important than the other two, because they derive from it; yet this third aspect is often neglected. Since we believe that the Bible is most fundamentally God's revelation of himself, the most basic idea of the text's authority derives from its portrayal of God. When we submit to the authority of the text, we are embracing—without exception or qualification—its portrayal of God. We cannot adopt only the parts we like and reject the parts that we find disturbing. When something seems awry in his portrayal, we ought to give God the benefit of the doubt.

Furthermore, this authoritative picture of God insists that the God of the Old Testament is the same as the God of the New Testament—incarnate in Christ. Whatever we, in our limited humanity, might think looks like a flaw in God's character or an inconsistency in his behavior testifies only to our inadequacies, not to his. This remains true whether the supposed problems occur in the biblical stories or in our own experiences. If submitting to the authority of the Bible means the unqualified acceptance of its presentation of God, no room is left for us to justify ourselves at his expense, to think that we could do something better than God, or to suggest that we could be more compassionate, more merciful, more loving, or more just.

When we as Christians are asked to explain our understanding of God, we can point only to the testimony of the Bible. If we arbitrarily pick and choose acceptable texts, we illegitimately set ourselves over the authority of the Scripture. If we are willing to construct our own view of God from our perceptions and experiences, we are setting ourselves up as the authority rather than submitting to biblical authority. We thus admit that the pluralists are right: Anyone can construct their own view of God. What would make one person's reconstruction any more or less accurate than another's? If we accept the biblical view, then we can stand on its authority. If we waver, then any human authority is as good as another.

Those of other faiths sometimes inquire how Christians can arrogantly assert that Christianity is right and other religions are wrong (to some extent at least), or to maintain that Christ is the only way. Our only defense against these questions lies in biblical authority: These are not our ideas, but the Bible's revelation. We can only say that we take such difficult positions because of the testimony and authority of the Bible. If we do not consistently adopt the Bible's presentation of God, the argument crumbles.

Our determination not to justify ourselves at God's expense rests on our confession:

- When God's behavior does not make sense, we give him the benefit of the doubt.
- We cannot outdo God in any of his attributes.
- We take all or nothing of the Bible's portrayal of God.
- If we try to pick and choose to construe our own "mix 'n match" picture of God, we have set ourselves up as God.

This is what the authority of the Bible is about, and this is the faith position that we adopt when we accept its authority.

God's judgment. As we read Job 24, we might easily find ourselves sympathizing with Job's burning questions. Why *doesn't* God set times for judgment (24:1)? Why *doesn't* God charge people with wrongdoing when they are so obviously guilty (24:12)? It is no comfort to say that we all stand guilty before God—that is not the discussion here. Who enforces the system? Job wants to know—and so do we often enough. Oppression of every sort runs rampant while innocent people suffer. What is God doing? Nothing, we fear. What kind of God is this? Some reach the point of indifference, having concluded that God is not worthy of their recognition. If God truly weeps over the condition of the world, how can he adopt such a "hands-off" posture? Even when we are able to give God the benefit of the doubt (therefore not suggesting that he is flawed or that we are superior), we still have questions.

Though these questions can be addressed from a philosophical perspective, in terms of theodicy (defending the justice of God or investigating the origin of evil), we often are more interested in our own experiential understanding. In the end, the book of Job will offer answers that encourage us to trust the wisdom of God, but we will wait until we reach the conclusion to explore these answers in more depth. At this point our focus must turn to the fallen world in which we live.

A fallen world is intrinsically defined by wickedness. If there were no wickedness, the world would not be fallen. No matter how much wickedness God might eliminate, we could always find more wicked people to complain about (defining "the wicked" as anyone we see as more wicked than ourselves). If all wickedness were eliminated, the world would no longer be fallen and none of us would exist. We see this idea in Shakespeare's *Merchant of Venice*, when Portia, posing as a judge, addresses the Jew, Shylock:

Therefore, Jew,
Though justice be thy plea, consider this,
That, in the course of justice, none of us
Should see salvation: we do pray for mercy.[75]

Why does God mercifully maintain a fallen world?[76] Why did he not destroy Adam and Eve for their sin and start over? When examining Job 4 – 14, we asked whether some attributes of God trumped others, and we concluded this is not the case (p. 190). The question about the fallen world deals with the same issue. Is it more important or more natural for God to be just (having no tolerance for a fallen world) or to be compassionate (sparing his creatures despite their fallenness) and gracious (providing a means of reconciliation)? I would contend neither is the case. It is just as characteristic for God to be gracious as it is for him to execute justice. We cannot think that justice is the default while mercy requires a conscious departure from standard operating procedure. God's attributes carry equal sway within his being, and he operates with all of them held in perfect balance.

If it is not contradictory to the character of God to tolerate a degree of fallenness, is there a degree at which fallenness *would* become contradictory? Does God allow sin only to a certain limit?[77] How would the limits be defined? Answers to such questions would have to be premised on God's purposes rather than his character. To what end does God maintain a fallen world, and how does he ensure that it will accomplish his goals? We must seek answers to these questions through the revelation God has given us or through observations of what we and others experience (descriptive approach) rather than through logic (rationalistic approach designed to devise coherence).

That brings us back to the beginning with only our own bewildering observations. Does God intend our good? We would have to take the Bible's word for it that he does (Rom. 8:28). Should we be able to figure out how our experiences benefit us? Not necessarily (note Eccl. 6:12). Is our "good" defined by our comfort or our success? Often not. Consequently our normal criteria for judging what is for our good do not help us to draw sound conclusions. Yet still we ask, how could the prosperity of the wicked possibly contribute to our "good"?

Job's deteriorating concept of God. When life goes wrong, often one of the first results is that our concept of God deteriorates, and this is

---

75. Act IV, scene 1, 197 – 200; thanks to Joshua Valle for bringing this to my attention.

76. Of course, whenever we ask why God does anything, we can only speculate. C. S. Lewis observed that our conjectures concerning God's actions would be equivalent to our dogs' observations of us as we read the morning paper.

77. Gen. 18:20 – 21 and Jon. 1:2 suggest there *are* limits.

certainly the case for Job. The deterioration takes root in perhaps small misconceptions, but these gradually become major misrepresentations of the divine character. Tracking the path of decline in Job will help us to understand how our minds work.

Section and Theme	Reference	Divine Characteristic or Behavior
Narrative and lament Potential pettiness	1:4–5	Potentially petty
	1:21	Gave and took away
	2:10	Gives trouble as well as good
	3:23	Hedges in
Cycle 1 Uncontestable power Overdemanding	6:4; 7:14	Terrorizes him
	7:17–19; 10:14–17; 14:6	Overattentive
	7:21	Unforgiving
	9:2–3	Unapproachable, unrestrainable
	9:14–20	Power abuser
	9:22	Indiscriminate destroyer
	10:3	Not forthcoming about offense
	12:13–25; 14:20	All-powerful for good or ill
Cycle 2 Unrelenting assault Overaggressive	16:7–14	Assailant
	17:6	Ruined reputation
	19:6–20	Made a mess of life in his anger
Cycle 3 Unaccountable judge Inaccessible	23:8–9	Remote
	23:13	Unaccountable
	24:1, 12	Lax in execution of judgment
	26:7–14	Incomprehensibly powerful
	27:2	Denied plea, made bitter
	27:11–23	Devastating to the wicked

Job's ideas certainly do not develop as a systematic trajectory. Job is making the mistake that we would all make: inferring the nature of God from his experiences (and thus coming to many wrong conclusions). The divine attributes in the chart are neither taught in the Bible nor promoted/affirmed by the book. Likewise we can see that Job's concept of God cannot be considered above reproach. In one sense, Job's friends have a more orthodox approach, in that they do not adjust their view of God to accommodate Job's innocence. Instead, they are willing to question Job's innocence.

Job's thought progression reflects the common complaints that people make against God. In trying to please a holy God, many look through the Bible and conclude that God *asks* too much. Once we reach this conclusion, we can become critical when we perceive God acting on the basis of what he has asked and then conclude that he is too intrusive: God *does* too much. If we persuade ourselves that God is demanding and intrusive, we finally decide that he just doesn't care enough about us or our situation. Like the child who thinks that there are too many chores and rules and chafes when he or she receives discipline for falling short of expectations, our ultimate accusation becomes: "You don't love me." Even though Job is not undergoing discipline (though he and his friends all think he is), his comments proceed through the standard sequence.

Accommodationist hermeneutics. We have tried to demonstrate that Job's cosmic hymns (9:4–10; 26:7–13) follow closely the cosmology of the ancient Near East. If we look through the rest of the Old Testament, we should not be surprised to find that this is the case throughout. No passage speaks of the shape or operation of the cosmos in a manner inconsistent with the beliefs of the ancient world; it all conforms to what can be called "Old World Science."[78] God was in the business of revealing himself to his people, and to do so he did not need to give them a more advanced science. Such an action would have been problematic, because then we would have to decide which time period the science reflected. Science changes all the time, so to put revelation in terms of the science of one period would automatically make it anachronistic to earlier periods and obsolete to later periods. Science is not made of facts; it expresses society's consensual understanding of how the world works.[79]

Throughout the twentieth and into the twenty-first century, some biblical interpreters have adopted what is known as a concordist hermeneutic. This approach views the Bible as an expression of modern science. We can force an agreement between the Bible and science either by reading modern science between the lines of the biblical text, or by trying to construct a science from the interpretation of the biblical text. The drawback of these concordist approaches is that they typically end up making the Bible say a whole lot more than it said to the ancients, giving words and phrases new meanings that they never had. One could therefore question whether concordists actually dilute the authority of the Bible (built on authorial intent) in order to salvage "truth" (equated with modern scientific ways of thinking).

---

78. This is true even though some of it might also converge with modern science.

79. D. Ratzsch, *Science and Its Limits* (Downers Grove, Ill.: InterVarsity Press, 2000), esp. 26–27.

As an alternative hermeneutic to the concordist approach, one could adopt an accommodationist hermeneutic—the approach that I have taken here. The accommodationist hermeneutic asserts that to communicate effectively, God accommodated his revelation to the ideas of the day. For instance, if God wanted to communicate that he created everything, he would define "create" and "everything" in terms meaningful to the specific audience. After all, though the Bible was written *for* everyone, it was written *to* Israelites in the ancient world. If the Bible had been written to us, God would have used different terms to say that he created everything. Likewise, if God wanted to describe to us his construction of the cosmos, he would talk about the material world: the first event (big bang?); the way that he set up gravity and hung the planets in space by the laws of motion; the process of beginning life through the atomic, cellular, and molecular levels; all the way to the unique brain chemistry that makes humans the image of God.

But he was talking to ancient Israelites, and all of that would have been meaningless nonsense. This revelation was not intended to be mystical or obscure. Communication requires building on the familiar, so God used Old World Science as the template for communication. The ancients were far less interested in the material cosmos than in the functional cosmos.[80] God spoke in their terms—which are far different from ours—because he was not intending to reveal an authoritative cosmic geography. The point of God's revelation is to assert that, regardless of the details of one's cosmic geography, God set it up and makes it work.

Some have found this accommodationist hermeneutic problematic because it makes some statements of Scripture untrue. The sky is not a solid canopy holding up waters above the earth. The sun, moon, and stars are not inside this solid water barrier. The earth is not a flat disk. But before we let this bother us, we have to look again at our doctrine of biblical authority and inerrancy. Even the statement of the International Council on Biblical Inerrancy pointedly refused to include scientific accuracy in its understanding of the Bible as "inerrant in all that it affirms." God communicates his revelation with certain goals in mind, and it is those goals that constitute revelation and carry authority. Along the way God communicates many incidental matters that are not revelation and do not carry authority. The Bible communicates a spelling of "Nebuchadnezzar" and therefore could be said to tacitly affirm it—but God has no revelation on the spelling of Nebuchadnezzar (and in fact, the Bible spells it two different ways; Jeremiah prefers the more accurate Nebuchadrezzar, e.g., Jer. 21:2). This is an incidental detail and does not carry the burden of biblical authority.

---

80. I have treated this at length in *Lost World of Genesis One*, 23 – 36.

We as scientific human beings made the same kind of conclusions when we decided that we do not have to consider the earth as the center of the universe with the sun moving across the sky. We have also decided that, contrary to the statements of Scripture, cognitive and emotional processes are not carried out by the blood pumps in our chests or by our kidneys. Scriptural authority resides in God's revelatory message, not in the incidentals he uses to communicate that message. Inerrancy describes the nature of revelation and our confidence that it is true. God is who he says he is. He has done what he says he has done. His motives and purposes are what the Bible proclaims them to be. He interacted with the people that the text reports he did.

Nothing in this hermeneutic should surprise us; communication always requires accommodation. When I lecture to any group, whether graduate students in my classes at Wheaton or sixth graders in the classes I teach at church, I have to use words and ideas that they will understand or my communication will fail. God is an effective communicator; therefore, when God chose to reveal himself, to communicate to his creatures, he adopted a course of accommodation. He did not communicate in some universal language using only universal cultural elements; there are no such things (at least not since the Tower of Babel). He spoke to Israelites in an ancient culture, using expressions they understood. Our interpretation begins here.

Some concordists would say that within God's communication to that ancient culture, God was able to embed hints of more sophisticated information — hints that we can now decipher, since we possess advanced knowledge. In other words, the ancients would have comprehended the basic level of the text, but the text has multiple layers, just as we might imagine for prophecy and fulfillment or christological interpretation. Such a system could potentially work if the deeper levels simply build on the surface level, but it is not so easy when the supposed deeper levels contradict the surface level. Either the sun moves around the earth or the earth moves around the sun. Both cannot be true.[81] Furthermore, in prophecy and fulfillment, we typically only accept those adjustments that are confirmed by an authoritative source (i. e., the New Testament).

An accommodationist hermeneutic poses no problem for the doctrine of inerrancy. Inerrancy always requires us to interpret the meaning of the text so we can determine what is inerrant. The book of Job is a great exam-

---

81. Some might claim that the sun moving around the earth is true as a perception, but if that is the way the argument is going to go, one need move no further than the surface level. The truth of the text would not need to be "salvaged" by providing other levels of more scientifically accurate information.

ple because most of the details of the book are wrong: The Challenger is wrong; the friends are partially wrong; Job himself is partially wrong. Inerrancy comes in the interpretation of the book as a whole. The book has to be interpreted to determine what the inerrant message is.

At the same time, it must be admitted that, like any interpretive method, an accommodationist hermeneutic offers its challenges. Where does the accommodation stop and the revelation begin? Should we follow the Levitical dietary laws? Should women wear head coverings? Is homosexuality contrary to God's designs or just a practice despised in ancient culture? Is it permissible to have slaves? Is polygamy an acceptable practice? Should we stone adulterers? Yes, these sorts of questions challenge us, but they are not questions that only occur in the context of an accommodationist hermeneutic. In fact, an accommodationist hermeneutic may enable us to sort some of those out more consistently than we have in the past. But that discussion would exceed the scope of this book.

RIGHTEOUSNESS ALONE. HUMANS (ESPECIALLY Americans) tend to be motivated by self-interest: "What is in it for me?" we ask. We have not only adopted our own self-fulfillment and happiness as a goal, but nearly consider it a right (subconsciously emending the Declaration of Independence to indicate what to us is indeed self-evident, that we have inalienable rights to life, liberty and the pursuit of happiness). Not only has happiness become our ambition, it has often become a spiritual expectation. Our relationship to God looks much like the Great Symbiosis, in that our commitment is premised on anticipated benefits. Often in the process we expect much of God and little of ourselves.

If the book of Job promotes disinterested righteousness as a moral principle, we should explore what this value looks like for our faith to get beyond self-interests. If our righteousness is for righteousness' sake, what will it look like? Taking the lead from the book of Job, we would have to conclude that such a faith would not abandon belief even if life gets difficult. But it is important that we also consider the proper motives for our behavior and our choices. How should we discern what God expects of us and what we should expect of ourselves? How should we live if we want to pursue a faith not premised on self-interests?

In the college context in which I work, students often grapple with behavioral expectations. All the authorities in their lives (whether school, church, or parents) have imposed restrictions on the way they live, each somehow connecting these regulations to biblical authority. It is no wonder, then, that young people misconstrue the Bible as a compendium of rules. As with any set of rules, the challenge too often becomes: "How much can I get away with without getting in trouble?" or "What is the least I have to do to get by?" These sorts of reactions are not just true of teenagers; that mentality stretches easily into our adult lives.

The fact is, we have trouble looking beyond our own self-interests. The goal of our lives, and especially of our faith, is that we become more god-like, not that we become more successful or comfortable. There is nothing wrong with success or prosperity — these can be legitimately pursued, but not as our primary goals or as the motivations of our faith.

When I refer to being godlike, I am not speaking of what we often call piety, devotion, spirituality, or godliness, though such demeanors are not to be gainsaid. I am more concerned here about what motivates our faith and our choices. The pathway we find most natural to follow (as fallen humans) is what I would call the "benefits-driven minimalistic life of faith." It is framed by the two questions already mentioned:

1. What is in it for me? (benefits driven)
2. What is the least I have to do (or most I can get away with)? (minimalism)

Because we tend to see God's requirements in the Bible as "rules," we rationalize giving ourselves permission to do what it does not explicitly forbid. If we conclude that the Bible does not specifically speak against certain sorts of sexual behavior, against the activities we enjoy (but have been told are not spiritual), against the movies we want to watch, against the language we enjoy using, against the way we dress, and so on, we feel free to indulge ourselves with free conscience: "The Bible doesn't say I can't." We may take comfort in all of the dastardly offenses we have not committed and decide that we are "good enough." After all, we are not disobeying the Bible.

This is minimalism in its mature and virulent form. For instance, the Bible says nothing about drug abuse. Some might respond by pulling out a biblical injunction to respect your body, but that is the wrong approach, because it still assumes that we have to dredge up a biblical prohibition or command to regulate every aspect of our behavior. Attempts to explicate all the mandates of Scripture are criticized (truly enough at times) as illegitimate proof-texting that employs questionable hermeneutics and fails to consider cultural context. Let us consider briefly some of the ways that people seek behavioral guidance from the Bible.

Role models. People commonly read the characters of the Bible as role models to either imitate or avoid. Though any literary character can offer a model for behavior, we must ask whether the narrators of the Bible intend to use characters for this purpose. Without discussing this in detail, we must recognize that the biblical authors rarely note whether certain behavior should be imitated or not. Though it is true that narrators may choose the more subtle route of showing rather than telling, ambiguity in the text often leaves us with unanswered questions. Furthermore, motives often make the difference between commendable and repugnant behavior, but motives are rarely revealed. Suffice it to say, this approach cannot provide consistent guidance and fails to address many important considerations. We should look for the authoritative element of biblical narrative in its revelation of God rather than in the behavior of the characters.[82]

Law. We all know that Christians are not required to follow the Old Testament law; however, some Christians argue that we should still use the law as an ethical guide. This approach fails when the criteria for laws we should or should not follow become completely arbitrary. We must formulate a consistent hermeneutic to determine how any law, or the law in its entirety, figures into our ethical behavior. The law was given to the Israelites as a guide to holiness and, in the end, it is holiness that God requires. The law can only give us minimal standards and guidelines. It cannot provide a fully developed ethical system that communicates our full responsibility before God.[83]

Wisdom. Wisdom literature such as that found in the book of Proverbs provides many important guidelines for behavior. Two problems, however, must be noted. (1) The literature contains a combination of guidelines that could be considered universal and those that are more cultural. (2) The coverage of the material is spotty. The literature gives us examples of how we can order our lives based on the fear of the Lord, but it is far from comprehensive, systematic, or programmatic.

Prophets. As we read the indictments against Israel, the prophets give us some helpful information about behavior that displeases God. They help us to understand God's covenant expectations for Israel and his concern because these have been violated. But we are not included in this covenant, and though those prophecies can benefit us, they are not addressed directly

---

82. For more detailed treatment of the problems with this approach, see J. Walton, "Bible-Based Curricula and the Crisis of Scriptural Authority," *Christian Education Journal* 13 (1993): 83–94; J. Walton and A. Hill, *Old Testament Today* (Grand Rapids: Zondervan, 2004), 200–203; R. Chisholm, *Interpreting the Historical Books: An Exegetical Handbook* (Grand Rapids: Kregel, 2006), 28–32.

83. For guidelines of applying the law to ourselves a Christians, see Walton and Hill, *Old Testament Today*, 117–21.

to us. As a result, the prophets can teach us something about the nature of God, but they cannot give us an entire ethical code.

New Testament. We are often more inclined to look to the Gospels and Letters to find our guidelines for life, and well we should. Yet again, we must realize the limitations here. Neither corpus of literature is designed to offer a fully developed guide for behavior. Instead we find occasional exhortations and admonitions, reflections and confrontations. From these we can gain discernment, but even a compilation of all this information cannot give us anything that approaches comprehensive understanding. Furthermore, as with the Old Testament, there are many cultural elements that make direct appropriation problematic.

These brief observations make an important point: The Bible does not readily translate into a comprehensive list of "dos and don'ts for righteous living"; it is even difficult to find answers to particular questions of behavior. Instead of being clear or forthright, we might regularly find that the Bible gives us ambiguous or controversial guidance.

Those who attempt to enforce behavioral constraints, whether through proof-texting or any of these methods, demonstrate a misunderstanding of the problem and seek the solution in the wrong place. The Bible does not have to forbid a behavior for us to consider that behavior wrong. How do we determine parameters for appropriate conduct? What does it mean to be godlike and what it would it look like? How do we avoid the benefits-driven minimalistic life of faith? *Is* there anything in it for us?

Recently I was having a conversation with students who wanted to know how one could or should develop a biblical view of sexual ethics (encompassing everything from pornography and lust to sex outside of marriage and definitions of marriage). What biblical statements have universal validity, and what statements are culturally relative? After all, the institution of marriage was far different in the ancient world than it is today, and the issue of premarital sex is inevitably tied to the definition of marriage. Even as we recognize the need for definitions of purity, we realize that standards of modesty vary from one culture to another. What does godliness look like in this area of behavior? What does God want from us? How do we draw parameters without imposing potentially arbitrary rules? How does one develop biblical standards if the Bible does not yield specific information through role models, the law, or exhortations in the Proverbs or New Testament letters?

Consider these ten principles:

1. We should conscientiously pursue wisdom (in its Old Testament sense), godlikeness, and holiness.
2. Beyond what is clearly stated in revelation, we should not presume to draw parameters for others (e.g., for what constitutes

modesty, humility, appropriate entertainment), only for ourselves; these should reflect our goal (holiness) rather than the lowest common denominator that we can rationalize.

3. The boundaries may differ from culture to culture and perhaps from person to person, but there must *be* carefully thought-out parameters that reflect our desire for holiness.
4. We should not impose our boundaries on others, though we could hold them accountable to their own boundaries and challenge them to aim higher.
5. There must be discernable differences between Christian behavior and the world's behavior (Rom. 12:1–2).
6. We should not concede either to self-righteousness or to self-indulgence.
7. We should understand that God does not need what we give; our behavior can please him but does not benefit him.
8. Our behavior should not be motivated by expectation of material rewards; further, our behavior cannot save us.
9. We should aspire to be godlike, not just to keep rules (which inherently only lead us in the right direction).
10. Obedience is expected but represents the minimal level of godliness.

The path of wisdom, godlikeness, and holiness would rely on Scripture for guidance without necessarily looking to specific texts to lay down hard and fast rules (though it occasionally might and we dare not neglect them when it does). Wisdom brings order to life and relationships, and the wise take God seriously. Wisdom derives from biblical values, but it is not necessarily bound to Israelite culture. Holiness recognizes that aspects of our behavior will sharply distinguish us from those around us. God's holiness is embodied in his distinguishing attributes; we exhibit holiness by reflecting God's communicable attributes (e.g., by exhibiting the fruit of the Spirit). We can build ideas about godlikeness around the biblical text's portrayal of God. Obedience is important, but our end responsibility is to strive to be like God. Disobedience will impede us from reaching this goal, but obedience alone will not necessarily achieve it.

Ideally, we should aspire to holiness, not because of benefits we can gain as a result, but because God is God and our righteous behavior is one of the ways we honor him. Regardless of whether we experience any advantages in life because of these decisions, we choose this path because of who God is.

But could we ever say there isn't anything in it for us? We often experience good feelings when we act altruistically; self-congratulation and feelings of approval can be strong motivators and have their own payoff. As Screwtape comments to Wormwood, when the subject actually experiences true humility, be sure to point him to how self-satisfied and proud he is of his humility.[84]

Two qualifications will help us through this dilemma. (1) The main threat comes from *material* benefits. It is not unworthy to pursue holiness in life in order to achieve the accolade, "Well done, my good servant!" (Luke 19:17), or to run so as to win the prize (Phil. 3:14). No fault need be found in a desire to gain Christ (3:8) or "to attain to the resurrection from the dead" (3:11). (2) We must recall that we are primarily concerned with the *motives* for our actions, not the circumstantial results. We may well obtain a multitude of benefits, material and otherwise, but we must probe deeply into our own hearts to seek out and understand our motivations, asking the Holy Spirit to reveal and purify them.

Finally, we may return to the question that prompted this lengthy discussion: Can we accept our (presumably) innocent suffering and the success of the wicked, based on the opportunity they provide us to learn godliness: forgiveness, humility, patience, joy in adversity, resilience to circumstances, understanding of sin, reliance on God's strength, empathy with others, appreciation of simple joys, and any number of other character-building qualities? I would reply that they do not offer *reasons* for suffering, but they may give us some *recompense* for the fallen circumstances that we endure; bringing good out of evil does not redefine evil as being good. Suffering can produce personal growth like nothing else, but certainly there are times when suffering produces, not maturity, but loss of faith, loss of confidence in God, loss of resolve to pursue godliness, bitterness, and disposal of all virtue and values. In light of these two diverse responses, we might do well to ask, not "Will I suffer in life," but "What kind of sufferer will I be?"

Cole in the movie *The Sixth Sense* confesses to his psychologist, "I see dead people ... all the time ... walking around ... they don't know they are dead ... they see what they want to see." We are likewise surrounded by the dead; some are dead in their trespasses and sins, others are dead in their faith—perhaps embittered because of personal suffering or disillusioned because of the world's depravity. They may have drifted from a once-strong faith, or they may have never achieved a full understanding of faith's essence. There is also a third group of dead people: those who have died to self and sin, crucified with Christ. We are all dead people; the question is, what kind of dead person are you going to be?

---

84. C. S. Lewis, *Screwtape Letters* (1942; repr., New York: Macmillian, 1944), ch. 14.

Example to others. People's stories can have a powerful influence on those around them; the story of Job, told in the book that bears his name, can likewise shape our thinking. On one level we are inspired by the story of his perseverance in righteousness and his resolve in suffering. This is story at its best. Even so, story alone cannot explain the *reason* for his suffering. We don't suffer misfortune so that we can give testimony, though we can give testimony when we suffer misfortune. Testimony is a possible outcome, but not a cause.

Eliphaz encourages Job to give testimony at another level. He wants Job to repent and so gain restoration so that he can testify to others that they ought to respond similarly to their suffering or misfortune (22:28–30). This is no longer testimony about perseverance in difficult circumstances, but testimony of forgiveness and restoration following failure. If we were to use the parable of the prodigal son as an example, the older brother offers the testimony of the one who persevered without wavering, while the younger one offers the testimony of one who returned and was restored.

Our culture abounds with stories of celebrity penitents, moving deftly from depravity to repentance to talk shows and book contracts. We easily see the potential for acting in self-interest, another of the unworthy motivations that the friends offered to Job and that continues to tempt us today. When material gain and influence over others become potential motivators, we are again challenged by the question of disinterested righteousness. We have seen that Job's friends urge him to pursue multiple paths that would expose an underlying, worldly motive for his righteousness; we can identify with these because we know that people primarily act with their own self-interest in the fore.

Kelly's Story[85]

KELLY HAS SHARED SOME of the many opportunities she had to influence others in all the right ways. However, like many people who are suffering through misfortunes or difficult circumstances, she also experienced the often-harsh or frustrating perspectives of well-intentioned people.

JHW: Were there people who suggested your circumstances were somehow caused by sin? What perspectives did you find most frustrating? How did you respond, either verbally or in your own thinking?

Kelly: People have suggested many theories of why certain things in my life have panned out the way they have, but only one person has actually

---

85. Kelly interacts with parts of her story in each Contemporary Significance section. For the introduction to the details of her story, see Contemporary Significance in the commentary on ch. 1, pp. 87–97.

insinuated that my pain was a result of my sin and I was being punished. This conversation happened at a church service. The pastor opened up a time of prayer and encouraged the congregation to pray for others around them. So this woman approached me because she noticed my arm and asked if she could pray for my arm. After she prayed for healing, she began to ask me more questions about the injury.

After hearing more about the situation, you could see her face expression change and she became perplexed. I could almost see it in her face that what I was saying did not line up with her theological perspective. So she asked more questions and then came to the conclusion that all of these painful experiences had to be because of something I was doing. She paused and then looked at me, and in a very sweet tone encouraged me to really analyze myself and my actions, or sin as she saw it, to discover why God is — in so many words — punishing me. She asked me if I thought I had some sins in my life that I had not yet dealt with that were keeping me from being healed or if I were experiencing the pains of the sins of my parents.

Not only is this perspective frustrating because I disagree with it from a theological standpoint, but it is also insulting. I knew her intentions were not to be hurtful, but I was hurt by the carelessness with her words to make such a bold claim of someone she has only met for the first time. This perspective is angering because it says a lot about how that person viewed God and his character. I remember thinking, "Did she really just tell me that the reason I have nerve pain and my arm is paralyzed is because God is punishing me for sin in my life?" I was so surprised by what she had just implied that I was shocked. I didn't know how to react. Do I get into a theological discussion about the loaded statement she just made? I chose to skip that discussion for that day and thanked her for her prayer and went on my way.

JHW: Did some suggest that healing was withheld from you because of your lack of faith? How did you deal with that?

Kelly: In many of the encounters I've mentioned, that was the conclusion people came to. My lack of faith was the only thing that made sense to them as to why I had not been healed. They would feel frustrated and confused when they did not see the result they were expecting. Many would say, "Kelly, I think it is your lack of faith that is keeping you in this state of medical trauma. I think if you really believed God had the power to heal, you wouldn't be in the state you are in." Out of all of the "advice" I've received, I think this was the most hurtful. It really struck me at the core. They challenged my belief in God's healing power, implying it is my fault that I experience the pain that I do. One time I responded by reminding them of Paul, an example I go back to often to keep me in the right mind-set. I told them that Paul had prayed for his thorn to be removed. It was not removed and he was told, "No, my grace is sufficient." Unfortunately most of the time, I wouldn't say much, but I would mull over their words later.

JHW: Were you troubled by your own doubts and dark thoughts concerning these areas?

Kelly: There definitely were times I struggled with doubt. I would doubt myself and my faith at times. Often times I would get home from church after having one of these conversations and would pray, "God, is it my lack of faith or lack of confidence in your healing power that has kept me in this medical state?" I would pray, pleading with God to confront me if for some reason I was misled. But I knew that did not line up with my core beliefs of God and how he handles our world. I knew that God was not punishing me for my sin or my parents' sin, so I would usually dismiss those claims. I also was confident that I did not have a demon in me. My doubts and dark thoughts centered more around my faith—not my faith in regards to believing in Jesus, but rather my confidence in his healing power. I would confuse myself because I know that God does call us to pray with confidence and have faith and hope, but then I remind myself or am reminded that having faith in God's healing power does not mean that we always get the result we are praying for.

To be honest, I sometimes feel as if my life with its share of trials and suffering makes people uncomfortable with their "comfortable God." For some of the people I encountered, I realized that it was difficult for them to be confronted with a woman who is pursuing God and her faith and still experiencing horrible pain, without doubting the faith of the woman. How could God allow a woman who is pursuing him with her heart to experience trial after trial? My story rattled many people's thought patterns on how they viewed their God, and they had to explain my suffering to themselves to keep their image of a "comfortable" God intact.

Job 28

¹"There is a mine for silver
   and a place where gold is refined.
²Iron is taken from the earth,
   and copper is smelted from ore.
³Man puts an end to the darkness;
   he searches the farthest recesses
   for ore in the blackest darkness.
⁴Far from where people dwell he cuts a shaft,
   in places forgotten by the foot of man;
   far from men he dangles and sways.
⁵The earth, from which food comes,
   is transformed below as by fire;
⁶sapphires come from its rocks,
   and its dust contains nuggets of gold.
⁷No bird of prey knows that hidden path,
   no falcon's eye has seen it.
⁸Proud beasts do not set foot on it,
   and no lion prowls there.
⁹Man's hand assaults the flinty rock
   and lays bare the roots of the mountains.
¹⁰He tunnels through the rock;
   his eyes see all its treasures.
¹¹He searches the sources of the rivers
   and brings hidden things to light.

¹²"But where can wisdom be found?
   Where does understanding dwell?
¹³Man does not comprehend its worth;
   it cannot be found in the land of the living.
¹⁴The deep says, 'It is not in me';
   the sea says, 'It is not with me.'
¹⁵It cannot be bought with the finest gold,
   nor can its price be weighed in silver.
¹⁶It cannot be bought with the gold of Ophir,
   with precious onyx or sapphires.
¹⁷Neither gold nor crystal can compare with it,
   nor can it be had for jewels of gold.
¹⁸Coral and jasper are not worthy of mention;
   the price of wisdom is beyond rubies.

¹⁹The topaz of Cush cannot compare with it;
  it cannot be bought with pure gold.

²⁰"Where then does wisdom come from?
  Where does understanding dwell?
²¹It is hidden from the eyes of every
      living thing,
  concealed even from the birds of the air.
²²Destruction and Death say,
  'Only a rumor of it has reached our ears.'
²³God understands the way to it
  and he alone knows where it dwells,
²⁴for he views the ends of the earth
  and sees everything under the heavens.
²⁵When he established the force of
      the wind
  and measured out the waters,
²⁶when he made a decree for the rain
  and a path for the thunderstorm,
²⁷then he looked at wisdom and appraised it;
  he confirmed it and tested it.
²⁸And he said to man,
  'The fear of the Lord—that is wisdom,
  and to shun evil is understanding.'"

THE WISDOM HYMN FOUND in this chapter can be divided into three major sections. Verses 1–11 begins with an extended discussion of mining that serves as an introductory image in the consideration of the difficulty in discovering wisdom. Humankind exerts great effort to draw precious metals from the remote depths of the earth. In verses 12–19 two parallel rhetorical questions turn attention explicitly to something even more precious and more inaccessible: wisdom. This section expands beyond the confines of the opening metaphor, for wisdom is not merely difficult to find but appears utterly inaccessible. Verses 20–28 are also introduced by two parallel rhetorical questions, and these verses provide an answer: God provides the pathway to wisdom, and the fear of the Lord is the foundation on which wisdom is built. It is the key that opens the door to the path of wisdom.

Mining (28:1 – 11)

MINING WAS AN IMPORTANT industry in the ancient world.[1] Mined materials were imported and the products were used in a wide variety of practical and aesthetic undertakings. These materials served as the foundation for technological advancement, production of art, and accumulation of wealth. The discovery of mineral deposits, the technology for extracting them from the earth, and the techniques for refining them were all considered somewhat esoteric, evoking awe and wonder. As the passage outlines, mining requires deep delving in dark, obscure places and produces stunning products (sapphire/lapis lazuli, gold) from what looks common (dust, rock). These aspects will be applied to the search for wisdom; the last line, "brings hidden things to light," provides a summary and transition to the topic of wisdom.

Two issues that arise in this section require some attention. (1) We might ask what significance there is to mentioning the birds and beasts in 28:7 – 8. The reference to the birds of prey is understandable within the context, since they are known for having keen eyesight, and the surrounding verses concern places that are dark and undetectable. Lions, however, do not typically prowl around in such places. Of the numerous Hebrew words for "lion," the one used here is among the least common (seven total occurrences). It is often used in parallel with other words for lion, but in Psalm 91:13 it parallels words for serpent. Furthermore, the phrase at the beginning of Job 28:8 ("proud beasts") is used elsewhere only to refer to Leviathan, who is king of the proud beasts (41:34). These three observations have led to the suggestion that this word for lion could refer to a composite creature: part lion, part serpent.[2] While the suggestion is interesting and has advantages, the data are insufficient to establish the case.

(2) What is the significance of the sources of the rivers in 28:11? In Ugaritic literature the high god El dwells at the source of the two rivers.[3] This is not to say that Job 28:11 is referring to seeking out the dwelling place of deity. Rather, the Ugaritic text confirms that the sources of rivers were commonly considered to be places of cosmic significance. Even Genesis 2 speaks of the source of four rivers being located in sacred space (Eden). The end of this section, therefore, brings the reader to the ultimate cosmic mystery. The core issue of the book of Job is concerned with how

---

1. P. R. S. Moorey, *Ancient Mesopotamian Materials and Industries* (Winona Lake, Ind.: Eisenbrauns, 1999); J. D. Muhly, "Mining and Metalwork in Ancient Western Asia," *CANE*, 1501 – 21.

2. S. Mowinckel, "שׁחל," in *Hebrew and Semitic Studies* (ed. D. Winton Thomas and W. D. McHardy; Oxford: Clarendon, 1963), 95 – 103.

3. Epic of Baal, see *COS*, 1.86 (259), col. 4, line 21.

the cosmos works. The mining illustration speaks of human attempts to understand the inner workings of the cosmos. But the importance of the material cosmos diminishes in light of the question concerning the role of deep wisdom in the cosmos.

Elusive Wisdom (28:12–19)

ONE CAN SEARCH FOR precious metals and find them, given sufficient technology and knowledge. Likewise, though it is difficult, it is possible to explore and discover the sources of rivers. In contrast, wisdom cannot be found and cannot be purchased. It is inaccessible from a human vantage point and beyond value.

To say that wisdom "cannot be found in the land of the living" (28:13) is a bold statement and seems to be contradicted by the concluding statement in 28:28. The examples given in 28:14, however, suggest that 28:13 is an "under the sun" type of statement, similar to those common phrases found in Ecclesiastes. "Deep" and "Sea" are the most inaccessible places in the land of the living, and they confess that they do not harbor wisdom in their depths. The acquisition of wisdom is a human desire that is not attainable by human effort. This quest will not be fulfilled in the human realm by human ingenuity.

The references to "Deep" (*tehom*) and "Sea" (*yam*) are personifications (thus my capitalization here), but there is no reason to consider them deities. These two primary representatives of the cosmic waters were generally believed to have been the first primordial inhabitants of creation, which makes them logical sources for information about wisdom. As always, the author reflects on the cosmos in terms that are familiar to him and his world. The section concludes with a listing of the most precious metals and gems from exotic places. None of these is sufficient to purchase wisdom as if it were a commodity.

Source of Wisdom (28:19–28)

JOB 28:20 REITERATES 28:12 with a change in the verb ("Where can wisdom be found" in v. 12 and "Where then does wisdom come from" in v. 20). This crucial adjustment distinguishes the message of verses 12–19, in which wisdom cannot be "found," from verses 20–28, which suggests that wisdom "comes from" God. The first concerns a search—ultimately unsuccessful; the second concerns a source. In 28:14 it was the Deep and the Sea who answered; in 28:22 it is Destruction and Death who answer. The distinction is again an important one. In 28:12–19 the quest focused on the land of the living, where Deep and Sea are located. In 28:20–28, the quest is extended.

Since wisdom is hidden from every living thing, Destruction and Death are consulted. They have word of it, but they confess that wisdom is not to be found in their realm either. One does not achieve wisdom by moving into the next realm. Sheol offers no heightened levels of awareness.

The word translated "Destruction" is *'abaddon* and "Death" is the familiar *mawet*. As with Deep and Sea in the last section, these are personified but not deified (though in Ugaritic mythology Mot/Death [cf. *mawet*] is a deity who contends with Baal). Abaddon occurs only five times in the Old Testament.[4] In intertestamental literature (*1 En.* 20:2) it takes on the persona of an angel, also evidenced in the New Testament (Rev. 9:11) where its Greek name is Apollyon. Despite those later developments, in the Old Testament Abaddon is a place name, sometimes personified as here, not a demonic creature. Demonology is largely absent in the Old Testament; it developed in Hellenistic Judaism under the influence of the ancient Near Eastern and Persian worldviews (see Introduction, p. 36).

Finally the poem begins moving to its conclusion with the first reference to God in 28:23, who then becomes the subject of the remainder of the sentences. Previously the path to wisdom and its place of dwelling were unknown; now the poem affirms that God knows both path and place. God's relationship to wisdom is elaborated in 28:24–27. We will now evaluate these important theological affirmations one at a time.

28:24. "He views the ends of the earth and sees everything under the heavens." The closest statement made to this in the rest of the Old Testament is in Isaiah 40:28, where Yahweh is the Creator of the ends of the earth. In ancient Near Eastern literature it is typically the sun god from his vantage point in the heavens who is able to see the ends of the earth. From Mesopotamia, a Hymn to Shamash, the sun god, makes affirmations of a similar nature:

> 19 Your splendor covers the vast mountains,
> 20 Your fierce light fills the lands to their limits.
> 21 You climb to the mountains surveying the earth,
> 22 You suspend from the heavens the circle of the lands.
> 27 Regularly and without cease you traverse the heavens,
> 28 Every day you pass over the broad earth.
> 43 To unknown distant regions and for uncounted leagues
> 44 You press on, Shamash, going by day and returning by night.[5]

---

4. Besides here, Job 26:6 (par. to Sheol); 31:12; Ps. 88:11 (par. to *qeber*, "grave"); Prov. 15:11 (par. to Sheol). It most likely was also in the original of Prov. 27:20. For discussion, see M. Hutter, "Abaddon," *DDD*[2], 1.

5. Lambert, *Babylonian Wisdom Literature*, 126–29.

In earlier Sumerian literature, Enlil was praised for the extent of his power:

> Lord, as far as the edge of heaven, lord as far as the edge of the
>   earth,
> From the mountain of sunrise to the mountain of sunset.
> In the mountain/land, no (other) lord resides, you exercise
>   lordship.[6]

Egyptian hymns express similar praises:

> Primeval One (Amun) who created himself,
> Who oversees all his creation, alone,
> Who reaches the ends of the earth each day
> In the sight of all those who walk on it;
> Who shines from the sky, whose visible form is the sun.[7]

The sun god Aten is also praised in these terms:

> You are beautiful, great, dazzling, exalted above each land,
> Yet your rays encompass the lands
> To the limits of all which you have created;
> There in the Sun, you reach to their boundaries[8]

Even though Yahweh is not viewed specifically as the sun god, his attributes include those associated with sun gods in the rest of the ancient Near East.[9] As Clines and many others observe, however, the Wisdom poem here in Job does not identify the gaze of God as a daily occurrence (as it is with the sun gods) but as having taken place in the primordial past and serving as the basis for his creative work.[10] Consequently this statement does not offer a reconsideration of 28:13. Though the path to and the place of wisdom are indeed in the land of the living (the ends of the earth and that which is under heaven), ultimately the inaccessibility of wisdom is most related to its place in time rather than its place in space. Wisdom is to be found in the decisions made in the original arrangement of the cosmos, for wisdom is to be found in the ordering of the components of the cosmos.

---

6. M. Cohen, *Canonical Lamentations of Ancient Mesopotamia* (Potomac. Md.: CDL, 1988), 339–40, cited in Horowitz, *Mesopotamian Cosmic Geography*, 331.

7. J. L. Foster, *Hymns, Prayers and Songs* (SBLWAW 8; Atlanta: SBL, 1995), 57.

8. Ibid., 103.

9. See full treatment of the connections in J. G. Taylor, *Yahweh and the Sun* (JSOTSup 111; Sheffield: JSOT, 1993).

10. Clines, *Job 21–37*, 919–20. He makes a case for the two verbs in v. 24 to be analyzed as preterits (past) rather than continuous present.

Order is not readily observable in daily operations, but it was instrumental in the foundation of creation and is inherent in the ongoing operations. That primordial perspective is inaccessible to humans.

This is an important statement for the case the book of Job is making. Job and his friends think that they know how the cosmos is ordered (the RP with justice as the foundation). God will eventually demonstrate that their model is flawed. God's perspective on the foundation of the cosmos is based on causes (all instigated by him), not on effects (what humans experience). There *is* no foundational principle that runs the cosmos. The cosmos runs by God's continuous and ongoing activity. It is dynamic because he is dynamic; this is why he acts according to circumstance and not by a rigid set of strictures. This is why modern empirical science (which is based on constancy and laws) has to remove God from the equation before it can do anything.

28:25 – 26. "When he established the force of the wind and measured out the waters, when he made a decree for the rain and a path for the thunderstorm." The lead word "when" informs the reader of the point in time at which God was viewing the ends of the earth. He had the whole of the cosmos in mind as he undertook creation. The elements of the cosmos mentioned here are those that have the most impact, both positively and negatively, on human survival and existence, and Yahweh will return to these in his speech (38:8 – 11, 22 – 30). Obviously these statements do not embrace every aspect of the creation of the cosmos. By focusing on those forces whose effects too often appear to work independently of justice, justice and wisdom are juxtaposed.

28:27. "Then he looked at wisdom and appraised it; he confirmed it and tested it." Here God approves creation by the criterion of wisdom — not justice. In other words, when God surveyed the breadth and width of the cosmos and the way that the wind, waters, rain, and thunderstorm had been set up, he concluded that the operations as ordered were characterized by wisdom. This is similar to the Genesis 1 assessment that each aspect of creation was good. In this sense the cosmos was an assertion of his wisdom, and the execution of his creative work successfully reflected his wisdom.

Again it must be noted that this assessment stands in contrast to what Job, his friends, and most of the other people in their world expected. They expected that God would have appraised the cosmos in light of justice because that is what they valued above all else.

28:28. "And he said to man, 'The fear of the Lord—that is wisdom, and to shun evil is understanding." Here the poem reaches its climax and conclusion. Commentators have considered this verse trite, clichéd, contradictory, and anticlimactic, or they have dismissed it as a later addition.

Such reactions are unnecessary, as I will seek to demonstrate below. Also of interest is the fact that the protagonists we have met so far (Job's friends) all have reputations as being among the wisest that the world has to offer; yet somehow the "fear of the Lord" has not figured prominently in their discussions.[11]

Some observations need to be made about the wording of the verse. First, the conclusion is presented as an instruction to humankind ('*adam*); second, it refers to the "fear of Adonai" rather than "fear of Yahweh"; third, unlike the similar saying in Proverbs where fear of the Lord is the *beginning* of wisdom, here the fear of the Lord *is* wisdom; and finally, the phrase "fear of the Lord" is paralleled with an ethical exhortation to shun evil. Each of these requires some consideration.

(1) *Instruction.* Sea, Deep, Destruction, and Death have all had their "say" in which they confessed to knowing little to nothing about wisdom. Now God has his "say," clarifying what humans need to know. Syntactically the instruction can be seen as a result clause following the assessment of wisdom. That is, having appraised and tested wisdom, the result is that he instructs humans to fear Adonai. Fearing the Lord means to take him seriously as opposed to:

- thinking him detached (therefore to be ignored)
- thinking him incompetent (therefore to be treated with disdain)
- thinking him limited or impotent (therefore to be scorned)
- thinking him corrupt (therefore to be admonished)
- thinking him shortsighted (therefore to be advised)
- thinking him petty (therefore to be resented)

Were Job and his friends taking God seriously? Job is identified as one fearing God in the introduction to the book, but his fear of God demonstrated itself at the level of meticulous ritual and conscientious submission. The dialogues, however, show his perception of God to be lacking key components. He is unwilling to give God the benefit of the doubt and inclined to think that God is deficient in some way. The fear of God involves more than recognition that he has the *power* to act for or against people.

Of course God has power, but this context suggests that an issue of *trust* is involved. The fact that wisdom is inaccessible to humans except through God requires that we trust him — and this aspect of trust is therefore included in his instruction to "fear the Lord." We trust that he is not

---

11. Job is identified as fearing God in the introduction, and the term is used again with a variety of nuances in 4:6; 6:14; 9:35; 15:4; 22:4; and 37:24.

detached, incompetent, impotent, corrupt, shortsighted, or petty. Thus we can rest assured in the information that our wisdom is codependent on his and derived from it. This reality has not been expressed in the dialogues between Job and his friends, but it is an essential element for making further progress in the discussion.

(2) *Adonai.* As previously mentioned, the name Yahweh occurs only in the frame narrative and the Yahweh speeches (Job 1–2; 38–42) with the arguable exception of 12:9 (see p. 177 for discussion), so we would not necessarily expect this poem to speak of the fear of Yahweh. What we might expect is that it would refer to the fear of God (*'elohim*) (as in 1:1, 8, 9; 2:3). Adonai is a much vaguer term since it can also refer to human authorities. This is also the only occurrence of Adonai in the book. Furthermore, it is put in the mouth of God (i.e., it is the instruction he is giving); nowhere else in the Old Testament does God refer to himself simply by the title Adonai. This usage is therefore noteworthy and unique on several counts.

Job has already been identified as one who fears God, so to reiterate that concept here only serves to loop the reader back to the opening description of Job. "Fear of Yahweh" would anticipate Yahweh's forthcoming speeches at the end of the book, but Job has not yet encountered Yahweh and that would preempt the book's conclusion. It should be noted that the instruction is not addressed to Job but to humankind, and thus to the reader. For the Israelite reader, the term Adonai moves toward the name Yahweh (from the more general *'elohim*), yet still retains some ambiguity. Somewhere between piety (fear of God) and Yahwism (fear of Yahweh) is the recognition of one's submission to deity. This is what Job lacks, and the book will move to address this deficit. The title Adonai, "lord, master," draws out this element of submission.

(3) *Is Wisdom.* In the previous references to wisdom in the chapter (vv. 12, 20), the noun has a definite article: *the* Wisdom, indicating that it is both fundamental and transcendent. Here in verse 28 there is no definite article. These references must therefore be distinguished. Fear of Adonai is not then being identified as the Wisdom to which God understands the way and that is inaccessible to humans in the land of the living. Fearing Adonai will not give people that Wisdom; it is an act of wisdom as it opens up the path to *the* Wisdom. Furthermore, when people respond to God with the assumption that he is wise, they will enact the fear of Adonai. It is wise to trust God as the path to *the* Wisdom.

(4) *Ethical exhortation.* What comprises the wise fear of Adonai? Here it is equated with turning away from evil. That sounds obvious enough to us, but we have to think in terms of the ancient world. We might recall that Job's fear of God in the first chapter expressed itself in dutiful and

conscientious ritual observance (1:4–5). This was a common reflex in the ancient world. God's assessment of him, however, asserted that Job was a man who had also turned away from evil (1:8—the same vocabulary as used here in 28:28). If Job is already one who fits the criteria cited here, what is the point?

The most reasonable explanation is that this serves as an affirmation and vindication of the stance that Job has adopted as he withstands the assault of his friends. The argument in the dialogues concerns whether Job is going to make a principled stand on his righteousness (this is the integrity that he defended in 27:1–6) or whether he will accede to the advice of his friends and admit to offenses in a strategy designed to recover his prosperity. Fear of Adonai is expressed in righteous behavior—turning away from evil, but not in appeasement of deity presumed to respond to people based on the ways they meet his needs. In this way of thinking, fear of Adonai does not look for patronizing a needy god so that he will leave you alone (inherent in the Great Symbiosis); fear of Adonai looks for upright behavior—true ethical righteousness as Job has insisted.

IN THE INTRODUCTION TO this commentary (pp. 29–31) I have already discussed the difficulties surrounding the identification of the speaker in this Wisdom poem. For the reasons indicated there I am not persuaded that the speaker is Job, Zophar, or Elihu, as others have suggested. I believe that this chapter is best understood as a return to the compiler, the true author of the book whose voice we hear in the prose introduction and conclusion.

Role in the book. In this scenario, this Wisdom poem serves as a transition from the section of the book that has presented the case of the three friends, who in turn have been unwittingly pressing the case of the Challenger. Job has stood firmly against their pressure to pursue a path of regaining his prosperity. Consequently the Challenger's contention that he was motivated by desire for reward has been shown false—Job's *is* a disinterested righteousness.[12]

Nevertheless, this still leaves Job's complaint unaddressed. The Challenger had contended it was bad policy for the righteous to *prosper* because such a

---

12. Note again, as I have previously distinguished, his disinterested righteousness pertains to the fact that he is not motivated by material benefits. The book does not intend to address existential benefits of a subtle sort (e.g., the satisfaction that may derive from a coherent epistemology).

policy would corrupt their motives. Job has contended that it is bad policy for the righteous to *suffer* because that would undermine God's justice. The "wisdom" of the friends has not been wisdom at all, and Job himself has been groping to understand his experiences and how God and the world work.

This poem ultimately affirms that the friends are wrong and Job is right in the sense that wisdom is found in a fear of God that depends on a righteousness that turns away from evil, rather than on one that relies on piety and appeasement and results in divine favor and prosperity. Having concluded the consideration of the case argued by the friends and Challenger, the author turns attention to the contention of Job. The question in the first part of the book was: "Is Job's righteousness disinterested?" In the second part of the book, the question turns to: "Can there be coherence when righteous people suffer?" Real wisdom has not yet been brought to light, and doing so is not an easy task, as chapter 28 indicates.

Job 28 and its view of wisdom. Job and his friends have been assuming that there is a wisdom that humans can acquire that understands life's experiences as an expression of God's justice (the wisdom expressed in the RP). This wisdom that they seek will presumably bring coherency by providing an understanding of how justice is done both in general and in Job's specific situation.

Though wisdom is the key to this understanding, Job and his friends seek a wisdom that is inaccessible and will not fulfill their expectations. "Whatever Job thinks he is doing, his mistake is in presuming that human rationality can grasp and hold the structures of the world in intelligibility."[13]

The poem shifts the book from a search for justice to a search for wisdom. God should be viewed as a purveyor of wisdom rather than a simple purveyor of justice. This offers an alternative model by which to account for reality. C. Newsom captures this with the observation that Job is involved in "the search for something that is not only more precious than gold but beyond all other values. What he seeks, though he may not employ the term *hokmah* [wisdom] for it, is a point of coherency, a vantage point from which God, the world, and his own experience make sense."[14]

God and wisdom. The term used predominantly in Job 28 for wise/wisdom is *ḥakam/ḥokmah*. A study of the root *ḥkm* throughout the Old Testament turns up some surprising results. The Old Testament rarely suggests that God is wise.[15] The noun (*ḥokmah*) refers to that which belongs to God

---

13. C. Newsom, *The Book of Job: A Contest of Moral Imagination* (Oxford: Oxford Univ. Press, 2003), 177.

14. Ibid.

15. The closest possibilities are in Job 9:4 and Isa. 31:2. The stative verb and adjective are used of people. See Zerafa, *Wisdom of God in the Book of Job*, 188.

(Job 12:13) and which is given by God (1 Kings 3:28; 10:24; Prov. 2:6; Eccl. 2:26). God operates in wisdom (Ps. 104:24; Prov. 3:19). God is the one who brought wisdom forth (Prov. 8:22). M. Fox observes about Proverbs 8 that "God acquired/created wisdom as the first of his deeds. Wisdom was 'born' (vv 24, 25) at that time. She did not exist from eternity. Wisdom is therefore an accidental attribute of the godhead, not an essential or inherent one."[16]

Wisdom should be understood as that which brings order and coherence. Since before there was creation there was only God, there was nothing for God to provide coherence for and no one to seek coherence. Order implies a relationship of things and there was nothing else. God is the author of order and the foundation for coherence, but one would not speak of God himself, alone, as coherent or orderly. Only as creation was put in place could God envision order and inculcate it into the cosmos. One can then say that God was exercising wisdom to do so, but to say that God is wise understates God's nature. Affirmations such as "God is wise," "God is good," or "God is holy" are misleading and ultimately reductionistic, though the Bible makes such statements legitimately. The adjectives themselves find their definition in God, so one may as well say "God is God"—a philosophically meaningless tautology. Humans can only approach wisdom, goodness, or holiness by being like God—not because he is wise, but because any wisdom we might find has its foundations in him.

These observations help us to begin to understand the point being made in Job 28. The cosmos is permeated with wisdom because God made it that way. The poem does not suggest that God *is* wisdom or that he *has* wisdom. Certainly God understands and knows wisdom because it finds its source in him. One can only perceive order and coherence if one takes seriously that those qualities of wisdom emanate from God; thus fearing the Lord is wisdom. We are used to the saying, "All truth is God's truth." The variation of that saying that emerges from this discussion is "All order is God's order."

How does the presentation of God in 28:24–27 contrast with the picture of God given previously in the book? Through this point in the book Job has been seeking wisdom (a coherent understanding of his situation), and his friends have been offering the wisdom that they reputedly and presumably have. Job has a reputation as a wise man, but now he is stumped. His default understanding of coherence is not working, and he finds the suggestions of his friends inadequate.

The introduction indicates that Job fears God (1:8). This is demonstrated by his pious attention to ritual and his turning away from evil. But

---

16. Fox, *Proverbs 1–9*, 279.

there are other areas in which to express fear of the Lord. Does Job consider God to be the author of coherence? Fearing God in that manner would be demonstrated in giving him the benefit of the doubt even in the midst of perceived incoherence. For Job, coherence can only be found in justice. It would seem that if Job is unable to identify a coherence associated with justice, God becomes suspect and should be called to account. In this sense, Job at least tacitly believes that he knows the path to wisdom and the shape that it needs to take. Job's friends suffer the same overconfidence.

Job 28 therefore serves an important function at this juncture in the book. It serves notice that Job is not in the position of control and that his expectations should not dictate the direction in which the situation proceeds. It also serves notice that the friends' perception of coherence is flawed and simplistic.

 OUR DISCUSSION OF THE contemporary significance of this chapter can proceed differently than it has in the previous chapters. Throughout the dialogues we were well aware that the text was presenting flawed views rather than authoritative biblical teaching. Our strategy was therefore to interact with those views, identify them in our own responses, and critique them.

If I am right in reading this speech as from the mouth of the narrator, however, we here have biblical teaching on the proper way to think. In fact, this chapter offers some of the fundamental insights on which I base my interpretation of the book and its teaching. These insights challenge our own inclinations when we face suffering and suggest new models for thinking.

Role of Wisdom in the Cosmos

PAST NOT PRESENT. WHEN life goes wrong, we look for reasons. Where do we expect to find them? This poem suggests that the wisdom for finding such explanations is not available. We should not expect that we will ever deduce or receive a rationalization that justifies our suffering.[17] Consequently it is futile to spend time and energy trying to decipher the situation.

Our circumstances find their roots in the past, not in the present. In other words, our circumstances, for good or ill, are based in God's ordering

---

17. I would note the exceptions in which there is a direct and observable cause-and-effect relationship (you want to know why you are in jail—well, you broke the law). But in these the cause-and-effect situations are tangible and in the human realm.

of the cosmos of creation. Perhaps a mundane illustration will help. We can say that God created gravity at the beginning. God's wisdom is inherent in gravity. When any of us do something intentional or accidental that results in us leaving the ground, gravity will become evident. God's wisdom is not to be sought in every individual expression of gravity, though we dare not say that it operates without him (one form of deism). He could theoretically disengage it in a particular moment or instance, but we should not expect it. The explanation for gravity would therefore be sought at the beginning of time, not in the present expression of it. One could ask endlessly why gravity expressed itself in a particular situation, but such answers are inaccessible and reflect a wrongheaded question.

Are our questions about our suffering really any different? When God made gravity, it became inevitable that some people would fall, resulting in death or injury. When God created our nervous systems, it became inevitable that there would be pain. Each experience of pain finds its ultimate explanation in how the system was initially constructed. When we move from the question, "Why do I experience pain?" (nervous system) to "Why did this particular pain-causing experience happen to me?" we should not expect to discern an answer.

When I trip and experience gravity, I don't ask, "What did I do that resulted in God causing me to trip?" God did not cause me to trip, nor did he foreordain me to trip. In the same way, when I experience pain or suffering, it is fruitless to ask, "What did I do that resulted in God causing this pain and suffering for me?" This is what the text is addressing when it indicates that answers to those questions are not to be found in the land of the living. Some explanations may be found in relation to the way that God ordered the cosmos. In such cases, the answers are systemic, not personal—just as gravity is systemic, not personal.[18] We must resist, however, adopting this course of logic as a replacement system, for it too easily becomes reductionistic. Deism is not an alternative Scripture allows.

We might then wonder why God has set things up in such a way that suffering could happen. This is a better question and has a different sort of answer. It is different in that it is theological and focuses on the systems inherent in the cosmos instead of on my specific experiences. Instead of asking questions about whether I or a loved one deserves to suffer (situational justice), it asks whether it was wise or just for God to set up such a system so that these things could happen. The poem in Job 28 talks about

---

18. This is not to imply that comparison to gravity suffices as a comparison for how God's wisdom works in the cosmos. It is a metaphor that quickly breaks down under scrutiny, but it is adequate for the starting point.

God's wisdom as inherent in the causes that he initiated, and we cannot confidently trace those to the effects that can be observed day by day.

Wisdom and justice. The next question, then, becomes whether justice was the central element in God's creation of the cosmos. That is, did he set up the system so that justice would always be done? Again, using gravity as an illustration, God did not make gravity discerning. Gravity does not choose the path of justice. It makes no decision about whether it engages and is not based on any person's nature or circumstances. Furthermore, God does not micromanage the application of gravity to individual circumstances. In his wisdom he constructed the system, without justice in mind or as the criteria in its operation. That does not mean that justice is perverted (in the system's operation/creation) or that God is not just. If God had set up the cosmos so that justice would be the default, a fallen world could not exist. As it stands, however, there is more to the world than justice, and we should be glad of this reality. Otherwise none of us would exist.

We should not seek an explanation for our personal circumstances, and we should not seek an understanding of how the larger issue of justice is served in our suffering. Instead we should understand that we have experienced one of the consequences of the way that God organized the cosmos as well as the consequence of the fall and the curse. We should seek out the wisdom of the cosmos rather than seek out the justice behind our circumstances. We should not assume that there is justice, but we should assume that there is wisdom.

A. MacLeish, in the Pulitzer Prize–winning play, *J.B.*, tries to put the pieces together:

> God is God or we are nothing—
> Mayflies that leave their husks behind—
> Our tiny lives ridiculous—a suffering
> Not even sad that Someone Somewhere
> Laughs at as we laugh at apes.
> We have no choice but to be guilty.
> God is unthinkable if we are innocent.[19]

Can we agree with this assessment and the reasoning that underlies it? The first five lines identify the philosophical problem in what I believe would be accurate terms. But the final two lines are theologically shortsighted. Yes, of course, all have sinned and fall short of the glory of God; but MacLeish's reasoning still has the shortcoming of turning suffering into

---

19. MacLeish, *J.B.*, 111.

punishment for our generalized guilt. Like Job and his friends, his only and final foundation is justice. Rather than thinking of God's presumed injustice making him "unthinkable," we should turn our attention to his wisdom, which is beyond our knowledge or imagination. This is only possible as it is facilitated by the "fear of the Lord" to which we now turn.

Fear of the Lord

IN THE POP-CULTURE NOVEL *Memnoch the Devil: The Vampire Chronicles* by Ann Rice, a remarkable 150-page section offers Memnoch's (Satan's) perspective on his fall in self-justifying terms. In the course of that lengthy conversation is the following reflection from those in Sheol:

> We accept that our lives have been wondrous experiences and worth the pain and the suffering, and we cherish now the joy we knew, and the moments of harmony, and we have forgiven Him for not ever explaining it all to us, for not justifying it, not punishing the bad or rewarding the good, or whatever else it is that all these souls, living and dead, expect of Him. We forgive Him. We don't know, but we suspect that maybe he knows a great secret about how all this pain could come to pass and still be good. And if He doesn't want to tell, well, He is God. But whatever, we forgive Him and we Love Him in our forgiveness, even though we know He may never care about any of us, any more than He cares for the pebbles on the beach below.[20]

We could contest the theology on many points here, but I quote it for its expression of one implication of the fear of the Lord. I would not agree with the concept of forgiving God, for that implies some offense on his part. What is important here is the ability — or perhaps the decision — to look beyond our perceptions of justice and our demands for answers. I don't think that it is a matter of his having a "great secret" that turns every devastating experience into good. The key, not a secret at all, is that God can take all of the pain and devastation that might occur in our lives and bring good from it. That does not make the pain and devastation good. Rather than thinking in terms of forgiving him, we should think in terms of trusting his wisdom and loving him. He *does* care for us more than for the pebbles on the beach and experiences our pain along with us.

Can we acquire an understanding of the wisdom that underlies the cosmic system? Job 28 says no. We are not able to understand it and we are not

---

20. Ann Rice, *Memnoch the Devil: The Vampire Chronicles* (New York: Knopf, 1995), 254.

asked to understand it. It is no surprise that we are curious, but we should not expect that curiosity to be satisfied.

The alternative that the text offers is that we partake of the wisdom that is expressed in fearing the Lord. This is different from the fruitless search described (28:20–21) in that it requires we believe that God has set up and sustains the cosmos in wisdom, even if we cannot receive an explanation that makes sense to us. It is wise for us to believe that he is wise. This becomes a matter of trust rather than understanding. Adopting such a posture does not require us to affirm that "there is a reason even though I don't know what it is." Instead it asks us to move beyond reasons. Our confidence is not that there *is* an explanation. We trust that God has established the cosmos wisely and that whatever comes our way is reconcilable with his wisdom.

This should not be confused with deism. God did not just initiate creation and then leave everything to work by itself. But many aspects of the cosmos have been firmly established since the foundation of the world. In these God's wisdom was manifest, but justice was not the sole basis for its design. Furthermore, God does not tinker with it situation by situation even though he is thoroughly engaged in the operation of the cosmos moment by moment (but if he wants to tinker, he can). In him all things cohere, and without his sustaining hand all would cease to exist.

Power and trust. Some people might say that we fear God because he has the power to do us harm. This is illustrated in the comment made by one of the characters in the TV show *House*: "People pray so that God does not squash them like bugs." It is true that he has the power to do us harm, and it is true that we risk his powerful wrath when we spurn him in our thoughts or actions. But our fear of the Lord is not supposed to either begin or end with his power. The power of a powerful being is expressed most in his or her ability to refrain from using that power in inappropriate ways. Such restraint results in trust.

We express our fear of the Lord when we trust him with our circumstances — as uncomfortable or confusing as they may be. We trust him enough to accept that there need not be an explanation. We trust that his just nature is unassailable even though there is no identifiable justice in the circumstances in which we find ourselves. We trust that he has set up the system in the very best (= wisest) way possible even when we are suffering the consequences of a system broken by the fall.[21] We trust his love

---

21. We should be careful not to think that everything that we experience as negative is the result of the fall. We do not know very much about what the prefall situation in the cosmos looked like, and we cannot assume that the end situation will look the same. Consequently we cannot detail the results of the fall and we cannot compare "before" and "after" pictures. For more discussion of this, see below, pp. 411, 419.

for us, and we trust that even in our difficulties, he can show his love and strengthen us through the trials.[22]

Ethics and ritual. What does God expect of us? Once we accept that the fear of the Lord (trusting him) is wisdom, what implications does that have for us? It is not unusual for Christians to have a response similar to what we called the Great Symbiosis in the ancient world. When the people in the ancient Near East experienced uncomfortable circumstances, they sought explanations. Since human obligation was to serve the gods by providing for their needs, the conclusion was generally reached that deity had been offended by some ritual trespass (since rituals addressed the needs of the gods). To summarize the logic:

- They suffered because deity was angry.
- Deity was angry because of ritual failure.
- Divine wrath needed to be appeased.
- Appropriate ritual acts would hopefully accomplish appeasement and restoration.

Do Christians follow a similar train of thought? In many ways, yes. The following questions will help you test your "Great Symbiosis Quotient":

1. Have sins caused your suffering?
2. Does God have "reasons"?
3. Did God do these things to you?
4. Does God "allow" suffering and disaster?

If your answer to each question was an unqualified yes, your GSQ is high and you have a lot in common with the Babylonians. Let's take a look at each question.

1. Have sins caused your suffering?

Sin can result in suffering because God does take the punishment of sin seriously and suffering is one possible punishment. Examples can be found throughout the Bible: the people groups whom God exterminated in the Old Testament (Canaanites, Amorites, Amalekites); the unfaithful Israelites; individuals committing offenses (Achan, Uzzah, Ahab; and in New Testament Ananias and Sapphira) p. 105; plus many others.[23] Nevertheless, we

---

22. This advice has moved us beyond the book of Job and the wisdom poem. The book itself never addresses the relational issues between God and humans.

23. It is interesting to note that all of these are punished by death, not by illness or suffering, which are much more difficult to document in the text. One might point to general statements such as 1 Cor. 11:30 and statements that Jesus makes in healing people when he says that their sins are forgiven. Mention might be made of Miriam's leprosy, but that has a number of unique elements connected to it.

also learn from Scripture that not all suffering is punishment for evil (note esp. 1 Peter 4:12–19). If not all personal suffering is caused by personal sin, one cannot confidently conclude that any particular suffering is punishment for sin, unless there is clear evidence to the contrary. We can say that sin in the world causes suffering in the world, but is your particular suffering the result of your personal sin? Probably not.

2. Does God have "reasons"?

It would be incorrect to think of God as acting in arbitrary, capricious, or selfish ways. We have proposed that God acts in wisdom. When we seek reasons, we are generally seeking explanations that will reveal the justice underlying our situations—that is, we are looking for particular sorts of reasons, reasons rooted in our behavior, for our particular circumstances. That is the flaw that exposes our Great Symbiosis thinking. While we would never want to presume so much knowledge of God that we would claim he has no reasons, at the same time we should think neither that there must be reasons nor that we could ever discern them when there are. If God has reasons, and they are important for us to know, his Spirit is perfectly capable of revealing them to us. But we should not be manufacturing them to satisfy our desire for coherency and closure.

3. Did God do these things to you?

It would be to our theological peril to think that *anything* that happens to us is outside of God's realm of activity and involvement. All that happens is under his supervision and providence and nothing happens that we could claim he did not do. So regarding anything that happens, he "did" it in the same sense that he causes you to stay on the ground rather than float away with each step you take. But when we think of God doing things to us, we usually think of him acting with reasons stimulated by our behavior, and that if we acted differently, he would act differently. Therein lies the Great Symbiosis thinking.

In H. Kushner's popular book, *When Bad Things Happen to Good People*, he offers the choice he has made at horrible cost: "I can worship a God who hates suffering but cannot eliminate it, more easily than I can worship a God who chooses to make children suffer and die, for whatever exalted reason."[24] This is a false dichotomy. God is neither incapable nor cruel for a higher good. Trusting in his wisdom does not make him the efficient cause of all that we experience.

---

24. H. Kushner, *When Bad Things Happen to Good People* (New York: Schocken, 1981), 134.

4. Does God "allow" suffering and disaster?

Undoubtedly yes, but that is not an answer because if God is all-powerful, everything must be allowed by him in some sense. This cannot be treated as a question that is simply asking whether God is all-powerful. Instead, it is generally a question about whether God allows things *with reasons*. The idea some people have seems to be that arbitrary circumstances come to God's desk, as it were, on which he decides whether there is sufficient cause or benefit to let it through or not. If there is, then he "approves" it and it transpires. This supposedly has the advantage of removing God from "cause" but maintaining his providence and sovereignty and preserving accountability for humans who may have had a culpable role.

This reasoning contains three potential theological flaws in that it assumes (1) a broad range of independently operating causation that could lead to viewing God as contingent; (2) an overly simplistic "approval process"; and (3) the necessity of "reasons." None of these assumptions is sustainable. Both prosperity and adversity come from the hand of God (Eccl. 7:11–14).

Greg Boyd legitimately (I think) critiques what he calls the "blueprint view"—that God ordains or at least allows every tragedy with reasons in mind.[25] He questions this view as he considers examples of disease or tragedy on the personal level, and terrorism and war on a global scope. He concludes that God is not to be held responsible, but that these are reflections of warfare against people by the enemies of God. I think he has overstated the role of the enemies of God, but I do adopt the same sort of conclusion he does. We should not look for enemy explanations any more than we should look for God's reasons. Instead, we settle for no explanation and trust God's wisdom in how the world was constructed and how it is run. We cannot say that there *are* reasons or that there are *not*. At the same time, we should not view God as constrained by the cosmos that he made—it is constructed in his wisdom and he is not contingent on it.

Returning to the matter of ethical behavior, we can now assert that God does expect ethical behavior to result from fear of the Lord, but this is not part of a Great Symbiosis equation. We are neither to seek to appease some imagined wrath of God with ritual, nor are we to think that we can earn reward through good behavior. We deserve neither the suffering that comes our way nor the prosperity that some enjoy. The various times of life come as they will and are part of life under the sun, as Ecclesiastes tells us (Eccl. 3).

---

25. G. Boyd, *Is God to Blame?* (Downers Grove, Ill.: InterVarsity Press, 2003), 41–60; though I should note that he does so in order to promote his openness view, which I do not find persuasive.

Seeking coherency. So how should we make sense of God, the world, and our experience? Perhaps there is a prior question: Is coherency to be expected? My reading of Ecclesiastes would suggest that we should not expect coherency. God, despite the fact that he has revealed himself to us, remains mysterious and paradoxical. The world, though under the control of God, is fallen, and as it awaits redemption it is often more chaotic than coherent. Our experiences in this world, given what was just said about God and the world, will evade our vain attempts to be harnessed into some sustained and consistent coherence.

Path to Wisdom

IN CONCLUSION WE MUST take seriously the claim of the poem that the path to Wisdom is not open to us: "[God] alone knows where it dwells" (28:23). Though that ultimate Wisdom is not accessible to us (even in the Bible), God has made a wise course of action available to us as we fear him, submit to his wisdom, and turn aside from evil.

What does this path look like when life is going terribly wrong?

1. Trust God rather than blame him or make demands of him for explanations.
2. Trust God for strength to endure.
3. Don't expect it all to make sense.
4. Channel resentment toward the fallenness of the world, not the God who has given all to initiate its redemption.
5. Resist succumbing to the temptation to believe that you could run this world better than God does.
6. Above all, trust that he is wise.

Kelly's Story[26]

IT IS ONE THING to construct a bullet-point list of theoretical strategies and advice as that just given, but an entirely different matter to consider its merits when life is a mess. Does it really work? I wanted to get Kelly's perspective on it.

JHW: Kelly, as you read Job 28 and the present chapter and reflect on the list above, what makes sense and what doesn't? Have any of these worked for you as you have tried to struggle through your circumstances?

---

26. Kelly interacts with parts of her story in each Contemporary Significance section. For the introduction to the details of her story, see Contemporary Significance in the commentary on ch. 1, pp. 87–97.

We would even like to know specifically which ones work and maybe which ones don't.

Kelly: After reading Job 28 and meditating on the meaning of the text and then reading the list above, I think to myself there is so much depth and truth in each point on the list, but how do I convey to the reader the magnitude of each step without appearing clichéd? I guess I can start with stating that when I look at this list, I think every point is a great step on the path towards wisdom, but so many of these points seem almost impossible without God's power.

I know if I had looked at this list in the spring of 2009 or even after the recent disappointing trip to California, I would want to trust God and have strength, not demand an explanation, or not have resentment, but I would feel helpless and feel as though I did not have the power to do so. When you are in a place of brokenness, you desire to feel close to God, to trust him and his will, but so many times the cycle of destructive thoughts wins the battle and brings you back to a place of frustration. Well, I shouldn't say frustration, because I was once told that "frustration" is a secondary emotion to either anger or sadness. So I guess it is more accurate to state that when destructive thoughts won the battle over wisdom, it brought me back to a place of sadness. So I think a key component to following these points as you seek wisdom is first and foremost to pray and ask God to help you each step of the way. Now as clichéd as that might sound, the power of prayer is vital, especially during a period of great suffering.

I remember distinctly when I started to heal and get back on my own two feet, while still dealing with the same trials and pain, I had to let go fully of any type of control, which also relates to point 5, because it was not going to be by my strength or power that I was going to get through this. So if you are angry with God, turn to him and start approaching him — even in your anger. Start spending time in the Word and making time for the Lord, to get to a place where you can reach the goal of point 4, "Channel resentment toward the fallenness of the world, not the God who has given all to initiate its redemption." So I think what makes sense to me is making point 4 the first point on the list. I say this because in my experience, I don't believe that you can get to a place of fully trusting God if you have not first dealt with your anger and resentment toward him. After getting to a place where you have realized that your anger needs to be channeled toward the fallenness in our world, you can begin the process of fully trusting him.

So the process of pursuing wisdom in light of my trials started with praying for the power to do so: praying for the power to trust God and for the strength to endure, to let go of control, and to realize you can't run the world; and praying for faith and trusting that he is wise.

For me, when I am in this process of struggling with my circumstances and trying to trust God, I have had a hard time with the second part of point 1, to not "make demands of him for explanations." We know God can bring good from our suffering, but it is important to differentiate between having hope that God has a reason and purpose, and being content not knowing what it is. This is the process of simply trusting that God is good and wise rather than demanding the reason, or manufacturing a reason to "satisfy our desire for coherency."

When our focus is solely on the pain and "figuring out" the trial we are in, our prayer life can become a desperate plea for an escape. We can get consumed by praying for God to remove this thorn from our life instead of praying and trusting God for the strength to endure it.

So I would say each point makes sense and is one that I have wrestled with throughout the process, and I think that it is important to recognize that it is a process. It is not a "six easy steps to wisdom" crash course. It is a continual struggle, but God does reward you with wisdom and perspective the more time you spend meditating on those things.

JHW: Is there anything you can add to the list?

Kelly: After thinking about my struggle to follow the path of wisdom while in the fire, I decided that a couple more points or additions might be helpful for some. I would add a second part to point 3. "Don't expect it to all make sense, and pray for a heavenly perspective." Oftentimes when we are in a hardship, as I mentioned before, it consumes us and our thoughts. All we see, think, or feel is related to the pain or struggle we are in. We need to take a step back and look at this experience from a wider view angle. When we come to terms with the fact that we cannot expect everything to make sense, we need to pray for a heavenly perspective to be at peace with that uncertainty, which also relates back to trusting God and his will.

The one other point I would add is to be sure to stay connected and spend time with godly people and/or mentors in your life. In times of hard trials it is easy to isolate yourself, and that is usually when your darkest thoughts and doubts fill your mind. When my left arm was losing feeling and strength daily, I went through a period where I did not want to be around my friends, mentors, or community, and it was in that period that I felt the weakest. When we are alone, we can dwell on the pain that we are experiencing and often get into a dark downhill spiral of thoughts. God can use those people to remind you of truth and help you get out of an unhealthy thought pattern. But as we learned in Job, your friends do not always offer the best advice or encouragement, so be wise with the people you chose to play that role in your life.

Job 29–31

🌿

J ob continued his discourse:

²"How I long for the months gone by,
　　for the days when God watched over me,
³when his lamp shone upon my head
　　and by his light I walked through darkness!
⁴Oh, for the days when I was in my prime,
　　when God's intimate friendship blessed my house,
⁵when the Almighty was still with me
　　and my children were around me,
⁶when my path was drenched with cream
　　and the rock poured out for me streams of olive oil.

⁷"When I went to the gate of the city
　　and took my seat in the public square,
⁸the young men saw me and stepped aside
　　and the old men rose to their feet;
⁹the chief men refrained from speaking
　　and covered their mouths with their hands;
¹⁰the voices of the nobles were hushed,
　　and their tongues stuck to the roof of their
　　　　mouths.
¹¹Whoever heard me spoke well of me,
　　and those who saw me commended me,
¹²because I rescued the poor who cried for help,
　　and the fatherless who had none to assist him.
¹³The man who was dying blessed me;
　　I made the widow's heart sing.
¹⁴I put on righteousness as my clothing;
　　justice was my robe and my turban.
¹⁵I was eyes to the blind
　　and feet to the lame.
¹⁶I was a father to the needy;
　　I took up the case of the stranger.
¹⁷I broke the fangs of the wicked
　　and snatched the victims from their teeth.

¹⁸"I thought, 'I will die in my own house,
　　my days as numerous as the grains of sand.

307

¹⁹My roots will reach to the water,
   and the dew will lie all night on my branches.
²⁰My glory will remain fresh in me,
   the bow ever new in my hand.'

²¹"Men listened to me expectantly,
   waiting in silence for my counsel.
²²After I had spoken, they spoke no more;
   my words fell gently on their ears.
²³They waited for me as for showers
   and drank in my words as the spring rain.
²⁴When I smiled at them, they scarcely believed it;
   the light of my face was precious to them.
²⁵I chose the way for them and sat as their chief;
   I dwelt as a king among his troops;
   I was like one who comforts mourners.

³⁰:¹"But now they mock me,
   men younger than I,
whose fathers I would have disdained
   to put with my sheep dogs.
²Of what use was the strength of their hands to me,
   since their vigor had gone from them?
³Haggard from want and hunger,
   they roamed the parched land
   in desolate wastelands at night.
⁴In the brush they gathered salt herbs,
   and their food was the root of the broom tree.
⁵They were banished from their fellow men,
   shouted at as if they were thieves.
⁶They were forced to live in the dry stream beds,
   among the rocks and in holes in the ground.
⁷They brayed among the bushes
   and huddled in the undergrowth.
⁸A base and nameless brood,
   they were driven out of the land.

⁹"And now their sons mock me in song;
   I have become a byword among them.
¹⁰They detest me and keep their distance;
   they do not hesitate to spit in my face.
¹¹Now that God has unstrung my bow and afflicted me,
   they throw off restraint in my presence.

¹²On my right the tribe attacks;
    they lay snares for my feet,
    they build their siege ramps against me.
¹³They break up my road;
    they succeed in destroying me—
    without anyone's helping them.
¹⁴They advance as through a gaping breach;
    amid the ruins they come rolling in.
¹⁵Terrors overwhelm me;
    my dignity is driven away as by the wind,
    my safety vanishes like a cloud.

¹⁶"And now my life ebbs away;
    days of suffering grip me.
¹⁷Night pierces my bones;
    my gnawing pains never rest.
¹⁸In his great power ⌞God⌟ becomes like clothing
                    to me;
    he binds me like the neck of my garment.
¹⁹He throws me into the mud,
    and I am reduced to dust and ashes.

²⁰"I cry out to you, O God, but you do not answer;
    I stand up, but you merely look at me.
²¹You turn on me ruthlessly;
    with the might of your hand you attack me.
²²You snatch me up and drive me before the wind;
    you toss me about in the storm.
²³I know you will bring me down to death,
    to the place appointed for all the living.

²⁴"Surely no one lays a hand on a broken man
    when he cries for help in his distress.
²⁵Have I not wept for those in trouble?
    Has not my soul grieved for the poor?
²⁶Yet when I hoped for good, evil came;
    when I looked for light, then came darkness.
²⁷The churning inside me never stops;
    days of suffering confront me.
²⁸I go about blackened, but not by the sun;
    I stand up in the assembly and cry for help.
²⁹I have become a brother of jackals,
    a companion of owls.

³⁰My skin grows black and peels;
   my body burns with fever.
³¹My harp is tuned to mourning,
   and my flute to the sound of wailing.

^{31:1}"I made a covenant with my eyes
   not to look lustfully at a girl.
²For what is man's lot from God above,
   his heritage from the Almighty on high?
³Is it not ruin for the wicked,
   disaster for those who do wrong?
⁴Does he not see my ways
   and count my every step?

⁵"If I have walked in falsehood
   or my foot has hurried after deceit—
⁶let God weigh me in honest scales
   and he will know that I am blameless—
⁷if my steps have turned from the path,
   if my heart has been led by my eyes,
   or if my hands have been defiled,
⁸then may others eat what I have sown,
   and may my crops be uprooted.

⁹"If my heart has been enticed by a woman,
   or if I have lurked at my neighbor's door,
¹⁰then may my wife grind another man's grain,
   and may other men sleep with her.
¹¹For that would have been shameful,
   a sin to be judged.
¹²It is a fire that burns to Destruction;
   it would have uprooted my harvest.

¹³"If I have denied justice to my menservants and
       maidservants
   when they had a grievance against me,
¹⁴what will I do when God confronts me?
   What will I answer when called to account?
¹⁵Did not he who made me in the womb make them?
   Did not the same one form us both within our
       mothers?

¹⁶"If I have denied the desires of the poor
   or let the eyes of the widow grow weary,

¹⁷if I have kept my bread to myself,
　　not sharing it with the fatherless—
¹⁸but from my youth I reared him as would a father,
　　and from my birth I guided the widow—
¹⁹if I have seen anyone perishing for lack of clothing,
　　or a needy man without a garment,
²⁰and his heart did not bless me
　　for warming him with the fleece from my sheep,
²¹if I have raised my hand against the fatherless,
　　knowing that I had influence in court,
²²then let my arm fall from the shoulder,
　　let it be broken off at the joint.
²³For I dreaded destruction from God,
　　and for fear of his splendor I could not do such things.

²⁴"If I have put my trust in gold
　　or said to pure gold, 'You are my security,'
²⁵if I have rejoiced over my great wealth,
　　the fortune my hands had gained,
²⁶if I have regarded the sun in its radiance
　　or the moon moving in splendor,
²⁷so that my heart was secretly enticed
　　and my hand offered them a kiss of homage,
²⁸then these also would be sins to be judged,
　　for I would have been unfaithful to God on high.

²⁹"If I have rejoiced at my enemy's misfortune
　　or gloated over the trouble that came to him—
³⁰I have not allowed my mouth to sin
　　by invoking a curse against his life—
³¹if the men of my household have never said,
　　'Who has not had his fill of Job's meat?'—
³²but no stranger had to spend the night in the street,
　　for my door was always open to the traveler—
³³if I have concealed my sin as men do,
　　by hiding my guilt in my heart
³⁴because I so feared the crowd
　　and so dreaded the contempt of the clans
　　that I kept silent and would not go outside

³⁵("Oh, that I had someone to hear me!
　　I sign now my defense—let the Almighty answer me;
　　let my accuser put his indictment in writing.

---

³⁶Surely I would wear it on my shoulder,
    I would put it on like a crown.
³⁷I would give him an account of my every step;
    like a prince I would approach him.)—

³⁸"if my land cries out against me
    and all its furrows are wet with tears,
³⁹if I have devoured its yield without payment
    or broken the spirit of its tenants,
⁴⁰then let briers come up instead of wheat
    and weeds instead of barley."

The words of Job are ended.

Introduction

IN JOB'S DISCOURSE IN these chapters, the book's attention turns to his contention that it is poor policy for God to inflict suffering on righteous people. Throughout Job 29, Job wallows in nostalgia, pining for his lost prosperity, honor, and dignity. This melancholy focus contrasts with his indignant posture in the book's dialogue section, where he expounded on his righteousness rather than his lost prosperity. While his mood and subject matter have shifted, Job still refrains from attempting to regain prosperity and thus maintains his integrity.

In 29:1–6, Job acknowledges God as the source of his former prosperity. This is the last explicit reference to God in the discourse until Job begins his oath of innocence.[1] Job's attention is fixed on himself and his plight.

The perspective of an honor-based culture is evident in Job 29–30. Chapter 29 characterizes Job's former state as the epitome of honor, and chapter 30 depicts his current misery as the opposite—utter shame and disgrace. These descriptions reveal the aspects of an individual's life that reflected honor or shame.

The following are hallmarks of honor:

- protective deity (29:2–4)
- many children (29:5)

---

1. God is generally assumed and supplied as the subject and object of verbs in 30:11, 18–23, but he is never actually mentioned.

- successful exploitation of resources (29:6)
- position of prominence in society (29:7)
- respect from all, including young and old and the powerful (29:8 – 11)
- responsiveness to the poor and bereaved (29:12 – 13)
- righteousness and justice recognized (29:14)
- aiding the blind and lame (29:15)
- facilitating justice for the vulnerable (29:16)
- scourge of the wicked (29:17)
- long life (29:18)
- health and vigor into old age (29:19 – 20)
- wisdom recognized (29:21 – 23)
- supplicants for his favor (29:24)
- elevated status (29:25)

Clearly most items on this list are societal rather than ethical in nature. In an honor/shame-based culture, a person's role and status within the community defines his or her identity. Corporate identity takes precedence over individual identity,[2] with the result that selfhood is shaped primarily by social interaction, not private inward perception. In other words, "self" is defined in largely exterior terms.[3] Egyptologist J. Assmann describes the social constellation as most important for identity:

> A person comes into being, lives, grows, and exists by building up such a sphere of social and bodily "constellations." A constellative anthropology stresses the ties, roles, and functions that bind the constituent parts together. It abhors the ideas of isolation, solitude, self-sufficiency, and independence, and considers them symptoms of death, dissolution, and destruction. Life is interdependence, interconnection, and communication within those webs of interaction and interlocution that constitute reality.[4]

---

2. For a good presentation of how various types of societies function, see J. Pilch, *Introducing the Cultural Context of the Old Testament* (Mahwah, N.J.: Paulist, 1991), esp. 97.

3. See discussions in K. van der Toorn, *Family Religion in Babylonia, Syria and Israel: Continuity and Change in the Forms of Religious Life* (Leiden: Brill, 1996), 116 – 17; T. Abusch, "Ghost and God: Some Observations on a Babylonian Understanding of Human Nature," in *Self, Soul and Body in Religious Experience* (ed. A. Baumgarten, J. Assmann, and G. Stroumsa; Leiden: Brill, 1998), 380 – 81; Walton, *Ancient Near Eastern Thought*, 147 – 49.

4. J. Assmann, "Dialogue between Self and Soul: Papyrus Berlin 3024," in *Self, Soul and Body in Religious Experience* (ed. A. Baumgarten, J. Assmann, and G. Stroumsa; Leiden: Brill, 1998), 386.

Assmann further notes that social coherence is essential for maintaining personal coherence.[5] Within a culture of shame and honor, Job cannot attain coherence unless he is reintegrated into society, which in turn cannot happen until he is vindicated and his honor is restored. In the dialogue section of the book, Job sought to recover connection to God by reiterating his plea for audience. By contrast, Job's statements in 30:18–23 suggest that he has abandoned hope that God will intervene. His oath of innocence attempts to appropriate God's silence as an inferred vindication, which will enable Job's reconnection with society.

Just as Job described honor in social terms in ch. 29, in 30 he likewise depicts his shame as an exterior situation. Outcasts with no social status consider Job even more inferior than they are and treat him with disdain. Their fathers were nothing, and they are less than nothing, yet Job has become the object of their scorn. In 30:15, the summary of this section, Job identifies the crux of his shame: his safety and dignity are gone, leaving him vulnerable and disenfranchised. As noted, this state is external in nature and should not be interpreted as a purely emotional struggle stemming from guilt, low self-esteem, or regret.

In a culture of shame and honor, one gains nothing by affirming a positive self-image, and the admiration of others is not won by displaying poise amid suffering. Job has been dehumanized, and it is out of his power to change his status. In this context, Job's claims of innocence sound as pitiful as those of today's indicted politicians, whose peccadilloes and corruptions are documented so publicly that guilt is a foregone conclusion. Like them, Job desires to portray himself as a victim, but in an honor-based society, someone so utterly debased could never regain a status of respect.

Job 29

THE CHAPTER CAN BE divided into six sections:
    a 29:1–6: How Job perceived God's protection
      b 29:7–10: How city leaders respected Job
        c 29:11–17: How Job served a royal role on behalf of the vulnerable
    a´ 29:18–20: How Job perceived his own prospects
      b´ 29:21–23: How the people respected Job
        c´ 29:24–25: How Job served a royal role

Never in Job's description of God's blessing in his life does he suggest that he deserved or had earned such treatment. In evaluating the nature of Job's special blessing, the reference to God's "intimate friendship" (Heb.

---

5. Ibid., 401.

sod) in verse 4 is of particular interest. This noun occurs about twenty times in the Hebrew Bible and often concerns the operation of a council (cf. Gen. 49:6; Job 15:8; Pss. 89:7; 111:1; Jer. 23:18; Ezek. 13:9). It can also describe more personal interaction, such as private confidences between individuals (cf. Ps. 25:14; Prov. 11:13; 20:19) or fellowship (Ps. 55:14).

Previously, Job used *sod* in relation to his friends who betrayed him (19:19), with whom he once shared confidences, counsel, and trust. Here in 29:4, this word is grammatically linked to the word for God ('*eloah*), a combination that occurs in only four other contexts (Job 15:8; Ps. 25:14; Jer. 23:18, 22; Amos 3:7). Of these, all but Psalm 25:14 refer to the formal divine council. All of the above uses share the concept of confidentiality. Formal councils take place behind closed doors and treat private matters. Friends who confide in one another may be termed confidants. When enemies conspire together, they formulate confidential schemes.

Prophets were considered to have access to the privy council of Yahweh, where they received the messages or overheard information that they subsequently transmitted to the people (Jer. 23:18, 22; Amos 3:7). Psalm 25:14 applies the *sod* of Yahweh beyond the role of prophet to all those who fear him. Job 29:4 states that the *sod* of Eloah was upon, or more likely over, Job's tent. This description seems to indicate that Job enjoyed an "insider" relationship with God and had access to the divine council chamber.

In the ancient world, kings sought admittance to the divine council via dream incubation, which entailed sleeping in the temple, where the divine council met, in an attempt to overhear the proceedings or perhaps even to receive direct comment. Because the divine council met in sacred space (cf. Isaiah's throne vision in Isa. 6), Job's description here equates his tent with sacred space. This depiction would make the line parallel to the first line of the next verse, which refers to God's presence with Job.

Because of this connection between Job's tent and the divine council, Job 29:4 may not be used to support a discussion about friendship with God. Job describes being taken into God's confidence, but in conciliar rather than personal terms. More importantly, his privileged status stems from his close physical proximity to sacred space. Israelite readers would identify access to sacred space and the divine council with elite offices such as those of king, prophet, and priest. God's presence brought Job the blessings of family and excess provision — the cream flowed out all around his feet, and the rock of the olive press produced not just a trickle of olive oil, but streams (29:6).

In Job 29:7 – 10 and 21 – 23, Job describes the universal respect he received from leaders and the general populace. Job may well have been wise, kind, and upright, and his attractive qualities certainly may have contributed to the respect he enjoyed. Ultimately, however, his success and prosperity were the primary factors behind his social position. Presumably his wisdom and kindness did not change, but when he lost his prosperity, he lost respect from those around him.

Job himself does not acknowledge this point—he cites his track record of care for the vulnerable (29:11–17) as the source of his good repute. When he joined the ranks of the vulnerable, however, he lost his ability to aid them. His lifetime of charitable work merited nothing; memories are short when fortunes change.

Job's state of blessing meant that his future prospects were likewise ideal, as described in 29:18–20. This highly poetic passage details Job's anticipation of a long life filled with prosperity and youthful vigor. Perhaps the most intriguing imagery is found in verse 18, which refers to his "nest" (*qen;* NIV: "house"). The phrasing here is problematic; the preceding preposition (*'im*) generally means "with" rather than "in" and most naturally would indicate that Job expects to perish along with his nest.[6] The best solution is yielded by an investigation of the Akkadian cognate *qinnu*, which refers predominantly to a bird's nest, as in Hebrew, but in a few occurrences connected to human beings clearly means "family."[7] In Akkadian texts, speakers express hopes that their family (*qinnu*) will not be scattered or dispersed.[8] A similar sense seems to be in play here: Job expects to die with his children surrounding him (taking *'im* to indicate in the midst of, rather than along with, his family).

Job's musings conclude by equating his high social standing to the role of a chief or king. The passage's imagery nuances the specific form of control he exercised: he *chose* their way, and he was like a king *among his troops*. These phrases suggest unquestioned loyalty from his followers and portray Job as a compassionate leader, not an oppressive tyrant over unwilling subjects.

Job 30

THE SCENE SHIFTS AS Job's thoughts turn to his current state. His recent disasters have obliterated past glories, and Job details the shame that he now endures. He identifies his mockers in verse 1 and comments on their

---

6. The reference to a nest has led some scholars to conclude that the second line of the verse refers not to sand but to the phoenix, which expires on its nest and then is reborn (see discussion in Clines, *Job 21–37*, 939–40). Neither the contextual nor the lexical data are persuasive.

7. See H. Tawil, *An Akkadian Lexical Companion for Biblical Hebrew* (Jersey City, N.J.: KTAV, 2009), 340; *CAD* Q, 258–60.

8. *Šurpu* II, 53; *Tamitu* texts, see W. G. Lambert, *Babylonian Oracle Questions* (Winona Lake, Ind.: Eisenbrauns, 2007), 40–41 (lines 341–42).

shiftless fathers in 30:1–8. Lacking the ability to meet even basic needs, these men became outcasts scratching out a mean existence. They passed this ignoble heritage to their sons, who are disrespectful predators. It is noteworthy that in this passage Job does not encounter disdain from every-one who formerly respected and honored him. Rather, those who are by nature scoundrels take advantage of his ill fortune. It would be bad enough to be passively neglected by upstanding citizens, but it is far worse to be subject to abuse by the dregs of society.

Job 30:15 concludes the exposition of Job's sad state. Although the word "terrors" (*ballahot*) is grammatically feminine plural, here it takes a mascu-line singular verb form, suggesting that it may be a personification.[9] The same term was used in 18:14, when Bildad spoke of a "King of Terrors" parallel to the "Firstborn" of Mot (Death) in a string of personifications. If Terrors is indeed a personal entity, "Night" in 30:17 may also be a personi-fication parallel to Terrors, and either or both could serve as the subject of the masculine singular verbs in 30:18–19. Most translations supply "God" as the subject here, though he is not mentioned in the Hebrew text. I prefer the personification reading, and thus consider 30:16–19 as describing the actions of "Night" rather than the actions of God.

Regardless of whether this interpretation is accepted, by 30:20–23 Job has indeed returned his attention to God. Once again the text does not explicitly mention God, but it employs second person forms, and it is unlikely that Job here is beseeching personified Terrors and Night. Rather, in Job's perception, God has joined Terrors and Night in behaving toward Job as a chaos creature, as author of disorder and death.

The chapter ends with Job's summary reflections on his plight (vv. 27–31). The close proximity of these observations to his characteriza-tion of God as the actor causing his distress (vv. 21–23) underscores Job's fundamental accusation against God in verses 24–26. Not only has God brought disaster, he refuses to act on Job's behalf or respond to his pleas. As a result, Job himself has become an outcast (30:29), like the worthless men described earlier in the chapter. He is now the mourner (30:31), with no one to comfort him.

In addition to social loss, his suffering encompasses physical ailments. He describes himself as "blackened" (*qdr*, v. 28) and as having black, peel-ing skin (*šḥr*, v. 30) and fevered bones. Assyrian medical texts mention

---

9. Other commentators have pointed out that there are a number of places in the book that exhibit similar lack of agreement between sentence parts in number and gender. Grant-ing their point, we still must first examine whether the words should be understood differ-ently before opting for grammatical lack of agreement.

blackened skin (necrosis) frequently as a disease symptom, but the condition is too general to allow diagnosis.[10]

Job 31

THE FINAL CHAPTER OF Job's discourse features an oath of innocence in which he catalogues potential offenses and vows that he is innocent of each. Such an oath presumes that if Job swears falsely, God will be obliged to punish him for both the crime and the false oath.

Ancient Near Eastern literature includes a variety of declarations of innocence. Most are fairly brief, with just a few lines listing denied offenses.[11] In literature from Mesopotamia, the works most frequently cited as similar to Job's oath are the DINGIR.ŠA.DIB.BA incantations and the *šurpu* incantations. Both texts address an angry god in an attempt to appease his wrath and bring relief to the person suffering. The DINGIR.ŠA.DIB.BA incantations contain lines in which the sufferer claims innocence on certain points (e.g., "I have not held back from him [the deity] the sheep in the pen"), as well as long confessions of sins he is willing to admit (e.g., "I spoke lies ... I coveted your abundant property ... I raised my hand and desecrated what should not so be treated ... I have continually committed iniquities, known and unknown").[12] The *šurpu* incantations, by contrast, limit their scope to confessions of actual offenses — the opposite of Job's tack.[13] Besides the incantations a negative confession can be found in ritual texts. In the Babylonian New Year's festival (Akitu), the king expresses his eligibility for renewed kingship by narrating his care for Babylon and the temple and its rites, including proper treatment of subordinates.[14]

The most extensive ancient Near Eastern claim of innocence is found in spell 125 in the Egyptian Book of the Dead. The spell lists forty-two denied offenses, each addressed to one of the forty-two gods who will decide whether the deceased will enter the next life. The list[15] incorporates a wide variety of behaviors:

---

10. See Scurlock and Andersen, *Diagnoses in Assyrian and Babylonian Medicine*.

11. Cornelius, "Job," 5:286−88.

12. These examples are drawn from the publication of the texts in W. G. Lambert, "DINGIR.ŠA.DIB.BA Incantations," *JNES* 33 (1974): 267−322.

13. E. Reiner, *Šurpu: A Collection of Sumerian and Akkadian Incantations* (AfO 11; Graz: Ernest Weidner, 1958). See contrast developed in Magdalene, *Scales of Righteousness*, 183.

14. J. Bidmead, *The* Akitu *Festival* (Piscataway, N.J.: Gorgias, 2002), 71.

15. This list is from the papyrus of Ani, translated by R. O. Faulkner, *The Egyptian Book of the Dead: The Book of Going Forth by Day* (San Francisco: Chronicle Books, 1998), plate 31. M. Lichtheim, *Ancient Egyptian Literature* (Berkeley: Univ. of California Press, 1976), 2:126−27, has some variations in translation.

---

1. I have not done wrong.
2. I have not robbed.
3. I have not stolen.
4. I have not slain people.
5. I have not destroyed food offerings.
6. I have not reduced measures.
7. I have not stolen the god's property.
8. I have not told lies.
9. I have not stolen food.
10. I was not sullen.
11. I have not fornicated with the fornicator.
12. I have not caused anyone to weep.
13. I have not dissembled.
14. I have not transgressed.
15. I have not done grain-profiteering.
16. I have not robbed a parcel of land.
17. I have not discussed secrets.
18. I have brought no lawsuits.
19. I have not disputed at all about property.
20. I have not had intercourse with a married woman.
21. I have not wrongly copulated.
22. I have not struck terror.
23. I have not transgressed.
24. I have not been hot-tempered.
25. I have not been neglectful of truthful words.
26. I have not made disturbance.
27. I have not cursed.
28. I have not been violent.
29. I have not confounded truth.
30. I have not been impatient.
31. I have not discussed.
32. I have not been garrulous about matters.
33. I have not done evil.
34. I have not disputed the king.
35. I have not waded in the water.
36. My voice was not loud.
37. I have not cursed a god.
38. I have not made extolling.
39. I have not harmed the bread ration of the gods.
40. I have not stolen the Khenef-cakes from the Blessed.
41. I have not stolen Hefnu-cakes of a youth, nor have I fettered the god of my town.
42. I have not slain sacred cattle.

Denials	Book of the Dead	Job 31:	Decalogue #
Astral worship		26−27	
Betrayal	17, 31, 32		
Cheating	6		
Concealed sin		33−34	
Cruelty	12		
Cursing	27	30	3
Demeanor (e.g., anger)	10, 24, 30, 36		
Failure to care for needy		16−22, 31−32	
Falsehood/deception	8, 13, 25, 29	5−6	9
Comprehensive general misdemeanors	1, 14, 23, 33		
Greed		24−25	
Oppression	15, 18, 26	13−15	
Political intrigue	34		
Property/theft	2, 3, 9, 16, 19	39−40	8
Rejoicing over enemy's trouble		29	
Sacrilege/ritual offense	5, 7, 35, 37−42	7	2
Sexual misconduct	11, 20, 21	1, 9−10	7
Unfaithfulness to God		28	1
Violence	4, 22, 28		6

The preceding comparison results in few surprises. Items unique to the Book of the Dead represent interests and norms common in Egyptian society, whereas items unique to Job reflect standard biblical concerns. Areas of overlap constitute recognizable categories of misconduct that pervade ancient literature, including the Decalogue, which features examples from most of the overlapping categories. The only Decalogue topics omitted from Job's list are abstaining from idol use, honoring the Sabbath, and honoring parents. The first two are distinctively Israelite topics (although other uniquely Israelite topics such as the prohibition of astral worship can be found in the list). The Egyptian list emphasizes ritual offenses, while such are not of significant concern in Job, which lists only one vague ritual offense. By contrast, Job places priority on several matters concerning treatment of the poor, a category absent from the Egyptian list.

In addition to a comparison of content, differences in function must be noted. The Egyptian list is magical in nature and serves to ensure passage to the afterlife. Job's list is legal and attempts to secure vindication in this life. The Egyptian list ostensibly is concerned with vindication, but since it accomplishes its aim by means of magic, it reflects a very different view of such vindication. Indeed, the Egyptian deceased does not presume righteousness, but seeks to be counted among the righteous by manipulation. Job employs his list consistent with his established intentions—as a means to protest his innocence and righteousness.

When we turn our attention to the details of Job's oath, several elements require investigation. The most striking issue is visible upon a casual reading—the first verse and the last three verses seem displaced. The most suitable introduction occurs in 31:2—4, and the best conclusion is 31:35—37. Various commentators offer rearrangements or simply omit verses as later additions.

Misplacement of verses is not unheard of. For example, a comparison of 2 Kings 20 with its parallel in Isaiah 38 reveals that a line has been misplaced in the latter. Isaiah 38:21—22 belongs between verses 6—7, as it is situated in 2 Kings 20:7—8. Such displacement can occur when a copyist inadvertently omits a line and, upon checking the page, discovers the error. Rather than write the entire page once more by hand, he opts to note the missing portion in the margin of the page. The next copyist encounters the marginal line and must decide where to put it. If his Hebrew is sufficient, he may deduce the correct placement; more likely, however, he will simply relocate it at the beginning or end of the chapter, as in Isaiah 38. Such a process may well have occurred in Job 31, and I agree with other commentators that Job 31:1 and 31:38—40a probably belong elsewhere in the chapter.[16]

Job 31:1 opens with reference to a covenant. The noun and verb here are the standard Old Testament terminology for making a covenant. These two occur with the preposition used here about twenty-five times; in most cases the object of the preposition designates the other party in the covenant. We would furthermore expect that both parties would be named in a covenant context. All of this suggests that Job's eyes are being treated as vassals brought under a suzerain's control.

---

16. I accept this alternative reluctantly, because, for the most part, I have expressed my commitment to take the text as it is. This displacement is relatively minor in relation to moving whole chapters around as others often do. Such displacement would have had to occur quite early, because the LXX agrees with the Hebrew Masoretic text on the arrangement. It should also be noted that even critical scholars sometimes make a case for treating the text as it stands; see Habel, *Job*, 427—28.

Since this verse seems an obvious statement about sexual ethics, we must consider the textual details carefully. The verb in the second line describing the forbidden activity is *'etbonen*, the Hithpael form of the root *byn*, which occurs twenty-two times in the Old Testament (eight times in Job). Most of these instances describe close or careful examination of an object. In only one occurrence (Ps. 37:10) is the verb followed by this preposition (*'al*), and there it refers to seeking out (but not finding) the wicked. Neither this instance nor any other occurrence of the Hithpael form carries sexual nuance. The NIV has arrived at its translation by context, interpreting the gaze as lustful because its object is a virgin (*betulah*).

This interpretation does not satisfactorily explain why the prohibition to Job's eyes is limited to a *betulah*. If sexual ethics are truly at stake, it would be more natural for his covenant to extend to any woman. Furthermore, if a girl remains under her father's protection (as does a *betulah* by definition), she is a viable candidate for marriage—and society at this time was comfortably polygamous.

To reach a better understanding, we must begin fresh. Job has made a covenant regarding his eyes—that much is clear. The second part of the verse begins with a common interrogative particle, "what" (*mah*). Although Job's usage of this particle is consistent, most translations choose not to render it in this particular verse. Typically in Job this particle introduces a rhetorical question, which seems likely here as well. Psalm 37:10 employs the same verb as this verse to direct the reader to "look all around" for the location of the wicked; within its context, this directive suggests that if one inquires diligently after the status of the wicked, the search will yield nothing. If we apply this observation to Job's statement, the sense is as follows: "Since I have made a covenant with regard to my eyes, what interest would I have in inquiring after a *betulah* (i.e., investigating her availability)?"

Inquiring after a *betulah* is not the same as inquiring after a prostitute. If the text truly was speaking against lust, the verb *ḥmd* ("covet") would be a more likely word choice.[17] *Betulah* generally does indicate a virgin, but virginity is more circumstantial than truly representative of the word's core meaning. More to the point, a *betulah* is a marriageable girl still within the household of her father and under his protection.[18] One would inquire after a *betulah* in order to arrange a marriage. Such an inquiry could potentially be motivated by lust (cf. Judg. 14:2), but that is only one of several alternatives and may not be automatically inferred. In point of fact, *any* arranged marriage begins with inquiring after a *betulah*.

---

17. For another likely wording, see Job 31:9.
18. J. Walton, "בְּתוּלָה," *NIDOTTE*, 1:781–84.

In light of this discussion, Job's covenant regarding his eyes cannot be interpreted as a commitment to asceticism, because he already has a wife (as noted not only in ch. 2, but also in 31:10). The logical alternative is that the statement concerns the acquisition of a harem. A large harem was an indicator of power and status in the ancient world. Job eschews amassing multiple wives and concubines, and he characterizes this decision as a covenant regarding his eyes in order to underscore the point that he is not even "on the prowl." This avowal mirrors his statement in 31:24−25 that he is not absorbed in the pursuit of wealth. Job has undertaken neither a vow of poverty nor a vow of chastity, but rather avoids the obsessive pursuit of prestige. This interpretation takes account of each word choice the author has made and therefore presents the most likely interpretation. Accordingly, the verse has nothing to do with sexual ethics, as important as they may be. Instead, it accords with Job's many pronouncements that he has not attempted to consolidate or abuse his power—tempting actions for a person in his position (cf. Samuel's lecture in 1 Sam. 8:11−17 regarding the tactics of a king building a power base).

Verse 2 leads into the chapter's effectual introduction. Job demonstrates his ongoing commitment to the RP in his assertion that the wicked will suffer. Verse 4 combines the philosophical premise of verse 3 with the theological affirmation that God scrutinizes Job's actions. These two principles give Job's oath of innocence its bite: swearing a false oath, especially one so replete with claims, would be an evil worthy of punishment, and God is paying attention. Therefore, if God does not act against Job, Job may claim vindication.

Verse 5 launches the catalog itself. Commentators dispute how many items the list includes, but the number's significance is minimal. If we base the list's structure on the protases, we can identify eleven paragraphs from 31:5−34[19] and a twelfth in 31:38−40. Each paragraph begins with "if" (*'im*), the typical Hebrew introduction to a self-curse. In such a curse, the protasis of the conditional statement usually appears alone, with an implied apodosis of judgment, such as "may God strike me dead."[20] Yet four of the twelve paragraphs of Job's oath feature an explicit apodosis (vv. 8, 10, 22, 40; and a further quasi-apodosis in v. 28). These apodoses are extreme and accordingly should be understood hyperbolically. Their excessive force demonstrates Job's confidence in his innocence. The following formal outline, divided by protases, illuminates the variety of features contained in the twelve paragraphs.

---

19. Vv. 5−6, 7−8, 9−12, 13−15, 16−23, 24, 25, 26−28, 29−30, 31−32, 33−34.

20. For an example in which the apodosis is actually stated, see Ruth 1:17; 2 Kings 6:31. Even God uses the unstated apodosis style in Deut. 1:35.

31:5–6	Protasis: walking in falsehood, hurrying after deceit (two parts, 5a, b) Plea to God for fair consideration (6)
31:7–8	Protasis: steps turned from path, heart led by eyes, hands defiled (three parts, 7a, b, c) Apodosis: others eat of my labor, crops uprooted (two parts, 8a, b)
31:9–12	Protasis: heart enticed by woman, lurked at neighbor's door (two parts, 9a, b) Apodosis: wife grind another's grain, other men sleep with wife (two parts, 10a, b) Explanation indicating seriousness of crime (11) Wisdom saying (12)
31:13–15	Protasis: denied justice to servants (13) Accountability to God (14)—God will act Theological rationale for values and behavior (15)
31:16–23	Compound protasis: denied the poor, failed to share bread with fatherless, ignored needy, acted against fatherless (four parts, each beginning with the particle *'im*, 16, 17, 19–20, 21) Contrasting positive behavior (18) Apodosis: broken limb (22) Accountability to God (23)—fears God
31:24	Protasis: trust in gold (24)
31:25	Protasis: rejoiced in wealth (25)
31:26–28	Protasis: astral worship (three parts, 26–27) Quasi-apodosis: judged (28a) Explanation indicating seriousness of crime (28b)
31:29–30	Protasis: rejoiced at enemy's misfortune (29) Corresponding negative affirmation (30)
31:31–32	Protasis: treatment of strangers (complex, two parts, including negative affirmation, 31–32)
31:33–34	Protasis: concealed sin (33) Identification of projected motivation for crime he did not commit (34)
31:38–40	Compound protasis: land use (two parts, each beginning with the particle *'im*, 38, 39, the latter having two parts, 39a, b) Apodosis: weeds instead of crops (40)

The above outline clarifies that while the conditional self-curse form is employed throughout the chapter, other variables occur irregularly and prevent the formulaic chapter from becoming rhythmic.

The preceding analysis has rested on the protases. If we adopt an alternative chapter structuring based on the apodoses, we find that the number of sections reduces to five, and the subjects of discussion are conveniently grouped together:

Verses	Subject	Apodosis
31:5–8	Lack of integrity of character	Loss of means of provision (8)
31:9–12	Lack of sexual purity	Loss of wife (10)
31:13–23	Lack of compassion and charity to the vulnerable	Loss of power to do good or ill (22)
31:24–28	Lack of trust in God	Loss of favor with God (28)
31:29–32, 38–40	Lack of grace to outsiders (enemies, strangers, competitors)[21]	Loss of produce and prosperity (40)

Textual Explanations

31:5–8. THIS SECTION COULD be viewed as continuing the thought expressed in verse 4, since it also comments on Job's steps and path. Because God observes Job's steps (v. 4), he knows whether Job has gone astray (v. 5); therefore, Job asks to be judged accordingly (v. 6). If viewed as connected to verse 4, verses 5–6 can serve as an introduction to the entire chapter, as Job calls on God to affirm his innocence.

Job's request to be weighed in honest scales is reminiscent of the judgment scene in the Egyptian Book of the Dead. The forty-two statements of innocence before the forty-two gods of the tribunal are accompanied by the famous illustration in which Anubis brings the deceased before the scales of judgment and weighs the individual's heart against Maat (truth, justice), represented by her emblem feather, while Thoth records the results. If the declaration of the deceased is acceptable and the heart does not outweigh Maat, Horus ushers the deceased before Osiris, the god of the netherworld, and grants entry to the next life. If the deceased fails, the devouring gobbler waits hungrily nearby.

The second part of this section (31:7) continues the theme of Job's steps and path. The deviations that Job denies here and in the previous section involve a variety of general offenses that primarily concern issues of character, such as duplicity in the pursuit of selfish desires, and which are expressed in connection with body parts (feet, heart, eyes, hands). The

---

21. For this interpretation, see discussion below, pp. 328–29.

proposed punishment correlates to the sin. Had Job sought personal gain, he would suffer personal loss. Had he attempted to achieve his desires at the expense of integrity, he would lose his means for even basic survival. The apodosis suggests reversal of fortunes in the same area of life where the denied offense would have taken place.

31:9–12. The potential offense here concerns sexual purity. Being enticed by a woman entails falling prey to a second party's active advances.[22] Lurking at a neighbor's doorway exhibits a more active pursuit—solicitation of an adulterous liaison with the neighbor's wife. These two examples demonstrate the oath's application to a wide range of sexual misconduct and indicate that illicit sexual relationships, rather than merely any illicit sexual acts, are its target. The projected punishment is loss of legitimate sexual relationship. Another man would take Job's wife, and Job would become the injured party instead of the neighbor. The image of Job's wife "grinding another man's grain" is a sexual euphemism: She will process what another man produces (i.e., children).

The wisdom saying that closes the section (31:12) bears resemblance to the one that encapsulates the message of Song of Songs: "Love is as strong as death, its jealousy unyielding as the grave. It burns like a blazing fire, like a mighty flame" (Song 8:6). Passion cannot easily be extinguished and, as the text indicates, will burn to Destruction (Heb. *'abaddon*). When Job states that such passion would have uprooted his harvest, he acknowledges that sexual misconduct would have undermined all his positive effort and blessing. As many have discovered, it only takes a moment of sexual indiscretion to undo a lifetime of labor.

31:13–23. The broad range of activities in this section finds order within a rubric of justice. Per Job, the person who does justice shows compassion and performs acts of charity. His list of just behavior includes hearing grievances (v. 13); meeting the needs of the poor (v. 16a); comforting the bereaved (v. 16b); and providing bed and board for the orphan (vv. 17–18), clothing for the needy (vv. 19–20), and legal defense for the powerless (v. 21). Job's protases imply that he took every available opportunity to enact compassion and justice, as anyone who is able should, and therefore he considered himself above reproach.

The extreme consequence envisioned in the apodosis (v. 22) is loss of an arm. The ramifications of this idiomatic expression reach beyond anatomical casualty: both arm and hand are metaphors for power. If Job had possessed the power to help and failed to do so, his power would be revoked.

---

22. While we could imagine someone being enticed through his own imagination, unrelated to any activity by the woman in question, Hebrew usage of this verb suggests that the enticer's behavior is deliberate.

31:24 – 28. Attention now turns to sources of trust and security. Job raises two possibilities. The first is the familiar faith in material wealth. Job has not chosen a life of poverty or given away his property, but he insists that he exhibits an appropriate attitude toward his worldly goods. Job maintains that he has successfully held great wealth without finding security therein.

The second potential locus of trust is the gods, particularly the astral deities (sun and moon). The offense to which Job refers involves perception followed by a response of worship (v. 27b). In verse 29, the verb "enticed" is the same as in 31:9, although the verbal stem is different (Qal, four other occurrences: Deut. 11:16; Job 5:2; Prov. 20:19; Hos. 7:11). Contextual usage of this stem suggests a stative aspect,[23] "to be gullible or mindless; easily led astray." While some English translations render the act of worship as a hand offering a kiss of homage (NIV), the Hebrew is much more laconic and somewhat puzzling: "my hand kissed my mouth." The verb "kiss" (*nšq* in Qal plus prep. *l-*) appears in a worship context only one other time (1 Kings 19:13, kissing Baal).[24] In every instance of this phrase, the preposition *l-* takes a person as its object, never an anatomical part such as hand or lips. For the latter, *ʿal* would be used (cf. Gen. 41:40). In Job 31:27b, there is no person in view, only anatomical references. "My hand" must be the subject of the verb, because "my mouth" is introduced with the preposition. Every other occurrence of this verb has a person as its subject, so context is the only available guide to the potential meaning of "my hand kissed my mouth." The most plausible interpretation is suggested by ancient Near Eastern iconography, in which a worshiper often appears with hand over mouth in the presence of a deity, a pose commonly interpreted as a gesture of worship.[25] For example, Hammurabi's stele portrays Hammurabi before the sun god, Shamash, so in his case the gesture is an acknowledgment of the sun (god).

The apodosis comes in verse 28, where Job indicates the expected consequences of such misplaced trust and worship. The NIV refers to the actions in views as "sins to be judged," since they would render Job "unfaithful to God." The word translated "judged" (*pelili*) appears only in this chapter (see also v. 11). Because contextual data is limited, to better understand this word's meaning we may turn to root associations, which suggest that

---

23. R. Mosis, "פתה," *TDOT*, 12:164. The Qal describes a stative condition, whereas the Niphal describes a passive response to the action of another.

24. Hos. 13:2 refers to kissing the calf, but there is no preposition used.

25. For a few examples, see the "worshiper of Larsa" (*ZIBBCOT*, 5:289) and Hammurabi at the top of his stele of legal sayings (*ZIBBCOT*, 5:377). In the Persian period, similar deference was given to the king (*ZIBBCOT*, 3:424).

it refers to taking proactive steps to initiate a course of action. This word highlights a recurring theme of the section, because taking action is precisely the response that Job is attempting to elicit from God. In the midst of his oath, Job reminds God that he is obliged to take action if Job has committed any of these errors, including in this case "unfaithfulness" to God. The word rendered "unfaithfulness" is the root *kḥš*, which in the Piel stem often connotes dissociating or disowning. Job identifies such behavior as sufficiently serious to necessitate retribution from God.

This sin of dissociation is an example of an offense that carries much more weight in Israel than the rest of the ancient Near East. In a polytheistic setting, attention to another a deity is a nonissue. The very essence of polytheism is the recognition of the existence of many gods. But any given worshiper would have to choose which deities would be worthy of attention and worship. In a somewhat analogous manner, today people might choose to support a particular charity or mission organization. They may give occasionally or regularly, as influenced by a variety of factors. At some point, they may be impressed with one organization or disappointed by another, and adjust their giving patterns accordingly. Such a shift is not necessarily considered unfaithfulness, but it could involve dissociation. In the ancient Near East, acknowledgment of sun or moon would not equate to detachment from a city's patron deity or one's personal deities. But in an Israelite context of monotheism, recognition of any other deity involves an intrinsic dissociation with Yahweh, for he tolerates no rival.

31:29–32, 38–40. The overarching theme of this paragraph may be termed "grace to outsiders"—outsiders being identified as those who are not members in good standing in the community. The text references various categories of people: enemies (vv. 29–30), strangers (vv. 31–32), and landowners (vv. 38–39). The first two groups are defined clearly, and their outsider status is readily visible. The third category, however, is more problematic. The NIV translates "tenants," but the Hebrew word (*baʿal*) usually signifies owner or master. If the two lines of verse 39 are parallel, and there is every reason to believe they are, the verse describes Job as devouring landowners' property, not just its yield, without payment. Such confiscation would naturally bring grief, expressed here by a deep sigh, to the owners.

In the ancient world, the unpredictable climate often caused consecutive years of nonproductivity, resulting in debt and subsequent forfeiture of property for those with meager holdings. Large landholders too could be forced into insolvency and fall prey to powerful rivals. Any scenario of forced forfeiture makes sense within these verses, but if they are associated with verses 29–34 (a proposal open to question), the "outsider" status would be best filled by agricultural competitors, who could be forced out of business.

31:33–37. This section serves as a transition to the key verses of the chapter: Job's signature to his oath (31:35–37). In verse 33, Job comments that he has not hidden offense in the "fold of his garment" (pers. trans.); the word appears only here, so there is some uncertainty as to its exact meaning, but it is generally agreed that it refers to his clothing rather than physiology (e.g., NIV, "heart"). More significant is the interpretation of the first line's comparative phrase, which the NIV renders "as men do." An alternative reading understands the word *'adam* not as humankind in general, but as Adam in the Genesis narrative.[26] In this more specific reading, Job asserts that he did not conceal his sin as Adam did in the garden. The same question of whether *'adam* is general or specific occurs in two other Old Testament passages that compare a person's fate to that of *'adam* (Ps. 82:7; Hos. 6:7). In this instance, we should remember that Genesis refers to Adam concealing himself, not his sin.

While some build arguments based on Job's probable knowledge (or lack thereof) concerning the Genesis narrative, the better interpretive method is to evaluate what makes the best logical sense in the passage. In fact, the comparison to Adam makes no sense in this context—Job comments in the next verse that his motivations for hiding sin would have been fear of the crowd or the contempt of other families. These fears have no relevance to Adam's motivation, so it is unlikely that Job employs him as a comparison here. Job's allusion to fear of public scorn reminds us how central the opinion of family friends was to identity and self-perception.

Job's oath reaches its grand finale in 31:35–37. In the absence of an advocate or judge, he sets his signature to the dossier of oaths. The text includes no word for this dossier (NIV adds "defense" for clarification). His "signature" is an X mark—the Hebrew word is *taw*, the final letter of the alphabet, which in the earliest forms of the script took the shape of an X.

Job calls not only on El Shaddai to answer him (although he may not expect an answer), but also on anyone who wishes to contest his claims of innocence. Job employs legal language here; any potential litigant (*'iš ribi*; NIV: "accuser") must submit a formal claim (indictment). If no one, divine or mortal, steps forward with such a claim, Job will have secured his vindication and, consequently, the possibility of reintegration into society. In anticipation of that positive outcome, Job uses royal imagery ("prince" and "crown") to describe his willingness and ability to give full account for his actions. Job is no cringing defendant; he will receive any challenge with confident assurance of his innocence.

---

26. Clines, *Job 21–37*, 1030.

Job's imagery (bearing the indictment on his shoulder, donning it as a crown) also suggests that he will publicize any claims against him. Commentators have explored whether this language might represent a historical legal custom involving an actual physical enactment, but there is no available documentation of such a practice, and the description may well be metaphorical. Regardless, the significant implication is Job's eagerness for the opportunity to respond to formal legal charges.

Job's final formal speech thus concludes on one of the book's high points. He has adamantly denied any wrongdoing and has taken a decisive (and risky) step to try to force a response from God. If God remains silent, Job, though undoubtedly still dissatisfied, could at least theoretically claim vindication (i.e., God did not strike him dead for a false oath) in order to facilitate social reintegration and restoration of his status and identity. Such an accomplishment would enable Job to restore his sense of coherence.

Rhetorical Strategy

JOB'S DISCOURSE CONCERNS THEMES of coherence and equilibrium as he considers his plight:

- Chapter 29 recalls the coherence of the past.
- Chapter 30 describes the incoherence of the present.
- Chapter 31 seeks to regain coherence not by revising Job's expectations or his focus on justice, but by attempting to force God's hand through the oath of innocence. This strategy is not designed to regain Job's prosperity but to achieve vindication, albeit tacitly.

In the dialogues, Job's friends offered him a solution to find coherence and equilibrium, but at a cost. Their resolution required Job's righteousness to be motivated by gain. According to their worldview, the cosmos is founded on justice, and thus coherence is sustained by adopting the Great Symbiosis. Appeasement is the all-purpose equilibrator: find a path to appeasement, regain the favor of deity, and prosperity and blessing will be restored. If Job had taken this route to regain coherence, he would have been required to adopt a perspective of self-interested righteousness. The primary question underlying the dialogue section of the book is whether Job's righteousness is disinterested.

Having rejected his friends' solution, in Job 29–31, Job seeks his own path to coherence and equilibrium. The primary question becomes that familiar quandary: Why do God's policies allow righteous people to suffer? After juxtaposing his previous prosperity (ch. 29) and his current degradation (ch. 30) in stark contrast, Job presents the core of his case in the oath of chapter 31. If Job's plan is successful, he will demonstrate conclusively that God's policies are incoherent. In the dialogues, Job has prioritized his righteousness over prosperity. In this discourse, he demonstrates that he values his righteousness more than God's reputation.

Job's oath of innocence in chapter 31 addresses the passage's underlying question: Why does God allow the righteous to suffer? In his oath, Job seeks coherence based on himself rather than God. Job's oath is intended to vindicate him, and in that vindication he will find coherence and equilibrium. Although his life remains in shambles, he will attain a measure of peace if his innocence is declared. Additionally, he will have public evidence of vindication, which may provide the means to regain social integration. Although Job never demonstrates interest in regaining prosperity, he certainly desires to recover his status as a righteous person within his community. Because his desire is for a status based on recognition and approval of his righteousness, his righteousness may yet be characterized as disinterested. His desire for status can be classified as disinterested because it is his righteousness that motivates him. If he is recognized as righteous, the status will automatically follow. He is not pursuing office or honors but a reputation for righteousness, which has been tarnished.

How exactly does Job's attempt to regain coherence and equilibrium function, particularly in relation to previous discussions surrounding the RP? In the dialogues, coherence and equilibrium would be found when the RP was in evidence. Under the RP, if Job confessed sin, his prosperity would be restored, and all would be right in a just world. But Job is notably uncooperative. Had he cooperated, God's policies would have been revealed as inadequate, because Job's righteousness would have been motivated by gain, which would confirm the Challenger's suspicions. An RP-based worldview would have been preserved, but as pretense only, because Job's experience was not truly just.

In the oath of innocence in chapter 31, coherence and equilibrium would theoretically result from God's expected continued silence, which would tacitly vindicate Job. As noted, Job would not necessarily regain prosperity, but his reputation would be vindicated and his claim to righteousness upheld. The coherence attained here stems not from the RP, but Job's perception of himself as righteous. This scenario renders God's policies capricious and discredits his reputation—he is neither just nor wise.

This coherence comes at a high theological cost. The battle would have been won but the ramifications of the theological conclusions would be devastating. If Job prevails in the confrontation, God is reduced to a power-ful being who possesses neither wisdom nor justice. He is a chaos creature who is not just arbitrary, capricious, or inscrutable; rather, he is uncon-trolled even by himself. This result is worse than the result that could have come from the dialogue scenario. There God would have been reduced to a deity like any other in the ancient Near East. In Job's scenario, God is no God at all.

If we understand wisdom to be aligned with coherence and equilibrium, Job thinks he knows the way to it (contrary to the claim of the author of the Wisdom poem in ch. 28). As previously suggested, fearing Adonai (the heart of wisdom) involves an element of submission. Yet Job is the oppo-site of submissive; he is confrontational and demanding. Job's attempt at wisdom, entangled in his struggles for coherence, requires him to discount God's wisdom.

Theology: Job's View of God

AT THIS JUNCTURE, IT is helpful to consider how the view of God expressed in this section fits into Job's broader argument and whether this view differs from previous statements. Within the dialogue section, the strongest nega-tive statements about God appear in 16:9 – 14. There Job claims God has acted in anger (16:9) and without pity (16:13). By contrast, the accusation in 30:18 – 23 that God has behaved with reckless cruelty (*'akzar*, 30:21) is significantly more severe.[27] In the dialogues, Job infers that God is angry and portrays his actions as incomprehensible, yet he continues to seek the reasons for God's actions, as demonstrated by his repeated attempts to force God into court to defend his justice. Throughout the dialogues, Job never questions—and in fact affirms—God's wisdom (e.g., 12:13).

In Job's present discourse, however, he portrays God as a chaos creature (ch. 30) who brings disorder and who can be outmaneuvered (ch. 31). Job's case has ceased questioning God's justice and begun questioning his wis-dom—precisely the divine quality affirmed in chapter 28, providing fur-ther evidence that the Wisdom poem in chapter 28 should not be viewed as Job's speech. In a marked shift from the dialogues, God has become the author of disruption. In 7:12, Job wondered why God was treating him as a chaos creature; here he assigns that role to God.

---

27. The distinction is difficult, because in some passages, such as Isa. 13:9, the cruelty (*'akzar*) is characterized by anger, and in other passages, such as Jer. 50:42, it is character-ized by lack of compassion. Waltke defines the adjective as defining "an insensitive and merciless person who willfully, knowingly, and unrelentingly inflicts pain on others" (B. Waltke, *The Book of Proverbs 1 – 15* [Grand Rapids: Eerdmans, 2004], 312).

The oath of chapter 31 is intended to accomplish a forced coherence and equilibrium. If God does not strike Job dead for a false oath, the assumption would be that he is innocent. If Job is innocent, then God has acted unjustly in bringing disaster on him. The unanswered oath juxtaposed to the horrors Job has suffered would demonstrate that God's policies cannot be carried out consistently. If Job's oath stands unanswered, Job wins, and God's policies have been proven flawed with regard to the suffering of the righteous—Job's primary concern in this section.

Although the categories of denied offenses in Job's oath have been addressed, we have yet to consider the theology revealed in other parts of chapter 31. Job has demonstrated his *righteousness* to be disinterested, but that does not mean that his *theology* is disinterested. The primary question of the dialogues concerned what motivated Job: blessing or righteousness? In the discourse section, the question becomes who is in the right—Job or God? In effect, Job pits his reputation against God's. His view of the intrinsic importance of righteousness, as displayed in the dialogue section, is appropriate and biblical; his view of God as displayed in the discourse is not. Job is wrong about the nature of God. He himself is dissatisfied with his conclusions about God and would wish them otherwise, but his drive to achieve coherence can only reach its goal, he believes, if he adopts an alternative view of God. In this respect, Job mirrors the behavior of many Christians today, who make costly theological sacrifices in order to attain a measure of coherence in their world. Thus it is beneficial to examine the flawed theological underpinnings of Job's position.

Manipulation. The most significant flaw in Job's theology is his belief that God can be manipulated and outmaneuvered. Hints at this weakness appear as early as chapter 1, where we see that Job perhaps was treating God as if he were a petty deity who could be managed by ritual (Job 1:4–5)—a common practice in the ancient world. This type of manipulation is not limited to the ancient world, however. The belief that deity is limited and may be controlled in some manner lies behind any thought system that we label paganism. In this sense, a "pagan splinter" is lodged in each of our hearts, most likely as a consequence of the fall; we each are inclined to try to bring God to heel, however subtle or subconscious our attempts may be.

Job's clearest attempt to outmaneuver God appears in his strategic oath of innocence, in which God's reputation is forfeit while Job's is salvaged. This effort, however, is categorically different from ritual manipulation, since the latter supposes that the divine being in question has needs. Job does not treat God as needy, but as apathetic, preoccupied, or inept. The oath is evidence of Job's core theological problem, because it underestimates God's wisdom and undermines his character.

Trusting God—which is the same as fearing God—means accepting the fact that God does not need us or anything we possess or accomplish, and acknowledging that he is not lacking in any aspect of his character or nature. The God revealed in the Bible cannot be manipulated or outmaneuvered, and our petty attempts to do so only demonstrate our refusal to accept Scripture's presentation of God in favor of our own caricatures of him.

God as chaos creature. Job's revised portrayal of God as chaos creature is the inevitable conclusion of the philosophy Job adopts. If God does not have reasons for his choices, is not universally governed by justice, and influences human lives with his power, he logically falls into the category of chaos creature—a category well-known throughout the ancient world.[28]

Chaos creatures have no direct parallel in our modern worldview. They represent a cosmic element that works against order. They should not be equated with demons, although demons in the ancient world sometimes pose threats to order as well. The ancient world construed demons differently from what we do today; the ancients viewed them as amoral (as we would consider a tornado) and under the control of deity. Most demons could function for either good or evil, but if left unsupervised might run amok.

It is highly debatable whether the Old Testament contains any reference to demons. Notable biblical examples of chaos creatures in the contrast include Leviathan, Tannin, and Rahab. In biblical theology as well as the ancient Near East in general, these monsters do not pose a threat to God.[29] In ancient Near Eastern contexts, chaos creatures can adopt an adversarial role (as Anzu does, for example), and in the Old Testament, God at times opposes their influence. But overall, these creatures work against order, not against God, and they come into conflict with deity only when deity works to establish order.

To help us understand how Job thinks about God in this discourse, we may turn to an eighth-century myth known as the Poem of Erra, in which the deity Nergal takes on the role of chaos creature.[30] This work, also known as Erra and Ishum, is believed to be a mythological reflection of the political upheaval that took place in Babylon in the first half of the first millennium BC. Nergal, god of plague and the netherworld, tricks Marduk, chief god of Babylon, into leaving the city. Nergal then wreaks havoc until

---

28. See discussions in J. G. Westenholz, *Dragons, Monsters and Fabulous Beasts* (Jerusalem: Bible Lands Museum, 2004).

29. Note that Leviathan is created as part of the ordered cosmos in Gen. 1 and is for God's sport in Ps. 104:26; yet in Ps. 74:14, his heads are crushed.

30. For translation, see *COS*, 1.113: 404–16.

Marduk returns and restores order. While I am not persuaded that Job borrows from the Poem of Erra or that a point-by-point comparison may be sustained, the Poem of Erra demonstrates that a god acting as chaos creature as a known motif in the ancient world.[31] The key feature of this idea is the deity's lack of discrimination between the righteous and the wicked.[32]

In the Old Testament, God sometimes uses disorder as punishment (e.g., the flood of Noah, the destruction of the temple and Jerusalem by the Babylonians). In such cases, however, the text carefully notes that God's actions constituted just punishment of indictable evil. Prophets such as Habakkuk sometimes demand explanations for events apparently lacking rationale, and ultimately explanations are presented. In contrast, Job does not simply question—he accuses. As noted, this behavior demonstrates that Job has succumbed to a flawed view of deity common in the ancient Near East. Because he experiences what he perceives to be irrational disorder, he finally concludes that God must be the author of that disorder. Indeed, in some sense God is the agent of Job's distress, but Job has yet to comprehend God's role in a theologically appropriate manner.

Weighing in honest scales. The very nature of Job's plea to be evaluated accurately reveals a deep theological flaw. His request implies that there is an alternative—namely, that God might not assess Job's case honestly. To admit such a possibility is to establish ourselves as arbiters of God's policies; *our* judgment determines whether God does right or not. Yet if God does not always behave according to what is right, what becomes of the standard by which we may measure justice?

Job seeks to hold God accountable. This is poor theology. In the ancient Near East, it was necessary to hold the gods accountable for their actions, because they were not naturally inclined to behave appropriately. Yet even their accountability was to the divine council, not to human beings.

In his discourse, Job pictures God as a being who can be manipulated, who tends to be irrational and uncontrollable, and who must be called to accountability. The latter point inevitably assumes a standard outside of God, making God a contingent being. Just as the biblical text as a whole does not affirm this picture of God, the book of Job does not expect the reader to adopt it as revealed truth. At this stage in the book, Job's perspective is not refuted, but Elihu will eventually rebuke Job, and Yahweh will provide an alternate view. Consequently, we can conclude that the purpose of this section is not to teach us about God, but rather to illustrate how human beings in the throes of crisis might easily misconstrue God's nature.

---

31. S. A. Meier, "Destroyer," *DDD²*, 241.
32. See Erra and Ishum, 4:104–7; Erra and Ishum 5:6–10.

The book continues to explore the question of who is at fault for the mess that sometimes characterizes our lives, and in so doing, it exposes the selfishness inherent in our inclination to impugn God rather than ourselves.

MOTIVATION FOR RIGHTEOUSNESS. THE contrast between the innocence oaths in Job and the Egyptian Book of the Dead offers some insight into problems that persist in today's church. Is our behavior motivated by a desire to be righteous, or have we developed a social code that functions almost as a magical means of ensuring access to heaven (as the Egyptians did)?

It is easy to slip into a pragmatic mentality that views our religious and spiritual commitments as means for gaining benefits. Without a doubt our righteousness—though it be as filthy rags—brings important benefits, such as forgiveness of sin and eternal life, making it all the more difficult to ensure that our motives are pure as we pursue right living. Our righteousness does not earn these benefits, but Scripture traces a connection between the salvation we are granted and the righteousness that characterizes our life of faith (e.g., Matt. 25:31–46; Heb. 4:11; 10:19–31; James 2:14–26; 1 John 3:11–24). We may also be lured into believing that our righteousness does (or should) earn us special consideration from God. *It is critical that we as Christians understand that righteousness is solely an end, never a means.* Righteousness is not a bargaining chip but is rather the offering that God asks of us and which we owe to him as our Creator and Savior. Righteousness should be our natural response to the fact that God is God.

Biblical values. Although Job has assessed the situation incorrectly and reached false conclusions about God and the world, he demonstrates a firm grasp of values that are legitimately biblical. As indicated in the chart on p. 325, these values are integrity of character, sexual purity, compassion toward the vulnerable, trust in God, and grace to outsiders. We should seek to imitate these values, although the biblical text does not mandate them here. The values that Job upholds delineate a set of behaviors that continue to challenge us today.

In fact, the five categories that they represent could be considered among the most significant areas for Christian self-evaluation. Our struggles today relatively rarely take the form of theft, murder, idol worship, or polytheism. Most churches, however, are plagued by conflicts in which integrity of character is sadly lacking. We can easily recognize ourselves in Job's list. Too often churches must engage in discipline related to sexual sin.

Many churches insulate themselves from the needs of the world, neglecting compassion. In an established church culture, we may find it easier to rely on ourselves, our programs, and our strategies than to rely on God. Outsiders may enter the doors of the church once and never return, because they were treated coldly or ignored altogether, and too often the church's population itself is divided among social cliques, with lonely people held at arm's length. Fostering values such as Job's helps us honestly evaluate our shortcomings and avoid erosion of character within the church.

Faulty theology as a consequence of experiences. What theological price are we willing to pay in order to achieve coherence in our lives? Do we prioritize our coherence above God's reputation? Do we give more concern to our reputation than God's reputation? If we truly believe what we say we believe about the Bible—that it is God's revelation of himself, in which he offers an understanding of his character that is both right and true—then that biblical revelation takes precedence over our feeble attempts to discern coherence in our world and over any defense we may wish to make of our reputation.

Kelly's Story[33]

JHW: JOB RESORTED TO various strategies that revealed much about his perception of God. In times of hardship, our view of God is put to the test. I would like you to reflect on whether you found your experiences leading to such strategies, and how they put pressure on your view of God. Did you ever find yourself trying to manipulate God? What did that look like, and how did you move past that approach?

Kelly: I did find that my view of God was pressured during my own experiences of hardship, but it was a lie about his character that was so deeply buried that it was impossible to recognize until I started searching for it. We have seen throughout the book of Job that so often in our struggles, our first cry to God is, "Why? Why would you do this or allow this to happen?" Even by asking that common question, we are challenging God's character and how he runs the world. As we challenge him, it is a clear sign that it is not God's character that is flawed, but our view of him.

When I would confront God in pain or anger, I did not necessarily manipulate him or try to test him. The list described in the chapter about Job 28 states that when we fear the Lord, we do not think of him as "detached, incompetent, limited, corrupt, shortsighted, or petty." But I

---

33. Kelly interacts with parts of her story in each Contemporary Significance section. For the introduction to the details of her story, see Contemporary Significance in the commentary on ch. 1, pp. 87–97.

think that many people could identify with this way of thinking about God. After experiencing extreme pain and trials, it is easy to believe the lie that God fits one or many of those descriptions.

Personally, the lies that I had started to believe about God's character were more in relation to his love for me. I believed that God had the power to heal, but that he never would choose to or it would never be in his will for my life. Then God put an amazing Christian woman in my life as a mentor, who prayed with me and met with me, helping me struggle with the emotional pain I was dealing with. It was in one of my conversations with her, when she asked me to reflect on that angry conversation with God, that I realized that I was listening to the lie that God did not love me. When I finally realized the lie that was binding me, I could begin to pray against it. She would ask me to pray and go to him with that lie against his character and ask, "Now what does God's Word have to say about that lie."

JHW: Job was most interested in finding coherence for himself, even if it resulted in accepting a downgraded view of deity. Do you recognize that inclination in any of the ways that you responded to your suffering? What did that look like, and how did you move past it?

Kelly: Pursuing wisdom in times of suffering is a long process, and as I reflect back on different stages in the process, I can identify a time when I responded trying to find coherence, but at the cost of accepting a down-graded view of God's deity. In the spring of 2009, the season I continually refer back to, when I felt my health took a big turn for the worse, I remember coming to the conclusion that God must be causing all these things to happen at once, in order to strengthen my testimony to be a light for others. I found coherence or a "purpose" to hold on to that made some sort of sense in my mind; but if this statement was true, it meant that I would have to accept that God is a God that uses people for their testimonies at their expense. As I said before, I struggled with God's love for me. I knew the right words in my mind about Jesus' love, and at times I would feel his love at the surface but it did not sink into my heart.

Even the most recent trip to California caused me to have a difficult conversation with God. I had prayed for months for him to shut the door if this was not in his will. I asked the Lord to make all of the California plans difficult if it was not in his will and would not be successful. Not only did the clinic have a miraculous opening in their schedule during the exact time we were available to go, but we were also offered free housing in Los Angeles that turned out to be right next to where the clinic is, so it seemed each step in the planning period was being blessed by God.

Yet the trip only resulted in a huge financial burden that will take years to pay off, along with pain and confusion. I had an angry conversation with God on the long fifteen-hour drive home that really revealed to me how many lies I was still struggling with from my experiences and how that had affected my view of God. The idea arose yet again that God was "strengthening my testimony." Those words became very bitter. Some days—a lot of days actually—I would be grateful for how my testimony has encouraged people. But I definitely wrestled with God about when I was going to get a break. And if I truly analyzed what I was implying by saying that to God, it was as though he was detached, without deep love for me, just ready to do something else because he knew regardless, I'd still believe in him. I am embarrassed as I type these words to think of how I downgraded the deity of God.

Then I also found myself accepting a downgraded view of his deity during the recovery process of my left arm. Feeling and motion came and went, fluctuating. We would see improvement, and then randomly I'd lose control of my fingers while sitting in class and wouldn't be able to write notes. Then I would humbly have to ask a peer if I could copy their notes later. So I became fearful—fearful of the next thing God would do to "strengthen my testimony." So I began trying to not "give him more opportunities" to hurt me. This meant that I would avoid any medical procedure or medication that was said to help me because I did not want to risk God's allowing the procedure to fail, leaving me worse off. I believed if there was a risk of something going wrong, it would. That statement is full of lies about God's character.

When we realize how our view of God has been distorted, we need to ask ourselves what experience on earth led us to that conclusion about God. The biggest step in healing and correcting that mind-set is identifying what the lies are and where they come from. When I was in the thick of it, I couldn't tell you why I was so sad, hurt, confused—beyond the physical pain. It was a jumbled mess in my head. I just knew the pain I was feeling emotionally, physically, and spiritually was suffocating me. It wasn't until I started meeting with Beth, my mentor, to just talk about some of the things I was experiencing that I started to dissect it to find out what the roots were beyond some deep lies and wounds.

That process was not fun by any means. It took intentional effort. Who wants to sit in a room and talk about the things that hurt you the most or about your deepest fears? So many times I dragged my feet, dreading the conversation that was ahead, and it was on those days that I saw the most breakthroughs. So I think a huge contributing factor to getting past the approach of distorting God's character in response to your pain, is first, to be willing to address the pain and the circumstances. Second, seek a mentor. Find someone who can help you through this process, because for me, if I didn't have someone asking about me continuously, I would bottle all of my emotions, listening to the lies in my head because they sounded like truth based on my experiences. Finally, I learned we don't reflect on the past or the present pains to identify the lies that are binding us and then forget them; instead, we identify them so we can redeem them. Redeeming lies about our Father can only happen with the help of the Holy Spirit.

JHW: Job attempted to call God to account. Do you have thoughts on that?

Kelly: Calling God to account is one more thing that identifies your view of him as flawed, and I did have those weak moments where I thought I had some authority to do that. In the middle of my semester in my junior year at Wheaton, things were at their worst. I could no longer take notes in class, type papers, or use a camera—and I was attempting to double major in studio art photography and Spanish. With an eighteen-hour class load and not a functioning hand to get the thoughts in my head to paper, I was at my wit's end.

One blessing was, I was seeing an amazing chiropractor in Naperville, Dr. Scott Selby, to whom I give credit for helping me get the use of my left arm back. After learning more about the disc injury causing the loss of feeling and motion, I started seeing him three times a week. He would realign the disc and I would be able to use my hand for a day or so, then slowly I would lose feeling again as the disc slid back out of place. I had to reorganize my homework based on which days I could see Dr. Selby and be able to use my hand. So I'd try to type all of my homework, papers, and so on in that short period of time because it was uncertain how long I'd have use of fine motor skills in my hand.

I remember one night, after coming home from seeing Dr. Selby, that I was feeling hopeful we might be making progress. When I got to my apartment and pulled the Mai Thai's pad thai out of the fridge, I reached up in the cabinet to get a plate, and as I began to take it out, the weight became too much and my hand gave out, sending the plate crashing to the floor. It was one plate. I couldn't lift one plate. I sat on the floor in the broken glass around me and began to cry. I remember feeling as if God had me in the wilderness. I did not feel his presence, his comfort, his guidance, anything. I remember calling out to God as I sobbed on the floor, once again with limp arms saying, "God, you picked a really bad time to be silent or have me in the wilderness. This is when I need you the most and you choose to be silent. Please come! I NEED YOU! I need your help!"

God did show up, but I soon found out it was because I finally recognized that I needed him. My lack of trust in him, that he'd be there or that he'd help me, caused me to resort to use my own strength, and I created that distance. I remember feeling as if God was just saying, "Kelly . . . I have been waiting for you to say that. You do need me." I do believe that God oftentimes uses a famine in order to work up an appetite for him.

Job 32–37

❧

So these three men stopped answering Job, because he was righteous in his own eyes. ²But Elihu son of Barakel the Buzite, of the family of Ram, became very angry with Job for justifying himself rather than God. ³He was also angry with the three friends, because they had found no way to refute Job, and yet had condemned him. ⁴Now Elihu had waited before speaking to Job because they were older than he. ⁵But when he saw that the three men had nothing more to say, his anger was aroused.

⁶So Elihu son of Barakel the Buzite said:

"I am young in years,
  and you are old;
that is why I was fearful,
  not daring to tell you what I know.
⁷I thought, 'Age should speak;
  advanced years should teach wisdom.'
⁸But it is the spirit in a man,
  the breath of the Almighty, that gives him understanding.
⁹It is not only the old who are wise,
  not only the aged who understand what is right.

¹⁰"Therefore I say: Listen to me;
  I too will tell you what I know.
¹¹I waited while you spoke,
  I listened to your reasoning;
while you were searching for words,
  ¹²I gave you my full attention.
But not one of you has proved Job wrong;
  none of you has answered his arguments.
¹³Do not say, 'We have found wisdom;
  let God refute him, not man.'
¹⁴But Job has not marshaled his words against me,
  and I will not answer him with your arguments.

¹⁵"They are dismayed and have no more to say;
  words have failed them.
¹⁶Must I wait, now that they are silent,
  now that they stand there with no reply?

¹⁷I too will have my say;
   I too will tell what I know.
¹⁸For I am full of words,
   and the spirit within me compels me;
¹⁹inside I am like bottled-up wine,
   like new wineskins ready to burst.
²⁰I must speak and find relief;
   I must open my lips and reply.
²¹I will show partiality to no one,
   nor will I flatter any man;
²²for if I were skilled in flattery,
   my Maker would soon take me away.

^{33:1}"But now, Job, listen to my words;
   pay attention to everything I say.
²I am about to open my mouth;
   my words are on the tip of my tongue.
³My words come from an upright heart;
   my lips sincerely speak what I know.
⁴The Spirit of God has made me;
   the breath of the Almighty gives me life.
⁵Answer me then, if you can;
   prepare yourself and confront me.
⁶I am just like you before God;
   I too have been taken from clay.
⁷No fear of me should alarm you,
   nor should my hand be heavy upon you.

⁸"But you have said in my hearing—
   I heard the very words—
⁹'I am pure and without sin;
   I am clean and free from guilt.
¹⁰Yet God has found fault with me;
   he considers me his enemy.
¹¹He fastens my feet in shackles;
   he keeps close watch on all my paths.'

¹²"But I tell you, in this you are not right,
   for God is greater than man.
¹³Why do you complain to him
   that he answers none of man's words?
¹⁴For God does speak—now one way, now another—
   though man may not perceive it.

¹⁵In a dream, in a vision of the night,
  when deep sleep falls on men
  as they slumber in their beds,
¹⁶he may speak in their ears
  and terrify them with warnings,
¹⁷to turn man from wrongdoing
  and keep him from pride,
¹⁸to preserve his soul from the pit,
  his life from perishing by the sword.
¹⁹Or a man may be chastened on a bed of pain
  with constant distress in his bones,
²⁰so that his very being finds food repulsive
  and his soul loathes the choicest meal.
²¹His flesh wastes away to nothing,
  and his bones, once hidden, now stick out.
²²His soul draws near to the pit,
  and his life to the messengers of death.

²³"Yet if there is an angel on his side
  as a mediator, one out of a thousand,
  to tell a man what is right for him,
²⁴to be gracious to him and say,
  'Spare him from going down to the pit;
  I have found a ransom for him'—
²⁵then his flesh is renewed like a child's;
  it is restored as in the days of his youth.
²⁶He prays to God and finds favor with him,
  he sees God's face and shouts for joy;
  he is restored by God to his righteous state.
²⁷Then he comes to men and says,
  'I sinned, and perverted what was right,
  but I did not get what I deserved.
²⁸He redeemed my soul from going down to
    the pit,
  and I will live to enjoy the light.'

²⁹"God does all these things to a man—
  twice, even three times—
³⁰to turn back his soul from the pit,
  that the light of life may shine on him.
³¹"Pay attention, Job, and listen to me;
  be silent, and I will speak.

³²If you have anything to say, answer me;
    speak up, for I want you to be cleared.
³³But if not, then listen to me;
    be silent, and I will teach you wisdom."

^{34:1} Then Elihu said:

²"Hear my words, you wise men;
    listen to me, you men of learning.
³For the ear tests words
    as the tongue tastes food.
⁴Let us discern for ourselves what is right;
    let us learn together what is good.

⁵"Job says, 'I am innocent,
    but God denies me justice.
⁶Although I am right,
    I am considered a liar;
although I am guiltless,
    his arrow inflicts an incurable wound.'
⁷What man is like Job,
    who drinks scorn like water?
⁸He keeps company with evildoers;
    he associates with wicked men.
⁹For he says, 'It profits a man nothing
    when he tries to please God.'

¹⁰"So listen to me, you men of understanding.
    Far be it from God to do evil,
    from the Almighty to do wrong.
¹¹He repays a man for what he has done;
    he brings upon him what his conduct deserves.
¹²It is unthinkable that God would do wrong,
    that the Almighty would pervert justice.
¹³Who appointed him over the earth?
    Who put him in charge of the whole world?
¹⁴If it were his intention
    and he withdrew his spirit and breath,
¹⁵all mankind would perish together
    and man would return to the dust.

¹⁶"If you have understanding, hear this;
    listen to what I say.

¹⁷Can he who hates justice govern?
>   Will you condemn the just and mighty One?
¹⁸Is he not the One who says to kings, 'You are
>   worthless,'
>   and to nobles, 'You are wicked,'
¹⁹who shows no partiality to princes
>   and does not favor the rich over the poor,
for they are all the work of his hands?
²⁰They die in an instant, in the middle of the night;
>   the people are shaken and they pass away;
>   the mighty are removed without human hand.

²¹"His eyes are on the ways of men;
>   he sees their every step.
²²There is no dark place, no deep shadow,
>   where evildoers can hide.
²³God has no need to examine men further,
>   that they should come before him for judgment.
²⁴Without inquiry he shatters the mighty
>   and sets up others in their place.
²⁵Because he takes note of their deeds,
>   he overthrows them in the night and they are crushed.
²⁶He punishes them for their wickedness
>   where everyone can see them,
²⁷because they turned from following him
>   and had no regard for any of his ways.
²⁸They caused the cry of the poor to come before him,
>   so that he heard the cry of the needy.
²⁹But if he remains silent, who can condemn him?
>   If he hides his face, who can see him?
Yet he is over man and nation alike,
>   ³⁰to keep a godless man from ruling,
>   from laying snares for the people.

³¹"Suppose a man says to God,
>   'I am guilty but will offend no more.
³²Teach me what I cannot see;
>   if I have done wrong, I will not do so again.'
³³Should God then reward you on your terms,
>   when you refuse to repent?
You must decide, not I;
>   so tell me what you know.

³⁴"Men of understanding declare,
   wise men who hear me say to me,
³⁵'Job speaks without knowledge;
   his words lack insight.'
³⁶Oh, that Job might be tested to the utmost
   for answering like a wicked man!
³⁷To his sin he adds rebellion;
   scornfully he claps his hands among us
   and multiplies his words against God."

³⁵:¹Then Elihu said:

²"Do you think this is just?
   You say, 'I will be cleared by God.'
³Yet you ask him, 'What profit is it to me,
   and what do I gain by not sinning?'

⁴"I would like to reply to you
   and to your friends with you.
⁵Look up at the heavens and see;
   gaze at the clouds so high above you.
⁶If you sin, how does that affect him?
   If your sins are many, what does that do to him?
⁷If you are righteous, what do you give to him,
   or what does he receive from your hand?
⁸Your wickedness affects only a man like yourself,
   and your righteousness only the sons of men.

⁹"Men cry out under a load of oppression;
   they plead for relief from the arm of the powerful.
¹⁰But no one says, 'Where is God my Maker,
   who gives songs in the night,
¹¹who teaches more to us than to the beasts of the earth
   and makes us wiser than the birds of the air?'
¹²He does not answer when men cry out
   because of the arrogance of the wicked.
¹³Indeed, God does not listen to their empty plea;
   the Almighty pays no attention to it.
¹⁴How much less, then, will he listen
   when you say that you do not see him,
that your case is before him
   and you must wait for him,
¹⁵and further, that his anger never punishes
   and he does not take the least notice of wickedness.

---

¹⁶So Job opens his mouth with empty talk;
without knowledge he multiplies words."

^{36:1}Elihu continued:

²"Bear with me a little longer and I will show you
that there is more to be said in God's behalf.
³I get my knowledge from afar;
I will ascribe justice to my Maker.
⁴Be assured that my words are not false;
one perfect in knowledge is with you.

⁵"God is mighty, but does not despise men;
he is mighty, and firm in his purpose.
⁶He does not keep the wicked alive
but gives the afflicted their rights.
⁷He does not take his eyes off the righteous;
he enthrones them with kings
and exalts them forever.
⁸But if men are bound in chains,
held fast by cords of affliction,
⁹he tells them what they have done—
that they have sinned arrogantly.
¹⁰He makes them listen to correction
and commands them to repent of their evil.
¹¹If they obey and serve him,
they will spend the rest of their days in prosperity
and their years in contentment.
¹²But if they do not listen,
they will perish by the sword
and die without knowledge.

¹³"The godless in heart harbor resentment;
even when he fetters them, they do not cry for help.
¹⁴They die in their youth,
among male prostitutes of the shrines.
¹⁵But those who suffer he delivers in their suffering;
he speaks to them in their affliction.
¹⁶"He is wooing you from the jaws of distress
to a spacious place free from restriction,
to the comfort of your table laden with choice food.
¹⁷But now you are laden with the judgment due the wicked;
judgment and justice have taken hold of you.

¹⁸Be careful that no one entices you by riches;
   do not let a large bribe turn you aside.
¹⁹Would your wealth
   or even all your mighty efforts
   sustain you so you would not be in distress?
²⁰Do not long for the night,
   to drag people away from their homes.
²¹Beware of turning to evil,
   which you seem to prefer to affliction.

²²"God is exalted in his power.
   Who is a teacher like him?
²³Who has prescribed his ways for him,
   or said to him, 'You have done wrong'?
²⁴Remember to extol his work,
   which men have praised in song.
²⁵All mankind has seen it;
   men gaze on it from afar.
²⁶How great is God—beyond our understanding!
   The number of his years is past finding out.

²⁷"He draws up the drops of water,
   which distill as rain to the streams;
²⁸the clouds pour down their moisture
   and abundant showers fall on mankind.
²⁹Who can understand how he spreads out the clouds,
   how he thunders from his pavilion?
³⁰See how he scatters his lightning about him,
   bathing the depths of the sea.
³¹This is the way he governs the nations
   and provides food in abundance.
³²He fills his hands with lightning
   and commands it to strike its mark.
³³His thunder announces the coming storm;
   even the cattle make known its approach.

^{37:1}"At this my heart pounds
   and leaps from its place.
²Listen! Listen to the roar of his voice,
   to the rumbling that comes from his mouth.
³He unleashes his lightning beneath the whole
        heaven
   and sends it to the ends of the earth.

⁴After that comes the sound of his roar;
   he thunders with his majestic voice.
When his voice resounds,
   he holds nothing back.
⁵God's voice thunders in marvelous ways;
   he does great things beyond our
         understanding.
⁶He says to the snow, 'Fall on the earth,'
   and to the rain shower, 'Be a mighty downpour.'
⁷So that all men he has made may know his work,
   he stops every man from his labor.
⁸The animals take cover;
   they remain in their dens.
⁹The tempest comes out from its chamber,
   the cold from the driving winds.
¹⁰The breath of God produces ice,
   and the broad waters become frozen.
¹¹He loads the clouds with moisture;
   he scatters his lightning through them.
¹²At his direction they swirl around
   over the face of the whole earth
   to do whatever he commands them.
¹³He brings the clouds to punish men,
   or to water his earth and show his love.

¹⁴"Listen to this, Job;
   stop and consider God's wonders.
¹⁵Do you know how God controls the clouds
   and makes his lightning flash?
¹⁶Do you know how the clouds hang poised,
   those wonders of him who is perfect in
         knowledge?
¹⁷You who swelter in your clothes
   when the land lies hushed under the south wind,
¹⁸can you join him in spreading out the skies,
   hard as a mirror of cast bronze?

¹⁹"Tell us what we should say to him;
   we cannot draw up our case because of our
         darkness.
²⁰Should he be told that I want to speak?
   Would any man ask to be swallowed up?

²¹Now no one can look at the sun,
  bright as it is in the skies
  after the wind has swept them clean.
²²Out of the north he comes in golden splendor;
  God comes in awesome majesty.
²³The Almighty is beyond our reach and exalted in power;
  in his justice and great righteousness, he does not
    oppress.
²⁴Therefore, men revere him,
  for does he not have regard for all the wise in heart?'"

SUSPENSE IS RUNNING HIGH at this point in the book. Job has thrown down the gauntlet before God with his oath of innocence in chapter 31. It looks like a win-win situation for Job. If God strikes him dead for a false oath, Job's death wish (Job 3) is fulfilled. If God does nothing, Job is tacitly vindicated of wrongdoing because his oath stands. If God defends himself, Job gets the satisfaction of the dialogue he has been demanding. Job has constructed an alternative legal scenario by uttering his oath (where previously he was trying to subpoena God). He has chosen a risky strategy, and for the reading audience the atmosphere crackles with expectation. We have every indication that we have reached the climax and culmination of the drama.

What an odd time to introduce a new character. The resulting literary vertigo has led many interpreters to conclude that the Elihu speeches must be a later addition by a clumsy editor. They consider his bombastic speeches to be nonproductive repetitions of the points already covered. In contrast, however, as suggested in the Introduction, Elihu is the only character in the book who offers a cogent theodicy (I referred to it as an "educative theodicy"). He defends God's justice rather than a system, though he still accepts a modified version of the RP that the other characters accept. He accuses Job of self-righteousness, an accusation later verified by God (40:8). We can see, then, that Elihu offers a model for coherence while trying to maintain a justice orientation. It is a clever and noteworthy attempt that is more sophisticated than what was offered by the other characters, though it remains inadequate.

While Elihu pontificates against Job and spins his proposal, the audience is left suspended in the shadow of the delayed denouement, wondering how God will respond to Job's hubris.

Elihu's Identity and Status (32:1 – 5)

WHO IS ELIHU? HE does not come among the three friends introduced in 2:11. His pedigree is longer than any other in the book, and all the names would be appropriate Hebrew eponyms. This leads Hartley to identify him as Israelite,[1] an opinion that, while attractive, does not account for the fact that he is identified as a Buzite. Buz was a brother of Uz in Genesis 22:20 – 21, and thus Elihu is related to Israelites as part of the international family of Abram. Territorially, Jeremiah 25:23 locates the clan in Edom. Despite the ethnic relationship and territorial proximity, such identification still distances Elihu from national Israelites.

Nevertheless, the meaning of his name ("He is my God") draws him nearer and the position he adopts is one that a right-thinking Israelite could maintain. In this way, I might suggest that just as the friends represented the common logic of the ancient Near East, Elihu represents a more theologically sophisticated and nuanced opinion that might have predominated among the Israelites. Those Israelites who would have scoffed at the blatant attempts of the friends to prompt Job to action in order to restore his prosperity and favor with God would likely find Elihu's thinking more persuasive.

Elihu's character has been heavily criticized. Though descriptions of him as insufferably pompous are perhaps accurate, they should not lead to a dismissal of him as a buffoon (as some interpreters do). The other friends were also arrogant and insensitive, as people can be when they are not the ones in the difficult situation.

More than any other quality trait, however, Elihu is seen as a raging, angry young man. The narrator indicates this four times in the text itself (32:2 [2x], 3, 5). He directs his anger against Job because of Job's self-righteous attitude (32:2) and against the three friends because of their philosophical incompetence (32:3, 5). The text is clear that this anger is not just because Job considers himself righteous, for Job's righteousness has been repeatedly affirmed and Elihu would have no reason to be angry with that which is patently true. More specifically, Elihu is angry because Job regards his own righteousness more highly than he regards God's. This is the same accusation God will make in Job 40:8, so his anger on this point is justifiable.

Elihu directs his anger against the incompetence of the friends on two counts: (1) They have condemned Job without having found fault, and (2) they had run out of arguments without having succeeded. The first of

---

1. Hartley, *Job*, 429.

these has constituted the core of the book's message: Elihu's condemnation of the friends is nothing less than a condemnation of the Great Symbiosis in general and the traditional formulation of the RP in particular. They have functioned as unwitting agents of the Challenger by means of representing that philosophy in their arguments. The second count of his anger expresses his disappointment that they could not move beyond their simplistic paradigms to address what Elihu considers the real issues. Those issues are the ones to which he turns his attention.

Elihu's Premise (32:6–22)

ELIHU FIRST REFUTES WHAT is apparently traditional thinking, if not common sense, that in matters of wisdom, age should have priority. In contrast, he contends that while a certain wisdom can come with age, the most important wisdom comes from God and may be given to young or old (32:9, 18; 33:4).

In Job 32:8 Elihu asserts "But it is the spirit in a person, the breath of the Almighty, that gives them understanding" (NIV 2011). The word translated "breath" alludes to the concept expressed in Genesis 2:7, where God breathed into Adam the breath of life. That breath came from God, and so also here it denotes the "breath of the Almighty." In Genesis 2 that breath made Adam a living being, whereas here it gives understanding. In this sense, we might justifiably connect the breath of life/the Almighty with the image of God in Genesis 1, which could easily be associated with the human attribute of wisdom.[2] In this sense, Elihu's statement can be viewed as merging anthropological concepts found in Genesis 1 and 2.

Elihu goes further, however, to suggest that this "breath of the Almighty" serves as a person's spirit (*ruah*). It is true that some interpreters have preferred a capitalized reading of Spirit and considered it a (veiled) reference to the Holy Spirit.[3] Trinitarian theology would not be what Elihu would have had in mind, nor would it be something comprehended by Job or the Israelite audience, whatever we might decide the role of the Holy Spirit to be. If we are to contend for biblical authority, we must retain linkage to the author's understanding. Elihu's statement has more to say about his understanding of the human nature than about the divine nature.

We may infer from the Old Testament that the Israelites considered the human spirit to be "on loan" from God. In Israelite understanding, one would not say that humans are body, soul, and spirit. Rather, a human *is* a *nepeš* (self or soul; it ceases when one dies, see Gen. 35:18), who *has* a body (made by God to return to the earth) and *has* a spirit (*ruah*, given by

---

2. It should also be noted that the Spirit of God gives wisdom (Ex. 28:3; Isa. 11:2).
3. See NIV footnote with that alternative reading.

God as a portion of his own spirit to return to him upon death).[4] The idea that humans have no spirit of their own but only God's spirit "on loan" is primarily conveyed in the book of Job (27:3–5; 33:4; 34:14–15), but also indicated in Psalm 104:29 (people's *ruah* is gathered, presumably back to God who gave it, and they die; their bodies return to dust). God also speaks of his *ruah* in humankind in Genesis 6:3 (perhaps the only clear part of that difficult verse). Ecclesiastes 12:7 verifies this assertion: "The spirit returns to God who gave it."

Zechariah 12:1 potentially offers a different view referring to the "spirit of man" that God formed within a human being.[5] This is not contradictory, however, if we conclude that when God places his spirit in a human being, it becomes that person's spirit until he or she dies and it returns to God from whom it came. In Israelite thinking the spirit (whether described as God's or human's) is a vitalizing energy rather than a component part.[6] Here Elihu identifies the spirit particularly as the source of the wisdom that he declares he possesses. It is the spirit within him (not the Holy Spirit) that compels him in 32:18; he is energized and impatient to speak.

In 32:12–14 Elihu reiterates the failure of the friends to answer Job satisfactorily and proceeds to differentiate himself from the three friends. He anticipates their assessment of the current state of the discussion in 32:13: They believe they have done their job of making wisdom plain, but since Job has proven so intractable, further or more persuasive refutation will have to come from God. In contrast to their lame philosophical capitulation, Elihu declares that none of Job's arguments have addressed the direction his argument will take (32:14), and he is not going to be following the same tactic they have used.

In 32:15–22 Elihu's description of himself resembles Jeremiah's description of how he is compelled to deliver his prophetic message. Just as Elihu feels ready to burst and needs to find relief, Jeremiah reports that if he tries not to speak the prophetic message given to him, "his word is in my heart like a fire, a fire shut up in my bones. I am weary of holding it in; indeed, I cannot" (Jer. 20:9). We should not, however, conclude that Elihu is claiming a prophetic office or role. There is no sense of "This is what the LORD says" here.

Elihu concludes this part of his speech by insisting that he will not engage in flattery or show partiality. Readers will recall that when the

---

4. H.-J. Fabry, "רוּחַ," *TDOT*, 13:365–402; esp. 386–88. Fuller discussion in Walton, *Ancient Near Eastern Thought*, 210–14.

5. Note also the psalmist's reference to "my spirit" (Ps. 31:5 [6].).

6. Fabry, "רוּחַ," 13:387.

friends began their speeches, they acknowledged the wisdom and righteousness of Job. Only as the dialogues continued did they begin accusing. Elihu is not inclined to such diplomacy; he jumps directly to confrontation. The word translated "flattery" (32:22) is used elsewhere to refer to the bestowing of honorific titles (cf. Isa. 44:5; 45:4). Elihu thereby asserts that he has no intention of engaging in obsequious pandering. To use some modern clichés, he views this as a "no holds barred" situation and does not plan to "pull any punches." Intriguingly he claims that his integrity will not allow any other path. He says that if he did not do this, his Maker would soon take him away. Just as Job continually insists on keeping his integrity intact, Elihu identifies his own guiding mantra as boldly proclaiming hard truths.

Elihu's Theory Statement (Job 33)

IN CHAPTER 33 ELIHU presents the theology that provides the foundation for his understanding of Job's situation. In the following paragraphs I will clarify some of the phrasing and statements and then turn to his overall argument in the Bridging Contexts section.

"The Spirit of God has made me; the breath of the Almighty gives me life" (33:4). Even though the NIV capitalizes "Spirit," the parallel with "breath" suggests otherwise. Humans are viewed as invigorated by the breath of God. If this were to be viewed as a reference to the Holy Spirit, it would suggest that every human has been granted the presence of the Holy Spirit. Furthermore, the Israelites knew nothing of the Trinity and would not have used "the Spirit of God" for the third person of the Trinity. In the Old Testament the "spirit of God" is understood as an extension of the power of God. This statement by Elihu continues his claim in 32:8 that he is possessed of wisdom. The statement that the spirit "has made me" is parallel to the statement that God's breath "gives me life." Elihu is speaking of that aspect of creation that is focused on the functional rather than the material.[7] God "made" him by giving him life and wisdom. He is referring to the same role of God when he describes him as his "Maker" in 32:22. There he indicates that the Maker would virtually unmake him if he misused his wisdom in idle flattery.

Claims attributed to Job (33:8–11). Even though Elihu does not directly quote any of Job's lines, Elihu fairly summarizes Job's overall posi-

---

7. Note that when Elihu does make a passing reference to the material, he refers to "clay" rather than "dust" (33:6). In this he reflects a common ancient Near Eastern idea of people being fashioned from clay. See comments on 10:9; see also discussion in Walton, *Ancient Near Eastern Thought*, 205–6.

tion. Since we are in the discourse section of the book rather than the dialogue section, we never hear how Job would respond to Elihu, but most likely he would not object to this paraphrase. Job would not have considered himself free of any guilt whatsoever, and Elihu places the claim of innocence relative to the way that God has treated Job. That is, Job would claim that the suffering that has come his way can in no way be justified by his behavior.

Portrayal of God and his ways. Elihu begins by warning Job that no one can "out-God" God (33:12). Job seems to believe that he has caught God in an inconsistency—that his policies are somehow flawed or his execution of them lacking. To his credit, Elihu avers on principle that this can never be the case. This theological commitment is Elihu's strength and it is what makes his position more acceptable than Job's.

Specifically, Elihu contends that God has not been silent; rather, Job has not been listening on the right frequency. He presents dreams and visions as the first examples of the media God uses for communication (33:15–18). Everyone in the ancient world believed that dreams were communication from deity, and Job himself has referred to his dream experiences as one of the ways God has terrorized him (7:14). In ancient Near Eastern thinking, nightmares indicate that the gods are angry with the dreamer.[8] Thus, terrifying dreams constitute one form that suffering takes. Elihu adds physical pain to the list of divine communications in 33:19 along with distress (such as Job experienced in losing his property and family). He identifies all of these communication strategies as having corrective intentions (33:17–18).

In other words, Elihu considers these communications to be instructive and constructive rather than punitive. In this he offers a perspective not represented in the thinking of Job or his friends. Rather than restoring the sufferer to the path of life, however, such experiences often lead instead to depression and a decline toward death. On a technical point, it should be noted that the last word in 33:18 is now often understood to refer to the river of death that has to be crossed (see NIV text note) and is thus parallel to "the pit" in the first line of the verse.[9]

How can this discrepancy (decline toward death rather than restoration to life) be addressed and the cycle broken? Elihu offers his theory in 33:23–28, but it is not an easy one to sort out. Questions arise as to whether the messenger (NIV "angel") is an angelic mediator or a human one, whether the intercession involves communication to God or to the

---

8. Butler, *Mesopotamian Conceptions of Dreams*, specifically noted on 67, but addressed in several chapters throughout the book.

9. See Clines, *Job 21–37*, 733.

sufferer, and whether the "ransom" (33:24) is something specific or general. The procedure involves actions by all three parties: the messenger (33:23–24), God (33:25), and the sufferer (33:26–28). The messenger is identified specifically as a mediator (*meliṣ*), a term used in 16:20 for someone who intercedes with God on the behalf of someone who is suffering. Outside of Job the word is used only three times; in each it refers to humans (a human interpreter, Gen. 42:23; human envoys, 2 Chron. 32:31; most likely prophets in Isa. 43:27). In Job, "angel" (*mal'ak*) occurs only two other times, once referring to a human messenger (1:14) and once to supernatural beings (4:18). In this context, the messenger/mediator speaks both to the sufferer ("to tell a man what is right for him") and to God ("spare him")[10] regarding the situation and contributes to the solution by finding a "ransom." None of these dictates whether the messenger/mediator is human. In Job "ransom" (*koper*) is used as a monetary sum to be paid on one's behalf.[11]

Sorting through all of these variables, I would agree with those who believe that Elihu is referring to his own role.[12] He views himself as the messenger/mediator who is going to interpret Job's situation and advise him what he needs to do ("tell him what is right," as he does beginning in 34:4). He intercedes with God to spare Job's life (his intention as stated in 33:32),[13] and he provides a ransom, if that can be understood as a portion of the wealth of his wisdom. In that case, the ransom provides the reasoning that would allow Job to make progress toward a solution. The ransom is a strategy that would satisfy all parties. That is what diplomats (mediators) do when they attempt to bring two sides together.

If this is the case, rather than Job being provided the equivalent of a public defender (as he has requested numerous times), Elihu is serving in the role we might recognize as federal mediator to bring the sides to a mutual understanding. He proposes that God will restore Job to health (33:25–26;

---

10. The word here is problematic because its root would be *pd'* whereas the normal root for "spare" would be *pdh*. The root as stands is not known in Hebrew and most commentators and translations have accepted the emendation to the revised and more common root, as it seems to be what the context requires.

11. In Job 36:18, the NIV translates it "bribe." The same concepts are found in 6:22–23, but other synonyms are used instead of *koper*.

12. This is not a common view, but it is not unprecedented (e.g., Wilson, *Job*, 377, appears to accept it).

13. The uncommon Piel stem of the verb *ṣedeq* elsewhere used only in Ezek. 16:51–52. The Piel serves a factitive function when the Qal is stative as here. Since the Qal means "to be righteous," the Piel would refer to any activity that would make, declare, or consider someone to be righteous. Here Elihu wants to be able to declare Job righteous by virtue of Job's having taken the appropriate steps of reconciliation.

notice no reference to restoring prosperity) and that Job will reconcile with God (33:26) and confess in public to the nature of his wrongdoing and the grace of God's treatment of him (33:27). That Elihu considers himself to be in this role is supported by the fact that after he paints this scenario, he urges Job to listen to him (33:31–33) as he proceeds to do exactly what he just proposed more generally. Nevertheless, Elihu is hardly the sort of mediator whom Job has been seeking.

Verdict: The Justice of God (Job 34)

ELIHU'S ARTICULATION OF JOB'S position in 34:5–9 is confusing. It is certainly true that Job considers himself innocent and maintains that God has denied him justice (34:5; cf. 40:8, where God says something similar). He also considers his position to be truthful and the scourge of God to be disproportionate to his guilt (34:6; cf. 6:4, 28; 9:21). But what is Elihu referring to in 34:7–9? In 34:7 Job is said to "drink scorn." One could logically think that "drinking" refers to absorbing scorn—taking it in. This would be an accurate description of Job's position since he has been absorbing the scorn of people around him, including his friends. Alternatively, however, one could think of drinking as meeting a basic need and providing for one's own refreshment. In this approach Job indulges in mockery as easily and frequently as he drinks water. In this view, rather than being mocked by others, Job is being accused of engaging in mockery of God. The content of this mockery would be the accusations that Elihu has already identified in 34:5. The shape of the metaphor would thus favor seeing Job as the object of scorn, whereas the context would favor seeing Job as the one who is scorning.

The issue has to be resolved by sorting out 34:8–9. It has certainly not been proven that Job "keeps company with evildoers," and the purported position stated in 34:9 uses the language that was adopted by Eliphaz in 22:2 (though 34:9 does not reiterate the claim actually made by Eliphaz; see discussion on p. 244). Is 34:9 a claim that represents Job's thinking accurately? To answer that we have to make sure we understand the statement clearly. We have already treated the Hebrew verb *skn* in detail in its context in Job 22:2 (p. 245). It means to gain, profit, or benefit from something. The NIV renders the last phrase in 34:9 as "tries to please God," but we can be a little more specific. The Hebrew root *rṣh* generally means "to please or take delight," but here it is combined with the preposition '*im*. This collocation occurs elsewhere only in Psalm 50:18, where by context and parallel it clearly focuses on keeping company with someone (the "pleased" aspect would be represented in that one found the company of certain individuals to be pleasant and desirable).

We can now see, then, that Job 34:9 needs to be read as the complement of 34:8. Job has tacitly taken up company among the wicked when he concludes that associating with God does not produce personal benefit. Thus 34:8 is a logical deduction rather than an empirical observation; that is, Job is accused of aligning himself philosophically with evildoers by default when he sets himself against God.

In this deduction, Elihu is wrong. We should recall that the whole question of the book is whether Job's chosen behavior is based on potential gain. Job has "maintained his integrity" (27:1–6) by not pursuing regaining his prosperity. Elihu's statement assumes that if Job finds no benefit in throwing in his lot with God, he is therefore going to throw in his lot with the wicked. This would be a logical deduction only if Job's alignment with God were based on the expectation of benefit. Job in fact believes that it *should* work that way (i.e., the RP should work), but the whole book is designed to demonstrate that Job is not *motivated* by that expectation. After all, that had been the Challenger's claim from the beginning. This is important because in this sense, though Elihu is more justified in the sort of offense that he identifies in Job (self-righteousness), the accuracy of that assessment still does not compromise or undermine the central question of the book. Though Job *is* guilty of self-righteousness and disparaging God's justice (as Elihu contends), he is *not* guilty of pandering—following God only because of the benefit such a relationship brings. In this misrepresentation of Job, Elihu is no better than the friends. The difference is that he does not misrepresent God as the friends do. He is right about Job's offense; he is wrong in his inference about Job's motivation.

In 34:10–20 Elihu offers his basic presuppositions. In 34:10 he indicates that the justice of God is his bedrock. This is what differentiates him from the other protagonists. In 34:11 we see that his corollary includes a full affirmation of the RP. Elihu's worldview presupposes that if God is just, the RP must be carried out—an ideal he asserts directly in 34:12. In this way we can see that justice provides the framework for Elihu's worldview just as it does for everyone else in the book. Yahweh is going to offer another alternative through his speeches, so this is still a flaw in Elihu's position.

Elihu's insistence that God would not pervert justice echoes the words of Bildad's first speech (8:2). It is strong language, and in using it Elihu may be guilty of maintaining a simplistic tautology. In this tautology justice is defined by the RP; therefore, perversion of justice is the only possible assessment when the RP is not maintained.

Elihu continues to wax eloquent on the loftiness of God in 34:13–15. He affirms that God is not a contingent being (not accountable or dependent on another). In theological terms, he is asserting God's aseity (his existence has its source only in himself). Conversely, human beings are absolutely and totally contingent (34:14–15). If God withdrew from us, we would cease to exist. Elihu's affirmations of God's aseity and humanity's contingency contribute to his case in that they establish rank priority: God does not need us but we need him; God is not accountable to us but we are accountable to him. Consequently we do not surpass God in his attributes, including that of his justice.

Elihu continues by posing a rhetorical question in 34:17, but it again reflects reductionism. No one has suggested that God *hates* justice. Job, for his part, has wondered how important justice is to God and whether he carries it out consistently. So again, hyperbole, though perhaps rhetorically acceptable, here weakens Elihu's case. Yet as he returns to expressing the attributes of God, his affirmations are legitimate. In 34:17b–20 Elihu again addresses human contingency in reference to the most powerful humans. People cannot hold God accountable (v. 17b), but it is God who condemns wicked rulers, shows no partiality to the wealthy, and exacts punishment. It is true that God acts in this way. The question that Elihu fails to consider is whether his policies are defined by and grounded in such involvement. Does God have options?

What we are seeing is that just as Job has drawn false inferences about governance from his understanding of God (inferences about the centrality and execution of the RP), Elihu is drawing other inferences (based on his reinterpretation of the RP). Though both have a basically sound comprehension of the attributes of God, both are wrong (in different ways) about what inferences can therefore be drawn.

In 34:21–30 we find the next stage of Elihu's case for God. He begins by affirming God's omniscience, particularly as it relates to his omnipresence. God has access to every place, and thus, in his role as judge, he has immediate access to all pieces of evidence. He is omniscient and has no need to gather information, no need for research, testimony, or trial ("no need to examine," 34:23; "without inquiry," 34:24). He simply acts to carry out judgment. Some of the cases of judgment are final ("shatters," 34:24; "overthrows" or "crushes," 34:25) and may take place out of the public eye ("in the night," 34:25). Other types of punishment are done in public (34:26 uses a word specifically connected with public beatings).

In 34:29–30 Elihu turns his attention to an issue that is closer to home. Up to this point he has been talking about God taking responsibility to maintain justice, but what if God remains silent? Indeed, this is precisely the content of Job's complaint. He has noted God's silence in terms of his failure to respond to the deeds of the wicked and his inattention to the pleas of the suffering righteous. Elihu maintains that God has a right to such a silence and thus implies that Job is presumptuous to be critical of God on this count. Elihu also contends that God's silence does not allow one to conclude that God is an absentee landlord. Though one may not perceive it, God is still at work to prevent negative situations from developing.

Having offered a defense of God's apparent indifference (which addresses indirectly one of Job's major complaints), Elihu now proposes a hypothetical course of action (34:31—33). Commentators offer a wide variety of interpretations of verse 31 because the terseness of language creates confusion for the modern reader. The verb translated by the NIV as "I am guilty" (*naśa'ti*) is a common enough verb ("lift up, raise"), but it usually communicates its meaning through combination with an object (e.g., hand, head, face, sin, eyes, voice—all with their own idiomatic values), and here there is no object. What is Job supposed to lift up and with what purpose?

The decision must be made on the basis of 34:32—33. In verse 32 there is no admission of offense, only the willingness to be shown offense and the commitment to deal with it once it is made known. Furthermore, verse 33 speaks of the absence of repentance. We must therefore conclude that verse 31 does not contain repentance or admission of guilt. Instead, it would logically refer to the person adopting a posture of confidence—standing tall in the dock with head held high.

The last verb in verse 31 (NIV: "offend") is first person imperfect and therefore suggests the person is offering a statement about present or future behavior. It could not easily be read as a statement about the past (i.e., "I have committed no offense"). The verb is rarely used and the only other occurrence of the Qal is in Nehemiah 1:7. It may well be that this should be read as his determination not to act corruptly. Corrupt behavior would result in the kind of compromising of his integrity to which the friends have been urging him. If this is the case, then the attitude attributed to Job here is similar to that which he stated himself in 27:1—6.

Support for this view of 34:31 comes in 34:32. Here the person in the dock (presumably representing Job in Elihu's little vignette) requests that he be charged with specific offenses if they are known. He demands a formal accusation from the prosecution. In this sequence Elihu has characterized Job accurately in terms that are consistent with the dialogue section of the book. As Job has refused to repent, Elihu makes his case as he asks Job what he expects God to do (34:33). Elihu implies that he has expressed Job's expectations in this confrontation and thus insinuates that Job's request is impious. Though Elihu has characterized Job's posture correctly, has he rightly identified Job's expectation? What *does* Job expect to result from the legal confrontation that he requests?

Elihu's assessment is that Job wants God to "reward" him on Job's terms. The verb NIV translates "reward" (*šlm*, Piel) usually expresses something more along the line of compensation or recompense in legal contexts. Most agree that the thrust of the first line is to challenge Job concerning his apparent belief that he can call the shots and drive the process according to his understanding. Elihu's affirmations about God through the middle section of this chapter have led to this climax. God is in charge and cannot be called to heel as Job has been attempting. This posture of Job's is what Elihu then identifies in 34:36–37 as he summarizes what he perceives to be Job's offense. That offense is not something that occurred prior to his downfall, but it has become evident in his response to his downfall. Elihu's call, then, is: "Stand down, Job!" Now that he has issued his summary indictment, Elihu will develop his understanding of Job's offense in more detail in the next chapter.

Transcendence of God (Job 35)

ELIHU'S SUMMARY OF JOB'S putative position presents Job as expecting to benefit from his righteous behavior (35:3). As I indicated earlier, that may indeed be Job's expectation, but that does not mean it is his motivation. If, however, we could imagine Job's response to Elihu (which he never gives), he might object that he is *not* looking for profit or gain from not sinning; he *is* expecting that he would be protected from major devastations. The semantic distinction might be that any profit Job might expect would be in protection, not in material prosperity. Argue as we may, however, it is Elihu's rhetorical style to be reductionist and to engage in hyperbole.

Elihu's first point of reply is that any human being's righteousness or wickedness has no effect on God whatsoever. In these affirmations Elihu offers a concise refutation of the Great Symbiosis. As discussed in the Introduction, this symbiosis is benefit-focused: The gods reap benefits from the labor of humans, and the humans reap benefits from the favor of the gods. In its ancient Near Eastern form, people were providing material support for the gods (food, clothing, housing, etc.).

In Job, no one is advising Job that he should be more involved in the care and feeding of the gods, but there is still an element of the Great Symbiosis in the assumption that Job has offended God and therefore disrupted the Great Symbiosis. Offense would often take the form of intruding on divine prerogatives. In this way the other friends were encouraging Job to adopt the Great Symbiosis thinking; Elihu, by contrast, accuses him (as the Challenger had) of falling prey to that kind of thinking. Again, he is wrong about Job but right about God. The other friends spoke incorrectly about God because they viewed him as involved in the Great Symbiosis system. Elihu becomes the defender of God by denying the validity of the Great Symbiosis. The difference that righteous or wicked behavior makes must be viewed only horizontally (affecting the human world) rather than vertically (affecting God).

In 35:8–13 Elihu contrasts two different ways of approaching God. The first involves prayers for relief from oppression (35:9); the second involves a search for God and recognition of his grace as he teaches wisdom (35:10–11). Elihu suggests that God is not responsive to the former (35:12–13). In this he suggests that people should be more interested in coming to know God better rather than on trying to get God to solve their problems. He should be the object of our inquiry rather than the object of our complaints. He is not at our beck and call and cannot be called to heel like a dog—he is our *Maker!*

As Elihu thus emphasizes God's transcendence over his immanence (introduced in 35:5) he suggests that we need to show a little more recognition of our place. If God's "job" is not to field people's complaints, then Job should not expect God to be responsive to his calls for attention. Elihu would say that we should think in terms of responding to God rather than God responding to us. God responds according to his own purposes and timing. People cannot call him to account for the way he interacts with them nor to criticize him in accordance with their own expectations.

In this Elihu again offers a valid understanding of the nature of God. In Elihu's view Job has made the mistake of thinking that he is important. This sense of self-importance is out of proportion but is characteristic of people who think that God is micromanaging their personal circumstances (e.g., as Job does in 7:17–24). He believes that Job has diminished God by the way he thinks about him.

Summary and Closing Remarks—The Acts of God (Job 36–37)

As ELIHU INTRODUCES HIS last speech, he again indicates that he views himself as speaking on behalf of God. Elihu's insistence that people recognize God's transcendence (again the title "Maker"[14] in 36:3, to keep us in our place) is entirely appropriate and not open to discussion. At the same time we can see that he continues to believe that justice is the foundation of God's policies and behavior. In the end, this view is not going to be endorsed in the book. Ultimately, God does not defend his justice and does not posit justice alone as the foundation of his policies.

---

14. This word for "Maker" is derived from a different root than the one used in 35:10, but no difference in nuance is discernible.

Elihu appears to have an elevated view of himself ("knowledge from afar," 36:3a; "perfect in knowledge," 36:4b). The word translated "afar" (*lemerahoq*) refers sometimes to distance in relation to divine (2 Sam. 7:19; 2 Kings 19:25, information of an arcane nature). At other times, it refers to distance in relation to the human world (relative to sound, Ezra 3:13, or sight, Job 39:29). Elihu is claiming the former. This is consistent with his earlier claims that God has given him this understanding (32:8). It would mean little for him to claim that his knowledge is exotic (from faraway places). When he describes himself as "perfect [*tammim*] in knowledge," we easily misunderstand his claim. Even though he is prone to hyperbole and may be engaging in it here, he is only saying that his opinions (which he is about to put forward) are consistent and coherent. The adjective *tammim* is related to integrity.[15] Opinions that have an internal integrity are soundly reasoned and well-thought out.

In the remainder of Elihu's speech he waxes eloquent on the might of God, introducing the topic with the adjective *kabbir*. Of its ten occurrences in Hebrew Bible, seven are in Job and the remainder in Isaiah.[16] The contexts are widely disparate. Only one other occurrence in Job is used as a divine attribute (34:17). The other occurrences serve to modify wind, wealth, and years of life. In Isaiah it describes a loud roaring and the power of waves in flooding, and in its negation it refers to feeble survivors of Moab. An English adjective approaching a similar range of meaning might be "inexorable." It speaks of that which cannot be opposed or even withstood. Such things are relentless and overwhelming. Something so described represents a force to be reckoned with—a juggernaut.

The view of God that Elihu offers balances the ideas that though God is inexorable, he does not therefore simply run roughshod over humans indiscriminately. He is not incognizant of people and their situations (my interpretation of "he does not reject"—to care little for something or devalue it through disdain or neglect). In contrast, God's inexorability is guided by a "firm ... purpose" (NIV). The "strength of heart" (lit. trans.) with which God is characterized is the opposite of indiscriminate neglect. Instead, he has a determined posture and steadfast policy regarding his treatment of humanity, though that does not mean he is predictable. Again, Elihu identifies this divine policy as the RP—the wicked are punished while the righteous are rewarded (36:6–7). He elaborates by asserting that not only does God act according to this principle, but he also communicates (36:9–10),

---

15. Note, e.g., the usage in Josh. 24:14; note also that almost the exact phrase describes God in Job 37:16.

16. Job 8:2; 15:10; 31:25; 34:17, 24; 36:5 (2x); Isa. 16:14; 17:12; 28:2.

---

thus giving people opportunity to change their ways and their circumstances (36:11–12). As before, God's character is accurately perceived, but his policies are misrepresented.

After characterizing the wicked as unresponsive to God's promptings (36:13–14), Elihu makes a bold transition from third person plural forms to second person singular in 36:16–21 to draw out the implications for Job personally. The Hebrew is particularly difficult and interpretations range widely. In 36:16 Elihu suggests that God would like nothing better than to restore Job to a status of blessing. The verb that NIV translates as "woo" typically refers to trying to persuade someone to follow a course of action that they either do not want to pursue or should not pursue. Here the meaning would have to be the former—Elihu portrays Job as disinclined to accept the generous offer of God to resolve his situation. In Elihu's mind, Job has demonstrated this disinclination by refusing to back down and adopt a submissive posture before God. He considers Job's strident demands to be evidence of the intractable position he has adopted.

Job 36:17 then explains that Job has brought this judgment of God on himself—not by prior sin (as the other friends were persuaded) but by his self-righteous posture before God; yet evil is evil. In the remainder of this section Elihu turns to exhortation (36:18–21). We need to determine what courses of action Elihu is warning against and assess whether they realistically describe a behavior to which Job is prone.

In 36:18, the word translated "entice" is the same verb that was translated "woo" in 36:16 (*swt*). There it described a course of action offered by God that Job was disinclined to follow; here, the subject of the verb is someone who is presumably trying to lure Job into pursuing a course of action he should resist. Elihu expresses the idea that Job, in his present condition, is so attracted to wealth and power that he would be vulnerable to those who offered it in conjunction with oppressive schemes. If Job has found his righteous behavior incapable of delivering success and prosperity, he may be amenable to gaining it in other less honorable ways. As we have seen throughout Elihu's speeches, this is an inaccurate characterization of Job, who has demonstrated that his motivation is not wealth or power, but righteousness. As the other friends did, Elihu is representing a sort of thinking that one could pursue in seeking to understand suffering. Elihu's system differs from the friends, but as readers we see that Elihu's understanding is inadequate.

Elihu rightly observes that the short-term gain of accepting unrighteous profits would, in the end, have unsatisfactory results. This leads to his concluding admonition that Job should resist turning to evil, a course of action that Elihu alleges Job might soon opt for as a resolution to his affliction. Elihu has indicted Job for accusing God of injustice and adopting an attitude of self-importance and self-righteousness. He views this as only one step short of abandoning the idea of a just God and becoming an opportunist willing to take profit in a world where God is inattentive and justice is only an idle wish (Ezek. 9:9). The proverbial slippery slope Elihu presents begins with participating in get-rich schemes, then accepting bribes, and inevitably descends to displacing innocent people in the middle of the night.

In summary, Elihu suggests that if Job seeks to regain wealth and power through evil, he will simply be exchanging his current affliction for another one. It could not be fairly said that Job *chose* his current affliction, but if turning to evil is the choice he makes, he *will* be choosing the affliction that will inevitably result.

The description of God's cosmic power in 36:22–37:13 is one of the most eloquent in the Hebrew Bible. Elihu begins by identifying God's power as a means by which he teaches. The noun for "teacher" used here (*moreh*) occurs in only five other passages.[17] Syntactically, this passage presents the teaching as being accomplished by God's *exaltation* of his strength. This latter verbal form ("exalt," Heb. *śgb*) occurs approximately twenty times, but this is the only time it occurs in the Hiphil. In general the root refers to being lifted up for the purpose of security and protection. Usually the objects of the verbal action are vulnerable before they are secured (these occurrences use the Piel form) or are secure because they have been so lifted up (like a city that is lifted up and therefore secure in its defense, Isa. 26:5). When it is God or God's name that is lifted up, the verb describes the divine state (secure) and therefore its invulnerability (these occurrences use the Niphal form of the verb).

Presumably Elihu's speech uses the Hiphil because God's own strength, not an alternate outside force, secures his position. This secured, exalted position makes him an unsurpassable teacher because his instruction cannot be gainsaid. The next verse verifies this reading—no one can question him. This proclamation of the general greatness of God draws to a close with the exclamations in 36:26. When Elihu declares that God's years are unsearchable, we may prefer to translate *mispar* (NIV: "number") as "account" because the *count* of the years is ultimately insignificant. The question is, can they be accounted for?[18] That is, can God's biography be written? Elihu's few meager observations scarcely begin this report.

---

17. 2 Chron. 15:3 (priests); Prov. 5:13; Isa. 9:14 (prophets); 30:20 (voices in affliction); and Hab. 2:18 (image).

18. The same noun is used by Job in 31:37, where he claims that he can account for all his steps. Again, that has little to do with counting a number—it concerns assessing them.

Now we come to Elihu's recitation of some of the mighty acts of God, mostly related to precipitation, thunder, and lightning. His description of precipitation in 36:27–28 has drawn some interesting comments over the years. Some are inclined to see Elihu as offering a scientifically sophisticated understanding of the water cycle, including evaporation and condensation.[19] This idea would anticipate its scientific confirmation by millennia and one might wonder why, if that was what Elihu was understanding, that the scientific knowledge did not develop much earlier.

Much of this interpretation depends on the translation of the Hebrew verbs *grʿ* (NIV: "draws up") and *zqq* (NIV: "distill"). The first occurs only here and the second appears in this verbal stem only elsewhere in Job 28:1 (NIV: "refined").[20] This ought to make us cautious about concluding that they represent scientific innovation. We do not have a clear idea of what *grʿ* means, and *zqq*, with its connection to refining and filtering, most logically concerns how salt water in the cosmic seas (perhaps those above and below?) becomes fresh water in rain.

Before drawing conclusions such as these, we should explore what people in the ancient world thought about precipitation and see if Elihu offers a dramatically different conclusion. One author's assessment of the ancient worldview concludes that they believed that "the drops of water are taken from the celestial reservoirs, trickle through the firmament, and collect into clouds, which then finally cause the rain to fall."[21] This is as good a guess as any, but it is lacking clear, nonpoetic substantiation in the texts. The difficulty arises from the fact that the ancients did not concern themselves very much with material explanations since the phenomena were beyond their ability to investigate.[22] Not only were the means absent, so was the motivation.

In the ancient worldview, the germane questions concerned who controlled the weather, not how weather phenomena operated. They wanted to know who could send rain or withhold it and why they would do so. We might seek to control the weather by understanding the mechanics by which it works and then seeking to infiltrate those mechanics in order to manipulate the causes to produce more suitable results. Such manipulation is still largely beyond our capacity, so we content ourselves with reading the indicators and understanding the workings sufficiently to predict

---

19. H. Morris, *The Genesis Record* (Grand Rapids: Baker, 1976), 218.

20. These are Qal; there are a couple of occurrences of Piel and Pual (Isa. 25:6; Mal. 3:3) that mean "filter" or "refine."

21. H.-J. Zobel, "מָטָר," *TDOT*, 8:257.

22. The lack of such information can easily be inferred from Horowitz, *Mesopotamian Cosmic Geography*, whose comprehensive collection of information has almost nothing to offer about rain.

tolerably well what will happen. For the ancients, if they were to seek to control the weather by understanding the mechanics, they would be in the realm of theology, not meteorology. They did not believe there were material causes independent of deity, so why bother investigating them? Since the mechanics were ultimately theological, their attempts to infiltrate and manipulate the weather system were also theological.

Under these conditions, it is clear why the ancient world would have little concern for being able to describe the material processes. When they offer any thoughts on the matter, they are couched in poetry, as in Elihu's speech, and are related to divine activity. We might compare the brief and broken description in the Babylonian Creation Epic, *Enuma Elish* 5.49 – 50: "He [Marduk] collected it [presumably Tiamat's spittle, though the previous lines are broken] and rolled it into the clouds."[23]

In Elihu's comments we can see that he also is describing divine action, not material mechanisms ("*He* draws up ..."); in fact, he explicitly notes that it is beyond understanding ("Who can understand how he spreads out the clouds?" 36:29). He shows no inkling that he is receiving new revelation about the hydrologic cycle, and we would be surprised to find God introducing such a scientific innovation in this context.

The rain is ultimately delivered to the "streams" (NIV; Heb. 'ed). This is that same problematic word that occurs in Genesis 2:6 (its only other occurrence), where it refers to how the earth was watered. It may be instructive to excerpt from the study of this word that I included in my Genesis commentary in this same series.[24]

> The term has posed difficulties to translators on three counts: the context is obscure, the lexical base is small (only one other occurrence, Job 36:27), and the comparative Semitic data have been variously interpreted. Thus we find quite a variety of translations offered (e.g., "mist," "flood," "water," "streams"). Lacking contextual, synchronic, and diachronic information, it is no surprise that our exegesis must be considered tentative. Contextually 'ed can be distinguished from rain in that rain comes down while 'ed comes up. Synchronic information (that which is derived from how contemporary authors used the word) draws from Job 36:27 only that the 'ed was the recipient of rain.
>
> Diachronic information (that which is derived from the etymology, constituent parts, other uses of the root, or cognate usage of the word) is a generally unreliable source of information about a word,

---

23. Ibid., 118
24. Walton, *Genesis*, 164 – 65.

but must suffice when synchronic information is lacking.[25] Two connections have been suggested: one to the Sumerian *ID*, which refers to subterranean fresh waters (followed, e.g., by Westermann and Wenham); the second to Akkadian *edu*, which refers to waves or the swell of a body of water (followed, e.g., by Speiser and Hamilton).

Tsumura makes a case that *'ed* refers (among other things) to the regular inundation of the major river systems.[26] As such it stands in contrast to rain so that both represent the two major ways that water fertilized the land in the ancient Near East. The inundations would be mentioned in relation to people working the ground because the annual inundations were only made useful by the digging of irrigation canals to channel the water profitably. It is also true that the inundation rises (to match the verb in v. 6). In Akkadian usage *edu* was believed to arise from the *apsu*, the subterranean waters.[27]

The thrust of verses 5 – 6 in an interpretive paraphrase is as follows: "No shrubs or plants were yet growing wild (for food) because God had not yet sent rain; and people were not yet around to work the ground (for irrigation) so the regular inundations saturated the ground indiscriminately (thus no food was being grown)." A creation text from Nippur sets the scene for creation in a similar way by saying that waters did not yet flow through the opening in the earth and that nothing was growing and no furrow had been made.[28]

In the decade since that was written, little has changed in our ability to understand the word.

Elihu's discourse on the weather continues in 36:29 – 37:5 with discussion of thunder and lightning. The focus is still on God's control of these phenomena and the evidence they provide of his rule (36:31). His rule is expressed in providing the food supply necessary for survival. This is the way he governs the people (not NIV's "nations" — the present term does not refer to political rule). Furthermore, the Hebrew word that NIV translates "governs" (*dyn*) is one that typically refers to judging. It is by means of providing or withholding food that God brings justice on the people.

This reminds us that the focus of Elihu's discussion is on God's justice. We may not understand his justice (36:29), but even the cattle recognize

25. For methodological discussion, see J. Walton, "Principles for Productive Word Study," *NIDOTTE*, 1:161–71.

26. D. Tsumura, *The Earth and the Waters in Genesis 1 and 2* (JSOTSup 83; Sheffield: JSOT, 1989), 110–16.

27. Ibid., 111–12.

28. R. J. Clifford, *Creation Accounts in the Ancient Near East and in the Bible* (CBQMS 26; Washington, D.C.: Catholic Univ. of America, 1994), 28.

his hand at work (36:33). This is the conclusion that he draws in 37:5 — it is *God's* voice that thunders, and it is beyond human understanding. Elihu notes the unfathomable nature of all of this by assigning it to the category of *nipla'ot* (NIV: "marvelous ways"). This term is used when something is classified as divine and therefore impossible for humans to grasp (e.g., when God or his messenger's name is requested and is told it is "wonderful," as in Judg. 13:18; cf. Gen. 18:14).

Elihu illustrates the way this unfathomable instrument of judgment works in 37:6–13. Extreme weather is debilitating to agricultural work. All meteorological phenomena continue to be seen as the direct work of God (note particularly that his breath produces ice, 37:10, not the cold temperatures and their effect on molecules of H_2O). All of it takes place at his command (37:12).

Elihu concludes this section by returning to his main point: Through this activity God punishes or shows his favor — weather is an instrument of his justice (37:13). This is surely the sense of this line though the Hebrew is far from transparent. The main dilemma is whether the verse offers two possible scenarios or three. NIV treats it as two (punishment or love), but the syntax favors three (for a rod [= punishment], for his land [= neutrality with regard to people], or for his loyalty [= blessing]).

Elihu's speech concludes as he addresses Job directly again in 37:14–24 and urges him to consider the "wonders" (*nipla'ot*, as in 37:5) of God. This strategy is intended to cause Job to recognize his false presumption that he could comprehend what God was doing and critique his policies. Elihu's posing of rhetorical questions to prompt Job's recognition of God's great works in nature (37:15–16) foreshadows the approach of God in the next chapter. He also challenges Job to envision himself in God's role (37:18), which is likewise part of Yahweh's challenge (40:10–14). Yahweh's challenge concerns the enforcement of the RP, however, while Elihu's concerns involvement in creation.

The cosmological comments in 37:18 require some specific attention. In the first line Elihu poses the question to Job about whether he thinks he could join God in "spreading out the skies." Both the verb and its direct object are of interest here. The verb is from the root *rq'* (11x), which is related to the noun *raqia'*, used in Genesis 1:6 (NIV: "expanse"). The verb in some of its forms appears in metallurgical contexts, referencing the technical work of preparing metals for overlaying wood (e.g., Ex. 39:3; Num. 16:39).[29] In other contexts it refers to trampling (e.g., 2 Sam. 22:43; Ezek. 6:11).[30] The remaining three occurrences refer to cosmology

---

29. This is the use of the Piel and Pual, 4 occurrences.
30. Qal usage; 3 occurrences.

(Ps. 136:6; Isa. 42:5; 44:24 — all referring to God spreading out the earth on the waters).[31] Job 37:18 stands uniquely apart from these other occurrences in both its verbal form (the only Hiphil) and its direct object (connected with the "skies" instead of the earth). When the Qal form is active indicative, as it is with this root, the Hiphil typically involves a double direct object (someone causes D.O.[1] to do D.O.[2]). The use of the Hiphil thus suggests that the role posited by Elihu for Job is not as passive as "join with him" might imply. It rather puts Job in the position of control and cause with God as his instrument. The object (here, God) is viewed as participating in the event, to "participate indirectly as a second subject" rather than serving as the primary actor.[32] Job is thus hypothetically portrayed by Elihu as directing God in this cosmological process.

As Elihu concludes his speech, he confronts Job with a question that Job himself has considered: "What in the world do you think you would say to him if you got your request of a day in court?" (cf. 37:19). Job has already anticipated this problem (9:14–20) and, like Elihu, held out little hope for the prospect. Elihu wonders why anyone would ask for the inevitable trouble that would result (37:20). When God approaches, his majesty is overwhelming. Elihu's description of this in 37:22 anticipates Yahweh's entrance a few verses later.

Elihu, however, is mistaken in his assertion that God is beyond human reach, though he is right that God is exalted in power (37:23). God is going to demonstrate that he is both beyond human reach (transcendent), yet accessible in his immanence.

As interpreted in the NIV, Elihu ends with a rhetorical question (37:24).[33] Part of this decision is based on the identification of the "wise in heart." Is it referring to those who actually are wise or to those who think they are wise? To begin the discussion, we might inquire as to why Elihu uses "wise of heart" instead of just "the wise." M. Fox investigates the use of the combination of *hakam* and *leb* and suggests that it functions as a designation of those who have been given the wherewithal to exercise wisdom, though it has yet to be gained, developed, or exercised.[34] In many contexts this would make sense, but a previous use in 9:4 presents a problem for this analysis because it is traditionally translated as a reference to God. There is reason, however, to suggest an alternative translation. Rather than God

---

31. These three are all in the Qal. Note also that this verse offers a different view than Gen. 1, where the dry land emerges, rather than God spreading it out.

32. *IBHS*, 27.1d. In 27.3b it is stated that either object could potentially be marked by a preposition (as both are here in Job) rather than by a direct object marker.

33. This is interpretive because there is no signal in the syntax.

34. M. Fox, *Proverbs 10–31* (ABY; New Haven, Conn.: Yale Univ. Press), 515–16.

Excursus on *Šahaq*

The identification of the object being spread out also proves problematic. The word translated "skies" (*šehaqim* in the plural) is often rendered "clouds" in its twenty-one occurrences.[1] Nevertheless, it must be noticed that in this context, 37:21 (again, "skies") cannot possibly refer to the clouds since it specifically refers to a cloudless sky. Furthermore, 2 Samuel 22:12 speaks of the "clouds of the *šehaqim*," indicating that the clouds are part of the *šehaqim*, rather than the *šehaqim* being clouds. It would be nonsensical to say "clouds of the clouds." We should also note that in another cosmological context, it is obvious that establishing the *šehaqim* refers to an act of creation rather than to something God does now and then (Prov. 8:28).

In light of these data, we must undertake a fresh examination of the *šehaqim*. In terms of their role we find that they are never identified as the source of rain (as clouds would be), but are identified as the source of other forms of moisture. The verbs used to express this (*nzl*, Job 36:28; Isa. 45:8; and *r'p*, Job 36:28; Prov. 3:20) are connected with dew.

Structurally, the *šehaqim* are part of the heavens (*šamayim*) and can appear parallel to the heavens (Deut. 33:26; Job 35:5, as can *raqia'*). They are said to contain the doors of heaven through which manna came (Ps. 78:23). Their appearance is described as "hard as a mirror of cast bronze" (Job 37:18). From these structural data, I would propose that *šehaqim* pertains to the solid sky, a common component of ancient Near Eastern cosmology. It is commonly accepted that the Israelites also believed in a solid sky, but usually scholars identify that solid sky with the *raqia'*.

Given this fresh analysis of *šehaqim*, I would propose that *raqia'* refers to the space created when the *šehaqim* were put in place. This would explain why the birds and sun and moon are seen to be *in* the *raqia'*. Both *šehaqim* and *raqia'* can be used parallel to *šamayim*, and perhaps they could be viewed as constituting the plurality of *šamayim*. Some cosmological literature from Mesopotamia describes the solid sky as being composed of three levels of stone, and the texts detail what stone each is made of and which gods are associated with each.[2] The regular use of *šehaqim* in the plural may plausibly suggest that the Israelites also thought in similar terms.

This proposal requires an explanation of three potentially problematic passages in order to be confirmed. The customary translation of Job 38:37 indicates the *šeḥaqim* can be counted (Piel of *spr*). "Count" is certainly one of the possible meanings of this verb (though typically with the Qal, while this verse has a Piel), and if it is to be retained, we might consider whether it refers to counting the levels of heaven. The Piel and Pual forms of the verb regularly refer to giving an account through report or proclamation. In these occurrences, the context almost always indicates someone to whom the report or account is being given. Fortunately, Job 28:27 offers us a similar type of syntax and context in which wisdom is the object of the verb (NIV: "appraised").[3] I would therefore conclude that Job 38:37 is not referring to "counting the clouds" but to "appraising the nature of the [solid] skies."[4]

The next problem arises when we try to understand the significance of the two passages where the singular *šaḥaq* is used. In Psalm 89:6-7 the text describes *šaḥaq* as the place where God and the divine council reside. If we are right to think of the plural as referring to multiple levels of heaven as in Mesopotamia, we could suggest that, like the Babylonians, they associated a particular level with the location of God's heavenly residence. Thus the plural was used to refer to all the levels as a component of the cosmos, but one particular one was where God dwelt. Likewise, Psalm 89:37 would be seen as a reference to one particular level where the faithful witness was established.

Finally, by far the most difficult context is Isaiah 40:15. All translators have struggled with this because the context refers to the insignificance of the nations and clearly demands something like "dust" on the scales. This perception is strengthened by the parallel to a drop in a bucket in the previous line and to "fine dust" in the following line. Yet it is odd to take a word that otherwise refers to a macro-component of the cosmos and translate it as "dust."

The solution that I have to offer combines the needs of this context with the previously mentioned idea that the *šeḥaqim* were understood as the source of the dew. In ancient Near Eastern texts the source of dew is the stars,[5] which are believed to be engraved on the underside of the lowest level of the solid sky.[6] This would demonstrate that connections between the dew, the stars, and the solid sky were made in the ancient Near East. Based on the association with stars, another Akkadian term emerges as significant for this discussion. The Akkadian term *burumu* refers to the level of the skies that hold the night stars and specifically describes the appearance of the stars as specks.[7] In the context of Isaiah 40:15 the nations would then be likened to the appearance of the night sky (the starry *šaḥaq*—not all the levels, just that one) on the scales. They would thus be considered specks on the scale. The interpretation of the passage would not change, but this reading clarifies the metaphor. Isaiah refers to the great multitude of parts making up the whole (same as drops in a bucket) and the corresponding insignificance of each one. The scale metaphor introduces the concept of assessment—the nations are being weighed, measured, assessed, and judged.

---

1. In the singular 3x (Isa. 40:15; Ps. 89:7, 38), the remainder in the plural.

2. Horowitz, *Mesopotamian Cosmic Geography*, 243–67.

3. Similar usage can be seen in Ps. 26:7 and probably Ps. 50:16.

4. This solution is also suggested in R. Alter, *The Wisdom Books* (New York: Norton, 2010), 163.

5. Horowitz, *Mesopotamian Cosmic Geography*, 243–44.

6. Ibid., 13–15.

7. Ibid., 226. Horowitz points out that the noun derives from the verb *baramu*, "to be speckled."

being identified as the one whose "wisdom is profound and power is vast" (NIV), the description could be taken as a reference to the one who wishes to dispute with God (9:3). Even though such a one might be wise and powerful, he does not escape unscathed. It is the next verse that adopts God as its subject.

With this modification as caveat, Fox's assessment of the nature of the designation "wise of heart" suits well the sixteen contexts in which the two terms occur together.[35] The result of this analysis as it regards Elihu's statement is that rather than a rhetorical question, it is his final conclusion that God cannot be swayed by those who would qualify as the wisest among humanity (whether in the estimation of others or in their self-assessment). People fear (= respect) him because they are no match for him.

---

35. Ex. 28:3; 31:6; 35:10, 25; 36:1, 2, 8; 1 Kings 3:12; Job 9:4; Prov. 10:8; 11:29; 16:21, 23; Eccl. 7:4; 8:5; 10:2.

Elihu's Rhetorical Role in the Book

I HAVE SUGGESTED THAT the three friends are representatives of ancient Near Eastern thinking and that they unwittingly press the case of the Challenger. If the friends had persuaded Job to comply with their advice, the Challenger would have won his case. Job would have thus shown that prosperity was his highest priority rather than righteousness itself.

That is not so with the argument of Elihu. If Job were to accept Elihu's accusations as truth, he would not thereby betray self-interested motives (though Elihu does also believe that Job's motives are questionable). Elihu is not advising Job as to how he can get back in favor with God to have his prosperity restored (as the friends were). Elihu instead is holding Job accountable to God. This contrast demonstrates that Elihu's discourse properly belongs in this section of the book where Job's case against God is being treated ("It is bad policy for righteous people to suffer") rather than the Challenger's case ("It is bad policy for righteous people to prosper").[36] Elihu believes that Job deserves his treatment because of his self-righteous attitude in which he justifies himself at the expense of God's reputation.

We can identify the parameters of Elihu's claims from his speeches:

1. He defends God from the charge of evil (34:10, 12, 17).
2. He defends God's justice (36:3; 37:23).
3. He accepts the paradigm of the RP (34:11; 36:11–12).
4. He agrees with the Challenger about Job's motives (35:3).
5. He accuses Job of the sin of self-righteousness and considers that to be the reason for Job's suffering (34:35–37); this is the only point that differentiates him from the other accusers.
6. His emphasis is on righteousness, not the Great Symbiosis, though he questions whether God needs human righteousness (35:7–8).

To clarify Elihu's position we need to return to the triangle diagram offered in the Introduction (pp. 42–44). There I observed that Elihu seeks to defend the corner of the triangle that represents God's justice and thus to offer a theodicy. It is an "educative theodicy" that sees suffering as a means of bringing potential problems to our attention so that they can be remedied. Elihu modifies the RP even as he defends it. His modification is that suffering is not just God's response to past sin; it can also preempt future or potential sin. He also modifies the triangle with regard to his understand-

---

36. See Introduction, pp. 21–22.

ing of Job's righteousness. Having redefined the scope of the RP (preventive, not only remedial), he now faults Job for his self-righteous response to suffering. So God's justice is maintained (theodicy) because Job really has committed a serious offense (indictment) and the (revised) RP remains intact as the foundation of God's policies in the world. In this position he refutes the friends, whom he considers guilty of counseling Job to bribe God with repentance of things he did not do in order to gain his riches back (36:18), and he refutes Job, whom he considers guilty of undermining God's justice by subordinating God to his own sense of self-righteousness.

As we assess Elihu's position, we can affirm some of his beliefs about Job and God, but we must reject others. He is patently right in his condemnation of Job's self-righteous attitude — not suggesting Job has been deceptively hiding massive crimes against humanity and maintaining a duplicitous life that has finally caught up to him (the implications made by the friends). No, Elihu has rightly identified Job's willingness to defend himself at the expense of God.

At the same time, Elihu is wrong about Job's motivations. Elihu despises the Great Symbiosis attitude and believes that Job is still harboring a desire for benefits. Job has amply demonstrated that prosperity at any cost is not the driving motivation of his life.

Elihu is right about God when he insists that God is not accountable to us and that his justice, along with all other aspects of his character, is unassailable. We cannot question God; we cannot do his job better; we dare not impugn his governance. God is not contingent, and we should not think that his actions are subject to our evaluation or correction.

Though he is therefore right about the nature of God's person, Elihu is wrong about the nature of God's policies. He continues to have an inadequate theodicy and does not seem to realize that in attempting a theodicy, he is falling prey to the same fault of which he accuses Job — he overestimates his ability to bring coherence on the basis of justice. God will present his policies very differently in his own speeches, and we will find that human attempts at theodicy are inevitably presumptuous.

What is Elihu's contribution to the book? Could we do without him? Though we can affirm much of Elihu's theology, he is not intended to be a doctrinaire voice instructing the reader in sound theology. His theology simply forms another component of his rhetorical role, and it is that rhetorical role that is his raison d'être in the book. In turn, that rhetorical role is essential to the book and its message. Without Elihu's voice, readers might have a tendency to idealize Job and to conclude that his response to his suffering was impeccable. In light of Elihu's sound rebuke of Job's self-righteousness, however, we are all warned against thinking that our suffering should properly instigate a challenge of God. Job's other friends had discovered no cracks in the façade of Job's character; Elihu, in contrast, reveals gaping wounds.

Furthermore, the philosophical contribution of Elihu plays a significant role. He begins to call into question the RP insofar as he does not seek to identify sin in Job's behavior prior to the onset of suffering. Though he does not go far enough, through Elihu we, as readers, can begin to detect the philosophical vulnerability of the RP. Elihu's most important philosophical role, however, is that he is the sole figure to attempt a theodicy, and the failure of his attempt shows that a reasoned theodicy such as the one he proposes cannot be the answer to suffering. God is above reproach, but theodicies of our own devising easily fall short. Thus Elihu, in his failure, effectively shuts down a significant philosophical approach to understanding suffering in the world. At the same time, he has represented the third angle of the triangle. With all three angles having been defended and found wanting, the book has arrived at the point anticipated in Job 28, that a solution lies in a different direction than the triangle could provide.

Elihu's Theology

WE HAVE SUGGESTED THAT Elihu offers a largely accurate (biblically speaking) picture of God, but a flawed understanding of how God's policies work (specifically the issue of theodicy). In this section we will explore Elihu's theology and philosophy as we unpack its truths as well as its distortions.

Spirit of God and man. Elihu's understanding of the divine spirit is nonpersonal; that is, God's spirit is never articulated in trinitarian terms in which the Spirit is a distinct person of the godhead. As in the rest of the Old Testament, the spirit is an extension of God's power, presence, and authority.[37] It is viewed as part of God's person, but not as a distinct person.

Elihu's view of the human spirit appears to be that it is a gift on loan from God. This also is a view consistent with other Old Testament passages. In this view, the spirit in Elihu, for example, is God's spirit in Elihu, not Elihu's spirit. In these elements Elihu can be seen to have theological ideas that Israelites would have agreed with, but that have been superseded in modern theology. New Testament revelation about the Holy Spirit has given us new ways to think about the spirit of God in the Old Testament. On the human side of the equation, we continue to understand the human spirit as a gift from God, but we are more inclined to consider it more than

---

37. J. Walton, "The Ancient Near Eastern Background of the Spirit of the Lord in the Old Testament," in *Presence, Power and Promise: The Role of the Spirit of God in the Old Testament* (ed. D. Firth and P. Wegner; Leicester, UK: Inter-Varsity Press, 2011), 38–70.

just an invigorating power. It is often seen as bearing the identity of the human person beyond death into eternity. Christian theologians and philosophers continue to debate the constitution of the human person (e.g., monism vs. dualism), what survives death in eternity and what existence beyond death will be like. There is no unanimity on that issue, but none of the positions align with Israelite beliefs. Consequently, Elihu does not offer us guidance on how to formulate a comprehensive doctrine of either the Spirit or the human spirit.

Revelation and the word of God. Elihu does not make claims of special inspiration. He views his wisdom as like that of any wise person, for all wisdom finds its source in God (32:8). Like a prophet he feels ready to burst under the compulsion of his message (32:18–19), but he has no oracles to offer under the rubric of "this is what the LORD says," and it does not present his argument as having its source in revelation from God. Elihu takes the mantle of a sage, not of a prophet.

No one can "out-God" God (33:12). This is one of Elihu's strongest and most important points. Its message should ring in our souls. One of the most persistent human errors is the belief that God is not doing a very good job, which implies that given the chance, we could do it better. This is precisely the mentality evident in Job's responses throughout the book, and this is what Elihu attacks most vigorously.

When the world doesn't work the way that we think it should, we are inclined to manufacture solutions in our minds that will address either our situation or the situation that concerns us (famine in Africa, child prostitution in the Far East, oppressive tyranny in this country or that). We are inclined to make it seem like a simple fix. We are rarely able to imagine the complications or collateral damage—a problem portrayed in modern application by the movie *Bruce Almighty*.

The human plight is a consequence of our fallenness. No aspect of that human plight can be addressed in isolation. Addressing one aspect of it is insufficient, and the only true resolution is in eliminating human sin. Practically speaking, that means the problem would be addressed only by obliterating sin—which would mean obliterating humanity (or, of course, initiating a process to redeem it). Our shortsighted and inadequate solutions only register as naive hubris when visualized to scale in relation to the majesty of God and the magnitude of the problem. We are mistaken to think of God as handling it poorly; God is no bumbler.

We should not even imagine that it is complicated for God or that he is somehow fraught with anxiety wondering how he can manage it all. For us there would be constant angst in finding the line between justice and mercy. For God, however, his attributes intertwine and apply in seamless perfection. This is not an affirmation we can make because we understand how that all happens and can be explained; it is the conviction of our faith that it is so. Such is Elihu's insistence, and we can be grateful for the reminder and the challenge that it brings.

Perverting justice? Job and his friends believe that if the RP is not maintained, God could be accused of perverting justice. Elihu's modification of the RP in defense of God and his construction of a theodicy suggest that he agrees (34:12−15). Many people throughout history have thought the same way in response to their suffering. Consequently we must ask whether it is so.

If we were to believe that justice could be assessed by the RP, we would have to develop a complex understanding of the principle. Elihu gives us a good example as he seeks to include both preventative and remedial aspects in his attempt to address what constitutes the offense that stimulates God's response. It becomes even more complicated than Elihu's modifications address. Two other factors, timing and proportionality, must also be considered.

With regard to timing, we would have to determine how often the accounts must be balanced for justice and the RP to be maintained. Should judgment and reward be given decade by decade? Month by month? Day by day? Moment by moment? What would meet the demands of justice? The psalmist addresses this issue when he asks "How long?" in the midst of injustice (Pss. 13:1; 82:2), or when he accepts a longer span of time between action and retribution (Ps. 37:25−26).

With regard to proportionality, the principle is that great righteousness should bring great reward; inversely, great wickedness should bring great judgment. This is fine in theory, but how do humans, with all of their limitations, assess the scale of one's wickedness or righteousness? How do we measure what is enough reward or enough judgment for one's actions? All of these unknowns make it impossible for humans to make this assessment.

The result is that we may well recognize that we cannot discern how the RP should work in all cases, but we believe we can recognize a travesty of justice when we see it, or even more so, when our personal situations are involved. I would therefore suggest that most attempts to tie justice to the RP amount to little more than special pleading for our own circumstances to be worked out more conveniently and comfortably. We really have no inkling how to make a whole system work consistently; we only know that it is not working to our satisfaction. We may talk about theodicy, but God is less of a concern than our personal claims of unfairness and our (less than objective) assessment of what would constitute our "just deserts." Consequently I would suggest that the true issue when people today cite failure of the RP is not really a concern about the perversion of justice; it is purely and simply disappointment with God that he did not work things out better for us.

God as judge. When we think of God as judge, we might consider the issue of his gathering of evidence and then weighing that evidence to arrive at a verdict. We have some sense of how this works in a court of law, and the Israelites also had beliefs about how the judiciary system works. Though their system differed at many points from our own, all people would share the idea that a judge ought to gather all possible evidence and then sift through it to arrive at a just decision. Despite this ideal, we all recognize that a human judge has limitations that can undermine, if not cripple, his ability to do his job. People may do things in secret places hidden from view of any potential witness. At times the important factor of their motivations could be involved. Furthermore, it was not unusual for a case to come down to one person's word against another. Any of these can hinder a judge's work or invalidate his verdict.

In Job 34:21–24 Elihu suggests that God is not subject to such limitations. In Psalm 139 the psalmist confirms this as he affirms that God knows everything we think (139:2–4), that we can do nothing in secret (139:7–12), and that he knows us intimately (139:13–16, which presumably includes our motivations). In this psalm these affirmations are part of the claim that God is therefore not a judge who suffers under the limitations of human judges. He has all the necessary information at his disposal and therefore should be able to execute justice perfectly. Elihu concludes with an affirmation that God indeed does judge fairly. Though he has all power and is not accountable, "he does not oppress" (Job 37:23). He is respected among men not as a result of his intimidating power, but for his justice (37:24).

Aseity and contingency. We reiterate what was stated in Original Meaning: God does not need us but we need him; God is not accountable to us but we are accountable to him. The Great Symbiosis has been one of the background discussion points in the book. It is a system that was based on gods who had needs. The gods of the ancient Near East were contingent beings. They not only needed what human beings provided for their continued sustenance, they needed one another to ensure the continuing operations of the cosmos, as well as those principles that had been woven into the cosmos. Polytheism is a contingency network. Further contingency is evident in the positioning of the gods in the cosmos. The ancient Near Eastern gods were inside the cosmos, not outside it. Many aspects of the cosmos were not set up by them and not subject to their authority. Consequently, they were contingent with relation to the cosmos just as they were to humans and one another.

Another piece of the picture of Elihu's view of God's aseity is that he values transcendence over immanence (35:6–7). When we discuss transcendence and immanence today, we often think in terms of the level of God's involvement with us. In Elihu's elaboration, he is more interested in our potential involvement with God. Our wickedness has no impact on him and our justice adds nothing to him. Today we often talk about how our sin grieves God and our righteousness delights him. To an extent these are true descriptions of how our behavior succeeds or fails to coincide with God's character and wishes. But we go too far if we begin to think of God's emotional stability as dependent on human behavior. If we think that our behavior is something that can be dangled over his head to motivate him to certain sorts of action, we have again reduced him to a contingent being.

In Elihu's speech we find a notably Israelite-shaped theology that posits a noncontingent deity. The God whom Elihu defends has no accountability (35:9–15) and no subordination. This is sound theology and a needed element in the theology of the book.

Accessibility. If God is judge, then one might think he ought to be accessible because in human terms, what good is a court system if no one can ever have their case heard. Yet if God is transcendent, such that our wickedness or righteousness does not affect him significantly, why should he bother? It is fine to affirm that God is a competent, even perfect judge, but is he accessible?

In the book of Job, God's lack of accessibility has been one of Job's greatest complaints. Elihu's portrayal is of a God who is not accessible (37:23). Elihu's opinion would be that God does not need our prompting to do justice and he should not be bothered with our petty requests. "Don't worry, he is doing his job and he shouldn't be bothered with your challenges or demands." God should not be viewed as working the customer service desk. People should be content to view him from afar to learn about him and respect him. Job should not have thought for a moment that God would respond to his desire for a hearing. We should be more concerned with responding to God rather than trying to get him to respond to us.

Is this sound theology? I believe that we should see wisdom in it and be cautioned by it. God, of his own will, has drawn near to us. From the very beginning, he has loved us and wants to be in relationship with us; this came to clearest expression in the incarnation of Jesus Christ. This immanence, however, can be abused, and we must be careful not to impose on his grace and generosity. I do not refer to how close we feel to him, but to the sort of familiarity where we might feel we have an inside track to influence his behavior of receive special favors.

We often hear "It is not what you know, but who you know that counts" in our world, where power is wielded and influence-peddling accomplishes things. Our governments are beleaguered by lobbyists seeking influence for their clients to affect public policy and accomplish their corporate objectives. There is power in being an "insider."

It is not surprising, then, that a natural human inclination is to want to have "insider" status with God. This is the accessibility that Elihu would most denounce, and rightly so. God is not subject to our influence-peddling or our attempts to exploit a relationship with him to achieve our goals. We must not overstep our privileges or presume on his grace. We insult him with our demands for more information as if he needed to be reminded of his responsibilities or explain what we might think are questionable actions.

God's control of weather for justice.[38] Elihu suggests that God uses the weather as one of his instruments to carry out justice (37:13). Yahweh's speech to Job is going to qualify this (38:25 – 27), but not negate it. Our theology can affirm that God is able to use the weather for his purposes, but there are limits to our ability to determine when that is the case. The question then is not "What can God do?" but "How would we know whether any given weather-related phenomenon is communication of God's favor or disfavor?" To answer such a question we need to enter a discussion of divine communication specifically as it relates to epistemology (How we know what we know?), beginning with Elihu.

In Job 33 Elihu offers the theoretical underpinnings of his theology. He begins with Job's claim that he is righteous yet has become God's target (33:9 – 11). Elihu contends that Job is incorrect in his complaint that God has refused to answer his pleas (33:12 – 14), and here he gets to his main point: God communicates in a variety of ways (Elihu mentions dreams and pain as two examples), and he does so in a variety of circumstances (33:17, remedial [turn from wrongdoing] or preventative [keep from pride]).

One of the areas of sharpest distinction between the ancient world and our modern world concerns how we think God communicates. How do we believe that we can know how God communicates and know what he is saying? What convinces us that we know what we believe we know? Modern Christians believe that they can know about God through the Bible because of their beliefs about the nature of the Bible. We further believe that some information about God is available from the blunt facts observable in the world around us (Rom. 1:20). We also believe that God communicates through his Holy Spirit. These are three elements of our

---

38. For helpful discussion, see T. E. Fretheim, *Creation Untamed: The Bible, God, and Natural Disasters* (Grand Rapids: Baker, 2010).

epistemology that distinguish us from the world around us. Others in our world, more skeptical of the claims of Scripture and about the existence or involvement of God, might believe that we can only know things that our senses perceive or that can be demonstrated naturalistically or scientifically.

By contrast, the epistemology of people in the ancient world included many other ways that deity communicated. Some believed that he communicated through the movements of the heavenly bodies, through the configuration of the entrails of animals, through the strange behaviors of animals in the world around them, and through dreams—just to name a few. What we understand as meteorological phenomena were also seen as a means by which God communicated. Some continue to think that today when they interpret a tsunami, a hurricane, a tornado, or a flood as acts of God's judgment.

A middle ground position that is more common today is that it may well be true that God is judging through natural disasters, but we have no reliable interpretive methodology by which we can receive that communication. Consequently, the credibility we lend to those who claim such prophetic ability has greatly diminished. For Elihu and his audience, however, the epistemological premise is uncontested even when a variety of interpretations might be possible. Weather is a communicative instrument of God.

Are we supposed to adopt this epistemology as biblically mandated? We cannot do so on the strength of Elihu's assertions, because he is not always correct. Sound bites from Elihu's speech cannot be used for theological proof texts. What he says must be verified from other canonical texts before they can be taken as truth. In this case Yahweh's speech offers important qualifiers that must supersede Elihu's blunt statements (this will be discussed further in the next chapter, pp. 414–15).

SENSE OF SELF-IMPORTANCE. IN this topic we find one of the great mysteries that we struggle with all the time. Our theology tells us that God cares about every aspect of our lives. Scripture tells us he knows the number of hairs on our head. Our moment-by-moment circumstances are important to him. We believe that he is involved in our lives and that nothing that happens is outside of his control. This is all sound theology.

At the same time, we share Elihu's caution about thinking of God micromanaging every second of our lives. An illustration might help. Once after a Christmas visit to the east coast, my wife and I were driving back to the Midwest. In western Pennsylvania we encountered blizzard conditions and the roads became treacherous. As I tried to move carefully and gradually from a middle lane to the right lane I found that the car was not responding to my steering. When I tried to stop moving over, the car continued its slide toward the edge of the road. We slid past the shoulder and up onto a rocky embankment, which finally gave me sufficient traction that I was able to steer back toward the shoulder. However, the rocks of the terrain had given me a flat tire, and when I got back to the shoulder, that wheel stopped working and the car pivoted 180 degrees to end up facing the opposite direction, thankfully still on the shoulder. Shaken, but relieved that we had been spared injury or serious accident, we thanked God.

As we waited for the tow truck and thought back through the experience, we realized how very fortunate we had been. All along that stretch of highway there were sections with deep drop-offs and others with rock walls. Sliding off the road in places like those would have been disastrous. We were thankful that we slid off the road where we did rather than in more dangerous locations.

Now to the theology. When we thank God in such situations, what role are we imagining for him? If we think that he was involved in protecting us from sliding off the road where there was a cliff, does that mean he orchestrated our sliding off the road where we did? In that case, why didn't he prevent us from sliding off altogether? Would it be appropriate to think of him with control of the wheel or the tires or the road or the placement of rocks? On one hand, we might well be reluctant to say that God had nothing to do with any of those things. On the other hand, I suspect that we would all feel reticent about thinking of God as selecting the place, guiding the steering wheel, and making sure that certain rocks were hit. Where is the line between a deism that posits an uninvolved God, and a micromanagement of everyone's circumstances down to the smallest detail (a form of what is sometimes called "meticulous providence")?

Elihu's opinion was that when anyone thinks of God as paying close attention to the details of our lives and micromanaging our circumstances, we are giving ourselves too much importance and trivializing God's role in the cosmos. Yet what is the alternative? Do we believe that God is not really involved in the details and is only engaged in the larger issues? Here lies mystery. While we can err on the deism extreme or on the micromanagement extreme, we can also err by thinking we can sort it all out and figure out how God works or does not work. The error of "God too small" is committed when we misrepresent at one extreme or the other, but it is also committed when we think we can fully describe the nature of his involvement. To believe that his work could so easily be defined is to reduce him to something manageable. We must be content with mystery. I can thank

God for protecting us and be grateful that we did not slide off the road at a more dangerous spot. But I must stop short of trying to detail all of the aspects of his involvement.

Furthermore, Elihu is right that we should be reluctant to think of ourselves as at the center of God's attention and worthy of his continuous involvement in our circumstances. Yet we should not be surprised that we are never "off the radar" and on our own. Again, the line between is part of the mystery that we can never fully understand. We should be willing to think less of our own importance and always willing to give more credit to God.

Christian responses to natural disasters. The world was shocked at the devastation caused throughout the Far East by the tsunami that struck on the day after Christmas in 2004, caused by the Sumatra-Andaman earthquake (the third largest ever recorded) in the Indian Ocean. The death toll was nearly a quarter of a million people. Was that an act of God? Some were quick to affirm it as such; others were unpersuaded and echoed Abraham's comment to God, "Far be it from you to do such a thing—to kill the righteous with the wicked, treating the righteous and wicked alike. Far be it from you! Will not the Judge of all the earth do right?" (Gen. 18:25).

The following spring I had a student in my class from one of the devastated areas of Indonesia. In one conversation with her I asked whether she had lost family or loved ones in the tragedy. She replied that gratefully all were safe, and then she told me a remarkable story. In recent years there had been a thriving Christian community living in the coastal region, her family included. The dominant Muslim population of that area, however, had become belligerent and had begun persecuting the Christians, taking their homes and driving them from the area. Over several years the Christians were all driven inland. Then the tsunami struck and virtually wiped out the population of their oppressors.

It would be easy to see how the Christians of that community would conclude that justice had been done—God had used the tsunami to punish evildoers. They got what they deserved. That was indeed the immediate response, but the wise and godly pastor began to push their thinking in a different direction. The tsunami, he insisted, was an opportunity for the Christians to show love to their enemies by coming to the aid of those who had persecuted them. He urged his congregation to gather medical supplies, food, and clothing and to travel to their old community and help those who had survived. What a challenge!

That pastor offers a lesson to all of us. Though it may well be that God has used a disaster to execute justice, it is not our job to take a seat next to him on the judge's bench to proclaim his deeds and add our renunciation to what we perceive as his verdict. God's verdicts are often sealed, and we cannot know their content. Our job, rather than taking up a cry of renunciation, is to respond with grace and mercy. God is the one responsible for doing justice. We are asked to be forgiving and merciful. This was the model Jesus gave us. It is articulated in the Sermon on the Mount and is illustrated in his interaction with his own enemies.

One remarkable illustration of this balance of justice and mercy is in the contested story of the woman caught in adultery in John 8:3–11. The force of the story has been captured brilliantly by Orson Scott Card in his fantasy novel *Speaker for the Dead*.[39]

> A great rabbi stands teaching in the marketplace. It happens that a husband finds proof that morning of his wife's adultery, and a mob carries her to the marketplace to stone her to death. (There is a familiar version of this story, but a friend of mine, a speaker for the dead, has told me of two other rabbis who faced the same situation. Those are the ones I'm going to tell you.)
>
> The rabbi walks forward and stands beside the woman. Out of respect for him the mob forbears and waits with the stones heavy in their hands. "Is there anyone here," he says to them, "who has not desired another man's wife, another woman's husband?"
>
> They murmur and say, "We all know the desire. But, Rabbi, none of us has acted on it."
>
> The rabbi says, "Then kneel down and give thanks that God made you strong." He takes the woman by the hand and leads her out of the market. Just before he lets her go, he whispers to her, "Tell the lord magistrate who saved his mistress. Then he'll know I am his loyal servant."
>
> So the woman lives, because the community is too corrupt to protect itself from disorder.
>
> Another rabbi, another city. He goes to her and stops the mob, as in the other story, and says, "Which of you is without sin? Let him cast the first stone."
>
> The people are abashed, and they forget their unity of purpose in the memory of their own individual sins. Someday, they think, I may be like this woman, and I'll hope for forgiveness and another chance. I should treat her the way I wish to be treated.
>
> As they open their hands and let the stones fall to the ground, the rabbi picks up one of the fallen stones, lifts it high over the

---

39. O. S. Card, *Speaker for the Dead* (New York: Tom Doherty, 1986), 277–78.

woman's head, and throws it straight down with all his might. It crushes her skull and dashes her brains onto the cobblestones.

"Nor am I without sin," he says to the people. "But if we allow only perfect people to enforce the law, the law will soon be dead, and our city with it."

So the woman died because her community was too rigid to endure her deviance.

The famous version of this story is noteworthy because it is so startlingly rare in our experience. Most communities lurch between decay and rigor mortis, and when they veer too far, they die. Only one rabbi dared to expect of us such a perfect balance that we could preserve the law and still forgive the deviation. So, of course, we killed him.

It is not within our ability to decide what are acts of God or what are not. It is not our place to take up the role of prophet announcing doom. It is our responsibility to come alongside hurting people, even if they are enemies, and offer assistance in the name of Christ. We promote justice insofar as it is within our ability to establish it. God will do his part.

Pain as God's megaphone. In Job 36:9–10, 15, Elihu asserts that God communicates wrongdoing by inflicting suffering and pain. Again, we cannot take Elihu's theological pronouncements as reliable because of his role in the book, so we have to examine whether they are accurate or not.

C. S. Lewis is well-known for expressing a similar perspective on pain: "But pain insists on being attended to. God whispers to us in our pleasures, speaks to us in our conscience, but shouts to us in our pains: it is His megaphone to rouse a deaf world."[40] In the movie version of Lewis's life, *Shadowlands*, he is shown as repeating that line in several lectures, but coming to reject its insensitive naiveté when faced with the deep suffering of his friend, and eventual wife, Joy Davidman Gresham.

It is undeniably true that pain shouts to us and that it must be attended to. It is also biblically supportable and theologically sound that God can use pain and suffering as a response to wrongdoing. The problem comes when we seek to move from those observations to generalizations about what suffering intrinsically is and how God is characteristically related to it. We can readily and appropriately conclude that suffering and pain can serve to draw our attention to God, rely on him, and perhaps in self-evaluation, discover behaviors or attitudes that should be corrected. But we should be more cautious about suggesting that pain and suffering be always viewed as God's instrument for accomplishing any of those goals. We cannot adopt

---

40. C. S. Lewis *The Problem of Pain* (New York: Macmillan, 1977), 81.

a view of suffering that sets up those potential results as God's reasons for bringing suffering into our lives.

Kelly's Story[41]

ARMED WITH THESE REFLECTIONS, we turn back to Kelly to see how they function when people are actually suffering.

JHW: Does the idea of pain as God's megaphone appeal to you? Does it help you to process your experiences?

Kelly: When I think of the idea of pain being God's megaphone, I do not reject the idea, but I also don't relate to it either. I can relate to entertaining the thought that God is causing these things to happen to correct some major sin in my life. But the more I thought and prayed about that idea, the more I found that wasn't the case. As you said, there is biblical support that God can use pain to draw our attention to him, bring us closer, teach us things, refine us in the fire, if you will. But I see a big difference between God using the pain that occurs in your life, and God putting the pain in your life as a megaphone to communicate to you that things need to change.

I was in a car accident and suffered from an injury that has left me extreme amounts of pain. That statement is a sign of the reality that we live in a broken, fallen, and imperfect world. I don't believe that God caused my brother to fall asleep at the wheel and have a nearly fatal car accident in order to use that as his megaphone to correct sin in our lives. In the same tone, I don't believe the devastation of the unending pursuit of pain relief is God's megaphone either. So "pain as God's megaphone" approach is not one I relate to; rather, when I am in trials that have come from circumstances, I pray that God will use the trial to teach and prune me.

JHW: How does Elihu's position strike you? Do you feel that his assertions have the potential of offering any comfort or resolution as you deal with your day-to-day circumstances?

Kelly: Elihu's position, although it has some faults, strikes me as a strong and important perspective that was needed in the conversation with Job and in our conversation about suffering in the present day. His assertions are applicable to one in the midst of suffering or any believer because I think we can easily fall into these faulty mind-sets and views of God. Given how Elihu's position was written, I would not say that if I were Job, I'd feel "comforted," but we should be comforted that he was right about God's

---

41. Kelly interacts with parts of her story in each Contemporary Significance section. For the introduction to the details of her story see Contemporary Significance in the commentary on ch. 1, pp. 86–97.

character. We worship a God who is bigger than the box that we, and Job, create for him. I would much rather be corrected in my distorted view of God than worship a God who was in fact petty, accountable, or contingent in the way that Job's arguments imply, and we should take comfort in that.

Even though Elihu was not accurate about Job's motivations, he was right to correct Job's view of God. Elihu's attack on Job's mentality that he can "out-God" God was one that we so often need to correct in our own lives. Elihu's position is one that can help in the day-to-day circumstances because we have a choice in how we respond to our suffering, and I think Elihu's challenges to Job's view of God are ones to keep in our minds. So often we let our experiences on earth dictate God's character.

With these assertions in mind, we can check ourselves when we are in a deep trial to see if our perspective of God is aligning with Job's and needs to be corrected. During the spring of 2011, when I was on the long drive back from California, I was confused and upset that once again I felt the Lord had opened all these doors and led me in, only to experience pain and disappointment, and to waste thousands of dollars I didn't have on something that did nothing for me. I began seeing myself starting to challenge God, but this time I was in a trial and felt more equipped. I had been studying Job throughout this process as we have been writing this commentary and reflecting on how my suffering has distorted my view of God in the past, so I began to catch myself before forming more lies in my head about God's character.

I still have questions and days where I am frustrated that God did not close that door and protect me from yet another emotional and physical rollercoaster, but overall I noticed that the questions I was asking were different and my thought process had changed as I wrestled with the unknown. So Elihu's position is directly linked with Job's faulty views of God and his character, and I think it can be helpful day by day to keep these things in mind, but also in being careful not to adopt Elihu's entire position. We should focus on his assertions regarding how Job viewed and approached God.

JHW: In your long-time experience of suffering, how satisfying is the proposal that we have to be content with "mystery in the middle"?

Kelly: When we consider God's involvement, we have no choice but to rest with the "mystery in the middle," because drifting to either extreme downgrades God's deity once again. But as I read that question, "... how satisfying is the proposal," I guess if I am honest, I'd have to say that I'm not fully satisfied if I continue to ask the same questions and wrestle with that mystery. I logically see that I need to be satisfied because we are not going to get the answers to God's mysteries, yet I know that I still pray and question God at times hoping that maybe this time he'll clue me in and give me a different answer.

Our own "sense of self-importance," as you described above, can often lead us to misconstrue God's role in the cosmos as well as bring us to false conclusions about our own experiences. We tend to put our trial as the center focus not of just our universe, but of God's. The example that you gave about your family's near accident is one I feel is so common in Christians' thinking today. We can overspiritualize experiences and credit every positive detail to be of God's intentional involvement, but those who hold that belief struggle with holding it consistently. If God is involved in every detail of the blessings in our lives, that would mean he is also involved in every detail of the painful things in life. I struggled with falling to the extreme that God micromanages, because I remember believing that God purposefully kept every medication and treatment from working in order to strengthen my testimony. This thought process reveals that I was giving myself and my testimony too much importance by thinking that God is focusing solely on me and causing these painful situations in order to strengthen my testimony. If I rest in the middle, I might conclude that my situation is likely due to the unfortunate truth that in our fallen world we have pain, and science has not found a way to treat the pain that I suffer. God sees this occurring, mourns with me as I suffer, and wants to use it for his purpose. So even though I wrestle with it and at times question God, I do feel at peace that God is in the middle of the two extremes.

Job 38–41

🌿

Then the LORD answered Job out of the storm. He said:

²"Who is this that darkens my counsel
with words without knowledge?
³Brace yourself like a man;
I will question you,
and you shall answer me.

⁴"Where were you when I laid the earth's foundation?
Tell me, if you understand.
⁵Who marked off its dimensions? Surely you know!
Who stretched a measuring line across it?
⁶On what were its footings set,
or who laid its cornerstone—
⁷while the morning stars sang together
and all the angels shouted for joy?

⁸"Who shut up the sea behind doors
when it burst forth from the womb,
⁹when I made the clouds its garment
and wrapped it in thick darkness,
¹⁰when I fixed limits for it
and set its doors and bars in place,
¹¹when I said, 'This far you may come and no farther;
here is where your proud waves halt'?

¹²"Have you ever given orders to the morning,
or shown the dawn its place,
¹³that it might take the earth by the edges
and shake the wicked out of it?
¹⁴The earth takes shape like clay under a seal;
its features stand out like those of a garment.
¹⁵The wicked are denied their light,
and their upraised arm is broken.

¹⁶"Have you journeyed to the springs of the sea
or walked in the recesses of the deep?
¹⁷Have the gates of death been shown to you?
Have you seen the gates of the shadow of death?

¹⁸Have you comprehended the vast expanses of the earth?
　　Tell me, if you know all this.

¹⁹"What is the way to the abode of light?
　　And where does darkness reside?
²⁰Can you take them to their places?
　　Do you know the paths to their dwellings?
²¹Surely you know, for you were already born!
　　You have lived so many years!

²²"Have you entered the storehouses of the snow
　　or seen the storehouses of the hail,
²³which I reserve for times of trouble,
　　for days of war and battle?
²⁴What is the way to the place where the lightning is
　　　　dispersed,
　　or the place where the east winds are scattered over
　　　　the earth?
²⁵Who cuts a channel for the torrents of rain,
　　and a path for the thunderstorm,
²⁶to water a land where no man lives,
　　a desert with no one in it,
²⁷to satisfy a desolate wasteland
　　and make it sprout with grass?
²⁸Does the rain have a father?
　　Who fathers the drops of dew?
²⁹From whose womb comes the ice?
　　Who gives birth to the frost from the
　　　　heavens
³⁰when the waters become hard as stone,
　　when the surface of the deep is frozen?

³¹"Can you bind the beautiful Pleiades?
　　Can you loose the cords of Orion?
³²Can you bring forth the constellations in their seasons
　　or lead out the Bear with its cubs?
³³Do you know the laws of the heavens?
　　Can you set up ⌞God's⌟ dominion over the earth?

³⁴"Can you raise your voice to the clouds
　　and cover yourself with a flood of water?
³⁵Do you send the lightning bolts on their way?
　　Do they report to you, 'Here we are'?

³⁶Who endowed the heart with wisdom
 or gave understanding to the mind?
³⁷Who has the wisdom to count the clouds?
 Who can tip over the water jars of the heavens
³⁸when the dust becomes hard
 and the clods of earth stick together?

³⁹"Do you hunt the prey for the lioness
 and satisfy the hunger of the lions
⁴⁰when they crouch in their dens
 or lie in wait in a thicket?
⁴¹Who provides food for the raven
 when its young cry out to God
 and wander about for lack of food?

^{39:1}"Do you know when the mountain goats
   give birth?
 Do you watch when the doe bears her fawn?
²Do you count the months till they bear?
 Do you know the time they give birth?
³They crouch down and bring forth their young;
 their labor pains are ended.
⁴Their young thrive and grow strong in
   the wilds;
 they leave and do not return.

⁵"Who let the wild donkey go free?
 Who untied his ropes?
⁶I gave him the wasteland as his home,
 the salt flats as his habitat.
⁷He laughs at the commotion in the town;
 he does not hear a driver's shout.
⁸He ranges the hills for his pasture
 and searches for any green thing.

⁹"Will the wild ox consent to serve you?
 Will he stay by your manger at night?
¹⁰Can you hold him to the furrow with a harness?
 Will he till the valleys behind you?
¹¹Will you rely on him for his great strength?
 Will you leave your heavy work to him?
¹²Can you trust him to bring in your grain
 and gather it to your threshing floor?

¹³"The wings of the ostrich flap joyfully,
    but they cannot compare with the pinions and
        feathers of the stork.
¹⁴She lays her eggs on the ground
    and lets them warm in the sand,
¹⁵unmindful that a foot may crush them,
    that some wild animal may trample them.
¹⁶She treats her young harshly, as if they were
        not hers;
    she cares not that her labor was in vain,
¹⁷for God did not endow her with wisdom
    or give her a share of good sense.
¹⁸Yet when she spreads her feathers to run,
    she laughs at horse and rider.

¹⁹"Do you give the horse his strength
    or clothe his neck with a flowing mane?
²⁰Do you make him leap like a locust,
    striking terror with his proud snorting?
²¹He paws fiercely, rejoicing in his strength,
    and charges into the fray.
²²He laughs at fear, afraid of nothing;
    he does not shy away from the sword.
²³The quiver rattles against his side,
    along with the flashing spear and lance.
²⁴In frenzied excitement he eats up the ground;
    he cannot stand still when the trumpet sounds.
²⁵At the blast of the trumpet he snorts, 'Aha!'
    He catches the scent of battle from afar,
    the shout of commanders and the battle cry.

²⁶"Does the hawk take flight by your wisdom
    and spread his wings toward the south?
²⁷Does the eagle soar at your command
    and build his nest on high?
²⁸He dwells on a cliff and stays there at
        night;
    a rocky crag is his stronghold.
²⁹From there he seeks out his food;
    his eyes detect it from afar.
³⁰His young ones feast on blood,
    and where the slain are, there is he."

^{40:1} The LORD said to Job:

²"Will the one who contends with the Almighty
      correct him?
  Let him who accuses God answer him!"

³ Then Job answered the LORD:

⁴"I am unworthy—how can I reply to you?
  I put my hand over my mouth.
⁵I spoke once, but I have no answer—
  twice, but I will say no more."

⁶Then the LORD spoke to Job out of the storm:

⁷"Brace yourself like a man;
  I will question you,
  and you shall answer me.

⁸"Would you discredit my justice?
  Would you condemn me to justify yourself?
⁹Do you have an arm like God's,
  and can your voice thunder like his?
¹⁰Then adorn yourself with glory and splendor,
  and clothe yourself in honor and majesty.
¹¹Unleash the fury of your wrath,
  look at every proud man and bring him low,
¹²look at every proud man and humble him,
  crush the wicked where they stand.
¹³Bury them all in the dust together;
  shroud their faces in the grave.
¹⁴Then I myself will admit to you
  that your own right hand can save you.

¹⁵"Look at the behemoth,
  which I made along with you
  and which feeds on grass like an ox.
¹⁶What strength he has in his loins,
  what power in the muscles of his belly!
¹⁷His tail sways like a cedar;
  the sinews of his thighs are close-knit.
¹⁸His bones are tubes of bronze,
  his limbs like rods of iron.
¹⁹He ranks first among the works of God,
  yet his Maker can approach him with his sword.

²⁰The hills bring him their produce,
    and all the wild animals play nearby.
²¹Under the lotus plants he lies,
    hidden among the reeds in the marsh.
²²The lotuses conceal him in their shadow;
    the poplars by the stream surround him.
²³When the river rages, he is not alarmed;
    he is secure, though the Jordan should surge against
        his mouth.
²⁴Can anyone capture him by the eyes,
    or trap him and pierce his nose?

^{41:1}"Can you pull in the leviathan with a fishhook
    or tie down his tongue with a rope?
²Can you put a cord through his nose
    or pierce his jaw with a hook?
³Will he keep begging you for mercy?
    Will he speak to you with gentle words?
⁴Will he make an agreement with you
    for you to take him as your slave for life?
⁵Can you make a pet of him like a bird
    or put him on a leash for your girls?
⁶Will traders barter for him?
    Will they divide him up among the merchants?
⁷Can you fill his hide with harpoons
    or his head with fishing spears?
⁸If you lay a hand on him,
    you will remember the struggle and never do
        it again!
⁹Any hope of subduing him is false;
    the mere sight of him is overpowering.
¹⁰No one is fierce enough to rouse him.
    Who then is able to stand against me?
¹¹Who has a claim against me that I must pay?
    Everything under heaven belongs to me.

¹²"I will not fail to speak of his limbs,
    his strength and his graceful form.
¹³Who can strip off his outer coat?
    Who would approach him with a bridle?
¹⁴Who dares open the doors of his mouth,
    ringed about with his fearsome teeth?

¹⁵His back has rows of shields
   tightly sealed together;
¹⁶each is so close to the next
   that no air can pass between.
¹⁷They are joined fast to one another;
   they cling together and cannot be parted.
¹⁸His snorting throws out flashes of light;
   his eyes are like the rays of dawn.
¹⁹Firebrands stream from his mouth;
   sparks of fire shoot out.
²⁰Smoke pours from his nostrils
   as from a boiling pot over a fire of reeds.
²¹His breath sets coals ablaze,
   and flames dart from his mouth.
²²Strength resides in his neck;
   dismay goes before him.
²³The folds of his flesh are tightly joined;
   they are firm and immovable.
²⁴His chest is hard as rock,
   hard as a lower millstone.
²⁵When he rises up, the mighty are terrified;
   they retreat before his thrashing.
²⁶The sword that reaches him has no effect,
   nor does the spear or the dart or the javelin.
²⁷Iron he treats like straw
   and bronze like rotten wood.
²⁸Arrows do not make him flee;
   slingstones are like chaff to him.
²⁹A club seems to him but a piece of straw;
   he laughs at the rattling of the lance.
³⁰His undersides are jagged potsherds,
   leaving a trail in the mud like a threshing
         sledge.
³¹He makes the depths churn like a boiling
         caldron
   and stirs up the sea like a pot of ointment.
³²Behind him he leaves a glistening wake;
   one would think the deep had white hair.
³³Nothing on earth is his equal—
   a creature without fear.
³⁴He looks down on all that are haughty;
   he is king over all that are proud."

As CLINES OBSERVES, IN contrast to *Waiting for Godot*, in which Godot never comes, the waiting for God has now come to fruition.[1] Yet many readers have wondered whether this long-awaited appearance is a mere shadow of a solution rather than the epiphany that was expected. Some readers have found God's reply to be an exercise in obfuscation meant to distract and intimidate rather than to offer real answers. It is not surprising that an answer of "I am God and you are not" is considered unsatisfying, leading to responses such as Bernard Shaw's reputed quip: "If I complain that I am suffering unjustly, it is no answer to say, 'Can you make a hippopotamus?'"[2]

Yahweh's speech begins with a series of rhetorical questions, first dealing with larger operations of the cosmos (macrocosm, 38:4–38), then with the animal world (microcosm, 38:39–39:30), and finally with the cosmic creatures Behemoth and Leviathan (40:15–41:34). The use of rhetorical questions in a discussion about the wisdom and power of deity is also found in the Akkadian epic known as Erra and Ishum:[3]

> Who carries the pure axe of the sun, and knows ... timbers?
> Who makes [the night?] as radiant as day and makes [people?]
>   bow down beneath me?
> Where is Kusig-banda, creator of god and man, whose hands are
>   pure?
> Where are the precious stones, produce of the vast ocean, fitting
>   ornaments for crowns?
> Where are the seven sages of the Apsu, the holy carp, who are
>   perfect in lofty wisdom like Ea their lord, who can make my
>   body holy?

As in the book of Job, the rhetorical questions draw out the necessary relationship between wisdom and power in matters concerning justice.

---

1. Clines, *Job 21–37*, 711.
2. J. A. Baker, "The Book of Job: Unity and Meaning," in *Studia Biblica 1978* (ed. E. A. Livingstone; Sheffield: JSOT, 1979) 17–26; quote on 17.
3. See translation in *COS*, 1.113; the series of rhetorical questions is found in Tablet 1, lines 150–62. The epic dates to the eighth century BC. I have included only a selection of the lines here. The speaker is the god Marduk.

Introduction (38:1 – 3)

WE MUST FIRST NOTICE that it is *Yahweh* who speaks. This marks a shift in terms, because throughout the dialogues and discourses of the book, the deity has most often been identified as El Shaddai or Elohim.[4] The use of Yahweh in the prologue and now in the divine speeches may well have significance, but it is not transparent what it might be. One might note that Shaddai pertains to the power of God and the switch to Yahweh may signal a theological upgrade in how the audience ought to think about God. Such usage might suggest that when the audience only knows of God as El Shaddai, they are left with no answers to their questions. The revelation of Yahweh, however, offers greater insight. But such speculations cannot be verified.

A second observation is that Yahweh comes in the storm (*se'arah*, see also 40:6). This word has not occurred previously in Job and is found only sixteen times in the Old Testament.[5] It is often used as an instrument in the hand of Yahweh in an expression of his wrath. The storm sets the tone for the nature of the theophanic speeches of Yahweh. Another example of a storm theophany is found in Ezekiel 1:4,[6] but there we see much more detail. Even though the theophany in Ezekiel eventuates in the prophet's commissioning, the storm communicates God's anger at his people and, in Ezekiel 10, his departure from the temple. In Job, Yahweh's first words also suggest anger at Job's arrogance and presumption (supported by 40:1 – 14). The important point is that Yahweh is not simply taking up the role of wisdom instructor; the tone of his words should be understood as a rebuke. The storm does not simply convey his power; it conveys his wrath.

Consequently, as Yahweh characterizes Job, we see a clear distinction from the open admiration expressed in the prologue. There Yahweh described Job as "blameless and upright" (1:1); here he is one who "darkens my counsel" and utters "words without knowledge." The contrast is not contradictory but suggests that although Job's conduct is above reproach, his understanding is flawed. Job's perception of God is the issue that has

---

4. "Yahweh" is used consistently in the prologue (last occurrence in 2:7) and in Yahweh's speeches at the end of the book (38:1; 40:1, 3, 6; 42:1, 7, 9 – 12). Outside these occurrences it is used only once, in 12:9, and there some manuscripts have *'eloah* in its place. See the commentary on that passage for further discussion.

5. Most occurrences are in the prophets and Psalms, with the notable exception of those in 2 Kings 2:1, 11, describing how Elijah was taken.

6. The theophany of Yahweh on Mount Sinai manifests as a storm, but this word is not used there.

been under scrutiny since the opening verses of the book. Job's excessive action on behalf of his children first raised the question of how he viewed God. The Challenger's case focused on whether Job's conduct was properly motivated. Job's speeches demonstrated shortcomings in how he understood God and his operation in the world. Now, as God begins his speech, the negative characterization of Job is intended to indicate unambiguously that Job's assessment of God and his ways is not accurate. Yahweh is about to offer a corrective.

The assertion that Job has "darkened my counsel" uses a causative form of the familiar verb and noun (*ḥšk*) that contrasts with light. The other five occurrences of this causative form predictably refer to bringing night or trouble. The pairing with "counsel" is unique to this passage. Yahweh's use of this word characterizes Job as considering God's plan ("counsel") to be dark — that is, sinister, devious, or even evil. In Job's reiteration of this accusation in 42:3, he substitutes a verb that indicates obscuring or hiding. Job's word choice perhaps avers that though he may have been confused about God's plan, he is unwilling to own that he has portrayed God's plan as sinister. It is no surprise that Job would be confused because he lacked knowledge; what is unacceptable is that he spoke as if he did have knowledge. For this he is reprimanded.

The reprimand takes the form of an examination as Yahweh turns the tables. Instead of Job playing inquisitor, a role he has taken throughout the book, Yahweh will ask the questions. Although the queries that follow are rhetorical, Yahweh states that Job should answer. The answer expected is not a reply to specific questions, but a response to God that will reflect a reassessment of Job's perspective and beliefs.

Macrocosmic Operation (Job 38:4 – 38)

IN THESE VERSES YAHWEH expresses his control, which comprises his power and wisdom. He communicates about macrocosmic operations using the terminology and understanding of the ancient world — Job's world. In this worldview, we find a cosmic geography consistent with what we have seen throughout the book and with the general beliefs of the ancient world:[7]

- The earth has foundations (38:4), footings (38:6), and a cornerstone (38:6).
- The sea has been confined behind doors with bars (38:10).

---

7. For detailed discussion of beliefs about cosmic operations in the ancient world, see W. Horowitz, *Mesopotamian Cosmic Geography* (rev. 2nd ed.; Winona Lake, Ind.: Eisenbrauns, 2011).

- The netherworld has gates (38:17).
- Light and darkness have locations rather than sources (38:19).
- Snow and hail are kept in storehouses (38:22).
- Lightning and east winds are locations (38:24).
- Rain is stored in water jars (38:37).

Because of this passage's poetic nature, we can appreciate these statements as poetic, in contrast to our modern cosmic geography, and thus dispense with questions of scientific accuracy. But in the ancient world, this poetry expressed the reality of common understanding, not just metaphors severed from genuine perception. Furthermore, nothing here suggests that scientific truth is being offered that diverges from how the people of antiquity perceived the world. As is true throughout the Bible, God communicates to his people on the basis of their understanding when it comes to scientific matters. It is primarily in theological matters that he pushes them beyond their cultural understandings.

It should also be noted that this passage is a discussion of Yahweh's work as Creator, yet it deals not with manufacturing matter out of nothing, but with bringing organization and order to the operations of the cosmos. This supports what I have contended elsewhere, that in the ancient world people thought of creation largely in functional rather than material terms.[8]

We should pause for further comment on a few of the details of this section. In 38:7 we encounter one of the few references in the Old Testament to the *bene 'elohim* (lit., "sons of God"; the others are in Gen. 6:2, 4; Job 1:6; 2:1; the similar *bene 'elim* occurs in Pss. 29:1; 89:7). In our brief discussion of the term in Job 1:6 (pp. 63 – 64), the sons of God were seen as members of the divine council. Here we have additional information that presents them as parallel to "the morning stars." This association between the members of the divine council and the stars also occurs in ancient Near Eastern literature,[9] in which the gods are considered celestial bodies, the celestial bodies are considered images of the gods, and the celestial bodies are considered to have a divine nature.[10] In Ugaritic texts, the "sons of El" or "sons of the gods" are parallel to the "assembly of the stars."[11] In this

---

8. See Walton, *Lost World of Genesis One*, or the more technical presentation in Walton, *Genesis 1 as Ancient Cosmology*, 23 – 46.

9. Francesca Rochberg, "'The Stars and Their Likeness': Perspectives on the Relation between Celestial Bodies and Gods in Ancient Mesopotamia," in *What Is a God?* (ed. B. N. Porter; Winona Lake, Ind.: Eisenbrauns, 2009), 41 – 92.

10. Ibid., 46 – 47.

11. CAT 1.10:1:3 – 4, translated in Parker, *Ugaritic Narrative Poetry*, 182.

way, Yahweh's speech reflects common thinking in the ancient world. The difference is that in Israelite theology, the divine council (= sons of God = heavenly host = stars) is not composed of gods with whom Yahweh shares divine authority, though he may at times delegate tasks to them.[12]

A second issue of particular note arises in 38:25–27. Throughout the book, Job's expectations have been premised on the idea that he knows how the world operates. He has assumed the RP and therefore has embraced the belief that the world operates according to justice. These beliefs have been challenged by his experience, which cannot be explained as justice. His quandary, then, is that God, who runs the system, may not be just.

The flaw in this logic is that one cannot move automatically from the justice of God to the necessity of the world's operations being just. Yahweh makes this point in 38:25–27, where he notes that rain falls in places where no one lives. If justice reigned in the cosmos, rain, the provider of blessing and fertility, would target the deserving. By noting that rain falls on uninhabited lands, Yahweh demonstrates to Job that his logic does not account for reality. In effect, Yahweh asserts that justice is not the foundation of the world, nor does the cosmos operate by justice, despite the fact that he rules the cosmos and he is just. We can understand Job's confusion, yet we can also recognize the validity of the point. No one today would argue that gravity was just, for example, or that God makes decisions about when gravity should work and when it should not. Although we affirm God's control of the forces of nature, we don't believe that he micromanages the system with justice in mind for each moment's activity. Thus Job's perception of the cosmos is undermined, and his reliance on the RP crumbles under scrutiny.

A third note concerns the ancient Near Eastern context for the depictions of rain, dew, and ice in reproductive and familial terms in 38:28–30. In Ugaritic texts, "dew" is one of Baal's daughters.[13] Furthermore, some have suggested that rain was sometimes viewed as the semen of the sky god impregnating the earth with fertility.[14] Despite these notions, it is unlikely that Yahweh is refuting pagan fertility ideas; rather, he is addressing Job's misconceptions about philosophical foundations, and Job shows no inclination to believe the standard elements of pagan mythology. We can therefore posit that Yahweh is pointing out Job's lack of knowledge

---

12. For discussion of this distinction, see J. H. Walton, "Interpreting the Bible as an Ancient Near Eastern Document," in *Israel: Ancient Kingdom or Late Invention?* (ed. D. I. Block (Nashville: Broadman & Holman, 2008), 298–327.

13. *COS*, 1.111:398b.

14. Cf. Rochberg, "Stars and Their Likenesses," 78, though the passages she cites do not result in crops growing but in gods being born.

about the *source* of rain, dew, ice, and frost. Yahweh's use of the language of conception to do so demonstrates again that communication is taking place on the level of the popular thinking of the day.

Finally, a word should be said about the constellations. We have already discussed in some measure the constellations in relation to Job 9 (pp. 169 – 70). Mesopotamian cosmology held that the great gods had inscribed the stars and constellations on the underside of the heavenly dome.[15] As throughout this portion of his speech, Yahweh is challenging Job about his understanding of, or ability to perform, the deeds normally associated with deity. As the Babylonian text *Enuma anu Enlil* shows, the constellations and their movements were used as a source of omens and could thereby bring favor or disaster. These verses accordingly ask whether Job is able to bring about justice through the manipulation of constellations that theoretically determine fortunes on earth.

This thought finds its conclusion in 38:33, where Yahweh asks whether Job knows the laws of the heavens and can make decrees concerning the earth and its operation.[16] In the ancient world outside Israel, the divine council was responsible for making the decrees by which the cosmos, society, human lives, countries, and temples functioned. These decrees were made regularly and expressed the gods' control over the cosmos. In Old Testament theology, Yahweh is the one whose decrees determine operation of the cosmos.

In conclusion, this section about macrocosmic operations intends to show that Job is incapable of taking control of the cosmos to bring about justice. He has overestimated his ability to devise a cogent philosophy of the operation of the world and has underestimated the complexity of the system (note the inability to devise such systems in Eccl. 7:25 – 29). Yahweh's questions pertain to time (Where were you when? 38:4), to person (Who? e.g., 38:5, 8, 25, 36), and to place (On what? Where? e.g., 38:6, 19, 24). They include first person comments about what Yahweh has done (e.g., 38:9 – 11) and second person challenges regarding what Job cannot do or has not done. Job has questioned God's design and execution, so in this section God focuses on Job's faulty understanding of design and his inability to execute.[17]

---

15. Horowitz, *Mesopotamian Cosmic Geography*, 146 – 47. For discussion of the major constellations and their names, see U. Koch-Westenholz, *Mesopotamian Astronomy* (Carsten Niebuhr Institute of Near Eastern Studies 19; Copenhagen: Museum Tusculanum Press, Univ. of Copenhagen, 1995), 132 – 33.

16. This understanding deviates from the NIV's "dominion" and is supported in many of the commentaries.

17. Clifford, *Creation Accounts*, 193.

Microcosmic Operations (Job 38:39 – 39:30)

THIS SECTION COMMENTS ON eight animals, all but one of which are from
the wild or even the liminal world (the world that is near the boundaries
of the ordered world).

Verses	Animal	Subject
38:39 – 40	Lion	Providing food
38:41	Raven	Providing food
39:1 – 4	Nubian ibex	Mating and birthing
39:5 – 8	Wild donkey	Free ranging
39:9 – 12	Wild ox (aurochs)	Undomesticable nature
39:13 – 18	Ostrich	Treatment of eggs
39:19 – 25	Horse	Battle readiness
39:26 – 30	Hawk	Hunting prey

In the ancient world, it was a common academic exercise to make lists
of plants, animals, stars, and many other things (professions, words, etc.).
Such lists were a type of wisdom, so it is no surprise to find a list such as
this in a biblical wisdom book. Some of the earliest forms of wisdom literature had a fable aspect founded on the characteristics or behavior of plants
and animals. Hymns to gods likewise focus on the ways that they care for
animals. One section of a hymn to Amun reads as follows:

> Creator of the fodder on which cattle live and the tree of life for
>   people.
> He who creates what the fish in the river live on
> And the birds who populate the sky.
> He who gives breath to the one in the egg
> And sustains the young of the serpents,
> Who creates what gnats live on,
> And worms and fleas as well,
> Who provides for the mice in their holes,
> And sustains the beetles in every piece of wood.[18]

The eight sections in this portion of Job flow on the basis of concept
bridges. Lion and raven are connected by the concept of food; raven and
ibex by their young; ibex and donkey by their free-ranging nature; donkey
and ox by their untamable nature; ox and ostrich by their untrustworthiness;

---

18. Translated in J. Assmann, *The Search for God in Ancient Egypt* (Ithaca, N.Y.: Cornell Univ. Press, 2001), 58.

ostrich and horse by their relative speeds; horse and hawk by their senses from a distance; and, theoretically, hawk back to lion by their predation.

Though each of these animals could be discussed in turn, space demands that we narrow our focus. The most problematic section is the one addressing the ostrich (39:13 – 18). Some have objected that Yahweh's description does not accurately portray ostrich behavior, but it should be noted that the comments in the text deal with perception. Humans might observe the ostrich's behavior and draw conclusions that the bird is negligent of its young or that it treats them harshly — conclusions such as those reflected in this passage.[19] In reality, the ostrich behaves differently from other birds but is quite attentive to its very sturdy eggs.

The problem, then, is in 39:17. Yahweh does not say that the ostrich was given wisdom that humans cannot understand — a different kind of wisdom, as it were — but that he did not endow the ostrich with wisdom at all. In evaluating this verse, it should be noted that Yahweh here oddly speaks of himself in the third person: "God ['*eloah*] did not endow ..." (see also 38:41, though there God is object rather than subject; contrast to the first person in 39:6). The only solution to this conundrum that I see is the conclusion drawn in the section on the macrocosm: that Yahweh is adopting the perspective common to humans at the time rather than making universally verifiable statements about the ontological nature of ostriches.

Job's First Response (Job 40:1 – 14)

IN 40:1 – 2 Yahweh concludes his first discourse by again demanding an answer from Job. As in 38:2, it is clear that Yahweh is taking Job to task for the way that he has responded to his suffering. Three words characterize the criticism: Job is one who "contends" (*ryb*), seeks to "correct" (*ysr*), and "accuses" (*ykḥ*). The first verb is a legal term referring to a court dispute and is used both by Job in his inquiries about why *God* is contending with *him* (e.g., 10:2), and by Elihu describing Job's response to God (33:13). The NIV translates the second verb as if from the verb *ysr*, "to instruct," though this root is never used elsewhere in the Qal form of the verb. Other interpreters, with a slight repointing of the verb, understand it as related to the root *sur*, meaning to turn back, or, specific to this context, to withdraw or rescind a case. This suggestion makes sense in context, as "contend" in the first phrase would be parallel to "accuse" in the second, and "retract, rescind" in the first would be parallel to the expected direction of the "answer" in the second phrase.

---

19. For a thorough discussion of Ostrich habits, see Clines, *Job 38 – 42* (WBC 8A,; Nashville: Nelson, 2011), 89 – 90.

Job's reply (40:4–5) is appropriately one of submission and humility, but he stops short of recanting. He is speechless and has adopted a stance of neutrality: "I will say no more." Job has been cowed and intimidated—an outcome he had anticipated as early as 9:3, and which was not without a level of validity—but he has not yet understood the extent of his folly. Therefore Yahweh launches the second stage of his discourse.

As in 38:3, Yahweh opens in 40:7 by challenging Job to prepare to answer as one who has wisdom (as a *geber*).[20] In this second challenge, however, Job is identified as one who has discredited Yahweh's justice (40:8) in contrast to one who has questioned the wisdom of his design (38:2). Furthermore, Yahweh accuses Job of having defamed Yahweh in order to justify himself. We have noted from the beginning that Job considered his own righteousness the only factor of which he could be certain. Yahweh is taking Job to task for not valuing God's justice more than his own righteousness.

Yahweh offers a challenge: Let Job take up control of the cosmos using the RP that he has adopted and imposed on Yahweh. If Job were "God for a day," could he execute the RP consistently in bringing justice?

Two observations require our attention. (1) It is interesting that in 40:11–13 Yahweh speaks only of Job punishing the wicked with his endowment of power and makes no mention of ensuring that the righteous do not suffer. I suspect that this is because punishing the wicked would be much easier than ensuring that the righteous do not suffer, and the point will be made that Job cannot even do the former, let alone attempt the latter. (2) In 40:14 Yahweh concludes with the statement that if Job successfully meets his challenge, Yahweh will acknowledge that Job's own hand could save him. Why does Yahweh offer that conclusion given the previous verses?

Our interpretation begins with the recognition that 40:8 and 14 function as an inclusio to the section and therefore are parallel to one another. Job's "salvation" in 40:14 equates to a declaration of his righteousness (40:8). Throughout the book, Job's focus has been on his righteousness. He has not been interested in regaining his goods or his status, or in being relieved from his suffering. He wants to be declared righteous and receive acknowledgment that he did nothing to deserve the tragedies that he has experienced. Thus far in the book, he has attempted to establish his righteousness by defaming God's justice—or more precisely, the justice of God's policies for running the world.

---

20. *Geber* is used to designate someone of highest caliber in the contextual category. If the context is military, the *geber* is a warrior; if the context is societal, the *geber* is someone of responsibility in the community. Here in a wisdom context, the *geber* is the scholar par excellence, the respected philosopher.

In God's challenge, if Job could don the mantle of divine power and demonstrate that his concept of just cosmic operation could actually be sustained, his righteousness would be vindicated and he would be "saved." If he can consistently bring judgment on the wicked alone, he will vindicate his name by establishing a cosmic system operating solely on righteousness and justice. He must demonstrate that the system he envisions (and to which he wants God held accountable) can actually work. Only in such a system would suffering be taken as evidence of unrighteousness. Only in such a system would Job need vindication in the shadow of his suffering.

Cosmic Fringe Operations: Yahweh's Second Speech (40:15 – 41:34)

IN THIS SECTION THE discussion is no longer about Job being God for a day or Job's limitations. Instead, the focus moves to how God's system should properly be seen. The discussion shifts from reprimand to instruction, from what Job cannot do to what God has done ("I made," 40:15). In the dialogues, Job wonders why God is treating him like a chaos creature (7:12); in the discourses, Job suggests that God is acting like a chaos creature (ch. 30). Here in God's second set of speeches, Yahweh picks up both of Job's charges and alters Job's fundamental assumption: Chaos creatures are in fact part of God's ordered world.

Most of the ancient world believed that chaos creatures were outside of the established order and often viewed them as a threat to that order. In contrast, the Hebrew Bible consistently expresses God's control of chaos creatures and merges them into the ordered cosmos. For example, they are created (which entails being drawn into the ordered cosmos) in Genesis 1:21, and they are passive rather than threatening in Psalm 104:26.

The passages about Behemoth and Leviathan appropriately follow Yahweh's challenge to Job to bring low all the proud (40:11), for Leviathan is identified as the king over all who are proud (41:34). In the discussion of Leviathan in Job 3, I suggested that he should be labeled an "anti-cosmos creature" rather than a "chaos creature." These creatures exist on the fringes of the ordered world. Although creation entailed bringing order to the cosmos, the cosmos is not a totally ordered system. The fact that there is a garden of Eden, where a high level of order exists, but also space outside the garden, where order has yet to be established, evidences the distinction. Liminal creatures (such as coyote, owl, and ostrich) are near the boundaries of the ordered world. Nonzoological creatures such as Behemoth, Leviathan, Rahab, and Tannin are not viewed as unbridled threats, but neither are they drawn totally into the ordered sphere. Nahash, the serpent of

Genesis 3, is another example of an anti-cosmos creature.[21] Anti-cosmos creatures are creations of God but are the thorns and thistles of the animal world.

Identification. I do not find persuasive the suggestions that Behemoth and Leviathan are either zoological specimens or now-extinct creatures that once roamed the earth. In the former category, while Behemoth's location among the lotus plants in the reeds of the marsh (40:21–24) might bring to mind the mighty hippopotamus, the description of the tail (40:17) makes such identification impossible.[22] Likewise those who suggest some huge now-extinct plant-eating dinosaur would have trouble explaining how he is concealed among the lotus plants. In the same way, although Leviathan may have some characteristics of a Nile crocodile, his fire breathing (41:18–21) and multiple heads (Ps. 74:14) refute that identification.[23] I suspect those in antiquity would have viewed the hippopotamus and crocodile as reminiscent of Behemoth and Leviathan, and perhaps even as their spawn in some sense, but Behemoth and Leviathan are the archetypes and personify abstractions that the hippopotamus and crocodile do to a much lesser degree.

Alternatively, it is not uncommon to see Behemoth and Leviathan identified as throwbacks from ancient mythology. Behemoth would perhaps be represented in figurines and reliefs of a human-headed bison, and Leviathan, also referred to in Ugaritic texts (Litan), would be the seven-headed dragon that appears on seals and engravings in Mesopotamia.

A third direction taken by interpreters posits Behemoth and Leviathan as figures known from West Semitic mythology, primarily available in the Ugaritic texts. Collins associates them with Mot and Yamm,[24] while Day prefers to identify Behemoth with El's calf, Atik (Aršٰ), and Leviathan with the Ugaritic mythological sea dragon, Litan.[25]

It is no surprise that Behemoth and Leviathan evince connections to both the world of nature and the world of myth. These associations make

---

21. See R. Averbeck, "Ancient Near Eastern Mythography as It Relates to Historiography in the Hebrew Bible: Genesis 3 and the Cosmic Battle," in *The Future of Biblical Archaeology: Reassessing Methods and Assumptions* (ed. J. K. Hoffmeier and A. Millard; Grand Rapids: Eerdmans, 2004), 328–57.

22. Some have argued that the Hebrew word here does not refer to the tail but to the male member; see discussion in M. Pope, *Job*, 323–24.

23. Day, *God's Conflict with the Dragon*, 65–66, gives an extensive list of other differences between crocodiles and Leviathan and differences between hippopotami and Behemoth, 76–77.

24. Clifford, *Creation Accounts*, 194–95. See Wakeman, *God's Battle with the Monster*. Fyall, *Now My Eyes Have Seen You*, 126–37, accepts the connection of Behemoth with Mot, but considers Leviathan to be best identified with Satan.

25. Day, *God's Conflict with the Dragon*, 72–81.

them recognizable to the audience and inform their use. In the end, how-ever, it is not the roots of the ideas or the associations they may evoke that are most important; it is their literary use in Job.

Job is compared to Behemoth (40:15).[26] Job, like Behemoth, is the first of God's works (cf. 15:7) and withstands all turbulence. God brings his sword against Job (40:19) and by a snare he penetrates Job's anger (40:24). Yahweh does not speak of Job doing anything *to* Behemoth, but when the discussion switches to Leviathan, the first eight verses use the second per-son. I therefore suggest that Leviathan is to be compared to Yahweh (41:3, 10−11, 34)[27]—he won't beg you for mercy and won't speak with gentle words; you can't put him on a leash, subdue him, or rouse him. These all discuss what *Job* can't do to Leviathan, and they are also things that Job must learn he cannot do to Yahweh. The following summary identifies how Yahweh presents Behemoth as an illustration for Job to emulate and Leviathan as an illustration of how Job should think about Yahweh.

Behemoth.

40:15 Starts with a comparison—"along with you"[28]
40:15 Content and well-fed (as you have been)
40:16−18 Made strong (as I made you)
40:19 Ranks first among its kind (as you do)
40:20 Cared for (as you were)
40:21−22 Sheltered (as you were)
40:23 Not alarmed by raging river (as you should not be)

---

26. S. Balentine, "'What Are Human Beings, That You Make So Much of Them?' Divine Disclosure from the Whirlwind: 'Look at Behemoth,'" in *God in the Fray* (ed. Tod Linafelt and T. K. Beal; Minneapolis: Augsburg Fortress, 1998), 259−78, esp. 270−71; J. Gam-mie, "Behemoth and Leviathan: On the Didactic and Theological Significance of Job 40:15−41:26," in *Israelite Wisdom* (ed. J. G. Gammie et al.; New York: Union Theological Seminary, 1978), 217−31, esp. 221−22.

27. Habel, *Job*, 570−71, picks up a piece of this in his comment "Now Yahweh chal-lenges Job to consider how he could possibly take his stand before God's 'face' if he cannot survive a confrontation with Leviathan." But he does not follow that observation to the conclusions reached here. Likewise C. Newsom, *The Book of Job* (Oxford: Oxford Univ. Press, 2003), 252, also perceives it as she speaks of a "curious level of identification between God and Leviathan" but fails to follow this thought to its logical conclusion.

28. This is a unique collocation. Usually when the verb *'asa(h)* is used with the preposi-tion *'im* there is also an adjective (X) or longer descriptions of behavior, and the meaning is, e.g., "I have acted in X way toward you" (see other uses in Job 10:12; 13:20). Here there is no adjective, but the way God has acted toward Job could feasibly, though elliptically, be picked up in the opening reference to Behemoth: "Behold Behemoth, I have acted toward you [as if you were him]." Admittedly there are clearer ways that this could be said, but that would be true no matter how one interprets the verse.

40:23 Trusts and is secure (as you should be)

40:24 Cannot be captured or trapped (to which you should also be invulnerable)

40:24 Nose (= anger) cannot be "pierced" (difficult word — sometimes means named, designated, or penetrated) (to which you should also be invulnerable)

Note that the text does not say what Job can or cannot do with regard to Behemoth, or what God does with Behemoth.

Leviathan. The text switches immediately to "you," focusing on what Job cannot do to Leviathan (i.e., if you can't do this to Leviathan, why do you expect to do it to me?). Likewise this passage never talks about what God does to Leviathan (e.g., his control of him or defeat of him).[29]

41:1 – 2 Cannot be controlled (neither can Yahweh)

41:3 – 6 Will not submit or beg for mercy (neither will Yahweh)

41:7 – 9 Cannot be wounded or subdued; hopeless to struggle against him (same is true of Yahweh)

41:10 Outright comparison: can't rouse him, so who can stand against me?

41:11 No one (including you, Job) has a claim against *me*

41:12 – 18 Cannot force his mouth open to receive bridle (so Yahweh cannot be controlled or domesticated)

41:19 – 25 Dangerous when riled (as is Yahweh)

41:26 – 32 Invulnerable (as is Yahweh)

41:33 No creature is his equal (nor is Job Leviathan's equal, let alone Yahweh's equal)

41:34 Dominates all who are proud (cf. 40:11 – 14, where the section was introduced). Job cannot humble the proud (40:11 – 12), nor can he subdue the king over the proud (41:34); God is also king of the proud in the sense that he rules over them.

If this is what the text is doing, it does not matter what relationship these creatures have to zoology or mythology; rather, the point of the text lies elsewhere. Yahweh's message would be clear: "Job, be strong and content like Behemoth, and don't think that you can domesticate or subdue

---

29. Day, *God's Conflict with the Dragon*, 69, says: "One may therefore reasonably conclude that the list of things connected with the subduing of Leviathan ... which are impossible for Job, represents what God has actually done. The message therefore presupposes a battle in which God defeated Leviathan." One can see that Day imposes all of this on the text, which says nothing about God battling Leviathan or defeating him.

me any more than you can Leviathan." Job needs to have more respect for Yahweh. Yahweh now *is* addressing Job as if he (Job) were a chaos creature (cf. 7:12), and he *is* likening himself to a chaos creature (cf. ch. 30)—but all within the confines of his ordered world.

Obviously this interpretation is diametrically opposed to one like Fyall's, who views Behemoth and Leviathan as the "embodiment of cosmic evil."[30] One looks in vain to find any characterization of evil in either creature. Yet Fyall hits the mark when he comments, "Now he [Yahweh] is showing Job that it is unthinkable that he could confront Leviathan much less God."[31] The point is not that God can subdue Leviathan and therefore he can subdue Job—that was never in question. Rather, the passage indicates that since Job cannot bring Leviathan to heel, he cannot expect to domesticate Yahweh.

Rhetorical Strategy

IN THIS SECTION OF Job, we are finally offered the perspectives that the author wishes us as readers to adopt regarding our understanding of how God works in the world. By demonstrating to Job that there are many phenomena in nature that humans do not understand, God shows the folly of devising a simplistic system such as the RP, which is supposed to give consistent account of the way the natural world operates under God's sovereign control.

As noted in the introductory chapter (using the triangle illustration, pp. 42–44), God rejects the idea that the RP can provide a foundation for understanding how he works in the world, because it is an inadequate description of his policies. The RP is founded on principles of justice, but God urges a perspective founded on principles of wisdom. Instead of addressing his justice and attempting to give account of it, Yahweh's first speech addresses wisdom by drawing Job's attention to the macrocosm and microcosm so that Job can realize his inadequacy to formulate a theory encompassing everything (note Eccl. 8:17).

A view that attributes to God the things for which we have no explanation sometimes is called "God of the gaps." Many consider it a flawed way of thinking because it results in God growing smaller as more understanding is gained through science. We should note, however, that the modern

---

30. Fyall, *Now My Eyes Have Seen You*, 157.
31. Ibid., 160.

undertaking of classifying what can be explained without recourse to God is part of the logic used to try to demonstrate that there is a God, and that humans and their scientific endeavors cannot explain everything.

In this section of Job, Yahweh is not seeking to prove his existence. He is making the point that it is foolhardy to call him to task for his putative failure to conform to a system of human devising that has access to so little data. The issue at stake in the Old Testament is not whether God exists and what role he might have in the cosmos. Everyone believed there were gods and that they were thoroughly engaged in the operation and control of the cosmos. Consequently, there is no Old Testament comparison to today's "God of the gaps" discussions. Job is confronted with his inability to formulate an understanding of how the world works. If he cannot construct such a theory, he cannot presume to hold God accountable to work in certain ways.

As an aside, it is also important to note that several of the passage's examples show God's provision for predators. For many people today, predation constitutes an inexplicable aspect of creation that is commonly associated with the fall. One of the arguments against evolution or an old earth is that such views entail predation before the fall, a situation that some find irreconcilable with the nature of God or the statement in Genesis 1 that "it was good." In contrast to this argument, Yahweh's speech shows that he provides for predators just as he does for everyone else, so such provision is not contrary to his character. With regard to Genesis 1, as I have suggested elsewhere, the term "good" should be understood relative to proper functioning rather than to a standard of moral perfection.[32]

The first speech is intended to demonstrate Yahweh's knowledge and control of the macrocosm and the microcosm. Job, like us, has little understanding or power, but Yahweh's knowledge and power are unlimited. God has ordered the cosmos by his wisdom; justice is one of his attributes, but the cosmos does not mirror his attributes. Wisdom is at the heart of order.

Job's response to this first speech is silence (40:2–5) in acknowledgment that he is unworthy to devise a scheme for how the world works. He thereby acknowledges his lack of wisdom. But it is not enough for Yahweh to extract from Job this admission of inadequacy. A mere concession of Yahweh's divinity and Job's humanity ("You are God; I am not") is insufficient. Job, like us, needs direction in order to adopt a more proactive attitude. This is the focus of Yahweh's second speech.

As suggested in Original Meaning, I believe that Behemoth and Leviathan are offered as illustrations of how to think about God's policies, God's

---

32. Walton, *Lost World of Genesis One*, 149–51.

role, and our posture. Answers to questions regarding suffering and justice do not lie in our ability to devise a system in which the operations of the cosmos all fit a neat scheme. Instead we should acknowledge God's wisdom and realize that he controls the cosmos in accordance with that wisdom. Such a perspective goes beyond a simple assertion that we are not God—it warns us not to reduce God to less than he is.

In the movie *Patch Adams*, Robin Williams plays an idealistic medical student who wants to revolutionize the medical profession to focus on compassion more than profits. He starts a free clinic that predictably attracts some who not only are at risk themselves but endanger others. Patch's girlfriend works alongside him at the clinic and is tragically murdered by one of the unstable patients. This experience throws Patch into a crisis of philosophical and theological confusion. At one point in the movie, he finds himself looking down from a cliff and considering suicide. His poignant soliloquy addressed to God is illustrative of the experience of many who suffer:

> So answer me please—tell me what you're doing ... You create man; man suffers enormous amounts of pain; man dies. Maybe you should have had just a few more brainstorming sessions prior to creation. You rested on the seventh day—maybe you should have spent that day on compassion.

After this serious indictment against God, Patch looks down again as he considers throwing himself off, then turns his eyes back to heaven with his conclusion: "You know what? You're not worth it." And he walks away.

In this response, Patch reflects a conclusion common to those who suffer and those who are horrified by the needs of the world. They cannot reconcile a just and good God with a world gone awry. The book of Job encourages us to avoid the easy reductionism that makes God accountable to how we think the world ought to operate. His wisdom extends far beyond our shortsightedness; there is always more afoot than we can imagine. Our ideas of how things ought to work will always be naive and simplistic. God asks that we trust him.

The reader will recall that in the book of Job, accusations are made against God's policies from two directions: from the Challenger, who contends that it is bad policy for righteous people to prosper because that will subvert their motivations for righteousness, and from Job, who contends that it is bad policy for righteous people to suffer because that is inconsistent with God's just character. The Challenger's contention has been answered by the fact that Job maintained his integrity even when he was not prospering (see discussion in Job 27, p. 265).

But answering Job's contention is more difficult, and that has been the focus of the second part of the book. If the RP (the basis for Job's understanding of God's policies) were allowed to stand as the foundation for how God's policies work, God would lose the case. If God used the RP to give Job an explanation of his suffering, he would lose the case. No hint of the RP enters Yahweh's speeches except where he casts doubt on it indirectly in 38:25−27.

God's answer to Job's contention is not to explain when or why righteous people suffer. The cosmos is not designed to protect righteous people from suffering. Suffering is inevitable in a world where order has not been finally and fully established. A complete state of order cannot exist in a world where sin (one manifestation of disorder) is present at any level. Like Job, we may think that it is bad policy for righteous people to suffer, but we would, I suggest, be equally dissatisfied with the alternatives. The divine policy that we need to understand is not how God's justice is reflected in the operations of the cosmos, but that he has brought sufficient order into the cosmos for it to be functional for our existence as his creatures, and at the same time has allowed sufficient disorder to accommodate the continued existence of sinful humanity—one of the forms that disorder takes.

Job questioned God's design, and God responded that Job had insufficient knowledge of God's design to do so. Job questioned God's justice, and God responded that Job ought to be content and trusting, and that he should not be so bold as to think that God can be domesticated to conform to Job's feeble perceptions of how the cosmos should run. God asks for trust, not understanding, and the cosmos is founded on his wisdom, not his justice.

Notice that the comparisons to Behemoth and Leviathan do not comment on righteousness or justice. Job's speeches have been replete with claims about his own righteousness and claims against God's justice. Behemoth is not an example of righteousness, but an example of stability and trust. Leviathan is not an example of justice, but a picture of one who cannot be challenged. If Job is to understand the world, he must recognize these respective roles. Humans should respond to raging rivers (i.e., the crises of life, the metaphor drawn from 40:23) with security and trust, and they should not think that they can domesticate or challenge God.

In short, God offers information on three topics: Speech one, how we should think about the world; speech 2a (Behemoth), how we should think about ourselves; and speech 2b (Leviathan), how we should think about God.

We can contrast some of the answers offered throughout the book as follows:

RP (Job and his friends): Wickedness is God's reason for sending suffering.

Elihu: God's reasons for sending suffering may be more complex than the RP recognizes. Suffering has its cause either in wicked behavior or in an attempt to address potentially wicked behavior or attitudes. Elihu still sees suffering as having a cause rooted in wickedness.

God: Humans cannot assume that all suffering is caused by God with "reasons" in mind, though this in no way compromises his sovereignty. The RP, in its restrictive identifications of cause and its simplistic focus on justice as discernible by human observers, puts limitations on God's sovereignty by not giving enough room for his wisdom. Providence does not insist that God endowed nature with his attributes.

God's wisdom and justice cannot be comprehended in full by human beings, but at the same time, God cannot be considered inscrutable (i.e., illogical, inconsistent, arbitrary, or as having alternate criteria for justice). Rather, human inability to discern justice ought to be explained by our limitations in wisdom. The fact that we cannot discern the logic does not mean that there is no logic or that the logic is different from that under which we operate. The fact that Job does not understand the ordering of the cosmos is no proof that such ordering does not exist. The fact that Job does not understand the reasons for events in the natural world does not mean that there are none, though the existence of reasons cannot be assumed. Things that appear random or uncontrolled are not, but neither is everything explicable in terms of justice.

We must recall that it is not Job who is on trial, but God's policies. The book never intended to provide an explanation for human suffering. Rather, it offers a defense of God's policies, rejecting a wooden application of the RP in the process. This approach is not "inscrutability," which in the ancient Near East was the conclusion that God cannot be known. The only inscrutability here concerns "reasons," which cannot be known and cannot be inferred from the RP. It is important that Job is never told "why" he suffered (and the prologue does not tell *us* why he suffered either — the narrative scenario is not a reason). Assessment of justice requires all the facts. Since all the facts cannot be given or comprehended, we must depend on the wisdom of the judge. If Job were told *why*, his situation would cease to be realistic because no one receives answers, and the answer Job would receive would be an explanation of the scene in heaven, which would apply to no one else. Furthermore, offering an explanation would return the focus to the question of justice and would thus displace the focus on wisdom.

So, at long last, what answers does the book provide as it seeks to guide our understanding of God's policies in a world where suffering and evil may plague the righteous as well as the wicked? Yahweh does not defend his justice; he does not explain Job's suffering; and he does not enter the courtroom into which Job has summoned him. We should not expect him to perform any of these actions in our personal circumstances either, even though these often represent our deepest longings. He directs our thinking in an entirely different direction. If there is any part of Job's speeches that Yahweh addresses directly, it is Job's lament over the day of his birth, since Yahweh picks up many of the same terms and concepts that Job used.[33] This interconnection gives some indication of where God is trying to meet Job.

The message of Job is that we must trust God's wisdom when we encounter suffering or crises, rather than attempting to figure out answers to the "why" questions. We should not think that the cosmos itself reflects God's attribute of justice or that we can hold God accountable to running the cosmos according to justice moment by moment. If he were to do so, none of us would survive, for we all embody injustice at some level in our sinful condition. So justice would involve punishing us.

Trusting God's wisdom does not mean adopting a belief that everything that happens to us ultimately represents justice even though we cannot see why that is so. Trust is not the conviction that there is a good reason (= explanation that justifies the suffering) even when we cannot fathom it. In other words, the book does not suggest a hidden, deeper justice behind what we perceive as injustice. If we were to think in those terms, we would still be clinging to justice as the foundation of the system and simply theorizing alternative ways that it could function, as Elihu did.

Instead, the book posits that God, in his wisdom, is willing to allow injustice in this world—perhaps sometimes as a means to a greater end, but even that does not offer an explanation that justifies the suffering. We can assume that it grieves his heart, for he is just. In his wisdom, he elevates *purposes* above *reasons*, a concept that was elaborated briefly in the Introduction (pp. 47–48). Even here, however, we must tread carefully. We cannot *know* reasons, and we cannot assume that there *are* reasons. We should assume that there *are* purposes, but that does not mean that we can or will ever *know* those purposes. The injustice, suffering, trials, and crises that we experience shape us into the people we are and the people God desires us to be. This truth is not intended to bring comfort to those suffering, nor does it do so. It is meant to bring understanding that might prevent us from committing Job's error, which is the easy solution of blaming God. The alternative is to trust God.

---

33. Ticciati, *Job and the Disruption of Identity*, 102–9.

Theological Issues

MANY DEEPLY SIGNIFICANT THEOLOGICAL issues present themselves in the book of Job. These issues are not merely esoteric; they pertain to our deepest feelings and questions. We can only address a few of them briefly here, but the comments that follow provide some direction for further meditation and discussion.

God does not endow nature with his attributes. We affirm an important distinction between God's ability to use any aspect of the cosmos to effect his will and the idea that all of the cosmos reflects and operates by the character of God. In the ancient world, this distinction was not maintained. The polytheism and low view of deity that pervaded the ancient world could be thought of as resulting directly from the belief that all earthly events were a reflection of some divine will or attribute. Consequently, ancient people could not view the gods as intrinsically just (even though the gods were interested in justice). The world was not just, and therefore the gods were not just. This link between deity and cosmic operations lies at the very root of pagan thinking, and thus when we fail to clearly distinguish these two elements, we risk being drawn into thinking that is essentially pagan and degrading to the God of the Bible.

Pantheism sees the divine in everything and considers everything (rocks, trees, insects, etc.) to be in some way part of the divine. Animism moves a further step by divinizing everything. The polytheism of the ancient world is one step removed from animism in the linkage it assumes between the god and the actors in the cosmos (sun, moon, storm, etc.) The resulting homological relationship consists of inseparably linked pairs (e.g., sun and sun god).

The theology presented in the biblical text is the next step removed. God is now outside the cosmos, yet still controls it moment by moment. He is not a sun god or storm god, though he controls both sun and storm. The cosmos does not share or reflect his attributes, yet he governs the operations of the cosmos.[34] This view is one step (or perhaps several steps) short of deism, which removes God not only from linked identification, but also from cosmic operations. In deism, God is not only outside worldly operations (i.e., noncontingent), he is disengaged.

In the biblical view, God's attributes are not present in the rain (Job 38:25−27; cf. Matt. 5:45), nor in the storms, hurricanes, tsunamis, earthquakes, tornadoes, droughts, famines, plagues, and epidemics, nor in any of those phenomena that actively or passively bring trouble to our world, including mutation at the cellular level. That is not to suggest that these

---

34. For more information about this contrast, see my discussion in the chapter on the gods in *Ancient Near Eastern Thought and the Old Testament*, 87−112, esp. 97−99.

elements are impervious to God's control. They do not exist independently of him, but they cannot be viewed consistently as operating by his remote control. God can use such things to bring judgment, but not every occurrence of them can be considered an act of judgment. Just as people do not always reflect the attributes of God but operate according to their own nature and can be used by God in complex and subtle ways to accomplish his plan, so the elements of the cosmos are subject to his bidding.

The result of this conclusion is that we cannot evaluate God's nature based on events in the cosmos or in our experience. Here we must note how limited a statement Paul actually makes in Romans 1:20. He specifies that what has been evident in the created world is God's "power" (*dynamis*) and "divine nature" (*theiotes*). His point is that the cosmos offers sufficient evidence of a great God. It can be discerned that the Creator *has* a divine nature, but creation does not offer definition of the divine attributes. Paul stops short of suggesting that all of God's attributes can be deduced from the cosmos or that a full revelation of the nature of deity is available therein. Such beliefs constituted the most central misunderstandings of the polytheistic systems of the ancient and classical world, and Paul does not embrace them.

How *should* one reconcile the justice of God with a cosmos that, although under his control, is not just? Job found it easy to expect that if God is just and he rules the world, then the world ought to be just. This conclusion is logical enough, but we are well aware, and Job was no less so, that justice cannot be attributed to what we call the "natural" world. How then is it under the control of a just God?

We do not have to be persuaded that the cosmos we experience is not just. We affirm that God can at any time use earthquakes, rainfall, floods, or temperature to effect his will and to carry out justice. Yet even in that affirmation we must confess that we have no access to a prophetic voice to lead us to understand precisely when and how he is doing that. We cannot discern that any particular tsunami or epidemic is a judgment from God, or that those spared from such calamities are under his protection. But we are left with the question of how a just God can tolerate the operation of a cosmos that does not bend to his nature and will at all moments.

I believe that the answer is "grace." A cosmos totally conformed to his justice would have no room for sinners, even those whose sins stood forgiven. It is his mercy that stays his hand of justice. God is not incapable of imposing justice on humanity and the cosmos he created, but his love constrains him from doing so.[35] In his wisdom he acts in justice or mercy.

---

35. I would insist, however, that this factor still does not offer a reason or an explanation that justifies suffering.

He does not have to think deeply about which to apply at any given time or in any given situation. God does not have quandaries. He not only possesses the attributes that define him, he executes them in perfect harmony.

Some conclude as they look at the suffering around them or in their own lives that there must be a better way. How can a loving and merciful God not intervene to alleviate the horrors that people experience with such regularity? Again, these questions echo the flawed thinking of both Job and Patch Adams—the presumptuous belief that we could do a better job than God. We cannot afford to underestimate God or to overestimate our own abilities. In the film *Bruce Almighty* the character played by Jim Carrey was guilty of doing both. He thought it would be fun and easy to be God. He found that it was neither. Job learned that same lesson, and we need to assimilate it as well. God does not wield this message as intimidation ("I am God, you are not"), but as realism. We find it too easy to look at only one part of the problem, so our solutions can only be naive.

Is the cosmos fully ordered?[36] The essence of the idea of creation in the ancient world is that God brought order to the cosmos in his creative acts. In fact, the Greek word *kosmos*, from which we derive our English word, has the concept of order inherent within it. Order is imposed on the material of the cosmos as well as on the functions of the cosmos. In the ancient world, people were more interested in and focused on function, whereas we in the modern world are often more interested in and focused on the material cosmos when we talk about creation.[37]

Nevertheless, order has been imposed neither fully nor equally on the cosmos. As mentioned in passing in Original Meaning, this diverse state is evident in Genesis in the description of the garden of Eden, in the creation of the chaos creatures, and in the incorporation of darkness and the Sea. God's presence was located in the center of sacred space in the middle of the garden. The garden functioned much like the antechamber of the temple adjacent to the Holy of Holies. In the concept of sacred space represented in temples in the Bible and the ancient world, there were concentric circles of graduated holiness. In Israel, after the Holy of Holies and the antechamber, the next gradation of holiness was the courtyard surrounding the altar. Outside the temple courts, "the camp" had a lower level of sacredness, and "outside the camp" even lower. Those who did not meet the holiness or cleanliness requirements for the camp were sent outside the camp.

---

36. For discussion, see Fretheim, *Creation Untamed*, 9–17, 83.

37. See discussion of the significance of this for reading creation narratives in Walton, *Lost World of Genesis One*.

The area outside the camp was still ordered space, but beyond it was the liminal region of unordered space—the sea and the desert. In the ancient world these were sometimes described as "nonexistent," because existence was defined as having been brought into the ordered sphere.[38] Like the gradations of sacredness within and surrounding the temple, the order inside the garden of Eden can be contrasted to a lesser degree of order outside the garden. Thus Adam and Eve had the task of expanding the ordered cosmos (since they were to be fruitful and multiply, they would eventually need more ordered space),[39] and when they sinned they were driven from the ordered space to the area outside the garden, where things were much more difficult, for order was less evident.

That Adam and Eve failed in their commission to preserve the order of sacred space can be inferred from the presence of the serpent, a chaos creature, in the garden. This again demonstrates that disorder continued to exist in the partially ordered cosmos. The world was a work in progress that God expected humans, as his image, to help establish more fully.[40] Disorder had not been eliminated entirely by the imposition of order, but, as many biblical texts attest, especially in Psalms and Job, it had been pushed to the margins and contained, as Levenson contends:

> The confinement of chaos rather than its elimination is the essence of creation, and the survival of ordered reality hangs only upon God's vigilance in ensuring that those cosmic dikes do not fail, that the bars and doors of the Sea's jail cell do not give way, that the great fish does not slip his hook.[41]

Biblical theology substantiates in both Testaments the continued existence of disorder—both that which remained after creation and that brought about by sin—and amplifies the effects of disorder on the human world. Scripture occasionally refers to the impact of the fall rippling across the "natural" world (e.g., Rom. 8:18–25) and to the world's restoration (e.g., Hos. 2:18), but it offers little explanation of precisely what constitutes that fallen nature. Disorder, however, is not just the result of the fall, but the evidence of a creation in progress. Some believe that at the conclusion of history we will return to the prefall state. I think it more accurate to say that some of what we experience in eternity may represent a return to what was before the fall, but that there will be much more to the

---

38. Walton, *Ancient Near Eastern Thought*, 179–84.

39. See evidences offered in Walton, *Genesis*, 166–74, 180–87.

40. Not to be confused with process theology, in which God continues to develop.

41. J. Levenson, *Creation and the Persistence of Evil* (Princeton, N.J.: Princeton Univ. Press, 1988), 17.

experience. In eternity all will be brought into order (though Gehenna will continue to be a pocket of disorder), a situation that was not present in the prefall condition.

What does a biblical theology of suffering look like?[42] Randy Becton identifies five basic ways that people explain suffering:[43]

1. Suffering is divine punishment.
2. Suffering is a divine test or trial of faith.
3. Suffering is part of the gift of human freedom.
4. Suffering is part of the nature and function of the physical world.
5. Suffering is creation in process.

These are not mutually exclusive positions, and I will address them in the following series of propositions.

Suffering is one of the contingencies of creation in process. God created people with a nervous system. The pain we experience warns us of harm or potential harm. People who lose the use of their nervous system find themselves in dire jeopardy. God also created us with emotions, which make us subject to being hurt by others. If we love, we are subject to suffering. Physical and emotional suffering are not avoidable in the current state of creation because they are part of the ordered cosmos. The remainder of disorder in the cosmos also is at least partially responsible for the experience of suffering. Scripture does not suggest that we should expect to be free of these contingencies until the new heavens and new earth.

Suffering is not intrinsically connected to sin. The RP has been rejected as offering a theodicy. As suggested in the Introduction (p. 45), it is retained as sound theology (i.e., it accurately describes the nature of God as one who delights to extend his favor to his faithful people and who judges sin), but we dare not conclude that all suffering is a consequence of the sufferer's sin. We may "reap what we sow" (Gal. 6:7), but not everything a person "reaps" is something that they have "sown." It has never been appropriate for us to assume that if someone is suffering, they must have done something to deserve it.

Suffering is the lot of all humanity. Though some experience suffering more than others, no one should think oneself immune. No logic explains

---

42. I am using "suffering" in this section as a reference to the ordeals of emotional or physical distress we personally suffer, as well as the suffering that comes through the situations of those who are near and dear to us. I would likewise not rule out the suffering that we observe from afar that may baffle us.

43. R. Becton, *Does God Care When We Suffer and Will He Do Anything About It?* (Grand Rapids: Baker, 1988), 33–34, with fuller discussion on 43–53.

why some seem particularly prone or vulnerable to suffering. Some might take solace in the comfort of a suffering-free life, but that should only drive them to experience more the suffering of others and to prepare for the day when trouble will be their lot as well. This is not fatalism; it is realism and good theology insofar as it coincides with the larger composite picture offered throughout Scripture.

Suffering should be faced with trust in God's wisdom. This is difficult to achieve, particularly when certain cases of suffering make so little sense to us. Nevertheless, it is the only counsel Scripture offers. Trusting God's wisdom does not mean that we try to explore the question of "Why did God do this?" or "Why did God not prevent that?" We should not assume that God initiated the course of action resulting in a particular case of suffering, or even that he "signed off" on it (we often use terms such as "allowed" or "permitted").[44] These responses reflect an overly simplistic view.

We have no language to express the nature of God's involvement. He is neither disengaged from a world run amok, nor is he micromanaging a disastrous sequence of events. In his wisdom God created this world this way, not another way, and he therefore has chosen to operate in this kind of world.[45] Accepting this tension is integral to the kind of trust that God calls us to exercise. On this topic J. Polkinghorne suggests that terminology like "allow" should not be used in a way that suggests blame: "The suffering and evil of the world are not due to weakness, oversight, or callousness on God's part, but, rather, they are the inescapable cost of a creation allowed to be other than God."[46]

Suffering should be viewed as an opportunity to deepen our faith and spiritual maturity as we look forward to understand God's purposes, rather than backward in an attempt to discern reasons. Suffering shapes us — of this there is no doubt. What varies is whether it breaks us. Sometimes there is no visible silver lining, no redeeming value in sight. Sometimes those who endure difficulty feel that nothing is left but an empty shell. Some people never recover physically, emotionally, or spiritually. It is not guaranteed that we will emerge on the other side of pain strengthened by the experience. It would be naive to suggest that suffering universally results in growth. S. Cairns suggests a more nuanced perspective as he elaborates on Simone Weil's observation that "affliction compels us to recognize as real what we do not think possible." He observes:

---

44. Fretheim, *Creation Untamed*, 109.

45. P. Yancey, *Disappointment with God* (Grand Rapids: Zondervan, 1988), 63 – 64; Boyd, *Is God to Blame?* 112.

46. J. Polkinghorne, *Quarks, Chaos and Christianity: Questions to Science and Religion* (New York: Crossroad, 1994), 47.

The occasions of our suffering are capable of revealing what our habitual illusions often obscure, keeping us from knowing. Our afflictions drag us — more or less kicking — into a fresh and vivid awareness that we are not in control of our circumstances, that we are not quite whole, that our days are salted with affliction.[47]

I dare to suggest, however, that when we undergo trials, the biblical way to pray is for strength to carry on and acquit ourselves well. We should seek to honor God when life is at its lowest. We should strive to trust him even when hope is gone.

This is illustrated in the story Philip Yancey tells of a young woman dying a painful death from cystic fibrosis. She felt encouraged by William Barclay's statement that "endurance is not just the ability to bear a hard thing, but to turn it into glory."[48] In the case he recounts, as with many others, there was no opportunity for the young woman's afflictions to make her faith stronger and to bring greater maturity. Death was howling at the door. She was joined in her suffering by friends and family. For some their own faith was undoubtedly bolstered by the courageous faith of this woman dying in pain; others, just as assuredly, had their faith shaken. None, however, would miss the evidence of the frail world in which we live.

Suffering for the gospel gives us the opportunity to participate in Christ's sufferings. In one sense this may be the opportunity no one ever asks for, yet the testimony of the New Testament is clear on this point, from Jesus (Matt. 5:10 – 12; Luke 14:26), to Paul (Rom. 5:3; Phil. 3:10; Col. 1:24), to Peter (1 Pet. 2:19 – 25; 3:8 – 4:19), to the author of Hebrews (Heb. 11:32 – 40). We should count it all joy when we are called upon to suffer for Christ. This idea is counterintuitive to our natural thought and is the polar opposite of the RP. Under the RP, suffering is considered the judgment of God for evil. The New Testament turns suffering into a joyful means of being "in Christ." But this cannot be used to refurbish the RP — being in Christ gives us a response to suffering, not the reason for it.

We should further note that when God, in his wisdom decided to use a long process to bring order to the cosmos and to humanity and thereby chose to have a world with continuing disorder and resultant suffering, he also chose the world in which Jesus would have to suffer and die. His wisdom might seem foolishness to some (1 Cor. 1:18 – 21), but it includes suffering in a disordered world moving toward order.

---

47. S. Cairns, *The End of Suffering: Finding Purpose in Pain* (Brewster, Mass.: Paraclete, 2009), 7. Weil's quotation is taken from *Gravity and Grace* (London: Routledge, 2002), 73.
48. W. Barclasy quoted in Yancey, *Disappointment with God*, 172 – 75.

WE BEGAN THIS CHAPTER with a brief allusion to *Waiting for Godot*. In that work Godot never arrived, but in the book of Job, God did. Godot has been interpreted as a thinly disguised trope for God (among many other things). The play is an exercise in the absurd, and "nothing" is a key theme. Everywhere they look, the characters find "nothing"—a commentary on life in general and on the search for God in particular. Both main characters confess they know little to nothing about Godot, but they expect to recognize him when they see him. The play is punctuated by a false Godot (Pozzo, in several guises) and by a messenger who assures the waiting pair that Godot will indeed arrive shortly. In the messenger's second appearance, we are told that Godot does nothing and perhaps wears a long white beard.

If the play is viewed in relation to the book of Job, Pozzo could represent several different perspectives on God. He is not the Godot the characters are waiting for, but he is mistaken for him. In his first appearance, he keeps his slave on a leash, as God might be thought to treat humankind. In this guise, Pozzo is all talk and eats grandly, but has little to share with the two who are waiting and hungry. In his second appearance, he is blind and led by his slave—a picture reminiscent of a blind god created by humankind and totally at their disposal. Commentators have noticed that Pozzo's slave, Lucky, is consistently the one in charge. He is the one who thinks, and he meets the needs of Pozzo. This image is reminiscent of what we have called the Great Symbiosis in the ancient Near East.[49] Lucky dances and thinks on Pozzo's command, and that is how some would consider humanity's relationship to God, as puppets on a string. Like Lucky, we are on a long rope, totally controlled, but actually in charge in subtle ways.

I am not suggesting that Samuel Beckett meant to present these ideas in his play, only that when we read Job and *Godot* together, we may observe ways in which they align. The book of Job wants to correct the misconceptions about God to which we are so prone. God is not the do-nothing with the white beard who beats his servants; he is not the conceited Pozzo, incapable of thinking for himself, with humanity (whom he needs) dancing at the end of a leash; he is not the blind Pozzo totally controlled by his

---

49. Interestingly enough, Beckett himself is reported to have identified the meaning of the play as "symbiosis." Interview with Peter Woodthrope, 18 February 1994, quoted in J. Knowlson, *Damned to Fame: The Life of Samuel Beckett* (London: Bloomsbury, 1996), 371–72.

slave; and he is not the unknown, ever-awaited character who is forever offstage and disappointing in his absence.

We easily caricature God and construct our worldview around our misconceptions, as do the characters in both *Godot* and Job. Godot never arrives, and therefore no correctives are ever offered for the characters' perspectives. How is it different when Yahweh actually does arrive? How should Yahweh's speeches affect our misguided perspectives?

How Should We Think about God?

IN BRIDGING CONTEXTS I suggested that the book of Job is not intended to bring comfort to the suffering, but to bring understanding that might prevent us from simply blaming God. The alternative is to trust God, and the book gives us a focus for our faith. Too often we focus our faith on believing that God will heal, relieve our suffering, or protect us from pain. Sometimes our faith lies in the belief that God will somehow come to us and give us explanations. Other times we place our faith in our ability to force our experiences into a coherent, meaningful narrative. All these approaches are unrealistic. Our faith should be directed toward embracing an all-wise God and asking him for help to live well before him regardless of our plight in this world that continues to display both order and disorder.

We should recognize, then, that the book of Job does not seek to explain God to us—such an endeavor would be impossible, as the book demonstrates. The book instead exposes our false and misguided ideas about God, the world, and suffering. It does not replace the rejected concepts with a comprehensive list of particulars, but simply gives direction for thinking. If we can avoid the standard list of misperceptions and begin moving in the right direction, the book will have achieved its purpose.

Should we expect God to speak to us as he eventually did to Job? I suggest that this should not be our goal—the book has told us what he would say. The fulfillment of Job's hopes that God would come and speak took shape in a manner far different than he imagined. First, God came in wrath—that is not the sort of appearance most of us desire. Second, we again note that God did not answer Job's questions. If we ask whether Job was satisfied with God's resolution of his requests, I suspect the answer would be no. Finally, recall that I have suggested that much in Job is part of a "thought experiment" (see Introduction, pp. 26–27). If this is so, we need not think of God's appearance to Job as a precedent for our crises. The book does not offer paradigms for how God regularly acts. It does not give us a guide for what our experience might look like, but it tries to shape our thinking as we face suffering. Through the book, then, we have come to know God better by eliminating incorrect thinking.

How Should We Think about the World?

THE BOOK OF JOB has indicated our need to realize that the world is not set up to operate in accordance with God's attribute of justice (or any other constant principle). This realization, however, does not mean that we should cease pursuing justice. When God created human beings in his image, he gave them the charge to "subdue and rule."[50] One of the ways in which we do so is by seeking to establish justice and thus bring increased order to the world. God established sufficient order for us to exist in this world, but he did not complete the task—he gave it to us, his stewards, to continue. We cannot bring order to the macrocosm, though technology has made considerable advances over the centuries as we have learned to harness our environment. Technology is helping us to bring order out of disorder (though since we are wielding it, it can also create further disorder). More importantly, we can seek to bring order by establishing justice in society. This also is a task that God assigned from early times (Gen. 9:6), though also one that cannot be fully achieved.

Justice in the cosmos and in society is therefore our objective, not our experience. We must keep this distinction in mind when we face the results of living in an unjust world: Suffering is inevitable, and it does not discriminate.[51] Disorder is not to be thought of as "Chaos"—that is, a personified horror (whether as a flawed conception of God or an anti-God devil). Chaos simply represents an unfinished creation. It is unfinished by plan, not by negligence or incompetence. Humanity is a work in progress; each of us individually is a work in progress; and the cosmos is likewise a work in progress. Suffering is the by-product of our in-progress state, and new creation is the denouement of God's ongoing creative activity.

How Should We Respond to Suffering?

WHAT DOES A PROPER response to suffering look like "on the ground"? I find it interesting that Job never addresses a prayer to God, asking him to deliver or save, though that likely would have been our first inclination.[52] Its absence should not be taken as a tacit suggestion that such a response is misguided, but if the book is offering strategies, it is noteworthy that this particular strategy is lacking. Neither Job nor the Bible as a whole

---

50. Fretheim, *Creation Untamed*, 14, suggests that these verbs should be understood as a mandate to continue bringing order out of disorder.

51. Admittedly, however, some purveyors of injustice may discriminate as they target certain people or classes of people.

52. I would admit, however, that his desire to be vindicated may be a difference without a distinction.

suggests that the standard sequence is suffering-prayer-healing. We might notice that even the Lord's Prayer contains no prayers for healing or relief from suffering — only that we not be tempted and that we seek God's kingdom.[53]

Areas of temptation might easily include being tempted to think wrongly about God or about our suffering. Instead, we seek God's kingdom. We do so in at least two ways: first, by seeking to live well even during times of suffering so that we might bring honor to him; and second, by patiently waiting in faith for the new creation. Others could be added. For example, we continually seek God's kingdom by trying to establish justice and relieve the suffering of others. Our prayers certainly can request relief, but more importantly they should focus on how we respond to our suffering. We should be praying, "Lord, use this to help me become more trusting, more dependent on you, more patient with others, more aware of my weaknesses, and more full of grace rather than bitterness." We must use our suffering to push us nearer to Christ rather than allowing it to drive us away from God. As Simone Weil observes, "The extreme greatness of Christianity lies in the fact that it does not seek a supernatural remedy for suffering, but a supernatural use for it."[54]

The book argues against looking to the past to find reasons. That does not mean that there are never reasons for suffering that might need to be recognized. Sometimes we suffer the consequences of bad choices, and we need to acknowledge that and make changes. Overall, however, we are not encouraged to immerse ourselves in anguish over what may have caused our suffering. We definitely should not assume that if we are suffering, we must have done something to deserve it. People are often prone to respond to suffering with the question, "Why me?" I would propose that it is when we have *not* suffered or when we are unexpectedly granted *relief* from suffering that we should pose the puzzled question, "Why me?"

If we shouldn't expect explanations or relief, what should we expect? We should expect that God is able to sustain us through suffering and even strengthen us through it. We please and honor God by trusting him in faith. We find purpose in suffering if we allow it to draw us closer to him in dependence instead of driving us further from him (though this should not be confused with ultimate cause or treated as a reason). We serve and honor God by being people of faith and helping others who might also be suffering to find the same solutions.

---

53. Some would claim that it is covered in "deliver us from evil," but that would entail an identification of all suffering as evil, which I have been arguing against.

54. Weil, *Gravity and Grace*, 73.

Kelly's Story[55]

JHW: HAVE YOU DEVELOPED your own "theology of suffering" in light of your experiences? What does it look like?

Kelly: I would say, in light of my experiences and the opportunities I have had to look into this topic on a deeper level, that yes, I have developed such a theology—or maybe it is more accurate to state that I have adopted one that was already created. My theology with suffering starts with trusting God. From that follows knowing that God is good and God loves us. Those are statements that, even though they sound clichéd, were some of the core beliefs I struggled accepting with my whole heart, as you saw over the course of my story. I continually challenged God and viewed my experiences in a way that, if you boil it down, meant that I did not trust God or believe that he loved me.

So if I start the foundation of my theology with those three things— trusting God, acknowledging that God is good, and believing that God loves us—then I know my foundation is solid. As you noted, I acknowledge that there are biblical examples of when God brought about suffering to bring judgment or teach his people something, but I do not believe we can use those examples to draw a conclusion that says: "If there is suffering, then God brought it upon them as judgment or pruning." Rather, we live in a fallen world where things don't always work out; to be more specific, I live in a fallen world where a car accident occurred leaving me with an incredibly painful disability that doctors have failed to solve, despite their efforts.

I know God has the power to intercede, which at times is the part I still wrestle with. That is where trusting him comes into play. I have to trust God and accept that he is good even when I do not understand. I may not understand the purpose or why God didn't choose to intercede in different parts of my story, but I do know he has used my experiences to teach me something about wisdom and perspective, and to draw me closer to him in a way that he never could have if I hadn't gone through the experiences I did.

So I don't know if I'd state that this is my own theology on suffering; rather, it may be an assortment of what I believe to be wise and true teachings from people in my life that I respect. I have had the honor to discuss these questions regarding God and suffering, which are questions that Christians and non-Christians struggle with alike.

---

55. Kelly interacts with parts of her story in each Contemporary Significance section. For the introduction to the details of her story, see Contemporary Significance in the commentary on ch. 1, pp. 87–97.

The book of Job serves the purpose of providing training for the mind so we can be prepared for suffering and crises. When musicians prepare for a recital or concert, they engage in many long hours of practice. A pianist trains her fingers to know the music so that when it is time for the concert, they go through the right movements subconsciously. If the pianist has to think about each transition and each fingering, the recital will not be a success. The body must be trained to act instinctively. Such a feat can only be accomplished through mental and physical discipline.

The book of Job is intended to function like the scales and finger exercises that a pianist has to practice endlessly so that the concert pieces may be played with skill. The book of Job is not the musical score itself that serves as a script, and we do not turn to this book as a resource to walk us through our suffering. Job is the practice material that prepares us for the performance. We assimilate its truths now so that we will be mentally and spiritually prepared for suffering when it comes. Sight-reading music the day of the concert dooms one to failure. The book does not give us a step-by-step guide to ensure a flawless performance; instead, it gives us the tools necessary to prepare for a respectable performance. How embarrassing it would be to play a piece in the wrong key, or in three-four time when it should be four-four.

As I was writing these final chapters a number of situations unfolded in the lives of family members — serious illnesses, lost jobs, emotional stresses. As I interacted with them in their crises, I searched back in my mind through what I had written in the pages of this commentary to see how I could offer comfort. I came up empty, because the book offers no comfort to the suffering. Comfort would have to consist of explanations or hope, and neither of those is intended by the author. The book offers theological guidance, not an instrument for psychological, emotional, or spiritual counseling. I use the book to help me think right and well so I am prepared for suffering; I have not discovered how to use it to respond to people's needs when trouble strikes.

In summary, then:

1. Wisdom, not justice, is the foundation of how God has set up the world. Disorder exists alongside order, and we must trust God's wisdom and rely on him in faith when we experience disorder.
2. Our expectations in life should not be based on the RP. We can follow the advice found in Ecclesiastes: Live as if the RP is true, but don't expect it to work out consistently in experience (my summary of the thrust of Eccl. 8 – 9).
3. Purpose, not cause, should be the focus of our attention when we face difficult times. This is the direction that Jesus gives in John 9:3.

4. Above all, we must not underestimate God by imagining that we could do things better. Concluding that God is incompetent or less than what Scripture presents him as being is the first step to setting ourselves up as God—a transaction doomed to miserable failure.

All of this is inadequate and unsatisfying when we or our loved ones suffer, or when we are crushed by the suffering we see all around us. It is not meant to be satisfying but to drive us to faith. No explanation can suffice to alleviate our suffering, and no strategy can avoid or eliminate suffering, but, as Bonhoeffer observes, life with all its struggles, trials, and hardships is what develops us into people of faith:

> I thought I could acquire faith by endeavoring to lead what might be termed a holy life.... Later I discovered, and am still discovering to this day, that one can acquire faith only by leading an entirely worldly [as opposed to other-worldly] life. If we renounce any attempt to make something of ourselves, be it saint or penitent sinner or churchman (a so-called priestly type!), be it a righteous or unrighteous, sick or healthy individual—and by worldliness I mean living amid the [world's] abundance of duties and problems, successes and failures, experiences and perplexities—if we do that, we cast ourselves completely into the arms of God; we take seriously, not our own sufferings, but those of God in this world; and we share Christ's vigil in Gethsemane. That, I believe, is faith, is *metanoia*, and that is how one becomes a human being and a Christian.... I'm thankful to have recognized this, and I know that I could only have done so on the road I have traveled. That is why I reflect with gratitude and serenity on things past and present.[56]

Bonhoeffer shows us that beyond faith and trust, what God asks of us is humility: humility about our ability to discern how the cosmos works, and humility about our ability to fully comprehend God and his ways.

---

56. Dietrich Bonhoeffer, *Love Letters from Cell 92: The Correspondence between Dietrich Bonhoeffer and Maria von Wedemeyer, 1943–45* (ed. Ruth-Alice von Bismarck and Ulrich Kabitz; trans. John Brownjohn; Nashville: Abingdon, 1995 [German orig. 1992]), 259.

Job 42

⚜

Then Job replied to the LORD:

²"I know that you can do all things;
    no plan of yours can be thwarted.
³⌊You asked,⌋ 'Who is this that obscures my counsel without knowledge?'
    Surely I spoke of things I did not understand,
    things too wonderful for me to know.
⁴⌊"You said,⌋ 'Listen now, and I will speak;
    I will question you,
    and you shall answer me.'
⁵My ears had heard of you
    but now my eyes have seen you.
⁶Therefore I despise myself
    and repent in dust and ashes."

⁷After the LORD had said these things to Job, he said to Eliphaz the Temanite, "I am angry with you and your two friends, because you have not spoken of me what is right, as my servant Job has. ⁸So now take seven bulls and seven rams and go to my servant Job and sacrifice a burnt offering for yourselves. My servant Job will pray for you, and I will accept his prayer and not deal with you according to your folly. You have not spoken of me what is right, as my servant Job has." ⁹So Eliphaz the Temanite, Bildad the Shuhite and Zophar the Naamathite did what the LORD told them; and the LORD accepted Job's prayer.

¹⁰After Job had prayed for his friends, the LORD made him prosperous again and gave him twice as much as he had before. ¹¹All his brothers and sisters and everyone who had known him before came and ate with him in his house. They comforted and consoled him over all the trouble the LORD had brought upon him, and each one gave him a piece of silver and a gold ring.

¹²The LORD blessed the latter part of Job's life more than the first. He had fourteen thousand sheep, six thousand camels, a thousand yoke of oxen and a thousand donkeys. ¹³And he also had seven sons and three daughters. ¹⁴The first daughter he named Jemimah, the second Keziah and the

third Keren-Happuch. ¹⁵Nowhere in all the land were there found women as beautiful as Job's daughters, and their father granted them an inheritance along with their brothers.

¹⁶After this, Job lived a hundred and forty years; he saw his children and their children to the fourth generation. ¹⁷And so he died, old and full of years.

Job's Second Response

IN 40:4–5, Job responded to God's questioning concerning the macrocosm and microcosm with awed silence. He would no longer press his case. Yahweh deemed his silence inadequate, however, and followed up with a second speech featuring the mysterious Behemoth and Leviathan. Job now responds to this second speech by recanting and repenting.

Job here first acknowledges God's wisdom and power (42:2), then admits the validity of God's accusation that he (Job) has obscured knowledge and spoken ignorantly (42:3). He concedes that he spoke of things too "wonderful" to know. The Hebrew word here is *pele'*, which refers to information in the divine realm that is beyond human understanding. The same word describes knowledge of God's name (Judg. 13:18) and God's wondrous acts (Ex. 3:20; Josh. 3:5; Judg. 6:13; Ps. 139:6). An equivalent term today would be "supernatural."

No concept of natural existed in the ancient world, so there could be no distinction between natural and supernatural. All action was considered effected by God,[1] though people did recognize a difference between divine and human capabilities. In Job, the word *pele'* occurs five other times (5:9; 9:10; 10:16; 37:5, 14), and these instances provide a helpful profile of its usage. Job's use of the word here is particularly appropriate, as he acknowledges that God's ways are beyond his ability to comprehend and systematize.

In 42:5 Job distinguishes between secondhand experience ("my ears had heard") and firsthand experience ("now my eyes have seen"), and in light of the comparison, he "despises" (NIV; Heb. *m's*) and "repents" (NIV; Heb. *nḥm* in the Niphal). The first verb connotes considering something or someone as nothing or as having no value. Job previously used this verb to

---

1. Not quite the modern theological concept of God being the "efficient cause" of everything, but nearly so.

describe his low estimation of himself (7:16; 9:21).[2] The expression goes beyond humility to self-abasement. He is deeply ashamed of his former presumption in challenging God's ways.[3]

The second verb should be distinguished from others that can be translated "repent." Eliphaz, working under the assumption that Job was guilty of great sin, urged him to "repent" (NIV: "return" in 22:23; *šub*)—that is, to change his behavior. In 42:5, Job does not suggest behavior change, but rather wishes to retract his previous statements. He employs the same verb and form used when God "changes his mind" (e.g., Ex. 32:14; Jer. 4:28; 18:10; Joel 2:13; Jonah 3:10). While it is a difficult word to translate into English, many of its occurrences take place in situations involving regret. It would not be misguided to see in Job's statements that he regrets his previous statements, his characterization of God, his presumptuous belief in his own understanding, and his arrogant challenges.

Nevertheless, his statement here focuses elsewhere. When the Niphal form of the verb *nhm* is used with the preposition ʿ*al* (as here), it typically means to reconsider something or, more often, to put something out of mind—to forget all about it.[4] In this verse, that "something" is his dust and ashes. The preposition cannot be read as Job repenting *with* dust and ashes; rather, he "reconsiders dust and ashes," or "puts dust and ashes out of his mind." He has thereby announced the end to his mourning as he has accepted his reality.

Narrative Epilogue

THE EPILOGUE COMPRISES TWO parts: the reprimand and reconciliation of Job's friends (42:7–9), and the restoration of Job's prosperity (42:10–16). Both have their difficulties. The first section presents vocabulary problems, which we will address immediately, and the second raises concerns regarding the conclusion's theological and rhetorical logic, which we will address under Bridging Contexts.

After God expresses his anger at the three friends, he twice identifies the reason for his displeasure: "You have not spoken of me what is right, as my servant Job has." At this point in the book, we can see many ways in which the friends have spoken incorrectly, but it is more difficult to understand why Job seems to receive exoneration for his statements about God,

---

2. In 7:16 it lacks a direct object, as here.

3. See lengthy discussion in Clines, *Job 38–42*, 172–73. He chooses to translate it "submit."

4. Ex. 32:12, 14; 2 Sam. 13:39; 1 Chron. 21:15; Ps. 90:13; Isa. 57:6; Jer. 8:6; 18:8, 10; 31:15[14]; Ezek. 14:22; 32:31; Joel 2:13; Amos 7:3, 6; Jonah 3:10; 4:2.

particularly in light of the harsh indictment that immediately preceded this section.

Outside of God's statements in 42:7–8, neither God nor Job seems to consider Job's speech about God to be appropriate; indeed, passages such as 30:18–23 raise serious questions about the validity of Job's characterization of God. Furthermore, Job's oath of innocence in chapter 31 carries implications that are inherently devastating to God's character. As is often the case, clarity is found in a close reading of the Hebrew text, particularly an investigation of the narrator's choice of words.

The Hebrew combines the verb *dibber* (the common word for the act of speaking) with the preposition *'el* followed by the first person pronoun, ending with the adjective *nekonah* (NIV, "right"), and presents the entire phrase as a contrast to Job's behavior (*k-* preposition of comparison).

The versions and manuscripts testify that interpreters have long struggled with this line. Most notably, many Hebrew manuscripts substitute the Hebrew preposition *b-* for *k-* preceding the reference to Job. This change results in the translation: "because you have not spoken of me what is right *against* my servant Job" (instead of "*as* my servant Job"). Such a reading eliminates the suggestion that Job has spoken correctly about God.[5] Although this presents a possible solution, it may be a textual adjustment made in the transmission history in order to resolve a perceived problem rather than a reading that commends itself as original.

An alternative explanation relates to the word *nekonah* (Niphal fem. ptc. of *kwn*). As noted in the comments on Job 10:13 (p. 178), when this word concerns something that is expressed or discovered, it indicates that such expression or discovery is sensible, logical, or verifiable. A statement characterized as *nekonah* can be validated by evidence. In 10:13, I suggested the following conclusion: "Job believes that God is afflicting him without cause (9:17), a belief that God affirms is true (2:3); in contrast, Job's friends claim that God is afflicting Job with cause and press Job to confess his supposed crimes. This does not mean that Job's concept of God is unobjectionable or that all that he says of God is correct, but it does mean that Job has drawn logical conclusions." As this reading suggests, we may be able to differentiate between ways of "speaking what is right." In contrast to his friends, Job did speak what is right (or valid) in certain ways, even though in other ways he misspoke. I believe this offers the most profitable direction for interpretation. Regardless of which interpretive option we

---

5. For occurrences of *dibber b-* as "speak against," see Num. 12:8; 21:5, 8; Job 19:18; Ps. 50:20; Zech. 13:3. The LXX intriguingly translates the Hebrew *k-* in verse 7 (*hosper*), but the variant *b-* in v. 8 (*kata*).

choose, however, all commentators agree that although Job spoke more truly than his friends, God does not exonerate his behavior as a whole.[6]

We must address one more textual issue before turning our attention to rhetorical strategy in Bridging Contexts. In verse 8 God states that if Job offers a sacrifice and prays for the friends, "I will accept his prayer and not deal with you according to your folly" (NIV). This translation avoids a problem evident in the Hebrew text, which has no second person pronoun attached to the noun folly (*nebalah*). The Hebrew thus appears to require the translation "lest I commit folly in my treatment of you." The syntax (*lebilti* + ʿ*aśot* + uninflected noun, cf. Lev. 18:30; Ezek. 33:15, in this case, *nebalah*) suggests that Yahweh may act with folly (*nebalah*), a concept that is incompatible with his character (note *nebaloth* as a description of Job's wife in 2:10). Before adding words to the text (as the NIV does), we will attempt to understand the full semantic range of the word *nebalah*.

Some have suggested that *nebalah* refers to actions that are scandalously contrary to convention or to someone engaged in such behavior.[7] The word often describes strikingly immoral behavior (e.g., Gen. 34:7; Judg. 19:23; 2 Sam. 13:12) or disparagement of God's character (Isa. 9:17; Jer. 29:23). Such behavior is considered outrageous because it violates all sensibility, logic, and tradition. We readily translate *nebalah* as "folly," because characteristically it is a fool who commits such acts. The term involves not only unconventional comportment, but shocking iconoclasm and reversal of norms. Can God act this way? In light of preceding chapters, we must answer in the affirmative, for a reversal of norms is precisely the manner in which God has acted toward Job: God brought suffering on that righteous man even though convention dictated that he should prosper. Here, then, God threatens that Job's friends are not immune to similar treatment. They too are vulnerable to loss and misery, contrary to their confidence in the RP.

Finally, Job offers a prayer for his friends after they have offered the requisite sacrifices. This action serves as an inclusio with chapter 1, where Job offered sacrifices for his children. When Job acted as priest for his children, his behavior revealed flaws in his theology and exposed him to questions regarding his motivations, which led to his suffering. In contrast, when Job acts as intercessor for his friends at the end of the book, he does so in reflection of God's compassion, not in suspicion of God's unreasonable character; as a result, this behavior leads to Job's restoration (42:10). Job conducted his

---

6. Clines, *Job 38–42*, 196, offers a similar reading.

7. Ngwa, "Did Job Suffer for Nothing," 378. See J. Marböck, "נָבָל," *TDOT*, 9:167–71; his conclusion about the semantic location of the root is that it should be understood as "a breach or derangement of the bonds that unite human beings with each other or with God, whether expressed in status, attitude, word, or deed" (171).

former rituals in order to hedge against the possibility that his children had cursed God; now their rituals and his prayer are required because his friends did not speak what was right about Yahweh—a fact, not a vague suspicion.

Rhetorical Strategy

WE MUST ADDRESS TWO questions as we approach the rhetorical conclusion of the book:

1. How does Job's concluding statement serve as a logical response to God's second speech?
2. How does the epilogue serve as a legitimate conclusion to the book?

Job's response to Yahweh's second speech. We have already discussed the reasons for Yahweh's second speech and the ways in which Job's second response surpasses his first. We must now consider why Yahweh's second speech effectively elicits a more significant response from Job.

As previously suggested, in his second speech Yahweh employs Behemoth and Leviathan as illustrations for Job and himself, respectively. The lesson of Behemoth concerns stability and trust. The lesson of Leviathan is the utter folly of challenging God—one wouldn't dream of challenging Leviathan, and God is far greater than Leviathan. Job's second response, in which he recants his arrogant challenges, demonstrates that he has taken these lessons to heart. Presumably he is now prepared to place his trust in God rather than the RP.

Epilogue as fitting conclusion to the book. Many have been baffled by the conclusion for a number of reasons:

- Restoring Job's prosperity doesn't erase the suffering he experienced—this solution rings hollow.
- Providing Job with more children does not heal his grief for those he lost.
- Restoring Job's prosperity seems like a reinstallation of the RP, which makes little sense given that God has just established its inadequacy.

Any treatment of the book must address these issues in order to explain why the conclusion is appropriate.

To fully grasp the appropriateness of the conclusion, we must bear in mind the book's central concern: God's policies. The Challenger claims that it is poor policy for righteous people to prosper. Job claims that it is poor policy for righteous people to suffer. The first twenty-seven chapters of the book explore the Challenger's claim, throughout which Job maintains his belief that righteousness, not prosperity, matters most. We traced the integrity of Job's conviction chapter by chapter and concluded that, contrary to the Challenger's contention, prospering righteous people does not automatically subvert their motives. Job demonstrates that it is possible to be righteous for righteousness' sake—he indeed will serve God for nothing.

The book likewise addresses Job's claim and concludes that it is not God's *policy* to prosper righteous people invariably. While God delights in bringing good to those who are faithful, the world does not operate according to justice. The RP does not provide a theodicy.

By restoring Job's prosperity in the epilogue, God makes a clear statement that he will continue to act as he did before, with policies unchanged. The cases presented by the Challenger and by Job have proved untenable. God is not bound by the RP. Job can now understand his prosperity differently: Prosperity is not a reward he deserves or one that God is obliged to provide. It is rather a gift from God.

When we view the epilogue in this light, the objections raised earlier may be effectively addressed. The restoration of Job's prosperity is not intended to erase Job's pain, and it is not even primarily for Job's benefit. This is not about Job. Through Job's renewed prosperity, God's challenged policies are reinstated. Now, however, it can be understood that this prosperity of Job's is not a given, is not mechanical; it is not the obligation of God but the pleasure of God. This point is critical for an accurate understanding of the book's message. The epilogue does not suggest that when we suffer, we may console ourselves with an expectation of future satisfaction—that someday we will get it all back.

Similarly, the fact that Job is given more children is not meant to erase his grief over those who died. Like many Jews in the aftermath of the Holocaust, Elie Wiesel struggled to understand a God who could allow such devastation to his chosen people. In *Messengers of God: Biblical Portraits and Legends*, Wiesel makes the point that tragedies do not cancel one another out. Wiesel suggests that what Job should have asked at the end of the book was: "What about my dead children?"[8] Those losses were real and could not be ameliorated by replacements. But the epilogue does not suggest such an unrealistic way of thinking. Again, the restoration is not primarily for Job's benefit; rather, it demonstrates that God's policies

---

8. Elie Wiesel, *Messengers of God: Biblical Portraits and Legends* (New York: Simon and Schuster, 1985), 234.

are intact and unaltered in the aftermath of the challenges made to them. Wiesel is seeking reasons and explanations for suffering, which the epilogue does not offer.

If we consider the epilogue (or the book as a whole) and imagine how we would feel if we were Job or if we experienced Job-like suffering, we will miss the point. Our purpose is not to learn from Job as a character or from his experiences. The book does not ask us to put ourselves in his place or to model our responses after his behavior. Instead, the book prompts us to learn how to think about God more accurately, just as Job learns alongside us. God delights in showing favor to those who are faithful to him, but the world is not bound to operate on that premise.

The observations provided in response to the first two objections also give an answer to the third. The restoration of Job's prosperity does not equate to an unqualified reinstallation of the RP, and thus Job's blessings now may be considered in a different light. Neither God's policies nor the world's operations are founded on the RP applied as theodicy. Rather, when events appear to occur according to the RP, they should be viewed as the ripple effects of God's character as he intervenes to bring blessing and judgment.

In order to understand the strategy and import of the book, we must recognize that it does not offer us an explanation of why righteous people suffer. We should not base our expectations on Job's experiences. Job receives no explanation for his suffering, and the book does not fill that void for readers either. The only explanation the book offers concerns right thinking about God and his policies in a world where suffering is pervasive and inevitable.

In light of the preceding points, the epilogue is the perfect conclusion to the book. The challenges to God's policies have been addressed, and various misconceptions about God and the cosmos have been dispelled. In the process, we have gained wisdom. This wisdom does not ease our suffering, but it does help us to avoid the foolish thinking that might lead us to reject God when we need him most.

Theological Issues

RETRIBUTION PRINCIPLE REMIX. GIVEN the book's conclusion, we may reevaluate our view of the RP, especially in light of the positive affirmations found in Proverbs, wisdom psalms such as Psalm 37, and Deuteronomy's covenant blessings and curses. The Introduction (pp. 39–48) addressed this material at length, so we only reiterate it briefly here. The two key ideas are as follows:

1. The Bible affirms the RP as good theology, but it does not use it to construct a theodicy, despite the natural inclination to do so.

2. The Bible's affirmation of the RP is covenantal and proverbial. In covenantal terms, it operates collectively, not individually, and therefore is philosophically unproblematic when an individual faces a crisis. Wisdom literature presents the RP as proverbial truth, which by its genre constitutes a generalization about how things tend to be rather than a guarantee of universal reality.

As we consider the RP in collective covenantal terms, we may ponder Job's impact on corporate Israel. It is unlikely that Israelites in exile viewed themselves as a corporate righteous sufferer, but they may well have gained insight into the covenant's RP aspects in context of their national relationship to Yahweh.[9] Per the message of Job, the covenant asks Israel to trust God's wisdom rather than to apply a mechanical tally system suggested by a superficial reading of the covenant blessings and curses.

God's policies remix. Even when we accept the book's teaching that God's policies are sound and that the RP is not the foundation for the world's operations, we inevitably find ourselves with further questions about how God works. Why does God bring blessing to the righteous and judgment on the wicked inconsistently? Even if he did so only rarely, wouldn't such action require "overriding" the natural system of cause and effect in order to impose his will? If God overrides the system sometimes, why not all the time? How does he choose when to do so? We easily find ourselves at square one, questioning God's policies.

Our understanding of these issues will benefit if we can set aside our default conception of the post-Enlightenment Kantian divide between supernatural and natural, in which the natural world operates by an inexorable chain of cause and effect, and any supernatural element is a disruption. Instead, we must think in ancient categories of order and disorder, which were introduced in our investigation of Behemoth and Leviathan (p. 413). Suffering is part of the disorder that continues to exist in the cosmos. It has been left there by God's design, according to his purposes. God *can* send suffering as punishment, but suffering is also an automatic result of disorder. Human beings, made in God's image, can alleviate a measure of suffering as they follow their mandate to "subdue and rule." Such alleviation may be seen in technology employed on a global basis to maximize resources, and through the advance of medical technology to treat disease and reduce pain. This type of progress, however, is inevitably limited and cannot serve as a final solution to disorder. These same technologies can be exploited in harmful ways as they are wielded by fallen humans.

---

9. Ticciati, *Job and the Disruption of Identity*, 73.

God brings order in many ways besides human effort. Creation is the act of bringing order, and God is Creator. His creating work entails ongoing involvement, not merely a past burst of activity. Enactments of the RP are a manifestation of order. We cannot address why God chooses to enact the RP in some instances and not in others—this is where trust comes into play. God will eventually align all of creation with his attributes and establish absolute order in the new heavens and new earth. Until then, we should expect continued manifestations of disorder.

 WHEN I HAVE OPPORTUNITY for casual reading, fantasy is my genre of choice. I enjoy how it opens my imagination and offers truths about the world. Fantasy writers often indulge in philosophical and theological ruminations; in this and many other ways, they are indebted to the likes of J. R. R. Tolkien and C. S. Lewis. Sometimes their ideas ring true; other times, I find reason to disagree or to question whether they have put truth in the mouths of their characters.

In *The Astonishing Life of Octavian Nothing: Traitor to the Nation, Volume 1, The Pox Party*, by M. T. Anderson, one of the characters offers a remarkable commentary on the relationship between kindness and profit— precisely the issue addressed in the book of Job.

> Kindness without the promise of profit is an impossibility. You must want something if you are to act. Otherwise, it would be like movement without motivation. Reaction without action. Kinesis without stimulation. Motion without energy. Kindness without profit is like a teapot hovering over a table, held by nothing.[10]

It is not surprising that some people truly subscribe to this belief. Profit is undoubtedly a common motivation for kindness, and in our fallen state this observation easily shapes our mind-set, even if subconsciously. After all, we are not naturally inclined to be kind. The book of Job offers the good news that kindness (or righteousness) can be motivated by something other than profit.

This statement appropriately leads to a question we each should answer: Do we serve God for nothing? If our righteous or kind behavior is motivated primarily by a desire to ingratiate ourselves with God and/or others,

---

10. M. T. Anderson, *The Astonishing Life of Octavian Nothing: Traitor to the Nation, Volume 1, The Pox Party* (Cambridge, Mass.: Candlewick, 2006), 336.

to win approval, or to conform to expectations, we are missing the mark. Honest self-evaluation can be difficult, because these false motivations are often buried deeply in our psyche. To correct this tendency, we do not need to eliminate our desire for approval or our inclination to conform, but we do need to nurture right ways of thinking.

How do we do so, and how will we know if we are getting it right? Righteous behavior often *does* result in approval or even profit, and it is all too easy to view those results as incentives. In order to detach motivation from personal gain, therefore, we ought to seek opportunities to do what is right without hope of approval or profit. Even in anonymous acts of righteousness, however, we may feel satisfied that we are ingratiating ourselves with God, and we must dissuade ourselves from thinking in those terms. Righteousness and kindness certainly please God, and his pleasure is sound motivation. The key is to avoid expecting something in return; his approval should be enough. These are high ideals indeed, and they do not come naturally. We can work on them for our entire lives and still feel we have made little progress and failed frequently. Nevertheless, pure motivation should become the object of our prayers.

As the book of Job comes to a close, we should also take the opportunity to review our conception of an appropriate response to suffering. We have discussed this notion several times, but we have yet to address the various suggestions that are typically made. I begin with a quote from another fantasy novel, this one offering a perspective on suffering: "Every injury is a gift, every gift an injury."[11] When I encountered this statement by one of the characters in the book, I set the book down and spent some time pondering its validity. I recognize the statement as a generalization, and as such it need not be considered *always* true. But does it have a ring of truth to it as an observation of reality?

We could consider "every injury a gift" if we emphasize the way in which an injury to one part of the body sometimes strengthens other parts. Indeed, in the book the line was spoken by a blind character who experienced compensatory development via the sharpening of other senses. We could also consider the statement to be true in the sense that suffering may help us to mature, as pointed out earlier. In this way too, injuries could be accepted as gifts.

Correspondingly, we could consider "every gift an injury" because a gift may indebt us to the giver. Obligations place burdens on us, some of which we can never repay. In such cases, we may feel guilty or constrained. When gifts come with chains of conscience or duty attached, we may indeed view them as injuries.

---

11. T. Williams, *Otherland: Sea of Silver Light* (New York: Daw, 2001), 888.

It is inappropriate, however, to think of God's gifts as inflicting injury. The essential point of Job is that God does not run a mutual indebtedness scheme. His gifts to us impose no obligation. Undoubtedly some respond to God as if they are trapped in servitude, but that is not how God desires us to interact with him. We are to respond as his children, not as his slaves (Rom. 8:15–17). It is true that we are debtors to his grace, but that is a debt we can never repay, and in fact God does not expect repayment. Christ died because we could not independently rectify our situation, so if we serve him only out of a sense of guilt or duty, we miss the point entirely. Christ's death was not a relocation of guilt—guilt over sin to guilt over an impossible debt; rather, Christ died to free us from guilt so that we can serve him freely, out of love.

We may conclude, then, that the novel's saying contains some truth and demonstrates a potential perspective on suffering: suffering as a gift. Those who maintain that suffering is God's will and therefore worthy of a joyful response express the same concept. The notion of rejoicing in suffering has biblical support:

> Consider it pure joy, my brothers, whenever you face trials of many kinds, because you know that the testing of your faith develops perseverance. Perseverance must finish its work so that you may be mature and complete, not lacking anything. If any of you lacks wisdom, he should ask God, who gives generously to all without finding fault, and it will be given to him. (James 1:2–5)

These verses touch on many of the points we have presented throughout the book. Trials result in maturity, and God gives us wisdom to cope with the pain we experience. Notice also that James urges us to pray for wisdom rather than for relief.

At the same time, we may question whether James is addressing trials of suffering, for within the book's discussion of perseverance, the emphasis remains primarily on temptation and persecution. James likely would not exempt suffering from the larger category he labels "trials," for he mentions Job as an example of one who persevered (James 5:11). It is appropriate, then, that we try to find joy (which is distinct from "happiness") in suffering. Although such an attempt often feels impossible, it is nonetheless the perspective to which we should aspire.

I must make one final observation on this point: I am not convinced that we should view suffering as "God's will," by which I mean that it is not his desire for us to suffer. God desires that we learn perseverance and wisdom and that we mature. Suffering is part of the disorder in the world and God can bring good from it. Disorder has remained part of the cosmos as part of

God's plan. But instead of responding to this disorder righteously, we have responded to this disorder with sin, which sometimes results in suffering. We should not rejoice over our sin and over the chaos and suffering that ensue as a result. Positive results can follow sin when we recognize it, suffer the consequences, repent, and thereby grow strong against it—but that does not make sin God's will.

We should not think of suffering as God's way to teach us a lesson and that our continued suffering means we have not yet learned the intended lesson. God can teach lessons through our suffering, but we should not think of it as his will to do so. Likewise we should not think in terms of "blaming the world." We must resist finding a focus for blame, for that is not the point.

God's plan for history and the cosmos entails a gradual process of expanding order. While that process remains incomplete, we cope with the disorder that remains. God could have chosen to act differently, but it is not our role to second-guess God or to suggest better options, as the book of Job has taught us. When we distinguish between God's permissive will and his perfect sovereign will, we reflect our desire to craft theology to justify our experience. Such systematizations run the risk of committing the same fault as Job and his friends: reducing God's policies to a simple formula.

My reticence to label suffering as "God's will" does not entail agreement with those who label suffering as the work of the devil.[12] We often overstate the role of Satan in the world. When we portray him as the enemy of God, we must be careful not to elevate him above his pay grade. God has no enemies worthy of the title, and he is not in a struggle to retain power or control over the universe. Satan is *our* enemy, but he is entirely under God's control, as discussed in chapter 1 (pp. 64–67). Satan is only part of the disorder that continues to exist in the cosmos; he is neither the author of that disorder nor its sustainer. He has a role in the disorder, and his presence testifies to it, but every instance of disorder cannot be attributed to him.

Another common reaction to suffering is the conclusion that we suffer because we deserve it. For every natural disaster, there are unfortunately people willing to enumerate the sins of the victims (corporately if not individually). When Hurricane Katrina decimated a large section of New Orleans, self-styled prophets announced that the devastation was God's judgment on a sinful city. There is no question that God can use natural disasters to bring judgment, but no one today should dare claim a prophet's authority to expound the mind of God. Correlating suffering and sin too closely leads to overreliance on the RP's explanatory capacity. This is precisely the error critiqued by the book of Job, and we should seek to avoid it.

---

12. This is the inclination of Boyd in his book *Is God to Blame?*

This flaw also appears in the ever-popular "health-and-wealth" gospel. Instead of claiming that disasters are God's punishment for wickedness, this theological aberration proclaims great material rewards, often in the form of monetary gifts, for those who respond to God. This outlook is another misapplication of the RP. As noted, the RP appears within the context of wisdom literature and should be read as theological proverb; it cannot accurately or profitably be viewed as offering a promise or guarantee.

Other explanations of suffering emerge in contexts such as the dramatic production *God on Trial*, which portrays a court case held at Auschwitz.[13] God is put on trial for violating his covenant and abandoning his people. The play identifies various interpretations of suffering, including the ideas that God brings suffering to test the faith of righteous people (offered by the character named Kuhn) and that God brings suffering for the purpose of purification (offered by Schmidt). Neither of these options should be dismissed out of hand. Undoubtedly, either could be the *result* of suffering, but there is a significant difference between "result" and "reason." As we have learned from Job, we should be hesitant to believe that we can identify reasons for suffering or explanations for God's actions. Our job is to trust, not to explain. Our objective is faith and perseverance, not relief. Our determination is to refrain from reducing God to a manageable size by confining him to a philosophical box of our own design. And our commitment is to respond with humility rather than to defame his character or dismiss him.

In conclusion, I want to register a final objection to those who summarize the message of the book of Job as "I am God and you are not." I begin with a confession. When I was in my adolescent years, our home had a simple back patio made of stone slabs with spaces of soil between them. As is often the case, ants made their home in these dirt cracks, and the patio was often awash with their activity. For some reason that I still cannot fathom, I used to spend time out on the patio with a basketball, squashing ants. It did not occur to me that I should be reluctant to so casually remove life that God had created, with no reason or benefit—the ants brought no harm to the house or garden.

Sometimes we might be inclined to see ourselves as the ants and God as the mindless adolescent with the basketball. He is not simply exercising power because he can, or demonstrating cruelty, so that it impossible for us to either question him or explain his actions. This view does not represent sound biblical or theological thinking. We should not adopt any of the following elaborations of "I am God and you are not:"

---

13. Frank Cottrell Boyce, *God on Trial*, PBS Masterpiece Theater (2008).

- I am God, mind your own business.
- I am God, I can do whatever I want.
- I am God, you are worthless.

In light of the book of Job, the only acceptable elaboration would be: "I am God, I care deeply, and I want you to trust me even when you don't understand." By affirming such a view of God, we do not dismiss suffering as meaningless but try to understand it in the larger context of God's wisdom and the world in which we live.

Kelly's Story[14]

JHW: WE HAVE REACHED the end of the book, Kelly, but you still have your life before you. Could you conclude by reflecting on how the book of Job has changed your perspective about your situation and what the future looks like for you (both in terms of your physical condition and your perspectives on it)?

Kelly: This process has changed my perspective on suffering and my situation in so many ways, I am not sure where to begin. Looking back at the lunch conversation with you in the Wheaton College dining hall when you asked me to consider being a part of this commentary in the spring of 2009, I remember feeling honored, excited, horrified, way underqualified, and confused all at the same time. I remember thinking, "Why on earth is he asking me? I feel like the last person to be giving my thoughts on suffering for a Job commentary. Maybe he hasn't noticed that God and I are in a bit of a disagreement at the moment." It was as though you read my mind because you then said, "Struggling through the hard questions, wrestling with the unknown, and having someone share their raw and real emotions in the midst of trial will be what readers relate to."

When I think about the honor I have had to be a part of this project, I see God's involvement, or rather his purpose, written all over it. As I reflect on my testimony, there are still many unanswered questions, and I may never know the answers — nor am I entitled to. When it comes to this book on Job, however, it is clear how God used the timing of this opportunity for a greater purpose.

I was broken. I was in the thick of it. When I first started writing my section of this book, typing was still a difficult task since I had lost my fine motor skills in my left hand and was still recovering and trying to strengthen those muscles. I am grateful that as I type now, it is a task I can

---

14. Kelly interacts with parts of her story in each Contemporary Significance section. For the introduction to the details of her story, see Contemporary Significance in the commentary on ch. 1, pp. 87–97.

do with ease. As we know from what we learned in studying Job, God is not a God who micromanages every detail; but I do believe he is a God who answers prayers, equips us, and gives us the strength—or in my case, the project—to help us through our trials.

God knew that I was angry, confused, hurt, and suffering, and that I would most likely bottle all of my emotions. I would not talk about my questions to God, or even what I was struggling through, but then I willingly signed a contract stating that I *have* to talk about the trial I'm in and write out my questions and dialogue with God in the process. He may not have removed the thorn, but what a better way to carry me through the trial than to say: "Kelly, I'm going to have you sign a contract for a commentary on the book of Job. So while you are in these trials, you are going to study Job and the topics of suffering on earth and my involvement in it. You will then talk about how those themes are directly connected to your personal testimony, and then be forced to deal with deep-rooted issues in regard to the lies that you have believed about me as a result of your painful experiences." It has been a process for which I am grateful. There were times where you would send me questions that I would have to skip and return to later on, because I wasn't ready to address that area of my faith or my life.

So once I was in the process, how did studying the book of Job change my perspective? First, I learned how to pray while in suffering, which greatly impacted my perspective. I learned that in my moments of pain I should seek wisdom (as we talked about in Job 28), ask for the strength to endure, and pray for a heavenly perspective, rather than focusing solely on the trial and begging for an escape. I learned that when I was challenging God and asking him "Why?" it did not reveal God's distorted character, but my distorted view of him. This caused me to reflect on the lies that I was believing about my own worth and about God that were formed from painful experiences on earth. But the largest thing that changed my view on my situation was identifying my lack of trust in God. The restoration of my trust in him and knowing his love for me brought emotional and spiritual healing.

There were times where I felt like the ant that you described in your story. In times like those I felt as if God was carelessly causing me pain, but I had to remember his love for me and that in the midst of the pain, I must trust that his plan is good, because his character does not change.

A lot has changed in my life throughout this process. I graduated from Wheaton College with a degree in Fine Art Photography and Spanish, moved back to my home state of Colorado to start up my photography business, and I got married in the summer of 2011 to my best friend. I know I would be in a very different place if I had not restored my trust in God, which has allowed me to heal from the lies that were binding me in my suffering. The trials and the story continue. I still have excruciating nerve pain, failed medical procedures, and medical bills for those failed procedures, and I know that such experiences will most likely be a part of my life in the future. But the only reason I talk in the past tense when referring to my view of my situation is because even though the suffering remains today, the refreshed perspective acknowledges that God is sovereign, and I believe in him, and his love gives me a renewed strength to trust his wisdom, to overcome the trials, and to be content in the mystery of the unknown.

As I write these words I want to be careful because even though I am joyful for the healing that has taken place and for my refreshed perspective, that does not mean I do not still have days where I feel weak and struggle. The trials are just as real today as they have been over this past decade. So as I encounter trials and pain in my life, I have to continue to seek God and seek wisdom to retain that perspective. I guess what I am saying is that it is *not* a one quick fix. Doubts and lies can still creep into our way of thinking, so we need to be praying for strength and for discernment when thoughts come into our minds that distort our view of God.

I do not know what the future holds in terms of my physical condition. I am continuing to learn how to do new things with one arm (I learned how to rock climb recently, and this past summer I had a surfing lesson!), but nerve pain is a continual battle. But in it all, I can say that I trust God and his wisdom, and that he will equip me to persevere through whatever this next season will bring.

Kelly's story, like most of our own stories, has no neat tying up of loose ends — no quasi-happy endings like the one we find in Job. Her story continues to unfold. As she noted, the pain continues as does the disability; bills remain; medical solutions are evasive; people continue to offer unhelpful or even hurtful advice. Kelly has chosen not to include many additional hurts in some of her personal relationships, but the ripple effects of those continue as well. The trust that we are called upon to exercise is not trust that God will bring resolution. That would be the wrong conclusion to draw from the book of Job. Instead, we trust in God's goodness and love, even when our experiences cause us to question those attributes.

This key aspect of trust was also the direction promoted in William Paul Young's wildly popular 2007 novel, *The Shack,* which gained a number-one position on the *New York Times* bestseller list.[15] The center portion of the book contains lengthy discussions between God and the main character

---

15. William Paul Young, *The Shack* (Newbury Park, Calif.: Windblown Media, 2007).

about numerous theological topics, including, prominently, suffering. The following speech by God tracks well to what I have suggested is part of the teaching of the book of Job.

> You try to make sense of the world in which you live based on a very small and incomplete picture of reality. It is like looking at a parade through the tiny knothole of hurt, pain, self-centeredness, and power and believing you are on your own and insignificant. All of these thoughts contain powerful lies. You see pain and death as ultimate evils and God as the ultimate betrayer, or perhaps, at best, as fundamentally untrustworthy. You dictate the terms and judge my actions and find me guilty.
>
> The real underlying flaw in your life, MacKenzie, is that you don't think I am good. If you knew I was good and that everything — the means, the ends, and all the processes of individual lives — is all covered by my goodness, then while you might not always understand what I am doing, you would trust me. But you don't.[16]

This conversation is drawn to a powerful conclusion:

> MacKenzie, you cannot produce trust, just as you cannot "do" humility. It either is or is not. Trust is the fruit of a relationship in which you know you are loved. Because you do not know that I love you, you *cannot* trust me.[17]

So now we have reached the end of the matter: trust in the wisdom of God born of our absolute conviction that he loves us. That is the way through the struggles of life.

The fitting benediction comes from Romans 11:33–36 (with my italics for emphasis):

> Oh, the depth of the riches of the *wisdom* and *knowledge* of God!
>> How unsearchable his *judgments*,
>> and his paths beyond tracing out!
> "Who has known the mind of the Lord?
>> Or who has been his counselor?"
> "Who has ever given to God
>> that God should repay him?"
> For from him and through him and to him are all things.
>> To him be the glory forever! Amen.

---

16. Ibid., 128.
17. Ibid.

Technical Appendix

Job 2:3

The word translated "incited" is in a form that creates a play on words with *śatan*: *tesiteni*, though neither the *s* nor the *t* is the same Hebrew letter as in *śatan*, and the *n* in this verb is part of the pronominal suffix, not the root; thus there is no morphological relationship between the words. The verbal root, *swt*, makes an intriguing study. It occurs only 18x, always in the Hiphil form; we should begin our first level of analysis with the most similar uses, so we begin with those occurrences that combine the verb with the preposition *be*, as in Job. This phrase features both a direct and indirect object in a collocation that occurs only three other times (1 Sam. 26:19; 2 Sam. 24:1; Jer. 43:3). In each of these, person A (subject) incites person B (direct object) against person C (indirect object) into taking a course of action that is contrary to what is expected, beneficial, or desired by person C.

	Person A	Person B	Person C	Action
1 Sam. 26:19	Yahweh	Saul	David	Pursuing him
2 Sam. 24:1	Yahweh (or his anger)	David	Israel	Take census
Jer. 43:3	Baruch	Jeremiah	Israel	Deliver to Babylonians
Job 2:3	*śatan*	Yahweh	Job	Ruin him without cause

Another set of occurrences feature a subject (person A) of the verb and a direct object (person B) but no indirect object (person C).

	Person A	Person B	Action
Deut. 13:6 (Heb. 7)	Close relative	Israelite	Worship other gods
1 Kings 21:25	Jezebel	Ahab	Do evil (context: Naboth)
1 Chron. 21:1	*śatan*	David	Take census
2 Chron. 18:2	Ahab	Jehoshaphat	Attack Ramoth Gilead

2 Chronicles 32:11, 15; 2 Kings 18:32; Isaiah 36:18	Hezekiah	Israel	Oppose Assyria
Job 36:18	No one	Sufferer/Job	Pursue riches
Jeremiah 38:22	False prophets	Zedekiah	Oppose Babylon

In these passages, person A is in a position of influence behind the scenes and would be considered complicit and responsible for the action of person B. Person B, however, is the one who actually is held accountable and is not considered a victim taken advantage of.

In the first table, the incited action is always negative for person C, though it is not intrinsically a sinful or evil action. Do ill feelings in person A motivate him to incite someone against person C? In 1 Samuel 26, we may hypothetically ask whether David is truly out of favor with Yahweh; if so, the inciting of Saul would be a reflection of that disfavor. In 2 Samuel 24, the author specifically states that Yahweh is angry with Israel. In Jeremiah 43, it appears that there has been some tension between Baruch and the Israelites, since they cast blame on him, but there is not enough information for us to draw a definitive conclusion.

When we bring this information to Job 2:3, we can conclude most importantly that, as person B, Yahweh is accountable for the action against Job, though the Challenger has influenced the decision. In this case, Job as person C has no knowledge of the Challenger's role and never voices any suspicion that another party might be involved; therefore, any potential disfavor toward Job on the Challenger's part (as person A, usually the driving force in these scenarios) cannot be assumed and is not part of the plot. It is true that person A cannot be exonerated from harboring ill feelings against person C, but there are not enough data to allow us to conclude that such ill feelings are intrinsically involved. In fact, the context here argues against this, as Yahweh specifically says he has been incited against Job "without any reason."

Job 22:2–3

The commentaries and translations regularly take the Hebrew word *geber* (NIV, Hartley: "man"; Habel: "hero"; Clines: "human") as the subject of the verb in the first clause of 22:2. The occurrence of the same construction in 34:9 shows, however, that *geber* must be the object rather than the subject, as I have rendered it.

I have proposed the interpretive "wise mediator" as the subject of the first sentence, which is a translation of the noun *maśkil*, which both in the

Hebrew text and in most translations (NIV, Hartley: "wise man"; Habel, Clines: "sage") occurs in the second line. Evidence that it should be considered the subject of this sentence is based on Job 34:9 (NIV: "It profits a man nothing when he tries to please God"), which uses the same verb as 22:2 (*skn*). What is in effect the subject in 34:9 also comes in the following line, in the phrase "when he tries to please God" (i.e., his attempts to please God profit a man nothing).

If the *geber* in 22:2 refers to a human being, as seems probable, then the *maśkil* must be someone else; this is the primary evidence for my translation of *maśkil* as "wise mediator." It is possible that Eliphaz is referring to his own role, but it would be unusual for him to refer to himself in such an obtuse way. Since the next verse at least alludes to Job's case, I propose that Eliphaz refers to the mediator that Job has been requesting. Job has not used the noun *maśkil* to designate this individual, but it is not surprising that Eliphaz chooses a different word from the one Job has been using. I have suggested that Job thinks of his advocate as a heavenly being (p. 214), an idea that Eliphaz has already pronounced useless (5:1). Here Eliphaz indulges Job by considering the role of an intermediary, but does so by referring noncommittally to any prudent, insightful individual who could be called on to serve as mediator. By definition, this mediator would speak on behalf of God as well as advocate for the human being. The mediator role is suitably expressed by this noun, which does not just refer to a sage, but to a particular type of wise man. Fox describes the root word (*śekel*) as:

> Insight, the ability to grasp the meanings or implications of a situation or message ... the ability to understand practical matters and interpersonal relations and make beneficial decisions.[1]

Waltke agrees with this assessment and adds that this prudent person "gives attention to a threatening situation, has insight into its solution, acts decisively, and thereby effects success and life and prevents failure and death."[2] Such is the role of a mediator.

I have rendered the verb *skn* as "do any good."[3] The NIV, Hartley, and Clines go the same direction while Habel chooses "endanger" on the basis of some slight cognate evidence. From the words used in parallel with *skn* in other passages, translators have deduced that *skn* has to do with profit or benefit; whatever its specific nuance, this is certainly the general drift.

---

1. Fox, *Proverbs 1–9*, 36.

2. Waltke, *Book of Proverbs, chapters 1–15*, 94.

3. The Qal form of the verb that occurs here occurs only in Job (15:3; 34:9; 35:3). It also occurs in Hiphil forms in three additional locations (Num. 22:30; Job 22:21; Ps. 139:3).

The basic thrust of Eliphaz's statement would then be: "Do you really think that a mediator will do you any good?"

Unlike the other translators, I have not set God as the direct or indirect object ("benefit [to] God") but removed him grammatically one step further from the action ("on behalf of God"). I base this decision on the other two occurrences of this construction (13:7 and 21:22; nowhere else in the Old Testament). A comparison of these verses will help us to see the parallel constructions:

Job 13:7	*hale'el*	*tedabberu*	*'awlah*
	Is it on behalf of God	you speak	wickedness
Job 21:22	*hale'el*	*yelammed*	*da'at*
	Is it on behalf of God	he teaches	knowledge
Job 22:2	*hale'el*	*yiskan*	*gaber*
	Is it on behalf of God	he benefits	human being
Grammar	interrogative (*ha*) + preposition *l-* + God (*'el*)	verb (imperfect)	noun abstraction as direct object

It seems clear to me from 13:7 that this opening combination must be translated, "Is it on behalf of God ...?"[4]

We have already established that *geber* must be the object of the verb (see comments above), and I have already indicated that as an abstraction, it should be rendered "human being." This translation is confirmed by the other two occurrences of the same construction (shown in the chart), which also have abstractions as the object.[5]

The Hebrew text of 22:3 begins with the noun translated pleasure or desire (*hps*, NIV: "pleasure"; Habel: "favor"; Hartley, Clines: "asset") preceded by the interrogative particle. First Samuel 15:22 (and many other

---

4. When we apply this to the second occurrence in 21:22, it revises our understanding of that verse. The NIV translates, "Can anyone teach knowledge to God, since he judges even the highest?" But if the combination requires the opening "Is it on behalf of God ..." then the subject of the verb "teach" is the wicked man (from earlier in the context) and the second half of the verse switches the subject to God. This should then be translated: "Does he [the wicked man] teach knowledge on behalf of God, when he [God] is the one who judges even the highest?"

5. In 13:7 the abstraction "wickedness" (*'awlah*) is the object of the verb, and in 21:22, the abstraction "knowledge" (*da'at*) is the object of the verb.

passages) indicate that this noun refers to receiving something with pleasure or favor. Eliphaz's rhetorical question suggests that he does not think God will respond favorably at all, an assessment born out later in the book.[6]

Contrary to the others, who render the verb in the first line simply as "be righteous/innocent," I have rendered it as "justify yourself" on the evidence of Job 40:8. The Qal form of the verb *ṣdq* is furthermore used for vindication numerous times in Job (see, e.g., 11:2; 13:8).

Finally, the last verb in 22:3 (Hiph. of *tmm*) is challenging. The translations above treat it variably as an adjective (expressed as fact, "to be blameless," Clines, NIV; or as a claim of blamelessness, Hartley) or as a verb ("to perfect your ways," Habel). It *is* a verbal form, and the Hiphil only occurs eight times.[7] My translation, "Give full account of your ways," is based on the observation that in many of the other contexts, it roughly concerns paying off or rendering account of something (note esp. 2 Kings 22:4).[8]

Job 24:22-23

The verb *mašak* that occurs in 24:22 also occurs in 21:33 as all men "follow after" the wicked. In Judges 4:6 this verb indicates the manner in which God will draw out Sisera and the Canaanites into battle.[9] Here, the wicked man's influence on the mighty forms a merism with his treatment of the vulnerable in 24:21.

The noun *'abbir* (in 24:22 in the plural) is used of princes/warriors— people in high positions of power, whether oppressive or not (Job 34:20; Ps. 76:5; Isa. 10:13).[10] Here it is the direct object of verb *mašak*.

qum. This is the familiar word for arising. Based on other uses in Job, I would translate it as arising to a position of power: He "takes his stand" (in 15:29, "endure"; 19:25 "will stand"; 30:28, "stand up in the assembly").

---

6. In 40:8 God is not pleased that Job has condemned him in order to justify himself (same imperfect Qal used in 22:3).

7. Besides here, 2 Sam. 20:18; 2 Kings 22:4; Isa. 33:1; Ezek. 22:15; 24:10; Dan. 8:23; 9:24.

8. See 2 Sam. 20:18, resolving issues at Abel; 2 Kings 22:4, Hilkiah rendering an account of the funds; Isa. 33:1, bringing a final resolution to their destroying ways; Ezek. 22:15, bringing resolution to their uncleanness; Ezek. 24:10, the meat is not just cooked, it is rendered/ resolved into stew; Dan. 8:23, their rebellions have been fully rendered; Dan. 9:24, transgression drawn to a resolution (though there is a textual variant here). It is clear that none of these have anything to do with blamelessness or innocence. The other translations are making the mistake of construing the Hiphil as too dependent on the Qal and the adjective. This fallacy involves valuing diachronic information higher than synchronic information.

9. For other similar uses, see Song 1:4; Isa. 5:18; Jer. 31:3; Hos. 7:5; 11:4.

10. Refers to people in nine other contexts: 1 Sam. 21:7; Job 34:20; Pss. 22:12 (metaphor); 76:5; 78:25; Isa. 10:13; 46:12; Jer. 46:15; Lam. 1:15.

'amin bahayyin. I would change to 'amin behayyaw, as most do.[11] The combination also occurs in Deuternonomy 28:66 ("never sure of your life"), where it indicates, as here, a precarious position. In Job 24 the wicked rises in position and power but is never secure (always in danger from his fragile sway over powerful people).

Job 24:23 begins in Hebrew with the verb *yitten*, which can be indefinite ("there is"; see Job 3:20). The wicked person in his precarious position of power continues as the singular subject. He does everything that he can to ensure his own safety (*bth*), for he realizes how tenuous it is (presumably because he is involved in all sorts of manipulative schemes).

weyiššaʿen is perhaps the most problematic word in 24:22–23 because all other twenty-one uses of the Niphal form occur in collocation with a preposition, while here it stands alone; this leaves unanswered the question of what the wicked person is relying on. The root *šʿn* is used often enough in combination with *bth* (e.g., Prov. 3:5; Isa. 50:10) to clearly indicate "rely/depend" as the meaning; the context in Job 24 suggests that the wicked person is relying on himself and the measures that he has taken for his safety.

Nevertheless, the wicked person's eyes are "on their [the mighty ones'] ways." This phrase parallels the last phrase of the previous verse that spoke of his insecurity. Here he can never takes his eyes off those whom he has dragged along and continues to manipulate. This speaks of the paranoia of those who gain power at the expense of others.

---

11. The *nun* would be an Aramaic plural and totally out of place. The orthographic difference between *nun* and *waw* is negligible, making it easy to mistake them for one another.

Scripture Index

Genesis

1 . . .119, 334, 352, 411
1:2 251
1:3 119
1:6 369
1:7 250
1:8 295
1:21 . . . . . .85, 163, 406
1:26 63
2–3 . . . . .84, 211
2 . . . . .286, 352
2:6 367
2:7 172
3 . . . .81, 85, 259, 407
3:1 211
3:15 171
3:19 . . . . .172, 219
3:22 63
4:10 214
5:24 . . . . .129, 132
6:2 . . . . .63, 400
6:3 353
6:4 . . . . .63, 400
6:6–7 48
9:13–16 254
9:25 122
10:23 56
11:7 63
11:28 68
12:8 . . . . .166, 168
15:12–21 157
16:8 . . . . .64, 100
18:14 369
18:20–21 . . . . .163, 270
18:25 . . . . .187, 188, 384
18:27, 29 31
19:24 70
20:5 57
20:6 57
20:11 58
22:12 48
22:20–21 351

22:21 56
22:22 70
23:3 68
23:7 71
25:2 105
25:3, 14 69
26:22 166
26:25 168
27:28, 39 103
27:29 121
29:4 100
29:15 100
31:47 215
32:22 68
33:3–7 71
33:19 . . . . .23, 168
34 104
34:7 434
35:18 352
36:21, 28 56
37:35 126
40:19, 22 253
41:13 253
41:32 173
41:40 327
42:6 72
42:7 100
42:18 58
42:23 . . . . .215, 356
42:38 126
44:29, 31 126
47:18 162
47:31 71
49:6 315
50:1 68
50:17 164

Exodus

3:20 431
4:1 178
4:31 71
8:26 173

12 86
12:27 71
15:12 253
19:9 254
22:28 . . . . . .59, 60, 121
23:7 260
23:21 164
24:11 . . . . .129, 220
26:9 176
27:20 165
28:3 . . . . .352, 373
29:13 221
30:34 165
31:6 373
32 48
32:12, 14 432
33:19 68
34:6 68
34:7 164
35:10, 25 373
36:1, 2, 8 373
39:3 369

Leviticus

10:2 70
10:3 68
18:30 434
19:10 130
24:2, 7 165
24:10–16 60
24:11 59
25:25 218

Numbers

3:4 68
11:1 70
11:13 100
12:8 433
14:18 164
16:35 70
16:39 369
20:12 159

21:5, 8 433
22 76
22:6, 12 121
22:22 . . . . . . .65, 75, 76
22:30 . . . . .245, 451
22:32 . . . . . . .65, 75, 76
23:7 121
24:8, 17 258
35:19 218

Deuteronomy

book 437
1:35 323
4:7 267
6:18 57
8:17 . . . . .58, 60
9:4 60
9:19 124
11:16 327
13:6 449
13:14 173
18:21 58
19:6 – 12 218
21:22 – 23 253
25:1 260
25:8 160
28:31 – 35 70
28:60 124
28:66 454
29:19 60
32:4 57
32:8 64
32:10 251
32:22 . . . . .127, 128
32:34 – 35 180
32:39 258
33:11 258
33:26 371
33:29 169

Joshua

2:4 100
2:13 131
3:5 431
6:26 60
7:19 162
8:29 253
9:8 100
10:26 253

24:14 363
24:19 164
24:32 23

Judges

4:6 453
5:26 258
6:13 431
13:6 100
13:18 . . . . .369, 431
14:2 322
16:26, 29 173
17:6 57
17:9 100
19 – 20 104
19:17 100
19:23 434
21:25 57

Ruth

book 218
1:17 323
1:20 259

1 Samuel

2:6 41
3:17 – 18 162
4:21 246
8:11 – 17 323
10:23 158
12:21 251
15:22 452
19:5 101
19:11 131
20:9 – 14 160
20:20 213
21:7 453
23:23 173
25:11 100
25:28 164
25:31 101
26 450
26:4 173
26:19 449
28:13 253
29:4 65

2 Samuel

1:2 70

1:3 . . . . .64, 100
1:13 100
4:12 253
7:6 101
7:17 157
7:19 363
13 104
13:12 434
13:39 432
14:18 162
15:2 100
15:4 260
16:5 – 14 174
16:5 – 13 60
16:10 – 11 174
18:10 253
19:23 65
20:18 453
21:1 75
22:10 168
22:12 371
22:16 257
22:39 258
22:43 369
23:9 261
24 . . . . .75 – 76, 450
24:1 449
24:10 164

1 Kings

1:47 71
2:6 127
2:31 101
3:12 373
3:28 295
5:4 65
5:15 179
8:32 260
9:7 68
10:19 255
10:24 295
11 76
11:9 – 14 76
11:14, 23, 25 65
17:22 226
19:11 70
19:13 327
21:10, 13 59

21:25 449
22 . . . . .63, 76
22:19 – 23 76

2 Kings

1:12 70
2:1, 11 398
2:16 128
2:24 60
4:35 226
5:25 100
6:27 100
6:31 323
13:14 68
13:21 226
18:32 450
19:25 363
20 321
20:14 100
22:4 453

1 Chronicles

1:17 56
1:42 56
21 76
21:1 . . . . .65, 75, 449
21:15 432
27:24 75

2 Chronicles

6:23 260
15:3 365
18:2 449
24:2 57
32:11, 15 450
32:31 . . . . .215, 356

Ezra

3:13 363

Nehemiah

1:7 360

Esther

book 253

Job

1 – 2 . . . . 21, 65, 108,
110, 124, 292

1 . . . . . . .247, 333, 434
1:1 . . . 22, 104, 165, 259,
292, 398
1:4 – 5 . . . .124, 271, 293
1:6 400
1:7 – 8 100
1:7 100
1:8 . . .103, 104, 292, 293
1:9 . . . . .21, 101, 292
1:10 . . . . . . .21, 103, 134
1:11 109
1:12 109
1:14 356
1:15 23
1:17 23
1:21 . . . . 101, 102, 119,
247, 271
2 . . . . .185, 323
2:1 . . . . .63, 400
2:2 64
2:3 . . . . . 67, 70, 98, 174,
292, 433, 449 – 50
2:5 . . . . .59, 119
2:7 . . . . .57, 398
2:8 219
2:9 59
2:10 . . . 41, 96, 119, 135,
171, 187, 271, 434
2:11 . . . . .222, 351
3 . . . .29, 174, 350, 406
3:5 254
3:8, 9 74
3:8 167
3:20 454
3:23 271
4 – 27 29
4 – 14 . . . . .229, 266, 270
4 – 5 181
4:6 – 7 . . . . .43, 107
4:6 . . . . . . .210, 223, 291
4:8 106
4:12 – 21 212
4:12 – 16 106
4:12 264
4:15 68
4:17 . . .43, 107, 108, 212
4:18 – 21 43
4:18 . . . . .212, 356

5:1 . . . . .214, 451
5:2 327
5:3 106
5:8 – 16 . . . . .43, 108
5:8 . . . . . .107, 223, 263
5:9 431
5:12 . . . . .210, 211
5:17 – 19 107
5:18 – 27 43
5:18 258
6 – 7 181
6:4 357
6:14 . . . . .271, 291
6:18 251
6:22 – 23 356
6:24 261
6:28 357
6:30 . . . . .178, 260
7 246
7:9 . . . . .125, 254
7:11 210
7:12 . . . . . .332, 406, 410
7:13 210
7:14 . . . . .271, 355
7:16 . . . . .261, 432
7:17 – 24 362
7:17 – 21 . . . . . . .62, 245
7:17 – 19 271
7:17 212
7:20 213
7:21 . . . . .219, 271
8 181
8:2 . . . . .358, 363
8:3 . . . . . . .43, 108, 217
8:4 – 7 107
8:4 . . . . .43, 59
8:5 – 7 . . . . .43, 107
8:5 223
8:8 106
8:9 107
8:10 261
8:13 261
8:18 101
8:20 – 22 . . . . . . .43, 108
9 – 10 . . . . .181, 224
9 . . . . .246, 402
9:2 – 3 271
9:3 . . . . .373, 405

9:4–10 . . . . . .249, 272
9:4 . . . . . .294, 370, 373
9:5–9 224
9:6 257
9:8 252
9:10 431
9:14–20 . . . . . .271, 370
9:14 223
9:17 433
9:20 . . . . .57, 211
9:21 . . . . .357, 432
9:22 . . . . .57, 271
9:27 210
9:28 124
9:29 261
9:33 214
9:35 291
10:1 210
10:2 404
10:3 271
10:7–8 101
10:9 219
10:12 408
10:13 . . . . .224, 433
10:14–17 271
10:16 431
10:21–22 253
11 181
11:2 453
11:5 223
11:7–9 . . . . .43, 107
11:8 125
11:11 . . . . . .43, 103, 107
11:13–19 107
11:13–14 263
12–14 . . . . .181, 224
12:2–3 225
12:9 . . . . .292, 398
12:13–25 . . . . . .43, 271
12:13 . . . . .295, 332
12:24 251
13:7 . . . . . .248, 260, 452
13:8 453
13:15 218
13:16 261
13:20 408
14:6 271
14:12 . . . . .219, 220

14:13 125
14:20 271
15–21 . . . . .184, 266
15:3 451
15:4 291
15:7–16 43
15:7 408
15:8 315
15:10 363
15:14 . . . . .107, 165, 166
15:15 162
15:18 162
15:20–35 . . . . . .43, 107
15:29 453
15:34 261
16:7–14 271
16:7 165
16:9–14 332
16:9 109
16:17 165
16:19–21 172
16:20 356
17:6 271
17:8 261
17:13, 16 125
18:5–21 . . . . . . .43, 107
18:14 . . . . .74, 317
19:6–20 271
19:6 . . . . .43, 165
19:7 188
19:18 433
19:19 315
19:21 109
19:25 453
20:4–29 . . . . . . .43, 107
20:5 261
20:27 261
21 246
21:13–16 245
21:13 125
21:14–16 245
21:22 . . . . .222, 244–45,
                          452
21:23–26 245
21:31–33 245
21:31 68
21:33 453
21:34 261

22–27 184
22:2–3 450–53
22:2 . . . . .357, 452
22:3 . . .38, 107, 452, 453
22:4 . . . . .161, 291
22:5–9 . . . . .43, 107
22:12–14 . . . . . .43, 108
22:15–20 . . . . . .43, 107
22:19 175
22:21 . . . . .107, 451
22:23 . . . . .107, 432
23:4 161
23:8–9 178
24 454
24:12 . . . . .43, 71
24:19 125
24:21 453
24:22–23 453–54
25:2 . . . . .43, 108
25:4–6 43
25:4 . . . . . .107, 165, 166
25:5 213
26:3 176
26:6 . . . . .125, 288
26:10 256
26:12 171
27–28 31
27 30–31
27:1–6 . . .293, 358, 360
27:1 30
27:2–6 34
27:2 188
27:3–5 353
27:4 . . . . .177, 178
27:6 163
27:7–23 30
27:11–12 162
28 . . . . .29, 30–31,
                   332, 337, 445
28:1 366
28:10 256
28:12 100
28:22 250
28:27 372
28:28 29
29–41 29
29–31 30–31
29:1 30

29:14 166
30 . . . . .406, 410
30:18 – 23 433
30:19 187
30:22 176
30:28 453
31 . . . . .350, 433
31:12 . . . . .250, 288
31:15 187
31:23 124
31:24 157
31:25 363
31:26 – 28 38
31:37 365
32:11 178
32:12 172
32:16 . . . . .103, 178
33:9 165
33:13 404
33:15 157
33:18 74
33:23 215
33:33 211
34:5 188
34:9 . . . . .450, 451
34:12 . . . . .165, 188
34:15 219
34:17 188
34:20 453
35:3 451
35:11 211
35:16 261
36 – 37 30
36:1 30
36:18 450
37:5 431
37:9 170
37:11 254
37:14 431
37:15 254
37:24 . . . . .103, 291
38 – 42 292
38 – 41 177
38 186
38:1 57
38:7 . . . . .63, 73
38:8 – 11 290
38:8 256

38:9 . . . . .254, 256
38:10 . . . . .215, 256
38:11 256
38:12 120
38:15 245
38:16 – 17 250
38:22 – 30 290
38:22 170
38:31 – 32 169
38:32 170
38:37 372
39:14 130
39:29 363
40:1 57
40:2 . . . . . .73, 162, 172
40:3 57
40:4 – 5 431
40:6 57
40:7 – 14 111
40:8 . . . . . 43, 171, 188,
          210, 267, 350,
          351, 357, 453
40:10 – 14 369
40:23 178
41 121
41:4 175
41:33 219
41:34 286
42 . . . . .173, 188
42:1 – 6 29
42:1 57
42:3 . . . . .174, 398
42:6 . . . . .186, 219
42:7 – 8 . . . . . . .173, 230
42:7 . . .57, 177, 178, 188
42:8 104
42:9 – 12 57
42:11 . . . . .23, 109
42:12 59
42:14 24

Psalms
book 419
1 42
2:4 175
3:3 129
5:9 173
6:5 131

6:6 127
7:9 221
8 . . . . .163 – 64
8:4 212
9:20 68
10:3 59
11:7 . . . . .128, 129, 220
13:1 378
13:2 131
14:1 . . . . .60, 104
16 131
16:9 – 11 . . . . . .128, 130
16:10 . . . . .126, 131
16:11 131
17:7 261
17:15 . . . . .129, 220
18 132
18:9 168
18:15 257
18:16 – 19 132
18:38 258
19:14 218
21:9 101
22:7 175
22:12 453
24:1 253
25:14 315
26:7 373
27:4 . . . . .129, 220
27:12 218
27:13 42
29:1 . . . . .63, 400
30:2 – 3 131
31:5, 6 353
32:1 164
34:18 267
37 437
37:7 44
37:10 322
37:25 – 26 378
37:25 44
38:20 65
40:10 162
44 42
49:13 157
49:14 – 15 131
49:14 130
49:15 . . . . .129, 132

50:16 373
50:18 357
50:20 433
51:6 165
53:1 60
55:14 315
55:15 126
55:19–20 179
59:12 261
63:2 . . . . .129, 220
63:3 129
68:21, 23 258
69:10 261
71:13 65
72:13 131
73:13 165
73:23–24 132
73:24 . . . . .129, 132
74:3 131
74:13–14 163
74:14 . . . .121, 334, 407
75:3 167
76:5 453
76:9 218
78:4 162
78:7 157
78:18 58
78:23 371
78:25 453
78:26 170
78:35 218
80:17 130
81:3 255
82 . . . . .64, 159
82:1 64
82:2 378
82:3 260
82:6 64
82:7 329
85:8 157
87:4 171
88:3, 10–12 127
88:11 . . . . .250, 288
89:6–7 372
89:7 . . .63, 315, 373, 400
89:11 171
89:37 372
89:38 373

90:13 432
91:13 286
104:2–3 252
104:2 . . . . . . .168, 253
104:7–8 255
104:7 257
104:9 256
104:24 295
104:26 . . . .121, 334, 406
104:29 353
106:9 257
107:40 251
109:4, 6, 20, 29 65
110:1 130
110:5, 6 258
111:1 315
118:15–18 130
119:9 165
119:39 124
119:42 261
119:78 . . . . . . .165, 217
119:97, 99 210
121:1 100
136:6 . . . . .253, 370
139 379
139:1–6 172
139:3 . . . . .245, 451
139:6 431
139:8 127
139:11 171
139:12 158
139:13 . . . . . . .191, 221
139:18 129
139:21 261
143:2 158
144:5–6 168
145:18 267
146:9 165

Proverbs
book 437
1:11–12 101
2:6 295
2:7 176
2:18 250
3:4 58
3:5 454
3:19 . . . . .258, 295

3:20 371
3:21 176
3:26 157
5:13 365
7:20 255
8 . . . . .257, 295
8:14 176
8:27–29 . . . . . .255, 256
8:28 371
9:18 250
10:8 373
10:9 57
11:13 315
11:29 373
15:11 . . . . .127, 250, 288
16:2 165
16:21, 23 373
17:15 260
18:1 176
19:28 101
20:9, 11 165
20:19 . . . . .315, 327
21:8 165
21:20 101
22:25 211
23:16 221
27:11 261
27:20 288
28:18 57

Ecclesiastes
book 45
1:15 165
2:2 159
2:26 295
3 303
3:21 253
5:19 236
6:6 127
6:12 270
7:4 373
7:7 159
7:11–14 303
7:13 165
7:14 41
7:25–29 402
7:25 . . . . .157, 159
7:29 57

8–9 428
8:5 373
8:17 410
10:2 373
10:13 159
12:3 165
12:7 353

Song of Songs
1:4 453
4:4 253
8:6 326

Isaiah
1:16 165
3:9 162
5:18 453
5:23 260
6 315
6:8 63
8:21 60
9:12 168
9:14 365
9:17 . . . . .168, 434
9:21 168
10:13 453
10:34 220
11:2 352
13:9 332
14 . . . . . . 79–80, 81, 83
14:5 78
14:9–11 . . . . . . .78, 125
14:9 250
14:12–15 78
14:12 79
14:13 60
16:6 175
16:14 363
17:6 220
17:12 363
19:1 254
21:4 167
22:1, 5 157
22:24 253
23:8 101
24:10 251
24:13 220
25:6 366
26:5 365

26:14 . . . . .227, 250
26:15 227
26:19 . . . . 129, 227,
                250, 253
27:1 . . . . .121, 259
28:2 363
28:15 126
28:29 176
29:21 251
30:7 171
30:20 365
31:2 294
32:6–7 104
33:1 453
34:11 251
36:18 450
38 321
38:18 127
39:3 100
40–49 251
40:13–14 . . . . . .63, 80
40:15 372–73
40:17 251
40:22 . . . . .168, 252, 256
40:23 251
40:26 . . . . .120, 168
40:28 288
41:13 100
41:29 251
42:5 . . . . .252, 370
43:27 . . . . .215, 356
44:5 354
44:6 218
44:9 251
44:22 254
44:24 . . . . .252, 370
44:25 176
45:4 354
45:7 41
45:8 371
45:12 . . . . .168, 252
45:18 251
45:19 251
46:12 453
47:1 219
47:8 . . . . .60, 80
47:10 60
48:12 218

49:4 251
49:7, 26 218
50:2 257
50:8 260
50:10 454
51:9 . . . . .171, 258
51:13 252
51:15 258
53:11 260
55:8–9 135
57:6 432
59:3 . . . . .177, 178
59:4 . . . . .178, 251
59:8 57

Jeremiah
4:13 254
4:23 251–52
4:28 432
5:22 256
8:6 432
10:12 . . . . .252, 258
11:20 221
15:18 131
17:10 221
18:8, 10 432
18:10 432
20:9 353
20:12 221
21:2 273
23:13 71
23:18, 22 315
23:23 267
25:20 56
25:23 351
29:23 434
31:3 453
31:15 432
31:35 258
32:7–8 218
38:14 162
38:22 450
38:25 162
43 450
43:3 449
46:15 453
48:30 175
50:2 162

50:34 258
50:36 175
50:42 332
51:15 252

Lamentations

1:15 453
2:2, 5, 8, 16 101
3:12 213
3:36 . . . . .165, 217
4:21 56

Ezekiel

1:4 398
3:14 128
6:10 100
6:11 369
8:3 128
9:9 365
10 398
13:9 315
14:14, 20 . . . . . . .24, 98
14:22 432
15:3 253
16:51 – 52 356
22:15 453
24:10 453
28 . . . . .83, 84
28:12 – 19 . . . 78, 80 – 83
28:12 211
28:14 82
32:7 254
32:10 68
32:31 432
33:15 434
37 227

Daniel

4:3 164
7:2 258
8:23 453
9:24 453
12 215
12:1 – 3 . . . 133, 227 – 28
12:2 129
12:3 260

Hosea

2:6 137

2:18 419
6:3 173
6:7 329
7:5 453
7:11 327
11:4 453
13:2 327
13:12 180
13:15 70

Joel

2:13 432
2:28 157

Amos

1:11 131
3:7 315
4:13 169
5:8 169
7:3, 6 432
8:5 165
9:2 . . . . .126, 127

Jonah

1:2 . . . . .163, 270
1:8 100
2:2 250
2:6 253
3:5 159
3:10 . . . . .48, 432
4:2 432
4:8 70

Micah

1:3 168
3:9 57
6:9 176
6:11 165

Nahum

1:4 257
3:7 100
3:8 158

Habakkuk

2:18 365
3:13 258
3:19 169

Zephaniah

1:12 60
2:15 80
3:8 218

Haggai

2:23 83

Zechariah

3:1 – 2 . . . . .65, 75
3:4 164
12:1 . . . . .252, 353
13:3 433
13:4 157

Malachi

3:3 366
4:1 130

Matthew

4 87
5:10 – 12 422
5:11 – 12 236
5:45 416
10:22 226
19:21 – 30 236
25:31 – 46 336

Luke

6:35 236
8:14 137
10:17 83
10:18 83
13:1 – 5 47
14:26 . . . . .236, 422
16 133
19:17 280

John

8:3 – 11 385
8:44 84
9 48
9:1 – 3 47
9:3 428
12:31 83
16:33 236

Acts

3 20

13:35 131
14:22 236

Romans
1:20 . . . . .381, 417
3:23 192
5:3 422
8:15–17 441
8:18–25 419
8:28 270
11:33–36 447
12:1–2 279
16:20 . . . . .85, 171

1 Corinthians
1:18–21 422
11:30 301

2 Corinthians
11:14 83
12:9–10 236

Galatians
6:7 . . . . .48, 230, 420

Philippians
1:29–30 236
3:8 280
3:10 . . . . .236, 422
3:11 280
3:14 280

Colossians
1:24 422

1 Timothy
2:5 . . . . .225, 267
3:6 84

Hebrews
4:11 336
8:6 225
9:15 225
10:19–31 336
10:32–34 236
11:32–40 . . . . .236, 422
12:7 236
12:24 225

James
1:2–5 441
1:2–4 236
2:14–26 336
5:11 . . . . . .24, 188, 441

1 Peter
2:19–25 422
2:19–21 236
3:8–4:19 422
3:14–17 236
4:12–19 . . . . . .236, 302

2 Peter
2:4 83

1 John
3:11–24 336

Revelation
9:11 288
12:9 . . . . .83, 85
20:2 85

Subject Index

abaddon, see Destruction/*abaddon*
accommodationist hermeneutics,
    272–75, *see also* concordist herme-
    neutics; Old World Science
Adapa, 25, 211
advocate, *see* mediator
afterlife, 41–42, 123, 125–34,
    139–41, 179, 184, 215, 220,
    227–28, 250–51, 321, *see also*
    Destruction/*abaddon*; resurrection;
    Sheol/netherworld
ancient authors, 23–25
ancient Near East, court documents
    from, 215, 244, 263, 371; creation
    accounts/cosmology, 172–73,
    272, 401; friends as representa-
    tives of, 106–8, 160, 374; sages,
    122; texts related to Job, 31–33;
    theology of, 33–41, 43, 61–63,
    72, 74, 85, 106–8, 157–58, 160,
    170, 172–73, 180, 192, 250, 253,
    257–58, 265, 272, 288–89, 301,
    316, 318, 327–28, 334–35, 351,
    355, 361, 368, 379, 400, 414; *see
    also* cosmic geography; gods; Great
    Symbiosis
angels 63, 83, 159, 164; *see also* demons;
    Sons of God
appeasement, *see* gods, appeasement of
authority of the Bible, 24, 86, 226, 266,
    268–69, 272–77, 352

Behemoth, 397, 406–11, 413, 431,
    435, 438
benefits, *see* righteousness, disinterested
blessing, *see* Retribution Principle (RP)

Chaldeans, 23, 69–70
Challenger, the, 20, 21, 22, 27, 31, 34,
    36, 48, 59, 62–69, 71, 73–75, 78,
    86, 98, 100–101, 106–9, 118, 123,
    134, 161, 171, 182, 184, 186–88,
    198, 214, 259, 262, 265–67, 275,
    293–94, 331, 352, 358, 374, 399,
    412, 436, 450; *see also* Sons of God
chaos, 85, 119, 167, 175, 257–58, 425;
    see also cosmic order
chaos creatures, 120–21, 163, 168,
    171, 259, 317, 332, 334–35, 406,
    410, 418–19; *see also* Behemoth;
    Leviathan; Rahab
children of Job, 24, 43, 58–62, 68–70,
    98, 182, 302, 316, 434–36
Christ, 47–48, 83, 96, 113, 128, 131,
    137, 139–40, 180, 189, 192, 199,
    218, 225–26, 229, 233, 235–36,
    267–68, 280, 338, 380, 385, 422,
    441
concordist hermeneutics, 251, 272–74,
    290; *see also* accommodationist
    hermeneutics; Old World Science
constellations, 169–70, 402
corporate identity, 313–14
cosmic geography, 166–75, 191,
    251–54, 256–57, 273, 287,
    399–400
cosmic laws, 39
cosmic mountain, 252
cosmic order, 29, 43, 104, 119–22,
    167–68, 171, 175, 249, 252,
    256–59, 264–65, 279, 290,
    295–97, 334–35, 400, 406,
    410–11, 413–14, 418–19, 422,
    424–25, 428, 438–39, 441–42; *see
    also* chaos; God, wisdom of
covenant, 23, 25, 41–42, 57, 70, 180,
    189, 267, 277, 321–23, 437–38; *see
    also* Retribution Principle (RP)
courtroom, *see* legal proceedings
cultic feasts, 58–59, 61; *see also* ritual
cursing, day of birth, 118–23; God,
    58–61, 68, 71, 102–5, 186–87,
    189, 435; others, 174, 261, 265, 319;
    self, 323–24

declarative praise genre, 35

Death/*mawet*/Mot, 74, 121, 216, 252, 258, 288, 317, 407

Deep/*tehom*, 163, 255, 257, 287; *see also* Sea/*yam*

demons, 33, 36, 38, 78, 86, 122, 157, 172, 191, 196–97, 217, 283, 288, 334; *see also* Challenger, the

Destruction/*'abaddon*, 250, 288, 326; *see also* Sheol/netherworld

dialogue section [chs. 4–27], 29, 243, 265, 312, 314, 330, 332–33, 355, 360

disciplinary correction, 137, 161, 181, 272; *see also* Elihu

discourse section [chs. 29–41], 29, 333, 355

disinterested righteousness, *see* righteousness, disinterested

divine council, *see* Sons of God/divine council

dreams/visions, 32, 129, 157, 160–61, 220, 315, 355, 381–82; *see also* revelation

Elihu, 28–30, 43–44, 165, 178, 188, 215, 293, 335, 350–88, 414–15

Enlil, 167, 289

Enki/Ea, 122, 167, 256, 397

Erra/Nergal, 122, 171, 334–35

Etana, 25

evil, 36, 39–41, 67, 74, 77–78, 85, 104–5, 280, 302, 399, 410, 421, 447; *see also* Challenger, the

faith/trust, 22–23, 41, 47, 96–97, 110–12, 134, 137, 139–40, 157, 178, 180–81, 190, 195, 197, 198–99, 233, 235, 269, 275–76, 282–83, 291–92, 300, 301, 303–6, 315, 325, 327, 336, 340, 412–13, 415, 420–22, 424, 426–29, 435, 438–39, 443–47; *see also* fear of the Lord

fear of the Lord, 29, 124, 277, 285, 290–91, 296, 299–304

forgiveness, 35, 75, 164–65, 271, 280–81, 299, 301, 336, 385–86, 417

friends of Job, accusing Job, 21, 31, 98, 210–11, 223–25, 244–46, 260, 354; agents of the Challenger, 108, 161, 184, 186, 198, 262, 266, 294, 374; historicity, 26–27; in the narrative, 105, 432–35; Job's response to, 30, 34, 161–63, 177–78, 183, 189, 217, 224, 259–61, 265, 293; reflecting traditional ancient Near Eastern dogma, 36, 38, 43, 106, 351, 374; theology of (and critique), 29, 42–43, 72–74, 86, 104, 106–8, 122, 173–74, 176, 178, 181–85, 198, 216, 222–25, 230, 260–62, 266, 271, 275, 281, 290–91, 294, 296, 299, 330, 351–53, 360–61, 364, 375, 378, 414, 433, 442; *see also* Elihu; Great Symbiosis; Retribution Principle (RP); traditional dogma

Gilgamesh, 25, 126

God, anger of 34, 75–76, 224, 230, 271, 332, 398, 432, 450; accessibility, 271, 370, 380–81; as a watcher of men, 164; as mediator, 214; attributes of, 41, 111, 113, 190, 267, 269–71, 279, 289, 295, 359, 363, 377, 411, 414–18, 425, 439, 446; breath/Spirit of, 259, 280, 302, 340, 352–54, 369, 376–77, 381; cause of suffering 109, 112, 116, 173–74, 187, 196–97, 236, 259, 302–4, 331, 414; contingency/aseity of, 40, 303, 335, 358–59, 362, 375, 379–80, 388, 416; grace of, 111, 136–37, 140, 180, 189–90, 194, 270, 283, 357, 362, 380–81, 417, 441; inscrutable, 38, 97, 107, 176, 182, 332, 414; justice of, 22–23, 35, 38–39, 41–43, 46–47, 73, 108, 111, 125, 130, 134, 140, 165, 172, 182, 185–90, 210, 220, 230, 259, 269–71, 290, 294, 298–300, 332, 334–35, 350, 357–62, 368–69, 374–75, 377–81, 384–85, 401, 405, 410–17, 425–26, 428; names of, 60, 73–74, 291–92, 398; policies of, 21–23, 27, 42, 44, 48,

63, 66–69, 72–75, 106, 108–10,
171, 182, 185–86, 188, 198, 225,
245, 265–66, 331, 333, 335, 355,
359, 362, 364, 369, 375–76, 405,
410–14, 435–38, 442; power of,
23, 36, 41, 43, 71, 131, 140, 166,
170–71, 183, 187, 191, 197–98,
249, 251, 255, 258–59, 264–65,
271, 282–83, 291, 300, 305, 332,
334, 338, 354, 365, 370, 376,
379, 398–99, 411, 417, 427, 431,
442–43; protector, 43, 121, 123,
131, 134–37, 314, 383–84, 417,
424; reputation of, 48, 68, 331,
333, 337, 374; role in the cosmos,
190–92, 302, 361, 380, 382–84,
388–89, 402, 411, 416, 421, 431,
439; Spirit of, 354, 376–77; viewed
as petty, 171, 189–90, 192–95,
229–30, 271, 291–92, 333, 337,
388; wisdom of, 22–23, 32, 38,
44, 46–47, 135, 176, 191–92,
258, 269, 292, 294–95, 299–300,
302–4, 332–33, 399, 411–15,
417, 421–22, 428, 431, 438, 444,
446–47
"God of the gaps," 410–11
gods, 32, 63, 252, 379, 400, 403;
appeasement of, 32, 34–35, 38,
62–63, 75, 107, 160–61, 225, 262,
293–94, 301, 303, 318, 330; justice/
policies of, 33, 35–37, 39–41, 62,
122, 160, 191, 263, 265, 355, 402,
411, 416; responsibility of humans
for, 34, 37, 62, 265, 301, 361; see also
Great Symbiosis
Great Symbiosis, 34–38, 62–63, 74,
108–9, 180, 186, 235, 265, 275,
293, 301–3, 330, 352, 361–62,
374–75, 379, 423

harem, 323
"health-and-wealth," 443
historicity, see friends of Job, historicity;
Job (book), historicity; Job (character), historicity
honor, 60, 312–14, 317, 331, 354; see
also shame

hope, 129, 133–34, 137, 140–41, 179,
197–98, 283, 306, 422, 428; Job's,
125, 157, 159–63, 172, 178–79,
181, 185, 210, 214–15, 218–20,
224, 226, 229, 246, 264, 314, 424;
see also afterlife; faith/trust
humility, 115, 233, 279–80, 405, 429,
432, 443, 447; see also pride

illness, see sickness
Intelligent Design, 27

Jesus, see Christ
Job (book), artistry, 21; author of,
23–24, 26–27, 57–58, 61, 80,
86, 293, 352; central question of,
20–23, 27, 188–89, 294, 415,
436; composition history, 28; date,
23–24; Israelite provenance, 36,
38, 70, 74; genre, 24–27; historicity, 24–25; language, 23–24; see also
wisdom literature
Job (character), accusations against
God/flawed view of God, 86,
188–90, 213, 223–24, 229, 259,
267–68, 270–71, 332–35, 398–99,
401–2, 410, 418, 433–34; as not an
Israelite, 23, 57–58, 74, 133, 167,
180, 320; as plaintiff or defendant,
108, 182, 329; as role model, 20,
97–98, 188, 276, 278; as star witness for the defense, 182, 186, 266;
motivations of, 20, 21, 23, 62–63,
68–69, 74, 98, 124, 179–80,
184–86, 211, 293, 324, 329–31,
333, 358, 361, 364, 374–75, 388,
399, 434, 436; name, 25; repentance, 161, 183, 263–64, 281, 360,
375, 431–32; restoration, 33, 44,
59, 161, 166, 177, 180, 182–87,
198, 221, 225, 245–46, 261–64,
314, 330–31, 351, 356–57, 364,
374, 432–37; innocence/righteous-
ness of, 25, 35–36, 38, 42–48,
57–58, 62, 66–69, 72, 100–101,
105, 108, 119, 161, 163, 180,
182, 185–88, 198, 223–25, 230,
246–48, 260–61, 264–67, 293–94,

312, 318, 320–21, 330–31, 333, 350–51, 354, 358, 361, 364–65, 375, 381, 405–6, 413, 436; signature of, 329; suffering of, 22, 42, 69–70, 101, 105, 109, 116, 186, 189, 218, 246, 259, 262, 317, 355, 375–76, 404–6, 415, 434–35, 437; view of God in general, 62, 165, 171, 173, 230, 271, 332–36; *see also* righteousness, disinterested

Job's lament [ch. 3], 29, 118, 162, 174, 415

justice, *see* God, justice of; gods, justice/policies of

Kirtu, 25

lament genre, 27, 29, 34–35, 40, 118, 124–26, 134, 138, 271; *see also* Job's lament [ch. 3]

law of Moses, 23, 57, 136, 189, 277–78; *see also* covenant

Leviathan, 85, 120–23, 163, 259, 286, 334, 397, 406–11, 413, 431, 435, 438; *see also* chaos creatures

legal proceedings, 211, 246, 379–80, 404; God on trial, 20–21, 42, 72, 178, 182, 414, 443; in ancient Near East, 66, 164, 244, 263; Job seeking legal action, 73, 125, 160–61, 164–66, 171–72, 174, 176–79, 183–84, 186–87, 211, 214–15, 218, 222–26, 233, 246, 259, 263, 266, 321, 329–32, 350, 360, 370, 415, 431; *see also* mediator

life's transience, 163

literary artifice, 24–27

Ludlul bel nemeqi, 25, 32, 37, 158, 160, 182, 219

Marduk, 32, 122, 250, 254, 258, 334–35, 367, 397

mediator, 158, 214, 223–26, 244, 262, 266–67, 355–57, 434, 450–52; *see also* God, as mediator

monotheism, 39–40, 42, 45, 63, 74, 328

Moses, 23, 48

Mot, *see* Death/*mawet*/Mot

mourning, 70–71, 102, 105, 126, 214, 219–20, 317, 432

narrative frame [chs. 1–3, 42], 28–29, 59, 124, 177, 271, 292, 432

netherworld, *see* Sheol/netherworld

oaths, 60–61, 259, 312, 314, 318, 321, 323, 326, 329–31, 333, 336, 350, 433

Old World Science, 191, 272–73; *see also* accommodationist hermeneutics, concordist hermeneutics

Open Theism, 48

order, *see* cosmic order

patriarchal period, 23

Plato, 26–27, 198–99

philosophy, 26, 31–33, 36, 40–41, 67, 73, 97, 104, 107–10, 140, 185, 190, 193–94, 225, 228, 266, 269, 298, 334, 351–53, 358, 376–77, 401–2, 412, 438, 443

piety, 32, 34, 36, 37, 58, 124–25, 157, 181, 210, 223, 244, 276, 292, 294

polytheism, *see* gods

pride, 84, 175, 222, 224–25, 233, 280, 406, 409; *see also* humility

prosperity/wealth, 21, 22, 33, 35, 36, 38, 39, 44, 58, 61, 69, 87, 101, 107, 115, 134, 161, 177, 181–182, 186, 213, 216, 227, 235, 245, 246, 259, 261, 276, 286, 293–94, 303, 312, 316, 323–24, 327, 330–31, 357, 361, 364–65, 375, 432, 435–36, 443; *see also* righteousness, disinterested

priest, 10–11, 23, 215, 226, 315, 434; *see also* cultic feasts; ritual

Qoheleth, 45–47

Rahab, 171, 258–59, 334, 406; *see also* chaos creatures

repentance, *see* Job (character), repentance

Rephaim, 250

responsibility, *see* God, cause of suffering; Job (character), innocence/righteousness of

resurrection, 128, 131, 133–34, 179, 219–20, 226–29, 280; *see also* afterlife

Retribution Principle (RP), 21, 23, 32, 33, 38, 39–48, 59, 67–68, 73, 98, 101, 108–9, 125, 134, 137, 157, 166, 172, 181–3, 185–86, 189–90, 216, 225, 230–31, 236, 247, 249, 259, 262, 264, 266, 290, 294, 323, 331, 350, 352, 358–59, 363, 369, 374–76, 378–79, 384–85, 401, 405, 410, 413–14, 420, 422, 428, 434–39, 443; *see also* God, justice of; traditional dogma

revelation, 34, 73, 111, 158, 181, 189–90, 212, 215, 267–70, 272–75, 277–78, 302, 304, 334–35, 337, 376–77, 381–82, 398, 417; *see also* authority of the Bible; dreams/visions

rewards, *see* righteousness, disinterested

righteous, the, 21–23; *see also* Retribution Principle (RP)

righteousness, 34–35, 38, 63, 159; disinterested, 23, 67, 107, 185, 188–89, 199, 216, 221, 235–36, 247, 260–61, 265–66, 275–81, 293–94, 330–31, 333, 336, 364; *see also* Job (character) innocence/righteousness of; prosperity/wealth; Retribution Principle (RP)

ritual, 34–38, 43, 58–59, 61–63, 67–68, 107, 121–22, 158–61, 163, 180, 210, 213, 226, 291, 293, 295, 301, 303, 318, 320, 333, 435; see cultic feasts; piety; priest

Sabeans, 23, 69

sacred space, 35, 62, 252, 254, 286, 315, 418–19

Satan, *see* Challenger, the

Sea/*yam*, 120, 163, 287–88, 291, 418–19; *see also* Deep/*tehom*

Shamash, 35, 257, 288, 327

shame, 133, 227, 312–14, 316, 432; *see also* honor

Sheol/netherworld, 78, 118, 120, 123, 125–28, 130–31, 133–34, 174–75, 179, 215, 228, 250–53, 256–57, 288, 299, 325, 334, 400; *see also* afterlife, resurrection

sickness, 32–33, 61, 101–2, 106, 137, 182, 216, 235, 301, 303, 318, 429

silence, 105, 162, 178–79, 183–84, 243, 262, 266, 314, 330–31, 355, 359–60, 411, 431

sin, *see* friends of Job, accusing Job; Job (character), innocence/righteousness of

Socrates, *see* Plato

Sons of God/divine council, 63–64, 74, 110, 160, 212, 214–15, 221, 315, 335, 372, 400–402

spirit, *see* God, Spirit of

suffering, 19–20, 22–23, 26–27, 37, 39–40, 43, 47, 73, 87, 97–98, 107, 116, 140–41, 192, 216, 231–34, 280–81, 296–303, 374, 376, 386–88, 397, 412–15, 418, 420–22, 424–29, 437–38, 440–44; in the ancient Near East, 31, 33, 36–37, 40, 43; *see also* evil; God, cause of suffering; Job (character), suffering of

tehom, see Deep/*tehom*

temple, 23, 57, 129, 315, 318, 335, 402, 418–19; *see also* sacred space

theodicy, 20, 21, 39–45, 47, 186, 269, 350, 374–76, 378, 420, 436–37, *see also* Elihu; Retribution Principle (RP)

theophany, 129, 168, 398

thought experiment, 26–27, 48, 69, 110, 424

traditional dogma, 36, 104, 106, 162, 181–83, 216, 222, 249, 262, 352; see friends of Job, Retribution Principle (RP)

trust, *see* faith/trust

Tsevat's triangle, 43–44, 108, 165, 185, 225, 262, 374, 376, 410

Uz, 23, 56–57, 351

wealth, *see* prosperity/wealth

weather, 170, 191, 254, 259, 290, 366–69, 371, 381–82, 398, 400–402, 416; *see* cosmic geography

wicked, the, *see* Retribution Principle (RP)

wife of Job, 45, 59, 102–6, 186, 323, 325–26, 434

wisdom, 31, 42, 57, 279; as inaccessible, 285, 287, 304; produces creation, 289–90, 300; source of, 183, 287–88, 352–54, 362, 377, 441; *see also* God, wisdom of

wisdom hymn [ch. 28], 29–30, 285, 332

wisdom literature, 26–27, 45, 58, 110, 277, 403, 438, 443

Joshua

Reading Joshua can be, frankly, a jarring experience. Serious, troubling questions about God's attitude toward his created peoples arise—questions with no easy answer. But the book of Joshua presents itself, warts (and wars!) and all, and asks readers to let it tell its story from its point of view and out of its ancient context.

Robert L. Hubbard Jr.   ISBN: 978-0-310-20934-8

Judges, Ruth

This commentary helps readers learn how the messages of Judges and Ruth can have the same powerful impact today that they did when they were first written. Judges reveals a God who employs very human deliverers but refuses to gloss over their sins and the consequences of those sins. Ruth demonstrates the far-reaching impact of a righteous character.

K. Lawson Younger Jr.   ISBN: 978-0-310-20636-1

1&2 Samuel

In Samuel, we meet Saul, David, Goliath, Jonathan, Bathsheba, the witch of Endor, and other unforgettable characters. And we encounter ourselves. For while the culture and conditions of Israel under its first kings are vastly different from our own, the basic issues of humans in relation to God, the Great King, have not changed. Sin, repentance, forgiveness, adversity, prayer, faith, and the promises of God — these continue to play out in our lives today.

Bill T. Arnold   ISBN: 978-0-310-21086-3

1&2 Kings

It is God's interaction with his people by way of his prophets and their kings—his pleadings, his warnings, and the fulfillment of his words—that comes across again and again with forcefulness and clarity. God speaks; now will his people hear, believe, and respond? August Konkel connects past context to our contemporary circumstances, helping us grasp the meaning of this question today.

August H. Konkel   ISBN: 978-0-310-21129-7

1&2 Chronicles

First and Second Chronicles are a narrative steeped in the best and worst of the human heart — but they are also a revelation of Yahweh at work, forwarding his purposes in the midst of fallible people, but a people who trust in the Lord and his word through the prophets. God has a plan to which he is committed.

Andrew E. Hill   ISBN: 978-0-310-20610-1

Esther

Karen H. Jobes shows what a biblical narrative that never mentions God tells Christians about him today.

Karen H. Jobes   ISBN: 978-0-310-20672-9

Psalms Volume 1

Gerald Wilson examines Books 1 and 2 of the Psalter. His seminal work on the shaping of the Hebrew Psalter has opened a new avenue of psalms research by shifting focus from exclusive attention to individual psalms to the arrangement of the psalms into groups.

Gerald H. Wilson   ISBN: 978-0-310-20635-4

Proverbs

Few people can remember when they last heard a sermon from Proverbs or looked together at its chapters. In this NIV Application Commentary on Proverbs, Paul Koptak gives numerous aids to pastors and church leaders on how to study, reflect on, and apply this book on biblical wisdom as part of the educational ministry of their churches.

Paul Koptak   ISBN: 978-0-310-21852-4

Ecclesiastes, Song of Songs

Ecclesiastes and Songs of Songs have always presented particular challenges to their readers, especially if those readers are seeking to understand them as part of Christian Scripture. Revealing the links between the Scriptures and our own times, Iain Provan shows how these wisdom books speak to us today with relevance and conviction.

Iain Provan   ISBN: 978-0-310-21372-7

Isaiah

Isaiah wrestles with the realities of people who are not convicted by the truth but actually hardened by it, and with a God whose actions sometimes seem unintelligible, or even worse, appears to be absent. Yet Isaiah penetrates beyond these experiences to an even greater reality. Isaiah sees God's rule over history and his capacity to take the worst of human actions and use it for good. He declares the truth that even in the darkest hours, the Holy One of Israel is infinitely trustworthy.

John N. Oswalt   ISBN: 978-0-310-20613-2

Jeremiah/Lamentations

These two books cannot be separated from the political conditions of ancient Judah. Beginning with the time of King Josiah, who introduced religious reform, Jeremiah reflects the close link between spiritual and political prosperity or disaster for the nation as a whole.

J. Andrew Dearman   ISBN: 978-0-310-20616-3

Ezekiel

Discover how, properly understood, this mysterious book with its obscure images offers profound comfort to us today.

Iain M. Duguid   ISBN: 978-0-310-21047-4

Daniel

Tremper Longman III reveals how the practical stories and spellbinding apocalyptic imagery of Daniel contain principles that are as relevant now as they were in the days of the Babylonian Captivity.

Tremper Longman III   ISBN: 978-0-310-20608-8

Hosea, Amos, Micah

Scratch beneath the surface of today's culture and you'll find we're not so different from ancient Israel. Revealing the links between Israel eight centuries B.C. and our own times, Gary V. Smith shows how the prophetic writings of Hosea, Amos, and Micah speak to us today with relevance and conviction.

Gary V. Smith   ISBN: 978-0-310-20614-9

Joel, Obadiah, Malachi

These books give a full picture of God, one who despises and rightly judges sin and rebellion, but who also lovingly invites people to return to him so that he might bestow his wonderful grace and blessings. It is a message no less timely today than when these books were first written, and David W. Baker skillfully bridges the centuries in helping believers today understand and apply it.

David W. Baker   ISBN: 978-0-310-20723-8

Jonah, Nahum, Habakkuk, Zephaniah

James Bruckner shows how the messages of these four Old Testament prophets, who lived during some of Israel and Judah's most turbulent times, are as powerful in today's turbulent times as when first written.

James Bruckner   ISBN: 978-0-310-20637-8

Haggai, Zechariah

This commentary on Haggai and Zechariah helps readers learn how the message of these two prophets who challenged and encouraged the people of God after the return from Babylon can have the same powerful impact on the community of faith today.

Mark J. Boda   ISBN: 978-0-310-20615-6

Matthew

Matthew helps readers learn how the message of Matthew's gospel can have the same powerful impact today that it did when the author first wrote it.

Michael J. Wilkins   ISBN: 978-0-310-49310-5

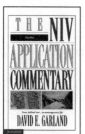

Mark

Learn how the challenging gospel of Mark can leave recipients with the same powerful questions and answers it did when it was written.

David E. Garland   ISBN: 978-0-310-49350-1

Luke

Focus on the most important application of all: "the person of Jesus and the nature of God's work through him to deliver humanity."

Darrell L. Bock   ISBN: 978-0-310-49330-3

John

Learn both halves of the interpretive task. Gary M. Burge shows readers how to bring the ancient message of John into a modern context. He also explains not only what the book of John meant to its original readers but also how it can speak powerfully today.

Gary M. Burge   ISBN: 978-0-310-49750-9

Acts

Study the first portraits of the church in action around the world with someone whose ministry mirrors many of the events in Acts. Biblical scholar and worldwide evangelist Ajith Fernando applies the story of the church's early development to the global mission of believers today.

Ajith Fernando   ISBN: 978-0-310-49410-2

Romans

Paul's letter to the Romans remains one of the most important expressions of Christian truth ever written. Douglas Moo comments on the text and then explores issues in Paul's culture and in ours that help us understand the ultimate meaning of each paragraph.

Douglas J. Moo   ISBN: 978-0-310-49400-3

1 Corinthians

Is your church struggling with the problem of divisiveness and fragmentation? See the solution Paul gave the Corinthian Christians over 2,000 years ago. It still works today!

Craig Blomberg   ISBN: 978-0-310-48490-5

2 Corinthians

Often recognized as the most difficult of Paul's letters to understand, 2 Corinthians can have the same powerful impact today that it did when it was first written.

Scott J. Hafemann   ISBN: 978-0-310-49420-1

Galatians

A pastor's message is true not because of his preaching or people-management skills, but because of Christ. Learn how to apply Paul's example of visionary church leadership to your own congregation.

Scot McKnight   ISBN: 978-0-310-48470-7

Ephesians

Explore what the author calls "a surprisingly comprehensive statement about God and his work, about Christ and the gospel, about life with God's Spirit, and about the right way to live."

Klyne Snodgrass   ISBN: 978-0-310-49340-2

Philippians

The best lesson Philippians provides is how to encourage people who actually are doing quite well. Learn why not all the New Testament letters are reactions to theological crises.

Frank Thielman   ISBN: 978-0-310-49300-6

Colossians/Philemon

The temptation to trust in the wrong things has always been strong. Use this commentary to learn the importance of trusting only in Jesus, God's Son, in whom all the fullness of God lives. No message is more important for our postmodern culture.

David E. Garland   ISBN: 978-0-310-48480-6

1&2 Thessalonians

Paul's letters to the Thessalonians say as much to us today about Christ's return and our resurrection as they did in the early church. This volume skillfully reveals Paul's answers to these questions and how they address the needs of contemporary Christians.

Michael W. Holmes   ISBN: 978-0-310-49380-8

1&2 Timothy, Titus

Reveals the context and meanings of Paul's letters to two leaders in the early Christian Church and explores their present-day implications to help you to accurately apply the principles they contain to contemporary issues.

Walter L. Liefeld   ISBN: 978-0-310-50110-7

Hebrews

The message of Hebrews can be summed up in a single phrase: "God speaks effectively to us through Jesus." Unpack the theological meaning of those seven words and learn why the gospel still demands a hearing today.

George H. Guthrie   ISBN: 978-0-310-49390-7

James

Give your church the best antidote for a culture of people who say they believe one thing but act in ways that either ignore or contradict their belief. More than just saying, "Practice what you preach," James gives solid reasons why faith and action must coexist.

David P. Nystrom   ISBN: 978-0-310-49360-0

1 Peter

The issue of the church's relationship to the state hits the news media in some form nearly every day. Learn how Peter answered the question for Christians surviving under Roman rule and how it applies similarly to believers living amid the secular institutions of the modern world.

Scot McKnight   ISBN: 978-0-310-49290-0

2 Peter, Jude

Introduce your modern audience to letters they may not be familiar with and show why they'll want to get to know them.

Douglas J. Moo

ISBN: 978-0-310-20104-5

Letters of John

Like the community in John's time, which faced disputes over erroneous "secret knowledge," today's church needs discernment in affirming new ideas supported by Scripture and weeding out harmful notions. This volume will help you show today's Christians how to use John's example.

Gary M. Burge

ISBN: 978-0-310-48620-6

Revelation

Craig Keener offers a "new" approach to the book of Revelation by focusing on the "old." He stresses the need for believers to prepare for the possibility of suffering for the sake of Jesus.

Craig S. Keener

ISBN: 978-0-310-23192-9

We want to hear from you. Please send your comments about this book to us in care of zreview@zondervan.com. Thank you.

ZONDERVAN.com/
AUTHORTRACKER
follow your favorite authors